WESTERN
CIVILIZATIONS

W·W·NORTON & COMPANY · NEW YORK LONDON

EDWARD MCNALL BURNS
ROBERT E. LERNER
STANDISH MEACHAM

WESTERN CIVILIZATIONS

Their History and Their Culture

VOLUME II / NINTH EDITION

For Dietlind and Olivia;
Edith, Louisa, and Samuel

W. W. Norton & Company, Inc., 500 Fifth Avenue,
New York, N.Y. 10110
W. W. Norton & Company, Ltd., 37 Great Russell Street,
London WC1B 3NU

Ninth Edition © 1980

First Edition, Copyright 1941
Second Edition, Copyright 1947
Third Edition, Copyright 1949
Fourth Edition, Copyright 1954
Fifth Edition, Copyright © 1958
Sixth Edition, Copyright © 1963
Seventh Edition, Copyright © 1968
Eighth Edition, Copyright © 1973

By W. W. NORTON & COMPANY, INC.

Book Design by Antonina Krass

Layout by Ben Gamit

Cartography by Harold K. Faye

3 4 5 6 7 8 9 0

ISBN 0-393-95087-5

CONTENTS

Part Five THE FRENCH AND INDUSTRIAL
REVOLUTIONS AND THEIR
CONSEQUENCES

Part Six   THE WEST AT THE WORLD'S
CENTER

ILLUSTRATIONS IN COLOR

(Illustrations appear facing or following the pages indicated)

ILLUSTRATIONS IN THE TEXT

MAPS

PREFACE

Edward McNall Burns wrote one of the most successful of all history textbooks ever published in the United States. His *Western Civilizations* first appeared in 1941 and was reissued with revisions in 1947, 1949, 1954, 1958, 1963, 1968, and 1973. Men and women who read it in a college course continue to refer to it, and new admirers come to it every day. The reasons for its popularity are manifold: it is clearly and forcefully written, it covers the whole history of the West in relatively brief compass, and it presents an excellent balance between narrative and analysis. The text also gained readers because it was conceived from the start as a history of *civilizations* rather than a chronicle of events. Professor Burns covered political history fully, but he believed that "the effects of the Black Death were no less important than the Hundred Years' War, and that, in the long run, the teachings of Aristotle and the Stoics transcended in significance the rise of the Bourbons or the decline of the Holy Roman Empire." Accordingly *Western Civilizations* has always laid great stress on the development of ideas and institutions. With Professor Burns's death in 1972, it was imperative that the careful balance he had struck be preserved by the authors chosen to succeed him.

In accepting the assignment to revise such an excellent textbook we had no doubts whatsoever that we wished to retain its basic physiognomy. But the expansion of historical research over previously neglected subject matters as well as the progress of research in more traditional areas have accomplished so much in recent years that we have found it necessary to revise substantial portions of the text. Throughout we have paid much more attention to the history of women and minorities than before, but since the text already devoted a good deal of space to social history we did not have to accomplish this at the expense of political or intellectual coverage. Although we pride ourselves in keeping the length of the book roughly the same as it was before by dint of editorial admonition and heroic self-restraint, we have also made numerous changes in organizational strategies and interpretative schemes, with the greatest amount of revision falling in the medieval period and the nineteenth century.

In the earliest parts of the book (chapters 1–8) the major changes have been to summarize the most recent findings concerning prehistoric peoples, to consider the relations between Minoan and Mycenaean civilizations on the basis of new insights provided by the decipherment of Linear B, and generally to alter the chronology to conform to the findings of the most recent research. More fundamental changes have been made in the late-Roman and medieval coverage, resulting in five substantially new chapters (9–13). Instead of treating Roman history after Diocletian as part of Roman civilization proper, the present edition follows recent approaches by devoting a chapter (9) to the "world of late antiquity" from the time of Diocletian to the end of the sixth century. Chapter 10 treats the three heirs of Rome—Byzantium, Islam, and the early-medieval Christian West—from a comparative perspective. Replacing the chronological division of the Middle Ages into two periods—early (500–1050) and late (1050–1350)—the present volume follows the more conventional scheme of dividing the Middle Ages into early (500–1050), high (1050–1300) and late (1300–1500) periods. Two chapters (11 and 12) are devoted to the High Middle Ages. These are almost chronologically co-extensive with the two chapters on what was previously called the late Middle Ages, but they introduce new subjects, such as the dynamic progress of medieval agriculture and the rise and fall of papal monarchy, as well as differences in descriptive vocabularies and interpretation. A full chapter on the later Middle Ages has no equivalent in the previous edition although this chapter does incorporate some of the subject matter that was included under the heading of the Renaissance. Shifting some of the Renaissance material made it possible to have a single chapter on the Renaissance as a whole instead of the previous two on the Renaissance in Italy and the Renaissance beyond Italy. The Reformation chapter (15) is largely unchanged, the Commercial Revolution chapter (16) adds the results of research on the agricultural revolution of the eighteenth century (the witchcraft material being removed to chapter 18), and the Absolutism chapter (17) introduces treatment of England from the Glorious Revolution to the reign of George III.

In revising chapters 19 through 26 we have attempted to unify the analysis of nineteenth-century western civilization around three major themes: 1) the manner in which both the French and Industrial Revolutions combined to produce the dramatic changes that occurred during that period; 2) the importance of class consciousness—a major factor in both of those revolutions—to an understanding of the period; and 3) the need to know more about the everyday life of men and women from all classes who experienced the changes described.

Throughout we have relied heavily on recent scholarship that has taken these themes as it subject.

In order to treat the legacies of the French revolution more coherently, material on Napoleon has been moved to Chapter 19. The Industrial Revolution is now discussed in two chapters. The first (20) includes expanded sections on European industrialization and the railway age; the second (24) deals with the technological changes that characterized the so-called "second" industrial revolution and with the effect of those changes in human terms. Chapters 21, 22, and 23 outline the manner in which the two revolutions altered the course of history. These chapters differ from the previous edition by attempting to define and describe class consciousness; by summarizing recent scholarly findings on the subjects of agricultural change and the standard of living; by stressing the connections between romanticism and nationalism and between nationalism and nation-building; by presenting liberalism as the characteristic political credo of the industrial middle class; and by describing in some detail the lives of men—and women—in middle and working-class homes and neighborhoods. Material on the various challenges to the industrial middle class has been concentrated in Chapters 21, 25, and 26. The remaining chapters (27–31), though in some parts extensively revised, retain the same general organizational outline employed in the Eighth Edition. The most significant alterations occur in Chapter 28, where material on interwar culture has been added, and in the last two chapters, where problems and trends of the post-World War II period have been reorganized and up-dated in a way that we hope makes sense of a constantly changing and very complex set of world conditions and movements.

In conjunction with the textual revisions the map and illustration programs have received serious attention. Most of the nearly fifty maps are either new or thoroughly amended. Virtually sixty percent of the seven hundred illustrations are new to this edition, having been culled from a wide range of European and American archives. The text was the first to include color illustrations and continues to include far more color plates than any other book in the field. The new edition, like its predecessors, has been brought out in a one-volume and a two-volume edition. Available for use with either is an entirely new Instructor's Manual and a revised Study Guide, whose most distinctive feature is the inclusion of numerous extracts from original and secondary sources.

Robert Lerner has had primary responsibility for the first half of the revision (inclusive of chapter 17) and Standish Meacham for the second half. Invaluable suggestions for improving the chapters on ancient history were made by Kenneth Sacks and George Szemler. Among the numerous experts who cheerfully submitted to bombardments of questioning were T. W. Heyck, David Joravsky, E. William Monter, James E. Packer, Carl Petry, and Susan Solway. Helen Feng, Erdmut Lerner, Oscar Lerner, Vita Maniscalco, James Murray, and Richard Wells provided extremely helpful aid in critical reading and research. At W. W. Norton & Company Ruth Mandel has been an expert picture-gatherer, Ben Gamit a superb make-up artist, and Robert E. Kehoe and Donald S. Lamm gracious and savvy producers. Michelle Cliff, our editor, counts not just as our chastizing angel but as our collaborator: to her we owe the greatest of our debts.

Robert E. Lerner
Standish Meacham

Evanston, Illinois
Austin, Texas

WESTERN
CIVILIZATIONS

Chapter 16

THE COMMERCIAL REVOLUTION AND THE NEW SOCIETY (c. 1450–c. 1800)

Although a Kingdom may be enriched by gifts received, or by purchases taken from some other Nations, yet these are things uncertain and of small consideration when they happen. The ordinary means therefore to encrease our wealth and treasure is by *Forraign Trade,* wherein wee must ever observe this rule: to sell more to strangers yearly than wee consume of theirs in value.

—Thomas Mun, *England's Treasure by Forraign Trade*

I n the three and a half centuries between 1450 and 1800 enormous changes took place in European economic life which are often described as the Commercial Revolution. While there is much room for disagreement in detail about what these changes entailed, certain basic generalizations are commonly agreed upon. Above all, the Commercial Revolution encompassed a change from the semi-static, localized, and largely subsistence economy of the Middle Ages to the dynamic, worldwide, capitalist regime of modern times. Recovery from the fourteenth-century economic catastrophes was spurred by overseas discoveries, the influx of new articles of consumption and precious metals, the establishment of overseas markets, and advances in banking and trade. Larger numbers of people began to live off commerce and industry, and the profit motive became more pronounced than ever before. Also during the period of the Commercial Revolution, first Spain and Portugal, and then the north Atlantic states of England, France, and Holland replaced the northern Italian cities as the centers of European economic initiative and prosperity. Finally, in the eighteenth century revolutionary developments in European agriculture brought the European economy to the threshold of the Industrial Revolution. Taken together, all these changes meant unprecedented

Major changes in European economic life

new wealth for Europe and carried in their train important changes in social organization and material culture.

1. THE NATURE AND EFFECTS OF OVERSEAS EXPANSION

Causes of the voyages of discovery

We have already seen in Chapter 13 that the European economy was beginning to expand around 1450 after about a century and a half of severe depression. No doubt expansion would have progressed steadily, but it was greatly accelerated in the sixteenth and subsequent centuries by the effects of overseas discoveries and conquests. The initial voyages of discovery were due primarily to Spanish and Portuguese ambitions for a share in the trade with the Orient. For some time this trade had been monopolized by the Italian cities of Venice and Genoa, with the result that the people of the Iberian peninsula had to pay high prices for the spices, silks, and drugs that were imported from the East. It was therefore quite natural that attempts should be made by sailors commissioned by Spanish and Portuguese monarchs to discover a new route to the Orient independent of Italian control. A second cause of the voyages of discovery was the missionary fervor of the Spaniards. The successful Spanish reconquest of the Iberian peninsula from the forces of Islam had generated a surplus of religious zeal, which spilled over into a desire to convert the overseas "heathen." To these causes should be added the fact that advances in geographical knowledge and technological expertise allowed mariners to venture more fearlessly into the open seas. It should be borne in mind, however, that these advances did not all transpire suddenly around 1490. The popular idea that all Europeans before Columbus believed that the earth was flat is simply not true: it would have been impossible after the twelfth century to have found an educated person who did not accept the fact that the earth is a sphere. Furthermore, technological aids like the compass and the astrolabe (a device used for measuring the position of heavenly bodies) were known long before Columbus's voyage. In fact, the Portuguese had already sailed boldly out into the Atlantic to reach the Azores Islands (one-third of the way to the New World) before 1350. Most likely, Europeans would have reached America and the Far East much earlier than they actually did had they not been held back by the depression and political upheavals of the later Middle Ages.

Spanish and Portuguese successes

If we except the Norsemen, who discovered the North American continent about 1000 A.D., the pioneers in oceanic navigation were the Portuguese. By the middle of the fifteenth century they had explored the African coast as far south as Guinea. In 1497 their most successful navigator, Vasco da Gama, rounded the tip of Africa and sailed on the next year to India. In the meantime, the Genoese mariner, Christopher Columbus (1451–1506), became convinced of the feasibility of reaching India by sailing west. Rebuffed by the Portuguese, he turned to the Spanish sovereigns, Ferdinand and Isabella, and enlisted their support of his plan. The story of his epochal voyage and its result is a familiar one and need not be recounted here. Though he died ignorant of his real achievement, his discoveries laid the foundations for the Spanish claim to nearly all of the New World. Other discoverers representing the Spanish crown followed Columbus, and soon afterward the conquerors, Cortes and Pizarro. The result was the establishment of a vast colonial empire including what is now the southwestern portion of the United States, Florida, Mexico, and the West Indies, Central America, and all of South America with the exception of Brazil, which was taken by Portugal.

The English and the French were not slow in following the Spanish example. The voyages of John Cabot and his son Sebastian in 1497–1498 provided the basis for the English claim to North America, though there was nothing that could be called a British empire in the New World until after the settlement of Virginia in 1607. Early in the sixteenth century the French explorer Cartier sailed up the St. Lawrence, thereby furnishing his native land with some shadow of a title to eastern Canada. More than a hundred years later the explorations of Joliet, La Salle, and Father Marquette gave the French a foothold in the Mississippi valley and in the region of the Great Lakes. Following their victory in their war for independence in the early seventeenth century, the Dutch also took a hand in the struggle for colonial empire. The voyage of Henry Hudson up the river which bears his name enabled them to found New Netherland in 1623, which they were forced to surrender to the English some forty years later. But the most valuable possessions of the Dutch were Malacca, the Spice Islands, and the ports of India and Africa taken from Portugal in the early seventeenth century.

The results of these voyages of discovery and the founding of colonial empires were almost incalculable. To begin with, they expanded commerce from its narrow limits of Mediterranean trade into a world enterprise. For the first time in history the ships of the great maritime powers now sailed the seven seas. The tight little monopoly of Oriental trade maintained by the Italian cities was thoroughly punctured. Genoa and Venice gradually sank into relative obscurity, while the harbors of Lisbon, Bordeaux, Liverpool, Bristol, and Amsterdam were crowded with vessels and the shelves of their merchants piled high with goods. A second result was a tremendous increase in the volume of commerce and in the variety of articles of consumption. To the spices and textiles from the Orient were now added tobacco from North America; molasses and rum from the West Indies; cocoa, chocolate, quinine, and cochineal dye from South America; and ivory, slaves, and ostrich feathers from Africa. In addition to these commod-

Cortes

The British, French, and Dutch

The expansion of commerce into a world enterprise

Aden. A sixteenth-century woodcut of the seaport which was a base for merchants and travelers sailing to India.

ities hitherto unknown or obtainable only in limited quantities, the supply of certain older products was greatly increased. This was especially true of sugar, coffee, rice, and cotton, which were imported in such amounts from the Western Hemisphere that they ceased to be articles of luxury.

The increase in the supply of precious metals

Another significant result of the discovery and conquest of lands overseas was an expansion of the supply of precious metals. When Columbus first sailed to America, the quantities of gold and silver in Europe were scarcely sufficient to support a dynamic economy. Indeed, it was nearly fifty years before the full impact of wealth from America made itself felt. For some time gold was the more abundant metal and was relatively cheap in relation to silver. About 1540 this relation was reversed. Massive imports of silver from the mines of Mexico, Bolivia, and Peru produced such a depreciation in the value of silver that quantities of gold had to be hoarded for critical transactions. Henceforth, for about eighty years, the European economy ran on silver. The result was a tremendous inflation. Prices and wages rose to fantastic heights in what may be considered an artificial prosperity. It did not affect all parts of Europe alike. The German silver-mining industry was ruined by the flood of silver from the Americas. As a consequence, the position of Germany declined, while England and the Netherlands rose to preeminence. For a brief period Spain shared this preeminence, but it was ill-fitted to continue it. Spanish industrial development was too feeble to supply the demand for manufactured products from the European settlers in the Western Hemisphere. Accordingly, they turned to the north of Europe for the textiles, cutlery, and similar products they urgently needed. By the end of the sixteenth century the Spanish economy, which had first seemed to be prospering greatly from the discoveries, lay almost completely in ruins.

2. THE MAIN FEATURES OF THE COMMERCIAL REVOLUTION

The major traits of the Commercial Revolution have been partly suggested by the foregoing discussion of overseas expansion. The outstanding characteristic was the rise of capitalism. Reduced to its simplest terms, capitalism may be defined as a system of production, distribution, and exchange, in which accumulated wealth is invested by private owners for the sake of gain. Its essential features are private enterprise, competition for markets, and business for profit. Generally it involves also the wage system as a method of payment of workers; that is, a mode of payment based not upon the amount of wealth they create, but rather upon their ability to compete with one another for jobs. As indicated already, capitalism is the direct antithesis of the semi-static economy of the medieval guilds, in which production and trade were supposed to be conducted for the benefit of society and with only a reasonable charge for the service rendered, instead of unlimited profits. Although capitalism did not come to its full maturity until the nineteenth century, most of its cardinal features were developed during the Commercial Revolution.

*Incidents of the
Commercial Revolution:
(1) the rise of capitalism*

A second important feature of the Commercial Revolution was the growth of banking. Because of the strong religious and moral disapproval of usury, banking had scarcely been a respectable business during the Middle Ages. For centuries the little that was carried on was

(2) the growth of banking

Sixteenth-Century Mining. The greater complexity of new mining techniques called for greater sophistication of capitalistic organization.

Jacob Fugger

*(3) the expansion of credit
facilities*

virtually monopolized by Jews. Nevertheless, exceptions did exist. As we have seen in Chapter 11, the Church did come to allow profit-making on commercial risks. The result was that several Italian families began to profit greatly from banking enterprises as early as the thirteenth century. The greatest Italian banks were ruined by the blows of the fourteenth-century depression, but afterwards newer and better managed Italian houses, like the bank of the Medici, took their place. By the fifteenth century the banking business had spread to southern Germany and France. The leading firm in the north was that of the Fuggers of Augsburg. The Fuggers lent money to kings and bishops, served as brokers for the pope in the sale of indulgences, and provided the funds that enabled Charles V to buy his election to the throne of the Holy Roman Empire. The rise of these private financial houses was followed by the establishment of government banks, intended to serve the monetary needs of the national states. The first in order of time was the Bank of Sweden (1657), but the one which was destined for the role of greatest importance in economic history was the Bank of England, founded in 1694. Although not technically under government control until 1946, it was the bank of issue for the government and the depositary of public funds.

The growth of banking was necessarily accompanied by the adoption of various aids to financial transactions on a large scale. Credit facilities were extended in such a way that a merchant in Amsterdam could purchase goods from a merchant in Venice by means of a bill of exchange issued by an Amsterdam bank. The Venetian merchant would obtain his money by depositing the bill of exchange in his local bank. Later, the two banks would settle their accounts by comparing balances. Among the other facilities for the expansion of credit were the adoption of a system of payment by check in local transactions and the issuance of bank notes as a substitute for gold and silver. Both of these devices were invented by the Italians and were gradually adopted

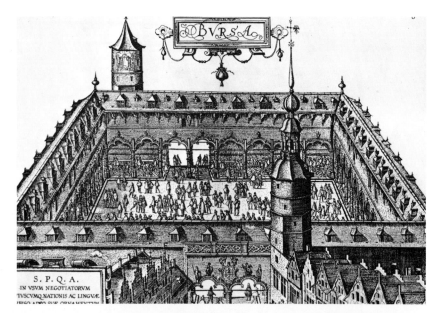

The Antwerp Bourse. Built in the sixteenth century, this was the place of exchange for merchants from all countries.

in northern Europe. The system of payment by check was particularly important in increasing the volume of trade, since the credit resources of the banks could now be expanded far beyond the actual amounts of cash in their vaults.

The Commercial Revolution was not confined, of course, to the growth of trade and banking. Included in it also were fundamental changes in methods of production. The system of manufacture developed by the craft guilds in the later Middle Ages was rapidly becoming defunct. The guilds themselves, dominated by the master craftsmen, had grown selfish and exclusive. Membership in them was commonly restricted to a few privileged families. Besides, they were so completely choked by tradition that they were unable to make adjustments to changing conditions. Moreover, new industries had sprung up entirely outside the guild system. Characteristic examples were mining and smelting and the woolen industry. The rapid development of these enterprises was stimulated by technological advances, such as the invention of the spinning wheel and the stocking frame and the discovery of a new method of making brass, which saved about half of the fuel previously used. In the mining and smelting industries a form of organization was adopted similar to that which has prevailed ever since. The tools and plant facilities belonged to capitalists, while the workers were mere wage-laborers subject to hazards of accident, unemployment, and occupational disease.

But the most typical form of industrial production in the period of the Commercial Revolution was the domestic system, developed first of all in the woolen industry. The domestic system derives its name from the fact that the work was done in the homes of individual artisans instead of in the shop of a master craftsman. Since the various jobs in the manufacture of a product were given out on contract, the system is also known as the putting-out system. Notwithstanding the petty scale of production, the organization was basically capitalist. The raw material was purchased by an entrepreneur (known as a clothier in the woolen industry) and assigned to individual workers, each of whom would complete his or her allotted task for a stipulated payment. In the case of the woolen industry the yarn would be given out first of all to the spinners, then to the weavers, fullers, and dyers in succession. When the cloth was finally finished, it would be taken by the clothier and sold in the open market for the highest price it would bring. The domestic system was, of course, not restricted to the manufacture of woolen cloth. As time went on, it was extended into many other fields of production. It tied in well with the new glorification of riches and with the conception of a dynamic economy. The capitalist could now thumb his nose at the old restrictions on profits. No association of his rivals could judge the quality of his product or the wages he paid to his workers. Perhaps best of all he could expand his business as he saw fit and introduce new techniques that would reduce costs or increase the volume of production.

Merchants' Houses in Amsterdam, Seventeenth Century. Several of the principal thoroughfares of Amsterdam are canals.

Advantages and disadvantages of the domestic system

Undoubtedly, the domestic system had advantages for the workers themselves, especially as compared to its successor, the factory system. Though wages were low, there was no regular schedule of hours, and it was generally possible for the laborer to supplement the family income by cultivating a small plot of land and raising a few vegetables. Furthermore, conditions of work in the homes were more healthful than in factories, and the artisan had his family to assist him with the simpler tasks. Freedom from the supervision of a foreman and from the fear of discharge for petty reasons were also definite advantages. On the other hand, it must not be forgotten that the workers were too widely scattered to organize effectively for common action. As a consequence they had no means of protecting themselves from dishonest employers, who cheated them out of part of their wages or forced them to accept payment in goods. It is also true that toward the end of the Commercial Revolution the workers became more and more dependent upon the capitalists, who now furnished not only the raw materials but the tools and equipment as well. In some cases the laborers were herded into large central shops and compelled to work under a fixed routine. The difference between this and the high-pressure methods of the factory system was only a matter of degree.

That the Commercial Revolution would involve extensive changes in business organization was practically assured from the start. The prevailing unit of production and trade in the Middle Ages was the shop or store owned by an individual or a family. The partnership was also quite common, in spite of its grave disadvantage of unlimited liability of each of its members for the debts of the entire firm. Obviously no one of these units was well adapted to business involving heavy risks and a huge investment of capital. The first result of the attempt to devise a more suitable business organization was the formation of *regulated companies*. The regulated company was an association of merchants banded together for a common venture. The members did not pool their resources but agreed merely to cooperate for their mutual advantage and to abide by certain definite regulations. Usually the purpose of the combination was to maintain a monopoly of trade in some part of the world. Assessments were often paid by the members for the upkeep of docks and warehouses and especially for protection against "interlopers," as those traders were called who attempted to break into the monopoly. A leading example of this type of organization was an English company known as the Merchant Adventurers, established for the purpose of trade with the Netherlands and Germany.

*(6) changes in business
organization; the growth
of regulated companies*

In the seventeenth century the regulated company was largely superseded by a new type of organization at once more compact and broader in scope. This was the *joint-stock company*, formed through the issuance of shares of capital to a considerable number of investors. Those who purchased the shares might or might not take part in the work of the company, but whether they did or not they were joint owners of the business and therefore entitled to share in its profits in accordance with the amount they had invested. The joint-stock company had numerous advantages over the partnership and the regulated company. First, it was a permanent unit, not subject to reorganization every time one of its members died or withdrew. And second, it made possible a much larger accumulation of capital, through a wide distribution of shares. In short, it possessed nearly every advantage of the modern corporation except that it was not a person in the eyes of the law with the rights and privileges guaranteed to individuals. While most of the early joint-stock companies were founded for commercial ventures, some were organized later in industry. A number of the outstanding trading combinations were also *chartered companies*. This means that they held charters from the government granting a monopoly of the trade in a certain locality and conferring extensive authority over the inhabitants. Through a charter of this kind the British East India Company ruled over India as if it were a private estate until 1784, and even in a sense until 1858. Other famous chartered companies were the Dutch East India Company, the Hudson's Bay Company, the Plymouth Company, and the London Company. The last of these founded the colony of Virginia and governed it for a time as company property.

*(7) the joint-stock
company*

The remaining feature of the Commercial Revolution which needs to be considered was the growth of a more efficient money economy. Money, of course, had been widely in use ever since the revival of

*The Spanish Milled Dollar or
"Piece of Eight."* This was one of
the first coins to have its cir-
cumference scored or "milled."
It was cut into halves and quarters to make change.

trade in the eleventh century. Nevertheless, there were few coins with a value that was recognized other than locally. By 1300, the gold ducat of Venice and the gold florin of Florence had come to be accepted in Italy and also in the international markets of northern Europe. But no country could be said to have had a uniform monetary system. Nearly everywhere there was great confusion. Coins issued by kings circulated side by side with the money of foreign states. Moreover, the types of currency were modified frequently, and the coins themselves were often debased. A common method by which kings expanded their own personal revenues was to increase the proportion of cheaper metals in the coins they minted. But the growth of trade and industry in the Commercial Revolution accentuated the need for more stable and uniform monetary systems. The problem was solved by the adoption of a standard system of money by every important state to be used for all transactions within its borders. Much time elapsed, however, before the reform was complete. England began the construction of a uniform coinage during the reign of Queen Elizabeth, but the task was not finished until late in the seventeenth century. The French did not succeed in reducing their money to its modern standard of simplicity and convenience until the time of Napoleon. In spite of these long delays it appears safe to conclude that national currencies were really an achievement of the Commercial Revolution.

3. MERCANTILISM IN THEORY AND PRACTICE

*The meaning of
mercantilism*

The Commercial Revolution in its later stages was accompanied by the adoption of a new set of doctrines and practices known as mercantilism. In its broadest meaning, mercantilism may be defined as a system of government intervention to promote national prosperity and increase the power of the state. Though frequently considered as a program of economic policy exclusively, its objectives were quite largely political. The purpose of the intervention in economic affairs was not merely to expand the volume of manufacturing and trade, but also to bring more money into the treasury of the king, which would enable him to build fleets, equip armies, and make his government feared and respected throughout the world. Because of this close association with the ambitions of princes to increase their own power and the power of the states over which they ruled, mercantilism has sometimes been called *statism*. Certainly the system would never have come into existence had it not been for the growth of absolute monarchy in place of the weak, decentralized structure of feudalism. But kings alone did not create it. Naturally the new magnates of business lent support, since they would obviously derive great advantages from active encouragement of trade by the state. The heyday of mercantilism was the period between 1600 and 1700, but many of its features survived until the end of the eighteenth century.

If there was any one principle which held the central place in mercantilist theory, it was the doctrine of bullionism. This doctrine means that the prosperity of a nation is determined by the quantity of precious metals within its borders. The greater the amount of gold and silver a country contains, the more money the government can collect in taxes, and the richer and more powerful the state will become. But what of those countries that owned no bullion-producing colonies? How were *they* to achieve riches and power? For these questions the mercantilists had a ready answer. A nation without access to gold and silver directly should attempt to increase its trade with the rest of the world. If its government took steps to ensure that the value of exports would always exceed the value of imports, more gold and silver would come into the country than would have to be shipped out. This was called maintaining a "favorable balance of trade." To preserve this balance, three main devices would be necessary: first, high tariffs to reduce the general level of imports and to shut out some products entirely; second, bounties on exports; and third, extensive encouragement of manufactures in order that the nation might have as many goods to sell abroad as possible.

The theory of mercantilism also included certain elements of economic nationalism, paternalism, and imperialism. By the first is meant the ideal of a self-sufficient nation. The policy of fostering new industries was not intended merely as a device for increasing exports, but also as a means of making the nation independent of foreign supplies. In similar fashion, the mercantilists argued that the government should exercise the functions of a watchful guardian over the lives of its citizens. Relief should be provided for the poor, including free medical attention if they were unable to pay for it. These things were

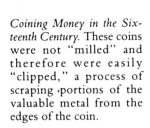

Coining Money in the Sixteenth Century. These coins were not "milled" and therefore were easily "clipped," a process of scraping portions of the valuable metal from the edges of the coin.

to be done, however, not with any view to charity or justice, but mainly in order that the state might rest upon a secure economic foundation and have the support of a numerous and healthy citizenry in case of war. Finally, the mercantilists advocated the acquisition of colonies. Again, the primary purpose was not to benefit individual citizens of the mother country, but to make the nation strong and independent. The types of possessions most ardently desired were those that would enlarge the nation's hoard of bullion. If these could not be obtained, then colonies providing tropical products, naval stores, or any other commodities which the mother country could not produce would be acceptable. The theory which underlay this imperialism was the notion that colonies existed for the benefit of the state that owned them. For this reason they were not allowed to engage in manufacturing or shipping. Their function was to produce raw materials and to consume as large a proportion of manufactured products as possible. In this way they would infuse lifeblood into the industries of the mother country and thus give it an advantage in the struggle for world trade.

*The defenders of
mercantilism*

The majority of those who wrote on mercantilist theory were philosophers and men of action in the world of business. Among the former were such advocates of political absolutism as the Frenchman Jean Bodin (1530–1596) and the Englishman Thomas Hobbes (1588–1679), who were naturally disposed to favor any policy that would increase the wealth and power of the ruler. While most of the apologists for mercantilism were interested in it mainly as a device for promoting a favorable balance of trade, others conceived it as a species of paternalism for increasing prosperity within the country. Some, for example, advocated a policy somewhat similar to contemporary ideas of government spending, by recommending that the state should appropriate a huge fund for the relief of the poor and for the construction of public works as a means of stimulating business.

*Mercantilism in practice:
in Spain and in England*

Attempts to put various mercantilist doctrines into practice characterized the history of many of the nations of western Europe in the sixteenth and seventeenth centuries. The theories, however, were not universally applied. Spain, of course, had the initial advantage by reason of the flow of bullion from its American empire. And while the Spaniards did not need to resort to artificial devices in order to bring money into their country, their government nevertheless maintained a rigid control over commerce and industry. The policies of other nations were designed to make up for the lack of bullion-producing colonies by capturing a larger share of export trade. This naturally involved a program of bounties, tariffs, and extensive regulation of manufacturing and shipping. Mercantilist policies were largely adopted in England during the reign of Queen Elizabeth I and were continued by the Stuart monarchs and by Oliver Cromwell. Most of these rulers engaged in a furious scramble for colonies, bestowed monopolistic privileges upon trading companies, and sought in a wide variety of ways to control the economic activities of their citizens. The most interesting examples of mercantilist legislation in England were, first, the Elizabethan laws designed to eliminate idleness and stimulate production and, second, the Navigation Acts. By a series of laws enacted toward the end of the sixteenth century, Queen Elizabeth gave to the justices of the peace the authority to fix prices, regulate hours of labor, and compel every able-bodied citizen to work at some useful trade. The first of the Navigation Acts was passed in 1651 under Oliver Cromwell. With the aim of destroying Dutch predominance in the carrying trade, it required that all colonial exports to the mother country should be carried in English ships. A second Navigation Act was passed in 1660, which provided not merely that colonial exports should be shipped in British vessels but prohibited the sending of certain "enumerated articles," especially tobacco and sugar, directly to continental European ports. They were to be sent first of all to England, whence, after the payment of customs duties, they could be reshipped elsewhere. Both of these laws were based upon the principle that colonies should serve for the enrichment of the mother country.

The Germanic states during the Commercial Revolution were too completely occupied with internal problems to take an active part in the struggle for colonies and overseas trade. As a consequence, German mercantilism was concerned primarily with increasing the strength of the state from within. It partook of the dual character of economic nationalism and a program for a planned society. But, of course, the planning was done chiefly for the benefit of the government and only incidentally for that of the people as a whole. Because of their dominant purpose of increasing the revenues of the state, the German mercantilists are known as cameralists (from *Kammer,* a name given to the royal treasury). Most of them were lawyers and professors of finance. Cameralist ideas were put into practice by the Hohenzollern kings of Prussia, notably by Frederick William I (1713–1740) and Frederick the Great (1740–1786). The policies of these monarchs embraced a many-sided scheme of intervention and control in the economic sphere for the purpose of increasing taxable wealth and bolstering the power of the state. Marshes were drained, canals dug, new industries established with the aid of the government, and farmers instructed as to what crops they should plant. In order that the nation might become self-sufficient as soon as possible, exports of raw materials and imports of manufactured products were prohibited. The bulk of the revenues gained from these various policies went for military purposes. The standing army of Prussia was increased by Frederick the Great to 160,000 men.

The most thorough, if not the most deliberate, application of mercantilism was probably to be found in France during the reign of Louis XIV (1643–1715). This was due partly to the fact that the French

Mercantilism in Germany: the cameralists

Jean Baptiste Colbert

*French mercantilism under
Colbert*

state was the fullest incarnation of absolutism and partly to the policies of Jean Baptiste Colbert, chief minister under Louis from 1661 until his death in 1683. Colbert was no theorist but rather a practical politician, ambitious for personal power and intent upon magnifying the opportunities for wealth of the middle class, to which he belonged. He accepted mercantilism, not as an end in itself, but simply as a convenient means for increasing the wealth and power of the state and thereby gaining the approval of his sovereign. He firmly believed that France must acquire as large an amount of the precious metals as possible. To this end he prohibited the export of money, levied high tariffs on foreign manufactures, and gave liberal bounties to encourage French shipping. It was largely for this purpose also that Colbert fostered imperialism, hoping to increase the favorable balance of trade through the sale of manufactured goods to the colonies. Accordingly, he purchased islands in the West Indies, encouraged settlements in Canada and Louisiana, and established trading posts in India and Africa. Furthermore, he was as devoted to the ideal of self-sufficiency as any of the cameralists in Prussia. He gave subsidies to new enterprises, established a number of state-owned industries, and even had the government purchase goods which were not really needed in order to keep struggling companies on their feet. But he was determined to keep the manufacturing industry under strict control, so as to make sure that companies would buy their raw materials only from French or colonial sources and produce the commodities necessary for national greatness. Consequently, he clamped upon industry an elaborate set of regulations prescribing nearly every detail of the manufacturing process. Finally, it should be mentioned that Colbert took a number of steps to augment the political strength of the nation directly. He provided France with a navy of nearly 300 ships, drafting citizens from the maritime provinces and even criminals to man them. He sought to promote a rapid growth of population by discouraging young people from becoming monks or nuns and by exempting families with ten or more children from taxation.

4. THE RESULTS OF THE COMMERCIAL REVOLUTION

*The foundation for
modern capitalism*

It goes without saying that the Commercial Revolution was one of the most significant developments in the history of the Western world. The whole pattern of modern economic life would have been impossible without it, for it changed the basis of commerce from the local and regional plane of the Middle Ages to the worldwide scale it has occupied ever since. Moreover, it exalted the power of money, inaugurated business for profit, sanctified the accumulation of wealth, and established competitive enterprise as the foundation of production and trade. In short, the Commercial Revolution was responsible for a large number of the elements that go to make up the capitalist regime.

But these were not the only results. The Commercial Revolution brought into being wide fluctuations of economic activity. What we now call booms and recessions alternated with startling rapidity. The inflow of precious metals, combined with a rise in population, led to rising prices and an unprecedented demand for goods. Businessmen were tempted to expand their enterprises too rapidly; bankers extended credit so liberally that their principal borrowers, especially nobles, often defaulted on loans. Spain and Italy were among the first to suffer setbacks. In both, failure of wages to keep pace with rising prices brought incredible hardships to the lower classes. Impoverishment was rife in the cities, and bandits flourished in the rural areas. In Spain, some ruined aristocrats were not too proud to join the throngs of vagrants who wandered from city to city. At the end of the fifteenth century the great Florentine bank of the Medici closed its doors. The middle of the century that followed saw numerous bankruptcies in Spain and the decline of the Fuggers in Germany. Meanwhile, England, Holland, and to some extent France, waxed prosperous. This prosperity was especially characteristic of the "age of silver," which lasted from about 1540 to 1620. In the seventeenth century decline set in once more after inflation had spent its force, and as a consequence of religious and international wars and civil strife.

Booms and recessions

The alternation of booms and recessions was followed by outbreaks of feverish speculation. These reached their climax early in the eighteenth century. The most notorious were the South Sea Bubble and the Mississippi Bubble. The former was the result of inflation of the stock of the South Sea Company in England. The promoters of this company agreed to take over a large part of the national debt and in return received from the English government an exclusive right to trade with South America and the Pacific islands. The prospects for profit seemed almost unlimited. The stock of the company rose rapidly in value until it was selling for more than ten times its original price. The higher it rose, the more gullible the public became. But gradually suspicion developed that the possibilities of the enterprise had been overrated. Buoyant hopes gave way to fears, and investors made frantic attempts to dispose of their shares for whatever they would bring. A crash which came in 1720 was the inevitable result.

The South Sea Bubble

During the years when the South Sea Bubble was being inflated in England, the French were going through a similar wave of speculative madness. In 1715 a Scotsman by the name of John Law, who had been compelled to flee from British soil for killing his rival in a love intrigue, settled in Paris, after various successful gambling adventures in other cities. He persuaded the regent of France to adopt his scheme for paying off the national debt through the issuance of paper money and to grant him the privilege of organizing the Mississippi Company for the colonization and exploitation of Louisiana. As the government loans were redeemed, the people who received the money were encouraged to buy stock in the company. Soon the shares began to soar,

The Mississippi Bubble

ultimately reaching a price forty times their original value. Nearly eve-ryone who could scrape together a bit of surplus cash rushed forward to participate in the scramble for riches. Stories were told of butchers and tailors who were supposed to have become millionaires by buying a few shares and holding them for a rise in price. But as the realization grew that the company would never be able to pay more than a nom-inal dividend on the stock at its inflated value, the more cautious in-vestors began selling their holdings. The alarm spread, and soon all were as anxious to sell as they had been to buy. In 1720 the Mississippi Bubble burst in a wild panic. Thousands of people who had sold good property to buy the shares at fantastic prices were ruined. The collapse of the South Sea and Mississippi companies gave a temporary chill to the public ardor for speculation. It was not long, however, until the appetite for speculative profits revived, and the stock-buying waves that followed in the wake of the Commercial Revolution were re-peated many times over during the nineteenth and twentieth cen-turies.

*The rise of a new class
and the Europeanization
of the world*

Among other results of the Commercial Revolution were the rise of the middle class to economic power, the beginning of Europeaniza-tion of the world, and the revival of slavery. Each of these requires brief comment. By the end of the seventeenth century the middle class had become an influential group in nearly every country of western Europe. Its ranks included the merchants, the bankers, the shipown-ers, the principal investors, and the industrial entrepreneurs. Their rise to power was mainly the result of increasing wealth and their ten-dency to ally themselves with the king against the aristocracy. But as yet their power was purely economic. Not until the nineteenth cen-tury did middle-class supremacy in politics become a reality. By the Europeanization of the world is meant the transplanting of European manners and culture in other continents. As a result of the work of traders, missionaries, and colonists, North and South America were rapidly stamped with the character of appendages of Europe. No more than a beginning was made in the transformation of Asia, but enough was done to foreshadow the trend of later times when even Japanese and Chinese would adopt Western locomotives and shell-rimmed spectacles.

Slavery

The most tragic, and humanly reprehensible, result of the Com-mercial Revolution was the revival of slavery—i.e., the buying and selling of human beings for forced labor and profit. Slavery had prac-tically disappeared from European civilization around the year 1000. But the development of mining and plantation farming in the English, Spanish, and Portuguese colonies led to a tremendous demand for unskilled labor. At first the colonizers attempted to enslave Native Americans, but they usually proved too susceptible to European infec-tious diseases. The need was filled in the sixteenth century, and another "commodity" added to the system of colonial trade, by the importation of Africans. From then until the nineteenth century, slavery was an integral part of the European colonial system, especially in those regions producing tropical agricultural products: e.g., sugar cane, tobacco, and, after about 1780, cotton.

Finally, the Commercial Revolution was exceedingly important in preparing the way for the Industrial Revolution. This was true for a number of reasons. First, the Commercial Revolution created a class of capitalists who were constantly seeking new opportunities to invest their surplus profits. Second, the mercantilist policy, with its emphasis upon protection for infant industries and production of goods for export, gave a powerful stimulus to the growth of manufactures. Third, the founding of colonial empires flooded Europe with new raw materials and greatly increased the supply of certain products which had hitherto been luxuries. Most of these required fabrication before they were available for consumption. As a consequence, new industries sprang up wholly independent of any guild regulations that still survived. The outstanding example was the manufacture of cotton textiles, which, significantly enough, was one of the first of the industries to become mechanized. Last of all, the Commercial Revolution was marked by a trend toward the adoption of factory methods in certain lines of production, together with technological improvements, such as the discovery of more efficient processes of refining ores. Thus the Commercial Revolution led inevitably to the Industrial Revolution, as we shall see.

Effects of the Commercial Revolution in preparing the way for the Industrial Revolution

5. REVOLUTIONARY DEVELOPMENTS IN AGRICULTURE

In the late seventeenth century and, above all, in the eighteenth century, sweeping changes occurred in European agriculture that may be regarded in part as effects of the Commercial Revolution. The rise in prices and increase in urban population brought about by commercial developments made agriculture an ever more profitable business and thus tended to stimulate agricultural improvements. In addition, one effect of overseas expansion was to familiarize Europeans with important new crops, above all, Indian corn and potatoes, which they could raise at home. But probably the most important influence of the Commercial Revolution on agricultural history was the triumph of the capitalist mentality. Landlords who had hitherto let peasants farm their lands inefficiently, now followed the model of businessmen in seeking a maximum of efficiency and profits. So long as these landlords were prepared to be ruthless, there were many revolutionary changes that they were able to bring about.

The countries that led the way in agricultural advance were Holland and England, no doubt largely because these countries had already

Relations between the Commercial Revolution and changes in agriculture

*Agricultural developments
in England*

participated to the fullest in the Commercial Revolution. Since England was able to advance rapidly beyond Holland, owing to its greater size and natural resources, we may limit our remarks here to English developments. It will be recalled from Chapter 11 that the typical medieval agricultural regime was one in which groups of peasants collectively cultivated long and narrow unfenced strips of land. Of those, one-third would lie fallow in any given year in order to restore fertility. Other neighboring lands would be given over to pastures and meadows for the grazing of collectively owned peasant herds. Most often, the actual ownership of all these lands was ill-defined or almost randomly parceled out; usually, however, there would be a prominent landlord in each area who could lay claim to owning a large percentage of the land even though peasants farmed it for him. The same individual might also claim legal title to the pastures and meadows. In England most of these landlords decided to "enclose" their lands in order to make them more profitable.

Enclosure in England

The earliest "enclosures" in England took place in the fifteenth and sixteenth centuries and entailed the conversion of lands into fenced-off sheep meadows. Because of the great profits to be accrued from wool, some landlords decided to convert common pastures that hitherto had supported peasant livestock into their own preserves for sheep-raising. Sometimes they also succeeded in converting grain fields into sheep pastures by evicting peasants whose leaseholds were none too secure. This caused grave hardships for the peasants concerned. As Thomas More wrote in his *Utopia* (1516) "sheep that used to be so meek and eat so little now are becoming so greedy and wild that they devour men themselves . . . for they leave no land free for the plough." The humanitarian More, however, was exaggerating somewhat. In fact, no more than about 3 percent of arable land had been enclosed before 1525 and part of that was not for sheep pasturage.

Scientific farming

The really dramatic enclosure movement in England took place between 1710 and 1810 and aimed not to free land for sheep but to increase the efficiency of crop-raising. In this period landlords became convinced of the necessity for "scientific farming." Above all, they realized that by introducing new crops and farming methods they could reduce the amount of fallow lands and bring in higher yields. Some of the important new crops with which they experimented were clover, alfalfa, and related varieties of leguminous plants. These reduced fertility much less than cereal grains and actually helped to improve the quality of the soil by gathering nitrogen and making the ground more porous. Another new crop that had a similar effect was the turnip. The greatest propagandist for the planting of this unattractive vegetable was Viscount Charles Townshend (1674–1738), a prominent aristocrat and politician, who toward the end of his life left the royal court to experiment with agriculture. In this he became a model for subsequent aristocratic interest in scientific farming. Townshend gained the nickname of "Turnip" Townshend because he was so dedicated to converting people to the use of the turnip in new crop rotation systems.

Clover, alfalfa, and turnips not only helped in doing away with the fallow but they provided excellent winter food for animals, thereby aiding the production of more and better livestock. And more livestock also meant more manure. Accordingly, intensive manuring became another way in which scientific farmers could eliminate the need for letting land lie fallow. Other improvements in farming methods introduced in the period were more intensive hoeing and weeding, and the use of the seed drill for planting grain. The latter eliminated the old wasteful method of sowing grain broadcast by hand, most of it remaining on top to be eaten by birds.

A Ball-and-Chain Pump. Men walking in the treadmill at the left powered this mid–sixteenth-century irrigation device.

Scientific farming dictated the necessity of enclosures because the "improving" landlord needed flexibility to experiment as he wished. He simply could not try to plant one narrow open strip with turnips while peasants were continuing to rotate all the contiguous areas on the basis of the age-old three-field system. Instead, it was necessary for him to have fenced-off compact plots to leave no doubt as to which territory was his own, to maximize efficiency in experimentation, and to keep away stray grazing animals. It must also be added that when the enclosure movement gathered momentum, landlords were not above using the principle of reorganizing and enclosing territories to gain new lands from the peasantry that hitherto had in no way belonged to them. In all this they had the government on their side. Parliament stopped trying to prohibit enclosures in 1640 and actually started directing them in 1710. Thereafter, throughout the eighteenth century, parliamentary "acts of enclosure" provided that all the lands of a given village be completely redistributed into compact, fenced parcels, with the leading landlords of an area gaining far and away the most land. (Parliament did this because it was dominated by the landowning aristocracy.) The result was that many peasants were driven off the land but also that productivity soared. In eighteenth-century England wheat production, for example, increased by one-third, and the average weight of livestock doubled. All told, the increased abundance and concentration of wealth brought about by the agricultural revolution and enclosure movement was a necessary prerequisite for the Industrial Revolution that began in England around 1780.

Consolidation of holdings

On the continent of Europe, aside from the minor exception of Holland, there was nothing comparable to the English advance in scientific farming. In most parts of the Continent agricultural change transpired more slowly and the real breakthrough in scientific methods came only in the nineteenth, or in some places the twentieth century. But the eighteenth century was nonetheless an important epoch in continental agriculture from the point of view of the introduction of new crops. Most important was the cultivation of maize

New Crops

Interior of a French Peasant's Cottage, Seventeenth Century. Virtually all activities centered about the hearth, the only source of heat for the entire dwelling.

(Indian corn) and the potato, both introduced from the New World. Since maize can only be grown in areas with substantial periods of sunny and dry weather, it was not planted in north Atlantic regions of Europe, but in the seventeenth and eighteenth centuries its cultivation spread through Italy and the southeastern part of the Continent. Its enormous attraction was that whereas an average ear of grain would yield only about four seeds for every one planted, an ear of maize would yield about seventy or eighty. That made it a "miracle" crop, filling granaries where they had been almost empty before. The potato was an equally miraculous innovation for the European north. Its great advantages were numerous: one was that potatoes could be grown on the poorest, sandiest, or wettest of lands where nothing else could be raised; another was that they could be fitted into the smallest of patches. Raising potatoes even on small patches was profitable because the yield of potatoes was extraordinarily abundant. Finally, the potato was an excellent food for the human diet: it is rich in calories, has many vitamins and minerals, and contains some protein as well. At first northern European peasants resisted growing potatoes because the plant is not mentioned in the Bible, but in the course of the eighteenth century they became accustomed to it, sometimes after considerable governmental pressure. Frederick the Great of Prussia at first practically forced potatoes down his peasants' throats, but soon the crop became a staple there and in the rest of northern Germany. By about 1800 the average northern German peasant family would be eating potatoes as a main course at least once a day. In the same period the potato was also introduced into Ireland and England: as late as the 1960s an English playwright could entitle his play about the lower classes *Chips* [i.e., fried potatoes] *with Everything.*

Probably the single most noteworthy fact about the economic history of the European continent in the eighteenth century was that poor people gradually stopped dying from famine. Until about 1700 about half of all European peasants could expect to see someone in their immediate family die from starvation about once every ten years. Often when periodic famines came whole families would be decimated. But the introduction of new crops like maize and the potato helped change all this. The result was that population began to soar as never before and that labor was ultimately freed for industrialization. At last, people in Europe were literally learning that they did not have to live by bread alone.

End of famine

6. THE NEW SOCIETY

Profound changes in the texture of society inevitably accompany economic revolutions. The society which was brought into being by the Commercial Revolution, though retaining characteristics of the Middle Ages, was markedly different in certain features. For one thing the population of Europe was becoming considerably larger. All told, the European population in 1500 is estimated to have numbered about 80 million; by 1800 it had more than doubled, to reach about 190 million. In 1378 London had a population of about 50,000; by 1600 the total had reached more than 200,000; and by 1800 more than 1 million! The reasons for these increases are closely related to the religious and economic developments of the time. In northern Protestant countries the overthrow of clerical celibacy and the encouragement of marriage were factors partly responsible. But far more important was the increase in means of subsistence brought about by the Commercial Rev-

Population growth

A Peasants' Meal by Louis Le Nain. This French painting of 1642 shows that the chief item of consumption was still bread and that grown men were often so poor that they had to go barefoot.

olution and agricultural improvements. Not only were new products, such as potatoes, maize, and tomatoes added to the food supply, but older commodities, especially sugar and rice, were now made available to Europeans in larger quantities.

Increased urbanization

As the figures for London suggest, Europe was becoming not just more populous but also more heavily urbanized. In 1500 there were only three cities in Europe—excluding Turkish Istanbul—with populations of more than 100,000; in 1800 there were twenty-two. Certainly the growth of new opportunities for earning a living in commerce and industry enabled most countries to support a larger population; it is significant that the bulk of these increases occurred in cities and towns. Nonetheless, the extent of urbanization before 1800 should not be exaggerated. In the seventeenth century 70 to 80 percent of all laborers were still agricultural workers; and most industrial labor remained handicraft labor. As one historian, R. S. Dunn, has observed, *"manufacture* still retained its Latin meaning: to make by hand." Even as late as 1800 most industries were centered around small shops, not mechanized factories. Although cities and towns had grown in size, only 3 percent of the European population lived in large cities of over 100,000 people. In short, the Industrial Revolution was only just beginning and the triumph of modern urbanism was yet to come.

The middle class

Just as urbanism had not yet fully triumphed, neither had the social status of the middle class. Historians used to talk of an ever "rising" middle class, but they now realize that this trend is too easily exaggerated. Without doubt, throughout most of the period there were great opportunities for ambitious and talented merchants to pile up fortunes and thereby climb some of the higher rungs of the social ladder. Yet merchants were never as respected as aristocrats: the French playwright Molière (1622–1673) for example, ridiculed "the bourgeois gentleman"—a rich merchant who clumsily tried to ape the ways of his "betters." Some of the professions, it is true, gained more wealth and dignity than they had enjoyed in the Middle Ages. Specifically, the artist, the writer, the lawyer, the university professor, and the physician emerged into positions of importance roughly comparable to what they now hold in modern society. But in general the age was by no means one of economic or social leveling. Indeed the aristocracy, which gained most of its livelihood from land, was as much economically and socially entrenched towards the end of the period as it was at the beginning.

Lack of compassion

The new egoism that characterized the middle and upper classes stood as a barrier to more generous treatment of the least fortunate human beings. Hearing a disturbance outside his quarters, the Emperor Charles V, in 1552, was reported to have asked who were causing the commotion. When told that they were poor soldiers, he said, "Let them die," and compared them to caterpillars, locusts, and june-

Slaves Being Ordered into the Hold of a Ship. Thousands of slaves died in the holds of ships during the long voyage to the Americas. Sympathetic but stylized illustrations such as this were designed to move the newspaper-reading public in the eighteenth century.

bugs that eat the good things of the earth. As a rule, the most pitiable fate was reserved for slaves and serfs. For the sake of big profits, blacks were hunted on the coast of Africa, captured and imprisoned in dungeons called "holding pens," and shipped to the American colonies. It may be of interest to note that one of the earliest Englishmen who engaged in this body-snatching business, Captain John Hawkins, called the ship in which he transported the victims the *Jesus*.

While black slaves were seldom employed in Europe proper, native Europeans were pitiably exploited as serfs. The institution of serfdom had died out in western Europe during the later Middle Ages, but after about 1600 it was revived and gained strength in those parts of Europe east of the Elbe river. There the desire for profit in agriculture and the collusion of the state with the aristocracy led to the growth of the "second serfdom"—a serf system much stronger than ever before. In East Prussia serfs often had to work from three to six days a week for their lord, and some had only late evening or night hours to cultivate their own lands. Worse, in Russia landlords had the power of life and death over their serfs and could sell them apart from the land and even apart from their families.

The second serfdom

Putting aside the plight of eastern European serfs, the eighteenth century did witness definite improvements in the living conditions of most Europeans. We have already seen that new items in the diet helped eliminate famine. Otherwise the poor stayed about as wretched as they had always been—the triumph over epidemic diseases like smallpox and malaria for the most part came about only in the nineteenth century—but there were improvements in the standard of living of the middle and upper classes. This is evidenced by the increasing per capita consumption of sugar, chocolate, coffee, and tea, which were not merely substituted for other foods and beverages but were additions to the average diet. The growing demand for linen and cot-

Changes in the standard of living

Effects of the coffee and tobacco habits

ton cloth, and for such articles of luxury as mahogany furniture designed by such masters as Chippendale, Hepplewhite, and Sheraton, may be taken as a further indication of rising prosperity.

The widespread adoption of the tobacco and coffee habits in the seventeenth and eighteenth centuries had interesting social and perhaps physiological effects. Although the tobacco plant was brought into Europe by the Spaniards about fifty years after the discovery of America, another half-century passed before many Europeans adopted the practice of smoking. At first the plant was believed to possess miraculous healing powers and was referred to as "divine tobacco" and "our holy herb nicotian." (The word nicotine is derived from Jean Nicot, the French ambassador to Portugal who brought the tobacco plant into France.) The habit of smoking was popularized by English explorers, especially by Sir Walter Raleigh, who had learned it from the Indians of Virginia. It spread rapidly through all classes of European society despite the condemnation of the clergy and the "counterblaste" of James I against it. The enormous popularity of coffee-drinking in the seventeenth century had even more important social effects. Coffee houses or "cafés" sprang up all over Europe and rapidly evolved into leading institutions. They provided not merely an escape for the majority of men from a cribbed and monotonous home life, but they took others away from the excesses of the tavern and the gambling den. In addition, they fostered a sharpening of wits and promoted more polished manners, especially inasmuch as they became favorite meeting places for the literary lions of the time. If we can believe the testimony of English historians, there was scarcely a social or political enterprise which did not have its intimate connections with the establishments where coffee was sold.

The coexistence of genteel coffee houses with the rise of slavery reflects the fact that the Commercial Revolution was founded on the pursuit of self-interest and maintained by indifference to intense human suffering. Nonetheless, the economic advances achieved by the Commercial Revolution did bring great benefits to many and would lead to still greater economic advances in subsequent ages.

SELECTED READINGS

- *Items so designated are available in paperback editions.*
- Braudel, F., *Capitalism and Material Life, 1400–1800,* London, 1973. A fascinating review of evidence pertaining to the entire world by one of the greatest of living historians.
- ———, *The Mediterranean and the Mediterranean World in the Age of Philip II,* New York, 1972. One of the most important and brilliant history

books of our age. Treats life in the Mediterranean regions in the second half of the sixteenth century with particular emphasis on how geography determines the course of human history.

- Burke, Peter, *Popular Culture in Early Modern Europe,* London, 1978. Synthesizes the most recent work on the period between 1500 and 1800. Fascinating.

  Chambers, J. D., and G. E. Mingay, *The Agricultural Revolution, 1750–1880,* London, 1966. Now the standard work.

- Cipolla, C. M., *Before the Industrial Revolution: European Society and Economy, 1000–1700,* 2nd ed. New York, 1980. Wide-ranging and full of deft observations.

- Davis, Natalie Z., *Society and Culture in Early Modern France,* Stanford, Calif. 1975. Eight scintillating essays by a pioneer in the use of anthropological methods for the study of early modern European history.

- Goubert, P., *The Ancien Régime: French Society, 1600–1750,* London, 1973. Particularly strong in its descriptions of rural life. Includes selections from illuminating documents.

- Hale, J. R., *Renaissance Exploration,* New York, 1968. A magnificent short introduction.

  Heckscher, E., *Mercantilism,* rev. ed., London, 1955. The most influential, but controversial, work on the subject.

- Hill, Christopher, *Reformation to Industrial Revolution* (The Pelican Economic History of Britain, vol. 2), rev. ed., Baltimore, 1969. Comprehensive.

  Hufton, O. W., *The Poor of Eighteenth-Century France,* New York, 1974.

  Kamen, Henry, *The Iron Century: Social Change in Europe, 1550–1660,* New York, 1971. Supports the recent view that there was an economic crisis in this period that interrupted preceding and succeeding periods of prosperity.

- Laslett, Peter, *The World We Have Lost: England Before the Industrial Age,* 2nd ed., New York, 1971. A very readable introduction to preindustrial social history, but controversial in parts.

- Mandrou, R., *Introduction to Modern France, 1500–1640: An Essay in Historical Psychology,* London, 1975. Assumes some prior knowledge of French history and culture, but full of fascinating information about daily life.

  Minchinton, W. E., ed., *Mercantilism: System or Expediency?* Lexington, Mass., 1969. A collection of readings that provides a valuable corrective to Heckscher.

- Morison, S. E., *Christopher Columbus, Mariner,* New York, 1955. A good shorter version of this master storyteller's definitive *Admiral of the Ocean Sea* (1942).

- Parry, J. H., *The Age of Reconnaissance,* London, 1963. The best history of the discoveries that emphasizes the details of shipbuilding and navigation.

- Penrose, B., *Travel and Discovery in the Renaissance,* Cambridge, Mass., 1952. Engrossing.

- de Roover, R., *The Rise and Decline of the Medici Bank, 1397–1494,* Cambridge, Mass., 1963. Authoritative, often very technical.

  Rudé, George, *Hanoverian London, 1714–1808,* Berkeley, Calif. 1971.

SOURCE MATERIALS

Barnett, G. E., ed., *Two Tracts by Gregory King,* Baltimore, 1936. An introduction to the work of the modern world's first real statistician.

Mun, Thomas, *England's Treasure by Foreign Trade,* Oxford, 1928. (Reprint of the original edition of 1664.) A vigorous early argument in favor of the balance of trade.

Parry, J. H., *The European Reconnaissance: Selected Documents,* New York, 1968.

Young, Arthur, *Travels in France During the Years 1787, 1788, 1789,* London, 1912. Vivid observations by an English traveler.

Chapter 17

THE AGE OF ABSOLUTISM
(c. 1500–1789)

There are four essential characteristics or qualities of royal authority.
First, royal authority is sacred.
Second, it is paternal.
Third, it is absolute.
Fourth, it is subject to reason.

—Jacques Bossuet, *Politics Drawn from the
Very Words of Holy Scripture*

I t now becomes necessary to go back and attempt to analyze the
major political developments which accompanied the birth of
modern civilization. During the fourteenth and fifteenth centuries
the power of the medieval national monarchies had been gradually
tested by the upheavals of the later Middle Ages. But, as we saw in
Chapter 13, monarchical power was ultimately not found wanting. In
the last quarter of the fifteenth century strong monarchs in the leading
states of western Europe—England, France, and Spain—overcame
threats of fragmentation and started to make royal power stronger
than ever. Thereafter most of Europe experienced the fullest flower-
ing of royal "absolutism," or untrammeled monarchy. The age of
absolutism lasted in England until the middle of the seventeenth century, in France until 1789, and elsewhere on the European continent
into the nineteenth century. There were several reasons why absolutism predominated in the period after 1500. One was that new wealth
helped monarchs to pay for expanding bureaucracies and new departments of government, above all departments that directed military organization and the conduct of foreign policy. Another was that international warfare lasted throughout most of the period, and warfare
tended to strengthen the power of the state because it allowed monarchs to maintain standing armies that could enforce peace at home as
well as abroad. Finally, the Protestant Revolution contributed consid-

The age of absolutism

erably to the growth of royal omnipotence. It broke the unity of the Christian Church, abolished papal overlordship over secular rulers, fostered nationalism, revived the doctrine of the Apostle Paul that "the powers that be are ordained of God," and encouraged the rulers of northern Europe to extend their authority over religious as well as over civil affairs.

Character of absolute monarchy

Although government was certainly becoming stronger than ever, it is well not to confuse early modern western European absolutism with either despotism or totalitarianism. Western European kings were not really despots because no matter how strong they were they seldom ruled arbitrarily like Oriental pharaohs or caliphs. Owing to the strength of their aristocracies and merchant classes they could not whimsically issue decrees to be carried out by a few henchmen; instead they usually had to justify their policies to hundreds or even thousands before they could be implemented. Moreover, absolute monarchs usually respected due process of law and broke with traditions only in exceptional circumstances. Even less were the absolute monarchs similar to modern dictators. Quite obviously, before the nineteenth and twentieth centuries the state could not interfere very efficiently in the lives of its citizens; it lacked mechanized transportation and communications systems, as well as radio, film, and television for propaganda, and sophisticated instruments of terror. Throughout the period of royal absolutism there were hardly even any policemen. Today most of us fear that the state will become too strong—if it has not already—but between 1500 and 1789 in western Europe it was still only distantly shaping the lives of its subjects.

1. THE GROWTH AND DEFEAT OF ABSOLUTE MONARCHY IN ENGLAND

Reasons for defeat in England

England was the only European country in which absolutism was defeated before 1789. The reasons for this were political, economic, and religious. As we have seen, the principle of consent to royal decision-making was stronger in medieval England than elsewhere. Only in England did a body like Parliament emerge from the Middle Ages to stand as a potential barrier to absolutism. Throughout the sixteenth century, the English Crown knew how to use Parliament to serve its own interests, but in the seventeenth century royal personalities and policies began to provoke parliamentary resistance. When that happened, the economic strength of many members of the parliamentary opposition, which had been brought about by England's major participation in the Commercial Revolution, greatly aided them in fighting and finally defeating the monarchy. The major immediate cause of the revolt against royal absolutism was religious. Radical Protestants strongly objected to royal religious policy and ultimately made their objections a cause for civil war.

Before that happened, it might have seemed that England was moving toward absolutism in the same fashion as the states of the Continent. The Tudor dynasty, initiated by Henry VII in 1485, had gained remarkable success in regulating the consciences of its subjects and in binding the nation to its will. It should be added that the most celebrated Tudors, Henry VIII (1509–1547) and Elizabeth I (1558–1603), gained some of their power through shrewdly maintaining a semblance of popular government. When they desired to enact measures of doubtful popularity, they regularly went through the formality of obtaining parliamentary approval. Or when they wanted more money, they manipulated procedure in such a way as to make the appropriations appear to be voluntary grants by the representatives of the people. But the legislative branch of the government under these sovereigns was little more than a rubber stamp. They limited parliamentary sessions to only three or four months of the year; they interfered with elections and packed the two houses with their own favorites; and they cajoled, flattered, or bullied the members as the case might require in order to obtain their support.

The Tudors

In 1603 Elizabeth I, the last of the Tudors, died, leaving no direct descendants. Her nearest relative was her cousin, James VI of Scotland, who now became the sovereign of both England and Scotland under the name of James I. His accession marked the beginning of the troubled history of the Stuarts, the second and last of the absolute dynasties in England. A curious mixture of stubbornness, vanity, and

The establishment of divine-right monarchy by James I

Queen Elizabeth I. Elizabeth, known to her admiring subjects as "Gloriana," is here depicted standing on a map of Britain.

James I. "The wisest fool in Christendom."

erudition, James was appropriately called by Henry IV of France "the wisest fool in Christendom." Though he loved to have his courtiers flatter him as the English Solomon, he did not even have sense enough to emulate his Tudor predecessors in being satisfied with the substance of absolute power; he insisted upon the theory as well. From France he appropriated the doctrine of the divine right of kings, contending that "as it is atheism and blasphemy to dispute what God can do, so it is presumption and high contempt in a subject to dispute what a king can do." Although he himself was most undignified in appearance and behavior, in his speech to Parliament in 1609 he declared that "kings are justly called gods, for they exercise a manner of resemblance of divine power upon earth."

That such ridiculous pretensions to divine authority would arouse opposition among the English people was a result which even James himself should have been able to foresee, for England still had traditions of liberty which could not be ignored. The ideal of limited government expressed in Magna Carta had never been entirely destroyed. Moreover, the policies of the new king were of such a character as to antagonize even some of his most conservative subjects. He insisted upon supplementing his income by modes of taxation which had never been sanctioned by Parliament; and when the leaders of that body remonstrated, he angrily tore up their protests and dissolved the two houses. He interfered with the freedom of business by granting monopolies and extravagant privileges to favored companies. He conducted foreign relations in disregard for the economic interests of some of the most powerful citizens. Ever since the days of the Elizabethan sea captains Sir John Hawkins and Sir Francis Drake, English merchants had been ambitious to destroy the commercial empire of Spain. They openly desired a renewal of the war, begun during Elizabeth's reign, for that purpose. But James made peace with Spain and entered into negotiations for marriage alliances favorable to Catholic sovereigns.

It was not marriage alliances alone that involved James in religious troubles. The Elizabethan Compromise, which brought the Reformation in England to a close, had not been satisfactory to the more radical Protestants. They believed that it did not depart widely enough from the forms and doctrines of the Roman Church. During the reign of Queen Mary many of them had been in exile in France and had come under the influence of Calvinism. When Elizabeth's compromise policy took shape, they denounced it as representing too great a concession to Catholicism. Gradually they came to be called Puritans from their desire to "purify" the Anglican Church of all traces of "popish" ritual and observances. In addition, they preached an ascetic morality and condemned the episcopal system of church government. However, they did not form a united group. One faction believed that it could transform the Anglican Church by working within that organization. The other preferred to withdraw from the Anglican fold and

AGE OF ABSOLUTISM

establish separate congregations where they could worship as they
pleased. The members of this latter group came to be designated Separatists. They achieved fame in American history as the so-called Pil-
grims, who founded Plymouth Colony.

Any brand or faction of Puritans was anathema to King James because he distrusted any religion that did not fit in with his own ideas of
relations between church and state. In his estimation the Puritans, by
repudiating the episcopal system of church government, were threatening to pull down one of the chief pillars of monarchy itself. Refusal
to submit to the authority of bishops appointed by the king was identical in his mind with disloyalty to the sovereign. For this reason he
regarded the Puritans as the equivalent of traitors and threatened to
"harry them out of the land." He showed little more wisdom in his
dealings with the Catholics. For the most part, he favored them,
though he could not resist the temptation to levy fines upon them
from time to time for violating the severe code which came down
from the Reformation. In 1605 a group of fanatical adherents of the
Roman faith organized the Gunpowder Plot. They planned to blow

*Relations with Puritans
and Catholics*

up the Parliament building while the king and the legislators were assembled in it, and, in the resulting confusion, seize control of the government. The plot was discovered, and Parliament enacted even more stringent laws against the Catholics. James, however, allowed the measures to go unenforced. Needless to say, his persistent leniency antagonized his Protestant subjects and made him more unpopular than ever.

Sir Edward Coke

From 1611 to 1621 James ruled virtually without Parliament. But this did not mean that his troubles were over. In 1613 the rights of the people found a new champion when Sir Edward Coke (pronounced Cook) was appointed chief justice. Coke was no democrat, but he did have a profound reverence for the common law and for the basic liberties inferred from Magna Carta. Moreover, he was a staunch defender of the privileged position of lawyers and judges. When the king insisted that he also had the faculty of reason and could interpret the law as well as the judges, Coke reminded him that he was not learned in the law, and that causes which concerned the lives and fortunes of his subjects were not to be decided by natural reason but only on the basis of long study and experience. Furthermore, the chief justice developed a rudimentary concept of judicial review. In the celebrated Dr. Bonham's case, he held that "when an act of Parliament is against common right and reason, or repugnant, or impossible to be performed, the common law will control it, and adjudge such act to be void." There is evidence that this opinion was highly regarded in colonial America, and that it was one of the factors which later gave rise to the idea that the Supreme Court of the United States has the authority to nullify laws of Congress which conflict with the Constitution.

The first of the Stuart kings died in 1625 and was succeeded by his son, Charles I (1625–1649). The new monarch was more regal in appearance than his father, but he held the same inflated notions of royal power. As a consequence, he was soon at odds with the Puritans and the leaders of the parliamentary opposition. As in the case of his father, religious tensions were exacerbated by questions of taxation. Soon after his accession to the throne Charles became involved in a war with France. His need for revenue was desperate. When Parliament refused to make more than the customary grants, he resorted to forced loans from his subjects, punishing those who failed to comply by quartering soldiers in their homes or throwing them into prison without a trial. The upshot of this tyranny was the Petition of Right, forced upon Charles by the leaders of Parliament in 1628. This document declared all taxes not voted by Parliament illegal. It condemned also the quartering of soldiers in private houses and prohibited arbitrary imprisonment and the establishment of martial law in time of peace.

Charles I. This portrait by Van Dyck vividly captures the ill-fated monarch's arrogance.

But acceptance of the Petition of Right did not end the conflict. Charles soon resumed his old practices of raising money by various irregular means. He revived obsolete feudal laws and collected fines from all who violated them. He compelled rich burghers to apply for knighthood and then charged them high fees for their titles. He sold monopolies at exorbitant rates and admonished his judges to increase the fines in criminal cases. But the most unpopular of all his expedients for raising revenue was his collection of ship money. Under an ancient custom the English seaboard towns had been required to contribute ships for the royal navy. Since the needs of the fleet were now provided for in other ways, Charles maintained that the towns should contribute money; and he proceeded to apply the new tax not merely to the coastal cities but to the inland counties as well. The levies of ship money were particularly irritating to the merchant class and served to crystallize the opposition of that group to monarchical tyranny. Many refused to pay, and the king's attorney general finally decided to prosecute. A wealthy squire by the name of John Hampden was haled into court in a test case. When convicted by a vote of seven to five, he acquired a sort of martyrdom. For years he was venerated by many as a symbol of resistance to royal autocracy.

The continued tyranny of Charles I

Like his blundering father before him, Charles also aroused the antagonism of the Calvinists. He appointed as archbishop of Canterbury a clergyman by the name of William Laud, whose sympathies were decidedly High Anglican. He outraged the Sabbatarianism of the Puritans by authorizing public games on Sunday. Worse still, he attempted to impose the episcopal system of church government upon the Scottish Presbyterians, who were radical Calvinists. The result was an armed rebellion by his northern subjects and the first step toward full-scale civil war.

Conflict with the Calvinists

In order to get money to punish the Scots for their resistance, Charles was finally compelled in 1640 to summon Parliament, after more than eleven years of autocratic rule. Knowing full well that the king was helpless without money, the leaders of the House of Commons determined to take the government of the country into their own hands. They abolished ship money and the special tribunals which had been used as agencies of tyranny. They impeached and sent to imprisonment in the Tower of London the king's chief subordinates, Archbishop Laud and the earl of Strafford. They enacted a law forbidding the monarch to dissolve Parliament and requiring sessions at least every three years. Charles replied to these acts by a show of force. He marched with his guard into the House of Commons and attempted to arrest five of its leaders. All of them escaped, but the issue was now sharply drawn between king and Parliament, and an open conflict could no longer be avoided. Both sides collected troops and prepared for an appeal to the sword.

The outbreak of civil war

These events ushered in a period of civil strife, which lasted from 1642 to 1649. It was a struggle at once political, economic, and religious. Arrayed on the side of the king were most of the chief nobles

Oliver Cromwell

and landowners, the Catholics, and the staunch Anglicans. The followers of Parliament included, in general, the small landholders, tradesmen, and manufacturers. The majority were Puritans and Presbyterians. The members of the king's party were commonly known by the aristocratic name of Cavaliers. Their opponents, who cut their hair short in contempt for the fashionable custom of wearing curls, were called in derision Roundheads. At first the party of the royalists, having obvious advantages of military experience, won most of the victories. In 1644, however, the parliamentary army was reorganized, and soon afterward the fortune of battle shifted. The Cavalier forces were badly beaten, and in 1646 the king was compelled to surrender. The struggle would now have ended had not a quarrel developed within the parliamentary party. The majority of its members, who were now Presbyterians, were ready to restore Charles to the throne as a limited monarch under an arrangement whereby the Presbyterian faith would be imposed upon England as the state religion. But a radical minority of Puritans, made up principally of Separatists but now more commonly known as Independents, distrusted Charles and insisted upon religious toleration for themselves and all other Protestants. Their leader was Oliver Cromwell (1599–1658), who had risen to command of the Roundhead army. Taking advantage of the dissension within the ranks of his opponents, Charles renewed the war in 1648, but after a brief campaign was forced to concede that his cause was hopeless.

The second defeat of the king gave an indisputable mastery of the situation to the Independents. Cromwell and his friends now resolved to put an end to "that man of blood," the Stuart monarch, and remodel the political system in accordance with their own desires. They conducted a purge of the legislative body by military force, ejecting 143 Presbyterians from the House of Commons; and then with the "Rump Parliament" that remained—numbering about 60 members—they proceeded to eliminate the monarchy. An act was passed redefining treason so as to apply to the offenses of the king. Next, a special High Court of Justice was established, and Charles was brought to trial before it. His conviction was a mere matter of form. On January 30, 1649, he was beheaded in front of his palace of Whitehall. A short time later the House of Lords was abolished, and England became an oligarchic republic. The first stage in the so-called Puritan Revolution was now completed.

The work of organizing the new state, which was given the name of the Commonwealth, was entirely in the hands of the Independents. Since the Rump Parliament continued as the legislative body, the really fundamental change was in the nature of the executive. In place of the king there was set up a Council of State composed of forty-one members. Cromwell, with the army at his back, soon came to dominate both of these bodies. However, as time went on he became exas-

Cromwell Felling the Royal Oak of England. A Royalist print of 1656 which portrays Oliver Cromwell as a destructive villain.

perated by the attempts of the legislators to perpetuate themselves in power and to profit from confiscation of the wealth of their opponents. Accordingly, in 1653, he marched a detachment of troops into the Rump and ordered the members to disperse. This action was followed by the establishment of a virtual dictatorship under a constitution drafted by officers of the army. Called the Instrument of Government, it was the nearest approach to a written constitution Britain has ever had. Extensive powers were given to Cromwell as Lord Protector for life, and his office was made hereditary. At first a Parliament exercised limited authority in making laws and levying taxes, but in 1655 its members were abruptly dismissed by the Lord Protector. Thereafter the government was but a thinly disguised autocracy. Cromwell now wielded a sovereignty even more absolute than any the Stuart monarchs would have dared to claim. In declaring his authority to be from God he even revived what practically amounted to the divine right of kings.

That Cromwell's regime would have its difficulties was certainly to be expected, since it rested upon the support of only a few people. He was opposed not only by royalists and Anglicans but by various dissenters, including some more radical than he. Like all upheavals of a similar character, the Puritan Revolution tended to move farther and farther in an extremist direction. Some of the Puritans became Levelers, who derived their name from their advocacy of equal political rights and privileges for all classes. Expressly disclaiming any intention of equalizing property, they confined their radicalism to the political sphere. They insisted that sovereignty inheres in the people and that government should rest upon the consent of the governed. Long in advance of any other party, they demanded a written constitution,

Levelers and Diggers

Charles II

The Restoration

Causes of the Glorious Revolution of 1688–1689

universal manhood suffrage, and the supremacy of Parliament. The Levelers were especially powerful in the army and through it exerted some influence upon the government. Still farther to the left were the Diggers, so called from their attempt to seize and cultivate unenclosed common land and distribute the produce to the poor. Though in common with the Levelers the Diggers appealed to the law of nature as a source of rights, they were more interested in economic than in political equality. They espoused a kind of primitive communism based upon the idea that the land is the "common treasury" of all. Every ablebodied man would be required to work at productive labor, and all persons would be permitted to draw from the common fund of wealth produced in proportion to their needs. The Church would be transformed into an educational institution and the clergy would become schoolmasters, giving instruction every seventh day in public affairs, history, and the arts and sciences.

In September 1658, the stout-hearted Lord Protector died. He was succeeded by his well-meaning but irresolute son Richard, who managed to hold office only until May of the following year. Perhaps even a man of much sterner fiber would also have failed eventually, for the country had grown tired of the austerities of Calvinist rule. Neither the Commonwealth nor the Protectorate had ever had the support of a majority of the English nation. Royalists regarded the Independents as usurpers. Republicans hated the disguised monarchy which Oliver Cromwell had set up. Catholics and Anglicans resented the branding of their acts of worship as criminal offenses. Even some members of the merchant class gradually came to suspect that Cromwell's war with Spain had done more harm than good by endangering English commerce with the West Indies. For these and similar reasons there was general rejoicing when in 1660 a newly elected Parliament proclaimed Charles I's exiled son king and invited him to return to England and occupy the throne of his father. The new king, Charles II, had gained a reputation for joyous living and easy morality, and his accession was hailed as a welcome relief from the somber rule of soldiers and zealots. Besides, he pledged himself not to reign as a despot, but to respect Parliament and to observe Magna Carta and the Petition of Right, for he admitted that he was not anxious to "resume his travels." England now entered upon a period known as the Restoration, covered by the reigns of Charles II (1660–1685) and his brother James II (1685–1688). Despite its auspicious beginning, many of the old problems had not really been solved but were simply concealed by the fond belief that the nation had regained its former stability.

Toward the end of the seventeenth century England went through a second political upheaval, the so-called Glorious Revolution of 1688–1689. Several of the causes were grounded in the policies of Charles II. That amiable sovereign was extravagant and carefree but determined on occasion to let the country know whose word was law.

His pro-Catholic attitude aroused the fears of patriotic Englishmen that their nation might once again be brought into subservience to Rome. Worse still, he showed a disposition, in spite of earlier pledges, to defy the authority of Parliament. In 1672 he suspended the laws against Catholics and Protestant Dissenters (i.e., all but Anglicans) and nine years later resolved to dispense with the legislative branch entirely. The policies of Charles II were continued in more extreme form by his brother, who succeeded him in 1685. James II was an avowed Catholic and seemed bent upon making that faith the established religion of England. He openly violated an act of Parliament requiring that all holders of public office should adhere to the Anglican church, and proceeded to fill important positions in the army and the civil service with his Romanist followers. He continued his brother's practice of exempting Catholics from the disabilities imposed upon them by Parliament, even going so far as to demand that the Anglican bishops should read his decrees for this purpose in their churches. As long as his opponents could expect that James II would be succeeded by one of his two Protestant daughters, they were inclined to tolerate his arbitrary rule, lest the country be plunged again into civil war. But when the king acquired a son by his second wife, who was a Catholic, the die of revolution was cast. It was feared that the young prince would be infected with his father's doctrines, and that, as a consequence, England would be fettered with the shackles of despotic and "papist"

Left: *The Trial of Charles I (1649)*. Right: *The Arrival of the First Course at James II's Coronation Dinner (1685)*. Both of these events took place at Westminster Hall: the first shows English royal power at its low point and the second at its apparent zenith. But James II was to be overthrown even more quickly than Charles I.

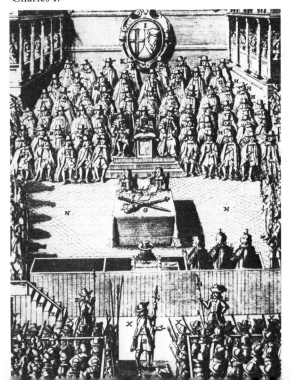

rule for an indefinite time to come. To forestall such a result it seemed necessary to depose the king.

The "Glorious Revolution" of 1688–1689 was an entirely bloodless affair. A group of politicians from the upper classes secretly invited Prince William of Orange and his wife Mary, the elder daughter of James II, to become joint rulers of England. William crossed over from Holland with an army and occupied London without firing a shot. Deserted even by those whom he had counted as loyal supporters, King James took refuge in France. The English throne was now declared vacant by Parliament and the crown presented to the new sovereigns. But their enthronement did not complete the revolution. Throughout the year 1689 Parliament passed numerous laws designed to safeguard the rights of Englishmen and to protect its own power from monarchical invasion. First came an act requiring that appropriations should be made for one year only. Next the Toleration Act was passed, granting religious liberty to all Christians except Catholics and Unitarians. Finally, on the sixteenth of December the famous Bill of Rights was enacted into law. It provided for trial by jury and affirmed the right of Englishmen to petition the government for a redress of grievances. It condemned excessive bail, cruel punishments, and exorbitant fines. And it forbade the king to suspend laws or to levy taxes without the consent of Parliament. More sweeping in its provisions than the Petition of Right of 1628, it was backed by a Parliament that now had the power to see that it was obeyed.

The significance of the revolution of 1688–1689 was very great. Since it marked the final triumph of Parliament over the king, it therefore spelled the doom of absolute monarchy in England. Never again was any crowned head in Britain able to defy the legislative branch of the government as the Stuart monarchs had done. The revolution also dealt a death blow to the theory of the divine right of kings. It would have been impossible for William and Mary to have denied the fact that they received their crowns from Parliament. And the authority of Parliament to determine who should be king was made more emphatic by the passage of the Act of Settlement in 1701. This law provided that upon the death of the heiress-presumptive Anne, younger sister of Mary, the crown should go to the Electress Sophia of Hanover or to the eldest of her heirs who might be Protestant. There were some forty men or women with better claim to the throne than Sophia, but all were eliminated by Parliament on the ground of their being Catholics. Finally, the Glorious Revolution contributed much to the American and French Revolutions at the end of the eighteenth century. The example of the English in overthrowing absolute rule was a powerful inspiration to the opponents of absolutism elsewhere. It was the British ideal of limited government which furnished the substance of the political theory of Voltaire, Jefferson, and Paine. And a considerable portion of the English Bill of Rights was incorporated in the French Declaration of the Rights of Man in 1789 and in the first ten amendments to the American Constitution.

In the eighteenth century English political life became far more stable. In 1714 the Electress Sophia's son succeeded Queen Anne as George I (1714–1727) and initiated the reign of the House of Hanover, which continued in England until 1901. Because George, who came to the throne at the age of fifty four, could speak no English and continued to spend much time in his German possession of Hanover, he was content to leave the real government of England to the leader of Parliament, Sir Robert Walpole (1676–1745). The latter deserves to be called the first English prime minister. During his supremacy Parliament became the real executive as well as legislative organ of England, and Walpole as parliamentary leader was the chief executive. Walpole ruled through a new system he devised, forever after called the cabinet system (originally because "cabinet" members met in a small room known as a cabinet). This meant that the leader of the parliamentary party in power (Walpole was a Whig, his opponents Tories) would work together with a group of like-minded parliamentary colleagues to push through legislation in Parliament and for practical purposes run the country. When the dominant party lost control, the opposition party would bring in a new prime minister and a new cabinet. The cabinet system continues in England until the present day.

Walpole, first prime minister

Walpole remained prime minister until 1742 by following a policy of cautious conservatism. Acting on his motto of *quieta non movere* ("let sleeping dogs lie") he kept England out of war for most of his supremacy and supported the financial interests of the upper classes.

George III

Sir Robert Walpole with Members of His Cabinet

New prime ministers continued to rule England more or less along the lines set down by Walpole throughout the rest of the reign of George II (1727–1760). They faced no interference from that monarch because, like his father, George II was really more German than English. But difficulties ensued at the beginning of the reign of George III (1760–1820). The latter was born in England and legend has it that his mother encouraged him to take an active role in English government by constantly saying "George, be king." Desiring to rule as well as reign, George III succeeded for a time in ensuring that only his favorites became prime ministers. But misrule followed. After England lost its American colonies and the king began to suffer from fits of insanity, Parliament regained the unimpeded initiative in governing the country which it has never lost since then.

2. ABSOLUTE MONARCHY IN FRANCE AND SPAIN

Contrasting conditions in England and France

The development of absolutism in France followed a course similar in some respects to early absolutism in England. Although France remained Catholic, its rulers had to contend with a Calvinist (Huguenot) opposition as formidable as that of the Puritans in England. Both nations had their staunch defenders of absolutism among lawyers and political philosophers. But there was one notable difference. England enjoyed an advantage of geographic isolation that sheltered it from foreign danger. It had not been invaded since the Norman Conquest in 1066. As a consequence, the English felt secure, and their rulers found it difficult to justify a huge professional army. They did, of course, maintain large fleets of war vessels, but a navy could not be used in the same manner as an army stationed in inland garrisons to overawe subjects or to stifle incipient revolutions. France, on the other hand, like most continental nations, faced almost constant threats of invasion. France's northeastern and eastern frontiers were poorly protected by geographic barriers and had been penetrated several times. As a result, it was easy for French kings to argue the need for massive armies of professional soldiers. And such troops could readily be utilized to nip domestic disturbances in the bud. It would doubtless be a mistake to give all of the credit to this difference in geographic position for the longer persistence of absolute government in France, but it was certainly a major factor.

The origins of absolutism in France

The growth of royal absolutism in France was the product of a gradual evolution. The most important antecedents were medieval. By 1300 the French kings were perfecting an efficient bureaucratic system of government. By 1450, largely owing to the results of the Hundred Years' War, they had introduced a standing army and had gained the right to collect national taxes. And by 1500 they had reduced regional separatism and the opposition of the provincial nobility. As royal power grew, the nobles were gradually reduced to the level of courtiers, dependent mainly upon the monarch for their titles and prestige. In the reign of Francis I (1515–1547) the crown became even stronger because it gained new control over ecclesiastics. By the Concordat of Bologna, an agreement struck with the papacy in 1516, the king gained the right to choose all French bishops and abbots. Although the pope was granted the first year's income from each new appointment, the agreement greatly favored the monarchy because it virtually conceded to it full political authority over the French Church.

The trend toward absolutism was interrupted during the sixteenth century when France was involved in a war with Spain and torn by a bloody struggle between Catholics and Huguenots at home. Ambitious nobles took advantage of the confusion to assert their power and contested the succession to the throne. Peace was restored to the exhausted kingdom in 1593 by Henry of Navarre (1589–1610), who four years before had proclaimed himself king as Henry IV. He was the founder of the Bourbon dynasty. Though at one time a leader of the Huguenot faction, Henry perceived that the nation would never accept him unless he renounced the Calvinist religion. Flippantly remarking that Paris was worth a Mass, he formally adopted the Catholic faith. In 1598 he issued the Edict of Nantes, guaranteeing freedom of conscience and political rights to all Protestants. With the grounds for religious controversy thus removed, Henry could turn his attention to rebuilding his kingdom. In this work, he had the able assistance of his chief minister, the duke of Sully. Grim, energetic, and penurious, Sully was a worthy forerunner of Colbert in the seventeenth century. For years the king and his faithful servant labored to repair the shattered fortunes of France. Sully devoted his efforts primarily to fiscal reform, so as to eliminate corruption and waste and bring more revenue into the royal treasury. He endeavored also to promote the prosperity of agriculture by draining swamps, improving devastated lands, subsidizing stock-raising, and opening up foreign markets for the products of the soil. The king gave most of his attention to fostering industry and commerce. He introduced the manufacture of silk into France, encouraged other industries by subsidies and monopolies, and made favorable commercial treaties with England and Spain. But Henry did not stop with economic reforms. He was deeply concerned with crushing the reborn power of the nobility, and so successful were his efforts in this direction that he restored the monarchy to the dominant position it had held under Francis I. He was active also in sponsoring the development of a colonial empire in America. During his reign the French acquired a foothold in Canada and began their exploration in the region of the Great Lakes and the Mississippi Valley. In short, his rule was intelligent and benevolent.

The reign of Henry IV was brought to an end by the dagger of a fa-

Francis I of France

Henry IV and the duke of Sully

The Assassination of Henry IV. This contemporary engraving shows Ravaillac climbing on the wheel of Henry's carriage in order to stab the French ruler.

Cardinal Richelieu

natic in 1610. Since the new king, Louis XIII, was only nine years old, the country was ruled by his mother, Marie de'Medici, as regent. In 1624 Louis XIII, no longer under the regency, entrusted the management of his kingdom to a brilliant but domineering cleric, Cardinal Richelieu, whom he made his chief minister. Richelieu dedicated himself to two objectives: (1) to destroy all limitations upon the authority of the king; and (2) to make France the chief power in Europe. In the pursuit of these aims he allowed nothing to stand in his way. He ruthlessly suppressed the nobility, destroying its most dangerous members and rendering the others harmless by attaching them as pensioners to the royal court. Though he fostered education and patronized literature, he neglected the interests of commerce and allowed graft and extravagance to flourish in the government. His main constructive achievements were the creation of a postal service and the establishment of a system under which *intendants,* or agents of the king, took charge of local government. Both were conceived as devices for consolidating the nation under the control of the crown, thereby eradicating surviving traces of independent local authority.

Richelieu's foreign policy

Richelieu's ambitions were not limited to domestic affairs. To make France the most powerful nation in Europe it was necessary to pursue an aggressive diplomacy and eventually to enter into war. France was still surrounded by what Henry IV had referred to as a "Hapsburg ring." On its southern border was Spain, ruled since 1516 by a branch of the Hapsburg family. To the north, less than a hundred miles from Paris, were the Spanish Netherlands. Other centers of Hapsburg power included Luxemburg, the Franche-Comté, and Milan, and still farther to the east the great Austrian Empire itself (see map, p. 517 above). Cardinal Richelieu eagerly awaited an opportunity to break this ring. As we shall see, he finally found it in the Thirty Years' War. Though engaged in suppressing Protestants at home, he did not hesitate to ally himself with Gustavus Adolphus, king of Sweden and leader of a coalition of Protestant states. Long before his death in 1642 the great cardinal-statesman had forged to the front as the most powerful individual in Europe.

Cardinal Richelieu

Absolute monarchy in France attained its zenith during the reigns of the last three Bourbon kings before the French Revolution. The first of the rulers of this series was Louis XIV (1643–1715), known as the "Grand Monarch," who epitomized the ideal of absolutism more completely than any other sovereign of his age. Proud, extravagant, and domineering, Louis entertained the most exalted notions of his position as king. Not only did he believe that he was commissioned by God to reign, but he also regarded the welfare of the state as intimately bound up with his own personality. The famous phrase imputed to him, *l'état c'est moi* (I am the state), may not represent his exact words, but it expresses very clearly the conception he held of his own authority. He chose the sun as his official emblem to indicate his belief that the nation derived its glory and sustenance from him as the planets do theirs from the actual sun. He gave personal supervision to every department and regarded his ministers as mere clerks with no duty but to obey his orders. In general, he followed the policies of Henry IV and Richelieu in consolidating national power at the expense of local officials and in trying to reduce the nobles to mere parasites of the court. But any possible good he may have done was completely overshadowed by his extravagant wars and his reactionary policy in religion. In 1685 he revoked the Edict of Nantes, which had granted freedom of conscience to the Huguenots. As a result, numbers of his most inventive and prosperous subjects fled the country.

Louis XIV, the supreme incarnation of absolute rule

Until the beginning of the revolution in 1789 the form of the French government remained essentially as Louis XIV had left it. His successors, Louis XV (1715–1774) and Louis XVI (1774–1792), also claimed to rule by divine right. But neither of these kings had the desire to emulate the Grand Monarch in his enthusiasm for work and his meticulous attention to the business of state. Louis XV was lazy and incompetent and allowed himself to be dominated by a succession of mistresses. Problems of government bored him, and when obliged to preside at the council table he "opened his mouth, said little, and thought not at all." His grandson, the ill-fated Louis XVI, was weak in character and mentally dull. Indifferent to politics, he amused himself by shooting deer from the palace window and playing at his hobbies of lock-making and masonry. On July 14, 1789 when mobs stormed the Bastille, he wrote in his diary "Nothing." Yet both of these monarchs maintained a government which was more arbitrary

Louis XIV by Rigaud

Philip II of Spain. This painting by Coello shows the famous protruding chin and lower lip which were characteristic features of the Hapsburg family.

Absolutism in Spain

Philip II

than had ever been the case before. They permitted their ministers to imprison without a trial persons suspected of disloyalty; they suppressed the courts for refusing to approve their decrees; and they brought the country to the verge of bankruptcy by their costly wars and by their reckless extravagance for the benefit of their mistresses and favorites. If they had deliberately planned to provoke revolution, they could scarcely have succeeded better.

The growth of absolute monarchy in Spain was less interrupted than was true in France. As we have seen in Chapter 13, by 1500 Ferdinand and Isabella had united Spain and made it a very powerful kingdom. In 1516 the realm was inherited by their grandson Charles I, whose father had been a Hapsburg. Three years later Charles was elected Holy Roman Emperor as Charles V, thereby uniting Spain with central Europe and southern Italy. Charles was interested not merely in the destinies of Spain but in the welfare of the Church and in the politics of Europe as a whole. He dreamed that he might be the instrument of restoring the religious unity of Christendom, broken by the Protestant Revolution, and of making the empire over which he presided a worthy successor of imperial Rome. Though successful in holding his disjointed domain together and in fighting off attempts of the French to conquer his Italian possessions and of the Turks to overrun Europe, he failed in the achievement of his larger objectives. At the age of fifty-six, overcome with a sense of discouragement and futility, he abdicated and retired to a monastery. The German princes chose his brother, Ferdinand I, to succeed him as Holy Roman Emperor. His Spanish and Italian possessions, including the colonies overseas, passed to his son, who became king as Philip II (1556–1598).

Philip II came to the throne of Spain at the height of its glory. But he also witnessed, and to a considerable extent was responsible for, the beginning of its decline. His policies were mainly an intensification of those of his predecessors. He was narrow, despotic, and cruel. Determined to enforce a strict conformity in matters of religion upon all of his subjects, he is reputed to have boasted that he would gather faggots to burn his own son if the latter were guilty of heresy. Therefore, he encouraged the ruthlessness of the Spanish Inquisition and launched the war for suppression of the religious revolt in the Netherlands. Philip was equally shortsighted in his colonial policy. Indigenous peoples were butchered and their territories greedily despoiled of their gold and silver, which were dragged off to Spain in the mistaken belief that this was the surest means of increasing the nation's wealth. No thought was given to the development of new industries in either the colonies or the mother country. Instead, the gold and silver were largely squandered in furthering Philip's military and political ambitions. It can be said, however, in the king's defense that he was following the accepted theories of the time. Doubtless most other monarchs with a like opportunity would have imitated his example.

The Escorial. Built in the sixteenth century by Philip II of Spain, this palace originally served as his retreat.

Philip II's crowning mistake was his war against England. Angered by the attacks of English ships upon Spanish commerce and frustrated in his schemes to bring England back into the Catholic faith, he sent a great fleet in 1588, the "Invincible Armada," to destroy Queen Elizabeth's navy. But Philip had little knowledge of either the new techniques of naval warfare or of the robust patriotism of the English. A combination of fighting seamanship and disastrous storms (the "Protestant Wind") sent many of his 130 ships to the bottom of the Channel and the rest back home in disarray. Spain never recovered from the blow. Though a brilliant cultural afterglow, exemplified the work of great writers and artists like Cervantes and Velasquez, continued for some years, the greatness of Spain as a nation was approaching its end.

The Armada

3. ABSOLUTISM IN CENTRAL EUROPE

The chief countries in central Europe where absolutism flourished most were Prussia and Austria. The founder of absolute rule in Prussia (a state made up primarily of Brandenburg, in north-central Germany, and Prussia, far to the east, near Russia) was the Great Elector, Frederick William, who ruled from 1640 to 1688. He was the first member of the Hohenzollern family to acquire full sovereignty over Prussia and to introduce a standing army. In addition, he began to bring all his dominions under centralized rule. The work of the Great Elector was continued and extended by his grandson, known as Frederick William I (1713–1740), since he now had the title of *king* of Prussia. Frederick William's major concerns were to build up the Prussian bureaucracy and the Prussian army. His bureaucratic officials ran Prussia extremely efficiently and at such small expense that Prussia

Frederick William I of Prussia

Frederick William I

Frederick the Great

Absolutism in Austria: Maria Theresa and Joseph II

was the only continental state in the middle of the eighteenth century with a budgetary surplus, even though the country had very limited natural resources. But Frederick William's really consuming passion was his army. This he more than doubled in size and drilled to a machinelike efficiency. Since he could hardly count on volunteers, he introduced conscription and supplemented that by sending gangs of kidnappers to drag back forced recruits from neighboring German lands. Frederick William had a strange love for particularly tall soldiers: his own private regiment of "Potsdam Giants" was comprised exclusively of soldiers over six feet in height. The king traded musicians and prize stallions for such choice specimens and then spent the bulk of his time marching his "giants" around his palace grounds.

The style but not the substance of Frederick William's militarism was altered by his noted successor, Frederick II (1740–1786), commonly known as Frederick the Great. An earnest disciple of the reformist doctrines of the new rationalist philosophy, Frederick was the leading figure among the "enlightened despots" of the eighteenth century. Declaring himself not the master but merely the "first servant of the state," he wrote essays to prove that Machiavelli was wrong and rose at five in the morning to begin a Spartan routine of personal management of public affairs. He made Prussia in many ways the best-governed state in Europe, abolishing torture of accused criminals and bribery of judges, establishing elementary schools, and promoting the prosperity of industry and agriculture. He fostered scientific forestry and the cultivation of new crops such as the potato. He opened up new lands in Silesia and brought in thousands of immigrants to cultivate them. When wars ruined their farms, he supplied the peasants with new livestock and tools. As an admirer of the French philosopher Voltaire, whom he entertained for some time at his court, he tolerated all sorts of religious beliefs. He declared that he would build a mosque in Berlin if enough Muslims wished to locate there. Yet he was strongly anti-Semitic. He levied special taxes on the Jews and made efforts to close the professions and the civil service to them. Moreover, Frederick continued to invest heavily in his army, and such benevolence as he showed in internal affairs was not carried over into foreign relations. Frederick robbed Austria of Silesia, conspired with Catherine of Russia to dismember Poland, and contributed at least his full share to the bloody wars of the eighteenth century.

The full bloom of absolutism in Austria came during the reigns of Maria Theresa (1740–1780) and Joseph II (1780–1790). Maria Theresa was one of the most capable of all eighteenth-century monarchs. She played the role of a flighty woman when it suited her advantage, but actually ruled with great common sense and determination. During her reign a national army was established, the powers of the Church were curtailed in the interest of consolidated government, and elementary and higher education was greatly expanded. Unlike the rulers of most other countries, Maria Theresa was sincerely devoted to Christian morality. Though she participated in the dismemberment of Poland to make up for the loss of Silesia, she did so with grave misgivings—an attitude which prompted the scornful remark of Frederick the Great: "She weeps, but she takes her share." The reforms of Maria Theresa were extended, at least on paper, by her son Joseph II. Inspired by the teachings of French philosophers, Joseph determined to remake his empire in accordance with the highest ideals of justice and reason. Not only did he plan to reduce the powers of the Church by confiscating its lands and abolishing monasteries, but he aspired to humble the nobles and improve the condition of the masses. He decreed that serfs should become free and promised to relieve them of the obligations owed to their masters. He aimed to make education universal and to force the nobles to pay their proper share of taxes. But most of his magnificent plans ended in failure. He antagonized not merely the nobles and clergy but also the Hungarians, who were deprived of all rights of self-government. He alienated the sympathies of the peasants by making them liable to compulsory military service. He was scarcely any more willing than Louis XIV or Frederick the Great to sacrifice personal power and national glory even for the sake of his lofty ideals.

Maria Theresa of Austria

4. ABSOLUTISM IN RUSSIA

Russia at the beginning of the early modern age was a composite of European and Oriental characteristics. Much of its territory had been colonized by the Norsemen in the early Middle Ages. The Russian religion, calendar, and system of writing had been derived from Byzantium. Even the governing regime, with its boyars, or magnates, and serfs, was not greatly dissimilar to that of western Europe. On the other hand, much of Russia's culture, and many of its customs, were distinctly not European. Russian arts were limited almost entirely to icon painting and religious architecture, characterized by the onion dome. There was practically no literature in the Russian language, arithmetic was barely known, Arabic numerals were not used, and merchants made their calculations with the abacus. Nor were manners and customs comparable to those of the West. Women of the upper classes were veiled and secluded. Flowing beards and skirted garments were universal for men. Table manners were considered superfluous. Seasons of wild revelry alternated with periods of repentance and morbid atonement. It would be a mistake, however, to suppose that Russia was totally cut off from Europe. As early as the fourteenth century, German merchants of the Hanseatic League conducted some trade in Russian furs and amber. In the 1550s English merchants discovered the White Sea and made Archangel a port of entry through

Russia at the beginning of the modern age

which military supplies could be exchanged for a few Russian goods and even products from Persia and China. But with Archangel frozen most of the year, the volume of this trade was undoubtedly small.

As late as the thirteenth century Russia was a collection of small principalities. They were attacked from the west by Lithuanians, Poles, and the Teutonic Knights. The last were members of one of several religious and military organizations that sprang from the Crusades. Established originally for charitable purposes, their order developed into a military one which adopted as its mission the conversion and conquest of lands on Germany's eastern frontier. The operations of the Teutonic Knights were part of the famous *Drang nach Osten* (Drive to the East) which occupied such a prominent place in German history. From the east Russia was threatened by the Mongols (Tartars), who had established a great empire in central Asia, eventually including both northern India and China. In 1237 the Mongols began an invasion which led to their conquest of nearly all of Russia. Mongol rule was in several ways a disaster. It marked the development of a stronger Asiatic orientation. Henceforth Russia turned more and more away from Europe and looked beyond the Urals as the arena of its future development. Its inhabitants intermarried with Mongols and adopted some elements of their way of life.

Eventually, Mongol power declined. In 1380 a Russian army defeated the Mongols and thus initiated a movement to drive them back into Asia. The state which assumed the leadership of this movement was the Grand Duchy of Moscow. Under strong rulers it had been increasing its power for some time. Located near the sources of the great rivers flowing both north and south, it had geographic advantages surpassing those of the other states. Moreover, it had recently been made the headquarters of the Russian Church. The first of the princes of Moscow to put himself forward as tsar (caesar) of Russia was Ivan the Great (1462–1505). Taking as his bride the niece of the last of the Byzantine emperors, who had perished in the capture of Constantinople in 1453, he proclaimed himself his successor by the grace of God. He adopted as his insignia the Byzantine double-headed eagle and imported Italian architects to work on an enormous building complex, the Kremlin, in demonstration of Russia's new independence and greatness. Avowing his intention to recover the ancient lands that had been lost to foreign invaders, Ivan forced the prince of Lithuania to acknowledge him as sovereign of "all the Russias" and pushed the Tartars out of northern Russia and beyond the Urals.

The first of the tsars to attempt the Europeanization of Russia was Peter the Great (1682–1725). He stands out as the most powerful and probably the most intelligent autocrat yet to occupy the Russian throne. With a reckless disregard for ancient customs, Peter endeavored to force his subjects to change their ways of living. He forbade the Oriental seclusion of women and commanded both sexes to adopt European styles of dress. He made the use of tobacco compul-

Peter the Great. An eighteenth-century mosaic.

sory among the members of his court. He summoned the great nobles before him and clipped their flowing beards with his own hand. In order to make sure of his own absolute power, he abolished all traces of local self-government and established a system of national police. For the same reason, he annihilated the authority of the patriarch of the Orthodox church and placed all religious affairs under a Holy Synod subject to his own control. Deeply interested in Western technology, he made journeys to Holland and England to learn about shipbuilding and industry. He imitated the mercantilist policies of Western nations by improving agriculture and fostering manufactures and commerce. In order to get "windows to the west" he conquered territory along the Baltic shore and transferred his capital from Moscow to St. Petersburg, his new city at the mouth of the Neva river. But the good that he did was greatly outweighed by his extravagant wars and his fiendish cruelty. He put thousands to death for alleged conspiracies against him. He murdered his own son and heir because the latter boasted that when *he* became tsar he would return Russia to the ways of its fathers. To raise money for his expensive wars he debased the currency, sold valuable concessions to foreigners, established government monopolies on the production of salt, oil, caviar, and coffins, and imposed taxes on almost everything, from baths to beehives.

Peter the Great

The significance of Peter the Great is not easy to evaluate. He did not singlehandedly transform Russia into a Western nation. Western influences had been seeping into the country as a consequence of trade contacts for many years. But Peter accelerated the process and gave it a more radical direction. Evidence abounds that he really did aim to

Results of Peter's reign

Peter the Great's Execution of Conspirators. This contemporary print shows scores of corpses gibbeted outside the walls of the Kremlin. Peter kept the rotting bodies on display for months to discourage his subjects from opposing his efforts to westernize Russian society.

The Winter Palace. This contemporary engraving shows the palace built by Peter the Great in the town that bore his name, St. Petersburg.

remake the nation and to give it at least a veneer of cultivation. He sent many of his countrymen abroad to study. He simplified the ancient alphabet and established the first newspaper to be published in Russia. He ordered the publication of a book on polite behavior, teaching his subjects not to spit on the floor or to scratch themselves or gnaw bones at dinner. He encouraged exports, built a fleet on the Baltic, and fostered new industries such as textiles and mining. Though a reaction set in after Peter's death against many of his innovations, some of them survived for at least two centuries. The Church, for example, continued as essentially an arm of the stage, governed by a procurator of the Holy Synod appointed by the tsar himself. Serfdom continued in the extended forms required or authorized by Peter. No longer were serfs bound to the soil; they could be bought and sold at any time, even for work in factories and mines. Finally, the absolutism developed by Peter showed few signs of abating until the early twentieth century. It was an absolutism based upon force, with a secret police, an extensive bureaucracy, and a subordinated Church as instruments for imposing the autocrat's will.

Catherine the Great

The other most noted of the Russian monarchs in the age of absolutism was Catherine the Great (1762–1796), who before her marriage was a German princess. Frequently classified as one of the "enlightened despots," Catherine corresponded with French philosophers, founded hospitals and orphanages, and expressed the hope that someday the serfs might be liberated. Ambitious to gain for herself a place in intellectual history, she rose at five in the morning to engage in scholarship. She wrote plays, published a digest of Blackstone's *Commentaries on the Laws of England,* and even began a history of Russia. Her accomplishments as a reformer, however, had only a limited scope. She took steps toward a codification of the Russian laws, restricted the use of torture, and remodeled and consolidated local government. Any plans she may have had, however, for improving the lot of the peasants were abruptly canceled after a violent serf rebellion in 1773–1774. Landlords and priests were murdered and the ruling classes terrified as the revolt swept through the Urals and the valley of the Volga. Catherine responded with stern repression. The captured leader of the peasants was drawn and quartered, and, as a guaranty against future outbreaks, the nobles were given increased powers over their serfs. They were permitted to deal with them virtually as if they were chattel slaves. Catherine's chief significance lies in the fact that she continued the work of Peter the Great in introducing Russia to Western ideas and in making the country a formidable power in European affairs. She managed to extend the boundaries of her country to include not only eastern Poland but lands on the Black Sea.

Catherine the Great

5. THE WARS OF THE EARLY MODERN PERIOD

Between 1500 and 1789 the years of peace in Europe were outnumbered by the years of war. The earlier conflicts were largely religious in character and have already been dealt with in Chapter 15. The majority of the wars after 1600 partook of the nature of struggles for supremacy among the powerful autocrats of the principal countries. But religion was also a factor in some of them, and so was the greed of the commercial classes. In general, nationalistic motives were much less important than in the wars of the nineteenth and twentieth centuries. Peoples and territories were so many pawns to be moved back and forth in the game of dynastic aggrandizement.

Character of the wars in the age of absolutism for the despots

The major warfare of the seventeenth century revolved around a titanic duel between Hapsburgs and Bourbons. Originally the rulers of Austria, the Hapsburgs had gradually extended their power over Hungary and Bohemia as well. In addition, the head of the family enjoyed what was left of the distinction of being Holy Roman Emperor. Since the time of Charles V (1519–1556) branches of the Hapsburgs had ruled over Spain, the Netherlands, the Franche-Comté, Milan, and the Kingdom of the Two Sicilies. For many years this expansion of Hapsburg power had been a source of profound disturbance to the rulers of France. They regarded their country as encircled, and longed to break through the enclosing ring. But tensions were building up in other parts of Europe also. The princes of Germany looked with alarm upon the growing power of the Holy Roman Emperor and sought opportunities to restrict him in ways that would increase their own stature. The kings of Denmark and Sweden were also developing expansionist ambitions, which could hardly be realized except at the expense of the Hapsburg Empire. Finally, the seeds of religious conflict, sown by the Reformation, were about ready to germinate in a new crop of hostilities. In 1608–1609 two opposing alliances had been formed, based upon principles of religious antagonism. The existence of these mutually hostile leagues added to the tension in central Europe and

Underlying causes of conflict

The Thirty Years' War

contributed toward making an eventual explosion almost a certainty. The conflict that followed, known as the Thirty Years' War (1618–1648), was one of the most tragic in history.

The immediate cause of the Thirty Years' War was an attempt of the Holy Roman Emperor, Matthias, to consolidate his power in Bohemia. Though the Hapsburgs had been overlords of Bohemia for a century, the Czech inhabitants of the country had retained their own king. When the Bohemian throne became vacant in 1618, Matthias conspired to obtain the position for one of his relatives, Duke Ferdinand of Styria. By exerting pressure he induced the Bohemian Diet to elect Ferdinand king. The Czech leaders resented this, since both nationalist and Protestant traditions were strong in the country. The upshot was the invasion of the emperor's headquarters in Prague by Czech noblemen and the proclamation of Bohemia as an independent state with Frederick, the Calvinist Elector Palatine, as king. The war now began in earnest. The success of the Hapsburgs in suppressing the Bohemian revolt and in punishing Frederick by seizing his lands in the valley of the Rhine galvanized the Protestant rulers of northern Europe into action. Not only the German princes but King Christian IV of Denmark and Gustavus Adolphus of Sweden joined the war against Austrian aggression—with the additional purpose, of course, of expanding their own dominions. In 1630 the French intervened with donations of arms and money to the Protestant allies, and after 1632, when Gustavus Adolphus was killed in battle, France bore the brunt of the struggle. The war was no longer a religious conflict, but essentially a contest between the Bourbon and Hapsburg houses for domination of the continent of Europe. The immediate objectives of Cardinal Richelieu, who was directing affairs for Louis XIII, were to wrest parts of Germany from the Holy Roman Empire and to weaken

Two Artistic Broadsides from the Thirty Years' War. On the left the German peasantry is ridden by the soldiery; on the right is an allegorical representation of "the monstrous beast of war."

A Swearing of Oaths at the Peace of Westphalia, 1648

the hold of the Spanish Hapsburgs on the Netherlands. For a time the French armies suffered reverses, but the organizing genius of Richelieu and of Cardinal Mazarin, who succeeded him in 1648, ultimately brought victory to France and its allies. Peace was restored to a distracted Europe by the Treaty of Westphalia in 1648.

Most of the results of the Thirty Years' War were unmitigated evils. By the Treaty of Westphalia France was confirmed in the possession of formerly German territories in Lorraine and Alsace. Sweden also received territory in Germany; the independence of Holland and Switzerland was formally acknowledged, and the Holy Roman Empire was reduced to a complete fiction, since each of the German princes was now recognized as a sovereign ruler with power to make war and peace and to govern his state as he chose. But most of these changes merely laid the foundations for bitter international squabbles in the future. In addition, the war wrought terrible havoc in central Europe. Probably few military conflicts since the dawn of history had caused so much misery to the civilian population. It is estimated that fully one-third of the people in Germany and Bohemia lost their lives as a consequence of famine and disease and the marauding attacks of brutal soldiers. The armies of both sides pillaged, tortured, burned, and killed in such manner as to convert whole regions into veritable desert. In Saxony one-third of the land went out of cultivation, and packs of wolves roamed through areas where thriving villages once had stood. In the midst of such misery, intellectual achievement of every description was bound to decline, with the result that civilization in Germany was retarded by at least a century. Nonetheless, the settlement of 1648 put an end to religious warfare in Europe for all time and initiated a half-century of comparative peace.

In 1700 the French king saw what appeared to be a new opportunity for expanding Bourbon power. In that year Charles II, king of Spain,

Results of the Thirty Years' War

died with neither children nor brothers to succeed him, and willed his dominion to the grandson of Louis XIV. The Austrians denounced this settlement, and formed a new alliance with England, Holland, and Brandenburg. The War of the Spanish Succession, which broke out in 1702 when Louis attempted to enforce the claim of his grandson, was the last important stage in the struggle between Bourbons and Hapsburgs.[1] By the Peace of Utrecht (1713–1714) the grandson of Louis XIV was permitted to occupy the Spanish throne, on condition that France and Spain should never be united. Nova Scotia and Newfoundland were transferred to England from France, and Gibraltar from Spain. The Belgian Netherlands, the Kingdom of the Two Sicilies, and Milan were given to the Austrian Hapsburgs.

It would be difficult to exaggerate the significance of the War of the Spanish Succession. Since it involved most of the nations of Europe and also lands overseas, it was the first of what can be called "world wars." It was fought, however, not by mass armies but chiefly by professional soldiers. It was the prototype, therefore, of most of the wars of the eighteenth century. These were wars between kings, in which the masses of the people were involved only indirectly. Among large-scale conflicts the War of the Spanish Succession was the first in which religion played almost no part. Secular rivalries over commerce and sea power were the major bones of contention. The war put an end to the claims of the smaller states to rank equally with their larger neighbors. Brandenburg and Savoy were the only important exceptions. The first came to be called Prussia and the second, Sardinia. Aside from Sardinia, the rest of the Italian states dwindled into insignificance, and Prussia started to play an important role on the German scene. Holland suffered such a strain from the war that it ceased to be a prime factor in the competition for world power. With a Bourbon king on the throne, Spain was reduced to subservience to France. The Spanish Bourbon dynasty continued to rule, with brief interruptions, until the overthrow of Alphonso XIII in 1931, and the dynasty has returned to Spain since 1975. The War of the Spanish Succession left France and Great Britain as the two major powers in Europe. Of these, the latter was the principal victor. Not only did it acquire valuable possessions, but the British muscled their way into the Spanish commercial empire. By an agreement known as the Asiento, Britain gained the privilege of providing Spanish America with African slaves. This privilege opened the way to the smuggling of all kinds of goods into the Spanish colonies, and contributed toward making Great Britain the richest nation on earth.

The most important of the wars between the War of the Spanish

---

[1] The War of the Austrian Succession (1740–1748), in which France fought on the side of Prussia against Great Britain and Austria, also involved a struggle between Bourbons and Hapsburgs. But the results for France were indecisive: the war was mainly a duel between Prussia and Austria.

Succession and the French Revolution was the Seven Years' War (1756–1763), known in American history as the French and Indian War. The causes of this struggle were closely related to some of the earlier conflicts already discussed. A chief factor in several of these wars had been commercial rivalry between England and France. Each had been striving for supremacy in the development of overseas trade and colonial empires. The Seven Years' War was simply the climax of a struggle which had been going on for nearly a century. Hostilities began, appropriately enough, in America as the result of a dispute over possession of the Ohio valley. Soon the whole question of British or French domination of the North American continent was involved. Eventually, nearly every major country of Europe was drawn in on one side or the other. Louis XV of France enlisted the aid of his relative, the Bourbon king of Spain. A struggle begun in 1740 between Frederick the Great of Prussia and Maria Theresa of Austria over possession of Silesia was quickly merged with the larger contest. The Seven Years' War thus reached the proportions of what virtually amounted to another world conflict, with France, Spain, Austria, and Russia arrayed against Great Britain and Prussia in Europe, and with English and French colonial forces striving for mastery not only in America but also in India.

The Seven Years' War

The outcome of the Seven Years' War was exceedingly significant for the later history of Europe. Frederick the Great won a decisive victory over the Austrians and forced Maria Theresa to surrender all claims to Silesia. The acquisition of this territory increased the area of Prussia by more than a third, thereby raising the Hohenzollern kingdom to the status of a first-rank power. In the struggle for colonial supremacy, the British emerged with a sensational triumph. Of their once magnificent empire in America, the French lost all but two tiny islands off the coast of Newfoundland, Guadeloupe and a few other possessions in the West Indies, and a portion of Guiana in South America. All of the territory given up by the French was acquired by Great Britain, with the exception of Louisiana, which France turned over to Spain as a reward for its part in the war. France was allowed to retain its trading privileges in India, but was forbidden to build any forts or maintain any troops in that country. France's treasury was now depleted, its trade almost ruined, and its chances of dominance on the Continent badly shattered. These disasters, brought on by the stupid policies of the French kings, had much to do with preparing the ground for the revolution of 1789. By contrast, Britain was now riding the crest of the wave—in a literal as well as figurative sense, for its triumph in the Seven Years' War was a milestone in its struggle for supremacy on the seas. The wealth from its expanded trade enriched British merchants, thereby enhancing their prestige in political and social affairs. But perhaps most important of all, its victory in the struggle for colonies gave England an abundance of raw materials which enabled it to take the lead in the Industrial Revolution.

*Results of the Seven
Years' War*

6. THE POLITICAL THEORY OF ABSOLUTISM

The influence of political philosophers in buttressing absolute rule

The autocratic behavior of the rulers of the sixteenth, seventeenth, and eighteenth centuries was sanctioned by the influence of political theory. Several of the Stuart and Bourbon kings, for example, derived justification for their policies from philosophers who expressed the prevailing ideas of their time in systematic and forceful writings.

Jean Bodin

One of the first of the philosophers to lend encouragement to the absolutist ambitions of monarchs was the Frenchman Jean Bodin (1530–1596). He agreed with the medieval philosophers that rulers were bound by the law of God, and he acknowledged that the prince had a moral duty to respect the treaties he had signed. But Bodin had no use for parliaments of any description. He emphatically denied the right of a legislative body to impose any limits upon royal power. And while he admitted that princes who violated the divine law or the law of nature were tyrants, he refused to concede that their subjects had any right of rebellion against them. The authority of the prince is from God, and the supreme obligation of the people is passive obedience. Revolution must be avoided at all costs, for it destroys that stability which is a necessary condition for progress. The main contribution of Bodin, if such it can be called, was his doctrine of sovereignty, which he defined as "supreme power over citizens and subjects, unrestrained by the laws." By this he meant that the prince, who is the only sovereign, is not bound by manmade laws. There is no *legal* restriction upon his authority whatever—nothing except obedience to the natural or moral law ordained by God.

The most noted of all the apostles of absolute government was Thomas Hobbes (1588–1679). Writing during and after the English Civil War and in close association with the royalists, Hobbes was disgusted with the turn which events had taken in England and longed for a revival of the monarchy. However, his materialism and his doctrine of the secular origin of the kingship made him none too popular with the Stuarts. For the title of his chief work Hobbes chose the name *Leviathan,* to indicate his conception of the state as an all-powerful monster. (In the Book of Job, Leviathan is the monster that ruled over the primeval chaos.) All associations within the state, he declared, are mere "worms in the entrails of Leviathan." The essence of Hobbes's political philosophy is directly related to his theory of the origin of government. He taught that in the beginning all human beings lived in a state of nature, subject to no law but brutal self-interest. Far from being a paradise of innocence and bliss, the state of nature was a condition of universal misery. As Hobbes said, "man is a wolf toward man." Life for the individual was "solitary, poor, nasty, brutish, and short." In order to escape from this war of each against all, people eventually united with one another to form a civil society. They drew

The Title Page of Hobbes's *Leviathan*

up a contract surrendering all of their rights to a sovereign, who would be strong enough to protect his subjects from violence. Thus the sovereign, while not a party to the contract, was made the recipient of absolute authority. The people gave up *everything* for the one great blessing of security. In contrast with Bodin, Hobbes did not recognize any law of nature or of God as a limitation upon the authority of the prince. Absolute government, he maintained, had been established by the people themselves, and therefore they would have no ground for complaint if their ruler became a tyrant. On the basis of pure deduction, without any appeal to religion or history, Hobbes arrived at the conclusion that the king is entitled to rule despotically— not because he has been appointed by God, but because the people have *given* him absolute power.

In a sense, the great Dutchman Hugo Grotius (1583–1645) may also be considered an exponent of absolutism; though with him the question of power within the state was more or less incidental to the larger question of relations among states. Living during the period of the revolt of the Netherlands and the Thirty Years' War, Grotius was impressed by the need for a body of rules that would reduce the dealings of governments with one another to a pattern of reason and order. He wrote his famous *Law of War and Peace* to prove that the principles of elemental justice and morality ought to prevail among nations. Some of these principles he derived from the Roman "law of peoples" and some from the medieval law of nature. So well did he present his case that he has been regarded ever since as one of the chief founders of international law. Grotius's revulsion against turbulence also inspired him to advocate absolutist government. He did not see how order could be preserved within the state unless the ruler possessed unlimited authority. He maintained that in the beginning the people had either surrendered to a ruler voluntarily or had been compelled to submit to superior force; but in either case, having once established a government, they were bound to obey it unquestioningly forever.

The theories just discussed were not simply those of a few isolated philosophers, but rather the widely accepted ideas of an age when order and security were considered more important than liberty. They reflected the desire of the commercial classes, especially, for the utmost degree of stability and protection in the interest of business. Mercantilism and the policies of rulers went hand in hand with the new theories of absolutism. The dictum, "I am the state," attributed to Louis XIV, was not just the brazen boast of a tyrant, but came close to expressing the prevailing conception of government in continental Europe. Those who had a stake in society really believed that the monarch *was* the state. They could hardly conceive of a government able to protect and assist their economic activities except in terms of centralized and unbridled authority. Their attitude was not so far dif-

*The significance of
philosophers' attempts to
justify absolutism*

ferent from that of some people today who believe that a dictatorship of one form or another is the only means for security and plenty.

7. SIGNIFICANCE OF THE AGE OF ABSOLUTISM

Beginnings of the modern state system

The age of absolutism was important not merely for the establishment of absolute monarchies. It bears even greater significance for its effects upon international relations. It was during this period that the modern state system came into existence. During the era of approximately a thousand years after the fall of Rome, states, in the sense in which we now understand the term, scarcely existed in Europe west of the Byzantine Empire. True, there were kings in England and France, but until almost the end of the Middle Ages, their relations with their subjects were essentially those of lords with their vassals. They had *dominium* but not sovereignty. In other words, they had the highest proprietary rights over the lands which constituted their fiefs; they did not necessarily possess supreme political authority over all the persons who lived on their lands. Only through extension of the taxing power, the judicial power, and the establishment of professional armies, did medieval rulers take steps toward becoming sovereigns in the modern sense.

Causes of the rise of the state system

Some historians consider the beginnings of the modern state system to date from the invasion of Italy in 1494 by King Charles VIII of France. Involved in this war for conquest of foreign territory were considerations of dynastic prestige, the balance of power, elaborate diplomacy, and alliances and counteralliances. It was in no sense a religious or ideological war but a struggle for power and territorial aggrandizement. Other historians conceive of the Reformation as the primary cause of the modern state system. The Protestant Revolution broke the unity of Western Christendom. It facilitated the determination of kings and princes to make their own power complete by repudiating the authority of a universal Church. As early as 1555 the Peace of Augsburg gave to each German prince the right to decide whether Lutheranism or Catholicism should be the faith of his people. It was probably the Treaty of Westphalia, however, that played the dominant role in making the modern state system a political reality. This treaty, which ended the Thirty Years' War in 1648, transferred territories from one rule to another with no regard for the nationality of their inhabitants. It recognized the independence of Holland and Switzerland and reduced the Holy Roman Empire to a fiction. Each of the German princes was acknowledged as a sovereign ruler with power to make war and peace and to govern his domain as he chose. Finally, the treaty introduced the principle that *all* states, regardless of their size or power, were equal under international law and endowed with full and complete control over their territories and inhabitants.

Whatever its origins, the modern state system may be considered to embody the following elements: (1) the legal equality and independence of all states; (2) the right of each state to pursue a foreign policy of its own making, to form alliances and counteralliances, and to wage war for its own advantage; (3) the use of diplomacy as a substitute for war, often involving intrigue and espionage to the extent necessary for political advantage; (4) the balance of power as a device for preventing war or for assuring the support of allies if war becomes necessary. Most of these elements of the state system have continued to the present day. Even the establishment of the League of Nations and the United Nations brought no substantial change, for both were founded upon the principle of the sovereign equality of independent states. Some observers believe that there will be no genuine prospect of world peace until the system of sovereign independent states is recognized as obsolete and is replaced by a world community of nations organized on a federal basis.

Elements of the modern state system

SELECTED READINGS

• *Items so designated are available in paperback editions.*
  Ashton, Robert, *The English Civil War: Conservatism and Revolution, 1603–1649*, New York, 1978.
• Birn, Raymond, *Crisis, Absolutism, Revolution: Europe, 1648–1789/91*, Hinsdale, Ill., 1977. A good college-level survey for the second half of the period covered in this chapter.
  Carsten, F. L., *The Origins of Prussia*, London, 1954. Standard work, through the reign of the Great Elector.
  Cherniavsky, M., *Tsar and People: Studies in Russian Myths*, 2nd ed., New York, 1969. Imaginative study of the symbolism of rulership.
  Church, William F., *Louis XIV in Historical Thought*, New York, 1976.
  Dorn, W., *The Competition for Empire, 1740–63*, New York, 1940. Excellent old-fashioned study of Europe in the mid–eighteenth century. Particularly strong on military affairs.
• Dunn, Richard S., *The Age of Religious Wars, 1559–1715*, 2nd ed., New York, 1979. The best college level text on this period. Extremely well written.
• Elliott, J. H., *Imperial Spain, 1469–1716*, London, 1963. A masterpiece of sophisticated synthesis.
  Elton, G. R., *England under the Tudors*, 2nd ed., London, 1977. Engagingly written and authoritative.
  Florinsky, M. T., *Russia: A History and an Interpretation*, Vol. I, New York, 1955. The best textbook on Russian history. Reviews divergent interpretations and emphasizes politics.
• Fraser, Lady Antonia, *Oliver Cromwell*, London, 1973. A popular biography.
  Friedrich, Carl J., *The Age of the Baroque, 1610–1660*, New York, 1952.
• Goubert, P., *Louis XIV and Twenty Million Frenchmen*, New York, 1970.

Events of the reign seen against the background of economic and social conditions.

Hatton, Ragnhild, *Europe in the Age of Louis XIV,* London, 1969.

Holborn, H., *A History of Modern Germany: 1648–1840,* New York, 1964.

• Jones, J. R., *Britain and Europe in the Seventeenth Century,* New York, 1966.

———, *Country and Court: England, 1658–1714,* London, 1978. Now the best survey of the period surrounding the Glorious Revolution.

• ———, *The Revolution of 1688 in England,* New York, 1972.

• Mattingly, Garrett, *The Armada,* Boston, 1959. Fascinating narrative; thoroughly reliable but reads like a novel.

Nussbaum, F. L., *The Triumph of Science and Reason, 1660–1685,* New York, 1953.

• Pennington, D. H., *Seventeenth-Century Europe,* London, 1970.

• Rabb, T. K., *The Struggle for Stability in Early Modern Europe,* New York, 1975. A stimulating essay arguing for a shift from crisis to stability around 1650.

Roberts, Penfield, *The Quest for Security, 1715–1740,* New York, 1947.

• Roots, Ivan, ed., *Cromwell, A Profile,* New York, 1973. A collection of readings on problems in interpretation; complements Fraser.

• Rosenberg, Hans, *Bureaucracy, Aristocracy, and Autocracy: The Prussian Experience, 1660–1815,* Cambridge, Mass., 1958. Difficult but rewarding.

• Russell, Conrad, *The Crisis of Parliaments: English History, 1509–1660,* New York, 1971. The best survey covering this broad range of time.

Sabine, George H., *A History of Political Theory,* 3rd ed., New York, 1951. An older work, particularly good on thought of this age.

Smith, Lacey B., *Henry VIII: The Mask of Royalty,* Boston, 1971. A breathtaking interpretation of the last years of Henry VIII and the age in which he lived.

Speck, W. A., *Stability and Strife: England, 1714–1760,* Cambridge, Mass., 1977.

• Steinberg, S. H., *The Thirty Years' War and the Conflict for European Hegemony, 1600–1660,* New York, 1966. The best account.

• Stone, Lawrence, *The Causes of the English Revolution, 1529–1642,* New York, 1972.

• Sumner, B. H., *Peter the Great and the Emergence of Russia,* London, 1950. A good short introduction.

Wedgwood, C. V., *The Thirty Years' War,* London, 1938. More attention to narrative than Steinberg.

Wolf, John B., *The Emergence of the Great Powers, 1685–1715,* New York, 1951.

• ———, *Louis XIV,* New York, 1968. The standard biography in English.

SOURCE MATERIALS

Bodin, Jean, *Six Books Concerning the State,* Cambridge, 1962.

Grotius, Hugo, *The Law of War and Peace,* New York, 1963.

• Hobbes, Thomas, *Leviathan.* (Many editions.)

Chapter 18

THE INTELLECTUAL REVOLU-TION OF THE SEVENTEENTH AND EIGHTEENTH CENTURIES

We are to admit no more causes of natural things than such as are both true and sufficient to explain their appearances. To this purpose the philosophers say that nature does nothing in vain, and more is in vain when less will serve; for nature is pleased with simplicity, and affects not the pomp of superfluous cause.

—Isaac Newton, *The Mathematical Principles of Natural Philosophy*

The years which witnessed the rise of absolutism in Europe were witness, as well, to what can fairly be described as an intellectual revolution. Traditional ideas concerning God, human existence, and the universe were challenged and, to a large extent, either drastically modified or totally cast aside. In their place, philosophers and scientists constructed a new worldview, rational, mechanistic, and largely impersonal, yet at the same time humane, tolerant, and therefore understanding of both the foibles and aspirations of humanity. This intellectual revolution was rooted in the history of the Renaissance and the beginnings of the Commercial Revolution; it derived from the widened intellectual horizons and increased general prosperity that those movements had produced.

The nature of the revolution

The extraordinary galaxy of men and ideas that constitute the revolution make it worth examining in its own right. It must also be studied, however, in order to understand the origins of ideas, institutions, and movements still current today. The self-confidence that compelled men and women to examine their world critically, and the belief in progress that encouraged them to change that world—both characteristic attitudes of this revolution—in turn helped foster the French and Industrial Revolutions, and thus the modern world.

Reasons for examining the intellectual revolution

Engraved Title Page from Bacon's *Novum Organum*

René Descartes

1. THE PHILOSOPHICAL FOUNDATIONS OF THE INTELLECTUAL REVOLUTION

The progenitors of the intellectual revolution were four men: Francis Bacon, René Descartes, John Locke, and Isaac Newton. All four were willing to attack fundamental assumptions about the universe and the human mind; all four were able not only to demolish the old, but to construct new ideas and theories to replace those they had discarded. The son of an Elizabethan government official, Francis Bacon (1561–1626) was both a philosopher and an ambitious courtier, who, as lord chancellor, was sentenced to imprisonment on charges of bribery. Attention to his political career prevented his fully developing those ideas which were to be his intellectual legacy. Yet even granting their limitations, Bacon's conclusions were of immense influence in the history of modern thought. In his two most important works, *Novum Organum* (a treatise on the method of acquiring knowledge, published in 1620) and *The Advancement of Learning* (1623) he insisted upon the importance of doubting all received knowledge.

Bacon's most important contribution to philosophy was the glorification of the inductive method as the basis of accurate knowledge. He believed that all seekers of truth in the past were slaves of preconceived ideas or prisoners of Scholastic logic. He argued that the philosopher should turn to the direct observation of nature, to the accumulation of facts about things and the discovery of the laws that govern them. Induction alone, he believed, was the magic key that would unlock the secrets of knowledge. Authority, tradition, and syllogistic logic should be as sedulously avoided as the plague. Bacon also argued that the worth of any idea depended on its usefulness. The ideas generated and debated by medieval scholastics were, in his opinion, worthless, because they could be put to no real use. Scientific discoveries were a part of "true" knowledge only when they could be applied practically.

René Descartes (1596–1650), like Bacon, constructed a philosophy on the basis of a systematic questioning of received truths. Unlike Bacon, however, his system of belief was built by means of the mathematical instrument of pure deduction. In his famous *Discourse on Method* (1637), and in other scientific writings, he began with simple, self-evident truths or axioms, like those found in geometry, and reasoned from these to particular conclusions. Descartes believed that he had found such an axiom in his famous principle: "I think, therefore I am." From this he maintained that it is possible to deduce a sound body of universal knowledge—to prove, for example, that God exists, and that men and women are thinking animals. These "truths," he declared, are just as infallible as the truths of geometry, for they are products of the same unerring method.

But Descartes is important not only as the founder of the new rationalism. He was also partly responsible for introducing the conception of a mechanistic universe. He taught that the whole world of matter, organic and inorganic alike, could be defined in terms of extension and motion. "Give me extension and motion," he once declared, "and I will construct the universe." Every individual thing—a solar system, a star, the earth itself—is a self-operating machine propelled by a force arising from the original motion given to the universe by God. Descartes did not even exclude the bodies of animals and humans from this general mechanistic pattern. He declared that the whole world of physical nature is one, and that the behavior of animals and humans flow automatically from internal or external stimuli. Yet Descartes was unwilling to include the human mind as part of his mechanistic system. Mind was not a form of matter, but an entirely separate substance implanted in the body by God. The world was therefore *dualistic:* i.e., composed of mind and matter. As a corollary to this assumption, Descartes believed in the existence of innate ideas. He taught that self-evident truths having no relation to sensory experience must be inherent in the mind itself. They are not learned through the use of the senses, but are part of the human mind from birth.

The implications of the thought of Bacon and Descartes were of enormous significance. Those now living, they argued, not only possessed the right but were charged with a duty to reassess the past and, when warranted, to reject its assumptions. They must have the courage to experiment, in order to reveal and understand the mechanical nature of the universe. Such reasoning would have a practical end, since it would result in humanity's mastery of the world. "Understanding the forces and actions of fire, water, air, the stars and heavens," Descartes wrote in the *Discourse,* "we can use these forces . . . for all purposes for which they are appropriate, and so make ourselves masters and possessors of nature."

The principles of rationalism and mechanism were adopted in some form or other by the majority of the philosophers of the seventeenth century. The most noted of Descartes's intellectual successors were the Dutch Jew Benedict Spinoza and the Englishman Thomas Hobbes, whom we have already encountered as a political theorist. Benedict (or Baruch) Spinoza was born in Amsterdam in 1632 and died an outcast from his native community forty-five years later. His parents were members of a group of Jewish immigrants who had fled from persecution in Portugal and Spain and had taken refuge in the Netherlands. At an early age Spinoza came under the influence of a disciple of Descartes and as a result grew critical of some of the dogmas of the Hebrew faith. For this he was expelled from the synagogue and banished from the community of his people. From 1656 till his death he lived in various cities of Holland, eking out a meager existence by grinding lenses. During these years he developed a philoso-

A Diagram Illustrating Cartesian Dualism. The eyes perceive the arrow; the soul, in the pineal gland, transmits an impulse to the muscles, causing the finger to point to the arrow. From the 1677 edition of Descartes's *De Homine.*

phy which incorporated the rationalism and mechanism but not the dualism of Descartes. Spinoza maintained that there is only one essential substance in the universe, of which mind and matter are but different aspects. This single substance is God, who is identical with nature itself. Such a conception of the universe was pure pantheism; but it was grounded upon reason rather than upon faith, and it was intended to express the scientific notions of the unity of nature and the continuity of cause and effect.

Spinoza's ethics

Much more than Descartes, Spinoza was interested in ethical questions. Having come to the conclusion early in life that the things people prize most highly—wealth, pleasure, power, and fame—are empty and vain, he set out to inquire whether there was any perfect good which would give lasting and unmitigated happiness to all who attained it. By a process of geometric reasoning he attempted to prove that this perfect good consists in "love of God"—that is, in worship of the order and harmony of nature. If people would but realize that the universe is a beautiful machine, whose operation cannot be interrupted for the benefit of particular persons, they would gain that serenity of mind for which philosophers have yearned through the ages. We can only be delivered from impossible hopes and cringing fears by acknowledging to ourselves that the order of nature is unalterably fixed, and that human beings cannot change their fate. In other words, we gain true freedom by realizing that we are not free. But with all his determinism, Spinoza was an earnest apostle of tolerance, justice, and rational living. He wrote in defense of religious liberty and, in the face of cruel mistreatment, set a noble example in his personal life of kindliness, humanity, and freedom from vengeful passions.

Hobbes

Another of the great rationalists of the seventeenth century was Thomas Hobbes. Born before either Descartes or Spinoza, he outlived both. Hobbes agreed with his two contemporaries in the belief that geometry furnished the only proper method of discovering philosophic truth. But he denied the Cartesian doctrine of innate ideas, maintaining that the origin of all knowledge is in sense perception. He refused to accept either the dualism of Descartes or the pantheism of Spinoza. According to Hobbes, nothing exists except matter. Mind is simply motion in the brain or perhaps a subtle form of matter, but in no sense a distinct substance. God, also, if we can believe that He exists, must be assumed to have a physical body. There is nothing spiritual anywhere in the universe of which the mind can conceive. This was the most thoroughgoing materialism to make its appearance since the days of the Roman Lucretius. It was combined with mechanism, as materialism usually is. Hobbes contended that not only the universe but humanity as well can be explained mechanically. All that human beings do is determined by appetites or aversions, and these in turn are either inherited or acquired through experience. In similar fashion, Hobbes maintained that there are no absolute standards of good and evil. Good is merely that which gives pleasure; evil, that which brings pain.

Spinoza and Hobbes, though important as recruits in the army of intellectual revolutionaries, were not, like Bacon and Descartes, primary instigators of that revolution. John Locke (1632–1704), the English philosopher, was. Locke, in his *Treatise of Civil Government,* posited a political philosophy based upon natural law which was used to justify the Glorious Revolution of 1688, and, later, the American and French Revolutions of the eighteenth century. He was, as well, the author of an extremely influential new theory of knowledge. Rejecting Descartes's doctrine of innate ideas, Locke maintained that all knowledge originates from sense perception. This theory had already been asserted by Hobbes; but Locke systematized and enlarged it. In his *Essay Concerning Human Understanding* (1690), he insisted that the human mind at birth is a blank tablet, a *tabula rasa,* upon which absolutely nothing is inscribed. It does not contain the idea of God or any notions of right and wrong. Not until the newborn child begins to have experiences, to perceive the external world with its senses, is anything registered in its mind. But the simple ideas which result directly from sense perception are merely the foundations of knowledge; no human being could live intelligently on the basis of them alone. These simple ideas must be integrated and fused into complex ideas. This is the function of reason or understanding, which has the power to combine, coordinate, and organize the impressions received from the senses and thus to build a usable body of general truth. Sensation and reason are both indispensable—the one for furnishing the mind with the raw materials of knowledge, the other for working them into meaningful form.

John Locke

Locke

Locke's theory of knowledge was as effective as were the ideas of Bacon and Descartes in freeing men and women from the restraints of received beliefs. If there was evil in the world, Locke's argument implied, it was not the result of some divine plan but rather of an environment and educational system that men and women had made and that men and women could change. Improve society, Locke was saying, and you will improve human behavior, since the latter takes its shape from the former. The optimism implicit in Locke grew explicit in the writings of other theorists as the eighteenth century progressed.

Locke's optimism

The fourth "founding father" of the intellectual revolution was the English scientist Isaac Newton (1642–1727). With the publication in 1687 of his *Mathematical Principles of Natural Philosophy,* Newton offered the world for the first time a single, coherent mechanical theory for the understanding of the universe. All measurable motion could be described by the same formulas. "Every particle of matter in the universe attracts every other particle with a force varying inversely as the square of the distance between them and directly proportional to the product of their masses." This force was gravity, which Newton dis-

Newton

Sir Isaac Newton

Implications of Newton's work

covered, and the proposition defining that force he held to be valid not only on the earth but throughout the endless expanse of the solar system. Newton's discoveries were "true" knowledge, in the Baconian sense, since they had been arrived at through observation, and since they were useful in assisting men and women in mastering the world in which they lived. The measurement of tides; the locating of ships on the ocean; the predictability of a cannon ball's trajectory—all this and much more was the practical result of Newton's scientific achievement.

The implications of Newton's work were those of the entire philosophical and scientific revolution to which he himself contributed so signally: first, that it is the task of philosophers and scientists—and of all thoughtful people—to challenge the received opinions of the past, to think matters out for themselves anew; second, that nature is governed neither by mysterious divine intervention nor by caprice, but by rational, universal laws, which can be formulated as precisely as mathematical principles. From this latter conclusion it was but one further step to the assumption that there exists a set of natural laws governing the politics of the nations of the earth. Those laws were presumed to be reasonable in the freedoms they afforded legitimately constituted authority, yet stern in their prohibitions against arbitrary power that operated against their fixed principles. Third, men and women, though subject to all the laws governing the universe, could, by discovering the way those laws worked, put them to use to ensure the progress of the human race.

2. THE PERSISTENCE OF SUPERSTITION

The strength of superstition

Despite remarkable achievements in thought, the period of the intellectual revolution was by no means free from superstitions. Numerous quaint and pernicious delusions continued to be accepted as valid truths. The illiterate masses clung to their beliefs in goblins, satyrs, and wizards and to their fear of the devil, whose malevolence was assumed to be the cause of diseases, famine, storms, and insanity. But superstition was not harbored in the minds of the masses alone. The astronomer Kepler believed in astrology and depended upon the writing of almanacs, with predictions of the future according to signs and wonders in the heavens, as his chief source of income. Not only did Francis Bacon accept the current superstition of astrology, he also contributed his endorsement of the witchcraft delusion. Newton also lent his voice to superstition; for example, he searched the Bible for hidden references predicting the reign of Anti-Christ.

The worst of all the superstitions that flourished in this period was unquestionably the witchcraft delusion, under which women were tortured and burned as the assistants of Satan. Belief in witchcraft was by no means unknown in the Middle Ages or the Renaissance, but it never reached the proportions of a dangerous hysteria until after the beginning of the Protestant Revolution. The persecutions attained their most virulent form in the very countries where religious conflict raged the fiercest, that is, in Germany and France. The witchcraft superstition was a direct outgrowth of the belief in Satan which obsessed the minds of so many of the Reformers. In general, the tendency of each camp of theologians was to ascribe all the victories of their opponents to the uncanny powers of the Prince of Darkness. With such superstitions prevailing among religious leaders, it is not strange that the mass of their followers should have harbored bizarre and hideous notions. The belief grew that the devil was really more powerful than God, and that no one was safe from destruction. It was assumed that Satan not only tempted mortals to sin, but actually forced them to sin. This was the height of his malevolence, for it jeopardized chances of salvation.

According to the definition of the theologians, witchcraft consisted in selling one's soul to the devil in return for supernatural powers. It was believed that a woman who had concluded such a bargain was thereby enabled to work all manner of spiteful magic against her neighbors—to cause their cattle to sicken and die, their crops to fail, or their children to fall into the fire. But the most valuable gifts bestowed by Satan were the power to blind husbands to their wives' misconduct or to cause women to give birth to idiots or deformed infants. It is commonly assumed that the so-called witches were toothless old hags whose cranky habits and venomous tongues had made them objects of suspicion and dread to all who knew them. However, the writers on the Continent and in England generally imagined the witch to be a "fair and wicked young woman," and a large percentage of those put to death in Germany and France were adolescent girls and women not yet thirty.

The earliest persecutions for witchcraft were those initiated by Pope Innocent VIII in 1484, who instructed his inquisitors to use torture in procuring convictions. But it was not until after the beginning of the Protestant Revolution that witchcraft persecution became a mass hysteria. Luther himself provided some of the impetus by recommending that witches should be put to death with fewer considerations of mercy than were shown to ordinary criminals. Other Reformers quickly followed Luther's example. Under Calvin's administration in Geneva, twenty-one women first had their right hands cut off and were then burned for the alleged crime in 1545. From this time on the persecutions spread like a pestilence. Women, young girls, and even mere children were tortured by driving needles under their nails, roasting their feet in the fire, or crushing their legs under heavy weights until the marrow spurted from their bones, in order to force them to confess filthy orgies with demons. To what extent the persecutions were due to sheer sadism or to the greed of magistrates, who were sometimes permitted to confiscate the property of those con-

Burning of Witches at Dernberg in 1555. From a sixteenth-century German pamphlet denouncing witchcraft.

victed, is impossible to say. There were few people who did not believe that the burning of witches was justifiable. One of the most zealous defenders of the trials was the French political philosopher, Jean Bodin. The final number of victims will never be known. In the 1620s there was an average of 1,000 burnings a year in the German cities of Würzburg and Bamberg, and around the same time it was said the town square of Wolfenbüttel "looked like a little forest, so crowded were the stakes."

Decline of witchcraft

After about 1650 the mania gradually began to subside. The reasons for the decline are difficult to discern. Most likely the principal causes were the revival of reason and the influence of scientists and skeptical philosophers. At the very zenith of the witch-burning frenzy certain lawyers began to have doubts as to the value of the evidence admitted at the trials. In 1584 an English jurist by the name of Reginald Scot published a book condemning the belief in witchcraft as irrational and asserting that most of the lurid crimes confessed by accused women were mere figments of disordered minds. Such eminent scientists as Pierre Gassendi (1592–1655) and William Harvey also denounced the persecutions. The physician Harvey coolly dissected a toad that was alleged to be a witch's accomplice in order to show that it was just like any other and that there was no devil in it. Such appeals to scientific demonstration finally put the witch-hunting mania to an end.

3. THE ENLIGHTENMENT

Enlightenment concepts

The eighteenth-century cultural climate known as the Enlightenment was grounded on the rational, optimistic foundations laid by the seventeenth-century thinkers of the intellectual revolution. Enlightenment philosophy, as expressed in the writings of its leading exponents and popularizers, embodied among its principal tenets the following ideas and assertions:

The place of men and women within the universe: Men and women were no longer perceived as the explanation for the existence of the universe, as they had been in the theologically conceived worldview of the medieval period. Instead, they were considered only one link in a rationally ordered chain of being that included all living things. Yet their subjection to universal ordering by no means rendered them powerless or without purpose. Men and women, recognizing the extent to which their senses could ensnare them in acts of individual folly, were urged to exercise their reason as responsible beings in campaigns to eradicate folly from human society as a whole.

Attitudes toward God and organized religion: A rationally ordered universe, subject to invariable laws, precluded the existence of a capricious God, who could intervene through the agency of miracles to contradict those laws. If God did exist, as most Enlightenment philosophers believed, it was simply as a prime mover, as the force which had devised the laws, set them in motion, and ensured their continued functioning. Men and women who held to this view called themselves Deists. They attacked the biblical foundations of Christianity by subjecting the Bible to scholarly criticism and then arguing that it was no more than mythology. They joined a larger body of critics in denouncing institutionalized religions as instruments of exploitation, devised by rogues and scoundrels to enable them to prey upon the ignorant masses. They rejected the prayers and sacraments of organized Christianity as useless; God, they argued, cannot be persuaded to disregard natural law for the benefit of particular persons. They condemned the doctrine of original sin as pernicious. Men and women have the freedom and the rational ability to choose between good and evil; the notion that some are predestined for salvation and others for damnation denies humanity the dignity with which its reason has endowed it.

Classical civilization as exemplar: Enlightenment philosophers, having for the most part rejected the moral pronouncements of organized Christianity as an inspiration for right living, sought guidance instead in the history of the classical civilizations of Greece and Rome. By making the Greeks and Romans the arbiters of civilized behavior, Enlightenment thinkers were helping to deny to Christianity its claim as the central fact of human history. They rifled the vast store of ancient wisdom for precepts from writers as diverse as Socrates and Marcus Aurelius. They delighted in those passages where the Greeks and Romans attacked superstition and praised toleration; but they exercised extreme selectivity, ignoring the fact that classical civilization, taken as a whole, was more prey to irrationality and intolerance than was that of eighteenth-century Europe.

Emphasis upon the affairs and concerns of this world: The substitution of earthly for divine models of behavior was part of a broader movement, characteristic of the Enlightenment, which stressed the importance of thoroughly understanding the workings of this world, while dismissing as either unknowable or inconceivable the existence of some heavenly world-to-come. Travel to distant parts of the globe, which increased considerably during the eighteenth century, encouraged men and women to study other contemporary civilizations. As they observed the Chinese, the Persians, or the Tahitians, they began to argue the relative virtue of various ways of life, very often praising the attitudes of the supposedly inferior "natives"—toward sex and religion, for example—as superior to those characteristic of "civilized" western Europe. Concentration on the life of this world was a reflection of the attitudes expressed by Bacon when he defined "true" knowledge, and by Locke when he expounded his theory of knowledge. Truth was derived from the here-and-now, the practical concrete business of daily life. Knowledge came with the daily experiences imprinted upon the "blank tablet" of one's mind.

Humanitarianism: True understanding of the present world could lead, Enlightenment thinkers insisted, to an improved world in the future. A more perfect society could be realized once men and women applied reason to the task of banishing superstition and inhumanity. Happiness was perceived as a goal attainable on earth. As we shall see, this belief translated itself into practical programs of reform which went some way toward eliminating social evils and improving the general lot of humanity.

Although the Enlightenment derived much of its inspiration from the work of Englishmen, and although it was a general European phenomenon, it blossomed to its fullest glory in France, where its ideas were expressed in the writings of a group calling themselves *philosophes.* Without question, its leading exponent and propagandist in France was François Marie Arouet, a writer who signed himself Voltaire. Voltaire epitomized the Enlightenment as Luther did the Reformation or Michelangelo the Italian Renaissance. Voltaire was born in 1694 and, despite his delicate physique, lived until 1778, within eleven years of the outbreak of the French Revolution. He developed a taste for satiric writing early in his life and got himself into numerous scrapes by his ridicule of noblemen and pompous officials. As a consequence of one of his lampoons he was sent to prison and afterwards exiled to England. Here he remained for three years, acquiring a deep admiration for British institutions, and composing his first philosophic work, which he entitled *Letters on the English.* In this work he popularized the ideas of Newton and Locke, whom he had come to regard as two of the greatest geniuses who ever lived. Most of his later writings—the *Philosophical Dictionary, Candide,* his histories, and many of his poems and essays—were also concerned with exposition of the doctrine that the world is governed by natural laws, and that reason and concrete experience are the only dependable guides for men and women to follow. Voltaire had contempt for the smug optimism of some Enlightenment thinkers, who taught that the ills of

Voltaire by Houdon

each make up the good of all, and that everything is for the best in the best of all possible worlds. He saw, on the contrary, universal misery, hatred, strife, and oppression. Only in his utopia of El Dorado, which he described in his novel *Candide* and placed somewhere in South America, were freedom and peace conceivable. Here there were no priests, no lawsuits, and no prisons. The inhabitants dwelt together without malice or greed, worshiping God in accordance with the dictates of reason, and solving their problems by logic and science. But this idyllic life was made possible only by the fact that the land was cut off by impassable mountains from the "regimented assassins of Europe."

Voltaire is best known as a champion of individual freedom. He regarded all restrictions upon liberty of speech and opinion as barbarous. In a letter to one of his opponents he wrote what has often been quoted as the highest criterion of intellectual tolerance: "I do not agree with a word that you say, but I will defend to the death your right to say it." But if there was any one form of repression that Voltaire abhorred more than others, it was the tyranny of organized religion. He blasted the cruelty of the Church in torturing and burning those who dared to question its dogmas. With reference to the whole system of persecuting and privileged orthodoxy, he adopted as his slogan, "Crush the infamous thing." He was almost as unsparing in his attacks upon political tyranny, especially when it resulted in the slaughter of thousands to satisfy the ambitions of despots. "It is forbidden to kill," he sarcastically asserted, "therefore all murderers are punished unless they kill in large numbers and to the sound of trumpets."

Religious toleration

Among the other philosophers of the Enlightenment in France were Denis Diderot (1713–1784), Jean d'Alembert (1717–1783), and the marquis de Condorcet (1743–1794). Diderot and d'Alembert were the chief members of a group known as the Encyclopedists, so-called from their contributions to the *Encyclopedia,* which was intended to be a complete summation of the philosophic and scientific knowledge of the age. In general, both of them agreed with the rationalism and liberalism of Voltaire. Diderot, for example, maintained that "men will never be free till the last king is strangled with the entrails of the last priest." D'Alembert, while accepting the rationalist and individualist tendencies of the Enlightenment, differed from most of his associates in advocating a diffusion of the new doctrines among all the people. The general attitude of his contemporaries, notably Voltaire, was to despise the common people, to regard them as fools beyond redemption from ignorance and grossness. But for d'Alembert the only assurance of progress lay in universal enlightenment. Accordingly, he maintained that the truths of reason and science should be taught to the masses in the hope that eventually the whole world might be freed from darkness and tyranny. Condorcet, who committed suicide during the course of the French Revolution, was, like

Diderot, d'Alembert, and Condorcet

See color map facing page 576

The *Philosophes* at Supper. An imaginary convocation of some of the greatest of the French Enlightenment thinkers. The seated figures are Voltaire, with his left hand raised, and, moving to his left, Diderot, Père Adam, Condorcet, d'Alembert; Abbé Maury, and La Harpe.

d'Alembert, a devout believer in the theory of human progress. His book, *The Outline of the Progress of the Human Mind,* written while he was in hiding from revolutionary extremists, argued the possibility of general social improvement as a result of the application of reason to the problems of the world.[1]

Lessing

Although the Enlightenment had much less influence in Germany than in France or England, it did give birth there to significant and progressive ideas. The most widely recognized of its German leaders was Gotthold Lessing (1729–1781), primarily a dramatist and critic but also a philosopher of humane and far-sighted views. The essence of his philosophy was tolerance, founded upon a sincere conviction that no one religion has a monopoly of truth. In his play, *Nathan the Wise,* he expounded the idea that nobility of character has no particular relation to theological creeds. Largely for this reason he condemned adherence to any one system of dogma and taught that the development of each of the world's great religions (Christianity included) was simply a step in the spiritual evolution of humanity.

Hume

Two other philosophers commonly given a place in the Enlightenment—the Scotsman David Hume (1711–1776) and the Frenchman Jean-Jacques Rousseau (1712–1778)—were neither of them in full agreement with the majority of their contemporaries. Hume is noted above all for his skepticism. Like Hobbes, he taught that the mind is a bundle of impressions, derived exclusively from the senses and tied together by habits of association. That is, we learn from experience to associate warmth with fire and nourishment with bread. If we had

[1] The political and economic doctrines of the Enlightenment will be treated more fully in the following chapter on the French Revolution.

never actually experienced the sensation of warmth, no reasoning faculty in our minds would enable us to draw the conclusion that fire produces heat. But constant repetition of the fact that when we see a flame we generally experience warmth leads to the habit of associating the two in our minds. Impressions and associations are all that there is to knowing. Since every idea in the mind is nothing but a copy of a sense impression, it follows that we can know nothing of final causes, the nature of substance, or the origin of the universe. We cannot be sure of any of the conclusions of reason except those which, like the principles of mathematics, can be verified by actual experience. All others are likely to be the products of feelings and desires, of animal urges and fears. In his challenge to preconceived ideas, Hume was following Enlightenment practice. Yet in denying the competence of reason, Hume placed himself almost entirely outside the mainstream of contemporary thoughts.

In similar measure, Rousseau repudiated many of the basic assumptions which originated with Newton and Locke. An unhappy man, Rousseau failed in nearly every occupation he undertook. He preached lofty ideals of educational reform, but abandoned his own children to a foundling asylum. He quarreled with everybody and reveled in morbid self-disclosures. Undoubtedly it was these qualities of temperament which were largely responsible for his revolt against the coldly intellectual doctrines of his contemporaries. He maintained that to worship reason as the infallible guide to conduct and truth is to lean upon a broken reed. In the really vital problems of life it is much safer to rely upon feelings, to follow our instincts and emotions. These are the ways of nature and are therefore more conducive to happiness than the artificial lucubrations of the intellect. The "thinking man is a depraved animal." Yet notwithstanding his contempt for reason, Rousseau was in other ways thoroughly in agreement with the viewpoint of the Enlightenment. He extolled the life of primitive civilizations more fervently than did any of his associates. He shared the impatience of the Enlightenment with every sort of restriction upon individual freedom, though he was much more concerned about the liberty and equality of the masses than were the other reformers of his time. Rousseau's dogmas of equality and popular sovereignty, though frequently misinterpreted, became the rallying cries of late–eighteenth-century revolutionaries and of thousands of more moderate opponents of the existing regime. And, as the chapter on the French Revolution will show, it was Rousseau's political philosophy that provided the inspiration for the modern ideal of majority rule.

Jean-Jacques Rousseau

A movement as profoundly disturbing to Western society as the Enlightenment was bound to have its effects upon social customs and individual habits. Not all of the social progress of this time can be traced to intellectual influences; much of it derived from the prosperity induced by the expansion of trade in the Commercial Revolution.

Broader effects of the Enlightenment

Humanitarianism

Nevertheless, the progress of philosophy and science had more than incidental effects in clearing away ancient prejudice and in building a more humane society.

Mention has already been made of the influence of the Enlightenment in promoting the cause of social reform. A characteristic expression of this influence was agitation for revision of drastic criminal codes and for more liberal treatment of prisoners. With regard to both, the need for reform was urgent. Penalties even for minor offenses were exceedingly severe in practically all countries, death being the punishment for stealing a horse or a sheep or for the theft of as little as five shillings in money. During the first half of the eighteenth century no fewer than sixty crimes were added to the capital list in England. The treatment accorded to bankrupts and debtors was also extremely harsh. Beaten and starved by their jailers, they died by the thousands in filthy prisons. Conditions such as these eventually challenged the sympathies of several reformers. Foremost among them was Cesare Beccaria (1738–1794), a jurist of Milan, who had been deeply influenced by the writings of French rationalist philosophers. In 1764 he published his famed treatise *Crimes and Punishments,* in which he condemned the common theory that penalties should be made as severe as possible in order to deter potential offenders. Insisting that the purpose of criminal codes should be the prevention of crime and the reform of the wayward, rather than vengeance, he urged the abolition of torture as unworthy of civilized nations. He likewise condemned capital punishment as contrary to the natural rights of humans, since it cannot be revoked in case of error. Beccaria's book created a sensation. It was translated into a dozen languages, and stimulated efforts to improve conditions in many countries. By the end of the eighteenth century some progress had been made in reducing the severity of penalties, in relieving debtors from punishment, and in providing work and better food for prisoners.

Antislavery

The humanitarian spirit of the Enlightenment found an outlet also in other directions. Several of the scientists and philosophers denounced the evils of slavery. Many more condemned the slave trade. The efforts of intellectuals in this regard were warmly seconded by the leaders of certain religious groups, especially by prominent Quakers in America. Pacifism was another ideal of many of the Enlightenment thinkers. Voltaire's strictures on war were by no means the only example of such sentiments. Rousseau attacked as illogical attempts to draw a distinction between just and unjust wars. From the pens of other *philosophes* emanated various ingenious plans for insuring perpetual peace, including a scheme drafted by a Frenchman, the Abbé de Saint-Pierre (1658–1743), for a league of nations to take concerted action against aggressors.

Influential though the ideas of the Enlightenment were, they were not all-pervading, nor did everyone who encountered them find them

persuasive. The intellectual revolution we have been describing occurred within a society the majority of whose members was illiterate
and, as we have seen, deeply superstitious. When Halley's comet,
named for the English astronomer Edmund Halley, made its appearance in 1682, popular imagination took it as an omen of impending
cataclysm, much as it interpreted the devastating Lisbon earthquake of
1755 as a sign of divine displeasure. Men and women, literate or not,
found it exceedingly difficult to surrender the reassuring idea that
humankind and its activities were the center upon which the world was
fixed. They continued to believe, despite what philosophers might tell
them, that God was interested in their individual plight, and that their
supplications would bring them the relief and support they sought.
The ignorant still resorted to the full demonology and mythology of
medieval folklore. The more thoughtful, dissatisfied with the theological and spiritual thinness of Deism or, indeed, of conventionally practiced orthodoxies, had recourse to an evangelicalism whose beliefs
were the antithesis of Enlightenment rationalism. Quietists, whose
greatest strength was in France, argued that God spoke directly to
them of salvation. They denied the need for institutionalized religion,
but for reasons far different from those of the Deists. The Jansenists,
another French sect, revived a belief in predestination. And in England, John Wesley (1703–1791), the founder of Methodism, stirred
mass meetings of thousands from mid-century on by preaching salvation through faith in God's love for sinful men and women.

Rejection of the ideas of the
Enlightenment

Yet the impact of the Enlightenment, qualified though it must be,
was nevertheless profound, both upon individuals and upon society as
a whole. Those who read and accepted its doctrines and discoveries
found their perceptions of themselves and their universe vastly altered. Its rationalism undoubtedly helped in some measure to improve
the human condition. And its insistence upon a social order controlled
by natural law and governed according to the practical experiences of
this world was eventually instrumental in bringing an end to the remaining vestiges of feudalism and the monopolies of unearned privilege.

The Enlightenment's
impact

4. SCIENCE AND THE INTELLECTUAL REVOLUTION

The intellectual revolution celebrated the triumph not only of reason
but of science as well. Prior to the seventeenth century, scientists had
worked in isolation from one another and in opposition to a worldview which was inclined to regard their work as suspect, if not as outright blasphemy. From the mid–seventeenth century on, however,
science became an international enterprise, encouraged by that willingness we have already noted to challenge accepted ideas, and supported by governments, as anxious as scientists themselves to put new

The prestige of science

An Illustration of a Laboratory from an Eighteenth-Century Edition of Diderot's *Encyclopedia*. The Enlightenment stressed the importance of scientific experiment.

discoveries to practical use. The Royal Society of London, founded in 1662 with King Charles II as its patron, and the French Academy of Sciences, founded four years later, stimulated the publication of scientific treatises and the exchange of scientific knowledge. Science was no longer seen as an esoteric field of inquiry, existing apart from the everyday business of the world. Instead it was welcomed for the very reason that its discoveries were proving to be of great value to humanity. Scientists themselves worked to apply their researach to the needs of society. Newton, for example, devised a series of navigational tables, by which the changing positions of the moon among the stars could be accurately predicted. And he invented the sextant for measuring these positions and thereby determining latitude and longitude.

Electricity
Some preliminary progress was made during this period in the understanding of electrical phenomena. At the beginning of the seventeenth century the Englishman William Gilbert (1540–1603), discovered the properties of lodestones and introduced the word "electricity" into the language.[2] Other scientists quickly became interested, and sensational results were anticipated from experiments with the marvelous "fluid." A learned Jesuit even suggested that two persons might communicate at a distance by means of magnetized needles which would point simultaneously to identical letters of the alphabet. Late in the eighteenth century Alessandro Volta (1745–1827) constructed the first battery. Still another important achievement in elec-

[2] "Electric" comes from the Greek word for amber. Gilbert and others had observed that amber rubbed on fur will attract paper, hair, straw, and various other things.

trical physics was the invention in 1746 of the Leyden jar for the storage of electric energy. It was mainly as a result of this invention that the American Benjamin Franklin (1706–1790) was able to show that lightning and electricity are identical. In his celebrated kite experiment in 1752 he succeeded in charging a Leyden jar from a thunderstorm.

Almost as spectacular as the progress in physics was the development of chemistry. If any one scientist can be called the founder of modern chemistry, it is Robert Boyle (1627–1691). The son of an Irish nobleman, Boyle achieved distinction in 1661 with the publication of his *Sceptical Chymist, or Chymico-Physical Doubts and Paradoxes.* In this work he rejected the theories of the alchemists and thereby contributed toward the establishment of chemistry as a pure science. In addition, he distinguished between a mixture and a compound, learned a great deal about the nature of phosphorus, produced alcohol from wood, suggested the idea of chemical elements, and reviewed the atomic theory. No scientist before his time had foreshadowed so much of the knowledge of modern chemistry.

Chemistry: Boyle

Despite the work of Boyle, little further development of chemistry occurred for almost a hundred years. The reason lay partly in the wide acceptance of errors concerning such matters as heat, flame, air, and the phenomenon of combustion. The most common of these errors was the so-called phlogiston theory. The theory was based on the idea that phlogiston was the substance of fire—i.e., when an object burned, phlogiston was supposed to be given off. The remaining ash was said to be the "true" material. In the second half of the eighteenth century important discoveries were made which ultimately overthrew this theory and cleared the way for a real understanding of some of the most familiar chemical reactions. In 1766 the Englishman Henry Cavendish reported the discovery of a new kind of gas obtained by treating iron, zinc, and other metals with sulphuric acid. He showed that this gas, now known as hydrogen, would not of itself support combustion, and yet would be rapidly consumed by a fire with access to the air. In 1774 oxygen was discovered by another Englishman, the Unitarian minister Joseph Priestley. He found that a candle would burn with extraordinary vigor when placed in the new gas—a fact which indicated clearly that combustion was not caused by any mysterious principle or substance in the flame itself. A few years after this discovery, Cavendish demonstrated that air and water, long supposed to be elements, are actually a mixture and a compound, respectively, the first being composed principally of oxygen and nitrogen and the second of oxygen and hydrogen.

Cavendish and Priestley

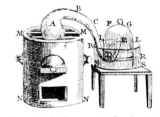

Lavoisier's Apparatus for the Decomposition of Air

The final blow to the phlogiston theory was administered by the Frenchman Antoine Lavoisier (1743–1794), one of the greatest of all scientists of the intellectual revolution, who later lost his life in the French Revolution. Lavoisier proved that both combustion and respiration involve oxidation, the one being rapid and the other slow. He

Lavoisier

provided the names for oxygen and hydrogen, demonstrated that the diamond is a form of carbon, and argued that life itself is essentially a chemical process. But undoubtedly his greatest accomplishment was his discovery of the law of the conservation of mass. He found evidence that "although matter may alter its state in a series of chemical actions, it does not change in amount; the quantity of matter is the same at the end as at the beginning of every operation, and can be traced by its weight." This "law" has, of course, been modified by later discoveries regarding the structure of the atom and the conversion of some forms of matter into energy. It is hardly too much to say, however, that as a result of Lavoisier's genius chemistry became a true science.

Biology

Although the physical sciences received the major attention in the intellectual revolution, the biological sciences were by no means neglected. One of the greatest of the early biologists was the Englishman Robert Hooke (1635–1703), the first to see and describe the cellular structure of plants. This achievement was soon followed by the work of Marcello Malpighi (1628–1694) in demonstrating the sexuality of plants and in comparing the breathing function of vegetable leaves with that of the lungs of animals. About the same time a Dutch businessman and amateur scientist, Anthony van Leeuwenhoek (1632–1723), discovered protozoa and bacteria and wrote the first description of human sperm. The seventeenth century also witnessed some progress in embryology. About 1670 the Dutch physician, Jan Swammerdam (1637–1680), carefully described the life history of certain insects from the caterpillar stage to maturity and compared the change of tadpole into frog with the development of the human embryo.

Linnaean classification

In many ways the end of the seventeenth century appeared to mark a decline of originality in the sciences that deal with living things. During the next hundred years biologists were inclined more and more to center their efforts upon description and classification of knowledge already in existence. The most brilliant classifier of biological knowledge was the Swedish scientist, Carl von Linné (1707–1778), more commonly known by his Latinized name of Linnaeus. In his *System of Nature* and in his *Botanical Philosophy* Linnaeus divided all natural objects into three kingdoms: stone, animal, and vegetable. Each of these kingdoms he subdivided into classes, genera, and species. He invented the system of biological nomenclature still in use, by which every plant and animal is designated by two scientific names, the first denoting the genus and the second the species. Thus he called humans *Homo sapiens*. Linnaeus's system of classification was widely adopted even in his own time.

Buffon

The second great genius of descriptive biology in the eighteenth century was the Frenchman Georges Buffon (1707–1788). His *Natural History* in forty-four volumes, though intended as a general summation of science, dealt mainly with humans and other vertebrates. While much of the material in this work was taken from the writings of other scientists and from the accounts of travelers, the author was able to reduce a vast body of knowledge to orderly arrangement and enliven it with his own interpretations. Buffon recognized the close relationship between humans and the higher animals. Though he could never quite bring himself to accept the full implications of a theory that linked human evolution directly to that of other animals, he was nonetheless strongly impressed by the striking resemblances among all of the higher species. He admitted the possibility that the entire range of organic forms had descended from a single species.

Despite the notable scientific advances of the seventeenth and eighteenth centuries, the development of physiology and medicine progressed rather slowly during the same period, and for several reasons. One was the inadequate preparation of physicians, many of whom had begun their professional careers with little more training than a kind of apprenticeship under an older practitioner. Another was the common disrepute in which surgery was held as a mere trade, like that of a barber or blacksmith. Perhaps the most serious of all was the prejudice against dissection of human bodies for use in anatomical study. As late as 1750 medical schools which engaged in this practice were in danger of destruction by irate mobs. Despite these obstacles some progress was still possible. About 1670 Malpighi and Leeuwenhoek confirmed the famous discovery of the Englishman William Harvey by observing the actual flow of blood through the network of capillaries connecting the arteries and veins. At approximately the same time an eminent physician of London, Thomas Sydenham, proposed a new theory of fever as a natural process by which diseased material is expelled from the system.

Medicine

Medical progress during the eighteenth century was somewhat more rapid. Among the noteworthy achievements were the discovery of blood pressure, the founding of histology or microscopic anatomy, the development of the autopsy as an aid to the study of disease, and the recognition of scarlet fever as a malady distinct from smallpox and measles. But the chief milestones of medical advancement in this period were the adoption of inoculation and the development of vaccination for smallpox. Knowledge of inoculation came originally from the Near East, where it had long been employed by the Muslims. Information concerning its use was relayed to England in 1717 through the letters of Lady Montagu, wife of the British ambassador to Turkey. The first systematic application of the practice in the Western world, however, was due to the efforts of the American Puritan leaders, Cotton and Increase Mather, who implored the physicians of Boston to inoculate their patients in the hope of curbing an epidemic of smallpox which had broken out in 1721. By the middle of the century inoculation was quite generally employed by physicians in Europe and in

Inoculation

America. In 1796 a milder method of vaccination was discovered by the Englishman Edward Jenner. It was now revealed that direct inoculation of human beings with the deadly virus of smallpox was unnecessary: a vaccine manufactured in the body of an animal would be just as effective and much less likely to have disastrous results. The vast possibilities thus opened up for the elimination of contagious diseases appeared to confirm the Enlightenment belief in the ability of men and women to make nature's laws work for the betterment of the human condition.

5. CLASSICISM IN ART AND LITERATURE

Classical models

The history of European art and literature during the seventeenth and eighteenth centuries reflects the respect for the classical world which we have noted as a particular characteristic of Enlightenment thought. Artists and writers strove to imitate classical models. They chose classical titles and themes for many of their works and embellished them wherever possible with allusions to antique mythology. Deploring the destruction of ancient civilization by "Christian barbarians," they were unable to see much value in the cultural achievements of later centuries. In particular, they despised what they termed the "Middle Ages" as a long night of barbaric darkness stretching between the classical period and their own. Most would have agreed with the dictum of Rousseau that the Gothic cathedrals were "a disgrace to those who had the patience to build them."

Left: *St. Peter's Cathedral, Rome.* The sweeping colonnades, designed by Bernini and begun in 1656, express the dramatic splendor that was characteristic of baroque architecture. Right: *St. Paul's Cathedral, London.* Designed by Christopher Wren, the boldness of the structure reflected the emergence of England as a world power.

The Chateau of Versailles. Dramatically expanded by Louis XIV in the 1660s from a hunting lodge to the principal royal residence and the seat of government, the chateau became the standard of secular baroque architecture and a monument to the international power and prestige of the Grand Monarch.

These attitudes were an inheritance from the Renaissance humanists. Yet the classicism of the seventeenth and eighteenth centuries was no mere copy of that espoused by earlier artists and writers. As adopted by architects, painters, and sculptors, classicism emerged in new forms as the baroque style. This style was initially developed as part of the Catholic Reformation of the late sixteenth century. Churches were built in a manner designed to inspire renewed reverence and respect for the Church of Rome. Classical elements such as columns, domes, and architectural sculpture were combined in such a way as to express both aggressive restlessness and extraordinary power. The results are clearly visible in a structure such as Giovanni Lorenzo Bernini's (1598–1680) colonnades at St. Peter's in Rome. The Englishman Christopher Wren (1632–1723), with Bernini among the most gifted of baroque architects, employed the same style in his design for St. Paul's Cathedral in Protestant London, an architectural statement whose grandeur challenged the authority claimed by Roman Catholicism.

The baroque style

The baroque style was soon adopted by the absolutist monarchs of seventeenth-century Europe to symbolize their power and magnificence. The palace of Louis XIV at Versailles is undoubtedly the supreme example of secular baroque architecture. Buildings and grounds together are a remarkable expression of the formality and hierarchy of the autocratic state, and of the power invested in the person of the monarch. Other European rulers commissioned royal residences in the style of Versailles: Peter the Great, for example, built the Peterhof at his capital of St. Petersburg; King William of England employed Wren to embellish the already standing palace of Hampton Court. None of these structures, however, could rival Versailles, ei-

Royal Baroque

Left: *The Petit Trianon, Versailles.* Added as a royal retreat in the gardens of Versailles by Louis XV, this structure expresses the refined elegance that characterized rococo architecture. Right: *The Interior of the Pilgrimage Church, Bavaria.* An example of the flamboyance of the late baroque architectural style.

ther in its grandeur or its total devotion to the harmony and proportion which characterized the baroque.

During the eighteenth century the baroque style gradually gave way to further adaptations of the classical. On the Continent, the baroque *Rococo* was succeeded by the rococo, a term perhaps derived from the French words for rock and shell (*rocaille* and *coquille*), two natural forms often employed in both exterior and interior rococo ornamentation. The rococo differed from the baroque in several ways: it was lighter, less majestic; it created an impression of grace and refinement. In place of a struggle for dynastic power and colonial empire, much of European society by now focused its attention on the dilletantism and elegance of the court of Louis XV, which set the standard for continental behavior among the ruling classes. The rococo both represented and reflected this change in focus. Well-known examples of the rococo are the Petit Trianon, a small palace built on the grounds of Versailles, which was designed as a royal retreat, and the palace of Sans Souci (literally, "Without Care") at Potsdam, built by Frederick the Great.

In England reaction to the baroque took the form of a return to the severer classicism of Renaissance architecture, adapted from the de-*Palladianism* signs of the Italian architect, Andrea Palladio (1508–1580) and from those of the seventeenth-century Englishman, Inigo Jones. Most of the imposing country houses built by the landed gentry in this period displayed a fidelity to the precise mathematical equations of neo-Palladianism. As such they reflected the general Enlightenment worship of reason and order.

To a certain extent the evolution of painting during the seventeenth and eighteenth centuries paralleled that of architecture. The greatest painters in the baroque tradition were the Flemish artists, Peter Paul Rubens (1577–1640) and Anthony Van Dyck (1599–1641), and the Spaniard, Diego Velásquez (1599–1660). Rubens was the outstanding genius among these three. In such works as *The Fates Spinning* and *Venus and Adonis,* he combined classical themes with sumptuous baroque color and richness pleasing to the affluent merchants and nobles of his day. The pink and rounded flesh of his full-blown nudes is thoroughly in keeping with the robust vitality of the age. Both Rubens and his gifted pupil, Anthony Van Dyck, are noted for their portraits of rulers and nobles, with full attention paid to the gorgeous details of elegant apparel and opulent furnishings in the background. Van Dyck's best-known portraits are those of the English kings, James I and Charles I, and their families. Velásquez, the third great artist of the baroque tradition, was the court painter to Philip IV of Spain. Much of his work consisted of royal portraits, suffused in soft and silvery light but fundamentally empty of meaning or emotional expression, a testimony, perhaps, to the waning power of the Spanish Empire.

Rubens's Portrait of His Son Nicolaus

See color plates following page 576

Venus and Adonis by Peter Paul Rubens. Rubens often painted classical themes, which he conceived on a grand scale and executed with sweeping vigor.

Rembrandt

Self-Portrait by Rembrandt

Classical literature

All of the painters mentioned thus far were exponents in some degree of the classical influence. But there were others in both the seventeenth and eighteenth centuries who refused to be bound by the prevailing artistic conventions. Foremost among them was Rembrandt van Rijn (1606–1669), now universally considered one of the greatest painters of all time. The son of a well-to-do miller of Leyden, Rembrandt was allowed to begin his artistic education at an early age. Under a series of native masters he learned the technique of subtle coloring and a skillful depiction of natural phenomena. Famous by the time he was twenty-five, he fell upon evil days later in his life, mainly as a consequence of bad investments and the failure of critics to appreciate his more recondite works. In 1656 he was stripped by his creditors of all he possessed and driven from his house. Apparently these reverses served mainly to broaden and deepen his philosophy, for in this very same year he produced some of his greatest achievements. As a painter Rembrandt surpassed all the other members of the Dutch school and deserves to be ranked with the painters of the High Renaissance in Italy like Titian and Leonardo. No artist had a keener understanding of the problems and trials of human nature or a stronger perception of the mysteries of life. His portraits, including those of himself, are imbued with an introspective quality and with a suggestion that the half is not being told. Rembrandt departed from the subjects of classical mythology, preferring to portray solemn rabbis, tattered beggars, and scenes from the Old and New Testaments, rich in drama and in human interest. Some of his best-known works include *The Good Samaritan, The Woman Taken in Adultery, The Marriage of Samson,* and *The Night Watch.*

The history of literature in the seventeenth and eighteenth centuries exhibited tendencies quite similar to those of art. The most popular literary ideal was classicism, which generally meant not only a studied imitation of classical forms but also an earnest devotion to reason as a way of life. Although literary classicism was not confined to any one country, its principal center was France. The most noted member of the French group of poets and dramatists was Jean-Baptiste Poquelin (1622–1673), who is much better known by his adopted name of Molière. Less respectful of ancient formalism than any of his associates, Molière was the most original of French comedians. Few keener critics of human nature have ever lived. "The business of comedy," he once declared, "is to represent in general all the defects of men and especially of the men of our time." The mortal weakness he delighted most to ridicule was pretentiousness, as he did so brilliantly in plays such as *Tartuffe.* But with all of this penchant for satire, Molière had a measure of pity for the evil fortunes of humankind. In a number of his plays sympathy and even melancholy go hand in hand with clever wit and pungent scorn. His genius was probably broader in scope than that of any other dramatist since Shakespeare. Two French play-

Aristotle Contemplating the Bust of Homer by Rembrandt. A fine example of Rembrandt's obsession with the effects of light and shade as means of expression.

wrights whose work more directly mirrored the classical tradition were Pierre Corneille (1606–1684) and Jean Racine (1639–1699). Both took as their subjects the heroes and heroines of ancient literature and history—Medea, Pompey, and Phaedra, for example; and both chose as their literary models the poets and dramatists of classical Greece and Rome.

Seventeenth-century England also produced writers in the classical style. The greatest was the renowned Puritan poet, John Milton (1608–1674). The leading philosopher of Cromwell's Commonwealth, Milton wrote the official defense of the beheading of Charles I. Nearly all of his writings were phrased in the reasoned and formal expression of the classical tradition, while many of the lesser ones took their themes from Greek mythology. But Milton was as much a Puritan as he was a classicist. He could never escape from the idea that the essence of beauty is morality. Moreover, he was deeply interested in theological problems. His greatest work, *Paradise Lost,* is a synthesis of the religious beliefs of his age, a majestic epic of the Protestant faith. In spite of the fact that Milton was a Puritan, his views reflected ideas characteristic of the intellectual revolution. The principal themes of *Paradise Lost* are the moral responsibility of the individual and the importance of knowledge as an instrument of virtue. Paradise is lost repeatedly in human life to the extent that men and women allow passion to triumph over reason in determining the course of their actions.

Milton

Classicism in English literature reached its zenith in the eighteenth century with the poetry of Alexander Pope (1688–1744). Pope was a great exponent in verse of the mechanistic and Deist doctrines of the Enlightenment. In such poetic works as his *Essay on Man* and his *Essay on Criticism* he set forth the view that nature is governed by inflexible laws, and that men and women must study and follow nature if they

John Milton. From the First Edition of his poems, 1645.

Gin Lane by William Hogarth. Hogarth, like his friend Henry Fielding, believed in portraying human nature as he found it. In this famous engraving, he is preaching a sermon against the gin trade, one of the besetting evils of eighteenth-century London.

Literature in eighteenth-century England

would bring any semblance of order into human affairs. Other English writers, however, turned from classical models to describe, castigate, and celebrate present-day eighteenth-century society. Jonathan Swift (1667–1745), Daniel Defoe (1660–1737), and Henry Fielding (1707–1754) all took as their subjects human nature as it manifested itself in the lives of their contemporaries. Swift, in *Gulliver's Travels,* ridiculed current human pretensions and political realities by contrasting them with the perceptions of a series of mythical races. Defoe, in *Robinson Crusoe,* the tale of one man's survival on a desert island, extolled practical ingenuity and defended the subjugation of indigenous peoples by Europeans. Fielding, in *Tom Jones,* the first modern novel, and one of the greatest, declared that men and women, if they are to be portrayed as they should be, must be depicted not as impossibly virtuous heroes and heroines, but simply as real people, responsible for their actions.

6. MUSIC IN THE SEVENTEENTH AND EIGHTEENTH CENTURIES

Italian opera

The seventeenth century witnessed a dramatic change in the form of musical structure and composition, one which reflected shifts occurring elsewhere in the intellectual world. As we have previously observed, the end of the sixteenth century had marked the culmination of a long era of choral, polyphonic music. Almost immediately, however, a reaction set in, so powerful that the polyphonic style became obsolete within twenty-five years of the death of its most gifted and advanced practitioner, Palestrina, in 1594. A new ideal, that of primary voice accompanied by one of several musical instruments, swept Italy in a remarkably short time, and became known as monody. One of the major reasons for this change was a growing and characteristically baroque insistence upon the dramatic, and a realization on the part of Italian composers that the intense feelings of an individual cannot be adequately expressed by a many-voiced chorus. The same impulses that produced the architecture of Bernini and the paintings of Rubens led to the creation of opera, which reached its first powerful manifestation in *Orfeo* (1607) by the Italian Claudio Monteverdi (1567–1643), the dominating musical personality in the first half of the new century. Within a generation operas were performed in most important cities in Italy; by 1736 Venice boasted an opera house for every parish. Opera, staged within magnificent settings, and calling upon the talents of singers, musicians, artists, dramatists, and as master of the grand design—the conductor—expressed as clearly as any art form the dedication of the baroque to grandeur, complexity, and display.

During this same period, the instrumental tradition of the Renaissance began to produce works for organ, harpsichord, and the various string and wind instruments. In the last third of the century instrumental music created the concerto, along with opera one of the greatest original stylistic accomplishments of the Italian baroque. Both opera and concerto soon spread beyond the Alps. Though the seventeenth century was preoccupied with musical experiments, it created an impressive synthesis upon which the first half of the eighteenth century could build the final great achievements of late baroque music.

The concerto

The late baroque culminated in two towering composers: Johann Sebastian Bach (1685–1750) and George Frederick Handel (1685–1759). Though both were born in Saxony, Bach became the epitome of German musical genius, while Handel, who lived for almost half a century in London and became a British subject, embodied an English national style. Bach combined an unbounded imagination and a capacious intellect with heroic powers of discipline and an unquenchable zeal for work. By lifelong study he made himself the master of most existing types and styles of music, from little dance pieces for the clavichord to gigantic choral works. As a church musician, Bach's duty was to provide new music for elaborate Sunday and holy day services. Therefore the bulk of his work is made up of cantatas (over 200 preserved), oratorios, Passions, and Masses. His settings of the Gospels according to St. John and St. Matthew represent the unsurpassable peak of this genre. Fundamentally, though, Bach was an instrumental composer, the creator of tremendous works for organ and harpsichord, and of spacious concertos and sonatas for various combinations of instruments, and suites for orchestra. Bach was steeped in German Protestantism in a way that makes him, in one sense, uncharacteristic of the generally antireligious Enlightenment.

Johann Sebastian Bach

"The Charming Brute." A contemporary caricature of Handel, engraved by Joseph Groupy, 1754.

Classical music

Mozart

Yet no one who has heard Bach's music or studied his scores can deny the extent to which they reflect the attention to rational order and mathematical harmony that lay at the heart of the intellectual revolution.

Handel was the absolute antithesis of his great fellow-Saxon. After four years spent in Italy he completely absorbed Italian techniques and modes of composition, subsequently settling in England, where for years he ran an opera company that produced nothing but Italian operas, mostly his own. Italian opera did not suit the English middle class public, however, and after decades spent in composing and producing dozens of operas, Handel realized that he must turn to something more acceptable to the English taste. This he found in the "oratorio," a musical drama intended for performance in concert form. With the exception of *Messiah,* the most famous of his oratios, these works were not religious music, although their themes came from the Old Testament. Undoubtedly one reason for Handel's success in his adopted country was the fact that his virile and heroic oratorios could be said to symbolize the English people, their pride in their institutions and their attainment of national greatness.

After the mid–eighteenth century, the center of the musical world shifted to Vienna, where a group of highly gifted composers achieved a remarkable stylistic synthesis by reconciling baroque weightiness, rococo charm, and preromantic excitement into the form that has been labeled classical. Christoph Willibald von Gluck (1714–1787) reformed the declining "serious" opera into a noble drama that recalls the tone of classical antiquity. The appeal of the mischievous, Italian comic opera, the *opera buffa,* forced a fusion with serious opera which reached its greatest height in the operas of Wolfgang Amadeus Mozart (1756–1791), while chamber and orchestral music achieved a new formal and expressive level under the leadership of Joseph Haydn (1732–1809).

The eighteenth century was full of music, but its social organization severely hampered the creative artist. Handel, who ran his own business and left behind a respectable estate, was an exception to the general rule. In most instances, if a composer or musician was not employed by a court, noble house, church, or municipality, or if he was not an internationally acclaimed virtuoso or a renowned teacher, he ran the risk of being ground down in an effort to make a living. Mozart was among the first to shed the security of a position as "musical lackey" and to try the free artistic economy of the metropolis. While a child prodigy he was adored and admired, but when he left the employ of the archbishop of Salzburg to take up the career of a freelance artist in Vienna, he could support himself only with the greatest difficulty. Although the remaining ten years of his life were spent in bountiful productivity, he had to live from hand to mouth. Financial troubles pursued him until his death at the age of thirty-five.

Mozart, at the Age of Six, Plays Before Empress Maria Theresa. This contemporary illustration suggests the importance of royal patronage and the often demeaning relationship between artists and patrons in this era.

When appraising the music of the classical era we must realize that in spite of its magnificent sonatas and symphonies, the stylistic core of the era was still in the dramatic music of the opera. Mozart used the operatic form to shape the characters, fates, and conflicts of human beings in a way that other forms too became permanent. Each great Mozart opera—*The Marriage of Figaro, Don Giovanni, The Magic Flute*—provides a center from which the form of piano sonatas, quartets, quintets, concertos, and symphonies were subsequently derived by his successors.

Mozart's operas

Haydn was carved from sterner timber than Mozart; his peasant background made him tenacious and stubborn. If Mozart embodied the aristocratic spirit, Haydn did that of the liberated plebeian. It was because of their diametrically opposed personalities that the two musicians got along so well; they complemented each other, learned from each other, and, in fact, were friends. Haydn had a sharp intellect and acquired his extensive knowledge of music through incessant study and experimentation. His art conveys the impressions of the village and the countryside, but also the elegance of the princely Austrian household that patronized him for many years. Haydn's compositions are so numerous that a complete edition of them has never been made. They include many operas and Masses, oratorios, concertos, over eighty string quartets, and more than 100 symphonies. It was Haydn who firmly established the technical and stylistic principles of symphonic construction, creating, with Mozart, the pattern of the symphony orchestra which remained the basis for all future musical developments.

Joseph Haydn

The careers of Mozart and Haydn suggest both the achievements and limitations of the revolution we have traced. Their compositional innovations were a part of that broad series of intellectual changes that assisted in carrying Europe forward into the modern world. Yet

Haydn's dependence upon aristocratic patronage, and Mozart's inability to live apart from it, make clear the extent to which the world of the Enlightenment remained a world bound together by rank and privilege. Only at the very end of the eighteenth century, with the coming of the French and Industrial Revolutions, did the ideas of the intellectual revolution begin to play an active role in altering, in any major way, the structure of the social and political institutions of the West.

SELECTED READINGS

- *Items so designated are available in paperback editions.*
- Carl Becker, *The Heavenly City of the Eighteenth-Century Philosophers,* New Haven, Conn., 1932. Relates the Enlightenment to its medieval origins.
- Burford, W. H., *Germany in the Eighteenth Century: The Social Background of the Literary Revival,* London, 1935. A combination of social and intellectual history, this work remains the best introduction in English to the German Enlightenment.

  Cassirer, Ernst, *The Philosophy of the Enlightenment,* Princeton, N.Y., 1951. Emphasizes the role of critical thinking on the part of the *philosophes* and the nature of reason in the Enlightenment.

  Cobban, Alfred, *In Search of Humanity: The Role of the Enlightenment in Modern History,* London, 1960.
- Gay, Peter, *The Enlightenment: An Interpretation;* Vol. I, *The Rise of Modern Paganism;* Vol. II, *The Science of Freedom,* New York, 1966–69. A brilliant work by the leading authority on the eighteenth-century intellectual world. Argues that the Enlightenment represented a complete break with the medieval past and the first stage of the modern world. Contains superb bibliographies.

  Gillespie, C. C., *The Edge of Objectivity: An Essay in the History of Scientific Ideas,* Princeton, N.J., 1960.
- Grimsley, Ronald, *Jean-Jacques Rousseau: A Study in Self-Awareness,* Cardiff, 1961. An excellent biography concerned with Rousseau's psychological development.

  Haldane, E. S., *Descartes, His Life and Times,* London, 1905. An old but thorough biography.
- Hall, A. R., *The Scientific Revolution, 1500–1800: The Formation of the Modern Scientific Attitude,* rev. ed., New York, 1966.
- Hampshire, Stuart, *Spinoza,* London, 1952.

  Havens, George R., *The Age of Ideas: From Reaction to Revolution in Eighteenth-Century France,* New York, 1955. Short biographies of the major French *philosophes.*

  Humphreys, A. R., *The Augustan World: Society, Thought, and Letters in Eighteenth-Century England,* London, 1954.

  Manuel, Frank E., *A Portrait of Isaac Newton,* Cambridge, Mass., 1968. A psychoanalytic interpretation.

  Mellone, S. H., *The Dawn of Modern Thought: Descartes, Spinoza, Leibniz,* London, 1930. Explains the Cartesian system and its influence.

0   500 miles

SCOTLAND   • ADAM SMITH, 1723
     • △ Edinburgh
BURNS,   HUME,
1759   1711
GOLDSMITH,   ENGLAND
1728 •   • Dublin   • PRIESTLEY, 1733
  SWIFT,   Liverpool
IRELAND   1667   RICHARDSON,   NEWTON, 1642
     1689   PAINE,   LEEUWENHOUK,
BOYLE,   DRYDEN,   1737   1632
1627   S. JOHNSON,   1631   VERMEER,   NETHERLANDS
   1709   WREN, GAINSBOROUGH,   1632   SPINOZA, 1632
LOCKE, 1632   1632   1727   Delft • Leiden
FIELDING,   London • JENNER, 1749   REMBRANDT,   Göttingen
1707   HOBBES,   1606   RUBENS,   BACH,
   1588   HARVEY,   1577   1685
   HOOKE,   1578   VAN DYCK,   HOLY   ROMAN
   1635   CORNEILLE,   1599
BACON, 1561   1606   WATTEAU,   GOETHE, 1749
DEFOE, 1659   1684   Frankfurt
GIBBON, 1737   CONDORCET,   Mannheim   EMPIRE
MILTON, 1608   1743   RACINE,   Vienna
POPE, 1688   VOLTAIRE, 1694   Paris 1639   GLUCK
   LAVOISIER, 1743   MOLIERE,   1714
     1623   DIDEROT,   KEPLER,   Munich   HAYDN,
  DESCARTES,   • 1713   1571   Salzburg   1732
  1596   △ • Dijon   SWITZ.   MOZART,   AUSTRIA
     FRANCE   ROUSSEAU, Geneva   1756   HUNGARY
     1712
PASCAL,   Verona   MONTEVERDE,   OTTOMAN
1623   1567   EMPIRE
MONTESQUIEU,   Turin •   Bologna
Bordeaux   1689   • Genoa   MALPIGHI,
     1628 • Florence
     • Toulouse   Marseilles   GALILEO,   ITALY
     1564

ATLANTIC

OCEAN

CORSICA   • Rome △
     BERNINI,
• Barcelona   1598
     SARDINIA   • Naples
PORTUGAL   Tagus R.   • Madrid
   BALEARIC
△ • Lisbon   SPAIN   ISLANDS
   VELAZQUEZ,
   1599   SICILY
   • Seville

SEA

DENMARK   LINNAEUS,
     1707
   • △ Copenhagen   BALTIC   SEA
     KANT, 1724
     Königsberg •
• Hamburg
   Elbe R.
   HANDEL,   • Berlin   POLAND
   1685   Oder R.   Vistula R.

Garonne R.   Seine R.   Loire R.   Rhine R.   Rhone R.   Danube R.

MEDITERRANEAN   SEA

ADRIATIC SEA

THE INTELLECTUAL REVOLUTION
OF THE SEVENTEENTH AND EIGHTEENTH CENTURIES

•   Birthplaces of scientists, artists, and writers
△   Scientific academies
–·–·–   Boundaries ca. 1740

The Last Judgment, Peter Paul Rubens (1577–1640). Vivid colors, voluptuous figures, and classical themes are typical of Rubens' work. (Alte Pinakothek, Munich)

England and Scotland Crowning Charles I, Rubens. This scene was part of a series painted in Whitehall Palace, London, to glorify the Stuart family. (Minneapolis Institute of Art)

Pope Innocent X, Velásquez. (Doria-Pamphili Collection)

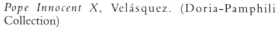

The Marchessa Durazzo, Anthony Van Dyck (1599–1641). This portrait of a Genoese noblewoman suggests the Italian Renaissance sophistication admired by the Flemish burghers. (MMA)

The Night Watch, Rembrandt. (The Rijksmuseum)

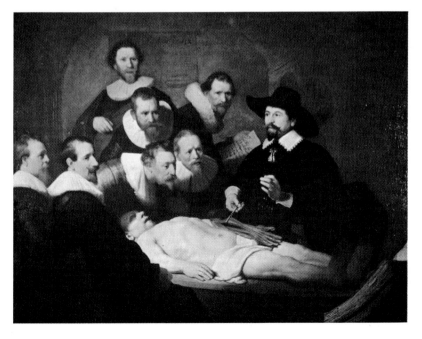

The Anatomy Lesson, Rembrandt van Rijn (1606–1669). Rembrandt scorned the classical themes of his contemporaries and turned to character analysis and the portrayal of life. (Mauritshuis, The Hague)

The Stonemason's Yard, Canaletto (1697–1768). A quiet scene of everyday life, in strong contrast to the portrait below. (National Gallery, London)

Marriage à la Mode, William Hogarth (1697–1764). A satirical look at the arranged marriage: the financial needs of the nobleman and the social aspirations of his middle class counterpart dominate the negotiations. (National Gallery, London)

Le Mezzetin, Antoine Watteau (1684–1721). Mezzetin was a popular character in Italian comedy who was much liked in France. Watteau enjoyed portraying the make-believe world of the court with its festivals and formalized elegance. (MMA)

The Blue Boy, Thomas Gainsborough (1727–1788). Though the costume suggests the romantic ideal of Prince Charming, the face is a penetrating study of the moodiness and uncertainty of adolescence. (Huntington Library)

Sarah Siddons as the Tragic Muse, Sir Joshua Reynolds (1723–1792). Mrs. Siddons, a famous actress of the XVIII cent., is here portrayed as the Queen of Tragedy, in accordance with Reynolds' habit of depicting wealthy patrons in impressive classical poses. (Huntington Library)

Madame de Pompadour, François Boucher (1703–1770). This portrait idealizes the favorite mistress of Louis XV. (The Wallace Collection, London)

Madame Recamier, Jacques Louis David (1748–1825). David was the exponent of a new classicism during and after the French Revolution. The couch, the lamp, and the costume are copied from Rome and Pompeii. (Louvre)

Execution of the Rioters, Francisco Goya (1746–1828). Unlike most artists of his time, Goya dealt unflinchingly with suffering, violence, fear, and death. Depicted here is the execution of Spanish rebels by Napoleon's soldiers in 1808. This harshness caused the rebellion to spread over the whole peninsula. (Prado)

The Raft of the Medusa, Théodore Géricault. Agony and suffering is vividly portrayed in Géricault's realistic figures. (Louvre)

THE EMPIRE OF NAPOLEON
AT ITS GREATEST EXTENT • 1812

French territory

French dependencies

Allied with
Napoleon

Independent
states

RUSSIA

Moscow

Borodino

NAPOLEON 1812

Tilsit

Friedland

Warsaw

DUCHY
OF
WARSAW

PRUSSIA

Berlin

Copenhagen

DENMARK

SWEDEN

NORWAY

BALTIC SEA

Leipzig

Elbe R.

Austerlitz

Vienna

AUSTRIAN
EMPIRE

CONFEDERATION
OF THE
RHINE

Ulm

HOLLAND

Amsterdam

Rhine R.

HELVETIC
REPUBLIC

KINGDOM
OF
ITALY

Po R.

ILLYRIAN PROVINCES

ADRIATIC SEA

PAPAL
STATES

Rome

Naples

KINGDOM
OF
NAPLES

KDM. OF
SICILY

CORSICA

KDM.
OF
SARDINIA

Marseilles

FRENCH
EMPIRE

Paris

Waterloo

Brussels

Bordeaux

ENGLAND

London

IRELAND

English Channel

NORTH
SEA

ATLANTIC
OCEAN

Madrid

SPAIN

KDM. OF
PORTUGAL

Lisbon

MEDITERRANEAN SEA

BLACK SEA

OTTOMAN
EMPIRE

AEGEAN
SEA

500 miles

Monter, E. W., ed., *European Witchcraft*, New York, 1969. Selected readings with fine introductions by one of the world's leading experts.

More, L. T., *Isaac Newton: A Biography*, New York, 1934. The standard biography.

Ornstein, Martha, *The Role of Scientific Societies in the Seventeenth Century*, rev. ed., Hamden, Conn., 1963.

Palmer, R. R., *Catholics and Unbelievers in Eighteenth-Century France*, New York, 1939. Argues that Catholic thinkers were as enlightened as the *philosophes*, and that, ironically, their very tolerance contributed to the anticlericalism of the age.

• Phillipson, Coleman, *Three Criminal Law Reformers: Beccaria, Bentham, Romilly*, rev. ed., London, 1970.

Shackleton, Robert, *Montesquieu: A Critical Biography* London, 1961. The man and his thought.

Shryock, Richard H., *The Development of Modern Medicine: An Interpretation of the Social and Scientific Factors Involved*, London, 1948.

• Thomas, Keith, *Religion and the Decline of Magic*, London, 1971. A marvelously insightful study of popular belief in England.

SOURCE MATERIALS

Beccaria, Cesare, *An Essay on Crimes and Punishments, with a Commentary by M. de Voltaire*, Stanford, 1953. A reprint of the 1767 edition. Beccaria advocates a rational approach to punishment, with the good of the state outweighing motives for revenge. Voltaire's Commentary contains some interesting remarks on witchcraft.

• Boswell, James, *Life of Johnson*, London, 1970. The classic biography of the English man of letters, Samuel Johnson, written by his protégé; contains a superb portrait of eighteenth-century London.

Gibbon, Edward, *Autobiography*, London, 1961.

• ———, *The Decline and Fall of the Roman Empire*, 3 vols., New York, 1960. Published in 1776, this classic work exemplifies the skeptical, anticlerical nature of much of Enlightenment thought of the eighteenth century, especially Chapters 15 and 16 of Volume I.

• Kors, Alan C., and E. Peters, eds., *Witchcraft in Europe, 1100–1700: A Documentary History*, Philadelphia, 1972.

• Kramer, Heinrich, and James Sprenger, *The Malleus Maleficarum*, New York, 1971. An extraordinary work, the *Malleus* ("The Hammer of Witches") was the handbook of the witchcraft prosecutors of the Inquisition.

• Locke, John, *Two Treatises of Government*, ed. by Peter Laslett, London, 1960. Locke's celebrated tracts invoking the concept of the contractual nature of government and the sanctity of private property. An excellent introductory essay by Laslett.

• Voltaire, *Candide*, New York, 1956. Voltaire's satirical critique of the contemporary philosophy that "this is the best of all possible worlds," traced through a series of disasters experienced by his protagonist. First published in 1759.

Part Five

THE FRENCH AND INDUSTRIAL REVOLUTIONS AND THEIR CONSEQUENCES

No two events more profoundly altered the shape of Western civilization than the French and Industrial Revolutions. "Modern" history begins with their occurrence. The major happenings of the nineteenth and early twentieth centuries—the spread of middle-class liberalism and economic success; the decline of the old, landed aristocracies; the growth of class consciousness among urban workers—all had their roots in these two revolutions.

The French and Industrial Revolutions took place at about the same time and affected many of the same people—though in different ways and to varying degrees. Together they resulted in the overthrow of absolutism, mercantilism, and the last vestiges of manorialism. Together they produced the theory and practice of economic individualism and political liberalism. And together they ensured the growth of class consciousness, and the culmination of those tensions between the middle and working classes that imparted new vitality to European history after 1800.

Each revolution, of course, produced results peculiarly its own. The French Revolution encouraged the growth of nationalism and its unattractive step-child, authoritarianism. The Industrial Revolution compelled the design of a new, urban social order. Yet despite their unique contributions, the two revolutions must be studied together and understood as the joint progenitors of Western history in the nineteenth and early twentieth centuries.

The French and Industrial Revolutions and Their Consequences

POLITICS	SCIENCE & INDUSTRY

1770

James Watt's steam engine, 1763
Spinning jenny patented, 1770

American War of Independence, 1775–1783

Beginning of factory system, 1780s

French Revolution begins, 1789

Lavoisier discovers the indestructibility of matter, 1789

France declared a republic, 1792
Declaration of Pillnitz, 1792
Reign of Terror, 1793–1794

Cotton gin invented, 1793
Edward Jenner develops smallpox vaccine, 1796

Treaty of Campo Formio, 1797

1800

Napoleon, first consul of France, 1799
Treaty of Lunéville, 1801
Napoleon declared first consul for life, 1802
Napoleon crowns himself emperor of the French, 1804
Continental System established, 1806

Reforms of Hardenberg and Stein, Prussia, 1808

Napoleon's invasion of Russia, 1812
Congress of Vienna, 1814–1815

Battle of Waterloo, 1815

"Peterloo Massacre," England, 1819
Congress of Verona, 1822
Monroe Doctrine, 1823

Louis Pasteur, 1822–1895

1825

"Decembrist" Revolt, Russia, 1825
Greek Independence, 1829
Revolution in France, 1830
"Young Italy," 1831
Reform Bill of 1832, England
Slavery abolished, British colonies, 1833
Poor Law reform, England, 1834
Chartist movement, England, 1838–1848

First railway, England, 1825

Corn Laws repealed, England, 1846
Revolutions in Europe, 1848
Karl Marx, *Communist Manifesto,* 1848
Second Republic, France, 1848
Frankfurt Assembly, Germany, 1848–1849
Reign of Louis Napoleon, 1851–1870

Great Exhibition, London, 1851
Invention of the sewing machine, 1850s

ECONOMICS & SOCIETY	ARTS & LETTERS	
Jean-Jacques Rousseau, *The Social Contract,* 1762		*1770*
	Ludwig van Beethoven, 1770–1827	
Adam Smith, *Wealth of Nations,* 1776		
	Immanuel Kant, *Critique of Pure Reason,* 1781	
Jeremy Bentham, *The Principles of Morals and Legislation,* 1789		
Utilitarianism, 1790–1870	Johann von Goethe, *Faust,* 1790–1808	
	Romantic movement, 1790–1850	
Tom Paine, *The Rights of Man,* 1791–1792		
Thomas Malthus, *An Essay on the Principle of Population,* 1798	William Wordsworth, *Lyrical Ballads,* 1798	
		1800
	G. W. Hegel, *Phenomenology of the Spirit,* 1807	
	J. G. Fichte, *Addresses to the German Nation,* 1808	
Louis Blanc, 1811–1882		
	Francisco Goya, *The Executions of the Third of May,* 1814	
Founding of Prussian Zollverein, 1818		
		1825
	Honoré de Balzac, *The Human Comedy,* 1829–1841	
	Eugène Delacroix, *Liberty Leading the People,* 1830	
	Realism in literature and art, 1840–1870	
Friedrich Engels, *The Condition of the Working Class,* 1844		
John Stuart Mill, *Principles of Political Economy,* 1848	Pre-Raphaelite Brotherhood formed, 1848	

POLITICS	SCIENCE & INDUSTRY

1850

Crimean War, 1854–1856

Invention of the Bessemer process, 1856

Unification of Italy, 1858–1866

Charles Darwin, *Origin of Species,* 1859

Civil War, United States, 1861–1865
Otto von Bismarck's accession to power, 1862
First International, 1864

Parliamentary Reform Bill, England, 1867

Suez Canal opened, 1869
Union Pacific railroad, United States, 1869

Franco-Prussian War, 1870

ECONOMICS & SOCIETY	ARTS & LETTERS	
		1850
	Giuseppe Verdi, *Il Trovatore,* 1853	
	Richard Wagner, *The Ring of the Nibelung,* 1854–1874	
	Charles Dickens, *Hard Times,* 1854	
	Gustave Flaubert, *Madame Bovary,* 1857	
Emancipation of the serfs, Russia, 1861		
	Leo Tolstoy, *War and Peace,* 1866–1869	
Karl Marx, *Capital,* 1867	Pope Pius IX, *Syllabus of Errors,* 1869	

Chapter 19

THE FRENCH REVOLUTION

Men are born, and always continue, free and equal in respect of their rights. Civil distinctions, therefore, can be founded only on public utility.

The nation is essentially the source of all sovereignty; nor can any individual, or any body of men, be entitled to any authority which is not expressly derived from it.

— *The Declaration of the Rights of Man and of the Citizen,* 1789

In 1789, one European out of every five lived in France. And most Europeans, French or not, who thought beyond the boundaries of their own immediate concerns, perceived of France as the center of European civilization. It followed, therefore, that a revolution in France would immediately command the attention of Europe, and would from the first assume far more than mere national significance. Yet the French Revolution attracted and disturbed men and women for reasons other than the fact that it was French. Both its philosophical ideals and its political realities mirrored attitudes, concerns, and conflicts that had occupied the minds of Europeans for several decades. When the revolutionaries pronounced in favor of liberty, they spoke not only with the voice of the eighteenth-century *philosophes,* but with those of the English aristocracy in 1688 and the American revolutionaries of 1776. Absolutism was the bane of continental noblemen, jealous to preserve their ancient freedoms from monarchical inroads; it was also the bane of continental merchants, chafing under the constraints of mercantilist authority. Across Europe, monarch, nobility, and middle class confronted each other in uneasy hostilities that varied in intensity, but reflected common mistrust and uncertainty.

The era of revolution

Louis XVI

Governmental structure

Financial problems

I. THE BACKGROUND OF THE FRENCH REVOLUTION

To understand why revolution came to France, we must first understand the major components of French society in the late eighteenth century and the manner in which they stood in opposition to each other. At the head of society stood the king, Louis XVI. Neither the most talented nor the most incompetent of the Bourbons, Louis XVI was attempting to rule France as he believed he should rule: absolutely in theory, yet in practice in consort with the most capable advisors willing to serve under him. He was hampered in his attempts to rule effectively by two major factors.

First, the governmental structure of France was both illogical and unsystematic. Confusion reigned in nearly every department, the product of a long and somewhat irregular growth extending back into the Middle Ages. New agencies had been established from time to time to meet some particular condition, often with a total disregard for those already in existence. As a result there was much overlapping of functions, and numerous useless officials drew salaries from the public purse. Conflicts of jurisdiction between rival departments frequently delayed action on vital problems for months at a stretch. In financial matters there was no more regularity than in other branches of public policy. The collection of public revenues was exceedingly haphazard. Instead of appointing official collectors, the king employed the old Roman system of farming out the collection of taxes to private corporations and individuals, permitting them to retain as profit all that they could obtain from the people in excess of a stipulated amount. Similar disorganized conditions prevailed in the realm of law and judicial procedure. Nearly every province of France had its special code based upon local custom. As a consequence, an act punishable as a crime in southern France might be no concern of the law in a central or northern province.

Louis XVI's second major difficulty was financial. England and France had been in conflict for most of the eighteenth century. In all but one of the wars between them, France had emerged the loser and had paid for those losses with surrendered colonies. Ironically, it was the war which the French had helped to win—the American War of Independence—that was now causing them the most immediate problems. The expense of maintaining fleets and armies in the Western Hemisphere had been particularly heavy and had demanded extensive borrowing. The result was a national debt which the inefficient and overly bureaucratic French government found it could not sustain, although it was no greater than that left by Louis XIV in 1714, and no more than half that incurred by the British. Louis pressed his advisors to devise new methods of retrenchment and taxation to keep the government afloat. Yet these men, and Louis with them, recognized that they could make no headway unless by some miracle they could induce the clergy and nobility to surrender the ancient privileges which allowed them to escape payment of an equitable share of the nation's taxes.

The likelihood of this surrender was remote. The system of privilege was one the nobility and the church, the first two of the three "estates" of the realm, were loath to alter. This remained the case despite the clamor of the third estate, the commoners, that they do so. Although many parish priests were as poor as their humble parishoners, the monsignors, bishops, archbishops, and cardinals of the Roman Catholic Church in France enjoyed large incomes, as did the institution of the Church itself. The Church rulers claimed the medieval right to evade taxes on their properties by the payment of a periodic "free gift" to the state, invariably far less than might have been obtained from direct taxation of church property.

The nobility was also protected by custom from the payment of anything like its proportionate share of taxes. Taxes in France, long before 1789, had come to consist of two main types, direct and indirect. The direct taxes included the *taille,* or tax on real and personal property; the poll tax; and the tax on incomes, originally at the rate of 5 percent, but in the eighteenth century more commonly at 10 or 11 percent. The indirect taxes, or taxes added to the price of commodities and paid by the ultimate consumer, embraced mainly the tariffs on articles imported from foreign countries and the tolls levied on goods shipped from one province of France to another. In addition, the *gabelle,* or tax on salt, was a form of indirect tax. For some time the production of salt had been a state monopoly in France; every individual inhabitant was required to buy at least seven pounds a year from the government works. To the cost of production was added a heavy tax, with the result that the price to the consumer was often as much as fifty or sixty times the actual value of the salt.

While exceedingly burdensome, the indirect taxes were not as a rule unfair distributed. It was difficult for anyone, regardless of social status, to avoid paying them. The case of most of the direct taxes, however, was far otherwise. The clergy escaped payment of both the *taille* and the income tax. The nobles, especially those of higher rank, made use of their influence with the king to obtain exemption from practically all direct levies. As a result, the main task of providing funds for the government fell upon the common people, or members of the third estate. And since few of the artisans and laborers had much that could be taxed, the chief burden had to be borne by the peasants and the middle class.

Not all the nobles opposed the king's plan to abolish their customary exemptions. Many of the most ardent reformers were the *nobles of the robe,* men who had acquired judicial office (hence the "robe") which conferred a title of nobility, as well as an opportunity to ac-

Le Hameau. This rustic villa was constructed in the gardens of Versailles to allow the French court to experiment with the "return to nature" advocated by some of the *philosophes.*

Nobles of robe and nobles of the sword

cumulate a substantial fortune in land and other property. Included in this group were such talented and concerned men as the philosopher the baron de Montesquieu, the lawyer the comte de Mirabeau, and the statesman the marquis de Lafayette, who had come to the aid of the American colonies. Among the nobles of the robe were men who would play prominent roles in the revolution itself. In contrast—and often in opposition—to this group stood the *nobles of the sword,* those whose titles extended back to the feudal lords of the Middle Ages. Many of these aristocrats looked with disdain upon their brethren of the robe. Though in general not nearly so widely representative a group as the nobles of the robe, those of the sword nevertheless held many of the leading positions in the government, delegating their work to subordinates. The nobles of the sword owned large estates, upon which they seldom resided, living instead at the court of Versailles, relying upon bailiffs and stewards to extract all they could from the peasants who lived under their jurisdiction at home. Theirs was an expensive, if not particularly purposeful, existence. Their polished, artificial style of life required increasingly large sums of money. Hence their natural unwillingness to surrender tax exemptions, no matter how hard pressed the government.

Aristocratic demands

To reinforce their political intransigence and economic independence, the nobles had insisted on a greater share in both central and local administration. They asserted their claim by making increased use of three governmental institutions—parliaments, provincial estates, and intendencies. The thirteen French parliaments were regional courts of appeal, but the nobility used them to play an increasingly political role. The provincial estates, also under the control of the nobility, claimed not only judicial but legislative power. Both parliaments and estates insisted, specifically, upon the right to consent to taxation. Both argued that they were exercising this right to protect the population from the never-ceasing demands of a greedy state treasury. In fact, the nobility used these bodies with increasing frequency to do no more than protect its own privileges. Finally, the nobility had entrenched itself in many of the intendencies, those offices from which the thirty-four generalities, or districts, of the country were administered. During the reign of Louis XIV, intendents had, for the most part, been commoners, whose assignment it was to keep the nobility in line. Now many were nobles themselves, less likely to come to the king's aid than to oppose his will.

Within the third estate the peasants, upon whom the nobility depended for much of their income, had come to resent their increasingly intolerable economic situation. A major source of the peasants' discontent were the customary duties that had survived the end of manorialism. True, a vast majority of peasants were free; a considerable proportion owned the lands they cultivated. Others were tenants or hired laborers; the largest percentage appear to have been sharecroppers, farming the lands of the nobles for a portion of the harvest, generally ranging from a third to a half. Even those peasants who were entirely free, however, were required to perform obligations inherited from the later Middle Ages. One of the most odious of these was the payment of an annual rental to the lord who had formerly controlled the land. Another was the donation to the local noble of a share of the price received whenever a tract of land was sold. In addition, the peasants were still required to contribute *banalités,* or fees for the use of various facilities owned by the noble. During the Middle Ages *banalités* had been paid for the use of the lord's flour mill, his wine press, and his bake oven. In spite of the fact that by the eighteenth century many of the peasants owned such equipment themselves and no longer benefited by the services provided by the noble, the *banalités* were still collected in the original amounts.

Probably the most exasperating of all the relics of manorialism were the *corvée* and the hunting privileges of the nobility. The *corvée,* formerly a requirement of labor on the lord's demesne and in the building of roads and bridges on the manorial estate, had become an obligation to the government. For several weeks each year the peasant was forced to put his own work aside and devote his labor to maintaining the public highways. No other class of the population was required to perform this service. Even greater inconvenience was suffered as a result of the hunting privileges of the nobles. From time immemorial the right to indulge in the diversions of the chase had been regarded as a distinctive badge of aristocracy. The property rights of the peasants were not allowed to stand in the way of this gentlemanly pastime. In some parts of France the peasants were forbidden to weed or mow in

The third estate: the peasants

The relics of manorial custom

breeding time lest they disturb the nests of partidges. Rabbits, crows, and foxes could not be killed regardless of how much damage they did to the crops or to domestic fowl and young animals. Furthermore, the peasant was expected to resign himself to having his fields trampled at any time by the horses of a thoughtless crew of noble hunters.

Enclosure of common land

Not only did the peasants suffer under the vestiges of manorial custom. During the eighteenth century they also came under pressure as a result of the increasingly frequent enclosure of what had been common land. Fields allowed to lie fallow, together with those tilled only infrequently, were considered "common," land on which all persons might graze their livestock. These common lands, particularly extensive in the west of France, were an important resource for the peasants. In addition to the above-mentioned right to pasturage, they enjoyed that of gathering wood and of gleaning cultivated fields following a harvest. Now the king's economic advisors—Charles Calonne, Étienne Loménie de Brienne, the Swiss banker Jacques Necker—declared these collective rights to be obstacles in the path of agricultural improvement. Anxious to increase their income by increasing the efficiency of their estates, the landlords agreed. The result was authorization, by the crown, of the breakup of common lands and their enclosure as private property.

Here, then, were peasants pressed on the one side to acknowledge the duties of an outmoded manorial system and on the other to acquiesce in the exactions of modern agricultural capitalism, all the while paying taxes from which their aristocratic neighbors were exempt.

The frustrations of the peasants mirrored those of the most dynamic element within French eighteenth-century society, the middle class. This group was by no means homogeneous; there were within it

A Gentleman of the Third Estate with His Family. A contemporary engraving which illustrates the respectability the Third Estate wished to see translated into political power.

many ranks, graded according to both occupation and income. At the top stood financiers and wholesale traders. Many of these men were also shareholders in various enterprises and in the government bonds which had been issued throughout the eighteenth century. (Noblemen invested in business as well; the economic line between the second and third estate was not as heavily drawn as was the social.) Professionals ranged throughout the ranks of the middle class: doctors and lawyers, many of the latter to play roles central to the revolution. Industry remained subordinate to trade: although a few factories existed in France prior to 1789, most manufacturing took place in homes, and most consumers were supplied by local craftsmen. For every capitalist entrepreneur, there were scores of small-scale masters, lodged somewhere in the lower reaches of the middle class, at home in the workshop yet removed by virtue of their ownership of that shop from the ranks of the laboring classes below them.

While these men acknowledged the gradations that separated them from each other, they resented the privileges that excluded them from any consequential participation in the affairs of state. No matter how much money a merchant, manufacturer, banker, or lawyer might acquire, he was still excluded from political privileges. He had almost no influence at the court; he could not share in the highest honors; and, except in the choice of a few petty local officers, he could not even vote. He was looked down upon as an inferior by the nobility. As the middle class rose in affluence and in consciousness of its own importance, its members were bound to resent such social discrimination. Above all, it was the demand of the commercial, financial, and industrial leaders for political power commensurate with their economic position that turned members of the middle class into revolutionaries.

A demand for political power was not the only consequence of the growing prosperity of the middle class; there was also an increasing clamor for the abandonment of mercantilist policies. In earlier times mercantilism had been welcomed by merchants and manufacturers because of its effects in procuring new markets and fostering trade. But those times occurred at the beginning of the Commercial Revolution, when business was still nascent. As commerce and industry flourished through succeeding centuries, the middle class became increasingly confident of its ability to stand on its own feet. The result was a growing tendency to look upon the regulations of mercantilism as oppressive restrictions. Merchants disliked the special monopolies granted to favored companies and the interference with their freedom to buy in foreign markets. Manufacturers chafed under the laws controlling wages, fixing prices, and restricting the purchase of raw materials outside of France and its colonies. These were only a few of the more annoying regulations enforced by a government operating under the twin objectives of paternalism and economic self-sufficiency.

Like the peasantry, the middle class saw itself bearing a major portion of the state's financial burdens. Unlike the peasants, however, the middle class—at any rate its upper echelons—represented an economic force that was compelling change in a new and untried direction. The peasants, opposing enclosure, wanted to return to what had been. The prosperous financiers, the frustrated lawyers, the emerging entrepreneurs wanted to play leading roles in encouraging an expansion of international trade and in moving France ahead in its commercial competition with Britain.

France on the eve of revolution was thus a country divided against itself. Monarchy struggled to exact money from an aristocracy increasingly determined not to pay and increasingly anxious in turn to exact what it could from a sullen peasantry. The middle classes resented a government that appeared at best an anachronism and at worst a tyranny, frustrated and furious that a country as prosperous as France should find it impossible to pay its debts. France did not fall to revolution because it was poor. It succumbed because those who knew best how rich it was were dissatisfied with the slow rate of its commercial progress.

No event as all-encompassing as the French Revolution occurs in a cultural vacuum. Although ideas may not have "caused" the revolution, they played a most important role in giving shape and substance to the discontent experienced by so many, particularly among the middle class. These ideas derived from the thought of the Enlightenment. Two theories, in particular, expressed the concerns and aspirations of the revolutionaries. The first was the *liberal* theory of such writers as Locke, Voltaire, and Montesquieu; and the second was the *democratic* theory of Rousseau. While the two were fundamentally opposed, they nevertheless had elements in common. Both were predicated upon the assumption that the state is a necessary evil and that government rests upon a contractual basis. Each had its doctrine of popular sovereignty, although with contrasting interpretations. Both upheld in some measure the fundamental rights of the individual. And both contained elements appealing to those who, for various reasons, were dissatisfied with things as they were.

The father of the liberal theory of the seventeenth and eighteenth centuries was John Locke. His philosophy of education, as we have seen, was intrinsic to the development of Enlightenment thinking. His political beliefs are contained chiefly in his *Second Treatise of Civil Government,* published in 1690. In this book he developed a theory of limited government, which was used to justify the new system of parliamentary rule set up in England as a result of the Glorious Revolution. He maintained that originally all humans had lived in a theoretical state of nature in which absolute freedom and equality prevailed, and in which there was no government of any kind. The only law was the law of nature, which each individual enforced for himself in order to protect his natural rights to life, liberty, and property. It was not long, however, until men began to perceive that the inconveniences of the state of nature greatly outweighed its advantages. With individuals attempting to enforce their own rights, confusion and insecurity were the unavoidable results. Accordingly, the people agreed among themselves to establish a civil society, to set up a government, and to surrender certain powers to it. But they did not make that government absolute. The only power they conferred upon it was the executive power of the law of nature. Since the state is nothing but the joint power of all the members of society, its authority "can be no more than those persons had in a state of nature before they entered into society, and gave it up to the community."[1] All powers not expressly surrendered are reserved to the people themselves. If the government exceeds or abuses the authority explicitly granted in the political contract, it becomes tyrannical; and the people then have the right to dissolve it or to rebel against it and overthrow it.

Locke condemned absolutism in every form. He denounced despotic monarchy, but he was no less severe in his strictures against the absolute sovereignty of parliaments. Though he defended the supremacy of the law-making branch, with the executive primarily an agent of the legislature, he nevertheless refused to concede to the representatives of the people an unlimited power. Arguing that government was instituted among people for the preservation of property (which he generally defined in the inclusive sense of life, liberty, and estate), he denied the authority of any political agency to invade the natural rights of a single individual. The law of nature, which embodies these rights, is an automatic limitation upon every branch of the government. Regardless of how large a majority of the people's representatives should demand the restriction of freedom of speech or the confiscation and redistribution of property, no such action could legally be taken. If taken illegally it would justify effective measures of resistance on the part of the majority of citizens. Locke was much more concerned with protecting individual liberty than he was with promoting stability or social progress. If forced to make a choice, he would have preferred the evils of anarchy to those of despotism in any form.

Locke's condemnation of absolutism

The appeal of Locke's ideas to the French middle class can be readily understood. His doctrines of natural rights, limited government, and the right of resistance to tyranny, as well as his stout defense of property, reflected the values of that element in French society. Like their American counterparts, who a decade earlier had incorporated Locke's theories into the Declaration of Independence, these middle-class Frenchmen opened their minds to Lockean suppositions and explanations.

Locke's appeal

In France the foremost exponents of the liberal political theory were Voltaire and Montesquieu (1689–1755). As was indicated earlier, Voltaire considered orthodox Christianity to be the worst of the enemies

[1] *Second Treatise of Civil Government* (Everyman Library ed.), p. 184.

The liberal political theory of Voltaire

Montesquieu

The separation of powers; checks and balances

of humanity; he reserved contempt for tyrannical government as well. During his exile in England he had studied the writings of Locke and had been deeply impressed by their vigorous assertions of individual freedom. In common with Locke he conceived of government as a necessary evil, with powers which ought to be limited to the enforcement of natural rights. He maintained that all are endowed by nature with equal rights to liberty, property, and the protection of the laws. But Voltaire was no democrat. He was inclined to think of the ideal form of government as either an enlightened monarchy or a republic dominated by the middle class.

A more systematic political thinker than Voltaire was his older contemporary, Montesquieu. Though, like Voltaire, a student of Locke and an ardent admirer of British institutions, Montesquieu was a unique figure among the political philosophers of the eighteenth century. In his celebrated *Spirit of Laws* he brought new methods and new conceptions to the theory of the state. Instead of attempting to found a science of government by pure deduction, he followed the Aristotelian method of studying actual political systems as they were supposed to have operated in the past. He denied that there is any one perfect form of government suitable for all peoples under all conditions. He maintained, on the contrary, that political institutions in order to be successful must harmonize with the physical conditions and the level of social advancement of the nations they are intended to serve. Thus he declared that despotism is best suited to countries of vast domain; limited monarchy to those of moderate size; and republican government to those of small extent. For his own country, France, he was disposed to think that a limited monarchy would be the most appropriate form, since he regarded the nation as too large to be made into a republic unless on some kind of federal plan.

Montesquieu is especially famous for his theory of the separation of powers. He avowed that it is a natural human tendency to abuse any power, and that consequently every government, regardless of its form, is liable to degenerate into despotism. To prevent such a result he argued that the authority of government should be broken up into its three natural divisions of legislative, executive, and judicial. Whenever any two or more of these are allowed to remain united in the same hands, liberty, he declared, is at an end. The only effective way to avoid tyranny is to enable each branch of the government to act as a check upon the other two. For example, the executive should have the power by means of the veto to curb the encroachments of the lawmaking branch. The legislature, in turn, should have the authority of impeachment in order to restrain the executive. And, finally, there should be an independent judiciary vested with power to protect individual rights against arbitrary acts of either the legislature or the executive. This favorite scheme of Montesquieu was not intended, of course, to facilitate democracy. Its purpose was largely the opposite: to prevent the absolute supremacy of the majority, expressed as it normally would be through the people's representatives in a legislature. Montesquieu's ideas thus appealed to both nobility and middle class. The nobility read his writings as a defense of their ancient privileges—elevated by Montesquieu into "liberties." The provincial estates, where noblemen exercised considerable political power, were the constituted bodies which would provide a check to royal power. The middle class welcomed further theoretical support to substantiate its preference for something other than the monarchical absolutism and centralized mercantilism of eighteenth-century France.

Additional arguments in favor of governmental nonintervention was provided by another group of libertarians—theoreticians who were redefining the study of economics.

In the second half of the eighteenth century a number of writers began attacking traditional assumptions with regard to public control over production and trade. Their special target of criticism was mercantilist policy. To a large extent the new economics was founded upon the basic conceptions of the Enlightenment, particularly the idea of a mechanistic universe governed by inflexible laws. The economists argued that the sphere of the production and distribution of wealth was subject to laws just as irresistible as those of physics and astronomy. The new economic theory was a counterpart of political liberalism. The cardinal aims of the two doctrines were quite similar: to reduce the powers of government to the lowest minimum consistent with safety and to preserve for the individual the largest possible measure of freedom in the pursuit of his own devices.

The new economists

The greatest of all the economists of the age of the Enlightenment and one of the most brilliant of all time was Adam Smith (1723–1790). A native of Scotland, Smith began his career as a lecturer on English literature at the University of Edinburgh. From this position he was soon advanced to a professorship of logic at Glasgow College. In 1776 he published his *Inquiry into the Nature and Causes of the Wealth of Nations*. In this work he maintained that labor, rather than agriculture or the bounty of nature, is the real source of wealth. While in general he accepted the principle of laissez faire, avowing that the prosperity of all can best be promoted by allowing all individuals to pursue their own interests, he nevertheless recognized the necessity for certain forms of governmental interference. The state should intervene for the prevention of injustice and oppression, for the advancement of education and the protection of public health, and for the maintenance of necessary enterprises which would never be established by private capital. Notwithstanding these rather broad limitations upon the principle of laissez faire, Smith's *Wealth of Nations* was adopted as holy writ by the economic individualists of the eighteenth and nineteenth centuries. Its influence in causing the French

The economics of Adam Smith

Revolution was indirect but nonetheless profound. It furnished the final answer to mercantilist argument and thereby strengthened the ambition of the middle class to have done with a political system which continued to block the path to economic freedom.

The second of the great political ideals which occupied an important place in the intellectual background of the French Revolution was the ideal of democracy. In contrast with liberalism, democracy, in its original meaning, was much less concerned with the defense of individual rights than with the enforcement of popular rule. What the majority of the citizens wills is the supreme law of the land, for the voice of the people is the voice of God.

The foremost theoretician of democracy in eighteenth-century Europe was Jean-Jacques Rousseau (1712–1778). The most significant of his writings on political theory were his *Social Contract* and his *Discourse on the Origin of Inequality*. In both of these he upheld the popular thesis that humans had originally existed in a state of nature. But in contrast with Locke he regarded this state of nature as a veritable paradise. People suffered no inconvenience from maintaining their own rights against others. Indeed, there were very few chances of conflict of any sort; for private property did not exist for a long time, and every person was the equal of every other. Eventually, however, evils arose, due primarily to the fact that some staked off plots of land and said to themselves, "This is mine." It was in such manner that various degrees of inequality developed; and, as a consequence, "cheating trickery," "insolent pomp," and "insatiable ambition" soon came to dominate the relations among men.[2] The only hope of security was now to establish a civil society and to surrender all rights to the community. This was accomplished by means of a social contract, in which each individual agreed with the whole body of individuals to submit to the will of the majority. Thus the state was brought into existence.

Rousseau developed an altogether different conception of sovereignty from that of the liberals. Whereas Locke and his followers had taught that only a portion of sovereign power is surrendered to the state, the rest being retained by the people themselves, Rousseau contended that sovereignty is indivisible, and that all of it became vested in the community when civil society was formed. He insisted further that each individual in becoming a party to the social contract gave up all rights to the people collectively and agreed to submit absolutely to the general will. It follows that the sovereign power of the state is subject to no limitations whatever. When Rousseau referred to the state he did not mean the government. He regarded the state as the politically organized community, which has the sovereign function of expressing the general will. The authority of the state cannot be repre-

[2] *Discourse on the Origin of Inequality* (Everyman Library ed.), p. 207.

sented, but must be expressed directly through the enactment of fundamental laws by the people themselves. The government, on the other hand, is simply the executive agent of the state. Its function is not to formulate the general will but merely to carry it out. Moreover, the community can set the government up or pull it down "whenever it likes."[3]

Rousseau's influence was great. His appeal, however, was not so much to those members of the middle class whose thoughts and actions dominated the first stage of the revolution. Although they might have agreed with Rousseau's opposition to hereditary privilege, they were, as convinced individualists, unmoved by arguments in favor of surrender to a "general will." Rousseau's influence upon the revolution was greatest during its second stage, when a more democratic and radical coterie emerged to lead events, first in the direction of democracy and then along a course toward an absolutism that nevertheless accorded with Rousseau's notions of the sovereign state.

Rousseau's appeal

2. THE DESTRUCTION OF THE ANCIEN RÉGIME

The French Revolution occurred when it did because of the government's inability to resolve its financial crisis. When the king's principal ministers Calonne and Loménie de Brienne attempted in 1787 and 1788 to institute a series of financial reforms in order to stave off bankruptcy, they encountered not just opposition but entrenched aristocratic determination to extract further governmental concessions from the king. To meet the mounting deficit, the ministers proposed new taxes, notably a stamp duty and a direct tax on the annual produce of the soil. The king summoned an assembly of notables from among the aristocracy, in the hope of persuading the nobles to agree to his demands. Far from acquiescing, however, the nobles insisted that to institute a general tax such as the stamp duty the king would first have to call together the Estates General, representative of the three estates of the realm.

The crisis of the monarchy

The summoning of this body, which had not met for over a century and a half, seemed to many the only solution to France's deepening problems. No doubt most of those aristocrats who argued for its calling did so from short-sighted and selfish motives. Yet the politically conscious population as a whole agreed with the idea in an unreasonable and desperate hope that this unusual event might, because of its very strangeness, work a miracle and save the country from ruin. During the period before the rise of monarchical absolutism, when the Estates General was convened more or less regularly, the representatives of each estate had met and voted as a body. Generally this meant that the first and second estates combined against the third.

The Estates General

[3] *The Social Contract* (Everyman Library ed.), p. 88.

 is preceded by these labels on the map:

ENGLAND

ENGLISH CHANNEL

HOLY ROMAN EMPIRE

AUSTRIAN NETH.

FLANDERS AND HAINAUT

ARTOIS

PICARDY

PALATINATE

Rouen

Varennes • METZ AND VERDUN

WÜRTTEMBERG

ISLE OF
Paris
Versailles

NORMANDY

CHAMPAGNE
AND
BRIE

FRANCE

LORRAINE

ALSACE

Seine R.

Rhine R.

BRITTANY

MAINE

ORLÉANAIS

FRANCHE COMTÉ

SWISS
CONFEDERATION

ANJOU

TOURAINE

NIVERNAIS

BERRY

BURGUNDY

SAU-
MUROIS

POITOU

BOURBONNAIS

DUCHY
OF
SAVOY

KINGDOM OF SARDINIA

ATLANTIC

AUNIS

MARCHE

Loire R.

LYONNAIS

SAINTONGE AND
ANGOUMOIS

LIMOUSIN

AUVERGNE

OCEAN

Bordeaux

Rhone R.

DAUPHINY

GUIENNE AND GASCONY

PROVENCE

Toulouse

LANGUEDOC

Marseilles

BEARN

FOIX

ROUSSILLON

MEDITERRANEAN SEA

CORSICA

ANDORRA

SPAIN

0   200 miles

FRANCE IN 1789 · THE "GOVERNMENTS"

By the late eighteenth century the third estate had attained such importance that it was not willing to tolerate such an arrangement. Consequently its leaders demanded that the three orders should sit together and vote as individuals. More important, it insisted that the representatives of the third estate should be double the number of the first and second. Leaving this issue unresolved, Louis XVI, in the summer of 1788, yielded to popular clamor and summoned the Estates General to meet in May of the following year.

In the intervening months, the question of "doubling the third" was fiercely debated. When the king pronounced against the idea, he lost support he might otherwise have obtained from the middle class, and virtually preordained the outcome of the convocation. Shortly after

*The new political role of
the third estate*

the opening of the Estates General at Versailles, in May 1789, the representatives of the third estate took the revolutionary step of leaving the body and declaring themselves the National Assembly. "What is the third estate?" asked the Abbé Sieyès, one of the most articulate spokesmen for a new order, in his famous pamphlet of January 1789. The answer he gave then—"everything"—was the answer the third estate itself gave when it constituted itself the National Assembly of France. Sieyès, unlike most other revolutionaries at this point, derived his argument from Rousseau, and claimed that the third estate was the nation and that as the nation it was its own sovereign. Now the middle-class lawyers and businessmen of the third estate acted on that claim. Locked out of their meeting hall on June 20, the commoners and a handful of sympathetic nobles and clergymen moved to a nearby indoor tennis court.

Here, under the leadership of Mirabeau and the Abbé Sieyès, they bound themselves by a solemn oath not to separate until they had drafted a constitution for France. This Oath of the Tennis Court, on June 20, 1789, was the real beginning of the French Revolution. By claiming the authority to remake the government in the name of the people, the Estates General was not merely protesting against the rule of Louis XVI but asserting its right to act as the highest sovereign power in the nation. On June 27 the king virtually conceded this right by ordering the remaining delegates of the privileged classes to meet with the third estate as members of the National Assembly.

The course of the French Revolution was marked by three stages, the first of which extended from June 1789 to August 1792. During most of this period the destinies of France were in the hands of the Na-

Abbé Sieyès

The Tennis Court Oath

The Opening of the Estates General in Versailles, May 5, 1789

The Tennis Court Oath by David. In the hall where royalty played a game known as *jeu de paume* (similar to tennis) leaders of the revolution swore to draft a constitution. In the center of this painting, with his arm extended, is Jean Bailly, president of the National Assembly. Seated at the table below him is Abbé Sieyès. Somewhat to the right of Sieyès, with both hands on his chest, is Robespierre. Mirabeau, with a hat in his left hand and wearing a black coat, stands somewhat farther to the right.

tional Assembly. In the main, this stage was moderate, its actions dominated by the leadership of liberal nobles and equally liberal men of the third estate. Yet three events in the summer and fall of 1789 furnished evidence that the revolution was to penetrate to the very heart of French society, ultimately touching both the urban populace and the rural peasants.

The first stage of the revolution

News of the events of late spring 1789 had spread quickly across France. From the very onset of debates on the nature of the political crisis, public attention was high. It was roused not merely by abstract interest in matters of political reform, however. Prices had risen to a point where the cost of bread alone consumed more than 50 percent of a poor family's income in August 1788, and 80 percent in February and July 1789. Belief was widespread that the aristocracy and king were together conspiring to punish an upstart third estate by encouraging scarcity and high prices. Rumors circulated in Paris during the latter days of June 1789. At their clubs and in their shops, those men and women who would come to be called the sans-culottes[4]—workshop masters, craftspeople, shopkeepers, petty tradespeople—worried about their fate. Determined to obtain arms to defend themselves from the threat of counterrevolution, they successfully stormed the ancient fortress of the Bastille on July 14, thereby establishing the fact of the king's impotence within his own capital. Built in the Middle Ages as a stronghold, the Bastille was no longer much used; but it symbolized royal authority to the masses. When crowds demanded

Fall of the Bastille

[4] So-called because the men did not wear upper-class breeches.

arms from its governor, he refused and opened fire. The crowd took revenge, not only by capturing the fortress but by murdering the governor.

The fall of the Bastille was the first of those events which were to demonstrate the commitment of the common people to revolutionary change. The second occurred in the countryside, where the peasants were suffering the direct effects of economic privation. They, too, feared a monarchical and aristocratic counterrevolution. Eager for news from Versailles, their anticipation turned to fear when they began to understand that a middle-class revolution might not address itself to their problems. Frightened and uncertain, peasants in many areas of France panicked in July and August, setting fire to manor houses and the records they contained, destroying monasteries and the residences of bishops, and murdering some of the nobles who offered resistance.

The third instance of popular uprising, in October 1789, was also brought on by economic crisis. This time women, angered by the price of bread and fired by rumors of the king's continuing unwillingness to cooperate with the assembly, marched to Versailles on October 5 and demanded to be heard. Not satisfied with its reception by the assembly, the crowd broke through the gates to the palace, calling for the king to return to Paris. On the afternoon of the following day the king yielded. The National Guard, sympathetic to the agitators, led the crowd back to Paris, the procession headed by a soldier holding aloft a loaf of bread on his bayonet.

In each case, these three popular uprisings produced a decided effect on the course of political events as they were unfolding at Versailles. The storming of the Bastille helped persuade the king and nobles to treat the National Assembly as the legislative body of the nation. The "Great Fear" inspired an equally great consternation among the debaters in the assembly. On August 4, with one sweep, the remnants of manorialism were largely obliterated. Ecclesiastical tithes and the *corvée* were formally abolished. Serfdom was eliminated. The hunting privileges of the nobles were declared at an end. Exemption from tax-

The "Great Fear"

The "October Days"

Achievements of the first stage: (1) the destruction of feudal privilege

The Departure of the Women of Paris for Versailles, October 1789. Note that the contemporary caption refers to the "heroines of Paris." An early example of revolutionary propaganda.

ation and monopolies of all kinds were sacrificed as contrary to natural equality. While the nobles did not surrender all of their rights, the ultimate effect of these reforms of the "August Days" was to annihilate distinctions of rank and class and to make all French citizens of an equal status in the eyes of the law.

(2) the Declaration of the Rights of Man

Following the destruction of privilege the assembly turned its attention to preparing a charter of liberties. The result was the Declaration of the Rights of Man and of the Citizen, issued in September 1789. Property was declared to be a natural right as well as liberty, security, and "resistance to oppression." Freedom of speech, religious toleration, and liberty of the press were held to be inviolable. All citizens were declared to be entitled to equality of treatment in the courts. No one was to be imprisoned or otherwise punished except in accordance with due process of law. Sovereignty was affirmed to reside in the people, and officers of the government were made subject to deposition if they abused the powers conferred upon them.

(3) secularization of the Church

The king's return to Paris during the October Days confirmed the reforms already underway and guaranteed further liberalization along lines decreed by the middle-class majority in the assembly. In November 1789, the National Assembly resolved to confiscate the lands of the Church and to use them as collateral for the issue of *assignats,* or paper money, which, it was hoped, would resolve the country's inflationary economic crisis. In July of the following year the Civil Constitution of the Clergy was enacted, providing that all bishops and priests should be elected by the people and should be subject to the authority of the state. Their salaries were to be paid out of the public treasury, and they were required to swear allegiance to the new legislation. The secularization of the Church also involved a partial separation from Rome. The aim of the assembly was to make the Catholic Church of France a truly national institution with no more than a nominal subjection to the papacy.

An Assignat

(4) constitution of 1791

Not until 1791 did the National Assembly manage to complete its primary task of drafting a new constitution for the nation. The constitution as it finally emerged gave eloquent testimony to the dominant position now held by the middle class. The government was converted into a limited monarchy, with the supreme power virtually a monopoly of the well-to-do. Although all citizens possessed the same civil rights, the vote was allowed only to those who paid a certain amount in taxes. About half the adult males in France made up this latter category of "active" citizen. Yet even their political power was curtailed, for they were to vote for electors, whose property ownership qualified them for that position. Those electors, in turn, chose department officials and delegates to the National—or, as it was now called, Constituent—Assembly. The king was deprived of the control he had formerly exercised over the army and local governments. His ministers were forbidden to sit in the assembly, and he was shorn of all power over the legislative process except a suspensive veto, which in fact could be overridden by the issuance of proclamations.

The economic and governmental changes the Constituent Assembly adopted were as much a reflection of Enlightenment liberalism as were its constitutional reforms. To raise money, it sold off Church lands, but in such large blocks that peasants seldom benefited by the sales as they had expected to. In opposition to the interests of the peasantry, the assembly proceeded with the enclosure of common lands in order to facilitate the development of capitalist agriculture. To encourage the growth of unfettered economic enterprise, guilds and trade unions were abolished. To rid the country of authoritarian centralization and of aristocratic domination, local governments were completely restructured. France was divided into eighty-three equal departments. All towns henceforth enjoyed the same form of municipal organization. All local officials were locally elected. This reorganization and decentralization expressed a liberal belief in the necessity of individual liberty and freedom from ancient privilege. As such these measures proclaimed, as did all the work of the assembly, that the "winners" of this first stage of the revolution were the men and women of the middle class.

*(5) economic and
governmental changes*

3. A NEW STAGE: RADICAL REVOLUTION

Their triumph did not go unchallenged, however. In the summer of 1792, the revolution entered a second stage, which saw the downfall of moderate middle-class leaders and their replacement by radical republicans claiming to rule on behalf of the common people. Two major reasons accounted for this abrupt and drastic alteration in the course of events. First, the politically literate lower classes grew disillusioned as they perceived that the revolution was not benefiting them. The uncontrolled free-enterprise economy of the government resulted in constantly fluctuating and generally rising prices. These increases particularly exasperated those elements of the Parisian population that had agitated for change in preceding years. Rioting urban mobs demanded bread at prerevolutionary prices, while their spokesmen called for governmental control of the ever-growing inflation. Their leaders articulated as well the frustrations of a mass of men and women who felt cheated by the constitution. Despite their major role in the creation of a new regime, they found themselves deprived of any effective voice in its operation.

*The second stage: (1)
disappointment of the
common people*

The second major reason for the dramatic turn of events was the fact that France now found itself at war with much of the rest of Europe. From the outset of the revolution, men and women across Europe had been compelled, by the very intensity of events in France, to take sides in the conflict. What we have called the first revolution

(2) the revolution abroad

A Contemporary Engraving of the September Massacres in Paris, 1792

won the support of a wide range of thoughtful intellectuals, politicians, businessmen, and artisans. Strikes and revolts broke out in Germany and Belgium. In England, philosophical radicals such as Joseph Priestley, the scientist, and Richard Price, a Unitarian minister, joined with businessmen such as James Watt and Matthew Boulton to welcome the overthrow of privilege and absolutism. Others opposed the course of the revolution from the start. Edmund Burke, in his famous pamphlet, *Reflections on the Revolution in France,* denounced the egalitarian actions of the revolutionaries. The monarchs of Europe responded with at least passive sympathy to the distressed clamorings of Louis XVI, Marie Antoinette, his impetuous, ultra-conservative queen, and the émigré nobles who soon fled to the courts of German principalities in pursuit of assistance for their doomed cause.

It is questionable, however, whether that sympathy would have turned to active opposition, had not the French soon appeared as a threat to international stability and the individual ambitions of the great powers. It was that threat which led to war in 1792, and which kept the Continent in arms for a generation.

The impact of international war

This state of war had a most important impact on the formation of political and social attitudes during this period in Europe. Once a country declared war with France, its citizens could no longer espouse sympathy with the revolution without paying severe consequences. Those who continued to support the revolution, as did a good many among the artisan and small tradespeople class, were persecuted and punished for their beliefs. To be found in Britain, for example, possessing a copy of Tom Paine's revolutionary tract, *The Rights of Man* (1791–1792), a prorevolutionary response to Burke's *Reflections,* was enough to warrant imprisonment. As the moderate nature of the early revolution turned to violent extension, entrepreneurs and businessmen eagerly sought to live down their radical sentiments of a few years past. The wars against revolutionary France came to be perceived as a matter of national survival; to ensure internal security, it seemed, particularly to the English, that patriotism demanded not only a condemnation of the French but of French ideas as well.

The first European states to express public concern about events in revolutionary France were Austria and Prussia. They were not anxious to declare war; their interests at the time centered upon the division of Poland between themselves. Nevertheless, they jointly issued the Declaration of Pillnitz in August 1791, in which they avowed that the restoration of order and of the rights of the monarch of France was a matter of "common interest to all sovereigns of Europe." The leaders of the French government at this time were the moderate Girondists, many of whom came from the mercantile Girondist department. The Girondists drew their support largely from regions outside Paris, and were inclined to mistrust urban radicals. Afraid of losing political support in France, they pronounced the Declaration of Pillnitz a threat to national security, hoping that enthusiasm for a war would unite the French and result also in enthusiasm for their continued rule. They were aided in their scheme by the activities of monarchists, both within and outside France, whose plottings and pronouncements could be made to appear an additional threat, though to a greater extent than they actually were. On April 20, 1792, the assembly declared war against Austria and Prussia.

Edmund Burke

Declaration of Pillnitz

Although the Girondist faction expected that military success would solidify the loyalty of the people to the regime, many anti-Girondist radicals were clamoring for war in the secret hope that the armies of France would suffer defeat, and that the monarchy would thereby be discredited. A republic could then be set up, and the heroic soldiers of the people would turn defeat into victory and carry the blessings of freedom to all the oppressed of Europe. As the radicals had hoped, the forces of the French met serious reverses. By August 1792 the allied armies of Austria and Prussia had crossed the frontier and were threatening the capture of Paris. A fury of rage and despair seized the capital. The belief prevailed that the military disasters had been the result of treasonable dealings with the enemy on the part of the king and his conservative followers. As a consequence, a vigorous demand arose from the radicals for drastic action against all who were suspected of disloyalty to the revolution. It was this situation more than anything else which brought the extremists to the fore and enabled them to gain control of the assembly and to put an end to the monarchy.

The course of war

Thomas Paine

From this point, the country's leadership passed into the hands of an equalitarian-minded "middle" middle class. These new leaders called themselves Jacobins, after the Parisian political club to which they belonged. The hallmarks of the Jacobin, or second, stage of the French Revolution were its radical republicanism and its "Reign of Terror."

*The government during
the second stage: the
national convention*

One of the Jacobins' first actions was to ask all Frenchmen to vote for delegates to a national convention, to draft a new and more republican constitution. This convention, which assembled in September 1792, became the effective governing body of the country for the next three years. It was composed entirely of republicans; 486 of its 749 members were men who had not sat in the old assembly. On September 21, the convention abolished the monarchy and declared France a republic. In December, the convention placed the former king, Louis XVI, on trial; in January he was, by one vote, condemned to death. He and his queen suffered death on the guillotine, the frightful mechanical headsman that was one of the most famous and feared instruments of revolutionary fervor.

Domestic reforms

   Meanwhile, the convention turned its attention to the enactment of further domestic reforms. Among its most significant accomplishments over the next three years were the abolition of slavery in French colonies; the prohibition of imprisonment for debt; the establishment of the metric system of weights and measures; and the repeal of primogeniture, so that property might not be inherited exclusively by the oldest son, but be divided in substantially equal portions among all immediate heirs. The convention also attempted to supplement the decrees of the assembly in abolishing the remnants of manorialism and in providing for greater freedom of economic opportunity for the commoner. The property of enemies of the revolution was confiscated for the benefit of the government and the lower classes. Great estates were broken up and offered for sale to poorer citizens on easy terms. The indemnities hitherto promised to the nobles for the loss of their privileges were abruptly canceled. To curb the rise in the cost of living, maximum prices for grain and other necessities were fixed by

The Execution of Louis XVI. A revolutionary displays the king's head moments after it had been severed by the guillotine in January 1793.

law, and merchants who profiteered at the expense of the poor were threatened with the guillotine. Still other measures of reform were those in the sphere of religion. At one time during the period, an effort was made to abolish Christianity and to substitute the worship of Reason in its place. In accordance with this purpose a new calendar was adopted, dating the year from the birth of the republic (September 22, 1792) and dividing the months in such a way as to eliminate the Christian Sunday. Later, this cult of Reason was replaced by a Deistic religion dedicated to the worship of a Supreme Being and to a belief in the immortality of the soul. Finally, in 1794, the convention decreed simply that religion was a private matter, that Church and State would therefore be separated, and that all beliefs not actually hostile to the government would be tolerated.

While effecting this political revolution in France, the convention's leadership at the same time accomplished an astonishingly successful reorganization of its armies. By February 1793, Britain, Holland, Spain, and Austria were in the field against the French. Britain's entrance into the war was dictated by both strategic and economic reasons. The English feared French penetration into the Low Countries directly across the Channel; they were also concerned that French expansion might pose a serious threat to Britain's own growing mercantile hegemony around the globe. The allied coalition ranged against France, though united only in its desire to somehow contain this puzzling, fearsome revolutionary phenomenon, was nevertheless a formidable force. To counter it, the French organized an army that was able to win engagement after engagement during these years. In August 1793, the revolutionary government imposed a levy on the entire male population capable of bearing arms. Fourteen hastily drafted armies were flung into battle under the leadership of young and inexperienced officers. What they lacked in training and discipline, they made up for in improvised organization, mobility, flexibility, courage, and morale. (In the navy, however, where skill was of paramount importance, the revolutionary French never succeeded in matching the performance of the British.) In 1793–1794, the French armies preserved their homeland. In 1794–1795, they occupied the Low Countries, the Rhineland, parts of Spain, Switzerland, and Savoy. In 1796, they invaded and occupied key parts of Italy and broke the coalition that had arrayed itself against them.

These achievements were not without their price, however. To insure their accomplishment, the rulers of France resorted to a bloody authoritarianism that has come to be known as the Reign of Terror. Although the convention succeeded in 1793 in drafting a new democratic constitution, based upon manhood suffrage, it deferred its introduction because of wartime emergency. Instead, the convention prolonged its own life year by year, and increasingly delegated its responsibilities to a group of twelve leaders known as the Committee of Public Safety. By this time the moderate, upper middle-class Giron-

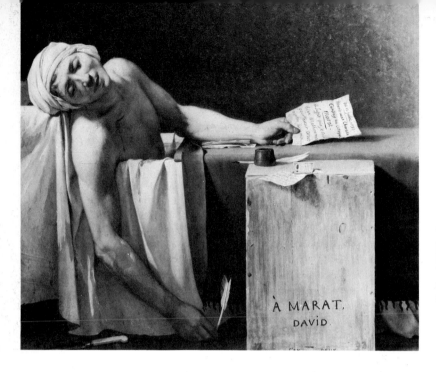

The Death of Marat. This painting by the French artist David immortalized Marat. The bloody towel, the box, and the tub were venerated as relics of the revolution.

dists had lost all influence within the convention. Complete power had passed to the Jacobins, who, though themselves from the middle class, were ardent disciples of Rousseau and champions of the urban workers.

Foremost among the leaders of the extremist faction and members of the Committee of Public Safety, were Marat, Danton, and Robespierre. Jean Paul Marat (1743–1793) was educated as a physician, and, by 1789, had already earned enough distinction in that profession to be awarded an honorary degree by St. Andrews University in Scotland. Almost from the beginning of the revolution he stood as a champion of the common people. He opposed nearly all of the dogmatic assumptions of his middle-class colleagues in the assembly, including the idea that France should pattern its government after that of Great Britain, which he recognized to be oligarchic in form. He was soon made a victim of persecution and was forced to find refuge in sewers and dungeons, but this did not stop him from his efforts to rouse the people to a defense of their rights. In 1793 he was stabbed through the heart by Charlotte Corday, a young woman who was fanatically devoted to the Girondists. In contrast with Marat, Georges Jacques Danton (1759–1794) did not come into prominence until the revolution was three years old; but, like Marat, he directed his activities toward goading the masses into rebellion. Elected a member of the Committee of Public Safety in 1793, he had much to do with organizing the Reign of Terror. As time went on he appears to have wearied of ruthlessness and displayed a tendency to compromise. This gave his opponents in the convention their opportunity, and in April 1794, he was sent to the guillotine. Upon mounting the scaffold he is reported

Marat and Danton

Danton

to have said: "Show my head to the people; they do not see the like every day."

The most famous and perhaps the greatest of all the extremist leaders was Maximilien Robespierre (1758–1794). Born of a family reputed to be of Irish descent, Robespierre was trained for the law and speedily achieved a modest success as an advocate. In 1782 he was appointed a criminal judge, but soon resigned because he could not bear to impose a sentence of death. Of a nervous and timid disposition, he was never able to display much executive ability, but he made up for this lack of talent by fanatical devotion to principle. He had adopted the belief that the philosophy of Rousseau held the one great hope of salvation for all mankind. To put this philosophy into practice he was ready to employ any means that would bring results, regardless of the cost to himself or to others. This passionate loyalty to a gospel that exalted the masses eventually won him a following. Indeed, he was so lionized by the public that he was allowed to wear the knee breeches, silk stockings, and powdered hair of the old society until the end of his life. In 1791 he was accepted as the oracle of the Jacobin Club, now purged of all but its most radical elements. Later he became president of the National Convention and a member of the Committee of Public Safety. Though he had little or nothing to do with originating the Reign of Terror, he was nevertheless responsible for enlarging its scope. He actually came to justify ruthlessness as a necessary and therefore laudable means to revolutionary progress. In the last six weeks of his virtual dictatorship, no fewer than 1,285 heads rolled from the scaffold in Paris.

Robespierre

The years of the Reign of Terror were years of ruthless dictatorship in France. Pressed by foreign enemies from without, the committee faced sabotage from both the political Right and Left at home. In 1793, a large band of peasants, opposed to military conscription and encouraged by British and royalist agents, revolted in the western area of the Vendée. Girondist fugitives helped fuel rebellions in the great provincial cities of Lyon, Bordeaux, and Marseilles. This harvest of the decentralizing policies of the National Assembly was bitter fruit to the committee. At the same time they met with the scornful criticism of revolutionaries even more radical than themselves. This latter group, known as the *enragés,* was led by the journalist Jacques Hébert, and threatened to topple not only the government but the country itself by its extremist crusades. Determined to stabilize France, whatever the necessary cost, the committee dispatched commissioners into the countryside to suppress the enemies of the state. During the period of the Terror, from September 1793 to July 1794, the most reliable estimates place the number of executions at approximately twenty thousand in France as a whole. A law of September 17, 1793, made every person who had been identified in any way with the Bourbon government or with the Girondists an object of suspicion; and no one who was a suspect or who was suspected of being a suspect was entirely

Jacobins. Contemporary drawings by Heuriot.

A Meeting of the Revolutionary Committee During the Reign of Terror

safe from persecution. When some time later the Abbé Sieyès was asked what he had done to distinguish himself during the Terror, he responded dryly, "I lived."

The achievements of the committee

Three points need to be made with regard to the Committee of Public Safety. First, it dramatically reversed the trend toward decentralization, which had characterized the reforms of the assembly. In addition to dispatching its own commissioners from Paris to quell provincial insurrection, the committee published a *Bulletin des loix,* to inform all citizens what laws were to be enforced and obeyed. And it replaced local officials, some of them still royalist in sympathy, with its own loyal "national agents." Second, by fostering, as it did, the interests of the lower middle class the committee significantly retarded the pace of industrial transformation in France. Through policies which assisted the peasant, the small craftsman, and the shopkeeper to acquire property, the government during this "second" revolution encouraged the entrenchment of a class at once devoted to the principle of republicanism while unalterably opposed to a large-scale capitalist transformation of the economy of France. Third, the ruthless Terror of the committee undoubtedly achieved its end, by saving France from defeat at the hands of the coalition of European states. Whether the human price extracted in return for that salvation was worth the paying is a matter historians—and indeed all thoughtful human beings—may well never finally resolve.

The Thermidorian reaction: stage three

The Committee of Public Safety, though able to save France, could not save itself. It failed to put a stop to inflation, thereby losing the support of those commoners whose dissatisfactions had helped bring the convention to power. The long string of military victories convinced growing numbers that the committee's demands for continuing self-sacrifice, as well as its insistence upon the necessity of the Terror, were no longer justified. By July 1794, the committee was virtually without allies. On July 27 (9 Thermidor, according to the new calendar) the convention "outlawed" Robespierre; on the following day he was executed. The only remaining leaders in the convention were men of moderate sympathies, who, as time went on, inclined toward increasing conservatism. Gradually, the revolution came once more to reflect the interests of the upper middle class. Much of the extremist work of the radicals was now undone. The law of maximum prices and the law against "suspects" were both repealed. Political prisoners were freed, the Jacobins driven into hiding, and the Committee of Public Safety shorn of its absolute powers. The new situation made possible the return of priests, royalists, and other émigrés from abroad to add the weight of their influence to the conservative trend.

In 1795 the National Convention adopted a new constitution, which lent the stamp of official approval to the victory of the prosperous classes. The constitution granted suffrage to all adult male citizens who could read and write. They were permitted to vote for electors, who in turn would choose the members of the legislative body. In order to be an elector, one had to be the proprietor of a farm or other establishment with an annual income equivalent to at least one hundred days of labor. The drafters of the constitution thus ensured that the authority of the government would actually be derived from citizens of considerable wealth. Since it was not practicable to restore the monarchy, lest the old aristocracy also come back into power, executive authority was vested in a board of five men known as the Directory, chosen by the legislative body. The new constitution included not only a bill of rights but also a declaration of the *duties* of the citizen. Conspicuous among the latter was the obligation to bear in

The 1795 constitution

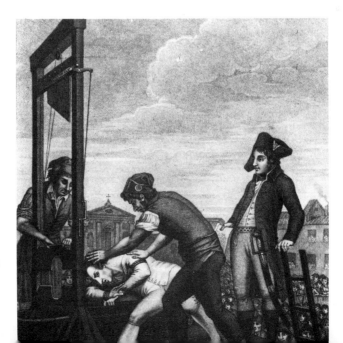

The Death of Robespierre

The Directory

Napoleon rescues the Directory

mind that "it is upon the maintenance of property . . . that the whole social order rests."

The reign of the Directory has not enjoyed a good historical press. The collection of *nouveau riche* speculators and profiteers who rose to prominence as they labored to make a good thing for themselves out of the war were not a particularly attractive crew. They were lampooned as ostentatious and vulgar *"merveilleuses"*—outrageously overdressed men and underdressed women. But however anxious they were to live down the self-denying excesses of the past several years by self-indulgent excesses of their own, they were in no mood to see the major accomplishments of the revolution undone. They had no difficulty in disposing of threats from the Left, despite their failure to resolve that bugbear of all revolutionary governments, inflation and rising living costs. When in 1796 the radical "Gracchus" Babeuf[5] launched a campaign to abolish private property and parliamentary government, his followers were arrested, executed, and deported.

To dispatch threats from the Right was not so easy. Elections in March 1797—the first free elections held in France as a republic—returned a large number of constitutional monarchists to the councils of government. Leading politicians, among them some who had voted for the execution of Louis XVI, took alarm. So too did the Directory's brilliant young general, Napoleon Bonaparte (1769–1821). His plans for permanent French expansion in Belgium and Italy were threatened by a promonarchist "peace" party that was urging an end to war, even if it meant the surrender of recent French conquests. Desperate to save republican France—and themselves—from the monarchists, the directors called for Napoleon's assistance. He sent a general to their aid. With the support of the army thus assured, the Directory in September 1797 annulled most of the election results of the previous

[5] Called "Gracchus" after the Roman tribune Gaius Gracchus, a hero of the people.

The Eighteenth Brumaire. A detail from a painting by Bronchet depicting Napoleon as the man of the hour.

spring. Its bold coup did little, however, to end the nation's political irresolution. Two years later, after a series of further abortive uprisings and purges, and with the country still plagued by severe inflation, Bonaparte seized his opportunity to fill the vacuum of French leadership. Leaving his army as it attempted to free itself from British naval domination in Egypt, Bonaparte appeared in France. Appealing to the desperate Directory, he descended upon them as the answer to their prayers: a strong popular leader who was not a king. Abbé Sieyès, who had once declared for revolution in the name of the third estate, now declared for counterrevolution in the name of virtual dictatorship: "Confidence from below, authority from above." With those words Sieyès foreshadowed the end of the revolutionary period.

4. NAPOLEON AND EUROPE

Few men in Western history have compelled the attention of the world as Napoleon Bonaparte did during the fifteen years of his absolutist rule in France. And few men have succeeded as he has in continuing to live on as myth in the consciousness, not just of his own country, but of all Europe. Without doubt, part of the success of the Napoleonic myth can be credited to the fact that Napoleon never attempted to disguise his less-than-gentlemanly background. Although born in Corsica into a family that held a title of nobility from the Republic of Genoa, he cultivated the rude manners of an *arriviste,* losing his temper, cheating at cards, taking what he could get without regard to the conventions of polite society. As such, he appealed to the new citizens of a triumphantly middle-class Europe. In the minds of his admirers he would remain the "little corporal" who, without the privileges of the aristocrat, had made it to the top on his own.

The character of Napoleon Bonaparte

Yet the myth was also grounded in the important fact of Bonaparte's undoubted abilities. Schooled in France and at the military academy in Paris, he possessed a mind congenial to the ideas of the Enlightenment—creative, imaginative, and ready to perceive things anew. His primary interests were history, law, and mathematics. His particular strengths as a leader lay in his ability to conceive of financial, legal, or military plans and then to master their every detail; his capacity for inspiring others, even those initially oppsed to him; and his belief in himself as the destined savior of the French. That last conviction eventually became the obsession that led to Napoleon's undoing. But supreme self-confidence was just what the French government had lacked since the first days of the revolution. Napoleon believed both in himself and in France. That latter belief was the tonic France now needed, and Napoleon proceeded to administer it in liberally revivifying doses.

His abilities

During the years from 1799 to 1804, Napoleon ruled under the title of first consul, but in reality as a dictator. Once again, France was given a new constitution. Though the document spoke of universal male suffrage, political power was retained, by the now familiar means of indirect election, in the hands of middle-class entrepreneurs and professionals. Recognizing, however, that his regime would derive additional substance if it could be made to appear the government of the people of France, Bonaparte instituted what has since become a common authoritarian device: the plebiscite. The voters were asked to approve the new constitution and did so by the loudly proclaimed vote of 3,011,107 in favor, 1,567 opposed.

Although the constitution provided for a legislative body, that body could neither initiate nor discuss legislation. The first consul made use of a Council of State to draft his laws; but in fact the government depended on the authority of one man. Bonaparte had no desire to undo the major egalitarian reforms of the revolution. He reconfirmed the abolition of estates, privileges, and local liberties, thereby reconfirming as well the notion of a meritocracy, of "careers open to talent," dear to the hearts of the middle class. Through centralization of the administrative departments, he achieved what no recent French regime had yet achieved, an orderly and generally fair system of taxation. His plan, by prohibiting the type of exemptions formerly granted the nobility and clergy, and by centralizing collection, enabled him to budget rationally for expenditures and consequent indebtedness. In this way he reduced the inflationary spiral that had entangled so many past governments.

Napoleon. A famous unfinished portrait by David.

Napoleon's most significant accomplishment was his completion of the educational and legal reforms begun during the revolutionary period. He ordered the establishment of *lycées* (high schools) in every major town and a school in Paris for the training of teachers. To supplement these changes, Napoleon brought the military and technical schools under state control and founded a national university to exercise supervision over the entire system. Like almost all his reforms, this one proved of particular benefit to the middle class; so did the new

legal code promulgated in 1810. The Code Napoleon, as the new body of laws was called, reflected two principles which had threaded their way through all the constitutional changes since 1789: uniformity and individualism. The code made French law uniform, declaring past customs and privileges forever abolished. By underscoring in various ways a private individual's right to property, by authorizing new methods for the drafting of contracts, leases, and stock companies, and by once again prohibiting trade unions, the code worked to the benefit of individually minded entrepreneurs and businessmen.

To accomplish these reforms Napoleon called upon the most talented men available to him, regardless of their past political affiliations. He admitted back into the country émigrés of all political stripes. His two fellow consuls—joint executives, but in name only—were a regicide of the Terror and bureaucrat of the Old Regime. His minister of police had been an extreme radical republi-

Coronation of Napoleon and Josephine by David. Napoleon crowned himself and his wife and assumed the title of Napoleon I, emperor of the French.

can; his minister of foreign affairs was the opportunist aristocrat Talleyrand. The work of political reconciliation was assisted by Napoleon's 1801 concordat with the pope, which reunited Church and State. Though the action disturbed former anti-Church Jacobins, Napoleon, ever the pragmatist, believed the reconciliation of Church and State necessary for reasons both of domestic harmony and of international solidarity. According to the terms of the concordat, the pope received the right to depose French bishops and to discipline the French clergy. At the same time, the Vatican agreed to lay to rest any claims against the expropriation of former Church lands. Hereafter, that property would remain unchallenged in the hands of its new middle-class rural and urban proprietors. In return, the clergy was guaranteed an income from the state. The concordat did nothing to revoke the principle of religious freedom established by the revolution. Although the Roman Catholic clergy received state money, so did Protestant clergy.

Napoleon's agreement won him the support of those conservatives who had feared for France's future as a Godless state. To prove to the old Jacobins, in turn, that he remained a child of their revolution, he invaded the independent state of Baden in 1804 to arrest and then execute the duke of Enghien, a relative of the Bourbons, whom Napoleon falsely accused of a plot against his life. (Three years before he had deported over one hundred Jacobins on a similar charge, but with no permanent political repercussions.) The balancing act only served to increase Napoleon's general popularity. By 1802 the people of France were prepared to accept him as "consul for life." In 1804, they rejoiced when, in the cathedral of Notre Dame, in Paris, he crowned himself Emperor Napoleon I.

Across the boundaries of France, the nations of Europe had watched, some in admiration, others in horror, all in astonishment, at

Napoleon crowned emperor

Anti-French alliances

Treaty of Lunéville

Napoleon's reforms in Europe

the phenomenon that was Napoleon. They had fought France since 1792 in hopes of maintaining European stability. Now they faced the greatest threat to that stability yet to arise. The detailed history of the wars fought to contain the French is complex, and of little direct relevance to the patterns of ideas, institutions, and societies we are tracing. Suffice it to say that from 1792 until 1795 France had been at war with a coalition of European powers—principally Austria, Prussia, and Britain. In 1795, Prussia retired from the fray, financially exhausted and at odds with Austria. In 1797, the Austrians, defeated by Bonaparte in northern Italy, withdrew as well, signing the Treaty of Campo Formio, which ceded to France territories in Belgium, recognized the Cisalpine Republic which Bonaparte had established in Italy, and agreed to France's occupation of the left bank of the Rhine.

By the following year, Britain was left to fight the French alone. In 1798 it formed a second coalition against the French, this one with Russia and Austria. The results did not differ significantly from those of the first allied attempt to contain France. Russia and Austria had no success in driving the French from Italy; the French likewise failed to break Britain's advantage at sea. By 1801, the coalition was in tatters, Russia having withdrawn two years previously. The Treaty of Lunéville, signed by France and Austria, confirmed the provisions of Campo Formio; in addition the so-called Batavian, Helvetian, Cisalpine, and Ligurian republics—established by Napoleon from territories in the Low Countries, Switzerland, Italy, and Piedmont—were legitimized. The Austrians also acquiesced to a general redrawing of the map of Germany, which resulted eventually in an amalgamation of semi-independent states under French domination into the Confederation of the Rhine. The following year Britain, no longer able to fight alone, settled with the French as well, returning all the territories it had captured in overseas colonial engagements except Trinidad and Ceylon.

Under Napoleon's reign, the territories of central Europe underwent a revolution. This revolution was a thorough governmental reorganization, one which imposed the major egalitarian reforms of the French Revolution upon lands outside the borders of France, while building a French empire. Most affected were territories in Italy (the "Kingdom of Italy" as it was now called); Germany (the Confederation of the Rhine, including the newly formed Kingdom of Westphalia); Dalmatia (the Illyrian provinces); and Holland. (Belgium had been integrated directly into the empire.) Into all these territories Napoleon introduced a carefully organized, deliberate system of administration, based upon the notion of careers open to talent, equality before the law, and the abolition of ancient customs and privileges. The Napoleonic program of reform in the empire represented an application of the principles that had already transformed postrevolutionary France. Manorial courts were liquidated, and Church courts abolished. Provinces were joined into an enormous bureaucratic network that reached directly back to Paris. Laws were codified, the tax system modernized, and everywhere individuals were freed to work at whatever trade they chose. The one freedom denied throughout this new grand hegemony was that of self-government: i.e., all governmental direction emanated from Paris, and therefore from Napoleon. Despite that fact, middle-class business and professional men, who had chafed against restrictions imposed upon them by petty despotic traditions, welcomed this chance to exercise their talents to a fuller degree than they had ever before enjoyed.

Napoleon's motives in introducing these various radical changes were by no means altruistic. He understood that the defense of his enormous domain depended on efficient administration and the rational collection and expenditure of funds for his armies. His boldest attempt at consolidation, however, a policy forbidding the importation into the Continent of British goods, proved a failure. This "Continental System," established in 1806, was designed as a strategic measure in Napoleon's continuing economic war against Britain. Its purpose was to destroy Britain's commerce and credit—to starve it economically into surrender. The system failed for several reasons. Foremost was the fact that throughout the war Britain retained control of the seas. The British naval blockade of the Continent, implemented in 1807, served, therefore, as an effective counter to Napoleon's system. While the empire labored to transport goods and raw materials overland to avoid the British blockade, the British worked with success to develop a lively trade with South America. Internal tariffs were a second reason for the failure of the system. Napoleon was unable to persuade individual territories to join a tariff-free customs union. As a result Europe remained divided into economic camps, fortified against each other by tariffs, and at odds with each other as they attempted to subsist on nothing more than what the Continent could produce and manufacture. The final reason for the system's collapse was the stark fact that the Continent had more to lose than Britain. Trade stagnated; ports and manufacturing centers grumbled as unemployment rose.

The Continental System

5. THE END OF THE REVOLUTIONARY ERA

The Continental System was Napoleon's first serious mistake. As such it was one of the causes of his ultimate downfall. A second cause of Napoleon's decline was his constantly growing ambition and increasing sense of self-importance. Napoleon's goal was a united Europe modeled after the Roman Empire. The symbols of his empire—reflected in painting, architecture, and the design of furniture and clothing—were deliberately Roman in origin. But Napoleon's Rome was without question imperial, dynastic Rome. The triumphal

The Empress Josephine

Reasons for Napoleon's fall

columns and arches he had erected to commemorate his victories recalled the ostentatious monuments of the Roman emperors. He made his brothers and sisters the monarchs of his newly created kingdoms, which Napoleon controlled from Paris. He divorced his first wife, the Empress Josephine, alleging her childlessness, and insured himself a successor of royal blood by marrying into the house of Hapsburg. Even his admirers began to question if Napoleon's empire was not simply a larger, more efficient, and, therefore, ultimately more dangerous despotism than the monarchies of the eighteenth century. War again broke out in 1805, with the Russians, Prussians, and Austrians joining the British in an attempt to contain France. But to no avail; Napoleon's military superiority led to defeats, in turn, of all three continental allies. Ultimately only the emperor's own unwillingness to recognize that his supply of men, materiel, and good fortune was not limitless brought military defeat upon him.

Invasion of Spain

In 1808, Napoleon invaded Spain on the pretext of guarding its coasts against the British, but with the intention of establishing his brother Joseph as king. Scarcely had the new monarch been crowned than the Spanish people rose in revolt. Though Napoleon sent an army against them, he was never able to crush the rebellion entirely. With encouragement and assistance from the British, the Spaniards kept up a series of guerilla attacks which caused no end of expense and annoyance to the great warlord of France. Further, the courage of Spain in resisting the invader promoted a spirit of defiance elsewhere, with the result that Napoleon could no longer count upon the docility of any of his victims.

See color map facing page 577

A more fateful stage in the downfall of the Corsican adventurer was

The Retreat from Russia. In this painting by Charlet the horrors of the Russian winter can be seen.

the disruption of his alliance with Russia. As a purely agricultural country, Russia had suffered a severe economic crisis when it was no longer able, as a result of the Continental System, to exchange its surplus grain for British manufactures. The consequence was that Tsar Alexander began to wink at trade with Britain and to ignore or evade the protests from Paris. By 1811 Napoleon decided that he could endure this flouting of the Continental System no longer. Accordingly, he collected an army of 600,000 men and set out in the spring of 1812 to punish the tsar. The project ended in disaster. The Russians refused to make a stand, thereby leading the French farther and farther into the heart of their country. They finally permitted Napoleon to occupy their ancient capital of Moscow. But on the very night of his entry, a fire of suspicious origin broke out in the city. When the flames subsided, little but the blackened walls of the Kremlin palaces remained to shelter the invading troops. Hoping that the tsar would eventually surrender, Napoleon lingered amid the ruins for more than a month, finally deciding on October 22 to begin the homeward march. The delay was a fatal blunder. Long before he had reached the border, the terrible Russian winter was upon his troops. Swollen streams, mountainous drifts of snow, and bottomless mud slowed the retreat almost to a halt. To add to the miseries of bitter cold, disease, and starvation, mounted Cossacks rode out of the blizzard to harry the exhausted army. Each morning the miserable remnant that pushed on left behind circles of corpses around the campfires of the night before. On December 13 a few thousand broken soldiers crossed the frontier into Germany—a miserable fraction of what had once been proudly styled the *Grande Armée*. The lives of nearly 300,000 men had been sacrificed in Napoleon's Russian adventure.

The allies now took advantage of Napoleon's depleted forces to engineer victory. By March of 1814 their armies were in Paris and Napoleon prepared for surrender. Exiled to the island of Elba, in the Mediterranean, he plotted return, while his successor Louis XVIII, brother of Louis XVI and the choice of the allies, attempted to fill a space far too great for his mediocre talents. In the spring of 1815, Napoleon returned to France, where he was received enthusiastically. But the rekindled loyalties could not outlast his final defeat at the Battle of Waterloo, in Belgium, on June 18, 1815. This time the allies exiled him to the tiny island of St. Helena, in the south Atlantic, where he died in 1821.

To appreciate the impact of this era of revolution upon Western civilization, one must trace the ideas and institutions it fostered as they work their way into the history of nineteenth- and twentieth-century Europe and America. Liberty—the right to act within the world with responsibility to no one but oneself—was a notion dear to those who made the French Revolution, and one which remained embodied in the reforms it produced. So was equality—the notion of rational laws

EXTRAIT DU MONITEUR.

ACTE
D'ABDICATION
DE
L'EMPEREUR NAPOLÉON.

Napoleon's Abdication Proclamation, 1814

The Russian campaign

The Battle of Waterloo

*The era of revolution:
liberty, equality,
nationality*

applied even-handedly to all, regardless of birth or position. National pride, the era's third legacy, was bred in the hearts of the French people as they watched their citizen armies repel attacks against their newly won freedoms. It was instilled, as well, into those whose opposition to the French made them more conscious of their own national identity. The three concepts—liberty, equality, and nationality—were now no longer merely ideas; as laws and as a new way of addressing life, they rested at the center of European reality. They were together one of the two elements upon which a new ruling class—the middle class—now rose to power. The other element—economic success—is the subject of the next chapter.

SELECTED READINGS

• *Items so designated are available in paperback editions.*
• Arendt, Hannah, *On Revolution,* New York, 1963. An analysis of the American and French Revolutions and their meaning for modern man.

Bosher, J. F., *French Finances, 1770–1795: From Business to Bureaucracy,* Cambridge, 1970. An impressive study concerned with the financial apparatus of Old Regime and revolutionary France.

• Breunig, C., *The Age of Revolution and Reaction, 1789–1850,* 2nd ed., New York, 1978.

• Brinton, Crane, *Anatomy of Revolution,* rev. ed., New York, 1961. Attempts to create a general model of revolutions by comparing the English, American, French and Russian Revolutions.

• ———, *A Decade of Revolution, 1789–1799,* New York, 1934. An excellent European survey.

• Bruun, Geoffrey, *Europe and the French Imperium, 1799–1814,* New York, 1938. Describes the impact of Napoleon upon Europe.

Cobban, Alfred, *The Social Interpretation of the French Revolution,* Cambridge, 1964. A penetrating critique of the radical interpretation of the revolution, more important for its questions than its conclusions.

Cone, Carl B., *The English Jacobins: Reformers in Late 18th-Century England,* New York, 1968.

Dansette, Adrien, *A Religious History of Modern France,* Vol. I, New York, 1961. Traces the position of the Catholic Church during the revolutionary and Napoleonic periods.

Ford, Franklin, *Robe and Sword: The Regrouping of the French Aristocracy after Louis XIV,* Cambridge, Mass., 1953. An important social study of the nobility of the robe and its striving for political dominance prior to the revolution.

• Gershoy, Leo, *The French Revolution and Napoleon,* rev. ed., New York, 1964. A good survey with annotated bibliography.

———, *From Despotism to Revolution, 1763–1789,* New York, 1944. Valuable for background on the revolution.

Geyl, Pieter, *Napoleon: For and Against,* rev. ed., New Haven, Conn., 1964. The ways in which Napoleon has been interpreted by French historians and political figures.

Gooch, G. P., *Germany and the French Revolution*, New York, 1920. An old but still valuable account of the German political and intellectual response to the French Revolution.

Goodwin, Albert, *The French Revolution*, rev. ed., London, 1958. A good introduction to the years 1789–1794.

Greer, Donald, *The Incidence of the Terror During the French Revolution: A Statistical Interpretation*, Cambridge, Mass., 1935. An important study which reveals that the lower classes suffered most during the Terror, rather than the nobility or the clergy.

• Hampson, Norman, *A Social History of the French Revolution*, London, 1963.

Herold, J. Christopher, *The Age of Napoleon*, New York, 1963.

• Lefebvre, Georges, *The Coming of the French Revolution*, Princeton, N.J., 1947. An excellent study of the causes and early events of the revolution.

———, *The French Revolution*, 2 vols., New York, 1963–64. An impressive synthesis by the greatest modern scholar of the revolution.

———, *Napoleon*, New York, 1969.

———, *The Thermidorians and the Directory*, New York, 1964.

McManners, John, *The French Revolution and the Church*, New York, 1969. Describes the impact of revolutionary anticlericalism upon the French Church.

Mathiez, Albert, *The French Revolution*, New York, 1928. Sympathetic to Robespierre.

• Palmer, R. R., *The Age of the Democratic Revolution: A Political History of Europe and America, 1760–1800*, 2 vols., Princeton, N.J., 1964. Impressive for its scope; places the French Revolution in the large context of a world-wide revolutionary movement.

———, *Twelve Who Ruled*, Princeton, 1958. Excellent biographical studies of the members of the Committee of Public Safety. Demonstrates that Robespierre's role has been exaggerated.

• Rudé, George, *The Crowd in the French Revolution*, Oxford, 1959. An important monograph which analyzes the composition of the crowds which participated in the great uprisings of the revolution.

Schapiro, J. S., *Condorcet and the Rise of Liberalism in France*, New York, 1934. A splendid study of revolutionary idealism.

Soboul, Albert, *The Sans-Culottes: The Popular Movement and Revolutionary Government, 1793–1794*, Garden City, N.Y., 1972. An outstanding example of "history from below"; analyzes the pressures upon the Convention in the year of the Terror.

Thompson, J. M., *Napoleon Bonaparte: His Rise and Fall*, Oxford, 1958. The standard work.

• ———, *Robespierre and the French Revolution*, London, 1953. An excellent short biography.

• Tilly, Charles, *The Vendée: A Sociological Analysis of the Counter-Revolution of 1793*, Cambridge, Mass., 1964. An important economic and social analysis of the factors that led to reaction in the Vendée.

• Tocqueville, Alexis de, *The Old Regime and French Revolution*. Originally written in 1856, this remains a classic analysis of the causes of the French Revolution.

• Williams, Gwyn A., *Artisans and Sans-Culottes*, New York, 1969.

SOURCE MATERIALS

• Burke, Edmund, *Reflections on the Revolution in France,* London, 1790. The great conservative statement against the revolution and its principles.
• Montesquieu, Baron de, *The Spirit of the Laws,* New York, 1945. See especially Books I, II, III, XI.
• Paine, Thomas, *The Rights of Man,* 1791. (Many editions.) Paine's eloquent response to Burke's *Reflections* resulted in his conviction for treason and banishment from England.
• Rousseau, Jean-Jacques, *Discourse on the Origin of Inequality,* 1754. (Many editions.)
——, *The Social Contract,* 1762, (Many editions.) Rousseau's *Social Contract* provided a philosophical justification for both the American and French Revolutions.
Sieyès, Abbé, *What Is the Third Estate?* 1789. The most important political pamphlet in the decisive year 1789.
Stewart, John Hall, *A Documentary Survey of the French Revolution,* New York, 1951.
Thompson, J. M., *French Revolution Documents, 1789–1794,* Oxford, 1948.
Young, Arthur, *Travels in France during the Years 1787, 1788, 1789,* London, 1912. France on the eve of revolution, as seen by a perceptive English observer.

Chapter 20

THE INDUSTRIAL REVOLUTION

Providence has assigned to man the glorious function of vastly improving
the productions of nature by judicious culture, of working them up into
objects of comfort and elegance with the least possible expenditure of
human labor—an undeniable position which forms the basis of our Factory System.

—Andrew Ure, *The Philosophy of Manufactures*

There have been many revolutions in industry during the history of Western civilization, and there will undoubtedly be
many more. Periods of rapid technological change are often
called revolutions, and justifiably so, But, historically, there is but one
Industrial Revolution. Occurring during the one hundred years after
1780, it witnessed the first breakthrough from a rural, handicraft
economy to one dominated by urban, machine-driven manufactuting.

The fact that it was a European revolution was not accidental. Although Europe was, in the mid–eighteenth century, a continent still
predominantly agricultural, although the majority of its people remained illiterate and destined to live out impoverished lives within
sight of the place they were born—despite these conditions, which in
our eyes might make Europe appear "underdeveloped," it was of
course no such thing. European merchants and men of commerce
were established as the world's foremost manufacturers and traders.
Rulers relied upon this class of men to provide them with the wherewithal to maintain the economy of their states, both in terms of
flourishing commercial activity and of victorious armies and navies.
Those men, in turn, had for the most part extracted from their rulers
the understanding that the property they possessed, whether invested
in land, or commerce, or both, was theirs outright. That understanding, substantiated by the written contracts that were replacing
unwritten, long-acknowledged custom, helped persuade merchants,
bankers, traders, and entrepreneurs that they lived in a world that was

*A European revolution:
the commercial class*

stable, rational, and predictable. Believing the world was so, they moved out into it with self-confidence and in hopes of prospering. Only in Europe does one find these presuppositions and this class of men in the eighteenth century; only through the activities of such a class could the Industrial Revolution have taken place.

Increasing markets

These capitalists could not have prospered without an expanding market for their goods. The existence of this market explains further why it was in Europe that the Industrial Revolution took place. Ever since the beginning of the seventeenth century, overseas commercial exploration and development had been opening new territories to European trade. India, Africa, North and South America—all had been woven into the pattern of European economic expansion. The colonies and commercial dependencies took economic shape at Europe's behest. Even the new United States had not been able to declare its economic independence. Whatever new design Europe might devise, all would be compelled to accomodate themselves to Europe's demands.

Population growth

A third factor helping to insure that the revolution would occur in Europe was the continuing growth of its population. In England, the population increased from about 4 million in 1600 to about 6 million in 1700, to 9 million in 1800. The population of France grew from 17 million in 1700 to 26 million a century later. Population growth on this scale provided, as did overseas expansion, an ever-increasing market for manufactured goods. It furnished, as well, an adequate pool—eventually a surplus—of laboring men, women, and children to work in the manufacture of those goods either at home or in factories.

Yet these factors—a thriving commercial class, growing markets, and an increasing population—while helping to explain why the Industrial Revolution took place in eighteenth-century Europe, fail to tell us enough about its origins. For that understanding, we must focus our attention from Europe as a whole to its most prosperous state, England.

1. THE INDUSTRIAL REVOLUTION IN ENGLAND

Why in England? (1) an economy of abundance

It was in England that the Industrial Revolution first took hold. England's economy had progressed further than that of any other country in the direction of abundance. In simplest terms: fewer people were engaged in the crude struggle to do no more than remain alive; more people were in a position to sell a surplus of the goods they produced to an increasingly expanding market; and more people had money enough to purchase the goods that market offered. English laborers, though poorly enough paid, enjoyed a higher standard of living than their continental counterparts. They ate white bread, not brown, and meat with some regularity. Because a smaller portion of their income was spent on food, they might occasionally have some to spare for articles which were bought rather than homemade.

Further evidence of this increasing abundance was the number of bills for the enclosure of agricultural land passed by an English Parliament sympathetic to capitalism during the last half of the eighteenth century. The enclosure of fields, pasture, and waste lands into large fenced tracts of land under the private ownership and individual management of capitalist landlords, although it deprived local agricultural laborers of the right to share in the use of common lands as they had in past times, meant an increased food supply to feed an increasing and increasingly urban population. Yet another sign of England's abundance was its growing supply of surplus capital, derived from investment in land or commerce, and available for further employment to finance new economic enterprises. Thus English capitalists had enough money on hand to underwrite and sustain an industrial revolution.

But the revolution required more than money. It required habits of mind that would encourage investments in enterprises at once risky, but with an enormous potential for gain. In England, far more than on the Continent, the pursuit of wealth was perceived to be a worthy end in life. The aristocracy of Europe had, from the period of the Renaissance, cultivated the notion of "gentlemanly" conduct, in part to hold the line against social encroachments from below. The English aristocrats, whose privileges were meager when compared with those of continental nobles, had never ceased to respect men who made money; nor had they disdained to make whatever they could for themselves. They invested and speculated. Their scramble to enclose their lands reflected this sympathy with aggressive capitalism. Below the aristocracy, there was even less of a barrier separating the world of urban commerce from that of the rural "gentry." Most of the men who pioneered as entrepreneurs in the early years of the Industrial Revolution sprang from the minor gentry or yeoman farmer class. To a degree unknown on the Continent, men from this sort of background felt themselves free to rise as high as their abilities might carry them on the social and economic ladder.

Eighteenth-century England was not by any means free of social snobbery, however: lords looked down upon bankers, as bankers looked down upon artisans. But a lord's disdain might well be tempered by the fact of his own grandfather's origins in the counting-house. And the banker would gladly lend money to the artisan if convinced that the artisan's invention might make them both a fortune. The English, as a nation, were not afraid of business. They respected the sensible, the practical, and the financially successful. Robinson Crusoe, that desert island entrepreneur, was one of their models. In the novel (1719) by Daniel Defoe, the hero had used his wits to master nature and become lord of a thriving economy. His triumph was not diminished because it was a worldly triumph; far from it. "It is our vanity which urges us on," the economist Adam Smith, defender of laissez faire capitalism, declared. And thank God, Smith implied, for our blessed vanity! An individual's desire to show himself a success worked to produce prosperity for the country as a whole.

(3) increasing markets

England's eighteenth-century prosperity was based upon an expanding market for whatever goods it manufactured. Its small size and the fact that it was an island encouraged the development of a nationwide domestic market. The absence of a system of internal tolls and tariffs, such as existed on the Continent, meant that goods could be moved freely to the place where they could fetch the best price. This freedom of movement was assisted by a constantly improving transportation system. Parliament in the years just before the Industrial Revolution passed acts to finance turnpike building at the rate of forty per year; the same period saw the construction of canals and the further opening up of harbors and navigable streams. Unlike the government of France, whose cumbrous mercantilist adventures as often as not thwarted economic growth, the English Parliament believed that the most effective way in which it could help businessmen was to assist them in helping themselves.

Overseas expansion

Parliament's members had every reason to promote England's economic fortunes. Some were businessmen themselves; others had invested heavily in commerce. Hence their eagerness to encourage by statute the construction of canals, the establishment of banks, and the enclosure of common lands. And hence their insistence, throughout the eighteenth century, that England's foreign policy respond to its commercial needs. At the end of every major eighteenth-century war, England wrested overseas territories from its enemies. At the same time, England was penetrating hitherto unexploited ports and territories, such as India and South America, in search of further potential markets and resources. The English possessed a merchant marine capable of transporting goods across the world, and a navy practiced in the art of protecting its commercial fleets. London, already a leading center for the world's trade, served as a headquarters for the transfer of raw material, capital, and manufactured products. By 1780 England's markets, together with its fleet and its established position at the center of world trade, combined to produce a potential for expansion so great as to compel the Industrial Revolution.

The cotton industry

English entrepreneurs and technicians responded to the compulsion by revolutionizing the production of cotton textile goods. Although far less cotton goods were made in eighteenth-century England than wool, the extent of their manufacture by 1760 was such as to make cotton more than an infant industry. Tariffs prohibiting the importation of East Indian cottons, imposed by Parliament to stimulate the sale of woolen goods, had instead served to spur the manufacture of domestic cotton goods. Thus the revolution, when it did occur, took place in an already well-established industry. Yet without the inven-

The Spinning Jenny. Invented by James
Hargreaves in 1767

tion of some sort of machinery which would improve the quality and
at the same time dramatically increase the quantity of spun cotton
thread, the necessary breakthrough would not have come. The invention of the fly-shuttle, which greatly speeded up the process of weaving, only made the bottleneck in the prior process of spinning the
more apparent. The problem was solved by the invention of a series of
comparatively simple mechanical devices, the most important of
which was the spinning jenny, invented by James Hargreaves, a car-
penter and hand-loom weaver, in 1767 (patented 1770). The spinning
jenny, named after the inventor's wife, was a compound spinning
wheel, capable of producing sixteen threads at once. The threads it
spun were not strong enough, however, to be used for the longi-
tudinal fibers, or warp, of cotton cloth. It was not until the invention
of the water frame by Richard Arkwright, a barber, in 1769, that
quantity production of both warp and woof (latitudinal fibers) became
possible. This invention, along with that of the spinning mule, conceived of by Samuel Crompton in 1779, and combining the features of
both the jenny and the frame, solved the problems that had heretofore
curtailed the output of cotton textiles. They increased the mechanical
advantage over the spinning wheel enormously. From six to twenty-
four times the amount of yarn could be spun on a jenny as on the
wheel; by the end of the century two to three hundred times as much
on the mule. Just as important, the quality of the thread improved not
only in terms of strength but also of fineness.

Once these machines came into general use, the revolution proceeded apace. Cotton suited the mule and the jenny because it was a
tougher thread than wool—fiber which could withstand the rough

Eli Whitney

Growth of factories

The extent of the cotton trade

treatment it received at the mechanical hands of the crude early machines. In addition, the supply of cotton was expandable in a way that the supply of wool was not. The cotton gin, invented by the American Eli Whitney in 1793, separated seeds from fiber, thereby making cotton available at a lower price. The invention kept America's slave plantations profitable, and meant that supply would be available to meet increased demand.

The first machinery was cheap enough to allow spinners to continue to work their own machines at home. But as the machinery increased in size, it was more and more frequently housed not in the cottages of individual spinners, but in workshops or mills located near water which could be used to power the machines. Eventually, with the further development of steam-driven equipment, the mills could be built wherever it might suit the entrepreneur—frequently in towns and cities in the north of England.

The transition from home to factory industry was of course not accomplished overnight. Cotton yarn continued to be spun at home at the same time that it was being produced in mills. Eventually, however, the low cost of building and operating a large plant, plus the efficiency realized by bringing workers together under one roof, meant that larger mills more and more frequently replaced smaller workshops. By 1851, three-fifths of those employed in cotton manufacture worked in medium- to large-sized mills. Weaving remained a home industry until the invention of a cheap, practical power loom convinced entrepreneurs that they could save money by moving the process from home to mill. Hand-loom weavers were probably the most obvious victims of the Industrial Revolution in England. Their unwillingness to surrender their livelihood to machinery meant that they continued to work for less and less—by 1830, no more than a pitiful six shillings a week. In 1815 they numbered about 250,000; by 1850, there remained only 40,000; by 1860, only 3,000.

English cotton textiles flooded the world market from the 1780s. Here was a light material, suitable for the climates of Africa, India, and the more temperate zones of North America. Here was a material cheap enough to make it possible for millions who had never before enjoyed the comfort of washable body clothes to do so. And here was material fine enough to tempt the rich to experiment with muslins and calicos in a way they had not done before. Figures speak eloquently of the revolutionary change wrought by the expanding industry. In 1760, England exported less than £250,000 worth of cotton goods; by 1800 it was exporting over £5 million worth. In 1760, England imported 2.5 million pounds of raw cotton; in 1787, 22 million pounds; in 1837, 366 million pounds. By 1800, cotton accounted for about 5 percent of the national income of the country; by 1812, from 7 to 8 percent. By 1815, the export of cotton textiles amounted to 40 percent of the value of all domestic goods exported from Great Britain. Although the price of manufactured cotton goods fell dramatically, the market expanded so rapidly that profits continued to increase.

Unlike the changes in the textile industry, those occurring in the manufacture of iron were not great enough to warrant their being labeled revolutionary. Yet they were most significant. Britain's abundant supply of coal, combined with its advanced transportation network, allowed the English, from the middle of the eighteenth century, to substitute coal for wood in the heating of molten metal. A series of discoveries made fuel savings possible, along with a higher quality of iron, and the manufacture of a greater variety of iron products. Demand rose sharply during the war years at the end of the century. It remained high as a result of calls for plant machinery, agricultural implements, and hardware; it rose dramatically with the coming of railways in the 1830s and 1840s. Britain was exporting 571,000 tons of iron in 1814; in 1852, it exported 1,036,000 tons out of a total of almost 2,000,000—more iron than was made by all the rest of the world combined.

The need for more coal required the mining of deeper and deeper veins. In 1712, Thomas Newcomen had devised a crude but effective steam engine for pumping water from mines. Though of value to the coal industry, it was of less use in other industries, since it was wasteful of both fuel and power. In 1763, James Watt, a maker of scientific instruments at the University of Glasgow, was asked to repair a model of the Newcomen engine. While engaged in this task he conceived the idea that the machine would be greatly improved if a separate chamber were added to condense the steam, so as to eliminate the necessity of cooling the cylinder. He patented his first engine incorporating this device in 1769. Unfortunately, Watt's genius as an inventor was not matched by his business ability. He admitted that he would "rather face a loaded cannon than settle a disputed account or make a bargain." As a consequence, he fell into debt in attempting to place his

The iron industry

The steam engine

James Watt Working on a Model of Thomas Newcomen's Steam Engine

The Staffordshire Collieries. In the building to the right is a whimsey, or coal-powered steam engine, used to lift loads of coal from the mines.

machines on the market. He was rescued by Matthew Boulton, a wealthy hardware manufacturer of Birmingham. The two men formed a partnership, with Boulton providing the capital. By 1800 the firm had sold 289 engines for use in factories and mines. One must not exaggerate the speed with which the steam engine replaced water as the principle motive force in industry. In 1850 more than a third of the power used in woolen manufacture and an eighth of that used in cotton was still produced by water. Despite those facts, there is no question that without the steam engine there could have been no expansion in those or other industries on the scale that we have described.

Other advances

Other industries experienced profound changes during the hundred years of the Industrial Revolution. Many of those changes came in response to the growth of textile manufacture. The chemical industry, for example, developed new methods of dyeing and bleaching, as well as improved methods of production in the fields of soap and glass-making. Production of goods increased across the board, as profits from the boom in manufacturing increased the demand for new and more sophisticated articles. Pottery, metalware—these and other trades expanded to meet demands, in the process adopting methods that in most instances reduced cost and speeded manufacture.

The limits of the Industrial Revolution

To understand fully the nature of the Industrial Revolution in England one must not lose sight of two important factors: the first is that dramatic as the revolution was, it happened over a period of two or three generations, at varying paces in different industries. Some men and women continued to work at home, much as their grandfathers and grandmothers had. Old tools and old methods were not immediately replaced by new ones, any more than populations fled the countryside overnight for the city. Second, the revolution was accomplished from a very limited technological and theoretical base. Except in the chemical industry, change was not the result of pure scientific research. It was the product of empirical experimentation—in some cases, of little more than creative tinkering. To say this is not to disparage the work of men such as Arkwright, Hargreaves, Watt, and their like. It is to suggest, however, the reason why England, without a national system of education on any level, was nonetheless able to accomplish the revolution it did. Nor are these remarks designed to belittle the magnitude of the change. What occurred in England was a revolution because of the way in which it reshaped the lives, not just of the English, but of people across the globe. By responding as it did to the demands of its apparently insatiable markets, England made a revolution every bit as profound and long-lasting as that which occurred simultaneously in France.

2. THE INDUSTRIAL REVOLUTION ON THE CONTINENT

The Industrial Revolution came in time to the Continent, but not to any important degree before about 1830. Manufacturing in eighteenth-century France and Germany clustered in regions whose proximity to raw materials, access to markets, and traditional attachment to particular skills had resulted in their development as industrial centers. Flanders and Normandy in France, and Saxony in Germany were centers for the manufacture of woolen cloth; Switzerland, southern Germany, and Normandy, of cottons; Wallonia (the area around Liège in Belgium), the Marne valley, and Silesia in Germany, of iron. Yet for a variety of reasons, these areas failed to experience the late-eighteenth-century breakthrough that occurred in Britain. Nor were they capable at first of imitating Britain's success, once they began to perceive the great economic advantages that its pronounced lead was bringing it. There were a number of reasons for the delay of continental industrialization, most of them opposite to those reasons which had brought the Industrial Revolution first to England. Whereas England's transportation system was highly developed, those of France and Germany were not. France was far bigger than England, its rivers were not as easily navigable, its seaports further apart. Central Europe was so divided into tiny principalities, each with its own set of tolls and tariffs, as to make the transportation of raw materials or manufactured goods over any considerable distance most impractical. Nor was France itself free of the sorts of regulations that thwarted easy shipments. In addition, the Continent was not as blessed with an abundance of raw materials as England. France, the Low Countries, and

Reasons for delay: (1) lack of transport and raw materials

Germany had to import wool. Europe, though richer than England in timber, lacked an abundant supply of the fuel that was the new source of industrial energy; few major coal deposits had as yet been discovered.

(2) lack of entrepreneurial spirit

Distances and distinctions between social and economic ranks were far greater on the Continent than in England. Money was not the social solvent in France and Germany that it was across the Channel. Before the French Revolution, continental aristocrats were unwilling to invest in commercial enterprises they believed would damage their social standing. More important, after the revolution middle-class Frenchmen, though free in theory to rise as high on the social and economic ladder as they might aspire, appear largely to have remained content to make only enough money to sustain a modest-sized business. Those revolutionary constitutional changes which had favored the lower middle class by encouraging its acquisition of property, prevented the growth of industry by dispersing capital into the hands of innumerable small-scale enterprises. The entrepreneurial spirit that compelled Englishmen to drive competitors to the wall was not as highly developed in France and Germany in the years after 1815. Exhausted by the competitiveness of war, and fearful of the disruptions that war brought in its train, continental businessmen remained far more willing than the English to keep on manufacturing and selling on the same scale they always had.[1]

(3) effect of wars

The Continent did not simply stand idle as England assumed its industrial lead. The pace of mechanization was increasing in the 1780s. But the French Revolution and the wars which followed disrupted the growth which might have otherwise taken place. Battles fought on French, German, and Italian soil destroyed factories and machinery. Although ironmaking increased to meet the demands of the wars, techniques remained what they had been. Commerce was badly hurt both by British destruction of French merchant shipping and by Napoleon's Continental System. Probably the revolutionary change most beneficial to industrial advance in Europe was the removal of previous restraints on the movement of capital and labor; for example, the abolition of trade guilds, and the reduction in the number of tariff barriers across the Continent. On balance, however, the revolutionary and Napoleonic wars clearly thwarted industrial development on the Continent, while at the same time intensifying it in England.

Increases after 1815: (1) population rise

A number of factors combined to produce a climate more generally conductive to industrialization on the Continent after 1815. Population continued to increase, not only throughout Europe, but in those areas now more and more dependent upon the importation of manufactured goods—Latin America, for example. These increases, which doubled the populations of most European countries between 1800 and 1850, meant that the Continent would be supplied with a growing

[1] On this point, see David S. Landes, *The Unbound Prometheus,* pp. 132–33.

A Swedish Mining Town, 1790

number of producers and consumers. More people did not necessarily mean further industrialization. In Ireland, for example, where other necessary factors were absent, more people meant less food. But in those countries with an already well-established commercial and industrial base—France and Germany, for example—increased population did encourage the adoption of the technologies and methods of production that had transformed Britain.

Transportation improved in the West both during and following the Napoleonic wars. The Austrian Empire added over 30,000 miles of roads between 1830 and 1847; Belgium almost doubled its road network in the same period; France built, in addition to roads, 2,000 miles of canals. In the United States, where industrialization was occurring at an increasingly rapid rate after 1830, road mileage jumped from 21,000 miles in 1800 to 170,000 in 1856. When these improvements were combined with the introduction of rail transport in the 1840s, the resulting increase in markets available to all Western countries encouraged them to introduce methods of manufacturing that would help meet new demands.

(2) improved transportation

In this endeavor, governments played a more direct role on the Continent than in Britain. Napoleon's rationalization of French and imperial institutions had introduced Europe to the practice of state intervention. His legal code, which guaranteed freedom of contract and facilitated the establishment of joint-stock enterprises, encouraged other rulers to provide a similar framework for commercial expansion. In Prussia, lack of private capital necessitated state operation of a large proportion of that country's mines. In no European country but Britain would railways be built without the financial assistance of the state. In the private sector, as well, more attention was given on the Continent than in England to the need for artificial stimulation to

(3) centralization

produce industrial change. It was in Belgium that the first joint-stock investment bank—the Société Générale—was founded, an institution designed to facilitate the accumulation of ready capital for investment in industry and commerce. Europeans were also willing for the state to establish educational systems whose aim, among others, was to produce a well-trained elite capable of assisting in the development of industrial technology. What Britain had produced almost by chance, the Europeans began to reproduce by design.

(4) the lack of technicians

Until the Continent produced its own technicians it was compelled to rely on British expertise. And another reason why the pace of continental, and also American, industrialization, even after 1815, remained far slower than in Britain was Britain's natural reluctance to see its methods of production pirated by others. Until 1825, British artisans were forbidden to emigrate; until 1842, much innovative machinery could not be exported. Laws did not, however, prevent the movement of creative technician-entrepreneurs and their particular skills; many Englishmen, during the first part of the nineteenth century, made fortunes as they taught others in Europe and America to do what they had taught themselves. But an initial shortage of home-grown experts undoubtedly hampered rapid industrial expansion on the Continent.

Textiles

The growth of the textile industry in Europe was patterned by the circumstances of the Napoleonic wars. The supply of cotton to the Continent had been interrupted, thanks to the British blockade, but the military's greater demand for woolen cloth meant that expansion occurred more rapidly in the latter than in the former industry. By 1820, the spinning of wool by machine was the common practice on the Continent; weaving, however, was still accomplished largely by hand. Centers for the production of wool were located at Rheims and in Alsace, in France; in what is now Belgium; and, in Germany, in

Silk Weavers of Lyon, 1850. The first significant working-class uprisings in nineteenth-century France occurred here in 1831 and 1834. Note the domestic character of the working conditions.

A German Textile Factory, 1848. This is an unusually large manufacturing facility for this period on the Continent.

Saxony and Silesia. Mechanization was retarded by the fact that hand labor was cheap, and by the important fact that since Britain's market was so large, continental profits too often depended upon the manufacture of some particular specialty not made in England, and therefore without broad commercial appeal. Cotton manufacture was curtailed by the same circumstances. In France, as a result, mechanization occurred first in the silk industry and those sections of the cotton industry which produced finer specialty materials—lace, for example. A tradition of prestige associated with the production of luxury goods, dating back to the reign of Louis XIV, encouraged entrepreneurs to invest in this branch of the textile industry. They were willing to forego mass markets in the hope that their products would not meet with British competition. France nevertheless remained the largest continental producer of cotton goods, followed, again, by Belgium, the German territories of the Rhine valley, Saxony, Silesia, and Bavaria.

In the area of heavy industry on the Continent, the picture was much the same as in textiles: i.e., gradual advances in the adoption of technological innovation against a background of more general resistance to change. Here, however, because change came later than in Britain, it coincided with an increased demand for various goods that had come into being as a result of industrialization and urbanization: iron pipe, much in use by 1830 in cities for gas, water, and drainage; metal machinery, now replacing earlier wooden prototypes. Con-

Heavy industry

sequently, the iron industry took the lead over textiles on the Continent, accompanied by an increase, where possible, in the production of coal. Coal was scarce, however; in the Rhineland wood was still used to manufacture iron. The result was an unwillingness on the part of entrepreneurs to make as extensive use of the steam engine as they might have otherwise; it used too much fuel. In France, as late as 1844, hydraulic (i.e., water-driven) engines were employed far more often for the manufacture of iron than were steam engines. One further problem hampered the development of continental heavy industry during the first half of the nineteenth century. British competition forced continental machine construction firms to scramble for whatever orders they could get. This need to respond to a variety of requests meant that it was difficult for firms to specialize in a single product. The result was a lack of standardization, and continued production to order, when rationalization and specialization would have resulted in an increased volume of production.

3. THE COMING OF RAILWAYS

Railways as a stimulus to the European and American economies

By about 1840, then, European countries, and to some degree, as well, the United States, were moving gradually along the course of industrialization traced by Britain, producing far more than they had, yet nothing like as much as their spectacular pace-setter. Within the next ten years, the coming of the railways was to alter that situation. Though Britain by no means lost its lead, the stimulus provided generally to Western economies by the introduction of railway systems throughout much of the world carried Europe and America far enough and fast enough to allow them to become genuine competitors with the British.

Railways as goods carriers

Railways came into being in answer to two needs. The first was the obvious desire on the part of entrepreneurs to transport their goods as quickly and cheaply as possible across long distances. Despite already mentioned improvements in transportation during the years before 1830, the movement of heavy materials, particularly coal, remained a problem. It is significant that the first modern railway was built in England in 1825 from the Durham coal field of Stockton to Darlington, near the coast. "Tramways"—parallel tracks along which coal carts were pulled by horses—had long been in use at pitheads to haul coal short distances. The Stockton-to-Darlington railway was a logical extension of this device, designed to answer the transportation needs produced by constantly expanding industrialization. The man primarily responsible for the design of the first steam railway was George Stephenson, a self-made engineer who had not learned to read until he was seventeen. He talked a group of North-of-England investors into the merits of steam traction and was given full liberty to carry out his plans. The locomotives on the Stockton-Darlington line traveled at fifteen miles per hour, the fastest rate at which human beings had yet moved overland.

Railways were also built in response to other than purely industrial needs: specifically, the need for capitalists to invest their money. Englishmen such as those who had made sizable fortunes in textiles, once they had paid out workers' wages and plowed back substantial capital in their factories, retained a surplus profit for which they wanted a decent yet reliable return. Railways provided them with the solution to their problem. Though by no means as reliable as had been hoped, railway investment proved capable of more than satisfying the capitalists' demands. No sooner did the first combined passenger and goods service open in 1830, on the Liverpool to Manchester line, than plans were formulated and money pledged to extend rail systems throughout Europe, the Americas, and beyond. In 1830, there were no more than a few dozen miles of railway in the world. By 1840, there were over 4,500 miles; by 1850, over 23,000. The English contractor, Thomas Brassey, the most famous, but by no means the only one of his kind, built railways in Italy, Canada, Argentina, India, and Australia.

Thomas Brassey

Railways as stimulus to industry

The railway boom was a boom to industrialization generally. Not only did it increase enormously the demand for coal and for a variety of heavy manufactured goods—rails, locomotives, carriages, signals, switches; by enabling goods to move faster from factory to salesroom, railways decreased the time it took to sell those goods. Quicker sales meant, in turn, a quicker return on capital investment, money which could then be reinvested in the manufacture of more goods. Finally, by opening up the world market as it had never been before, the railway boom stimulated the production of such a quantity of material goods as to insure the rapid completion of the West's industrialization.

The New Railway Age. Left: Stephenson's "Rocket." A reconstruction of the railway engine built by George Stephenson in 1829. Right: "The Railway Juggernaut of 1845." A cartoon from the English humor magazine *Punch* satirizing speculation—often financially disastrous—in railway stocks.

The building of a railway line was an undertaking on a scale infinitely greater than the building of a factory. Railway construction required capital investment beyond the capacity of any single individual. In Britain, a factory might be worth anything from £20,000 to £200,000. The average cost of twenty-seven of the more important railway lines constructed between 1830 and 1853 was £2 million. The average labor force of a factory ranged from 50 to 300. The average labor force of a railway, after construction, was 2,500. Because a railway crossed the property of a large number of individual landowners, each of whom would naturally demand as much remuneration as he thought he could get, the planning of an efficient and economical route was a tricky and time-consuming business. The entrepreneur and contractor had to concern themselves not only with the purchase of right-of-way. They also contended with problems raised by the destruction of sizable portions of already existing urban areas, to make room for stations and switching yards. And they had to select a route that would be as free as possible of the hills and valleys that would necessitate the construction of expensive tunnels, cuts, and embankments. Railway-builders ran tremendous risks. Portions of most lines were subcontracted at fixed bids to contractors of limited experience. A spate of bad weather might delay construction to the point where builders would be lucky to bring in the finished job within 25 percent of their original bid. Of the thirty major contractors on the London-to-Birmingham line, ten failed completely.

The "navvies"

If the business of a contractor was marked by uncertainty, that of the construction worker was characterized by back-breaking labor. The English "navvies," who built railways not only throughout Britain but around the world, were a remarkable breed. Their name derived from "navigator," a term applied to the construction workers on England's eighteenth-century canals. The work that they accomplished was prodigious. Because there is little friction between a train's wheels and its tracks, it can transport heavy loads easily. But

Construction of the London to Birmingham Railway, London, 1838. This drawing of the building of retaining walls in a new railway cut evokes the chaos created by railway construction within urban areas.

Railway Navvies. Without the aid of machinery, the burden of building Britain's railways fell on the backs of men such as these.

lack of friction ceases to be an advantage when a train has to climb or descend a grade, thereby running the risk of slippage. Hence the need for comparatively level roadbeds; and hence the need for laborers to construct those tunnels, cuts, and embankments that would keep the roadbeds level. In England and in much of the rest of the world, mid-nineteenth-century railways were constructed almost entirely without the aid of machinery. An assistant engineer on the London-to-Birmingham line, in calculating the magnitude of that particular construction, determined that the labor involved was the equivalent of lifting 25 billion cubic feet of earth and stone one foot high. This he compared with the feat of building the Great Pyramid, a task he estimated had involved the hoisting of some 16 billion tons. But whereas the building of the pyramid had required over 200,000 men and had taken twenty years, the construction of the London-to-Birmingham railway was accomplished by 20,000 men in less than five years. Translated into individual terms, a navvy was expected to move an average of twenty tons of earth per day. Railways were laid upon an almost infinite base of human muscle and sweat.

4. INDUSTRIALIZATION AFTER 1850

In the years between 1850 and 1870, Britain remained very much the industrial giant of the West. But France, Germany, Belgium, and the United States assumed the position of challengers. In the iron industry, Britain's rate of growth during these years was not as great as that of either France or Germany (5.2 percent for Britain, as against 6.7 percent for France and 10.2 percent for Germany). But in 1870 Britain

Britain still the leader

The Early Industrial Landscape. Stockport, England, in the 1840s.

Continuing European advance

See color map facing page 768

was still producing half the world's pig iron; 3.5 times as much as the United States, more than 4 times as much as Germany, and more than 5 times as much as France. Although the number of cotton spindles increased from 5.5 to 11.5 million in the United States between 1852 and 1861, and by significant but not as spectacular percentages in European countries, England in 1861 had 31 million spindles at work in comparison with France's 5.5 million, Germany's 2 million, Switzerland's 1.3 million, and Austria's 1.8 million.

Most of the gains experienced in Europe came as a result of continuing changes in those areas we have come to recognize as important for sustained industrial growth. The improved transportation systems that resulted from the spread of railways helped encourage an increase in the free movement of goods. International monetary unions were established, and restrictions removed on international waterways such as the Danube. The Prussian *Zollverein,* or tariff union, an organization designed to facilitate internal free trade, was established in 1818 and was extended over the next twenty years to include most of the German principalities outside Austria. Free trade went hand in hand with further removal of barriers to the freedom to enter trades and to practice business unhampered by restrictive regulation. Control of guilds and corporations over artisan production was abolished in Austria in 1859 and in most of Germany by the mid-1860s. Laws against usury, most of which had ceased to be enforced, were officially abandoned in Britain, Holland, Belgium, and in many parts of Germany. Governmental regulation of the operation of mines was surrendered by the Prussian state in the 1850s, freeing entrepreneurs to develop resources as they saw fit. The formation of investment banks proceeded apace, encouraged by an important increase in the money supply and therefore an easing of credit, following the opening of the California gold fields in 1849.

A further reason for increased European production was the growing trade in raw materials. Wool and hides imported from Australia helped diminish the consequences of the cotton shortage suffered after the outbreak of the United States Civil War and the Union blockade of the American South. Other importations—guano from the Pacific, vegetable oils from Africa, pyrites (sulphides) from Spain—stimulated the scale of food production and both altered and increased the manufacture of soap, candles, and finished textiles. Finally, discoveries of new sources of coal, particularly in the Pas-de-Calais region of France and in the Ruhr valley in Germany, had dramatic repercussions. Production of coal in France rose from 4.4 million to 13.3 million tons between 1850 and 1869; during the same years, German production increased from 4.2 million to 23.7 million tons.

Increased trade in raw materials

By 1870 Europe had by no means turned its back on agriculture. Fifty percent of France's labor force remained on farms. Agricultural laborers were the single largest occupational category in Britain during the 1860s. Great stretches of the Continent—Spain, southern Italy, eastern Europe—were almost untouched by the Industrial Revolution. And in the industrialized countries, much work was still accomplished in tiny workshops or at home. Yet if Europe was by no means wholly industrial, it was far and away the most industrially advanced portion of the globe—and not by accident. In order to maintain its position of producer to the world, Europe, and Britain particularly, made certain that no other areas stood a chance to compete. Europe used its economic and, when necessary, its military strength to insure that the world remained divided between the producers of manufactured goods—Europe itself—and suppliers of the necessary raw materials—everyone else. Often this arrangement suited those in other parts of the world who made their money by providing the raw materials that fueled the European economy. Cotton-growers in the southern United States, sugar-growers in the Caribbean, wheat-growers in the Ukraine—all remained content with arrangements as dictated by the industrialized West. Those countries which expressed their discontent—Egypt, for example, which in the 1830s attempted to establish its own cotton textile industry—were soon put in their place by a show of force. Western Europeans, believing in their right to industrial leadership in the world, saw nothing wrong with employing soldiers, if they had to, to make others understand their destiny.

Europe's economy within the world

SELECTED READINGS

• Items so designated are available in paperback editions.
• Ashton, T. S., *The Industrial Revolution, 1760–1830,* London, 1948. An excellent short introduction.
  Checkland, S. G., *The Rise of Industrial Society in England, 1815–1885,* New York, 1965. Emphasizes the economic organization of England.

• Deane, Phyllis, *The First Industrial Revolution*, Cambridge, 1965.

Henderson, W. O., *The Industrialization of Europe, 1780–1914*, New York, 1969.

———, *The State and the Industrial Revolution in Prussia, 1740–1870*, Liverpool, 1958. A biographical approach. Good on technical education.

• Hobsbawm, Eric, *Industry and Empire: 1750 to the Present Day*, New York, 1968. A general survey of industrialization in Britain.

Hoffman, Walther, *British Industry, 1700–1950*, Oxford 1955. A good source for statistics.

• Landes, David S., *The Unbound Prometheus*, London, 1969. An excellent treatment of the technological innovations and economic results of the Industrial Revolution.

McManners, John, *European History: Men, Machines and Freedom*, New York, 1967.

Mantoux, Paul, *The Industrial Revolution in the Eighteenth Century*, rev. ed., New York, 1961. The beginnings of the modern factory system in England.

• Rostow, Walt W., *The Stages of Economic Growth*, rev. ed., Cambridge, 1971. A synthesis by the exponent of the "take-off" theory of economic development.

• Taylor, George Rogers, *The Transportation Revolution, 1815–1860*, New York, 1968.

Usher, A. P., *A History of Mechanical Invention*, Cambridge, Mass., 1954.

SOURCE MATERIALS

Dodd, George, *Days at the Factories; or the Manufacturing Industry of Great Britain Described, and Illustrated by Numerous Engravings of Machines and Processes*, Totawa, N.J., 1975. A reprint of the 1850 edition.

Mitchell, Brian R., and Phyllis Deane, *Abstract of British Historical Statistics*, Cambridge, 1962. The single best source for statistics on population, trade, manufacturing, etc.

• Smith, Adam, *An Inquiry into the Nature and Causes of the Wealth of Nations*, Chicago, 1977. Written in 1776, this revolutionary work called for the end of mercantilism and the enshrinement of laissez faire.

Ward, J. T., *The Factory System, 1830–1855*, New York, 1970. Excerpts from contemporary documents describing, defending, and criticizing the factory system and industrialization.

Chapter 21

CONSEQUENCES OF INDUSTRIAL-IZATION: URBANIZATION AND CLASS CONSCIOUSNESS (1800–1850)

What Art was to the ancient world, Science is to the modern: The distinctive faculty. In the minds of men the useful has succeeded the beautiful. Yet rightly understood, Manchester is as great a human exploit as Athens.

—Benjamin Disraeli, *Coningsby*

The Industrial Revolution was more than an important event in the economic and technological history of the West. It helped to reshape the patterns of life for men and women, first in Britain, then in Europe and America, and eventually throughout much of the world. By increasing the scale of production, the Industrial Revolution brought about the factory system, which in turn compelled the migration of millions from the countryside and small towns into cities. Once in those cities, men and women had to learn a new way of life, and learn it quickly: how to discipline themselves to the factory whistle and survive in a slum, if they were first-generation urban workers; how to manage a work-force and achieve respectable prominence for themselves in the community, if they were businessmen and their wives. One particular lesson that industrialization and urbanization taught was that of class consciousness. Men and women, to a far greater degree than heretofore, began to perceive themselves as part of a class with interests of its own, and in opposition to the interests of men and women in other classes.

We shall examine this range of social and cultural changes as they occurred during the first fifty years or so of the nineteenth century, after looking briefly first at the condition of the bulk of the popula-

Consequences of the Industrial Revolution

tion, which, despite industrialization, remained on the land. Since the Industrial Revolution came first to Britain, our focus will be on that country. Yet the pattern set by the British was one that was repeated to a great extent in other European countries, as industrialization came to them in time.

1. PEOPLE ON THE LAND

Population increase

The dramatic story of the growth of industrialization and urbanization must not be allowed to obscure the fact that, in 1850, the population of Europe was still overwhelmingly a peasant population. Demographic pressures which helped produce chaos in the cities, likewise caused severe hardship in the countryside. The population increase which took place throughout Europe during this period appears to have been caused by two factors. The first was the occurrence of earlier and more frequent marriages. The second, from which the first followed, was the availability of cheaper food, the result of increased production, improved agricultural technology, and, in many places, the introduction of the potato. Coupled with these factors was a gradually decreasing deathrate. The populations of countries that were predominantly agricultural lept forward with those that were industrializing. The population of Ireland, despite famine, grew from 5.5 to 8 million, Russia's population from 39 to 60 million, in the years from 1800 to 1850.

Wretched rural conditions

Although conditions allowed a population increase, they were not such as to make the life of the poorer inhabitants of Europe anything other than bleak. Overpopulation brought underemployment, and hence poverty, in its train. Conditions in rural areas deteriorated sharply whenever there was a bad harvest, as there was with continuing regularity. Hunger, typhus, and near-starvation were not uncommon. The result was a standard of living—if one can dignify the condition with that name—that for many rural inhabitants of many areas in Europe declined in the first half of the nineteenth century, although not enough to reverse general population growth. Governments in some countries attempted to solve the related problems of population pressure and impoverishment by passing laws raising the age of marriage. In some of the states of southern and western Germany, as well as in Austria, men were forbidden to marry before the age of thirty, and were also required to prove their ability to support a family.

Agricultural capitalism

Even had such laws acted as an effective curb on population growth—which, in the main, they did not—they would nevertheless have failed to prevent the rural stresses that resulted from the continuing spread of agricultural capitalism. The pace of this change varied across Europe; it was furthest advanced in England and Prussia. Wherever landed proprietors determined to meet increased demand

Interior of an English Farm Laborer's Cottage, 1846. Note the wooden crate used as an infant's cradle.

for food by farming large areas as a capital investment, they imposed a series of transformations that were bound to affect the lives of agricultural laborers. First, land must be made a negotiable commodity. It must not, therefore, be tied to ancient customs which clouded its title—as was the case, for example, with common land, to which the poor within a community might have some right of access or cultivation. Second, land must be in the hands of those with capital enough to improve it, in order to make of it a profitable investment. It must be "enclosed"—"regulated" was the term in Prussia—so that it could be properly fertilized and drained, or, if it was grazing land, so that breeds might be scientifically improved without fear of mongrelization. Finally, a mobile force of agricultural laborers must be available to work at the capitalists' behest. They must not be "tied" to a particular piece of land, either through systems of customary rights or bondage. They must be free to go where they were told to go, to work whatever land would bring most profit to its owners.

These requirements, as they were imposed, produced dislocation and hardship. In Scotland, workers were cleared from land which they had farmed as tenants, in order to provide pasturage for the more profitable sheep. In Germany, those serfs emancipated by a reform-minded government in 1807 were compelled to forfeit somewhere between a third to a half of their land in return for their freedom; those who were able to retain small holdings were in most cases pressured to sell out to larger landholders. Not all landlords were ruthless. "Model" improvers among the wealthiest of the English landowners adjusted to capitalist competition without entirely forswearing traditional responsibilities. They built houses for tenants and laborers, and provided them with schools and churches. In eastern Europe there were among the Prussian landlords (Junkers) pietists who acknowledged obligations to their tenants as well as to the market.

Its results

The speed with which agricultural change occurred in various parts of Europe depended upon the nature of particular governments. Those more sympathetic to new capitalist impulses facilitated the transfer and reorganization of land by means of enabling legislation. They encouraged the elimination of small farms and an increase in larger, more efficient units of production. In England, over half the total area of the country, excluding waste land, was composed of estates of a thousand acres or more. In Spain, the fortunes of agricultural capitalism fluctuated with the political tenor of successive regimes: with the coming of a liberal party to power in 1820, came a law encouraging the free transfer of land; with the restoration of absolutism in 1823, came a repeal of the law. Russia was one of the countries least affected by agricultural change in the first half of the nineteenth century. There land was worked in vast blocks; some of the largest landowners possessed over half a million acres. But the institution of manorial serfdom, which bound hundreds of thousands of men, women, and children to particular estates for generations, prohibited the use of land as a negotiable commodity and therefore prevented the development of agricultural entrepreneurship. In France, despite the fact that manorialism had been abolished by the revolution, there was no rapid movement toward large-scale capitalist farming. An army of peasant proprietors, direct beneficiaries of the Jacobins' democratic constitution, continued to work the small farms they owned. The fact that France suffered far less agricultural distress, even in the 1840s, than did other European countries, and the fact that there was less migration in France from the country to the city and overseas than there was in Germany and England, are marks of the general success of this rural lower middle class in sustaining itself on the land. Its members were content to farm in the old way, opposed agricultural innovation, and, indeed, innovation generally. Despite their veneration of the revolution, they were among the most conservative elements in European society.

2. URBANIZATION AND THE STANDARD OF LIVING

If the countryside continued to hold the bulk of Europe's population in the years between 1800 and 1850, the growth of cities nevertheless remains one of the most important facts in the social history of that period. Cities grew in size and number once the steam engine made it practical to bring together large concentrations of men, women, and children to work in factories. Previously, workshops had been located throughout the countryside, close to the water power that provided the primary means of operating machinery. Steam engines freed entrepreneurs from their dependence on water power and allowed them to consolidate production in large cities. In cities, transportation was more accessible than in the countryside. Hence it was less costly to import raw materials and ship out finished goods. Workers were more readily available in cities, as well, attracted as they were in large numbers in the hope—often false—of finding steady work at higher wages than those paid agricultural laborers. Industrialization was not the only reason for the growth of cities in the early nineteenth century, however. General population growth combined with industrialization forced cities to expand at an alarming rate.

In the ten years between 1831 and 1841 London's population grew by 130,000, Manchester's by 70,000. Paris increased by 120,000 between 1841 and 1846. Vienna grew by 125,000 from 1827 to 1847, into a city of 400,000. Berlin had as large a population by 1848, having increased by 180,000 since 1815. The primary result in these and other fast-growing centers was dreadful overcrowding. Construction lagged far behind population growth. In Vienna, though population rose 42 percent during the twenty years before 1847, the increase in housing was only 11.5 percent. In many of the larger cities, old and new, working men and women lived in lodging houses, apart from families left behind in the country. The poorest workers in almost all European cities dwelt in wretched basement rooms, often without any light or drainage. Governments did their best to encourage emigration to ease the overcrowding, the majority of emigrants relocating in the Americas. Emigration from England rose from 57,000 in 1830, to 90,000 in 1840, to 280,000 in 1850. Ireland, in the early years of the nineteenth century, witnessed the departure of over 1.5 million before the great potato famine of 1846, which increased the flow to a flood. In that year, approximately three out of every four acres of potatoes were blighted. Over 1 million died between 1846 to 1851, either from starvation, or as a result of their weakened physical condition which left them prey to disease.

With cities as overcrowded as they were, it is no wonder that they were a menace to the health of those who lived within them. The middle classes moved as far as possible from disease and factory smoke, leaving the poorest members of the community isolated and a prey to the sickness which ravaged working-class sections. Cholera, typhus, and tuberculosis were natural predators in areas without adequate sewerage facilities and fresh water, and over which smoke from factories, railroads, and domestic chimneys hung heavily. Measures were gradually adopted by successive governments in an attempt to cure the worst of these ills, if only to prevent the spread of catastrophic epidemics. Legislation was designed to rid cities of their worst slums by tearing them down, and to improve sanitary conditions by supplying both water and drainage. Yet by 1850, these projects had only just begun. Paris, perhaps better supplied with water than any European city, had enough for no more than two baths per capita per year; in London, human waste remained uncollected in 250,000 do-

Wentworth Street by Gustav Doré. The artist was much concerned with the over-crowding squalor which resulted from early industrialization in London.

mestic cesspools; in Manchester, no more than a third of the dwellings were equipped with toilets of any sort.

The standard of living debate

Conditions such as these are important evidence in a debate which has occupied historians for the past several decades. The question is: Did the standard of living rise or fall in Europe during the first half-century of the Industrial Revolution? One school, the "optimists," argues that workers shared in the more general increase in living standards which occurred throughout Europe from 1800 onward. It is true, certainly, that some skilled workers within the new factories, along with some artisans in older trades as yet unaffected by industrialization, did benefit by a slight rise in wages and a decline in living costs. But regional variables, along with a constantly fluctuating demand for labor in all countries, have led most commentators to temper their conclusions.

Instability and unemployment

There is no evidence to suggest that the more lowly paid, unskilled worker, whether in England or on the Continent, led anything more than a precarious existence. Textile workers in England, if guaranteed something like full employment, could theoretically earn enough to support a family. Such was not the case in Switzerland, however, where similar work paid only half what was necessary, or in Saxony, where a large portion of the population was apparently dependent upon either poor relief or charity. One of the most depressing features of working-class life in these years was its instability. Economic depressions were common occurrences; when they happened, workers were laid off for weeks at a time, with no system of unemployment insurance to sustain them. Half the working population of England's industrial cities were out of work in the early 1840s. In Paris, 85,000 went on relief in 1840. One particularly hard-pressed district of Silesia reported 30,000 out of 40,000 citizens in need of relief in 1844. Nor must one overlook the plight of those whose skills had been replaced by machinery—the hand-loom weavers being the most notable examples. In the English manufacturing town of Bolton, a hand-loom weaver could earn no more than about three shillings per week in 1842, at a time when experts estimated it took at least twenty shillings a week to keep a family of five above the poverty line. On that kind of pay, workers were fortunate if they did not starve to death. Forced to spend something like 65 percent of their income on food, the per capita meat consumption of the average worker declined to about forty pounds per year in the early nineteenth century.

Such figures make the optimists' generalizations hard to countenance. Figures of whatever sort fail to take into account the stress that urban factory life extracted from the workers. Even workers making thirty shillings a week might well wonder if they were "better off," forced as they were to come to terms with the factory disciplines and living conditions imposed upon them. Though most of those who moved into factory towns migrated but a short distance from their place of birth, the psychological distance they traveled was tremendous. These qualitative factors, admittedly difficult to assess, must be weighed along with more easily quantifiable evidence before reaching any conclusion as to the increased standard of living in early–nineteenth-century cities. Whether or not life in cities was pleasant or ghastly, however, it was, for rapidly increasing numbers, a fact of life. Once we examine that life we will better understand the full impact of industrialization and urbanization upon those who first experienced it.

The quality of life

Soup Kitchen Run by Quakers, Manchester, England, 1862. Enterprises of this sort, which doled out charity "indiscriminately"—that is, without investigating the recipient's character — were condemned by many members of the middle class as encouraging the "worst" elements — idlers and loafers — among the poor.

3. THE LIFE OF THE URBAN MIDDLE CLASS

The urban middle class which emerged during this period was by no means one homogeneous unit, in terms of occupation or income. In a general category that includes merchant princes and humble shopkeepers, subdivisions are important. The middle class included families of industrialists, such as the Peels (cotton) in England and, at a later period, the Krupps (iron) in Germany. It included financiers like the internationally famed Rothschilds, and, on a descending scale of wealth and power, bankers and capitalists throughout the major money markets of Europe: London, Brussels, Paris, Berlin. It included entrepreneurs like Thomas Brassey, the British railway magnate, and technicians, like the engineer Isambard Kingdom Brunel, designer of the steamship *The Great Western*. It included bureaucrats, in growing demand when governments began to regulate the pace and direction of industrialization, and to ameliorate its harshest social and economic results. It included those in the already established professions—in law particularly, as lawyers put their expertise to the service of industrialists. It included the armies of managers and clerks necessary to the continuing momentum of industrial and financial expansion, and the equally large army of merchants and shopkeepers necessary to supply the wants of an increasingly affluent urban middle-class population. Finally, it included the families of all those who lived their lives in the various subcategories we have listed.

Isambard Kingdom Brunel. Behind him are lengths of anchor chain from the steamship *The Great Western*.

Movement within these ranks was often possible, in the course of one or two generations. Movement from the working class into the middle class, however, was far less common. Most middle-class successes originated within the middle class—the children of farmers, skilled artisans, or professionals. Upward mobility was almost impossible without education; education was an expensive, if not unattainable luxury for the children of a laborer. Careers open to talents, that goal achieved by the French Revolution, frequently meant middle-class jobs for middle-class young men who could pass exams. The examination system was an important path for ascendancy within governmental bureaucracies. If passage from working class to middle class *Social mobility* was not common, neither was the equally difficult social journey from middle class to aristocratic, landed society. This was particularly the case on the Continent, where the division between nobility and commoner had traditionally been most pronounced. In Britain, mobility of this sort was easier. Children from wealthy upper middle-class families, if they were sent, as occasionally they were, to elite schools and universities, and if they left the commercial or industrial world for a career in politics, might effect the change. William Gladstone, son of a Liverpool merchant, attended Eton and Oxford, exclusive educational preserves, married a connection of the aristocratic Grenville family, and became prime minister of England. Yet Gladstone was an

Young Gentlemen, 1834. It was to models such as these that the young men of the middle class aspired.

exception to the norm in Britain, and Britain was an exception to the Continent. Movement, when it occurred, did so in less spectacular degrees.

Nevertheless, the European middle class helped sustain itself with the belief that it was possible to get ahead by means of intelligence, pluck, and serious devotion to work. The Englishman Samuel Smiles, in his extraordinarily successful how-to-succeed book *Self Help,* preached a gospel dear to the middle class. Although the gospel declared that anyone willing to exert himself could rise to a position of responsibility and personal profit, however, and although some men actually did so, the notion remained no more than myth for the great majority.

Self-help

Seriousness of purpose was reflected in the middle-class devotion to the ideal of family and home. A practical importance attached to the institution of the family in those areas in England, France, and Germany where sons, sons-in-law, nephews, and cousins were expected to assume responsibility in family firms when it came their turn. Yet the worship of family ignored those practical considerations and assumed the proportions of a sacred belief. Away from the business and confusion of the world, sheltered behind solid masonry and amid the solid comfort of their ornate furnishings, middle-class fathers retired each evening to enjoy the fruits of their daily labors. Inside the home, life was enclosed in a hierarchical and ritualistic system under which the husband and father was absolute master. His wife was called his help-mate but was unquestionably his servant as well. Her task was to keep the household functioning smoothly and harmoniously. She maintained the accounts and directed the activities of the servants—

Family and home

Left: *A Salon in Vienna, 1830s.* A representation of middle-class home life on the Continent. Right: *A Victorian Family at Tea, 1860s*

usually two or three women. Because of the extent of her duties as overseer, she was excused from the everyday drudgeries of washing and cleaning. Called in Victorian England the "Angel in the House," the middle-class woman was responsible for the moral education of her children. Yet she probably spent no more than two or three hours a day at most with her offspring. Until sent to school, they were placed in the custody of a nursemaid or governess. Much of a middle-class woman's day was spent in the company of other women from similar households. An elaborate set of social customs involving "calls" and "at homes" was established in European middle-class society. Women were not expected to improve their minds. They were not expected to be the intellectual companions of their husbands. Rather, they were encouraged to be dabblers, education for them usually consisting of little more beyond reading and writing, a smattering of arithmetic, geography, history, and a foreign language, embellished with lessons in drawing, painting in watercolor, singing, or piano-playing.

Sexuality   Middle-class wives were indoctrinated to believe that they were superior to their husbands in one area only. A wife was "the better half" of a middle-class marriage because she was deemed pure—the untainted Vestal of the hearth, unsullied by cares of the world outside her home, and certainly untouched by those sexual desires which marked her husband, her natural moral inferior. A wife's charge was to encourage her husband's "higher nature." She must never respond to his sexual advances with equal passion; passion was, for her, a presumed impossibility. Instead she must persuade him to seek, through love of home and family, a substitute for the baser instincts with which nature had unhappily endowed the male. Should she fail—and the numberless prostitutes and courtesans in the streets and clandestine boudoirs of nineteenth-century cities suggest that she often did fail—she must accept the fact of her "failure" as she was bound to accept the rest of her life: uncomplainingly. Should she herself succumb to "unwomanly desires" and be discovered to have done so, she could expect nothing less than complete social banishment. The law tolerated a husband's infidelity and at all times respected a husband's rights both to his wife's person and to her property. It made quick work of an "unfaithful" wife, granting to her husband whatever he might desire in terms of divorce, property, and custody, to make him amends for the personal wrongs and embarrassments he had suffered at the hands of his "unnatural" spouse.

Middle-class family rituals helped to sustain this hierarchy. Daily meals, with the father at the head of the table, were cooked and brought to each place by servants, who were a constant reminder of the family's social position. Family vacations were a particularly nineteenth-century middle-class invention. Thanks to the advent of the railways, excursions of one or two weeks to the mountains or to the seashore were available to families of even moderate means. Entrepreneurs built large, ornate hotels, adorned with imposing names—Palace, Beau Rivage, Excelsior—and attracted middle-class customers by offering them on a grander scale exactly the same sort of comfortable and sheltered existence they enjoyed at home.

Domestic rituals

The Middle Class at Leisure. The "morning lounge" at Biarritz, a French resort on the Atlantic coast.

Houses

The houses and furnishings of the middle class were an expression of the material security the middle class valued. Solidly built, heavily decorated, they proclaimed the financial worth and social respectability of those who dwelt within. In provincial cities they were often free-standing "villas." In London, Paris, Berlin, or Vienna, they might be rows of five- or six-story townhouses, or large apartments. Whatever particular shape they took, they were built to last a long time. The rooms were certain to be crowded with furniture, art objects, carpets, and wall hangings. Chairs, tables, cabinets, and sofas might be of any or all periods; no matter, so long as they were adorned with their proper compliment of fringe, gilt, or other ornamentation. The size of the rooms, the elegance of the furniture, the number of servants, all depended, of course, on the extent of one's income. A bank clerk did not live as elegantly as a bank director. Yet in all likelihood both lived in obedience to the same set of standards and aspirations. And that obedience helped bind them, despite the differences in their material way of life, to the same class.

Cities and the middle class

The European middle class had no desire to confront the unpleasant urban by-products of its own success. Members of the middle class saw to it that they lived apart from the unpleasant sights and smells of industrialization. Their residential areas, usually built to the west of the cities, out of the path of the prevailing breeze, and therefore of industrial pollution, were havens from the congestion for which they were primarily responsible. When the members of the middle class rode into the urban centers they took care to do so over avenues lined with respectable shops, or across railway embankments that lifted them above monotonous working-class streets en route to their destination. Yet the middle class, though it turned its face from what it did not want to see, did not turn from the city. Middle-class men and women celebrated the city as their particular creation and the source of their profits. They even praised its smoke—as a sign of prosperity—so

The Paris Opera. An exterior view of the Opera. Designed by Charles Garnier, it was constructed between 1861 and 1875. This grandiose display of wealth and luxury epitomized the taste of the new industrial middle class.

long as they did not have to breathe it night and day. For the most part, it was they who managed their city's affairs. And it was they who provided new industrial cities with their proud architectural landmarks: city halls, stock exchanges, opera houses. These were the new cathedrals of the industrial age, proclamations of a triumphant middle class.

4. THE LIFE OF THE URBAN WORKING CLASS

Like the middle class, the working class was divided into various subgroups and categories, determined in this case by skill, wages, and workplace. The working class included skilled workers in crafts that were centuries old—glassblowing and cabinetmaking, for example. It included as well mechanics equally skilled in new industrial technology. It included the men who built textile machinery and the women and children who tended it. It included the men, women, and children who together worked in mines and quarries. And it included the countless millions who labored at unskilled jobs—railway navvies, coal porters, cleaning women, and the like. The nature of workers' experiences naturally varied, depending upon where they worked, where they lived, and, above all, how much they earned. A skilled textile worker lived a life far different from that of an unskilled dock laborer, the former able to afford the food, shelter, and clothing necessary for a decent existence, the latter so busy trying to keep himself and his family alive that he would have little time to think about anything but the source of their next meal.

Ranks within the working class

Some movement from the ranks of the unskilled to the skilled was possible, if children were provided, or provided themselves, with at least a rudimentary education. Yet education was considered by many parents a luxury, especially since children could be put to work at an early age to supplement a family's meager earnings. There was movement from skilled to unskilled also, as technological change—the introduction of the power loom, for example—drove highly paid workers into the ranks of the unskilled and destitute. Further variations within the working class were the result of the fact that though more men, women, and children were every year working in factories, the majority still labored either in workshops or at home. These variations mean that we cannot speak of a common European working-class experience during the years from 1800–1850. The life we shall be describing was most typical of English workers, during the first half-century of their exposure to industrialization. Only in the years 1850–1900 did continental workers undergo to anything like the same extent, this harsh process of urban acclimatization.

Social mobility

Life in industrial cities was, for almost all workers, uncomfortable at best and unbearably squalid at worst. Workers and their families

Left: *An Urban Courtyard in London.* Right: *A Working-Class Tenement in Glasgow, Scotland.* Courtyards such as these were frequently the only available dumping grounds for household sewage and garbage.

Housing

lived in housing that failed to answer the needs of its inhabitants. In older cities single-family dwellings were broken up into apartments of often no more than one room per family. In new manufacturing centers, rows of tiny houses, located close by smoking factories, were built back-to-back, thereby eliminating any cross-ventilation or space for gardens. Whether housing was old or new, it was generally poorly built. Old buildings were allowed by landlords to fall into disrepair; new houses, constructed of cheap material, decayed quickly. Water often came from an outdoor tap, shared by several houses and adjacent to an outdoor toilet. Crowding was commonplace. Families of as many as eight lived in two or, at the most, three rooms. Housewives could not rely, as in the country, on their own gardens to help supply them with food. Instead, they went to markets that catered to their needs with cheap goods, often stale or nearly rotten, or dangerously adulterated (formaldehyde was added to milk, for example) to prevent further spoilage.

The role of women

The life of working-class wives and mothers was hard. Lack of cheap contraceptive devices and a belief that these devices were immoral helped to keep women pregnant through most of their childbearing years, thus endangering their general health and adding to the burden of their lives. Wives were usually handed a portion of the weekly wage packet by their husbands, and were expected to house, feed, and clothe the family on the very little they were given. Their daily life was a constant round of cooking, cleaning, shopping, and washing—in a tiny space and without enough money. Their problems were compounded, of course, when they themselves had to work, and therefore had far less time to accomplish the household tasks they were still expected to perform.

Since many working-class families had only recently migrated from the country into the city, life there could be a lonely experience for them. If possible, they would live near relatives who had already made the transition and who could assist the newcomers in adjusting to their very different existence. In many cities working-class families lived in districts inhabited primarily by others working at the same trade—weavers in one place, miners in another—and in this way achieved some sense of commonality.

Loneliness

Adjustment to the demands of the factory was every bit as difficult for workers as was acceptance of urban living patterns. Factory hours were long, before 1850 usually twelve to fourteen hours a day. Conditions were dirty and dangerous. Textile mills remained unventilated, so that bits of material lodged in workers' lungs. Machines were unfenced and were a particular danger to child workers, often hired, because of their supposed agility, to clean under and around the moving parts. Manufacturing processes were unhealthy. The use of poison lead in the making of glazed pottery, for example, was a constant hazard to men and women workers in that industry.

Factory life

As upsetting as the physical working conditions in factories was the psychological readjustment demanded of the first-generation workers in them. Preindustrial laborers had had to work long hours and for very little monetary reward. Yet, at least to some degree, they were free to set their own hours and structure their own activities, to move from their home workshops to their small garden plots and back again as they wished. In a factory, all "hands" learned the discipline of the whistle. To function efficiently, a factory demanded that all employees begin and end work at the same time. Most workers could not tell time; fewer possessed clocks. None were accustomed to the relent-

Daily routine

A Laundress and Her Children. Note the cramped and cluttered living quarters.

less pace of the machine. In order to increase production, the factory system encouraged the breaking down of the manufacturing process into specialized steps, each with its own assigned time, an innovation that upset workers accustomed to completing a task at their own pace. The employment of women and children was a further disturbing innovation. In preindustrial communities, women and children had worked, as well as men, but more often than not, all together and at home. In factory towns women and children were frequently hired instead of men: they could be paid less and were declared to be easier to manage. When this happened, the pattern of family life was severely disrupted, and a further break with tradition had to be endured.

Escape

Faced with a drastic reordering of their lives, working-class men and women reacted in various ways. Some sought "the shortest way out of Manchester" by taking to drink (there were 1,200 public houses in that city in 1850). Some women turned to prostitution to supplement their meager wages. Many more men and women struggled to make some sort of community out of the street where they lived or the factory where they worked. It was a long and discouraging process. Yet by mid-century their experiences were beginning to make them conscious of themselves as different from and in opposition to the middle class that was imposing a new way of life on them.

5. THE MIDDLE-CLASS WORLDVIEW

The middle class was not unaware of the many social problems it was generating as it created an industrial society. Despite its general con-

"Capital and Labour." In its earliest years, *Punch,* though primarily a humorous weekly, manifested a strong social conscience. In this 1843 cartoon, the capitalists are seen revelling in the rewards of their investments while the workers—men, women, and children—who toiled in the mines under cruel and dangerous conditions are found crippled and starving.

The Interior of the Crystal Palace. This building of iron and glass was constructed to house exhibits sent to the Exhibition of the Works of Industry of All Nations, held in London in 1851. The exhibition celebrated the triumph of middle-class industrialization.

fidence that the world was progressing—and at its own behest—the middle class was beset by uncertainties. Its belief in its own undoubted abilities was shadowed by concern as to whether its particular talents might ultimately prove irrelevant to the preservation of prosperity. Self-assurance could dissolve in the face of bankruptcy and prosperity vanish in the abyss of economic catastrophe. Those who had risen by their own exertions might fall victim to someone else's ambitions. Nor was it always a simple matter for the middle class to reconcile its own affluence with the poverty of the thousands of workers exploited under its aegis. The middle class was responsible for having wrenched European society out of old patterns of living and thrust it into new ones. To those willing to acknowledge that responsibility, the realization was enough to temper confidence with apprehension. As a result, the middle class worked hard to rationalize its own prosperity, and to make legitimate its ascendancy over both the old society of the land and the urban working poor.

Uncertainty and the need for reassurance

To assist themselves in constructing this congenial worldview, the members of the new industrial middle class made use of the theories of a number of political economists. It is important to recognize that a factory-owner or a banker was not likely to have read the works of these theorists. He might, however, have encountered popular journalistic condensations of their ideas, or have participated in discussions at which the conclusions, if not the reasoned arguments, of the economists were aired. Because those conclusions supported his own inter-

Political economics and the worldview

ests, he grew familiar with them, until, in time, he could talk of the ideas of these men as if they were his own.

We have noted already the manner in which the writings of the economist Adam Smith sustained middle-class respect for individual enterprise. The writings of another group, the classical, or liberal, economists—particularly the Englishmen Thomas Malthus (1766–1834) and David Ricardo (1772–1823)—embodied principles appealing to businessmen who desired a free hand to remake the economies of their countries. The chief elements in the theories as formulated by liberal economists were:

(1) Economic individualism. Individuals are entitled to use for their own best interests the property they have inherited or acquired by any legitimate method. People must be allowed to do what they like so long as they do not trespass upon the equal right of others to do the same.

(2) Laissez faire. The functions of the state should be reduced to the lowest minimum consistent with public safety. The government should shrink itself into the role of a modest policeman, preserving order and protecting property, but never interfering with the operation of economic processes.

(3) Obedience to natural law. There are immutable laws operating in the realm of economics as in every sphere of the universe. Examples are the law of supply and demand, the law of diminishing returns, and so on. These laws must be recognized and respected; failure to do so is disastrous.

(4) Freedom of contract. Individuals should be free to negotiate the best kind of contract they can obtain from any other individual. In particular, the liberty of workers and employers to bargain with each other as to wages and hours should not be hampered by laws or by the collective power of labor unions.

(5) Free competition and free trade. Competition serves to keep prices down, to eliminate inefficient producers, and to ensure the maximum production in accordance with public demand. Therefore, no monopolies should be tolerated, nor any price-fixing laws for the benefit of incompetent enterprisers. Further, in order to force each country to engage in the production of those things it is best fitted to produce, all protective tariffs should be abolished. Free international trade will also help to keep prices down.

Businessmen naturally warmed to theories so congenial to their own desires and intentions. But Malthus and Ricardo made further contributions to the middle-class worldview, based upon their perceptions of conflicting interests within society. Malthus, in his well-known *Essay on Population,* first published in 1798, argued that nature has set stubborn limits to the progress of mankind in happiness and wealth. Because of the voracity of the sexual appetite there is a natural tendency for population to increase more rapidly than the supply of

Thomas Malthus

food. To be sure, there are powerful checks, such as war, famine, disease, and vice; but these, when they operate effectively, further augment the burden of human misery. It follows that poverty and pain are inescapable. Even if laws were passed distributing all wealth equally, the condition of the poor would be only temporarily improved; in a very short time they would begin to raise larger families, with the result that the last state of their class would be as bad as the first. In the second edition of his work, Malthus advocated postponement of marriage as a means of relief, but he continued to stress the danger that population would outrun any possible increase in the means of subsistence.

Malthus on population

Malthus's arguments allowed the middle class to acquiesce in the destruction of an older society which had made some attempt to care for its poor. In England, for example, officials in rural parishes had instituted a system of doles and subsidized wages to help sustain laborers and their families when unemployed. The attempt failed to prevent distress and was met with increasing resistance by taxpayers. Now Malthus told taxpayers that schemes designed to help the poor damaged both rich and poor alike. Poor relief took money, and therefore food, from the mouths of the more productive members of society and put it into the mouths of the least productive. Malthus helped shift the responsibility for poverty from society to the individual, a shift appealing to the middle class, which wished to be freed from the burden of supporting the urban unemployed.

The application of Malthusian doctrine

Malthusian assumptions played a large role in the development of the theories of the Scottish economist Ricardo. According to Ricardo, wages seek a level which is just sufficient to enable workers "to subsist and perpetuate their race, without either increase or diminution." This Ricardo held to be an iron law, from which there is no escape. If wages should rise temporarily above the subsistence standard, the population would increase, and the ensuing competition for jobs would quickly force the rate of pay down to its former level. Ricardo devised a law of rent as well as a law of wages. He maintained that rent is determined by the cost of production on the poorest land that must be brought under cultivation, and that, consequently, as a country fills up with people an ever-increasing proportion of the social income is taken by the landlords.

Ricardo on wages and rent

Here again, a theorist provided arguments useful to the middle class in its attempt to define and defend itself within a new social order. The law of wages gave employers a useful weapon to protect themselves from their workers' petitions for higher pay. The law of rent justified middle-class opposition to the continuing power of landed interests: a class which derived its income not from hard work but simply from its role as rent-collector was profiting unfairly at the expense of the rest of society and deserved to have its profit-making curtailed.

The uses of Ricardo's laws

As soon as the middle class began to argue in this fashion, however,

Jeremy Bentham

Benthamite utilitarianism

Utilitarianism's appeal to the middle class

it betrayed its devotion to the doctrine of laissez faire. Businessmen and entrepreneurs vehemently opposed to government intervention which might deny them the chance to make as much money as they could, were nevertheless prepared to see the government step in and prevent profiteering landlords from making what *they* could from their property. How could this apparent inconsistency be justified? The answer lay in the theories of the Englishman Jeremy Bentham (1748–1832), without doubt the mainstay of middle-class apologists. Bentham, whose major work, *The Principles of Morals and Legislation,* was published in 1789, argued against the eighteenth-century notion that a satisfactory theory of social order could be grounded in a belief in the natural harmony of human interests. Men and women were basically selfish beings. To suppose that a stable and beneficent society could emerge unassisted from a company of self-interested egos was, Bentham believed, to suppose the impossible. Society, if it was to function properly, needed an organizing principle that would both acknowledge humanity's basic selfishness and at the same time compel people to sacrifice at least a portion of their own interests for the good of the majority. That principle, called utilitarianism, stated that every institution, every law, must be measured according to its social usefulness. And a socially useful law was one which produced the greatest happiness of the greatest number. If a law passed this test, it could remain on the books; if it failed, it should be abandoned forthwith, no matter how venerable. A selfish man would accept this social yardstick, realizing that in the long run he would do himself serious harm by clinging to laws that might benefit him, but produce such general unhappiness as to result in disruptions detrimental to his own interests as well as to those of others.

In what ways did this philosophy particularly appeal to the industrial middle classes? First, it acknowledged the importance of the individual. The interests of the community were nothing more than the sum of the interests of those selfish egos who lived within it. Each individual best understood his or her own interests, and was therefore best left free, whenever possible, to pursue those interests as he or she saw fit. Only when they conflicted with the interests—the happiness—of the greatest number were they to be curtailed. Entrepreneurs could understand this doctrine as a license to proceed with the business of industrialization, since, they argued, industrialization was so clearly producing happiness for the majority of the world's population. At the same time, Bentham's doctrines could be used to justify those changes necessary to bring an industrial world into being. Was the greatest happiness produced, English factory-owners might ask, by an antiquated electoral system which denied representation to growing industrial cities? Obviously not. Let Parliament reform itself so that the weight of the manufacturing interests could be felt in the drafting of legislation.

Utilitarianism was thus a doctrine that could be used to cut two ways—in favor of laissez faire; in favor of governmental intervention. And the middle class proceeded to cut both ways at once. Benthamite utilitarianism provided the theoretical basis for many of the middle-class interventionist reforms, such as a revised poor law in Britain and an expanded educational system in France, achieved between 1815 and 1848.[1] At the same time utilitarianism, combined with the theories of Malthus and Ricardo, fortified the position of those businessmen who believed that unfettered individualism had produced the triumphs of the Industrial Revolution. To restrain that individualism was to jeopardize the further progress of industrialization and hence the greatest happiness of the greatest number.

Individualism and intervention

In arguing as it did, the middle class relied upon the conviction that industrialization and the factory system were together showering benefits on all—not just themselves. As we shall see, there were those who disagreed, who pressed, for example, for regulation of factory wages and hours. But the capitalists claimed intervention would inhibit the distribution of those benefits, and hence the proliferation of general happiness. In their support they could cite the English economist Nassau Senior, who claimed that the net profit of any industrial enterprise was derived solely from its last hour of daily operation. Reduce working hours, said Senior, and you eliminate profits, thereby compelling factories to close and workers to starve. The middle class believed Senior because it was clearly in its interest to do so. The middle class also believed him because the enterprise upon which it was embarked was so new and so uncharted that it was hard to prove him wrong. Their uncertainty led them to believe those theories which provided them with the most reassurance and encouraged them to think that what they were doing was of benefit to their fellow men.

Belief in improvement

Political economists and philosophers in France as well as in England helped provide the new middle class with a congenial worldview. Count Claude de Saint-Simon (1760–1825), while a proponent of utopian schemes for social reorganization, nevertheless preached the gospel of "industrialism" and "industrialists" (two words which he coined). Disciples of Saint-Simon were among the leading proponents in France of industrial entrepreneurship and a standardized and centralized financial system.

Far more generally influential was the Positivist philosophy of Auguste Comte (1798–1857). Comte's philosophy, like utilitarianism, insisted that all truth is derived from experience or observation of the physical world. Comte rejected metaphysics as utterly futile; no one can discover the hidden essences of things—why events happen as they do, or what is the ultimate meaning and goal of existence. All one can really know is how things happen, the laws which control their

Auguste Comte

---

[1] These and other similar reforms will be discussed in the following chapter.

The Positivism of Comte

occurrence, and the relations existing between them. Positivism derived its name from the assertion that the only knowledge of any current value was "positive," or scientific, knowledge. Comte argued that humankind's ability to analyze society scientifically and to predict its future had reached a point which would soon enable Europe to achieve a "positive" society, organized not in terms of belief but in terms of facts. Such an achievement would not be a simple matter, however; "positive" attitudes and institutions could not replace those of the "metaphysical" stage through which Europe had just passed without a struggle. By dividing the history of the world into progressive stages (a "religious" stage had preceded the "metaphysical"), and by declaring that the achievement of the highest stage was not possible without the turmoil of industrialization, Comte assured the middle class of its leading role in the better world that was to be.

6. EARLY CRITICS OF THE MIDDLE-CLASS WORLDVIEW

Honoré de Balzac

The middle-class worldview did not go unchallenged. Many writers deplored the social disintegration and moral hypocrisy they saw as the legacy of the Industrial Revolution. The Scot Thomas Carlyle (1795–1881), though a defender of the French Revolution and a believer in the need for a new aristocracy of industrialists ("captains of industry"), had nothing but contempt for the theories of the utilitarians. In Carlyle's view, they did no more than excuse the greed and acquisitiveness of the new middle class. Equally scathing in his attacks on the middle class was the English novelist Charles Dickens (1812–1870). In such novels as *Oliver Twist, Hard Times,* and *Dombey and Son,* he wrote with sympathy of the tyrannization of industrial workers by the new rich. In France, the Abbé Felicité Lamennais (1782–1854), though preaching respect for private property, nevertheless attacked self-interest. He argued, in his *Book of the People,* that the "little people" of the world enjoyed far too small a share in the direction of their lives. Honoré de Balzac (1799–1850) wrote *The Human Comedy* to expose the stupidity, greed, and baseness of the middle class. Gustave Flaubert (1821–1880) in his foremost novel *Madame Bovary,* depicted the banal, and literally fatal, nature of bourgeois existence for women.

Gustave Flaubert

One of the most trenchant critics of early industrialization was the English philosopher and economist John Stuart Mill (1806–1873). Though Mill as an economist is often considered a member of the classical school, he actually repudiated a number of its most sacred premises. First, he rejected the universality of economic laws. Though he admitted that there are unchangeable laws governing the field of production, he insisted that the distribution of wealth can be regulated by society for the benefit of the majority of its members. Second, he advocated more radical departures from laissez faire than any recommended by his forerunners. He favored legislation, under certain conditions, for shortening the working day, and he believed that the state might properly take preliminary steps toward the redistribution of wealth by taxing inheritances and by appropriating the unearned increment of land. In the fourth book of his *Principles of Political Economy* he urged the abolition of the wage system and looked forward to a society of producers' cooperatives in which the workers would own the factories and elect the managers to run them. On the other hand, Mill was no socialist. He distrusted the state, and his real reason for advocating producers' cooperatives was not to exalt the power of the workers but to give them the fruits of their labor.

Artists, too, attacked the values of industrial society in their painting and sculpture. The art preferred by the European middle class in the nineteenth century was that which in some way either told a story or, better still, preached a message. Beauty was surface decoration, which could be admired for its intrinsic richness and for what it therefore declared about its owner's wealth. Or beauty was a moralism, easily understood and, if possible, reassuring. When the Great Exhibition of the Works of Industry in All Nations was held at the Crystal Palace in London in 1851 to celebrate the triumph of industrialism, one of the most popular exhibits was *The Greek Slave,* a statue by the American sculptor Hiram Powers. Depicting a young Christian stripped bare and standing, according to the catalogue, before the gaze of an Eastern potentate, the work allowed its Victorian male admirers a chance to relish its salaciousness, while at the same time profiting from its depiction of the woman's righteous disdain for her captor.

Some of the artists most critical of the middle class, while repudiating the artificial and decorative, nevertheless reflected the middle-class obsession with art as morality. The self-designated Pre-Raphaelite Brotherhood of English painters was a group of men and women, led by the painter-poet Dante Gabriel Rossetti (1828–1882), determined to express its disdain for contemporary values. They called themselves Pre-Raphaelites as a way of announcing their admiration for the techniques of early Renaissance artists, untainted, supposedly, by corrupted artistic taste. Yet the works of the leading members of the Brotherhood exuded a degree of sentimentality that compromised their rebel nature and rendered them conventionally pietistic and ultimately innocuous as social protest. The same can be said, to a lesser degree, of the work of the Frenchman Jean François Millet (1814–1875). His *Man with the Hoe* is a stark, bitter statement about peasant life; his *The Angelus* softens the statement to sentiment. In both England and France, however, some of the most talented painters seriously questioned many of the values the middle class revered. Gustave Courbet (1819–1877) and Honoré Daumier (1808–1879)

John Stuart Mill

Middle-class art and its critics

The Pre-Raphaelites; Courbet and Daumier

See color plates following page 768

The Angelus by Jean-François Millet. The artist's peasants accept their humble lot in this sentimental portrayal.

both expressed sympathy toward the plight of the French working class, contrasting scenes of rural and urban misfortune with unflattering caricatures of the bourgeoisie. Daumier, in particular, was a powerful satirist of social and political evils, ridiculing the corruption of petty officials and the hypocritical piety of the rich. There was a harsh bite to most of the work of Daumier and Courbet that proscribed sentimentalizing.

Past or present? These writers and artists, while critical of the Industrial Revolution and middle-class values, proposed nothing very tangible in the way of radical reform. If they opposed the triumph of a materialistic middle class, they opposed, as well, the idea of complete democracy. Carlyle, in particular, criticized the present by comparing it with a rosy past that had never been. In this he was like one of the doughtiest critics of the new middle-class society, the Englishman William Cobbett (1763–1835). Cobbett, in his newspaper the *Political Register,* argued against industrialization itself as well as its effects. His propaganda mirrored the dilemma most critics had to face: Granted industrialization has brought great social and economic hardship in its train; does this mean that we should try to return to the life of preindustrial society, also often harsh, and always confining, though probably more secure?

Utopians For some time, a small band of thinkers had been answering that question with a resounding "no." They argued that there could be no return to old times and old ways, but that society could be at the same time both industrial and humane. These radical thinkers were often explicitly utopian. Two of the most persuasive were the Englishman

Robert Owen (1771–1858) and the Frenchman Charles Fourier (1772–1837). Though both writers are correctly seen as utopian, with all the practical limitations that label carries with it, in their day many of their followers believed in the possibility of instituting the programs Fourier and Owen propounded. Owen, himself the proprietor of a large cotton factory at New Lanark in Scotland, argued against the middle-class belief that the profit motive should be allowed to shape social and economic organization. Having reorganized his own mills to provide free schooling and a system of social security for his workers, he proceeded to advocate a general reorganization of society on the basis of cooperation, with communities rewarding workers solely on the basis of their actual labor. Fourier urged an even more far-reaching reconstitution, including the abolition of the wage system and the complete equality of the sexes. Followers of Owen and Fourier sought escape from the confusions of the contemporary world in idealist communities founded according to the principles of their leaders. All these attempts failed after a time, victims of faulty leadership and, in the case of Fourierist communities in France, of charges of moral turpitude resulting from Fourier's revolutionary sexual doctrines.

Louis Blanc

Blanc and Proudhon

Less utopian radical theories were proposed during the 1840s, years which witnessed recurring economic depressions and their horrifying consequences. The French politician and journalist Louis Blanc (1811–1882), stood, like many contemporary critics, against the competitiveness of the new industrial society and particularly opposed the exploitation of the working class. His solution was to campaign for universal male suffrage, which would give working-class men control of the state. Following their triumph, these workers would make the state the "banker of the poor" and institute "Associations of Production"—actually a system of workshops governed by workers—which would guarantee jobs and security for all. Once these associations became established, private enterprise would wither through competition, and with it the state, for which there would no longer be any need. As we shall see, these workshops were briefly instituted in Paris during the Revolution of 1848. Another Frenchman, Pierre Proudhon (1809–1865), condemned the profits accruing to employers at the expense of their employees. He, too, proposed new institutions, which he argued could be made to produce goods at a price fairer to the worker, a price based solely on the amount of labor devoted to the manufacture of any particular product.

The ideas contained in the works of Blanc and Proudhon and other radical writers received their clearest and most forceful expression by the German theorists Karl Marx (1818–1883) and Friedrich Engels (1820–1895). Both Marx and Engels were sons of wealthy middle class parents. Marx studied philosophy at the University of Berlin. Determined to play an active role in the transformation of a society he was growing to despise, he took a job as editor of the *Rhineland Gazette* in

Marx and Engels

1842. His radical policies soon put him at odds with his publishers. In 1843, he moved to Paris to devote further thought to the process and possibility of revolutionary change. From there he migrated to Brussels, where he was instrumental in founding the Communist League, a body whose declared aim was the overthrow of the middle class—or to use Marx's terminology, the bourgeoisie. While in Paris, Marx had renewed a former friendship with Engels, who had been living in Manchester where his family owned a cotton mill. While there, Engels wrote a devastating description of the effect of early industrialization upon the workers of England: *The Condition of the Working Class in England in 1844.* Together, Marx and Engels worked to produce a theory that would both explain how society had come to its present state and propose the means whereby it might be altered to benefit all. The theory was published by Marx at the request of the league in 1848, at the height of revolutionary agitation on the Continent, as *The Communist Manifesto.*

The Communist
Manifesto

In the *Manifesto* Marx outlined a theory of history which owed a good deal to the German philosopher Georg Wilhelm Hegel (see below, p. 702). Hegel had argued that ideas, the motive force of history, were in constant conflict with each other, and that this antithetical relationship between ideas in turn would produce an eventual synthesis, representing an advance in the history of the human race. Marx adopted this particular progressive notion of history to his own uses. Whereas Hegel perceived conflict and resolution (a dialectic) in terms of ideas, Marx saw them in terms of economic forces. Society, he argued, was at any time no more than the reflection of a hierarchy dictated by those who own the means of production and control the distribution of its material goods. As history has progressed, so have the means changed. Feudalism and manorialism were vanquished by capitalism. And capitalism, Marx declared, would be vanquished in turn by communism. That process, however, will first involve the concentration of capitalist economic power into fewer and fewer hands, and the consequent opposition of an ever-increasing and ever-debased working class (the proletariat). Once the proletariat overthrows the bourgeoisie by revolution, as it is bound to do eventually, society as a whole will be emancipated. An interim period in which a "dictatorship of the proletariat" rids the world of the last vestiges of bourgeois society will be followed by an end of the dialectical process and the emergence of a truly classless civilization.

Marx insisted that the *Manifesto* was not just another theory. His declaration that the proletariat together could consciously participate in the revolutionary process he described—could actually advance history through its own efforts—helps explain the document's appeal. The writings of Marx and Engels did not bring about an immediate proletarian revolution. Though the *Manifesto,* in its famous declaration, called upon the workers of the world to unite, Marx and Eng-

Karl Marx

els realized that this goal would not be achieved quickly. Marx and Engels, however, more than any other political thinkers of the 1830s and 1840s, provided workers with a potential sense of their worth as human beings and of their vital role in the historical process of the world. Engels made workers understand what factory work and urban living was doing to them: turning them from men and women into machines, alienated (a Marxian term) from themselves as human beings because they were alienated from the work over which they had no control. Marx gave workers the sense that those sufferings Engels described had an ultimate purpose, that they represented the workers' own particular contribution to the eventual and inevitable triumph of their class.

The theories of Marx and Engels spread throughout Europe after 1850. Like the theories of those other writers whom we have been considering—both the defenders and the opponents of the middle-class industrial world—they are historically important for two reasons. First, the ideas helped men and women better understand the new social order which had sprung up following the French and Industrial Revolutions, and the part they might play, as members of a class, in that new order. Second, the ideas themselves helped inspire the concrete political, social, and economic changes and events which are the subject of the next two chapters.

Friedrich Engels

SELECTED READINGS

• *Items so designated are available in paperback editions.*
• Berlin, Isaiah, *Karl Marx: His Life and Environment,* New York, 1948. The best short account.
  Briggs, Asa, *The Age of Improvement,* New York, 1959.
• ———, *Victorian People,* London, 1954.
• Burn, W. L., *The Age of Equipoise,* London, 1964. A charming account of the mid-Victorian years.
  Chevalier, Louis, *Laboring Classes and Dangerous Classes,* New York, 1973. An intriguing though controversial study of the quality of life in Paris between 1815 and 1848 which concludes that social mobility was downward and that the fear of crime dominated social consciousness.
  Gide, Charles, and Charles Rist, *A History of Economic Doctrines,* rev. ed., Boston, 1948. A good summary.
  Halevy, Elie, *The Growth of Philosophical Radicalism,* rev. ed., London, 1949. The best introduction to the thought of Malthus, Ricardo, Bentham, and their philosophical heirs.
  ———, *England in 1815,* London, 1949. The classic work by the greatest historian of nineteenth-century England.
• Hammond, J. L., and Barbara Hammond, *The Town Labourer, 1760–1832,* London, 1917. An impassioned account of the economic changes which affected the quality of life of the English worker.

Hobsbawm, Eric, *The Age of Capital, 1848–1875,* London, 1975. A perceptive world survey which traces the global triumph of capitalism and its impact upon the working classes.

• ———, *Labouring Men: Studies in the History of Labour,* London, 1964. A series of essays on workers and the working class in England.

• Langer, William L., *Political and Social Upheaval, 1832–1852,* New York, 1969. Comprehensive survey of European history, with excellent analytical chapters and thorough bibliographies.

Manuel, Frank E., *The Prophets of Paris,* Cambridge, Mass., 1962. An entertaining introduction to the philosophers of progress, from Turgot to Comte.

• Mehring, Franz, *Karl Marx: The Story of His Life,* New York, 1976.

• Rudé, George, *The Crowd in History,* New York, 1964.

• Thompson, E. P., *The Making of the English Working Class,* London, 1963. Argues that the coincidence of the French and Industrial Revolutions fostered the growth of working-class consciousness. A brilliant and important work.

Walker, Mack, *German Home Towns: Community, State, and General Estate, 1648–1871,* Ithaca, N.Y., 1971. Attempts to explain the absence of a strong middle class in Germany.

Zeldin, Theodore, *France, 1848–1951,* 2 vols., Oxford, 1973–77. A highly individualistic synthesis of French history, remarkable for its scope and insight.

SOURCE MATERIALS

• Engels, Friedrich, *The Condition of the Working Class in England,* New York, 1958. A much criticized, but reliable firsthand account by the later collaborator of Marx, written in 1844. Presents a devastating portrait of living and working conditions, especially in Manchester.

• Malthus, Thomas R., *An Essay on Population,* London, 1798 and 1803. Malthus's famous essay relating population growth and food production.

• Marx, Karl, *The Communist Manifesto,* 1848. Written under the spell of European revolutions, this was the young Marx's call for a revolution by the working class.

• Marx, Karl, and Friedrich Engels, *The Marx-Engels Reader,* 2nd ed., ed. by R. C. Tucker, New York, 1978.

• Mayhew, Henry, *London Labor and the London Poor,* New York, 1968. A reprint of the 1851 edition, provides a fascinating view of the population and trades of London. A good factual companion to Dickens.

Owen, Robert, *A New View of Society,* London, 1813. A proposed utopian society based upon cooperative villages by the founder of British socialism.

Chapter 22

THE RISE OF LIBERALISM
(1815–1870)

The general thought, the hope of France, has been order and liberty
reuniting under constitutional monarchy.

—François Guizot, "Speech on the State of the Nation," 1831

T he history of nineteenth-century Europe was to a great extent
shaped by the interplay of the forces of liberalism and nationalism. The middle classes of France and England, where liberalism was strongest, espoused a set of doctrines reflecting their concerns and interests. Liberalism to them meant (1) an efficient
government prepared to acknowledge the value of commercial and industrial development; (2) a government in which their interests would
be protected by their direct representation in the legislature—in all
probability, a constitutional monarchy, and most certainly not a democracy; (3) a foreign policy of peace and free trade; and (4) a belief in
individualism and the doctrines of the classical economists.

*The components of
liberalism*

Many middle-class men and women in other European countries
shared these beliefs and assumptions, and worked diligently and with
some success to carry through specific liberal reforms. But for them,
an equally important and often more immediate objective was the
achievement of some form of national unity. The middle classes in
Germany, Italy, Poland, and the Austrian Empire, however dedicated
they were to liberalism, believed that their chances of achieving liberal
goals would be greatly enhanced if they could unify the patchwork of
principalities that surrounded them into a vigorous, "modern" nation-state. In this chapter, we shall examine the phenomenon of liberalism, primarily as it affected the fortunes of England and France.
In the following chapter, we shall describe the way in which liberalism
combined with nationalism to reshape the history of central Europe.

*The compulsion of
nationalism*

1. CONSERVATIVE REACTION, 1815–1830

Congress of Vienna

The growth of liberalism occurred, in part, as a reaction to the conservative policies adopted by frightened governments anxious to restore domestic and international order following the Napoleonic wars. For a period of about fifteen years after 1815 the rulers of most European countries did their best to stem the advance of middle-class liberalism. In most instances, however, their repressive policies only made liberals more determined than ever to succeed. The primary concern of governments was to ensure that Europe would never again fall prey to the sort of revolutionary upheavals which it had experienced during the preceding quarter-century. To that end, when representatives of the European powers had met at the Congress of Vienna in 1814 to draw up a permanent peace settlement for Europe, they labored to produce an agreement that would as nearly as possible guarantee international tranquility. At the same time, however, they were by no means unwilling to advance the claims of their own countries to new territories, though such claims threatened conflict, or even war. Although the principle decisions of the congress were made by representatives of the major powers, it was attended by an array of dignitaries from almost all the principalities of Europe. No fewer than six monarchs attended: the tsar of Russia, the emperor of Austria, and the kings of Prussia, Denmark, Bavaria, and Württemberg. Great Britain was represented by Lord Castlereagh and the duke of Wellington. From France came the subtle intriguer Talleyrand, who had served as a bishop under Louis XVI, as foreign minister at the court of Napoleon, and who now stood ready to espouse the cause of reaction.

Alexander I

The dominant roles at the Congress of Vienna were played by Alexander I (1801–1825) and Metternich (1773–1859). The dynamic tsar is one of the most baffling figures in history. Reared at the court of Catherine the Great, he imbibed the doctrines of Rousseau from a French Jacobin tutor. In 1801 he succeeded his murdered father, Paul, as

The Congress of Vienna. The figure to the left of center is Metternich. Seated at the right, with his arms on the table, is Talleyrand.

tsar and for the next two decades disturbed the dreams of his fellow sovereigns by becoming the most liberal monarch in Europe. After the defeat of Napoleon in the Russian campaign, Alexander's mind turned more and more to mystical channels. He conceived of a mission to convert the rulers of all countries to the Christian ideals of justice and peace. But the chief effect of his voluble expressions of devotion to "liberty" and "enlightenment" was to frighten conservatives into suspecting a plot to extend his power over all of Europe. He was accused of intriguing with Jacobins everywhere to substitute an all-powerful Russia for an all-powerful France.

The most commanding figure at the congress was Klemens von Metternich, born at Coblenz in the Rhine valley, where his father was Austrian ambassador at the courts of three small German states. As a student at the University of Strassburg the young Metternich witnessed some excesses of mob violence connected with the outbreak of the French Revolution, and to these he attributed his life-long hatred of political innovation. After completing his education, he entered the field of diplomacy and served for nearly forty years as minister of foreign affairs. He was active in fomenting discord between Napoleon and Tsar Alexander, after the two became allies in 1807, and he played some part in arranging the marriage of Napoleon to the Austrian archduchess, Marie Louise. In 1813 he was made a hereditary prince of the Austrian Empire. At the Congress of Vienna Metternich distinguished himself for charm of manner and skillful intrigue. His two great obsessions were hatred of political and social change and fear of Russia. Actually the two were related. It was not simply that he feared revolutions as such; he feared, even more, revolutions inspired by the tsar for the sake of establishing Russian supremacy in Europe. For this reason he favored moderate terms for France in its hour of defeat, and was ready at one time to sponsor the restoration of Napoleon as emperor of the French under the protection and overlordship of the Hapsburg monarchy.

The basic idea that guided the work of the Congress of Vienna was the principle of *legitimacy*. This principle was invented by Talleyrand as a device for protecting France against drastic punishment by its conquerors, but it was ultimately adopted by Metternich as a convenient expression of the general policy of reaction. Legitimacy meant that the dynasties of Europe that had reigned in prerevolutionary days should be restored to their thrones, and that each country should regain essentially the same territories it had held in 1789. In accordance with this principle Louis XVIII, brother of Louis XVI,[1] was recognized as the "legitimate" sovereign of France, and the restoration of Bourbon rulers in Spain and the Two Sicilies was also confirmed. France was compelled to pay an indemnity of 700 million francs to the victorious

Tsar Alexander I

Metternich

Klemens von Metternich

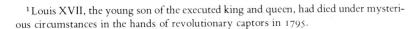

[1] Louis XVII, the young son of the executed king and queen, had died under mysterious circumstances in the hands of revolutionary captors in 1795.

Barriers to French expansion

The German settlement

allies, but its boundaries were to remain essentially the same as in 1789.

To ensure that the French would not soon again overrun their boundaries, however, a strong barrier was erected to contain them. The Dutch Republic, conquered by the French in 1795, was restored as the Kingdom of the Netherlands, with the house of Orange as its hereditary monarchy. To its territory was added that of Belgium, formerly the Austrian Netherlands, with the hope that this now substantial power would serve to discourage any future notions of French expansion. For the same reason the German left bank of the Rhine was ceded to Prussia, and Austria was established as a major power in northern Italy.

The principle of legitimacy was not extended to the German principalities, however. There, despite pleas from rulers of the sovereign bits and pieces that had existed before 1789, the great powers agreed to retain the boundaries as redrawn by Napoleon. Fear of an aggressive Russia led the other European nations to support the maintenance—as an anti-Russian bulwark—of the Napoleonic kingdoms of Bavaria, Würtemberg, and Saxony. At the same time, however, Tsar Alexander was demanding that Poland, partitioned into virtual extinction by Russia, Austria, and Prussia in the 1790s, be reconstituted a kingdom with himself as its constitutional monarch. Prussia was prepared to agree with this scheme, provided that it be allowed to swallow Saxony. National avarice for territorial expansion rapidly eclipsed legitimacy as a guiding principle in these negotiations. Metternich, horrified at the double threat thus presented to Austria by Prussia and Russia, allied himself with Talleyrand and Castlereagh, both of whom secretly agreed to go to war against Russia and Prussia, if necessary, in order to prevent them from consumating their Polish-Saxon deal. A compromise was eventually reached, allowing to Russia the major part of Poland and to Prussia a part of Saxony. Britain, no less anxious

"Dividing the Cake." A contemporary cartoonist's impression of the work of the congress diplomats.

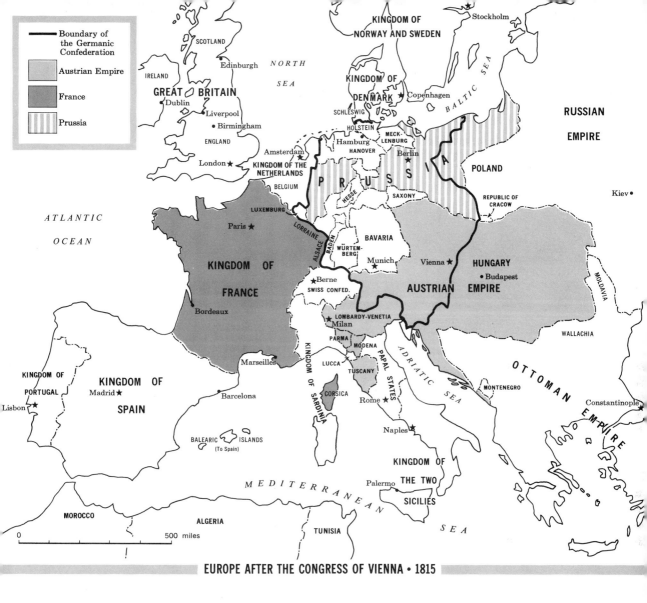

Map labels (as they appear):

Stockholm, KINGDOM OF NORWAY AND SWEDEN, SCOTLAND, Edinburgh, NORTH SEA, IRELAND, GREAT BRITAIN, Dublin, Liverpool, Birmingham, ENGLAND, KINGDOM OF DENMARK, Copenhagen, BALTIC SEA, SCHLESWIG, HOLSTEIN, Hamburg, MECK-LENBURG, Berlin, RUSSIAN EMPIRE, Amsterdam, HANOVER, KINGDOM OF THE NETHERLANDS, BELGIUM, P R U S S I A, POLAND, Kiev, London, HESSE, SAXONY, REPUBLIC OF CRACOW, ATLANTIC OCEAN, LUXEMBURG, LORRAINE, ALSACE, BADEN, WÜRTEM-BERG, BAVARIA, Munich, Vienna, HUNGARY, Paris, KINGDOM OF FRANCE, Berne, SWISS CONFED., AUSTRIAN EMPIRE, Budapest, MOLDAVIA, Bordeaux, LOMBARDY-VENETIA, Milan, PARMA, MODENA, PAPAL STATES, ADRIATIC SEA, WALLACHIA, Marseilles, KINGDOM OF SARDINIA, LUCCA, TUSCANY, MONTENEGRO, OTTOMAN EMPIRE, KINGDOM OF PORTUGAL, KINGDOM OF SPAIN, Madrid, Barcelona, CORSICA, Rome, Constantinople, Lisbon, BALEARIC ISLANDS (To Spain), Naples, KINGDOM OF THE TWO SICILIES, Palermo, MEDITERRANEAN SEA, MOROCCO, ALGERIA, TUNISIA, 0 — 500 miles

EUROPE AFTER THE CONGRESS OF VIENNA · 1815

than the other victorious powers to gain compensation for its long years at war, received territories principally under French dominion in South Africa and South America and the island of Ceylon, thus adding further to its commercial empire.

Following Napoleon's final defeat at Waterloo in 1815, the major powers reconfirmed the Vienna settlement in the hope that their efforts might result in a permanently stable "Concert of Europe." To further ensure an end to revolutionary disturbances, they formed the Quadruple Alliance—Britain, Austria, Prussia, and Russia; when France was admitted as a fifth member in 1818 it became the Quintuple Alliance. Its members pledged to cooperate in the suppression of any disturbances which might arise from attempts to overthrow legitimate governments or to alter international boundaries. At the same

The system of alliances

time, Tsar Alexander, his mystic nature now in the ascendant, persuaded the allies to join him in the declaration of another alliance—a "Holy Alliance"—dedicated to the precepts of justice, Christian charity, and peace. The only result of this second league was to confuse Europe's leaders as to Alexander's intentions. Was he a liberal—a Jacobin even, as Metternich feared—or a reliable conservative? The confusion was cleared away, as in one country after another, liberal uprisings were stifled by stern reactionary policies of the allied governments, Alexander's among them.

Suppression of liberal uprisings

Attacks against reactionary governments in Naples and in Spain brought the allies scurrying to a conference at Troppau in Austria in 1820. Secret brotherhoods of young liberals, many of them army officers, had spearheaded these revolts. These organizations, which originated in Italy, called themselves *Carbonari*. They were an active counterreactionary force, whose influence spread throughout Europe in the early 1820s. In both Naples and Spain, they succeeded in forcing the kings to take oaths to establish constitutions modeled on the liberal French constitution of 1789–1791. At Troppau, Austria, Prussia, and Russia reacted to these threats to international order and absolutism by pledging to come to each other's aid to suppress revolution. France and Britain declined to endorse the pledge, not so much because they opposed repression, but because they did not wish to curtail their freedom of action by binding themselves to detailed international treaties. Metternich nevertheless proceeded, with Russian and Prussian concurrence, in a repression of the *Carbonari* rebels through imprisonment or exile.

Defying the congress system

Two years later, in 1822, another congress was convened at Verona, this one to deal with the continuing liberal threat to stability in Spain, with the series of revolutions occurring in Spanish colonies in South America, and with an insurrection in the Near East. To resolve the Spanish problem, the French dispatched an army of 200,000 men to the Iberian peninsula in 1823. Without much difficulty, this force put an end to the Spanish liberals, who opposed King Ferdinand VII's attempt to undermine representative government. The French assisted Ferdinand in restoring his authority to rule as he pleased. Contrary to their experience in Spain, the defenders of the status quo were unable to succeed in stemming the move to independence and liberalism in the colonies. In 1823 President James Monroe of the United States issued the "Monroe Doctrine," which declared that attempts by European powers to intervene in the affairs of the New World would be looked upon as an unfriendly act by his government. Without British maritime support, the doctrine would have remained a dead letter. Britain was ready to recognize the independence of the South American republics, however, since as new countries they were prepared to trade with Britain instead of Spain. The British therefore used their navy to keep Spain from intervening to protect its vanishing empire.

In the Near East, a Greek soldier, Alexander Ypsilanti, was attempting to encourage the formation of a Greek "empire," to be constructed on vaguely liberal principles. In doing so, he had engaged his band of armed followers in battles against the Turks who ruled over Greece. Though Ypsilanti was soon defeated, his movement lived on. Five years later its aims had been narrowed to the more accessible goal of an independent Greece. Supported for reasons of Mediterranean naval strategy by a joint Anglo-French-Russian naval intervention, and by a Russian invasion of the Balkans, the rebels this time succeeded. Their success signaled the extent of changes that had occurred since the Congress of Verona. No longer could Metternich and other reactionaries build alliances on the assumption that, for the powers of Europe, preservation of the status quo was, before everything else, the major goal. Britain, in particular, could not be relied upon. There, by the late 1820s, the liberal movement was gaining momentum fast.

2. LIBERAL GAINS IN WESTERN EUROPE, 1815–1830

Liberal gains in Britain came after an era of reaction that paralleled that which occurred on the Continent. There the conservative Tory party had enjoyed almost unbroken political supremacy since the younger William Pitt had become first minister in 1783. Though Pitt had begun his career as something of a reformer, the French Revolution had turned him, along with his fellow-Tories, into a staunch defender of the status quo. The Tories' political opponents, the Whigs, had throughout the long years of the revolutionary and Napoleonic conflicts, remained to some degree conciliatory to the French. But Whigs were as unsympathetic as Tories to democratic notions and as defensive of their rights to the full fruits of their property.

British politics

Hence when rioting broke out in England after 1815 as a result of depression and consequent unemployment, there was general support among the well-to-do for the repressive measures adopted by the British government. Spies were hired to ferret out evidence against popular agitators. In the industrial north, where conditions were particularly severe, radical members of the middle and working classes capitalized on the general unrest to press their demands for increased representation in Parliament. At Manchester a crowd of 80,000, demonstrating for political reform in St. Peter's Fields, was fired upon by soldiers. Eleven persons were killed and over 400 injured, including 113 women. The massacre was thereafter called "Peterloo" by British radicals: i.e., a domestic Waterloo. It was the first of several repressive measures taken by the government to stifle reform. Another was the legislation known as the Six Acts, which was passed by Parliament in 1819, and outlawed "seditious and blasphemous" literature; levied a stamp tax on newspapers; allowed the searching of houses for arms; and restricted the rights of public meeting.

"Peterloo" and the Six Acts

Yet within a surprisingly short time British political leaders re-

The Peterloo Massacre, 1819. A contemporary rendering of the shootings which condemned the "wanton and furious attack by that brutal armed force The Manchester & Cheshire Yeomanry Cavalry."

The liberalizing Tories

versed their opposition to everything new. Instead, they displayed an ability to compromise which kept their country free from revolution. George Canning, the foreign minister, and Robert Peel, the home secretary, son of a rich cotton manufacturer, were both sensitive to the interests of Britain's liberal-minded capitalist entrepreneurs. Under their direction, the government retreated from its commitment to the intransigent Quintuple Alliance; it was Canning who took the lead in recognizing the new South American republics. At home, these same politicians began to make order of the inefficient tangle of British laws; for example, they abolished capital punishment for about a hundred different offenses. And Canning liberalized, though he did not abolish, the Corn Laws. These laws levied a tariff on the importation of cheap foreign grain. As such, they benefited English landlords, but hurt manufacturers, who had to pay higher factory wages to enable their workers to purchase more expensive bread. These "liberalizers" among the still essentially conservative Tories even succeeded in abolishing the laws which had kept both dissenting Protestants (members of Protestant sects—Baptist, Congregationalist, Methodist—other than Anglican) and Roman Catholics from full participation in public political life.

Parliamentary reform

What the conservatives would not do was reform the system of representation in the House of Commons, heavily weighted on the side of the landed interests. Here the Tories, the majority party in Parliament, drew the line and showed themselves still basically committed to the status quo. Yet members of the liberal middle class argued that such a reform was absolutely necessary before they could themselves play a constant and active role in shaping British policy to comply with their own interests. "Interest" was, indeed, the key word in the debate over parliamentary reform. For centuries Parliament had represented the interests of landowners, the major propertied class in England. About two-thirds of the members of the House of Commons were either directly nominated by or indirectly owed their election to the patronage of the richest landowners in the country. Many of the parliamentary electoral districts, or boroughs, which returned members to the House of Commons, were controlled by landowners who used the pressure of their local economic power—or, in many cases, outright bribery—to return candidates sympathetic to their interests. These were the "rotten" or "pocket" boroughs, so-called because they were said to be in the pockets of those men who controlled them. Those who favored the system as it was argued that it mattered little that electoral politics were corrupt, that electoral districts represented unequal numbers, or that very, very few (about one in a hundred) were enfranchised. What did matter, they claimed, was that the interests of the nation at large, which they perceived to coincide with the interests of landed property, were well looked after by a Parliament elected in this fashion.

Of course the new industrial middle class did not agree with the arguments of the landowners. They insisted, for example, that the Corn Laws did not coincide with the nation's best interest. (If they were followers of the theories of Jeremy Bentham, they might argue that the Corn Laws did not produce "the greatest happiness of the greatest number.") Rather, the Corn Laws worked only for the benefit of landlords, by keeping the price of grain high; and they worked to the disinterest of everyone else. Therefore, said members of the middle class, Parliament must be reformed to represent not only landlords but the interests of industrial England. It is important to note that the liberal middle class was *not* arguing in favor of reform on the basis of a belief in democracy. Some leaders within the emerging working class did make this argument—and, as we shall see, continued to make it after a reform bill was passed in 1832. Most of those who spoke in favor of reform, however, declared that the middle class was capable of representing the interests of the working class, as well as of itself, in Parliament. Reformers took this position either because they believed it; or because they were afraid of working-class representatives; or because they realized that to favor direct representation for the working class would frighten the more timid reformers and hence defeat their whole campaign.

The middle class and reform

Spurred by the example of liberal reformers on the Continent (see below, p. 681) and by the oratory and organizational abilities of middle-class and artisan radicals at home, the movement for reform intensified after 1830. It was strong enough to topple the Tories and to embolden the Whigs, under the leadership of Lord Grey, to bring in a bill to reform the electorate. The government was clearly frightened. Revolution, if it were ever to come in England, would come as a result of the alliance now threatening between middle-class industrialists and the artisan/tradesman leadership of the new working class. In Bir-

A working-class alliance

mingham, a middle-class banker, Thomas Attwood, organized a "Political Union of the Lower and Middle Classes of the People." By July 1830, there were similar organizations in Glasgow, Manchester, Liverpool, Sheffield, Newcastle, and Coventry. The king, William IV, wrote worriedly to Lord Grey that "miners, manufacturers, colliers, and labourers" appeared ready for some sort of open rebellion.[2] Sensing the grave danger of a possible union of the working and middle classes, the governing class once more accommodated to change, as it had in the 1820s.

The Reform Bill of 1832

The Reform Bill of 1832, however, was not a retreat from the notion of representation by interest. No attempt was made to create equal electoral districts. The franchise, though increased, was defined in terms of the amount of property owned and the length of time one had owned it. In the counties, for example, a man could vote if he paid at least ten pounds annual rental for land held on a long-term sixty-year lease. In other words, the vote was granted to the middle class, but to very few of the working class. Probably more significant than its extension of the franchise, was the bill's scheme for a redistribution of seats. One hundred and forty-three seats were reallocated, most of them from the rural south to the industrial north, thereby increasing representation in and around cities such as Manchester, Leeds, and Birmingham; and thereby increasing, in turn, the political power of the industrial middle classes. Though the bill was the product of change and itself brought change in its wake, it was understood as a conservative measure. It by no means destroyed the political strength of landed aristocratic interests, though it reduced that strength somewhat. And it preserved the notion of representation by interest. The liberal, industrial middle classes had been admitted into junior partnership with the landed oligarchy that had for centuries ruled Britain and was to rule it for at least one more generation.

Liberalism in other parts of the West

Efforts to introduce liberal political reforms were not limited to Britain during this period. In the United States, the rule of eastern landed and commercial interests was superseded by the antiprivilege Democratic party, led by the hero of the War of 1812, General Andrew Jackson. Across the world, in Russia, a group of army officers revolted, following the death of Tsar Alexander in 1825, in hopes of persuading his liberally minded brother, Constantine, to assume the throne and guarantee a constitution. In this case, however, the attempt at reform failed. Constantine was unwilling to usurp power from the rightful heir, a third brother, Nicholas. The officers, called Decembrists (because of the month of their rebellion), were harshly punished; Nicholas continued to rule in the severely autocratic ways Alexander had adopted toward the end of his life, creating the Third Section, a political police force, to prevent further domestic disorder.

Meanwhile autocracy also threatened the liberal revolutionary and

---

[2] Asa Briggs, *The Age of Improvement,* New York, 1959, p. 248.

Napoleonic heritage in France. The upper middle class in France had remained generally content with the domestic settlement agreed upon by the major powers in 1814 and confirmed at the Congress of Vienna the following year. Louis XVIII had issued a "constitutional charter" upon his succession to the French throne. While refusing to deny himself absolute power in theory, in practice Louis XVIII had willingly enough agreed to support those principles most desired by French middle-class liberals: legal equality; careers open to talent; and a two-chamber parliamentary government, with the vote confined to property-holders.

France

In 1824, Louis died and was succeeded by his reactionary brother Charles X. By his policies Charles immediately declared himself a foe of liberalism, modernization, and the general legacies of the revolutionary and Napoleonic eras. At his direction the French assembly voted indemnities to those aristocratic émigrés whose land had been confiscated by the state. The Church was allowed to reassert its traditionally exclusive right to teach in French classrooms. The upper middle class, strengthened by its role within the country's growing industrial economy, reacted by heading a rebellion against Charles's reactionary policies. In March 1830, members of the Chamber of Deputies, led by bankers, passed a vote of no confidence in the government. Charles dissolved the chamber, as he was constitutionally empowered to do, and called new elections for deputies. When those elections went against his candidates, Charles further retaliated by a series of ordinances, issued on his own authority, which (1) again dissolved the newly elected chamber before it had even met; (2) imposed strict censorship on the press; (3) further restricted suffrage so as to exclude the upper middle class almost completely; and (4) called for new elections.

Charles X and the threat
to liberalism

What Charles got in return for these measures was revolution. Led by republicans—workers, artisans, students, writers, and the like—Parisians took to the streets. For three days, behind hastily constructed barricades, they defied the army and the police, neither of which was anxious to fire into the crowds. Sensing the futility of further resistance, Charles abdicated. Those who had manned the barricades pressed for a genuine republic. But those with the power—bankers, merchants, and industrialists—wanted none of that. Instead they brought the duke of Orleans to the throne as King Louis-Philippe (1830–1848), after extracting a promise from him to abide by the constitution of 1814 which had so suited their particular liberal needs. The franchise was extended, from about 100,000 to 200,000 males. But the right to vote was still based upon property ownership. The major beneficiaries of the change were members of the middle class, those whose interests the Revolution of 1830 primarily served.

The Revolution of 1830
in France

Other countries in Europe caught the revolutionary fever in the summer of 1830. As we have already noted, middle- and working-class radicals in England were inspired by the French to press their

The July Revolution of 1830 in Paris. Workers construct street barricades to ward off government troops.

own case for liberal reform. In Belgium, an insurrection which combined elements of liberal and national sentiment put an end to the union of that country with the Dutch, instituted by the Congress of Vienna. The European powers strengthened Belgium's political structure, and hence its independence, by agreeing to the accession of Leopold of Saxe-Coburg, uncle of the future Queen Victoria of England, as king. Once again, a middle class had succeeded in establishing a constitutional monarchy to its liking, congenial to its liberal and entrepreneurial goals. No such fate awaited the liberal nationalists in Poland, who moved at this time to depose their ruler, the Russian Tsar Nicholas, whose hegemony extended to Poland as a result of the Vienna settlement of 1815. Western Europe did not intervene; Russian troops crushed the Polish liberal rebels, and Poland was merged into the tsarist empire.

Liberal revolts elsewhere

Liberal forces in Spain enjoyed a greater success. There middle-class liberalism was linked to the attempts of Queen Maria Christina, widow of King Ferdinand, to secure the throne for her daughter, Isabella. Though no liberal herself, the queen was prepared to court the favor of urban middle-class elites to win her struggle against her late husband's brother, Don Carlos. During the so-called Carlist Wars, which lasted from 1834 to 1840, liberals extracted from Isabella a constitution which ensured them a strong voice in the legislature, while restricting the franchise in such a way as to keep the more radical lower middle and artisan classes at bay. By mid-century, however, fear of these radicals led the middle class to acquiesce in a government that was nothing more or less than an authoritarian dictatorship, but that did not threaten directly their own economic interests.

Spain

3. LIBERALISM IN BRITAIN AND FRANCE, 1830–1848

The Revolution of 1830 in France and the Parliamentary Reform Bill of 1832 in England represented a setback for aristocratic power in both countries. Aristocrats and their supporters did not cease overnight to play an active role in politics, however. Lord Palmerston, for example, was one of England's most influential prime ministers at mid-century and one of Europe's most authoritative arbiters. But no longer would it be possible for the legislatures of France and England to ignore the particular interests of the middle class. Henceforth representatives would include members from that class in sufficient numbers to press successfully for programs which accorded with liberal beliefs.

Decline of aristocratic power

One of the major accomplishments of the first British Parliament elected after 1832 was passage of a new law governing the treatment of paupers. In accordance with the law passed in 1602 under Elizabeth I, each parish in England had been declared responsible for the maintenance of its own poor, either through accommodation in poorhouses, or through a system of doles, coupled with local public employment programs. This system, although it by no means eliminated the debilitating effects of poverty, did provide a kind of guarantee against actual starvation. But by 1830 it had broken down. Population growth and economic depressions had produced a far larger number of underemployed men and women in Britain than had ever before existed, placing tremendous strain upon those funds, levied as taxes, which each parish used to provide relief. Industrialization also demanded that families move in search of employment from one part of the country to another; yet the old poor law provided assistance only to those who applied in the parish of their birth. The old law did not accord with liberal notions of efficiency; the new Parliament set about to amend it. The result, drafted by Jeremy Bentham's former private secretary,

Liberal legislation in Britain: the new poor law

An English Workhouse for the Able-Bodied Poor. This workhouse in the county of Devon was built in the late 1830s.

Edwin Chadwick, and passed almost without dissent, clearly reflected the liberal, middle-class notion of how to achieve "the greatest happiness of the greatest number." Doles were to cease forthwith. Those who could not support themselves were to be confined in workhouses. Here conditions were to be made so severe as to all but compel inmates to depart and accept either whatever work they might find outside, no matter how poorly paid, or whatever charity their friends and relatives might be able to provide them. Parishes were to be grouped together into more efficient unions; the law was to be administered by a central board of commissioners in London. Inspiring this new legislation were the liberal belief that poverty was a person's own fault and the liberal assumption that capitalism, though unregulated, was capable of providing enough jobs for all who genuinely wanted them. Economic depressions in the early 1840s proved that latter assumption false, and wrecked the tidy schemes of the poor-law administrators. Doles were once more instituted, taxes once more increased. Yet the law's failure did not shake the liberal conviction that poverty was, in the end, an individual and not an institutional problem.

Even more symbolic of the political power of Britain's middle class than the new poor law was the repeal of the Corn Laws in 1846. The laws, even after their modification in the 1820s, continued to keep the price of bread artificially high, forcing employers, in turn, to pay wages high enough to allow workers to keep food on their tables. More than that, the Corn Laws symbolized to the middle classes the unwarranted privileges of an ancient and, to their minds, generally useless order: the landed aristocracy. The campaign to accomplish repeal was superbly orchestrated and relentless. The Anti–Corn Law League, an organization of middle-class industrialists and their supporters, held large meetings throughout the north of England, lobbied members of Parliament, and, in the end, managed to persuade Sir Robert Peel, now prime minister, of the inevitability of their goal. They were aided, as well, by the potato famine in Ireland, whose existence argued in favor of ending restrictions against the importation of cheap foodstuffs. That Peel was willing to split the Tory—or as it was now coming to be called, Conservative—party to introduce repeal suggests the power of the middle class and its belief in the gospel of free trade.

Legislation during this period reflected other middle-class concerns, and in some cases, directly conflicted with the liberal doctrine of nonintervention. Many members of the urban middle class professed devotion to the tenets of Christianity, particularly that doctrine which argued that all human beings have within themselves a soul which they must work to preserve from sin for their eternal salvation. This belief in the ability of an individual to achieve salvation, which contradicted the older Calvinist doctrine of a predestined "elect," accorded

Repeal of the Corn Laws

Robert Peel

well with more general middle-class notions about the importance of individualism and the responsibility of the individual for his or her own well-being. It produced legislation such as the abolition of the slave trade in British colonies (1833), and the series of Factory Acts which, in 1847, culminated in the curtailment of the workday in some trades to ten hours. Evangelicals such as William Wilberforce, who was throughout his life an eloquent spokesman for enslaved blacks, and Lord Shaftesbury, who campaigned to end the employment of women and children in mines, maintained that individual souls could not find God when imprisoned in the overworked bodies of plantation slaves or factory operatives. They were joined by others who argued, simply, that to keep people tied to their work for as long as twelve or fourteen hours a day was both inhuman and unnecessary. Middle-class liberals found the arguments confusing. The laws of classical economics pulled them in one direction; the ethics of Christianity in another. Their uncertainty mirrored the extent to which no one could discern a right course in this world of new difficulties and fresh options.

Humanitarian reforms

The years of Louis Philippe's reign in France were not so marked as those in England with significant reforms. In the first place, France was not confronted with anything like the same degree of rapid industrialization that was compelling legislative activity on a number of fronts in England. France had nothing to compare with the problems generated by the growth of urban manufacturing centers in the north of England. Though the Chamber of Deputies contained representatives from the upper middle class, they tended to be bankers and merchants, not industrialists. Some were willing to espouse the notion of free trade, though not with the general enthusiasm of their British counterparts, whose unrivaled position as the world's leading manufacturers gave them a vested interest in that cause. Under the succession of governments dominated by France's leading politician of the period, François Guizot (1787–1874), the French expanded their educational system, thereby further underwriting their belief in the liberal doctrine of a meritocracy, or careers open to talent. A French law of 1833 provided for the establishment of elementary schools in every village. Children of indigent parents were to receive a free education; all others would pay a modest fee. In addition, larger towns were to provide training schools for trade and industry, and departments, schools for teacher training. As a result, the number of pupils in France increased from about 2 million, in 1831, to about 3.25 million in 1846. Little else of lasting importance was accomplished during the liberal regime of Louis Philippe. Guizot became more and more an apologist for the status quo. Everyone was free, he argued, to rise to the upper middle class and thus to a position of political and economic power. His advice to those who criticized his complacency was: "enrich yourselves." Politicians followed his advice, finding in

Louis Philippe

*Growing dissatisfaction of
radicals*

Trade unionism

schemes for the modernization of Paris and the expansion of the railway system ample opportunities for graft. Louis Philippe did little to counteract the lifelessness and corruption that characterized his regime. Although he had played a minor part in the first stage of the revolution of 1789, he was no revolutionary. He did not have the dash and glamor of a Napoleon. He was a paunchy, fussy, and undistinguished person, easily caricatured by his enemies and without the talent necessary to rise above his stodgy public image.

Meanwhile radical members of the French and British lower middle and working classes who had assisted—if not propelled—the forces of liberalism to victory in 1830 and 1832 grew increasingly dissatisfied with the results of their efforts. In Britain they soon realized that the Reform Bill had done little to increase their chances for political participation. For a time they devoted their energies to the cause of trade unionism, believing that industrial, rather than political, action might bring them relief from the economic hardships they were suffering.

Trade union organization had been a goal of militant workers since the beginning of the century. Among the first workers' campaigns in the nineteenth century were those often riotous revolts organized both in England and, later, on the Continent against the introduction of machinery. In some instances, factories were attacked by workers and machines smashed, in the belief that machines, by replacing skilled workers, were producing widespread unemployment. In England, the rioters were called Luddites, after "Ned Ludd," who was the mythical leader of the movement. In other instances, the hostility of trade unionists was not directed so much toward machinery as toward those workers who refused to join in unions against their masters. Yet nowhere in Europe were trade unions able to organize themselves into effective bargaining agents before 1850. They came closest in England. There, artisans and skilled workers had banded together in the mid-1820s to form both Friendly Societies, really mutual aid and insurance organizations, and cooperatives, communal stores which cut prices by eliminating the middleman between producer and consumer. By 1831, there were about 500 cooperative societies in England, with a membership of something like 20,000. These organizations encouraged the parallel growth of trade unions, which, in the early 1830s, reached the peak of their early power and effectiveness. The National Association for the Protection of Labour comprised about 150 separate local unions in the textile and mining industries of the north; the Operative Builder's Union about 30,000 workers throughout the country. In 1834, a new and potentially far more radical organization, the Grand National Consolidated Trades Union of Great Britain and Ireland, was organized by a group of London artisans. Its leadership declared that only by bringing the country to a standstill with a general strike could workers compel the governing class to grant them a decent life. At that point, the governing class realized a serious threat to its existence and decided to put an end to

The Chartist Procession to the Houses of Parliament, April 1848

unions. Six organizers for the Grand National were convicted of administering secret oaths (unions were not themselves illegal) and sentenced to transportation (forced emigration to penal colonies in Australia). Subsequently employers demanded that their workers sign a document pledging their refusal to join a union, thereby stifling opportunities for further organization.

After the defeat of the Grand National, the efforts of radical democratic reformers in England turned back from trade union to political activity, centering on attempts to force further political reform upon the uninterested government through the device of the "People's Charter." This document, circulated across the country by committees of Chartists, as they were known, and signed by millions, contained six demands: universal manhood suffrage; institution of the secret ballot; abolition of property qualifications for membership in the House of Commons; annual parliamentary elections; payment of salaries to members of the House of Commons; and equal electoral districts.

Chartism

The fortunes of the Chartist movement waxed and waned. In some areas its strength depended upon economic conditions: Chartism spread with unemployment and depression. There were arguments among its leaders as to both ends and means: Did Chartism imply a reorganization of industry or, instead, a return to preindustrial society? Were its goals to be accomplished by petition only, or by more violent means if necessary? The Chartist William Lovett, a cabinet-maker, for example, was as fervent a believer in self-improvement as any member of the middle class. He advocated a union of educated workers to acquire their fair share of the nation's increasing industrial bounty. The Chartist Feargus O'Connor, on the other hand, appealed to the more impoverished and desperate class of workers. He urged a rejection of industrialization, and the resettlement of the poor on agri-

Varieties of Chartism

cultural allotments. These polarities and disagreements regarding the aims of the movement suggest the extent of the confusion within the working class, whose consciousness as a separate political force was only just beginning to develop. Events answered most of the Chartists' questions for them. In 1848, revolutionary outbreaks across the Continent inspired Chartist leaders to plan a major demonstration and show of force in London. A procession of 500,000 workers was called, to bear to Parliament a petition containing 6,000,000 signatures demanding the six points. Special constables and contingents of the regular army were marshaled under the now aged duke of Wellington to resist this threat to order. Less than 50,000 made the march to Parliament, however. Rain, poor management, and unwillingness on the part of many to do battle with the well-armed constabulary put an end to the Chartists' campaign, if not their cause.

In France, radical agitation produced very different results. There, as well, those who had manned the barricades in 1830 soon grew disgusted with the liberalism for which they had risked their lives. In their minds they carried memories or myths of the years of the first French Republic—its domestic accomplishments, its foreign victories, if not its Reign of Terror. They were opposed to constitutional monarchy, and only mildly enthusiastic about parliamentary government. They were prepared, if necessary, to use force in order to achieve their ends. Centered in Paris, they were for the most part either writers, students, or working-class leaders. They met in secret, studied the works of the radical theorist, Gracchus Babeuf (see above, p. 612), whose socialist *Conspiracy of Equals,* written during the French Revolution, became their Bible, and succeeded in making constant trouble for the liberal, middle-class governments of Louis Philippe. Their leading spokesman was the socialist Auguste Blanqui (1805–1881). He argued the victimization of the workers by the middle class, and helped organize secret societies which were to become the instruments of eventual insurrection. Radicals waged some of their most successful campaigns in the press. Honoré Daumier's savage caricatures of Louis

A Caricature of Louis Philippe by Daumier. The inscription reads "Louis Philippe, the Last King of France." It reflects a popular sentiment of the time.

Rue Transnomain. A drawing by Daumier to commemorate the victims of government repression in 1834.

The Revolution of 1848 in France.
A contemporary broadside celebrating the triumph of the people.

Philippe landed him in prison more than once. But radical campaigning took to the streets as well. In retaliation, the government in 1834 declared radical political organizations illegal. Rioting broke out in Lyon and Paris in protest, where for two days government troops massacred hundreds of insurgents, and arrested some 2,000 republican leaders. In 1835, following an attempt to assassinate Louis Philippe, the government passed a censorship law, which forbade the publication of articles attempting to inspire contempt for the king and which prohibited the printing of any drawing or emblem without prior governmental approval.

These repressive measures served only to increase dissatisfaction with the regime. Guizot was advised by more progressive members of the legislature to extend the franchise to professionals whose lack of wealth now denied them the vote, but whose general adherence to the doctrines of liberalism was unquestioned. Guizot unwisely refused, thereby driving these moderates into the camp of the more radical republicans. By 1847, various elements within the opposition were disaffected enough to instigate a general campaign of agitation throughout France. At political banquets, republicans such as the poet Alphonse de Lamartine (1790–1869) and socialist republicans such as Louis Blanc (see above, p. 667) preached drastic reform, though not outright revolution. Contrary to the expressed wishes of the king, a giant protest meeting was announced for February 22, 1848. The day before, the government forbade the meeting. Rioting and barricading during the following two days ended in the abdication of Louis Philippe and increased demands for a republic.

French republicans and socialists

The origins of the Revolution of 1848 in France

4. THE REVOLUTION OF 1848 IN FRANCE

The February revolution in France was a catalyst which, as we shall see, helped to produce uprisings in the succeeding months throughout much of Europe. Meanwhile, in Paris, a provisional government was

A National Workshop. When few could read, newspapers were heard rather than scanned. Under government auspices, these workshops achieved a good deal less than Louis Blanc had envisioned.

Republican-socialist split: Blanc's workshops

established consisting of ten men, seven of whom, including Lamartine, were middle-of-the-road republicans; three of whom, including Blanc, were socialists. The tensions between middle-class republicans and radical socialists, which had been masked by a common disgust with the government of Louis Philippe, now emerged to shape the political events of the ensuing months in several specific ways. Blanc insisted upon the establishment of national workshops, institutions he had championed as a writer, which were to be organized by trades as producers' cooperatives, where men and women workers would be trained if necessary, put to work, and paid two francs a day when employed and a smaller stipend when unemployed. Instead, the government established what it called workshops, but what amounted to nothing more than a program of public works in and around Paris, where economic conditions had resulted in widespread unemployment. Initially, plans had called for the employment of no more than ten or twelve thousand in projects throughout the city. But with unemployment running as high as 65 percent in construction trades and 51 percent in textiles and clothing, workers began to flood into the government's so-called workshops, as many as 66,000 by April, and 120,000 by June.

Continuing agitation

Paris meanwhile attracted numbers of radical writers, organizers, and agitators. The provisional government had removed all restrictions upon the formation of political clubs and the dissemination of political literature. As a result, 170 new journals and more than 200 clubs formed within weeks; the club headed by the socialist Auguste Blanqui claimed a membership of some 3,000. Delegations claiming to represent the oppressed of all European countries—Chartists, Hungarians, Poles—moved freely about the city, attracting attention, if not devoted followings, and contributing to tension which was convincing more and more members of the middle class that stern measures were needed to forestall further insurrectionary outbreaks. The middle-class side was strengthened as a result of elections held at the end of April. The provisional government had been pressured by Parisian radicals into decreeing universal manhood suffrage. Yet the election returned only a small proportion of radical socialists. The largest blocs consisted of "true," or moderate republicans and monarchists—this latter group was divided, however, between supporters of the Bourbon dynasty and the Orleanist Louis Philippe. The generally conservative tenor of the newly elected assembly strengthened the hand of those who pressed for the repression of the socialists. It also, naturally, convinced the socialists that once again, as in the 1790s, a potentially radical revolution had been betrayed by the timid, self-serving middle class.

By late spring, a majority of the assembly believed that the workshop system represented both an unbearable financial drain and a serious threat to social order. At the end of May, the workshops were closed to new enrollment as a first step toward barring membership to all who had resided for less than six months in Paris and sending all members between the ages of eighteen and twenty-five to the army. Thousands of workers lost their state-financed jobs, and with them their best chance for survival. Desperate, they and their supporters once more threw up barricades across Paris. From June 23–26, they defended themselves in an ultimately hopeless military battle against armed forces recruited, in part, from willing provincials eager enough to assist in the repression of the urban working class. Whether or not the Parisian insurrectionists were fighting as members of a beleaguered class, or simply as men and women on the brink of starvation, is a matter that historians continue to debate. That they were taken seriously as a revolutionary threat can be seen by the ferocity with which they were hunted out once the street fighting had ceased. About 3,000 were killed and 12,000 more arrested, the majority of whom were deported to Algerian labor camps.

The "June Days"

In the aftermath of the "June Days," the French government moved quickly to bring order to the country. The assembly, faced with the task of drafting a republican constitution, contained a large number of men to whom the idea of a republic was anathema. Assembly members therefore arranged for the immediate election of a president. Their hope was that a strong leader might assist in bringing dissidents to heel. Four candidates stood: Lamartine, the moderate republican; General Eugene Cavaignac, who had commanded the troops in June; Alexander Ledru-Rollin, a socialist; and Louis Napoleon Bonaparte, nephew of the emperor, who polled more than twice as many votes as the other three candidates combined.

The imposition of order

The astonishing upstart Louis Napoleon had spent most of his life in exile. Returning to France after the Revolution of 1830, he was imprisoned a few years later for attempting to provoke a local uprising. But in 1846 he escaped to England, where he was supplied with funds by

The rise of Louis Napoleon

A second emperor

both British and French reactionaries. By the summer of 1848 the situation in France was such that he knew it was safe to return. In fact, he was welcomed with open arms by members of all classes. Conservatives were looking for a savior to protect their property against the onslaughts of the radicals. Workers were beguiled by his glittering schemes for prosperity in his book, *The Extinction of Pauperism,* and by the fact that he had corresponded with Louis Blanc and with Pierre Proudhon, the anarchist. In between these two classes was a multitude of patriots and hero-worshipers to whom the very name Napoleon was a matchless symbol of glory and greatness. It was chiefly to this multitude that the nephew of the Corsican owed his astounding triumph. As one old peasant expressed it: "How could I help voting for this gentleman—I whose nose was frozen at Moscow?"

With grandiose dreams of emulating his uncle, Louis Napoleon was not long content to be merely president of France. Almost from the first he used his position to pave the way for a higher calling. He enlisted the support of the Catholics by permitting them to regain control over the schools and by sending an expedition to Rome to restore the pope to his temporal power. He courted the workers and the middle class by introducing old-age insurance and laws for the encouragement of business. In 1851, alleging the need for extraordinary measures to protect the rights of the masses, he proclaimed a temporary dictatorship and invited the people to grant him the power to draw up a new constitution. In the plebiscite held on December 21, 1851, he was authorized by an overwhelming majority (7,500,000 to 640,000) to proceed as he liked. The new constitution, which he put into effect in January 1852, made the president an actual dictator. After exactly one year Louis Napoleon Bonaparte ordered another plebiscite and, with the approval of over 95 percent of the voters, assumed the title of Napoleon III, emperor of the French.

What is the significance of the French Revolution of 1848 and its political aftermath in the history of middle-class liberalism, which is our subject? Two points need particular emphasis. First, we must recognize the pivotal role of the liberal middle class. Under Louis Philippe, it increasingly perceived itself and its particular interests as neglected. Denied a direct political voice because of a severely limited franchise, it swung to the left, allying itself with radicals who, by themselves, would probably have stood no chance of permanent success. Yet no sooner had Louis Philippe abdicated than the liberal middle class began to wonder if "success" was not about to bring disaster upon its heels. And so it swung again, this time to the right, where it found itself confronting the mysterious and yet not entirely unattractive prospect of Louis Napoleon. He, in turn, was clever enough to understand this first lesson of 1848, that in France no government could survive that did not cater to the interests of the middle class. By assisting it to achieve its liberal economic goals, the emperor helped it forget just how heavily he was trampling on its political liberties.

AU NOM DU PEUPLE FRANÇAIS.

LE PRÉSIDENT DE LA RÉPUBLIQUE

DÉCRÈTE:

Art. 1.
L'Assemblée nationale est dissoute.

Art. 2.
Le Suffrage universel est rétabli. La loi du 31 mai est abrogée.

Art. 3.
Le Peuple français est convoqué dans ses comices à partir du 14 décembre jusqu'au 21 décembre suivant.

Art. 4.
L'état de siége est décrété dans l'étendue de la 1ʳᵉ division militaire.

Art. 5.
Le Conseil d'État est dissous.

Art. 6.
Le Ministre de l'Intérieur est chargé de l'exécution du présent décret.

Fait au Palais de l'Élysée, le 2 décembre 1851.

LOUIS-NAPOLÉON BONAPARTE.

Le Ministre de l'Intérieur.

DE MORNY.

Napoleon III's Decree Dissolving the National Assembly

Yet 1848 proved that there was now in France another element—class consciousness may, at this point, not yet be the correct term—that governments ignored at their peril. If mid–nineteenth-century Europe saw the middle class closer than ever to the center of power, it saw the workers moving rapidly in from the edge. Their barricades could, if necessary, be destroyed, and their demands ignored, but only at an increasingly grave risk to the fabric of the state. Middle-class liberalism, if it was to thrive, would not only have to pay lip service to working-class demands, but in some measure accommodate to them as well.

Napoleon III

5. LIBERALISM IN FRANCE AND BRITAIN AFTER 1850

Napoleon III recognized the vital role that public opinion had now assumed in the management of affairs of state. He labored hard and successfully to sell his empire to the people of France. He argued that legislative assemblies only served to divide a nation along class lines. With power residing in him, he would unite the country as it had not been for generations. The French, who craved order following their recent political misadventures, bought the program he was selling willingly enough. Napoleon III modeled his constitution upon that of his uncle. An assembly, elected by universal manhood suffrage, in fact possessed almost no power. It could do no more than approve legislation drafted at the emperor's direction by a Council of State. Elections were manipulated by the government to insure the return of politically docile representatives. Control of finance, the army, and foreign affairs rested exclusively with the emperor. France was a democracy only in the sense that its people were periodically afforded a chance, through elections, to express their approval of Napoleon's regime.

*Napoleon III's
constitution*

In return for the gift of almost absolute power, Napoleon III gave the French what they appeared to want. For the middle class, he provided a chance to make a great deal of money. The device of the *Crédit Mobilier,* an investment banking institution, facilitated the expansion of industry by selling its shares to the public and using its income to underwrite various entrepreneurial schemes. In 1863 a limited liability law encouraged further investment by guaranteeing that stockholders could lose no more than the par value of their stock no matter how indebted the company in which they had invested. Railways, owned by the state, spread across the country, and spurred further industrial expansion. So prosperous did the French economy appear that Napoleon was prepared to follow Britain's lead in pressing for tariff-free trade between the two countries. A treaty was signed in 1860; though funds were set aside to compensate French industries for any loss they might suffer, they were never completely expended, suggesting that French manufacturers were now well enough established to meet the threat of British competition. The apparent satisfaction of the middle class with

*Napoleon III and the
middle class*

Paris Under the Second Empire. The Avenue de l'Imperatrice was designed for the enjoyment of the middle class.

Napoleon III and the workers

Napoleon's regime provides a measure with which to assess the state of liberalism in France after 1850. The fact that the country no longer enjoyed a free press, that universities were politically controlled, and that political opposition was repressed seemed to matter very little to most. Liberalism, if it existed at all, existed as the freedom to have one's own economic way.

Napoleon III, though he catered to the middle class, did not fail to court the favor of the workers as well. He encouraged the establishment of hospitals and instituted a program of free medical assistance. More important, he permitted, if he did nothing to encourage, the existence of trade unions and in 1864 introduced legislation to legalize strikes. Ultimately, he appealed to the workers much as he appealed to the middle class, as a glamorous, if not heroic symbol of his country's reemergence as a leading world power. The activities of his court, and of his glamorous empress, Eugenie, were well publicized. The reconstruction of Paris into a city of broad boulevards and grand open spaces was calculated to provide appropriate scenery for the theatre of empire—as well as to lessen the chances for successful proletarian barricade-building across narrow streets.

Grandeur, however, appeared to Napoleon III to demand an aggressive foreign policy. Although early in his regime he declared himself in favor of that central liberal tenet—international peace—he was soon at war: first against Russia in the Crimea; then in Italy; then in Mexico, where he attempted to assist in the establishment of another empire; and finally and disastrously with Prussia. The details of these adventures are part of the subject of the following chapter. It is enough at this point to remark that Napoleon III's foreign policy reflects clearly how far he—and the rest of France with him—had subordinated the liberal heritage of the first French Revolution to that of another of its legacies: national glory.

Empress Eugénie

What, meanwhile, of the liberal tradition in Britain? There the course of liberalism was altered by changes occurring within the working class. Industrialization had, by this time, begun to foster and sustain a growing stratum of labor "aristocrats," men whose particular skills, and the increasing demand for them, allowed them to demand wages high enough to insure them a fairly comfortable standard of living. These workers—concentrated for the most part within the building, engineering, and textile industries—turned from the tradition of militant radicalism that had characterized the so-called hungry forties. Having succeeded within the liberal economic system imposed upon Britain by the middle class, they were now prepared to accept many liberal, middle-class principles as their own. They believed in self-help, achieved by means of cooperative societies or through trade unions, whose major function was the accumulation of funds to be used as insurance against old age and unemployment. They believed in education as a tool for advancement, and patronized the Mechanics Institutes and other similar institutions either founded by them or on their behalf.

Yet the labor aristocracy, as it came to appreciate its ability to achieve a decent life for itself within the capitalist system, grew all the more dissatisfied with a political system which excluded it from any direct participation in the governmental process. Although some pressed for extension of the franchise as democrats, as many argued for it on the same grounds the middle class had used in 1832. They were responsible workers, whose loyalty to the state could not be questioned. As such, they were a bona fide "interest," as worthy of the vote and of direct representation as the middle class. They were joined in their campaign by many middle-class reformers who continued to chafe at the privileged position of national institutions which they associated with the landed society and the old order. Many middle-class men and women, for example, were dissenters from the Church of England; yet they were forced to pay taxes to support a church which was staffed, in the main, by sons of the gentry. Their sons were denied the facilities of the nation's ancient universities, Oxford and Cambridge, unless those sons subscribed to the articles of faith of the Anglican Church.

Together with working-class leaders, these middle-class dissidents organized a Reform League to campaign across the country for a new reform bill and a House of Commons responsive to their interests. Though by no means revolutionary, the reformers made it clear by their actions that they were determined to press their case to the utmost. Politicians in Britain in the 1860s were confronted by a situation not unlike that which had faced Guizot in France in 1848: middle class, lower middle class, and skilled workers discontented and demanding reform. Unlike Guizot, however, the leaders of both British political parties, Conservative (formerly Tory) and Liberal (formerly Whig), were prepared to concede what they recognized it would be dangerous to withhold. In fact, it was a Conservative government, with the future prime minister Benjamin Disraeli as its leader in the House of Commons, that enacted the second Reform Bill in 1867. The bill doubled the franchise by extending the vote to any males who paid poor rates or rent of ten pounds or more a year in urban areas (this would mean, in general, the skilled workers), and to tenants paying rent of twelve pounds or more in the counties. Seats were again redistributed as in 1832, with large northern cities gaining representation at the expense of the rural south. The "responsible" working class had been deemed worthy to participate in the affairs of state. For the next twenty years it showed its appreciation by accepting its apprentice position without demur, and by following the lead prescribed by the middle class.

The Triumph of British liberalism

The decade or so following the passage of the Reform Bill of 1867 marked the high point of British liberalism. The labor aristocracy was accommodated with the Education Act, virtually guaranteeing a primary education to all, with legalization of trade unions, and with a series of measures designed to improve living conditions in the great cities; yet it was the middle class that set the governmental tone. Under Disraeli and his Liberal counterpart William Gladstone, and with the cooperation of the newly enfranchised skilled workers, Britain celebrated the triumph of the liberal principles of free trade, representative—but not democratic—government, and general prosperity.

SELECTED READINGS

• *Items so designated are available in paperback editions.*

Anderson, R. D., *Education in France, 1848–1870*, New York, 1975. Covers every level of formal education and its practical and theoretical relationship to state and society.

• Artz, Frederick B., *Reaction and Revolution, 1814–1832*, New York, 1934. A European survey, dated but still useful.

• Binkley, Robert C., *Realism and Nationalism, 1852–1871*, New York, 1935.

Blake, Robert, *Disraeli*, London, 1966. A masterful biography.

Duveau, Georges, *1848: The Making of a Revolution*, New York, 1967. Focuses on the working class during the revolution in Paris: their unity at the outset, their division in the "June Days."

Finer, Samuel E., *The Life and Times of Edwin Chadwick*, London, 1952. An excellent biography of the great English Benthamite reformer.

Halèvy, Elie, *A History of the English People*, Vols. II–IV, London, 1949–52. The best survey of nineteenth-century England, comprehensive and analytical.

Harrison, Royden, *Before the Socialists: Studies in Labour and Politics, 1861–1881*, London, 1965. Examines the social and political background of franchise extension in Britain.

- Hobsbawm, E. and Rudé G., *Captain Swing: A Social History of the Great English Agricultural Uprising of 1830*, New York, 1975.
- Houghton, Walter, *The Victorian Frame of Mind, 1830–1870*, New Haven, Conn., 1957. An outstanding attempt to synthesize the Victorian middle-class mentality.
- Kissinger, Henry, *A World Restored: Metternich, Castlereagh, and the Problem of Peace, 1812–1822*, Boston, 1957. By an admirer of Metternich.
- Langer, William L., *Political and Social Upheaval, 1832–1852*, New York, 1969. (Several chapters have been published separately under the title *The Revolutions of 1848*.)
- McCord, Norman, *The Anti–Corn Law League*, London, 1955.

  Magnus, Philip, *Gladstone: A Biography*, London, 1955.

  Merriman, John M., ed., *1830 in France*, New York, 1975. Recent scholarship emphasizing the nature of revolution and examining events outside of Paris.
- Nicolson, Harold, *The Congress of Vienna, a Study in Allied Unity*, New York, 1946.
- Pinkney, David, *Napoleon III and the Rebuilding of Paris*, Princeton, N.J., 1958. An interesting account of the creation of modern Paris during the Second Empire.

  ———, *The French Revolution of 1830*, Princeton, N.J., 1972. A reinterpretation, now the best history of the revolution.

  Roberts, David, *Victorian Origins of the British Welfare State*, New Haven, Conn., 1960. Examines various nineteenth-century reforms in England.
- Robertson, Priscilla, *The Revolutions of 1848: A Social History*, Princeton, N.J., 1952.

  de Sauvigny, G. de Bertier, *The Bourbon Restoration*, New York, 1967. An outstanding work. The best history of a neglected period.
- Stearns, Peter N., *1848: The Revolutionary Tide in Europe*, New York, 1974.

  Thompson, J. M., *Louis Napoleon and the Second Empire*, Oxford, 1954. A good biography. Presents Louis Napoleon as a modern Hamlet.

  Woodward, E. L., *The Age of Reform*, Oxford, 1962. An excellent survey from the Oxford History of England series.
- Zeldin, Theodore, *The Political System of Napoleon III*, New York, 1958. Examines the processes by which Napoleon maintained power as the first modern dictator.

  ———, *France, 1848–1951*, 2 vols., Oxford, 1973–77.

SOURCE MATERIALS

- Flaubert, Gustave, *L'Education Sentimentale*, London, 1961. Contains an unsympathetic but memorable portrait of the Revolution of 1848 and of the bourgeois style of life that contributed to its outbreak.
- Greville, Charles Fulke, *Memoirs*, ed. by Roger Fulford, New York, 1963. Originally published in seven volumes in 1875, these comprise the diaries of the secretary to the Privy Council for the years 1821–1861. An excellent source for the court and politics of the period.

• Mill, John Stuart, *Autobiography,* London, 1873. The life of one of the germinal minds of the century. Serves as an excellent social history of the
period.

• ———, *On Liberty,* ed. by P. Appleman, New York, 1975. The classic
statement of liberalism first published in 1859.

• Price, Roger, ed., *1848 in France,* Ithaca, N.Y., 1975. An excellent collection
of eyewitness accounts, annotated.

Stewart, John Hall, *The Restoration Era in France, 1814–1830,* Princeton, N.J.,
1968. A brief narrative and a good collection of documents.

Chapter 23

NATIONALISM AND NATION-BUILDING (1815–1870)

The present problem, the first task . . . is simply to preserve the existence and continuance of what is German.

—Johann Fichte, *Addresses to the German Nation*

The great questions of the day will not be decided by speeches or by majority decisions—that was the mistake of 1848 and 1849—but by blood and iron.

—Otto von Bismarck, speech, 1862

I f the history of nineteenth-century Britain and France can be studied against a general background of middle-class liberalism, that of much of the rest of Europe during the same period must be understood in terms of a more complex combination of the forces of liberalism, nationalism, and nation-building. We shall define nationalism as a sentiment rooted in broad historical, geographical, linguistic, or cultural circumstances. It is characterized by a consciousness of belonging, in a group, to a tradition derived from those circumstances, which differs from the traditions of other groups. Nation-building is the political implementation of nationalism, the translation of sentiment into power.

Nationalism and nation-building defined

Men and women in Britain and France during the nineteenth century entertained national as well as liberal sentiments. When Britain's prime minister, Lord Palmerston, declared in 1850 that any British citizen, in any part of the world, had but to proclaim, like a citizen of the Roman Empire, "civis Romanus sum" ("I am a citizen of Rome") to summon up whatever force might be necessary to protect him from foreign depradations, he was echoing his countrymen's pride in the powers of their nationhood. When the French rejoiced in 1840 at the return of the Emperor Napoleon's remains from St. Helena to an elaborate shrine in Paris, they were reliving triumphs that had become

Nationalism in Britain and France

part of their nation's heritage. Palmerston's boast and Napoleon's bones were both artifacts of national traditions and sentiments bound up in the life of the English and the French.

Nineteenth-century nationalism in other areas of Europe was to be a more assertive phenomenon than it was in Britain and France, which had for centuries existed as particular geographical, cultural, and political entities. Elsewhere, common traditions and assumptions were less clearly articulated, because the political unity that might have helped define them did not exist. East Prussians or Venetians had no difficulty in perceiving of themselves as such; history had provided them with those identities. But history had not provided them, except in the most general way, with identities as Germans or Italians. They had to make a deliberate effort to think of themselves in those terms before the terms could have any political reality.

Neither nationalism nor nation-building stood in necessary opposition to liberalism. Indeed, to the extent that nationalism celebrated the achievements of a particular common people over those of a cosmopolitan aristocratic elite, it reflected liberalism's abhorrence of traditional privilege. Yet to liberalism's readiness to accept the new, nationalism responded with an appreciation, if not veneration, of the past. And to the liberals' insistence upon the value and importance of individualism, nation-builders replied that their vital task might require the sacrifice of some measure of each citizen's freedom. The success of nation-building rested upon the foundation of a general balance of international power, achieved by the European states during the half-century after 1815. The emergence of new nations—a unified Italy and Germany—would require readjustments to that balance. But accommodation remained possible, with only minor skirmishes marring the stability of the settlement achieved at the Congress of Vienna.

I. ROMANTICISM AND NATIONALISM

As we noted in the preceding chapter, nationalism was in part a child of the French Revolution. It was closely related, as well, to the intellectual movement that has been called "romanticism." Romanticism was so broad and so varied that it all but defies definition, if not analysis. Perhaps as much as anything, romanticism represented a reaction against the rationalism of the eighteenth-century Enlightenment. Where the eighteenth century relied on reason, the romantics put their faith in emotion. The eighteenth century understood the mind as a blank tablet, which received knowledge from impressions imprinted upon it through the senses by the external world. Romantics also believed in the importance of sense experience. But they insisted that innate sensibility—that which constituted a person's own particular personality—was inherited, and therefore present in the mind from birth. Knowledge, then, for the romantic, was the product of both innate feelings *and* external perceptions. Romanticism thus stressed individualism, and the individual creativity that resulted from the interaction of unique personality with external experience. At the same time, by stressing the inheritance of attitudes, it also celebrated the past. And that celebration was its link with nationalism.

Romanticism and nationalism were connected by their common belief that the past should be made to function as a means of understanding the present and planning for the future. It was in Germany that this notion received its fullest airing and most enthusiastic reception. One of the earliest and most influential German romantics was Johann von Herder (1744–1803). A Protestant pastor and theologian, his interest in past cultures led him, in the 1780s, to set out his reflections in a lengthy and detailed treatise, *Ideas for a Philosophy of Human History*. Herder traced what he perceived to be the progressive development of European society from the time of the Greeks through the Renaissance. He believed that civilization was not the product of an artificial, international elite—a criticism of Enlightenment thinking—but of the genuine culture of the common people, the *Volk*. No civilization could be considered sound which did not continue to express its own unique historical character, its *Volksgeist*. Herder did not argue that one *Volksgeist* was either better or worse than any other. He insisted only that each nation must be true to its own particular heritage. He broke dramatically with the Enlightenment idea that human beings could be expected to respond to human situations in more or less the same fashion, and with the assumption that the value of history was simply to teach by example.

Johann von Herder

Herder's intellectual heirs, men like the conservative German romantics Friedrich Schlegel (1772–1829) and Friedrich von Savigny (1779–1861) condemned the implantation of democratic and liberal ideas—"foreign" to Germany—in German cultural soil. History, they argued, taught that institutions must evolve organically—a favorite word of the political romantics, and that proper laws were the product of historical growth, not simply deductions from universal first principles. This idea was not peculiar to German romantics. The English romantic poet and philosopher Samuel Taylor Coleridge (1772–1834) argued against the utilitarian state and in favor of giving that ancient institution, the national church, a larger role in the shaping of society. The French conservative Chateaubriand (1768–1848) made much the same case in his treatise, *The Genius of Christianity,* published in 1802. The past is woven into the present, he declared. It cannot be unwoven without destroying the fabric of a nation's society. Religion, both as individual experience and as an expression of national heritage, played a large role in romantic thinking.

The role of history and religion

The theory of the organic evolution of society and the state received its fullest exposition in the writings of the German metaphysician

Georg Wilhelm Hegel

Fichte

Georg Wilhelm Hegel (1770–1831). Professor of philosophy at the University of Berlin, he attracted many adherents. Hegel wrote of history as development: Social and political institutions grew to maturity, achieved their purposes, and then gave way to others. Yet the new never entirely replaced the old, for the pattern of change was "dialectic." When new institutions challenged established ones, there was a clash of "thesis" and "antithesis" producing a "synthesis," a reordering of society that retained elements from the past while adapting to the present. Hegel expected, for example, that the present disunity among the German states (thesis), which generated the idea of unity (antithesis), would inevitably result in the creation of a nation-state (synthesis). Hegel had no use for the theory of a state of nature, so popular with philosophers like Rousseau and Hobbes. Men and women have always lived within some society or other, Hegel argued. The institution of the state was itself a natural historic organism; only within that institution, protected by its laws and customs from personal depradations, could men and women enjoy freedom, which Hegel defined not as the absence of restraint but as the absence of social disorder.

These theories of history and of historical development articulated by the romantics relate directly to the idea of nationalism formulated during the same period. The French Revolution provided an example of what a nation could achieve. Nationhood had encouraged the French to raise themselves to the level of citizenship; it had also allowed them to sustain attacks from the rest of Europe. Applying the historical lessons of the French Revolution and the theories of romantics, Germans, in particular, were roused to a sense of their own historical destiny. The works of the philosopher J. G. Fichte (1762–1814) are an example of this reawakening. As a young professor at the University of Jena, Fichte had at first advanced a belief in the importance of an individual's inner spirit, the creator of its own moral universe. Devoid of national feeling, he welcomed the French Revolution as an emancipator of the human spirit. Yet when France conquered much of Germany, Fichte's attitude changed dramatically. He adopted Herder's notion of a *Volksgeist;* what mattered was no longer the individual spirit, but the spirit of a whole people, expressed in its customs, traditions, and history. In 1808, Fichte delivered a series of *Addresses to the German Nation,* in which he declared the existence of a German spirit, not just one among many such spirits, but superior to the rest. The world had not yet heard from that spirit; he predicted it soon would. Although the French military commander in Berlin, where Fichte spoke, believed the addresses too academic to warrant censorship, they expressed a sentiment that aided the Prussians in their conscious attempt to rally themselves, and, as a political *Volk,* to drive out the French.

Nationalism, derived from romantic notions of historical development and destiny, manifested itself in a variety of ways. The brothers Grimm, editors of *Grimm's Fairy Tales* (1812) traveled across Germany to study native dialects, and collected folktales that were published as part of a national heritage. The poet Friedrich Schiller's (1759–1805) drama of *William Tell,* the Swiss hero (1804), became a rallying cry for German national consciousness. In Britain, Sir Walter Scott (1771–1832) retold in many of his novels the popular history of Scotland, while the poet William Wordsworth (1770–1850) consciously strove to express the simplicity and virtue of the English people in collections such as his *Lyrical Ballads* (1798). Throughout Europe, countries assiduously catalogued the relics of their historical past as in the society for publishing the *Monumenta Germaniae Historica* (Monuments of German History), founded in 1819; the French École des Chartes (1821); and the English Public Records Office (1838). In France, the neoclassical style, typified by the paintings of David, and used by Napoleon to exalt his image, gave way to the turbulent romanticism of painters like Eugène Delacroix, whose painting *Liberty Leading the People* (1830) was a proclamation not only of liberty, but of the courage of the French nation. Music, too, reflected national themes, though not until a generation or so after 1815. Many of Guiseppe Verdi's (1813–1901) operas, for example, *Don Carlo,* contained musical declarations of faith in the possibility of an Italian *risorgimento:* a resurrection of the Italian spirit. The operas of Richard Wagner (1813–1883)—in particular, those based on the German epic, *Song of the Nibelung*—managed to raise veneration for the myths of Nordic gods and goddesses to the level of pious exaltation. Architects, though they found it difficult to escape entirely from the neoclassicism of the eighteenth century, often tried to resurrect a "national" style in their designs. Sir Charles Barry, assigned the task of redesigning the British Houses of Parliament following their destruction by fire in 1836, managed to mask a

Giuseppe Verdi

Romanticism, nationalism, and the arts

See color plates following page 768

Houses of Parliament, London. Redesigned by Sir Charles Barry with a Gothic facade after the earlier structure was destroyed by fire.

*A William Blake Etching for a
Children's Book Written by Mary
Wollstonecraft*

George Sand

straightforward and symmetrical classical plan behind a Gothic screen, intended to acknowledge the country's debt to its own past. All this creative activity was the spontaneous result of artists' and writers' enthusiastic response to the romantic movement. Yet politicians soon perceived how historical romanticism might serve their nationalist ends. They understood how an individual work of art, whether a painting, a song, a drama, or a building, could translate into a national symbol. And they did not hesitate to assist in that translation when they deemed it useful.

Though romanticism and nationalism shared a common devotion to the past, romantics were not necessarily nationalists. Indeed, romanticism was explicitly international in its celebration of nature, and above all, of individual creativity. The romantics declared that nature was best perceived not by reason, but by the senses. And they respected those elements of nature which appeared the product of chance, not rational order. Whether as a single flower or a mountain range, nature was welcomed as it impressed itself directly on the senses. Men and women were declared free to interpret nature—and life as well—in terms of their individual reactions to it, not simply as it might reflect a set of general rational precepts. The English poet Percy Shelley (1792–1822), the German poet Heinrich Heine (1797–1856), the French novelist Victor Hugo (1802–1885), the Spanish painter Franciso Goya (1746–1828)—all characteristic figures of the romantic movement—expressed in their works romanticism's concern for the experiences of human individuals, a concern that transcended national boundaries. Human experience, romantics believed, was not linked to any one national tradition or *Volksgeist,* but rather to transcendant nature. The paintings of the Englishmen William Blake (1757–1827) and J. M. W. Turner (1775–1851), although they often reflect "Englishness," transcend nationalism by recording a communion with the fundamental elements of nature.

Romantics were internationalists because they enjoyed freedom from the confinement of any boundary—metaphysical or political—which tended to restrict a person's ability to realize his or her potential. In this way romanticism encouraged women to make themselves heard. The Englishwoman Mary Wollstonecraft (1759–1797), author of *A Vindication of the Rights of Woman;* Madame de Staël (1766–1817), an emigré from France to Germany during the revolutionary period, whose essay *De l'Allemagne* (On Germany) was steeped in romanticism; George Sand (1804–1876), whose novels, and whose life, proclaimed allegiance to the standards of radical individualism—these women exemplify romanticism's readiness to break with the past, and its assumptions and stereotypes, if they stood in the path of individual expression.

Romantics, as worshipers of individuality, worshiped "genius." The genius was possessed of a spirit which could not be analyzed and must be allowed to make its own rules. (It was the particular genius of an entire people, of course, that Herder extolled as the *Volksgeist*.) And the human spirit must never allow itself to be fettered by national prescriptions, any more than by social conventions, in such a way as to prevent enjoyment of its most precious possession, its freedom.

Freedom and the problem of self-recognition were major themes in the work of two of the giants of the romantic movement, the composer Ludwig van Beethoven (1770–1827) and the writer Johann Wolfgang von Goethe (1749–1832). The most remarkable quality about Beethoven's compositions is their uniqueness and individuality. In the Fifth Symphony Beethoven reaches the summit of symphonic logic, the Sixth is a glorification of nature, the Seventh a Dionysian revelry, the Eighth a genial conjuring up of the spirit of the eighteenth-century symphony. Then Beethoven, in his later years suffering from deafness, embarks on his last artistic journey: Five piano sonatas, five string quartets, the Ninth Symphony, and the great Mass, *Missa Solemnis,* constitute his final legacy. They fill the listener with awe not so much because of their unusual form or their vast proportions, but because they express boundless individual will and power.

Beethoven

Goethe's dedication to the idea of individual freedom was, in part, the product of his having been born and raised in the free imperial city of Frankfurt. Frankfurt was an international center, a trading place open to intellectual winds from all quarters. Goethe was, in terms of his environment, free from the particularist, nationalist influences which directed the work of other German romantics. Goethe's own "genius" drove him first to the study of law, then medicine, then the fine arts and natural sciences. In 1775 he took up residence at the court

Goethe

Left: *A Page from the Score of Beethoven's Piano Sonata Opus 109 in E Major.* Right: *Ludwig van Beethoven*

An Illustration from Goethe's
Sorrows of Werther

Immanuel Kant

of the young duke of Weimar. Weimar was a tiny German principality with a population of no more than half a million, another cosmopolitan community and in this respect not unlike Frankfurt. Influenced by Herder, Goethe had already published various romantically inclined works, including the immensely popular *Sorrows of Werther,* a novel expressive of Goethe's early restlessness and emotionalism. The almost excessive sensitivity characteristic of Goethe's earlier writings gave way, in his middle years, to the search for a new spirit, equally free and yet more ordered. This mode derived from his experiences in Italy and from his study of the ancient Romans and Greeks. In 1790 Goethe published the first part of his masterpiece, *Faust,* a drama in verse, which he completed a year before his death in 1831. The play, in its retelling of the German legend of the man who sold his soul to the devil in return for universal knowledge, reflects the romantic unwillingness to restrain the spirit; it also expresses Goethe's own recognition of the magnitude of humanity's daring in its desire for unlimited knowledge and its own fulfillment.

The theme of self-realization as humanity's ultimate goal, so characteristic of so much of romantic thinking, contrasted with the notions of those other romantics we have discussed, who, like Herder, insisted upon the subordination of one human spirit to the spirit of a whole people. Immanuel Kant (1724–1804), Goethe's only rival as a thinker during this period, expressed himself as opposed to the idea that unbounded individual freedom was the highest good. Kant, a retiring scholar who lived his life out in the city of Königsberg, where he was born, argued that there were limits to human knowledge, that beyond the world of appearances there lay an unknowable realm of what he called "things in themselves." This thesis, first expounded in his *Critique of Pure Reason* (1781), was further developed in his *Critique of Practical Reason* (1790), in which he attempted to establish proper criteria for personal behavior. If pure reason could neither prove nor disprove the existence of God, Kant argued, practical reason tells us that in the idea of God there exists an idea of moral perfection toward which all people must strive. They must live consistent with what Kant called the "categorical imperative": to act as if one's actions were to become a universal law of nature. Kant argued that only by living according to his categorical imperative could men and women enjoy true freedom. Freedom he defined in terms of self-imposed duty, rather than the absence of restraint or—as in Goethe's case—the compulsion to achieve self-fulfillment.

Whether or not Kant was a romantic is a question that historians have continued to debate. His devotion to reason has often led scholars to consider him a late Enlightenment figure. In one respect, however, Kant certainly thought with the romantics. His insistence that "things in themselves" were ultimately unknowable, reflected the romantics' willingness to surrender to the mysterious. "There is nothing beautiful, pleasing, or grand in life, but that which is more or less mysterious," Chateaubriand wrote, in his defense of Christianity. While Kant was not an explicit defender of Christianity, his philosophy helped perpetuate religious belief, and was thus one in its effect with romanticism. Certainly Kant was not a romantic nationalist, although nationalists used his arguments to support their claim that men and women had a duty to an authority higher than themselves. Kant himself, however, in his treatise *On Perpetual Peace,* published at the height of the revolutionary wars in 1795, argued vehemently against national aggrandizement and in favor of a kind of European federal union. *Kant as a romantic*

Romanticism and nationalism bear much the same relationship to each other in the history of nineteenth-century Europe as they do in the thought of the men and women we have just surveyed. At some points, as in England, they appear to run separate courses. At others they join together, as they did in Germany, whose own history lies at the center of the history of both romanticism and nationalism. *The relationship between romanticism and nationalism*

2. NATIONALISM AND NATION-BUILDING: 1800–1848

The humiliating French occupation of Prussia, combined with the growing sense of national destiny exemplified in Fichte's *Addresses,* resulted in a drive on the part of Prussian intellectuals and political reformers to bring their country once more to its former position among European powers. Prussia's crushing defeat by the French in 1806 had been the logical outcome of the inertia that had gripped the country during the half-century or so since the aggressive achievements of Frederick the Great. Unlike the rest of the German states, however, allied directly with France in the Confederation of the Rhine, the separate kingdom of Prussia consciously avoided French "contamination," participating unwillingly in the Continental System, and otherwise holding itself aloof. *Nationalism and reform in Prussia, 1806–1815*

Its major task was to rebuild its armies, since only by that means could Prussia reassert itself against Napoleon. To that end, two generals, Gerhard von Scharnhorst and August Gneisenau, instituted changes based on an essential lesson in nation-building they had learned from the French Revolution: that men were far more effective fighters if they believed themselves to have some direct stake in the wars they fought. A reconstituted national army, eventually based upon a system of universal military service, involved the country as a whole in its own defense and grew to become a far more consciously "Prussian" force than it had been heretofore. Officers were recruited and promoted on the basis of merit, not birth, although the large majority continued to come from the Junker (gentry) class. This breach with tradition encouraged the Prussian middle class to take a more ac- *Military reforms*

Baron Heinrich vom Stein

Stein's governmental reforms

Economic nationalism

tive and enthusiastic interest in its country's affairs. Old or inefficient officers, despite their social standing, were removed from positions of command; training at the royal cadet school in Berlin was modernized.

These reforms, which illustrate the way in which a liberal desire for modernization might combine with nationalism, paralleled similar changes instituted during the same period under the direction of Prussia's principal minister, Baron Heinrich vom Stein(1757–1831), and his successor, Karl von Hardenberg (1750–1822). Stein was not himself a Prussian; he was initially less interested in achieving a Prussian nation-state than in uniting by some means or other all the various principalities of Germany. Only after the disasters wrought upon the Germans by Napoleon did Stein turn to Prussia as a last resort. He had read Kant and Fichte, and was convinced by them that a state must somehow make its citizens aware of their obligations to the national interest. A sense of duty to the state could hardly be kindled, however, without first convincing men and women that loyalty meant reward as well as obligation. Stein therefore labored to dismantle the caste system which had until that time characterized Prussia, in order to permit individuals to rise within society. Stein's Municipal Ordinance of 1808 was a conscious attempt to increase the middle-class Germans' sense of themselves as citizens—again, a goal shared by both liberals and nationalists. All cities and towns were henceforth required to elect their councilmen, while local justice and security continued to be administered by the central government in Berlin; all other matters, including finance, were left to individual communities. Education played a vital role in nation-building. Schools were ideal agencies for the dissemination of the doctrines of national duty. Recognizing this fact, the Prussian reformers expanded facilities for both primary and secondary education. The University of Berlin, founded in 1808, numbered among its faculty such ardent nationalists as Fichte and Savigny, and was the institutional embodiment of the new spirit that contributed to Prussia's eventual victory over the French.

The history of Prussia between 1815 and 1850 can most easily be understood in terms of its continuing struggle to establish itself as an independent national power within Germany and in opposition to Austria. The most important Prussian victory in this respect was the establishment of the *Zollverein,* or customs union. By the 1840s, the union included almost all of Germany except German Austria. Meanwhile Prussia had produced in the work of the economist Friedrich List (1789–1846), a nationalist response to the internationalism of the liberal free-trade economists. List wrote that while free trade might suit the British, it did not suit Prussia. Economics, he argued, far from being an abstract science equally applicable everywhere, was a discipline which must be grounded in the particular national experience of individual countries. Germany's, and therefore Prussia's, experience demanded not free trade but high tariffs. Only when sheltered behind a protectionist system could Prussia build the factories and manufacture the goods that would guarantee its economic health.

The events which had altered the political shape of Britain and France in the early 1830s—revolution in the latter and liberal reforms in both—did not have lasting counterparts in Germany. A revolutionary movement of sorts, spawned in the universities and youthful secret societies, did result in temporary changes in a few German principalities. But Metternich, still in control of Austrian policy and determined to thwart Prussia's attempts to assert its nationality, used the occasion of those outbreaks to encourage a general antiliberal reaction throughout the German states by playing on the fears of the propertied classes. The diet of the German Confederation, the loose organization of sovereign powers that had replaced the finally defunct "Holy Roman Empire" after 1815, coordinated the repression. Prussia avoided revolution as a result of the reforms instituted a generation before by Stein and Hardenberg. In 1840 Frederick William IV succeeded to the Prussian throne. Apparently devoted to liberal principles, he relaxed censorship laws and encouraged participation in the central government by provincial diets. It soon became apparent, however, that the king was no liberal, but some sort of romantic-nationalist, and an authoritarian as well. He declared himself opposed to constitutionalism, that central doctrine in the liberal canon of beliefs. When middle-class Prussian liberals pressed, in 1847, for control over legislative and budgetary matters in the recently convened assembly of diets (the *Landtag*), the king saw to it that their request was denied. Frederick William then turned his attention to a scheme whereby Prussia might play a far larger role in the confederation. But before his plan could receive a hearing, it was overtaken by the revolutionary movement of 1848, which, as we shall see, engulfed central Europe as it had western Europe, though with different results.

National sentiment, the spirit which served to unite the Prussians, was at the same time operating to divide the heterogeneous elements within the Austrian Empire. Its people, who lived within three major geographical areas—Austria, Bohemia, and Hungary—were composed of a considerable number of different ethnic and language groups: Germans, Czechs, Magyars, Poles, Slovaks, Serbs, and Italians, to name the most prominent. In some parts of the empire, these people lived in isolation; elsewhere they dwelt in direct proximity, if not much harmony, with others. The Austrian Empire attempted to unite these groups by means of a reigning house, the Hapsburgs, and a supposedly benevolent bureaucracy. These devices failed increasingly to satisfy the various groups, in whom a spirit of cultural, if not political, nationalism grew persistently stronger in the years after 1815. In the Polish territories of the empire, where the gentry had for generations been conscious of themselves as Poles, the imperial government succeeded in stifling the sentiment by playing off the serfs against their masters, encouraging a class war as a means of preventing an ethnic one. Elsewhere within the empire they were less adroit. In Hungary, nationalism expressed itself in both cultural and political forms. In 1827, a Hungarian national theatre was established at Budapest. The year before, Magyar was substituted for Latin as the official language of government. A political movement, whose most formidable leader was the radical nationalist Louis Kossuth (1802–1894), was at the same time seeking independence and a parliamentary government for Hungary.

Pan-Slavism

The most widespread of the eastern European cultural nationalist movements was Pan-Slavism, at this period just beginning. Slavs included Russians, Poles, Czechs, Slovaks, Slovenes, Croats, Serbs, and Bulgars. Before 1848 Pan-Slavism was an almost exclusively cultural movement, united by a generalized anti-Western sentiment, yet divided by a tendency to quarrel as to the primacy of this or that particular language or tradition. These divisions did not substantially lessen the effect of Pan-Slavism as a further problem of the Austrian Empire. The literature of the movement—for example, the historian Francis Palacky's (1836–1867) *History of the Bohemian People* and the poetry of the revolutionary Pole Adam Mickiewiez (1798–1855), fed the desires of those who wished to rid themselves of what they considered a foreign yoke. In Russia, slavophilism had been held in check by the Western-looking Alexander I. After his death, however, the notion that the Russian people possessed its particular *Volksgeist* increased in general popularity.

Nationalism in Italy

Two other national movements were growing beyond infancy during the years before 1848: one in Italy, the other in Ireland. Among the organizations formed in the confused period at the end of the Napoleonic wars, none was louder in its nationalist proclamations than the Italian *Carbonari*. One member of that group, Joseph Mazzini (1805–1872) founded a society of his own in 1831, Young Italy, which was dedicated to the cause of uniting the peninsula. In 1834, from Switzerland, Mazzini launched a totally unsuccessful verbal assault against the Kingdom of Sardinia, in the hope that the rest of Italy would join with him. Mazzini subsequently contented himself with propagandizing for the cause of Italian nationalism and republicanism, attracting a devoted following, particularly among British liberals. Liberals in Italy, however, mistrusted him. Although they too wished to see Italy one nation, they were dismayed, as "good" liberals, and members of the middle class, by Mazzini's insistence upon a republic, hoping instead to merge existing principalities together into some sort of constitutional monarchy.

Nationalism in Ireland

If Italian nationalism was primarily a middle-class liberal phenomenon at this time, the same was not true of the Irish movement to repeal the union with England. Headed by Daniel O'Connell (1775–1847), it derived its strength from the support of Irish peasants. O'Connell's remarkably successful appeal was based on the hatred all Irish felt for the English, because of the centuries of oppression Irish Catholics had suffered under English Protestant rule. Both before and after the official union of 1801, the English had imposed on the Irish a foreign rule that had brought with it little but poverty and persecution. O'Connell's campaign for the repeal of the union was grounded in the hope that he would be able to negotiate some sort of moderate agreement with the English ruling class. The desires of his followers exceeded him in being far more radical in nature. Neither the separatist hopes of O'Connell, called by the Irish the "Liberator," nor the more genuinely nationalist hopes of his followers, however, were to achieve realization. Unlike the nationalist movements of central Europe, nationalism in Ireland faced a powerful and determined adversary—England—who would for a century deny it victory.

Joseph Mazzini

3. NATIONALISM, LIBERALISM, AND REVOLUTION, 1848

The history of the revolutions of 1848 in central Europe can most easily be understood in terms of two major themes: the first, the struggle of various nationalities, particularly within the Austrian Empire, to assert their own autonomy; the second, the contention between the forces of liberalism and nationalism in Germany.

News of the February revolution in France traveled quickly eastward. By the end of March the Austrian Empire was split apart. Hungary, with Kossuth in the lead, severed all but the most tenuous of links with the House of Hapsburg and prepared to draft its own constitution. In Vienna, workers and students imitated their counter-

The "March Days" in Austria

The March Days in Vienna, 1848

Counternationalism as an aid to restoration

parts in Paris, erecting barricades and invading the imperial palace. A measure of the political chaos was the fact that Metternich, veteran of a score of threats to the precarious stability he had crafted, found the pressure this time too great, and fled in disguise to Britain. Deserted by that tower of reactionary strength, the Hapsburg emperor, Ferdinand, yielded to nationalist demands from Bohemia and granted that kingdom its own constitution as well. To the south, Italians launched attacks against the Austrian-held territories in Milan, Naples, Venetia, and Lombardy, where the forces of the Sardinian ruler, King Charles Albert, routed the Austrians.

Yet the forces of national sentiment which had brought Austria to its knees then succeeded in allowing the empire to recoup its fortunes. The paradox of nationalism, as it manifested itself in central Europe, was that as soon as a cultural majority had declared itself an independent or semi-independent state, other cultural minorities within that new state complained bitterly about their newly institutionalized inferiority. This is precisely what happened in Bohemia. There the anti-German Czech majority refused to send delegates to an all-German assembly, meeting at Frankfurt to draft a German constitution. Instead, they summoned a confederation of Slavs to Prague. The delegates, most of them from within the boundaries of the old Austrian Empire, immediately recognized that the idea of a united Germany represented a far greater threat to their political and cultural autonomy than the fact of the empire ever had. The German minority in Bohemia, however, was naturally anxious to participate in discussions which might result in closer union with their ethnic counterparts. They resented the Bohemian government's refusal to do so. The resulting animosities made it all the easier for the Austrians to take advantage of a May 1848 insurrection in Prague, subdue the city, send the Slav congress packing, and reassert control in Bohemia. Although the Austrian government was at this time a liberal one, the product of the March revolution in Vienna, it was no less determined than its predecessor had been to prevent the total dismemberment of the empire. For this reason it was quick to restore Lombardy and Venetia to its realm when quarrels among the heretofore united Italian allies had sufficiently weakened their common stand against the Austrians.

Civil war in Hungary

Nationalism and counternationalism in Hungary set the stage for the final act of the restoration of Austrian hegemony. Kossuth's radical party was, above all, a Magyar nationalist party. Once in power, in early 1849 it moved the capital from Pressburg, near the Austrian border, to Budapest, and again proclaimed Magyar as the country's official language. These actions offended national minorities within Hungary, particularly the Croats, who prior to the revolution had enjoyed certain liberties under Austrian rule. The Croatians raised an insurgent army and launched a civil war. The Emperor Ferdinand, once more encouraging division along nationalist lines, named the Croatian rebel Josef von Jellachich his military commander against the

Maygars. By this time the Viennese liberals began to recognize—too late—that their turn might come next. They were right. Despite a second uprising in Vienna in October, the revolution was spent. Forces loyal to the emperor descended upon Vienna from Bohemia. On October 31, the liberal government capitulated.

Once the imperial government had reasserted itself, it labored to suppress nationalist impulses as thoroughly as possible. Austria's ministers recognized that, though tactically advantageous at times, nationalist movements operated generally to the detriment of imperial unity. The emperor's chief minister, Prince Felix von Schwarzenberg, and the minister of the interior, Alexander Bach, both nation-builders, together centralized the state within one united political system. Hungary and Bohemia no longer enjoyed separate rights. Peasants of all ethnic groups, liberated from serfdom as part of the general reform movement, were permitted to retain their freedom, on the grounds of their loyalty to the empire. The law was reformed, again to achieve uniformity, and railways and roads were constructed to link the empire. Tariff walls were erected around imperial boundaries to exclude foreign manufactures, while a free trade area within the empire encouraged home industries. Having done all it could to eradicate separatist movements, the Austrian government thus moved to secure its advantage by engaging in a vigorous campaign of nation-building.

In Prussia, revolution ran a similar course. In March, King Frederick William found himself compelled to yield to demands for a popularly elected legislative assembly. When it met, the body proved particularly sympathetic to the plight of the Polish minority within Prussia, and antagonistic toward the Russians, whom radical legislators saw as the major threat to the spread of enlightened political ideas in central Europe. When the assembly's sympathy with Polish nationalism extended to the granting of self-government to Prussian Poland, however, it generated the same feelings among the German minority there that we have seen arousing minorities within the Austrian Empire. In so doing, it precipitated the same eventual results. Germans in Posen, the major city of Prussian Poland, revolted against the newly established Polish government; not surprisingly, Prussian army units on duty sided with the Germans and helped them crush the new government. Power, it now became clear, lay with the army, professionalized since the days of Gneisenau and Scharnhorst, yet still dominated by the Junkers. Against the armed authority of the military, the radical legislators of Berlin were no match; revolution ended in Prussia as quickly as it had begun.

Meanwhile, at Frankfurt, Germans engaged in the debate that provides the history of central Europe in these revolutionary years with its second theme: liberalism vs. nationalism. Delegates had been chosen from across Germany and Austria to attend the Frankfurt Assembly. They were largely from the professional classes—professors, lawyers, administrators—and generally devoted to the cause of

Procession of the German National Assembly to Its Opening Session at St. Paul's Church, Frankfurt, May 1848

middle-class liberalism. Many had assumed that their task would resemble that of the assembly which had met in 1789 to draft a constitution for the French: i.e., they would draft a constitution for a liberal, unified Germany. That former convocation, however, had been grounded in the simple but all-important fact that a French nation-state already existed. The French assembly had been elected to give the nation a new shape and new direction. But a centralized sovereign power was there to reshape; there was an authority that could be either commandeered or, if necessary, usurped. The Frankfurt Assembly, in contrast, was grounded upon nothing but its own words. It was a collection of thoughtful, well-intentioned middle-class liberals, committed to a belief that a liberal-national German state could somehow be constituted out of abstract principles. These men, from the start of their deliberations, ruled out the use of violence to achieve their ends. At the same time, they failed to ally themselves with the urban workers. If by 1848 the workers were not yet a self-conscious and articulate class, they were nevertheless a force no reformer or revolutionary could reckon without. Yet the Frankfurt debaters by and large ignored them, and thus denied themselves the one source of power they might otherwise have called to their aid.

Almost from the start, the assembly found itself tangled in the problems of nationality. Who, they asked, were the Germans? A majority of the delegates argued that they were all those who, by language, culture, or geography, felt themselves bound to the enterprise now underway at Frankfurt. The German nation that was to be constituted must include as many of those "Germans" as possible. This point of view came to be known as the "Great German" position. Great Germans found themselves stymied, however, by the unwillingness of other nationalities to be included in their fold. The Czechs in Bohemia, as we have seen, wanted no part of Great Germany. In the end the Great Germans settled that the nation for which they were drafting a constitution should include, among other territories, all Austrian lands except Hungary. This decision meant that the crown of their new country might most logically be offered to the Hapsburg emperor. At this point the voice of the "Little Germans" began to be heard. Prussian nationalism took precedence over German nationalism; a minority argued that Austria should be excluded altogether and the crown instead offered to King Frederick William of Prussia.

The liberalism of the assembly was put to the test by events in Austria and Poland in the fall of 1848. When the imperial forces crushed the Czech and Hungarian rebellions, when the Prussian Junkers put an end to Polish self-government, liberals found themselves forced to cheer. They were compelled to support the suppression of minority nationalities; otherwise there would be no new Germany. But their cheers were for the forces not only of German nationalism but of antiliberal authoritarianism. The assembly's most embarrassing moment occurred when it found itself compelled to take shelter behind the Prussian army. Riots broke out in Frankfurt protesting the assembly's willingness to withdraw from a confrontation with the Danes over the future of Germans in Schleswig, a Danish province. That particular area, which many considered to be part of Germany, had been annexed by the Danes in March 1848. The Frankfurters had been unable to do more than ask the Prussians to win Schleswig back for them; and the Prussians had refused. Hence the riots; hence a second request, this time heeded, for Prussian assistance.

Reduced to the status of dependents, the Frankfurt delegates nevertheless, in the spring of 1849, produced a constitution. By this time Austria, fearing its Prussian rival, had decided to have no more to do with Frankfurt. The Little Germans thus won by default and offered their constitutional monarchy to Frederick William of Prussia. Though tempted, he turned them down, arguing that their constitution was too liberal, embodying as it did the revolutionary notion that a crown could be offered to a monarch. Frederick wanted the crown; but on his own terms. The delegates went home, disillusioned by their experience, many of them convinced that their dual goal of liberalism and nationalism was an impossible one. Some, who refused to surrender that goal, emigrated to the United States, where they believed the goal had already been achieved. Many of those who stayed behind convinced themselves that half the goal was better than none, and sacrificed their liberalism to nationalism.

4. NATION-BUILDING, 1850–1870

Bismarck

The twenty years between 1850 and 1870 were years of intense nation-building in the Western world. Of the master-builders, none was more accomplished than the man who brought Germany under Prussian rule, Otto von Bismarck (1815–1898). He was born into the Junker class. During the revolutionary period of 1848 and 1849, Bismarck had served in the Prussian parliament as a defender of the monarchy. Bismarck was really neither a liberal nor a nationalist; he was a Prussian. When he instituted domestic reforms, he did so not because he favored the "rights" of this or that particular group, but because he thought that his policies would result in a more united, and hence more powerful, Prussia. When he maneuvered to bring other German states under Prussian domination, he did so not in conformity with a grand Germanic design but because he believed that some sort of union was almost inevitable and, if so, that it must come about at Prussia's behest. He prided himself on being a realist; and he became a first-rate practitioner of what has come to be called *Realpolitik*—the politics, not of idealism, but of hard-headed reality.

Bismarck and the liberals

When Bismarck came to power as minister-president of Prussia in 1862, he was confronted by a liberal parliamentary majority which, since 1859, had opposed a campaign to increase military expenditures despite pressure from the king. This majority had been produced by an electoral system that was part of the constitution granted by Frederick William to Prussia in 1850, following the collapse of the assembly. The parliament was divided into two houses, the lower one elected by universal male suffrage. Votes were apportioned according to one's ability to pay taxes, however; those few who together paid one-third of the country's taxes elected one-third of the legislators. A large landowner or industrialist exercised about a hundred times the voting power of a poor man. Contrary to the king's expectations, however, under this constitution a liberal majority was succeeding in thwarting the plans of the sovereign and his advisors. It was to break this deadlock that King William I, who succeeded his brother Frederick William in 1861, summoned Bismarck. In Bismarck the liberals more than met their match. When they refused to levy taxes, he collected them anyway, claiming that the constitution, whatever its purposes, had not been designed to subvert the state. When liberals argued that Prussia was setting a poor example for the rest of Germany, Bismarck replied that Prussia was admired not for its liberalism but its power.

Whether or not the Germans—or the rest of Europe—admired Prussia's power, they soon found themselves confronted by it. Bismarck proceeded to build a nation that in the short space of eight years came into being as the German Empire. Bismarck was assisted in his task by his readiness to take advantage of international situations as

British Encampment Near Sebastopol, 1854–1855. Photograph taken by Roger Fenton. The Crimean War was the first to be reported to the world by photograph as well as by news dispatch.

they presented themselves, without concerning himself particularly with the ideological or moral implications of his actions. He was aided as well by developments over which he had no initial control but which he was able to turn to his advantage. The first of these, the Crimean War, had occurred in 1854–1856, prior to his taking office. Russia and Turkey, perennial European squabblers, had precipitated the hostilities. Russia invaded the territories of Moldavia and Wallachia (later Rumania) in an attempt to take advantage of the continuing political rot that made the Ottoman Empire an easy prey. In 1854 France and then Britain came to the aid of the Turks by invading Russia's Crimean peninsula. These allies were soon joined by Austria and Sardinia. The quarrel had by this time enlarged to include the question of who was to protect the Christians in Jerusalem from the Turks; it was fueled from the start as well by Britain's continuing determination to prohibit a strong Russian presence in the Near East. The allies' eventual victory was the result primarily of a British blockade of Russia. The peace settlement was a severe setback for Russia, whose influence in the Balkans was drastically curbed. Moldavia and Wallachia were united as Rumania, which, along with Serbia, was granted power as a self-governing principality. Austria, though it had sided with the victor, lost more than it gained from the war. Austrian military resources were severely taxed during the invasion and occupation of Moldavia and Wallachia. It was the subsequent weakness of both Russia and Austria, the result of the Crimean War, that Bismarck used to his advantage in the 1860s.

The Crimean War

In consolidating the German states into a union controlled by Prussia, Bismarck first moved to eliminate Austria from its commanding position in the Germanic Confederation. As a means to this end he inflamed the long-smoldering dispute with Denmark over the possession of Schleswig and Holstein. Inhabited largely by Germans, these two provinces had an anomalous status. Since 1815 Holstein had been

Steps to German unification: (1) weakening of Austria

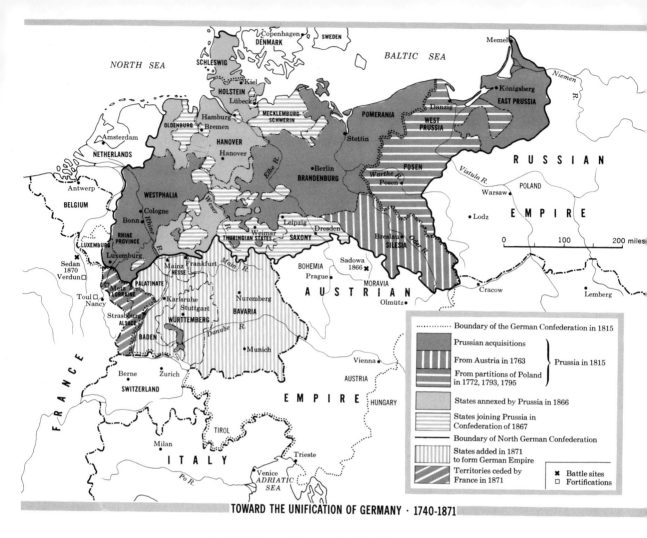

TOWARD THE UNIFICATION OF GERMANY · 1740-1871

included in the Germanic Confederation, but both were subject to the personal overlordship of the king of Denmark. When, in 1864, the Danish king attempted to annex them, Bismarck invited Austria to participate in a war against Denmark. A brief struggle followed, at the end of which the Danish ruler was compelled to renounce all his claims to Schleswig and Holstein in favor of Austria and Prussia. Then the very sequel occurred for which Bismarck ardently hoped: a quarrel between the victors over division of the spoils. The conflict which followed in 1866, known as the Seven Weeks' War, ended in an easy triumph for Prussia. Austria was forced to give up all claims to Schleswig and Holstein, to surrender Venetia, and to acquiesce in the dissolution of the Germanic Confederation. Immediately following the war Bismarck proceeded to unite all of the German states north of the Main River into the North German Confederation.

To achieve the confederation Bismarck willingly turned himself into a democrat. He saw that if he was to attain his end, which was a strong union with Prussia at its head, he would need to cultivate a constituency hitherto untapped by any German politicians: the masses. He appreciated the manner by which Napoleon III had reinforced his regime through plebiscites. And Bismarck understood that the majority of Germans were not particularly enthusiastic supporters of capitalist liberals, of the bureaucracies of their own small states, or of the Austrian Hapsburgs. The constitution he devised for his confederation provided for two chambers: the upper chamber represented the individual states within the union, though not equally; the lower chamber was elected by universal manhood suffrage. The liberal middle class, to say nothing of the Junkerdom, was astonished and dismayed, as well they might be. Bismarck's intention was to use popular support to strengthen the hand of the central government against the interests of both landlords and capitalists. To this end, he struck a bargain with German socialists, who agreed to exchange support for the confederation for universal suffrage.

Bismarck's final step in the completion of German unity was the Franco-Prussian War of 1870–1871. He hoped that a conflict with France would kindle the spirit of German nationalism in Bavaria, Würtemberg, and other southern states still outside the confederation. Taking advantage of a diplomatic tempest concerning the right of the Hohenzollerns (Prussia's ruling family) to occupy the Spanish throne, Bismarck worked hard to force a Franco-German misunderstanding. King William agreed to meet with the French ambassador at the resort spa of Ems in Prussia to discuss the Spanish succession. When William telegraphed Bismarck that the demands of the French for perpetual exclusion of the Hohenzollern family from the Spanish throne had been refused, Bismarck released portions of the message to the press so as to make it appear that King William had insulted the ambassador—which he had not done. When the garbled report of what happened at Ems was received in France, the nation reacted with a call for war. The call was echoed in Prussia, where Bismarck published evidence which he claimed proved French designs upon the Rhineland. Once war had been declared the south German states rallied to Prussia's side in the belief that it was the victim of aggression. The war was quickly fought. The French were no match for Prussia's professionally trained and superbly equipped forces. Nor did other European powers come to France's assistance. Austria, the most likely candidate, remained weakened by its recent war with Prussia. The Magyars, who at this time had assumed positions of influence within the Austrian government, were quite prepared to welcome a strengthened Prussia; Prussia's growing strength in Germany would further increase Austria's weakness there. And the weaker Austria was as a German power, the stronger would be the claims of the Magyars to predominance. Once more one nationalist consciousness was grinding against another. The war began in July; it ended in September with the defeat of the French and the capture of Napoleon III himself at Sedan in France.

(2) courting the masses

(3) the Franco-Prussian War

The German Empire

Italian unification

Following the collapse of the French imperial government, insurrectionary forces in Paris continued to hold out against the Germans until the winter of 1871. Bismarck meanwhile proceeded to consummate the German union toward which he had worked so assiduously. On January 18, 1871, in the great Hall of Mirrors at Versailles the German Empire was proclaimed. All those states, except Austria, which had not already been absorbed into Prussia declared their allegiance to William I, henceforth emperor or kaiser. Four months later, at Frankfurt, a treaty between the French and Germans ceded the border region of Alsace to the new empire, condemned the French to an indemnity of five billion francs, and thereby broadcast to the world the remarkable success of Bismarck's nation-building.

Events in Italy ran a course almost parallel to that which had led to the unification of Germany. Italy before 1848, it should be remembered, was a patchwork of petty states. The most important of those possessing independence were the Kingdom of Sardinia in the north, the Papal States in the central region, and the Kingdom of the Two Sicilies in the south. The former republics of Lombardy and Venetia were held by Austria, while Hapsburg dependents ruled in Tuscany, Parma, and Modena. As the revolutionary fervor of 1848 swept across the peninsula, one ruler after another granted democratic reforms. Charles Albert of Sardinia outdistanced all the others by providing for civil liberties and a parliamentary form of government. But it soon became evident that the Italians were as interested in nationalism as in liberalism. For some years romantic patriots had been dreaming of the *Risorgimento,* which would restore the nation to the position of glorious leadership it had held in Roman times and during the Renaissance. To achieve this, it was universally agreed that Italy must be welded into a single state. But opinions differed as to the form the new government should take. Young idealists followed the leadership of Mazzini. Religious-minded patriots believed that the most practicable solution would be to federate the state of Italy under the presidency of

Meeting to Arrange Peace Terms at the End of the Franco-Prussian War. On the left is Otto von Bismarck, chancellor of the new German Empire. In the center is Jules Favre and to his right Louis-Adolphe Thiers, both representing the provisional government set up after the overthrow of Napoleon III.

the pope. The majority of the more moderate nationalists advocated a constitutional monarchy built upon the foundations of the Kingdom of Sardinia. The aims of this third group gradually crystallized under the leadership of a shrewd Sardinian nobleman, Count Camillo di Cavour (1810–1861). In 1850 he was appointed minister of commerce and agriculture of his native state and in 1852 prime minister.

The campaign for unification of the Italian peninsula began with efforts to expel the Austrians. In 1848 revolts were organized in the territories under Hapsburg domination, and an army of liberation marched from Sardinia to aid the rebels; but the movement ended in failure. It was then that Cavour, as the new leader of the campaign, turned to less heroic but more practical methods. In 1855, to attract the favorable attention of Great Britain and France, he had entered the Crimean War on their side, despite the fact that he had no quarrel with Russia. In 1858 he held a secret meeting with Napoleon III and prepared the stage for an Italian War of Liberation. Napoleon agreed to cooperate in driving the Austrians from Italy for the price of the cession of Savoy and Nice by Sardinia to France. A war with Austria was duly provoked in 1859, and for a time all went well for the Franco-Italian allies. But after the conquest of Lombardy, Napoleon III suddenly withdrew, fearful of ultimate defeat and afraid of antagonizing the Catholics in his own country by aiding the avowedly anticlerical government of Cavour. Thus deserted by its ally, Sardinia was unable to expel the Austrians from Venetia. Nevertheless, extensive gains were made; Sardinia annexed Lombardy, and acquired by various means the duchies of Tuscany, Parma, and Modena, and the northern portion of the Papal States. Sardinia was now more than twice its original size and by far the most powerful state in Italy.

The second step in consolidating the unity of Italy was the conquest of the Kingdom of the Two Sicilies. This kingdom was ruled by a Bourbon, Francis II, who was thoroughly hated by his Italian subjects. In May 1860 a romantic adventurer, Giuseppe Garibaldi, set out with a regiment of one thousand "red shirts" to rescue his fellow Italians from oppression. Within three months he had conquered the island of Sicily and had then marched to the deliverance of Naples, where the people were already in revolt. By November the whole kingdom of Francis II had fallen to Garibaldi. He at first intended to convert the territory into an independent republic but was finally persuaded to surrender it to the Kingdom of Sardinia. With most of the peninsula now united under a single rule, Victor Emmanuel II, king of Sardinia, assumed the title of king of Italy (March 17, 1861). Venetia was still in the hands of the Austrians, but in 1866, following their defeat in the Seven Weeks' War, they were forced by the Prussians to cede it to Italy. All that remained to complete the unification of Italy was the annexation of Rome. The Eternal City had resisted conquest thus far, largely because of the military protection accorded the pope by Napoleon III. But in 1870 the outbreak of the Franco-Prussian War

Camillo di Cavour

Giuseppe Garibaldi

Garibaldi

THE UNIFICATION OF ITALY

Map labels:
SWITZERLAND
AUSTRIA
The Kingdom of Sardinia at the time of the Congress of Vienna, 1815
Territories acquired, 1859-1860
Territories acquired, 1860-1870
SAVOY (To France in 1860)
KINGDOM OF SARDINIA
PIEDMONT
LOMBARDY
• Milan
VENETIA
Venice
Po R.
• Turin
PARMA
FRANCE
Genoa •
MODENA
Bologna •
ROMAGNA
LUCCA
Florence •
Arno R.
PAPAL STATES
A D R I A T I C
S E A
TUSCANY
UMBRIA
Tiber R.
Rome ★
CORSICA (To France)
KINGDOM OF
★ Naples
KINGDOM OF SARDINIA
T Y R R H E N I A N
THE
S E A
TWO
0   200 miles
SICILIES
Palermo •
Messina •
M E D I T E R R A N E A N
SICILY
S E A

Italy and the Papal States

compelled Napoleon to withdraw his troops. In September 1870 Italian soldiers occupied Rome, and in July of the following year it was made the capital of the by now united kingdom.

The occupation of Rome brought the kingdom of Italy into conflict with the papacy. Indeed, the whole movement for unification had been characterized by hostility to the Church. Such was inevitably the case, with the pope ruling in the manner of a secular prince over the Papal States and opposing those who would rob him of his domain for the sake of a united Italy. Following the occupation of Rome in 1870, an attempt was made to solve the problem of relations between the state and the papacy. In 1871 the Italian parliament enacted the Law of

Papal Guaranties, purporting to define the status of the pope as a reigning sovereign. This law the reigning pontiff, Pius IX, promptly denounced on the ground that issues affecting the pope could be settled only by an international treaty to which he himself was a party. Whereupon he shut himself up in the Vatican and refused to have anything to do with a government which had so shamefully treated Christ's vicar on earth. His successors continued this practice of voluntary imprisonment until 1929, when a series of agreements between the Italian government and Pius XI effected settlement of the dispute.

Nation-building was the preoccupation of another major country in the first half of the nineteenth century: the United States. The history of the expansion and consolidation of this newly born country into a nation of remarkable economic potential in little over half a century can best be understood in terms of several major factors. The first is the growth of political democracy.

Nation-building in the U.S.: (1) the growth of democracy

The United States did not begin its history as a democracy. Although a few early leaders professed democratic ideals, these were not the doctrines of the most prominent. The authors of the Constitution were not interested in the rule of the masses. The primary aim of the founders of the United States was to establish a *republic* that would promote stability and protect the rights of private property against the leveling tendencies of majorities. For this reason they adopted checks and balances, devised the Electoral College for choosing the president, created a powerful judiciary, and entrusted the selection of senators to the legislatures of the several states.

Thomas Jefferson by Gilbert Stuart

Following the establishment of a new government under the Constitution of 1789, democratic ideals began to win acceptance in the United States. Until 1801 the Federalist party held the reins of power, representing big landowners, big money, and the conservatives generally. In the latter year the Democratic-Republicans gained control as a result of the election of Thomas Jefferson (1743–1826) to the presidency. This event is often referred to as the Jeffersonian Revolution, on the supposition that Jefferson was the champion of the masses and of the political power of the underprivileged. There is danger in carrying this interpretation too far. In several respects Jefferson's ideas were far removed from democracy in its historic meaning. He strenuously opposed the unlimited sovereignty of the majority. His conception of an ideal political system was an aristocracy of "virtue and talent," in which respect for personal liberty would be the guiding principle.

Yet the Jeffersonian movement had a number of democratic objectives of cardinal importance. Its leaders were vigorous opponents of special privilege, whether of birth or of wealth. They worked for the abolition of established churches. They led the campaign for the addition of a Bill of Rights to the Constitution and were almost exclusively responsible for its success. Although professing devotion to the principle of the separation of powers, they actually believed in the supremacy of the representatives of the people and viewed with abhor-

Jeffersonian principles

Jacksonian democracy

rence the attempts of the executive and judicial branches to increase their power.

By 1820, these notions were being expressed in more direct and forceful terms. Urban populations grew increasingly conscious of their political importance and demanded attention to their interests. The predominance of the agricultural Old South (the South of the original thirteen colonies) had declined. As a result of the Louisiana Purchase (a vast tract bought from the French in 1803) and of increased settlement in the area known as the Northwest Territory (western New York State and Ohio), a new frontier had come into existence. Life there was characterized by a rugged freedom that left little room for class distinctions. In the struggle to survive, hard work and sharp wits counted for more than birth and education. As a consequence a new democratic spirit, which eventually found its leader in Andrew Jackson (1767–1845), took shape around the principle of equality. The Jacksonian Democrats transformed the doctrines of liberalism into a more radical creed. They pronounced all (excluding slaves, American Indians, and women) politically equal, not merely in rights but in privileges. They were devoted adherents to the causes of suffrage for all white males; the election, rather than appointment, of all governmental office-holders; and the frequent rotation of men in positions of political power—a doctrine that served to put more Democratic politicians into federal office. These democratic beliefs helped encourage a spirit of unity within the United States during a period of rapid territorial expansion.

As the United States continued to acquire more territories in the West (the most notable addition resulting from the conquest of lands

"Meal Time." Between the decks on an immigrant ship to the United States in the mid–nineteenth century.

in the southwest from Mexico in 1846), it not only faced the task of binding those areas and their settlers into the nation. There was, as well, the problem of assimilating the thousands of immigrants who came to America from Europe in the first half of the century. Many were Scottish and English; for them the difficulties of adjusting to a new life in a new country were generally not difficult, since they spoke a common language with their fellow-citizens. For others the problems were far greater. For the Irish, who immigrated in great numbers, particularly during the 1840s, there was the fact of their alien religion, Roman Catholicism. For Germans and others from the Continent, there was the language barrier. The United States's policy towards its immigrants was directed against the creation of any foreign nationalist enclaves apart from the main body of its citizenry. Although foreign-language newspapers were tolerated, and immigrants were free to attend churches and social gatherings as they chose, English remained the language of the public schools, the police, the law courts, and the government. To hold a job, a person was almost always forced to learn at least some English. In this way, the United States encouraged immigrants to shed their "foreign" ways and to commit themselves to their adopted nation.

(2) immigration

If there were enclaves in the United States, they existed in the South, where the institution of slavery and the economic dependence of the planters upon England produced two distinct minorities, neither of which was to be assimilated without resort to war. During the nineteenth century, slavery had been abolished throughout much of the Western world, for both economic and humanitarian reasons. Southern planters continued to insist that without the slave system they would go bankrupt. To humanitarians they responded with arguments based upon theories of racial inferiority and upon their self-professed reputation as benevolent masters. The position of these southern spokesmen grew increasingly distasteful and unconvincing to the North. As the country opened to the west, North and South engaged in a protracted tug-of-war as to which new states were to be "free" and which "slave." Northerners were motivated by more than concern for the well-being of southern blacks. The North was industrializing fast. Capitalists there were demanding protective tariffs to assist them in their enterprises. Southerners favored free trade, since they wished to import British goods in return for the cotton they sold to the manufacturers of Lancashire.

(3) slavery and the South

The American Civil War, when it came in 1861, was a war not about the issue of slavery so much as it was about preserving the union of American states and territories. President Abraham Lincoln undertook the war to defend the unity of the United States. European governments, while never recognizing the Confederacy officially, nevertheless remained sympathetic to its cause. They hoped that the fragmentation of the United States would result in the opening up of markets for their manufactured goods, much as the dissolution of the

The Civil War

Nation-building in the West

Spanish Empire had proved a boon to European commercial interests. The victory of the North in 1865, however, insured the continued growth of the United States as a nation. The Fourteenth Amendment to the Constitution stated specifically that all were citizens of the United States, and not of an individual state or territory. In declaring that no citizen was to be deprived of life, liberty, or property without due process of law, it established that "due process" was to be defined by the national, and not the state or territorial governments.

The years following the American Civil War witnessed the binding together of the nation economically under the direction of northern private enterprise. The symbol of the North's triumph as nation-builder came with the driving of the final spike of the transcontinental Union Pacific railroad in 1869. Nation-building in Europe and the United States helped insure the continuing expansion of capitalism. Liberalism had provided a general climate of opinion and a set of attitudes toward government that encouraged industrialization. Nation-building, in its turn, produced the necessary economic units: large enough to generate the wherewithal to sustain economic growth; confident enough to enter into competition with the British Goliath.

SELECTED READINGS

• *Items so designated are available in paperback editions.*

Artz, Frederick B., *France under the Bourbon Restoration, 1814–1830,* New York, 1963. A basic survey with a good treatment of romanticism.

• Binkley, Robert C., *Realism and Nationalism, 1852–1871,* New York, 1935. An excellent synthesis.

Brunschwig, Henri, *Enlightenment and Romanticism in Eighteenth-Century Prussia,* rev. ed., Chicago, 1974.

• Craig, Gordon, *The Politics of the Prussian Army,* Oxford, 1955. Much more than the title implies. An excellent analysis of Prussian social structure and the role of the army in social reform and unification.

Deutsch, Karl W., and W. J. Folz, eds., *Nation-Building,* New York, 1963.

• Eyck, Erich, *Bismarck and the German Empire,* London, 1958. The best one-volume study of Bismarck.

Eyck, Frank, *The Frankfurt Parliament, 1848–49,* New York, 1968. A detailed study of its composition and procedure.

Ford, Guy Stanton, *Stein and the Era of Reform in Prussia, 1807–1815,* New York, 1922. An old but still valuable work on a leading Prussian reformer.

Gewehr, W. M., *The Rise of Nationalism in the Balkans, 1800–1930,* New York, 1931.

• Gleckner, R. F., and G. E. Ersco, eds., *Romanticism,* Englewood Cliffs, N.J., 1962.

Gooch, G. P., *Germany and the French Revolution,* New York, 1920. Examines the origins of reform in Germany in the aftermath of the French Revolution.

Griffith, G. O., *Mazzini: Prophet of Modern Europe*, London, 1931. The standard biography.

• Hamerow, Theodore, *Restoration, Revolution, Reaction*, Princeton, N.J., 1958. An excellent social and economic history of Germany between 1815 and 1871.

• ———, *The Social Foundations of German Unification, 1858–1871*, 2 vols., Princeton, N.J., 1969. Concentrates on economic factors which determined the solution to the unification question. An impressive synthesis.

Hayes, C. J. H., *The Historical Evolution of Modern Nationalism*, rev. ed., New York, 1968.

Holborn, Hajo, *History of Modern Germany*, Vols. II, III, New York, 1964. The best survey of German history in English.

• Kohn, Hans, *The Idea of Nationalism*, New York, 1944. A perceptive analysis.

———, *Panslavism: In History and Ideology*, South Bend, Ind., 1953.

• Langer, William L., *Political and Social Upheaval, 1832–1852*, New York, 1969.

Mack Smith, Dennis, *Garibaldi: A Great Life in Brief*, New York, 1956.

Namier, Lewis B., *1848: The Revolution of the Intellectuals*, London, 1947. A controversial analysis, highly critical of the Frankfurt Assembly.

Noyes, P. H., *Organization and Revolution: Working-Class Associations in the German Revolutions of 1848–49*, Princeton, N.J., 1966. An important monograph.

• Pflanze, Otto, *Bismarck and the Development of Germany, 1815–1871*, Princeton, N.J., 1963. An impressive analysis of Bismarck's aims and policies.

• Robertson, Priscilla, *The Revolutions of 1848: A Social History*, Princeton, N.J., 1952.

• Rosenberg, Hans, *Bureaucracy, Aristocracy, and Autocracy: The Prussian Experience, 1660–1815*, Cambridge, Mass., 1958. A difficult but valuable book explaining the forces that molded the modern Prussian state.

• Stearns, Peter N., *1848: The Revolutionary Tide in Europe*, New York, 1974.

• Taylor, A. J. P., *The Hapsburg Monarchy, 1809–1918*, rev. ed., London, 1960. An idiosyncratic account by an eminent historian.

SOURCE MATERIALS

Bismarck, Otto von, *Bismarck, the Man and the Statesman, Written and Dictated by Himself*, London, 1899. Bismarck's memoirs, written after his fall from power.

• Clausewitz, Karl von, *On War*, London, 1968. Published posthumously in 1831, this work, in reality a philosophy of war, was perceived by the Prussian military bureaucracy as a mandate for total war—for the subjugation of all interests of the state to war.

Fichte, Johann Gottlieb, *Addresses to the German Nation*, New York, 1968. Presented in 1808 while French armies occupied Prussia, these lectures helped stir a German nationalist spirit.

Schurz, Carl, *The Reminiscences of Carl Schurz*, 3 vols., New York, 1907–8. Especially valuable is Vol. I. A young German liberal in 1848 and a delegate to the Frankfurt Assembly, Schurz spent the rest of his life as an exile in the United States.

Part Six

THE WEST AT THE
WORLD'S CENTER

The years between 1870 and 1945 found the West at the center of global affairs. The industrial supremacy of western Europe and the United States gave them a combined power greater than that possessed by any nation or empire in previous times. Yet world domination was by no means accompanied by any sense of general world order. The economic might of the Western nations, while it resulted in their ability to dominate the less developed quarters of the globe, resulted, as well, in their concern lest one of their number overpower the others. The old system of the balance of power, designed to preserve peace by insuring that no one country achieved overwhelming predominance at the expense of its neighbors, was strained to the breaking point by economic rivalries that stretched around the world. Meanwhile, tensions mounted within each nation, as landed and middle classes, threatened by the possibility of social turmoil, tried to balance the mounting clamor for political concessions against their desire to retain power in their own hands. Twice during the period, in 1914 and 1939, international and domestic pressures exploded into global wars. Those wars and their results, generated by the rivalries and miscalculations of the Western nations, so sapped the strength of those nations as to depose them thereafter as the sole arbiters of the world's destinies.

POLITICS	SCIENCE & INDUSTRY

1870

First commercially practical electrical generator, 1870
Gilcrist-Thomas steel process, 1870s

Paris Commune, 1871
Kulturkampf, Germany, 1872
League of Three Emperors, 1873
Constitution for Third French Republic, 1875
End of First International, 1876
Congress of Berlin, 1878

Germ theory of disease, 1875
Invention of telephone, 1876

Triple Alliance, 1882
Berlin conference on imperialism, 1885
Second International formed, 1889
Pan-Slavism, 1890–1914

Dreyfus affair, 1894–1899

Discovery of the X-ray, 1895
Marie Curie, discovery of radium, 1898

Spanish-American War, 1898

Boer War, 1899–1902

Invention of wireless telegraph, 1899

1900

V. Lenin, *What Is to Be Done?,* 1902

First airplane flight, 1903
Ivan Pavlov, Nobel Prize for physiology, 1904
Albert Einstein, development of relativity theory, 1905–1910

Russo-Japanese War, 1904–1905
Revolution in Russia, 1905

Triple Entente, 1907
Bosnian Crisis, 1908
Revolt of the Young Turks, 1908

Model T Ford, 1908

Balkan Wars, 1912–1913

First World War, 1914–1918
Russian Revolution, 1917

Treaty of Versailles, 1919
Socialist revolution, Germany, 1919
League of Nations, 1920–1946

1920

NEP, Russia, 1921

Mussolini's March on Rome, 1922

Hitler's beer-hall putsch, 1923
New constitution, Soviet Union, 1924
Locarno agreements, 1925

Discovery of viruses, sulfa drugs, and penicillin, 1930s
World economic conference, 1933

Hitler, chancellor of Germany, 1933
New Deal, United States, 1933–1940

ECONOMICS & SOCIETY	ARTS & LETTERS	
	Impressionism in art, 1870–1900	*1870*
Growth of finance capitalism, 1880s		
Social welfare legislation, Germany, 1882–1884	Émile Zola, *Germinal,* 1885	
Sherman Anti-Trust Act, United States, 1890	Henrik Ibsen, *Hedda Gabler,* 1890	
Meline tariff, 1892	Paul Cézanne, *The Card Players,* 1890–1892	
	George Bernard Shaw, *Plays Pleasant* and *Unpleasant,* 1898	
Women's suffrage movement, England, 1900–1914	Sigmund Freud, *The Interpretation of Dreams,* 1900	*1900*
Social welfare legislation, France, 1904; 1910	Cubism in art 1905–1930	
Social welfare legislation, England, 1906–1912		
	Marcel Proust, *Remembrance of Things Past,* 1913–1918	
	Oswald Spengler, *The Decline of the West,* 1918	
	Bauhaus established, 1919	
German inflation, 1920s	Writers of the "Lost Generation," 1920–1930	*1920*
	Surrealism and Dadaism, 1920s	
	Ludwig Wittgenstein, *Tractatus Logico-philosophicus,* 1921	
	T. S. Eliot, *The Waste Land,* 1922	
	James Joyce, *Ulysses,* 1922	
Great Depression, 1929–1940	Neo-realism in art, 1930s	

POLITICS	SCIENCE & INDUSTRY
Italy conquers Ethiopia, 1935–1936	National rearmament programs, 1935
Rome-Berlin Axis, 1936	
Spanish Civil War, 1936–1939	
Germany annexes Austria, 1938	
Munich conference, 1938	
Nazi-Soviet pact, 1939	Discovery of atomic fission, 1939
Second World War, 1939–1945	
United States enters war, 1941	
Allied invasion of Normandy, 1944	
Bombing of Hiroshima and Nagasaki, 1945	First atomic bomb test, 1945
United Nations founded, 1946	

1940

ECONOMICS & SOCIETY	ARTS & LETTERS

J. M. Keynes, *General Theory of Employment, Interest, and Money,* 1936

Jean-Paul Sartre, *Being and Nothingness,* 1943

Chapter 24

THE PROGRESS OF
INDUSTRIALIZATION (1870–1914)

We have conquered for ourselves a place in the sun. It will now be my
task to see to it that this place in the sun shall remain our undisputed possession . . .

—Kaiser William II, speech, **1901**

I f most historians now speak of a second industrial revolution occurring during the years after 1870, they are quick to qualify the
term. Whatever the changes in technique and in scope—and they
were significant—they do not compare to those which characterized
the first revolution—*the* Industrial Revolution. There is, however,
good reason to distinguish a second period of industrial development
and advance from the first. Successful nation-building meant that the
years 1870–1914 would be characterized by sharply increased international economic rivalries, culminating in a scramble after imperial territories in Africa and Asia. Britain, if it did not actually surrender its
industrial lead during this period, failed to counter with any real success the energetic and determined challenges from Germany and the
United States to its constantly decreasing lead. New technology, particularly in the fields of metals, chemicals, and electricity, resulted in
new products. Improving standards of living produced greater demand, which, in turn, increased the volume of production. And the
need for increased production called forth significant reorganization to
provide a freer supply of capital and to ensure a more efficient labor
force. It is these changes that distinguish the second stage of industrialization from the first, and therefore warrant its separate treatment.
Yet they must be perceived as stemming not only from those economic conditions which were the result of the first stage, but also
from the more general political, social, and cultural climate whose history we have been tracing.

*A second industrial
revolution*

In analyzing the progress of industrialization, we shall deal with changes in three major areas: in technology; in scope and scale of production; and in the reorganization of the capitalist system. Finally we shall examine the phenomenon of late–nineteenth-century imperialism, and consider the extent to which that phenomenon can be attributed to increasing economic and industrial rivalries.

1. NEW TECHNOLOGIES

Technology in steel

A most important technological change in this period resulted in the mass production of steel. The advantages of steel over iron—a result of steel's lower carbon content—are its hardness, its malleability, and its strength. Steel can keep its cutting edge, where iron cannot; it can be worked more easily than iron, which is brittle and which, if it is to be used industrially, must almost always be cast (that is, poured into molds). And steel, because of its strength in proportion to its weight and volume, makes a particularly adaptable construction material. These advantages had been recognized by craftsmen for centuries. Until steel could be produced both cheaply and in mass, however, the advantages remained more theoretical than real. Two inventions, during the earlier years of the Industrial Revolution, had reduced the price and increased the output of steel to some degree. The crucible technique, discovered in the eighteenth century in England, called for the heating of relatively small amounts of iron ore to a point at which foreign matter could be removed by skimming, the carbon content reduced, and a proper proportion of carbon distributed evenly throughout the finished product. Although individual crucibles were not large, holding on the average no more than forty-five to sixty pounds, they could be poured together to produce steel ingots of several tons. A century later, in the early 1840s, two Germans adapted the puddling process, used in the production of iron, to the manufacture of steel. While it did not produce steel as hard as that made in crucibles, it reduced its price considerably.

Bessemer, Siemens-Martin, and Gilchrist-Thomas systems

Not until the invention of the Bessemer and Siemens-Martin processes, however, could steel begin to compete with iron. In the 1850s, an Englishman, Henry Bessemer, discovered that by blowing air into and through the molten metal he could achieve a more exact degree of decarbonization in much shorter time, and with far larger quantities of ore, than was possible with either the crucible or puddling methods. Bessemer soon found, however, that his "converters" were incapable of burning off sufficient quantities of phosphorous; and phosphorous in anything but the smallest quantities made the metal unworkable. A partial solution was achieved with the introduction of non-phosphoric hematite ores. Yet this was of little long-term use in most European countries, where supplies of hematite ore were not

The Manufacture of Steel by the Bessemer Process. An 1875 engraving.

abundant. This same problem plagued the German inventors Frederick and William Siemens, whose furnace made use of waste gases to increase heat. Not until Pierre Martin, a Frenchman, discovered that the introduction of scrap iron into the mix would induce proper decarbonization, could the Siemens furnace be used to make steel commercially. And not until the late 1870s was the problem of phosphoresence solved for both the Bessemer and the Siemens-Martin processes. The solution was a simple one, discovered by two Englishmen, a clerk and a chemist: Sidney Gilchrist Thomas and his cousin Sidney Gilchrist. They introduced limestone into the molten iron to combine with the phosphorous, which was then siphoned from the mix. And they lined the converter in such a way that the slag was prevented from eating away the walls and releasing phosphorous back into the molten metal.

Together, these three processes revolutionized the production of steel. Although the use of iron did not end overnight, steel soon moved into the lead. In the British shipbuilding industry, for example, steel had overtaken iron by 1890. In part because Siemens-Martin was particularly suited to the manufacture of steel plates used in shipbuilding, that process dominated the manufacture of steel in Britain, where shipbuilding was a major industry. Bessemer steel, which could be manufactured more cheaply and in larger plants, was more commonly produced on the Continent and in America. The result was a particular increase in the production of German steel: by 1901, German converters were capable of pouring an average of 34,000 tons, compared to Britain's 21,750. By 1914 Germany was producing twice as much steel as Britain, and the United States twice as much as Germany.

Increased steel production

A second and equally important technological development resulted in the availability of electric power for industrial, commercial, and domestic use. Electricity's particular advantages result from the fact

Electricity

that it can be easily transmitted as energy over long distances, and from the fact that it can be converted into other forms of energy—heat and light, for example. Although electricity had, of course, been discovered prior to the first Industrial Revolution, its advantages could not have been put to general use without a series of inventions which occurred during the nineteenth century. Of these, some of the most important were the invention of the chemical battery by the Italian Alessandro Volta in 1800; of electromagnetic induction by the Englishman Michael Faraday in 1831; of the electromagnetic generator in 1866; of the first commercially practical generator of direct current in 1870; and of alternators and transformers capable of producing high-voltage alternating current in the 1880s. These inventions meant that by the end of the century it was possible to send electric current from large power stations over comparatively long distances. Electric power could be manufactured by water—hence cheaply—and delivered from its source to the place where it was needed.

The uses of electricity

Once it had been delivered to its destination, the power was converted and put to use in myriad ways. Households quickly became one of the major users of electrical power. The invention by Thomas Edison of the incandescent filament lamp—or light bulb—was crucial in this regard. As individual houses were electrified to receive the power that was to be transformed into light, consumer demand for electricity resulted in further expansion of the electrical industry. Demand for electrical power was increasing in the industrial sector as well. Electric motors soon began to power subways, tramways, and, eventually, long-distance railways. Electricity made possible the development of new techniques in the chemical and metallurgical industries. Most important, electricity helped to transform the work patterns of the factory. Heavy steam engines had made equipment and machinery stationery; electric motors meant that comparatively lightweight power tools could be moved—often by hand—to the site of a particular piece of work. The result was far greater flexibility in terms of factory organization. Smaller workshop industries benefited as well; they could accommodate themselves to electrically powered motors and tools in a way they could not to steam.

An Early Dynamo Used for Lighting

Other technological advances

Steel and electricity were only two of the most important areas where technological changes were taking place. The chemical industry was significantly advanced by developments in the manufacture of alkali and organic compounds. Demand for alkali had increased with the demand for soaps and textiles, and with the changes in the manufacturing process of paper, which required large amounts of bleach. An older, more expensive and wasteful technique used extensively by the British was superseded after 1880 by a new process perfected by the Belgian Ernest Solvay. The result was, again, a rapid overtaking of the British by the Germans in the production not only of alkalis but of sulphuric acid, a by-product recoverable in the Solvay process, and used in the manufacture of fertilizers, petroleum refining, iron, steel, and textiles. In the field of organic compounds, the impetus for further discovery came as a result of demand for synthetic dyes. Although the British and French were the first successful pioneers in this area, the Germans once more moved ahead to a commanding lead by 1900. At the turn of the century German firms controlled about 90 percent of the world market.

The need for more and more power to meet increasing industrial demands resulted not only in developments in the field of electricity, already noted, but in the improved design and expanded capacity of steam engines. The most noteworthy invention in this area was the steam turbine, which permitted steam engines to run at speeds heretofore unobtainable. Internal combustion engines made their appearance during this period as well. Their major advantage lay in their efficiency; i.e., they could be powered automatically, and did not need to be stoked by hand like steam engines. Once liquid fuels—petroleum and distilled gasoline—became available, as they did increasingly with the discovery of oil fields in Russia, Borneo, and Texas about 1900, the internal combustion engine took hold as a serious competitor to steam. By 1914 most navies had converted from coal to oil, as had domestic steamship companies. The automobile and the airplane, both still in their infancies, made little impact upon the industrial world, however, before 1914.

2. CHANGES IN SCOPE AND SCALE

These technological changes must be understood as occurring against a background of—indeed in part as a result of—a generally increased standard of living for the majority of men and women in the Western

Improved engines

The First Successful Airplane Flight

The Interior of a Berlin Department Store, 1882

Increase in domestic consumption

world. There were, of course, still a great many very poor people, both in cities and in the country: casual laborers, the unemployed, those in declining industries and trades. Those skilled workers and their families whose real incomes did rise as a result of deflation and higher wage rates did not experience anything like the rate of increase enjoyed by most of the middle class. Nor could they expect to avoid altogether the stretches of unemployment that made life so chaotic for so many of their unskilled co-workers. Yet despite these qualifications, it is fair to say that more people enjoyed a higher standard of living than ever before. And a higher standard of living produced the demand for an increase in consumer goods.

New consumers

Increased consumption of manufactured goods was by no means uniform; it was higher in urban and industrialized areas than in the country. But even in the country, traditional thrift was challenged as farmers and their wives journeyed by train into the cities, saw what they had not imagined they could have, and then decided they must spend their savings to have it. To accommodate the new and largely middle-class consumers, department stores and chain stores designed their products and their advertising to make shopping as easy and inviting as possible. Behind large plate-glass windows goods were displayed attractively and temptingly; periodic sales encouraged householders to purchase "bargains"; catalogues and charge accounts made it easy for customers to spend money without leaving home. The result was an enormous increase in the volume of manufactured consumer goods produced for this rapidly expanding consumer market. Bicycles, clocks, appliances, furnishings—these and a great many other things were now being made in large quantities, and with new materials (cheap steel) and new techniques (electrical power). Many of these products were designed according to the correct assumption that women were more and more responsible for household purchases. Therefore, goods were fashioned to appeal directly to women, or to the children for whom women were responsible. The foot-powered sewing machine was a particular case in point—the first domestic appliance. Isaac Singer, the American responsible for the development of the treadle and straight needle in the 1850s, was as much an entrepreneur as an inventor. He was a pioneer in the field of advertising and promotion, encouraging purchase on the installment plan and providing courses for would-be domestic seamstresses.

Sewing machines changed far more than the sewing habits of housewives, however. They were cheap, lightweight tools, easily installed and easily operated. Workshop masters could set up several, employ a handful of young women at very low wages, and make a profit turning out cheap ready-made clothing in response to increasing markets. Here is just one of the ways in which the scale of manufacturing altered during the latter part of the nineteenth century, both demand and technology conspiring to produce the change. In metal-working, hard-edged steel allowed for the rapid cutting of patterns, which reduced price, which, in turn, encouraged the manufacture of a variety of inexpensive metal goods—kitchenware, for example. The sewing machine led to the development of other new tools that helped cut costs in the clothing industry: button-holers, lace-makers, leather-stitchers. Whereas it took one cobbler ten hours to make a pair of shoes in 1850 by hand, by the end of the century it took a team of cobblers but a few hours to produce ten pairs using machinery. In

The web of industrial change

Advertisement for a German Sewing Machine. The company proclaims the machine's versatility: unsurpassed for use in the home as well as in the workshop or factory.

Industrial expansion and consolidation

Effects of increase in scale on workers: (1) relearning

(2) efficiency

textiles, improved engines doubled the pace of mules and looms. In heavy industry, steam hammers performed the work of many men more precisely and with greater speed than before. New equipment of this sort was expensive. As a result, in heavy industry, it was the larger companies that prospered, and in the course of their prosperity, they grew even larger.

In all the countries of Europe, and in the United States, the pattern is one of expansion and consolidation. This was especially the case in Germany, where in the iron and steel industry nearly 75 percent of those employed worked in factories of a thousand or more, and where over 90 percent of the electrical equipment manufactured was made in factories with over fifty employees. Machinery was thus altering the scale of manufacturing in two directions at once. In the clothing industry, entrepreneurs could use inexpensive machines to make small workshops turn a profit. In steel foundries, the cost of new equipment forced small competitors to the wall, with the result that the foundries grew very much bigger.

The increase in the scale of manufacturing had important and often disturbing consequences for workers. The most obvious was the need for men and women to relearn their trades. They were compelled to adapt their older skills to the new machines. Very often this adaptation resulted in a loss of either pay or prestige, or both. Most machine work was not skilled work. A trainee could "pick up" a trade in a week or so. Workers who had prided themselves on a particular skill and had been paid according to their ability to perform it, had to face the fact that industrial change was not only forcing them to relearn, but was compelling them to tell themselves that their new "skills"—if they could be called that—did not amount to very much. For example, when the machine itself could cut metal with infinitesimal accuracy, there was far less need than there had been previously for the skills of a human "fitter." Even if workers were not forced to relearn in these ways in order to accommodate to increased scale, they often had at least to accommodate to factory reorganization and rationalization. In workplaces where the hand-carrying of materials had been a major factor in their final cost, mechanization to reduce that cost would produce a bewildering series of changes. Electric cranes, used together with huge magnets in the iron and steel industries, increased the speed with which goods could be moved, and demanded that workers defer to whatever changes their introduction might entail.

A second—and even more important—effect of the change in scale was the constant demand for further efficiency. The greater the scale of the operation, the more important it became to eliminate waste. One minute lost in the production of every ten pairs of shoes might not make much difference if only fifty pairs were produced in a day. But if hundreds were being made, it became crucial, in the eyes of management, to see that those minutes were no longer lost. In facto-

Technological Change and Production Speed-Up. An early assembly line of the Ford Motor Company, United States, 1913. Car bodies slid down the ramp and were attached to the chassis as they passed through the line below. One thousand cars were produced each day.

ries where capital had been spent on new machinery, the owners, conscious of the cost of their investment, increased output in order to realize a profit on their recent investment. In factories where older machinery was still in use, owners believed that the only way they could remain competitive with modernized operations was by extracting all they could from their less productive equipment. In both cases, workers were pressed to produce more and more. One result of this drive for efficiency was a restructuring of wage scales. Prior to this period, although there had been serious wage disputes, both management and labor appeared content to bargain from the traditional notion of "a fair day's wage for a fair day's work." Definitions of what was fair naturally varied. But the level of individual performance was generally set by custom. What workers produced in the course of a day continued to determine what they were expected to produce. From about 1870 onward, however, expectations and procedures began to change. Periodic economic depressions in the last quarter of the nineteenth century saw profits fall before wages. This pattern caused employers to insist on greater individual productivity from their employees. It was no longer enough to work at a job with customary speed. Workers were now asked to produce as much as the owners thought they were potentially capable of producing.

But who was to determine that potential? That question plagued industrial relations during these years. Employers, who were adopting precision tools in order to increase production, grew more and more convinced that worker output could be gauged with a like precision as well. The foremost theoretician of worker efficiency and what was called scientific management of labor was the American Frederick W.

Scientific management

Taylor (1865–1915). Taylor devised a three-step system whereby a worker's output could be "scientifically" measured, a system which, he argued, would provide a precise method for the determination of wage scales. First, he observed, timed, and analyzed workers' movements on the job, in order to determine how long a particular task should take. Second, he figured the labor costs of these movements. Third, he produced "norms," or general standards, which all workers were expected to maintain. These norms were invariably higher than those which had prevailed under traditional conditions.

Piece rates

In order to encourage workers to accept these increased standards, Taylor urged all factory-owners to adopt piece rates (i.e., payment to workers according to the specific amount produced) rather than hourly or daily wages. Payment by piece rate was already a growing practice in many European and American factories. In theory, at least, workers were not opposed to this method of payment; they reasoned that their only hope for a share in increasing output lay in their chance to be paid directly for what they made. But when they were told that their pay would not increase unless they measured up to predetermined—and, to their mind, unrealistic—norms, they rebelled. They argued that rates were set according to the performance of the speediest workers. Even though workers might earn more money if they agreed to the new rates, they resented the intrusion of management upon the pace of their working lives. Despite this opposition, scientific management spread throughout the industrialized West. In England, the United States, and on the Continent, particularly in the engineering trades, factory after factory subscribed to the new gospel. Where it could not entirely succeed in introducing "efficiency" on the shop floor, management proceeded to rationalize its own procedures. Accounting departments were expanded, and encouraged to attend closely to the problem of cost control in all areas of production and distribution. These reforms were no more than a reflection of the general move in the direction of greater efficiency. They were brought on by the vastly increased scale of production, the need to reduce waste wherever possible, and the desire to derive maximum profits from the elimination of unnecessary motions and unproductive habits.

3. THE NEW CAPITALISM

*The growth of
incorporation*

Responding to the increased scope of production and to the consequent pressures for further efficiency, the institutions of capitalism began to reorganize toward the end of the nineteenth century. Hitherto, most firms had been small or at most middle-sized; now, as firms grew and their need for capital increased, they began to incorporate. Limited liability laws, enacted by most countries in the course of the century, worked to encourage this incorporation. "Limited liability" meant that an individual owning stock in a particular corporation could be held liable only for the amount of his or her shares, should that corporation bankrupt itself. Once insured in this way, many thousands of middle-class men and women considered corporate investment a safe and financially promising way of making money for themselves. A stockholding, "rentier" class emerged, brought into existence by the willingness of governments to encourage capitalism through friendly legislation, and by the desire of capitalist businessmen to expand their industrial undertakings to meet increased demands. More and more companies incorporated. In doing so, their management tended to be removed from the direct control of family founders or of company-based boards of directors. The influence of bankers and financiers, often situated in cities far removed from the factories they invested in, grew accordingly. These men were not investing their own money but the money of their clients; their power to stimulate or to discourage the growth of particular industries and enterprises encouraged a kind of impersonal "finance" capital.

Corporate organization on a large scale facilitated the spread of industrial unification. Some industries—steel, for example—combined vertically. Steel companies, to ensure uninterrupted production, acquired their own coal and iron mines. By doing so, they could guarantee themselves a supply of raw materials at attractive prices. Often the same steel companies would obtain control of companies whose products were made of steel: for example, shipyards or railway factories. Now they would not only possess a ready stock of raw materials but an equally ready market for their manufactured products—steel plates, steel rails, whatever they might be. Such vertical integration was only

Vertical organization

The New York Stock Exchange, 1893

possible as a result of the money available for investment through the institutions of finance capital.

A second form of corporate organization was a horizontal formation: the cartel. These were combinations of individual companies producing the same kind of goods, joined for the purpose of controlling, if not eliminating, competition. Since their products were identical, an identical price could be charged. Companies involved in the production of coal and steel were especially suited to the organization of cartels because of the costs of initial capitalization. It is very expensive to build, equip, and man a steel foundry; thus there were relatively few of them. And because there were few, they were the more easily organized into a combine. Cartels were particularly strong in Germany; less so in France, where there was not as much heavy industry, where the tradition of the small family firm was particularly entrenched, and where there was long-standing opposition to competition in the form of price-cutting and general intra-industrial warfare. In Britain, though some cartels were formed, continuing subscription to the policy of free trade meant that companies would find it difficult to maintain fixed prices. How could they do so if they could not exclude, by means of a tariff, foreign competitors who wanted to undersell them? Germany had abandoned the policy of free trade in 1879; the United States, where cartels were known as trusts, did the same after the Civil War, though not all at once. Britain, however, clung to free trade until well into the twentieth century.

Defenders of the cartel argued that the elimination of competition brought more stable prices and more continuous employment. They pointed out as well that cartels almost always reduced the cost of production. Opponents questioned, however, whether those reduced costs were reflected in lower prices, or, as they charged, in higher stockholder profits. Critics of cartels were vocal in the United States, where the so-called captains of industry, most prominently the financier J. P. Morgan (1837–1913), were attacked as a new breed of feudal barons. The Sherman Anti-Trust Act was passed by Congress in 1890 to curb the practice of industrial combination. It had little effect in retarding the process, however, until the trust-busting presidency of Theodore Roosevelt (1901–1906). Elsewhere in the West, corporate cartels and combines of various sorts were either encouraged or at least tolerated as a natural stage in the growth of a capitalist system that, it was argued, was showering benefits on all classes of society.

J. P. Morgan

4. INTERNATIONAL COMPETITION: BRITAIN VS. GERMANY

Throughout the period we have been examining, Britain and Germany were locked in industrial competition. By 1914, both the United States and Germany were outproducing Britain in a number of areas. Yet the German challenge was, for the British, the more significant. Industrial competition with Germany helped reshape international political alliances at the end of the century. Britain, moving to align itself with its ancient enemy France against the Germans, found itself engaged in a contest of naval superiority with the latter, determined that in that field the British would not lose their age-old advantage to the upstart challenger.

To what degree did the Germans succeed in overtaking the British? By 1914, Britain's industrial-commercial day was by no means over. The volume of German trade at the turn of the century was no more than 60 percent as great. Britain, more mature industrially than Germany, was shifting resources to the service sector of the economy, into areas such as the wider distribution of goods. If Britain's output of manufactured goods did no more than double between 1870 and 1913, as compared to Germany's sixfold increase, it was in part for this reason. Nor should one suppose that all areas of German industry were functioning as efficient, modernized, and technologically advanced units. For every up-to-date chemical plant, for every thriving steel mill, there were many smaller workshops where manufacturing took place on little more than a domestic scale. Having said this, however, the fact remains that the Germans *were* a powerful threat to the British. Even before 1870, Germany had ceased to provide a ready market for British manufactures; the Germans were supplying their own needs. After 1870, Germany began to export to the rest of the world. Moving into markets that the British had considered exclusively their own, German salesmen promoted German goods in Australia, South America, China, and in Britain itself. In fields such as the manufacture of organic chemicals and electrical equipment, Germany outsold Britain across the globe.

How can Germany's success and, perhaps more important, Britain's inability to counter it be explained? To attempt an answer to the latter question first: Britain was handicapped because it had been the first nation to industrialize. Because of the capital they had invested in older factories and equipment, the British were reluctant to enter new fields or to exploit new methods. For example, because the British had constructed plants to manufacture alkali by an earlier, less efficient process, they found themselves trapped into continuing to produce in that way after the Solvay process had been discovered. Rather than make the expensive switch, British manufacturers attempted to make their alkali more competitive by cutting costs and improving worker efficiency. But when further refinements were introduced in the 1890s, British output not only failed to keep pace with German and also American increases, but actually decreased. The same difficulties arose with steel. Here again Britain was hampered by the problem of priority. Because the British were the first to industrialize, their manufacturing centers took shape in accordance with the scale of early- and mid–nineteenth-century production. Now there was need for

Interior of a Krupp Steel Mill, Essen, Germany

large tracts of land, close to transportation, to accommodate steel mills. Because of the cramped layout of Britain's industrial cities, it could not build mills as large as those in Germany or the United States. The result was that by 1900 the largest British steel mills were no bigger than the average-sized mills in Germany. Even new plants built for other manufacturing purposes in Britain were only a third as large as those constructed by its major rival. Because German plants were big, and because, therefore, they represented a large investment of capital, those who managed them did all they could to ensure their efficient operation. They rationalized design and standardized parts to an extent the British, with their smaller plants, continued to believe unnecessary. Smaller firms tended to receive smaller and more specialized orders which did not encourage standardization. Although standardization was accomplished by 1914 in Britain in some industries—notably iron and steel—in many others it remained more the exception than the rule.

(2) attitudes   Britain's industrial lead, which froze its urban areas into obsolete patterns and thus prevented growth, froze British attitudes as well. Because they had come so far so fast, the British had grown complacent. Nowhere is this fact more clearly reflected than in the British attitude toward education. If the achievements of the first Industrial Revolution—for example, the steam engine, the spinning jenny—were the result of what might be called creative tinkering, those of the second revolution were the product of a close and fruitful union of pure science with technology. Achievement now depended on a generally literate work-force, a trained body of mechanics, a scientifically grounded body of technicians, and a corps of highly trained, creative scientists. Germany was producing these cadres; Britain was not.

Only in 1870 was a system of public elementary education instituted in Britain, and not until ten years later was it made compulsory. In Germany, compulsory education dated from the eighteenth century. The British governing class believed the primary purpose of education was social control: teaching a boy or girl not only how to read and write, but to accept his or her particular place within the social structure. Though German elementary education was authoritarian in many respects as well, the fact that it had begun earlier and was directly joined to systems of secondary education encouraged the development of abilities; it was in this respect far less wasteful than the British. As Britain lagged in the area of elementary education, it lagged in the development of scientific and technological laboratories and training centers. In Germany, the state established an elaborate network of such technical institutions; in Britain there were almost none before the First World War.

Complacency was the major reason for this lack. The British tended to believe, wrongly, that practical experience and on-the-job training would produce the skills necessary to keep abreast of change. In addition, the British upper middle class convinced itself that the goal of education was not the production of creative technologists but of "gentlemen." Fathers who had made their fortunes as entrepreneurs during the first Industrial Revolution sent their sons to private boarding schools and to the ancient universities of Oxford and Cambridge to receive a "gentleman's" education—training in Greek and Latin, primarily. Those sons, whose creative talents might otherwise have been channeled into science and technology, chose careers in politics, or in the imperial or domestic bureaucracies instead. The result was a severe narrowing of the pool of creative technologists and dynamic entrepreneurs. There were fewer men than in either Germany or the United States interested in organizing the increasingly large amounts of capital necessary to engage in industrial expansion. It was easier to invest money overseas than to undertake the revitalization of various enterprises at home. A suspicion of what was new, encouraged by the British tendency to rely upon practical experience of the past, prevented Britain from rising in more than a fitful way to the German challenge.

Complacency

5. INTERNATIONAL COMPETITION: IMPERIALISM

The rivalry between Britain and Germany was only the most intense aspect of international competitiveness during the last decades of the nineteenth century. As nations proceeded with the business of industrialization, their search for markets brought them into direct opposition with one another. One result was that the dogma of free trade was abandoned by all save Britain. As we have seen, the Germans

A global economy

rejected the policy of low tariffs in 1879. Austria and Russia had already done so. Spain instituted new scales of import duties in 1877 and again in 1891. In France, two decades of gradual abandonment were climaxed by the passage of the Méline Tariff in 1892. Although individual nations attempted to isolate themselves from each other in this way, developments in international economics mandated the continuing growth and development of an interlocking, worldwide system of manufacturing, trade, and finance. For example, the general adoption by western Europe and the United States of the gold standard meant that the currencies of the so-called civilized world could be readily exchanged with each other against the measure of a common standard—the international price of gold. Hence countries needing to import from the United States, for example, did not have to sell goods directly to that country. They could sell to South America, exchange the money they received for gold, and then buy from America.

"Invisible" exports

Almost all European countries, dependent on vast supplies of raw materials to sustain their rate of industrial production, imported more than they exported. To avoid the mounting deficits that would otherwise have resulted from this practice, they relied upon "invisible" exports: i.e., shipping, insurance, and interest on money lent or invested. The extent of Britain's exportations in these areas was far greater than that of any other country. London was the money market of the world, to which would-be borrowers looked for assistance before turning elsewhere. By 1914, Britain had $20 billion invested overseas, compared with the $8.7 of the French and the $6 billion of the Germans. The insurance firm of Lloyds of London serviced clients around the world. The British merchant fleet transported the manufactured goods and raw materials of every trading nation. It was the volume of its "invisible" exports that permitted Britain to remain faithful to the doctrine of free trade while other European nations were forced to institute tariffs.

Effects on Africa and Asia

The competition between the principal economic powers of this worldwide marketplace affected not only their relationships with each other but also with those less developed areas upon which they were increasingly dependent for both raw materials and markets. Some of those areas, such as India and China, were the seats of ancient empires. Others, such as central Africa, sheltered less complex tribal soicieities. No matter what the nature of the indigenous civilization, the intrusion upon it of modern science and technology, systematic wage labor, financial and legal institutions caused enormous disruption. Though drawn into the world economy, these areas did not draw from it the benefits that the West did. Native industries such as Indian textile spinning and weaving stood no chance in competition with the factory-made products of Manchester. African herdsmen and hunters endured the disruption of their living habits by the activities of European ranchers and miners. Men who had made their living as boatmen and carters lost their livelihood to the railways constructed by Western nations. New jobs there might be; but they were jobs worked according to a Western style, dictated by Western economic demands, and threatened by Western economic disorders. In great measure the workers of this emerging world were assuming the role of a global unskilled working class under the hegemony of Western capitalism.

With this global background before us it is easier to understand the patterns of late–nineteenth-century imperialism. Imperialism we shall define simply as the domination of one people by another. So defined, imperialism had existed throughout the nineteenth century. The French had penetrated Algeria and the British, India. In other parts of the world, where Western powers did not govern directly, they often exercised an indirect influence so powerful as to preclude "native" defiance. When the West "opened" China beginning in 1834, it left the Chinese in nominal charge of their state. But it insured that affairs would be conducted to its advantage and within its "sphere of influence." Britain added to its "informal" empire in this way in South America, Africa, and south and east Asia.

Imperialism defined

As time passed, and rivalries increased, European powers moved with greater frequency and determination to control both the government and the economy of underdeveloped nations and territories. Although the primary reasons for the new imperialism were political and economic, support for imperial policy was motivated by a variety of sentiments. Some argued that it was Europe's duty to civilize—or to Christianize—the "barbaric" and "heathen" quarters of the globe. To combat slave-trading, famine, filth, and illiteracy seemed to many legitimate reason for invading the heart of Africa and the jungles of Asia. Hundreds of Europeans gave up comfortable middle-class lives to participate in what was without question a selfless mission. Others supported imperialism because the policy allowed them to celebrate their country's power. Men, women, and children took pleasure in pointing to those remote areas on the map colored with their particular hue. It was somehow reassuring to know that the sun never set on the British Empire.

Reasons for the new
imperialism

Those in charge of the imperial building process, however, although they welcomed support from whatever quarter and for whatever reason, decided policy in response to a combination of political and economic considerations, and as a corollary to the process of nation-building. National security and the preservation of a general balance of power were issues never far from the forefront of politicians' thinking and planning. Britain's domination of Egypt in the 1880s was the result, in large measure, of its fear of what might occur in the Near East should large portions of the decaying Ottoman Empire fall into Russian hands. Britain had purchased 44 percent of the shares in the Suez Canal Company in 1875, and considered the waterway a strategic lifeline to the east. The canal had been built by the French under the direction of the engineer Ferdinand de Lesseps. Begun in 1859 and completed in 1869, it was expected to assist France in its bid for com-

The politics of
imperialism

mercial expansion to the East. Britain obtained its shares from the spendthrift khedive (viceroy) of Egypt at a time when he was threatened with bankruptcy. When, in 1882, nationalist rebels protested continuing British intervention in the internal affairs of Egypt, the British claimed they had no choice but to bombard the port of Alexandria and place the Egyptian ruler under their protection. A continuing British presence in Egypt, and the willingness of the British government to support Egyptian claims to the Upper Nile, worried the French, who were growing to fear Britain's political domination of the entire African continent. Moving to correct what they perceived as a severe political imbalance, the French challenged the British and at Fashoda, in the Sudan, came close to war in 1898. The British called the French bluff, however, and war was averted. The power struggle over the Suez, Egypt, and the Sudan provides an excellent example of the manner in which international politics was directly related to the advancement of imperialism.

The economics of imperialism

Equally important as an explanation for imperialism are the facts of late–nineteenth-century world economics. There are those who have argued that imperialism was the result of the need for industrial Europe to invest surplus capital. This argument makes some sense when applied to Britain, about half of whose total of $20 billion in foreign investments was at work within its empire. But it fails to explain the imperial ambitions of the Germans and the French, who had much less capital to invest, and who invested that which they had in non-imperial enterprises. Only a very small portion of German capital was invested in German colonies by 1914; about one-fifth of French capital was so invested. The French had more capital in Russia, hoping to stabilize that ally against the Germans, than in all their colonial possessions.

A more important economic reason for imperial expansion lay in Europe's continuing need for imports. Demand for raw materials, far

Dredges and Elevators at Work on the Construction of the Suez Canal, 1869

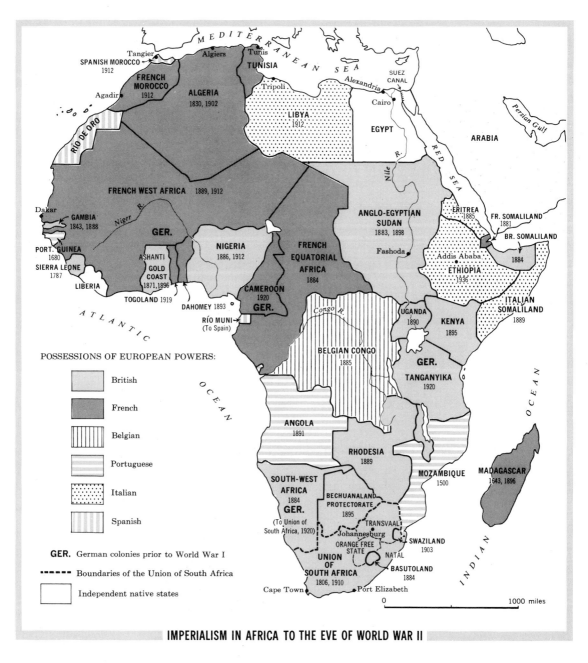

POSSESSIONS OF EUROPEAN POWERS:

British

French

Belgian

Portuguese

Italian

Spanish

GER. German colonies prior to World War I

- - - - Boundaries of the Union of South Africa

Independent native states

IMPERIALISM IN AFRICA TO THE EVE OF WORLD WAR II

more than the need to spend surplus capital, made colonies a necessary investment and imperialism, therefore, a worthwhile policy. Certainly Europe, and particularly Britain, continued to need more and more markets for manufactured goods. Yet those areas into which the imperially minded nations penetrated after 1870, though they afforded their colonial masters an opportunity to increase exports to some degree, were generally too poor to answer fully the market needs of Europe's manufacturers. In 1914, despite imperialism, the industrial

The need for imports

*The colonization of
Africa*

countries remained their own best customers. Economics, although an important explanation for the rise of imperialism, is by no means the only one.

Imperial competition centered in Africa. Germans pressed inward from the east; Frenchmen from the west. The Portuguese schemed to connect the ancient colonies of Angola, on the west, with Mozambique, on the east. Most active among the European powers during this initial period of late–nineteenth-century colonization was a privately financed group of Belgians under the leadership of that country's king, Leopold II. In association with H. M. Stanley, an American newspaperman and explorer, Leopold and a group of financiers founded the International Congo Association in 1878, which negotiated treaties with chieftains that opened the Congo River basin to commercial exploitation. A conference, called in Berlin in 1885 and attended by most European nations and the United States, attempted to establish certain ground rules for the game of imperial acquisition. The Congo was declared a Free State, under the trusteeship of Leopold (the first example of this later familiar device of protecting "backward" peoples). A European nation with holdings on the African coast was declared to have first rights to territory in the interior behind those coastal regions. Those rights, however, could be sustained only by what was termed "real" occupation—that is, the presence on the ground of either administrators or troops. The scramble was on! Occupation was accompanied by the exploitation of native labor. Agreements reached with local chieftains, whom the Europeans courted, authorized the employment of men and women as laborers under conditions little better than slavery. Often forced to live in compounds apart from their families, Africans were victimized by a system which rooted out prevailing custom without attempting to establish anything like a new civilization in its place.

The scramble for territory

The division of the geographical spoils proceeded apace. The Portuguese increased their hold in Angola and Mozambique. The Italians invaded Somaliland and Eritrea. They attempted to extend their controls to Ethiopia, but were repulsed by an army of 80,000 Ethiopians, the first instance of a major victory by native Africans over whites. Germany came relatively late to the game. Bismarck was reluctant to engage in an enterprise which, he believed, would do little to profit the empire either politically or economically. Eventually concluding, however, that they could not afford to let other powers divide the continent between them, the Germans established colonies in German East Africa, in the Cameroons and Togo on the west coast, and in the desertlike and economically valueless territory of South West Africa. The French controlled large areas in West Africa and, in the Red Sea, the port of Obok. It was to further their plan for an east-west link that the French had risked challenging the British at Fashoda. That scheme, however, fell afoul of Britain's need to dominate Egypt, and

"The Rhodes Colossus." The ambitions of Cecil Rhodes, the driving force behind British imperialism in South Africa, is satirized in this cartoon, which appeared in *Punch*.

of its plans for a north-south connection through the African continent.

Cecil Rhodes, the English entrepreneur and imperial visionary, promoted the notion of a Capetown-to-Cairo railway both before and after his assumption of the prime-ministership of the Cape Colony in 1890. His plans were thwarted in the south, however, by the presence of two independent neighboring republics, the Transvaal and the Orange Free State, both inhabited by descendents of the original Dutch settlers in South Africa. These Boers—the Dutch word for "farmers"—had fled from the British in the Cape Colony and established themselves in their agricultural states in defiant opposition to the freebooting and exploitationist spirit of the British economic adventurers who had driven them from the Cape. When diamonds and gold were discovered in the Transvaal in 1886, the tension between the British and the Boers grew. As British prospectors and entrepreneurs moved in, the Boers refused to pass laws permitting the exploitation of their resources by foreign firms. They also taxed the interlopers heavily. Rhodes retaliated by attempting to force a war with the republics. His first try, the dispatching of a force of irregular volunteers under the command of Dr. L. S. Jameson in 1895, failed to

The Boer War

Boer Commandos Under Louis Botha. Botha became the first prime minister of the Union of South Africa following the Boer War.

provoke a conflict, but precipitated general censure on the British for harassing a peaceful neighbor. Rhodes was forced to resign as prime minister of the Cape Colony in 1896. War broke out in 1899. Its course, however, did not run according to British plans. The Boers proved tough fighters. It took three years to secure an armistice; it took further long months and resort to brutal policies such as detention camps and farm-burning to bring the resilient republicans to heel. The major consequence of the Boer War was to reduce Britain's stature in the eyes of its own citizens and in the eyes of the world.

Britain in India

Britain's imperial record in India was more distinguished than it was in Africa. The "informal" rule of the commercially motivated East India Company had proved ineffective in 1857, when native Indian troops and a large number of other disaffected elements within the subcontinent rebelled in what the British chose to call "The Indian Mutiny," but which was in fact a far more serious and deep-seated challenge to foreign control. Henceforth the British determined to rule directly. But at the same time, they decided to rule through the Indian upper classes, and not, as in the past, in opposition to them. Although instruction in British-sponsored schools continued in English, Indian customs were tolerated as they had not been before, and princes and their bureaucracies were incorporated as protectorates into the general scheme of government. A class of westernized, and yet devotedly Indian, civil servants and businessmen thus emerged by the end of the nineteenth century, trained by the British yet burdened by no sense of obligation to their tutors. This group provided the leader-

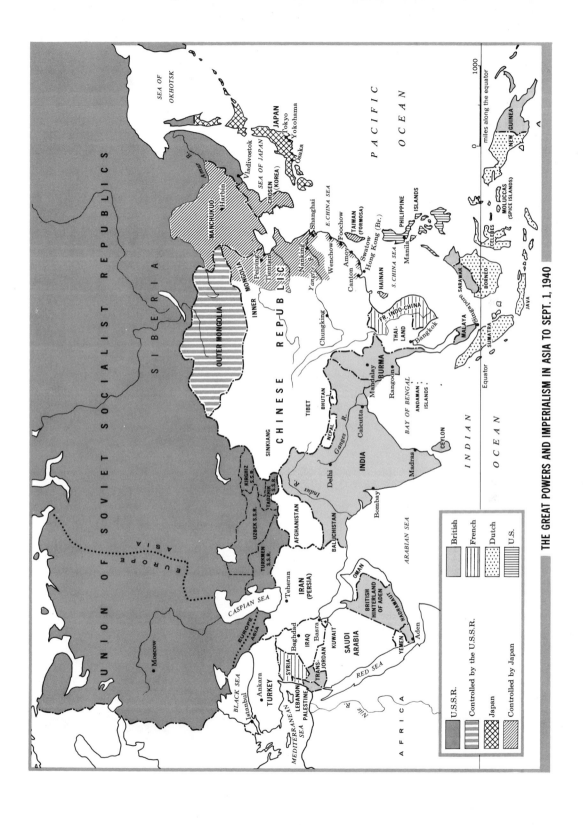

THE GREAT POWERS AND IMPERIALISM IN ASIA TO SEPT. 1, 1940

Imperialism. Left: Germans traveling in East Africa, 1907. Right: A British officer in India, c. 1900.

ship for the nationalist movement that was to challenge British rule in India in the mid–twentieth century.

Imperialism elsewhere

Elsewhere in the world, Western nations hastened to plant their colors upon those territories that promised rewards, either economic or strategic. Britain, France, Germany, and the Netherlands all staked claims in the East Indies, the Dutch achieving an overall hegemony there by 1900. China allowed itself to be victimized by a series of commercial treaties; among the predators was China's neighbor Japan, the only non-Western nation able to modernize in the nineteenth century. The United States played a double game. It acted as champion of the underdeveloped countries in the Western Hemisphere when they were threatened from Europe. Yet the Americans were willing, whenever it suited them, to prey on their neighbors, either "informally" or formally. When, at the end of the century, Spain's feeble hold on its Caribbean and Pacific colonies encouraged talk of rebellion, the United States stepped in to protect its investments and guarantee its maritime security. It declared and won a war against Spain in 1898 on trumped-up grounds. In the same year, the United States annexed Puerto Rico and the Philippines, and established a "protectorate" over Cuba. When Colombia's colony, Panama, threatened to rebel in 1903, the Americans quickly backed the rebels, recognized Panama as a republic, and then proceeded to grant it protection while Americans built the Panama Canal on land leased from the new government. Intervention in Santo Domingo and in Hawaii proved that the United States was no less an imperial power than the nations of western Europe. Together, by the end of the century, those countries had succeeded in binding the world together as it had never been before. The military and economic power with which they had accomplished that achievement meant that, for the time being at any rate, they would be the world's masters.

SELECTED READINGS

• *Items so designated are available in paperback editions.*
• Ashworth, W., *A Short History of the International Economy since 1850,* rev. ed., London, 1975.

Barkin, Kenneth D., *The Controversy Over German Industrialization, 1890–1902,* Chicago, 1970. The political and social struggles between agricultural and industrial interests. An important monograph.

Betts, Raymond F., *Europe Overseas: Phases of Imperialism,* New York, 1968.

Branschwig, H., *French Colonialism, 1871–1914,* New York, 1966.

Cameron, Rondo E., *France and the Economic Development of Europe, 1800–1914,* Princeton, N.J., 1961. Emphasizes the export of French capital and skill in the economic growth of Europe.

Clapham, John, *The Bank of England: A History,* Cambridge, 1944. The best history of this important institution.

Cooke, James J., *The New French Imperialism, 1880–1910; The Third Republic and Colonial Expansion,* Hamden, Conn., 1973.

• Fieldhouse, D. K., *The Colonial Empires,* London, 1966. A general survey from the eighteenth to the twentieth centuries.

• Gollwitzer, Heinz, *Europe in the Age of Imperialism, 1880–1914,* London, 1969.

Henderson, W. O., *Studies in German Colonial History,* Chicago, 1962.

• Hobsbawm, Eric, *Industry and Empire: The Making of Modern English Society, 1750 to the Present Day,* New York, 1968.

• Hodgart, Alan, *The Economics of European Imperialism,* New York, 1978.

• Kindleberger, C. P., *Economic Growth in France and Britain, 1851–1950,* Cambridge, Mass., 1963. A technical account.

• Landes, David S., *The Unbound Prometheus,* London, 1969. Particularly good on the Anglo-German rivalry.

Langer, William L., *The Diplomacy of Imperialism, 1890–1902,* New York, 1960.

Louis, William Roger, ed., *Imperialism: The Robinson and Gallagher Controversy,* New York, 1976. The best introduction to recent debate over the nature and causes of imperialism.

May, E. R., *American Imperialism,* New York, 1968.

Milward, Alan S., and S. B. Saul, *The Development of the Economies of Continental Europe, 1850–1914,* Cambridge, Mass., 1977. An excellent, comprehensive text, particularly good on the smaller European nations.

Platt, D. C. M., *Finance, Trade, and Politics in British Foreign Policy, 1815–1914,* Oxford, 1968.

Price, Roger, *The Economic Modernization of France,* New York, 1975. Rejects conventional periodizations; stresses the advent of railroads which transformed the market structure of France.

Robinson, Ronald, and J. Gallagher, *Africa and the Victorians: The Official Mind of Imperialism,* London, 1961. Contains their famous thesis that imperialism was not deliberately pursued as a policy of state, but rather was a response to events in colonial areas. The modern debate over imperialism begins with this work.

• Shannon, Richard, *The Crisis of Imperialism, 1865–1915,* St. Albans, Eng., 1976. An excellent survey of the transformation of British society in the wake of modern industrialization.

Stolper, Gustav, et al., *The German Economy, 1870 to the Present,* New York, 1967. A good introduction.

Thornton, A. P., *Doctrines of Imperialism,* New York, 1965.

SOURCE MATERIALS

Court, W. H. B., *British Economic History, 1870–1914: Commentary and Documents,* Cambridge, 1965. An excellent collection of documents.

Lenin, Vladimir, *Imperialism: The Highest Stage of Capitalism,* 1916. (Many English editions.) Lenin's most significant contribution to Marxist ideology. He saw the essence of imperialism as the export of capital rather than goods which led to worldwide competition, of which World War I was an inevitable result.

• ———, *The Lenin Anthology,* ed. by R. C. Tucker, New York, 1975.

Reitz, Deneys, *Commando: A Boer Journal of the Boer War,* London, 1929. A superb memoir of the Boer War.

Chapter 25

THE MIDDLE CLASS
CHALLENGED

The time of surprise attacks, of revolutions carried through by small conscious minorities at the head of unconscious masses, is past. Where it is a
question of a complete transformation of the social organization, the
masses themselves must also be in it, must themselves already have
grasped what is at stake, what they are going in for, with body and soul.
　　　—Friedrich Engels, *The Class Struggles in France, 1848–50*

Capitalism's continuing expansion encouraged middle-class men
and women at the end of the nineteenth century to believe
themselves the necessary key to the progress of the human
race. At the same time, however, that belief was being challenged
from several directions. In each case, the challenges called into question assumptions close to the core of middle-class consciousness. Socialist doctrine, which was for the first time receiving a widespread
hearing, pronounced capitalism a threat, rather than a boon, to society. New scientific theories—particularly the theory of evolution—
declared that the key to progress was not the well-laid schemes of humanity, but chance. Psychologists discovered the irrationality of
human beings and philosophers their ultimate helplessness. Paintings,
poetry, and music proclaimed an artists' revolution on behalf of the
idea of art for its own sake, not for the edification of a middle-class
public. Together, these various intellectual and cultural currents threatened the notion that society would most successfully advance under
middle-class auspices, setting its course in accordance with middle-
class moral and economic precepts, and placing its faith in a belief in
the importance and inevitability of continued material progress.

*The dimensions of the
challenge*

1. THE CHALLENGE OF SOCIALISM

Marx in England

The history of socialism in the latter half of nineteenth century is, to a great degree, the biography of its most famous propagandist and theoretician, Karl Marx (1818–1883). Marx was both a social thinker and a political leader. At certain times theory dictated his actions; at others, political events led him to alter doctrine. But always he was at the center of the socialist movement, his moral passion, as much as his scholarly research, shaping the course of its events. The fact of his continuing influence is particularly remarkable for two reasons. First, although a German, he lived from 1849 until his death in London, an exile from the mainstream of continental socialism, in a country whose toleration of socialists was a mark of its comparative immunity from their doctrines. Second, Marx was not a leader who readily took others into his confidence. His antisocial nature was due, in part, to the poverty in which he was forced to live. He and his family were kept alive by gifts of money from his faithful friend and collaborator, Friedrich Engels, who had gone to work for his father's Manchester textile firm, and by occasional stints as a political journalist—for a time Marx was a correspondent for the *New York Tribune*.

Capital

During the 1850s and 1860s Marx labored to produce his definitive analysis of capitalist economics, *Capital,* the first volume of which was published in 1867. In it Marx elaborated upon the theories first enunciated in his earlier economic tracts. He described in detail the processes of production, exchange, and distribution as they operated within the capitalist system. He argued that under capitalism, workers were denied their rightful share of profits. The value of any manufactured item, Marx claimed, was determined by the amount of labor necessary to produce it. Yet workers were hired at wages whose value was far less than the value of the goods they produced. The difference between the value of workers' wages and the value of their work as sold was pocketed by members of the capitalist class, who, according to Marx, made off with far more than a justifiable portion of the sale price. This so-called labor theory of value, borrowed from a somewhat similar doctrine held by Ricardo and other classical economists, was the basis for Marx's claim that the working class was compelled to suffer under the capitalist system. Because workers were forced to sell their labor they became nothing more than commodities in the economic market.

So long as capitalists refused to pay wages more nearly equal to the labor value of their employees' work, those employees would remain exploited. Marx preached that the only class which, under capitalism, produced more wealth than it enjoyed was the working class, the proletariat. The bourgeoisie, which owned the means of production and was therefore able to appropriate that which was rightfully the work-

Karl Marx

ers', had a vested interest in maintaining the status quo; hence its willingness to make use of political, social, religious, and legal institutions to keep the proletariat in its place.

Marx predicted that capitalism would eventually do itself in. He argued that as time passed, market competition would compel the formation of ever-larger industrial and financial combinations. As the smaller enterprenurial class—the petty bourgeoisie—was squeezed out by more powerful combines, its members would join with the proletariat, until society resembled a vast pyramid, with a much-enlarged proletariat at its base and an opposing force of a few powerful capitalists at its tip. At this point, Marx declared, the proletariat would rise in revolution against what was left of the bourgeoisie.

Marx as prophet

After capitalism had received its death blow at the hands of the workers, it would be followed by a stage of socialism. This would have three characteristics: the dictatorship of the proletariat; payment in accordance with work performed; and ownership and operation by the state of all means of production, distribution, and exchange. But socialism was intended to be merely a transition to something higher. In time it would be succeeded by communism, the goal of historical evolution. Communism would mean, first of all, the classless society. No one would live by owning, but solely by working. The state would now disappear, relegated to the museum of antiquities, "along with the bronze ax and the spinning wheel." Nothing would replace it except voluntary associations to operate the means of production and provide for social necessities. The *essence* of communism was payment in accordance with needs. The wage system would be completely abolished, and citizens would be expected to work in accordance with their faculties, entitled to receive from the total fund of wealth produced an amount in proportion to their needs.

The advent of communism

In the ten years after its publication, *Capital* was translated into English (Marx had written it in German), French, Russian, and Italian. It became the theoretical rallying point for a growing band of socialists who stood opposed to the world the middle class had made. For a time it breathed life into an organization of continental and British workers that had been founded in London in 1864: the International Workingmen's Association, usually referred to as the International. This body had been formed with the declared purpose of forging an international working-class alliance to overthrow capitalism and abolish private property. Marx delivered its inaugural address, in which he preached that workers must win political power for themselves if they were ever to escape their industrial bondage. Various difficulties had prevented the formation of a radically oriented workers' organization prior to this time. There was, first of all, fear of official reprisal. Second, the irregular pace of industrialization across Europe meant that workers in one country could have little understanding of the particular plight of their fellow-workers elsewhere. Finally, the period after

The First International

1850 had witnessed an increase in general prosperity which encouraged the more highly skilled—and more politically conscious—workers to forsake revolutionary goals and to pursue the more immediate end of accommodation with middle-class politicians. The German socialists' dealings with Bismarck (see below, p. 789), were a case in point. Meanwhile, however, the determination of a small band of dedicated radical socialists temporarily surmounted the problems to permit the formation of the first international workers' association.

Lassalle and Bakunin

Marx immediately assumed the direction of the International. He labored to exclude moderates from its councils and denounced the German socialists, and their leader Ferdinand Lassalle (1825–1864), for striking bargains with Bismarck. The duty of socialists, Marx argued, was not partnership with the state, but rather its overthrow. At the same time Marx battled the doctrines of the Russian anarchist Michael Bakunin (1814–1876), who opposed the socialist notion that social evil was the product of capitalism. Bakunin argued that the state was the ultimate villain, and preached its immediate destruction through isolated acts of terrorism. He also opposed centralization within the International, urging instead a kind of federal autonomy for each national workers' group. To Marx, these individualist notions represented nothing more than reversion to a kind of primitive rebellion, heroic but ultimately fruitless. He succeeded in having Bakunin banished from the International in 1872. The International prospered for a time during the 1860s. Individual trade unions in various countries were persuaded to join in this united campaign which preached revolution and, through the application of pressure both at the ballot box and in the factory, seemed to promise at least higher wages and shorter hours. Under Marx's direction the International was a highly organized and tightly controlled body, far more effective in this respect than any previous socialist organization.

The troubled International

Yet by 1876 it had faded from existence. Despite Marx's abilities as an authoritarian chief of staff, the International throughout its existence had to battle those same circumstances which delayed its foundation. In addition, Marx's insistence upon control from the center thwarted a growing desire on the part of individual socialist organizations to pursue programs of immediate benefit to themselves. These factors weakened the International. What probably brought about its demise was its association with events occurring in Paris after the defeat of France by Germany in 1870 in the Franco-Prussian War.

The Paris Commune

Following the collapse of Napoleon III, a new republic, generally conservative in tone, had been established by the French. In March 1871, the government attempted to disarm the Paris National Guard, a volunteer citizen army with radical political sympathies. The guard refused to surrender, declared its autonomy, deposed officials of the new government, and proclaimed a revolutionary committee—the Commune—as the true government of France. Though this move-

The Aftermath of the Paris Commune. A view of Champs Élysées showing damage resulting from the 1871 uprising. The Arc de Triomphe may be seen in the distance.

ment is commonly described as a rebellion of dangerous radicals intent upon the destruction of law and order, most of its members resembled the Jacobins of the first French Revolution and belonged largely to the lower middle class. They did not advocate the abolition of private property but rather its wider distribution. The movement was precipitated by bitterness over the defeat of Napoleon III and exhaustion by the long siege of Paris that followed. Added to these factors were fears that the central government would be dominated by the rural population to the disadvantage of the urban masses in the capital. After several weeks of frustrating disputation, the conflict turned into a bloody civil war. The Communards killed about sixty hostages, including the archbishop of Paris. The government numbered its victims by the thousands. The courts-martial which were set up executed twenty-six. Thousands of others were sentenced to imprisonment or banishment in New Caledonia, in the South Pacific.

While middle-class Europe reacted in horror at what it perceived as a second Reign of Terror, Marx, in the name of the International, extolled the courage of the Communards, who, he wrote, had fought the first pitched battle in the class war he had predicted. In a pamphlet entitled *The Civil War in France* (1871), Marx claimed that the Commune was an example of the transitional form of government through which the working class would have to pass on its way to emancipation. But many of the less radical members of the International were frightened and disturbed not only by the events of the Commune itself, but by the possibility of reprisals against members of an organization that openly praised men and women who were considered by the middle class to be little more than murderers. In 1872 Marx acknowl-

The Commune and the International

The Assassination of Hostages by the Communards in Paris, 1871

edged defeat by moving the seat of the International's council to the United States, a country far removed from the organization's affairs and from the criticisms that had begun to be heaped upon Marx for his misdirection. In 1876, the First International expired.

The spread of socialism

Although the International collapsed, socialism continued to gain ground as both a theory and a program. The German Social Democratic party was founded in 1875; a Belgian Socialist party in 1879; and in France, despite the disasters of the Commune, a Socialist party was established in 1905. In England, although socialism was much debated and discussed, no party proclaiming itself socialist emerged. When the Labour party came into being in 1901, however, various socialist societies were represented on its executive council, along with less radical, nonsocialist trade union groups. On the periphery of Europe—in Spain, Italy, and Russia—socialism made less headway. There the absence of widespread industrialization and the educational backwardness of large elements within the population retarded the development of a working-class consciousness, and of socialism as its political expression.

"Purists" vs. "revisionists"

During the years before the First World War, socialists continuously and often bitterly debated the course they should follow as they attempted to achieve their goal of radical change. One group, led by Marx himself until his death, urged socialists to avoid collaboration with other parties to achieve such immediate ends as higher wages, shorter working hours, unemployment insurance, etc. These reforms, the "purists" declared, were the means by which the bourgeoisie could buy off the proletariat and hence indefinitely postpone revolution. On the other hand, "revisionist" socialists urged their followers to take advantage of the fact that many of them now could vote for socialist candidates in elections. They argued that those candidates, if elected, could help them obtain a better life in the immediate future. Socialist theory might proclaim a worldwide struggle of the proletariat against the bourgeoisie; but was this any reason to turn one's back on a chance to make real headway through the ballot box in achieving reforms that would put a better life within reach of workers and their families?

Revisionism spread despite efforts of the "purists" to put a stop to it. In Germany the pattern had been established by Lassalle, whose opportunism had led him to bargain with Bismarck. Following his death, his place as theorist was taken by Eduard Bernstein, a Social Democrat and member of the German parliament, the Reichstag. Bernstein argued that capitalism could be gradually transformed to benefit the working class, and that revolution might not be necessary to achieve this end. Bernstein's most outspoken opponent in Germany was his fellow socialist Karl Kautsky, an orthodox Marxist who warned that collaboration would end in the total corruption and demoralization of the proletariat. In France, the same battle was waged by the "purist" Jules Guesde, who preached that the Socialist party's primary goal should be the development of proletarian class consciousness, and Jean Jaurès, socialist leader in the Chamber of Deputies, who advocated a revisionist course. In both Germany and France, revisionists outnumbered purists by a wide margin. This was, to an even greater degree, the case in Britain. There, Fabian socialists—so named from their policy of delay, in imitation of the tactics of Fabius, a Roman general—preached what they called "the inevitability of gradualism." They believed their country would evolve towards socialism by means of parliamentary democracy. Prominent among the Fabians were the social investigators Sidney and Beatrice Webb, the novelist H. G. Wells, and the playwright George Bernard Shaw.

The continued success of revisionism led its opponents to sharpen their attack and to advocate increasingly violent means to achieve their ends. Their campaigns, though they never managed to convince a majority of the working class, nevertheless attracted an increasing number of adherents. Some who had originally supported the revisionists grew disappointed when reforms did not come as quickly as expected. At the same time, in much of Europe, the cost of living began to rise for many workers. The comparative prosperity that some members of the working class had experienced vanished in the face of price rises that were not matched by wage increases. The result was a frustration which encouraged the adoption of a more militant stance. Germans rallied to the side of the radical socialists Rosa Luxemburg and Karl Liebknecht, while in France a new revolutionary socialist party disowned the reformist leader Alexandre Millerand, after he agreed to serve as cabinet member in a nonsocialist government.

Jean Jaurès

*Anarchism and
syndicalism*

Sorel

Georges Sorel

The Second International, which had been founded in 1889, demanded at a conference in 1906 that affiliated parties declare their goal to be the destruction of the bourgeois order and the state which served its interests.

This militant mood encouraged acceptance of the doctrines of anarchists and syndicalists. Anarchists preached the overthrow of capitalism by violence. They differed from socialists, however, in their hatred of the machinery of the state or any government based upon coercion. Socialists argued that until the communist millennium promised by Marx, the state would remain a necessary means to the achievement of that eventual end. Anarchists worked to see the immediate abolition of a state bureaucracy which, no matter who controlled it, they believed would result in tyranny. Bakunin, whom Marx had succeeded in expelling from the First International, was anarchism's most popular propagandist. Syndicalism, like anarchism, demanded the abolition of both capitalism and the state. It resembled socialism in its demand that workers share in the ownership of the means of production. Instead of making the state the owner and operator of the means of production, however, the syndicalist would delegate these functions to syndicates of producers. Thus all the steel mills would be owned and operated by the workers in the steel industry, the coal mines by the workers in the coal industry, and so on. These associations would take the place of the state, each one governing its own members in all of their activities as producers. In all other matters workers would be free from interference.

Syndicalism received its most sympathetic hearing in France, where a General Confederation of Labour, after 1902, resolved to seek solutions to economic problems outside the legally constituted framework of French politics. The most effective spokesman for syndicalism was the Frenchman Georges Sorel (1847–1922). Sorel, in his *Reflections on Violence,* published in 1908, argued that workers should be made to believe in the possibility of a general strike by the proletariat which would result in the end of bourgeois civilization. The general strike might be nothing more than myth, Sorel acknowledged. Yet, as myth, it remained a powerful weapon in the hands of those whose goal was the destruction of society and who must not shy from the employment of violent means to achieve that end.

Socialism before the First World War, then, was not a unified force. It was divided by quarrels between purists and revisionists, and challenged by the even more radical proposals of anarchists and syndicalists. Socialists, intent on their goal of international solidarity among working classes, ignored the appeal that nationalism and imperialism might make to workers in France, Germany, and Britain. Yet despite its divisions and weaknesses, socialism appeared to the middle classes of Europe as a real threat to their continued prosperity. Capitalism had provided the machinery by which the bourgeoisie had

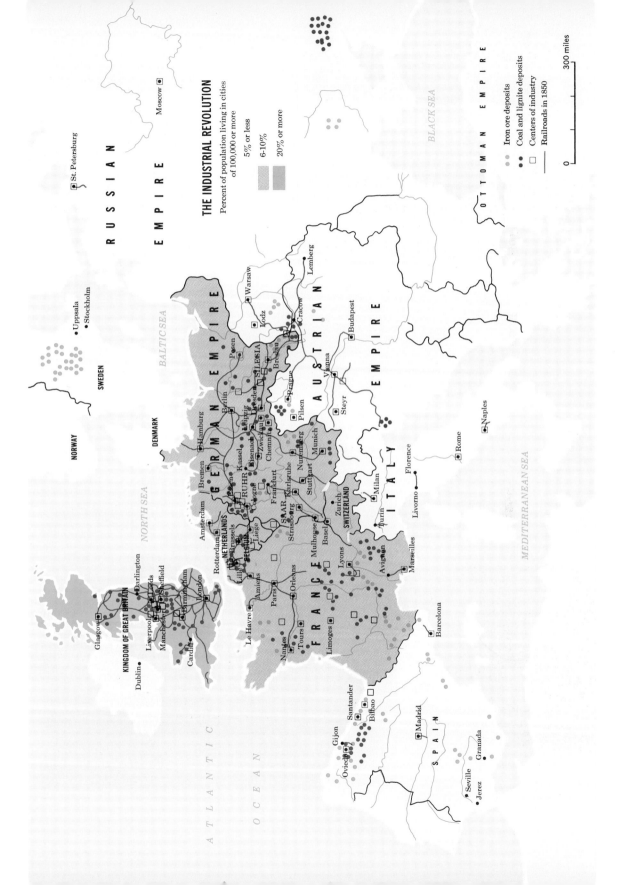

The Massacre of Chios, Eugène Delacroix (1798–1863). During the
Greek war for independence,
Turks slaughtered more than
20,000 Greeks in 1822, depicted in
this famous painting. (Louvre)

Liberty Leading the People, Eugène Delacroix (1798–1863). Delacroix was a
colorful painter of dramatic and emotional themes, as exemplified by this
imaginary scene from the Revolution
of 1830. (Louvre)

The Last of England, Ford Madox Brown (1821–1893). A haunting scene of a couple emigrating from England by one of the most noted pre-Raphaelites. (The City Museum and Art Gallery, Birmingham, England)

Valley of Aosta—Snowstorm, Avalanche, and Thunderstorm, Joseph M. W. Turner (1775–1851). Turner's complete absorption in light, color, and atmosphere helped to prepare the way for the French impressionists. (MMA)

Portrait of a Gentleman, Jean Auguste Ingres (1780–1867). A student of David, Ingres was a devoted admirer of classical antiquities. But he was also influenced by romanticism. (MMA)

A Woman Reading, Camille Corot (1796–1875). Corot was predominantly a naturalist, a painter of lifelike scenes of innocence and simplicity. He shared the romanticists' sentimental worship of woods and fields. (MMA)

The Port of La Rochelle, Corot. (Louvre)

Beatrice and Dante, William Blake (1757–1827). This painting is from Blake's series for *The Divine Comedy*. (The Tate Gallery, London)

The Gleaners, Jean François Millet (1814–1875). Sensuous colors and love of natural settings typifies Millet's work. (Louvre)

Above: *The Guitarist*, Édouard Manet (1832–1883). Right: *Émile Zola*, Manet. Though Manet is called the "father of impressionism," he was also a rebel against the traditions of sweetness and artificiality that dominated the XIX cent. He liberated painting, as his friend Zola emancipated literature. (MMA) (Louvre)

Village Girls, Gustave Courbet (1819–1877). One of the first of the realists, Courbet often portrayed life in a bitter and disparaging light. He eschewed imagination and painted only what he saw. (MMA)

The Third-Class Carriage, Honoré Daumier (1808–1879). Though Daumier was noted for his realistic caricatures and satires, his attitude toward common folk was one of sympathy and understanding. (MMA)

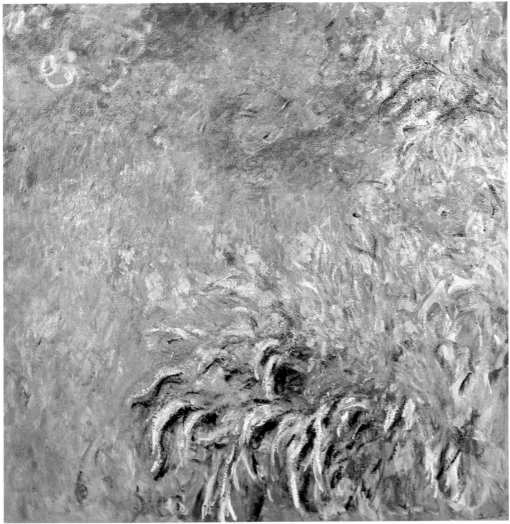

Iris beside a Pond, Claude Monet (1840–1926). Monet called some of his paintings Impressions, and the name soon came to designate a school. (Art Institute of Chicago)

Pink and Green, Edgar Degas (1834–1917). Degas was an impressionist to the extent of his interest in fleeting motion. But as an admirer of the classicist Ingres, he emphasized line and careful composition. (MMA)

Still Life, Cézanne. It has been said that when the impressionists painted a haystack, there was light, but there was no haystack. When Cézanne painted an apple, there was the play of light; there was also the apple. (MMA)

Montagne Sainte-Victoire with Aqueduct, Paul Cézanne (1839–1906). This landscape has been a source of inspiration for many of the tendencies of so-called "modern" art. The composition is as structurally balanced and proportioned as a Greek temple. (MMA)

The Card Players, Cézanne. Here are exemplified Cézanne's skill in composition, his discriminating sense of color, and the sculptured qualities of solidity and depth he gave to his figures. (Stephen C. Clark)

The Japanese Divan, Henri de Toulouse-Lautrec (1864–1901). Toulouse-Lautrec found his chief source of inspiration in the night life of Paris. *Divan Japonais* was a noted Paris café. (MMA)

Portrait of the Artist, Vincent van Gogh (1853–1890). This self-portrait shows a deep serious-ness and intense concentration. (V. W. van Gogh)

Ia Orana Maria, Paul Gauguin (1848–1903). Gauguin re-volted not only against the complexity and artificiality of European life, but against civilization itself. He finally fled to Tahiti to paint the lush, colorful life of an uncorrupted society. (MMA)

The Starry Night, van Gogh. This painting gives vivid expression to van Gogh's bold conceptions. (Museum of Modern Art)

Sunflowers in a Vase, van Gogh. The feverish technique seems to have endowed the flowers with rhythmic motion. (V. W. van Gogh)

Balzac, Auguste Rodin (1840–1917). Rodin was the great realist of XIX-cent. sculpture. He concentrated most of his attention upon facial detail, no matter how unflattering the result might be. (MMA)

A Young Woman in the Sun, Auguste Renoir (1841–1919). Though Renoir used impressionist techniques, the results sometimes bore little resemblance to the work of other impressionists. He believed that "a picture ought to be a lovable thing, joyous and pretty." (Jeu de Paume)

Luncheon of the Boating Party, Renoir. (Phillips Memorial Gallery)

The Piano Lesson, Henri Matisse (1869–1954). Matisse conveyed a freshness of approach and a vitality of line and color. (Museum of Modern Art)

Portrait of Gertrude Stein, Pablo Picasso (1881–1973). Picasso seems to have given this portrait of the great experimenter in poetry some elements of the distortion of form characteristic of the work of both. (Museum of Modern Art)

Three Musicians, Pablo Picasso. This painting, regarded by many as the masterpiece of cubism, sums up the final stage of the movement. (Museum of Modern Art)

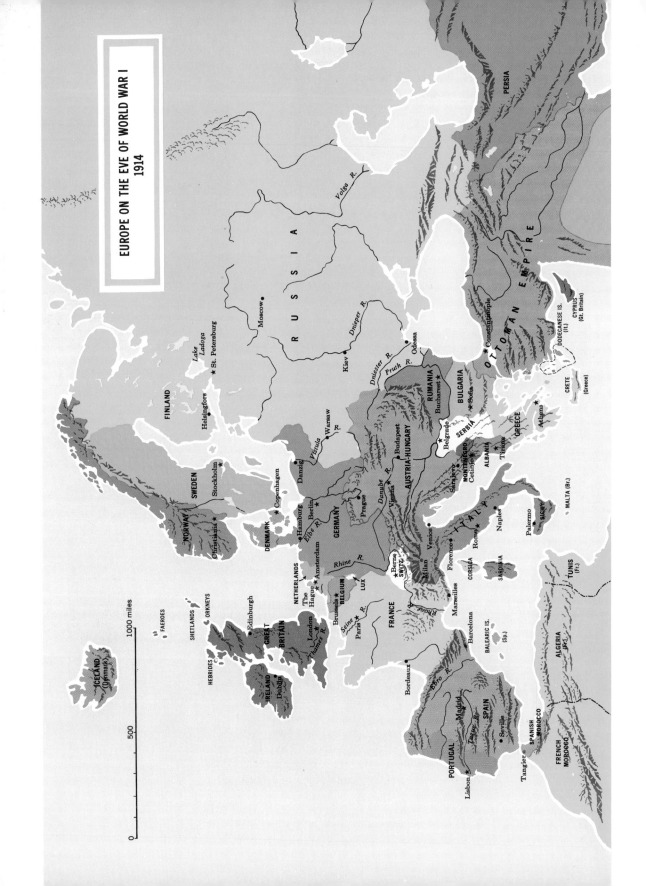

EUROPE ON THE EVE OF WORLD WAR I
1914

The Haymarket Riots, Chicago, 1886. A comtemporary illustration depicting the results of attempts to unionize workers at the McCormick Harvester works.

achieved power. Socialism attacked capitalism and hence those who were its direct beneficiaries. Although most socialists disapproved of violence, violent acts were attributed by middle-class men and women to an amorphous, anticapitalist body easily labeled "socialist." Riots by trade unionists in Chicago's Haymarket Square in 1886 and in London's Trafalgar Square in 1887; the assassinations of President Sadi Carnot of France in 1894, of King Humbert of Italy in 1900, and of President William McKinley of the United States in 1901; strikes which grew in number and violence throughout Europe and America after 1900—all these events were perceived by members of the middle class as part of a larger movement whose professed goal was to tear from them their economic, political, and social security.

Socialism as a threat to the middle class

2. THE CHALLENGE OF SCIENCE AND PHILOSOPHY

While socialism challenged middle-class self-confidence from one quarter, science and philosophy threatened from another. The fact that science might undermine, rather than sustain, certainty was all the more difficult to comprehend, given the manner in which science and technology had together assisted in the birth and continued development of industrialization. This is not to say that science abandoned its role as an instrument for the solving of human problems and as a vital aid to continuing progress. There were striking improvements in the field of medicine, for example. The Frenchman Louis Pasteur (1822–1895) proved that all forms of life, no matter how small, are reproduced only by living beings. Hitherto, according to the theory of spontaneous generation, it had commonly been supposed that bacte-

Science and progress

Louis Pasteur

Marie Curie

Darwin

ria and other microscopic organisms originated from water or from other decaying vegetable and animal matter. By locating the source of bacteria, Pasteur's discovery opened the way for major improvements in the areas of public sanitation and health, among others, the process of ridding food of objectionable bacteria by sterilization—pasteurization—that was named for him. Pasteur, along with the German Robert Koch (1843–1910), also proved conclusively that germs were not, as was commonly supposed, the result but rather the cause of disease. The discovery of the X-ray by the German Wilhelm von Röntgen in 1895 and of radium by the Polish scientist Marie Curie in 1898 not only altered perceptions as to the nature of energy, but suggested ways in which energy could be put to use for medical purposes. These discoveries—along with similarly important ones in the areas of cell theory, anesthetics, and antiseptics—worked to convince the educated public that science was a friend of humanity, and that it was also predictable, operating in accordance with laws which had only to be discovered in order to be put to use. Isaac Newton's law of gravitation continued to reign supreme, arguing that the universe was orderly, and essentially timeless, and that the passage of time brought with it no fundamental change.

Against this psychologically reassuring fortress of a harmonious universe, biological scientists hurled the bomb of evolutionary theory. We have seen that this theory was at least as old as Anaximander in the sixth century B.C., and that it was accepted by many of the great minds of antiquity. We have learned also that it was revived in the eighteenth century by the scientists Buffon and Linnaeus. But neither of these men offered much proof or explained how the process of evolution works. The first to develop a systematic hypothesis of evolution was the French biologist, Jean Lamarck (1744–1829). The essential principle in Lamarck's hypothesis, published in 1809, was the inheritance of acquired characteristics. He maintained that an animal, subjected to a change in environment, acquired new habits, which in turn were reflected in structural changes. These acquired characteristics of body structure, he believed, were transmissible to the offspring, with the result that after a series of generations a new species of animal was eventually produced. Lamarck's successors found little evidence to confirm this hypothesis, but it dominated biological thought for nearly fifty years.

A much more convincing hypothesis of organic evolution was that of the English naturalist Charles Darwin (1809–1882), published in 1859. The son of a small-town physician, Darwin began the study of medicine at the University of Edinburgh, but soon withdrew and entered Cambridge to prepare for the ministry. Here he gave most of his time to natural history. In 1831 Darwin obtained an appointment as naturalist without pay on H.M.S. *Beagle,* which had been chartered for a scientific expedition around the world. The voyage lasted nearly five years and gave Darwin an unparalleled opportunity to become acquainted at first hand with the manifold variations of animal life. He noted the differences between animals inhabiting islands and related species on nearby continents, and observed the resemblances between living animals and the fossilized remains of extinct species in the same locality. It was a magnificent preparation for his life's work. Upon returning from the voyage he read Malthus's essay on population, and was struck by the author's contention that throughout the world of nature many more individuals are born than can ever survive, and that consequently the weaker ones must perish in the struggle for food. Finally, after twenty more years of careful and extensive research, he issued his *Origin of Species* (1859).

Darwin's hypothesis was that of natural selection. He argued that it is nature, or the environment, which selects those variants among offspring that are to survive and reproduce. Darwin pointed out, first of all, that the parents of every species beget more offspring than can possibly survive. He maintained that, consequently, a struggle takes place among these offspring for food, shelter, warmth, and other conditions necessary for life. In this struggle for existence certain individuals have the advantage because of the factor of *variation,* which means that no two of the offspring are exactly alike. Some are born strong, others weak; some have longer horns or sharper claws than their brothers and sisters or perhaps a body coloration which enables them better to blend with their surroundings and thus to evade their enemies. It is these favored members of the species that win out in the struggle for existence and survive as the "fittest" of their generation; the others are eliminated generally before they have lived long enough to reproduce. Darwin regarded variation and natural selection as the primary factors in the origin of new species. In other words, he taught that individuals with favorable characteristics would transmit their inherited qualities to their descendants through countless generations, and that successive eliminations of the least fit would eventually produce a new species. Darwin applied his concept of evolution not only to plant and animal species but also to humans. In his second great work, *The Descent of Man* (1871), he attempted to show that the human race originally sprang from some apelike ancestor, long since extinct, but probably a common forebear of the existing anthropoid apes and humans.

The Darwinian hypothesis was elaborated and improved by several later biologists. The German August Weismann (1834–1914) flatly rejected the idea that acquired characteristics could be inherited. He conducted experiments to show that body cells and reproductive cells are entirely distinct, and that there is no way in which changes in the former can effect the latter. He concluded, therefore, that the only qualities transmissible to the offspring are those which have always been present in the reproductive cells of the parents. In 1901 the Dutch botanist Hugo De Vries (1848–1935) published his celebrated mutation hypothesis, based upon Darwin's original hypothesis and, in

Charles Darwin

Illustrations from Darwin's First Edition of *The Descent of Man*. The drawings were used to point up the similarities between a human embryo *(top)* and that of a dog *(bottom).*

large part, upon laws of heredity discovered by the Austrian monk Gregor Mendel (1822–1884). De Vries asserted that evolution results not from minor variations, as Darwin had assumed, but from radical differences or mutations, which appear in more or less definite ratio among the offspring. When any of these mutations are favorable to survival in a given environment, the individuals possessing them naturally emerge triumphant in the struggle for existence. Not only do their descendants inherit these qualities, but from time to time new mutants appear, some of which are even better adapted for survival than their parents. Thus in a limited number of generations a new species may be brought into existence. The mutation theory of De Vries corrected one of the chief weaknesses in the Darwinian hypothesis. The variations which Darwin assumed to be the source of evolutionary changes are so small that an incredibly long time would be necessary to produce a new species. De Vries made it possible to conceive of evolution as proceeding by sudden leaps.

Evolution and chance

Clearly, the implications of this new theory were deeply disturbing for those who had until now believed in an orderly universe, or had taken as literal the words of the Bible. For the latter the task of reconciling Darwin's account of creation with the first chapter of Genesis, though troublesome, was often not insuperable. Outside fundamentalist sects, the Bible was, at this time, perceived by growing numbers as containing a combination of myths, legends, history, and profoundly important moral truths. The work of the German theologian David Friedrich Strauss (1808–1874) and of the French historian Ernest Renan (1832–1892) had cast doubt on the historical accuracy of the Bible, and dealt with its inconsistencies. These writers had defended the intentions of the Bible's various authors, while firmly insisting upon their human fallibilities. Their searching yet nevertheless sensitive critiques helped people understand that they need not abandon their Christian faith simply because Darwin insisted that the world and all that lived within it had been created over millions of years and not in six days. Far more difficult to deal with was the notion, explicit in Darwin, that nature was not a changeless harmony, but instead a constant and apparently undirected struggle. Chance, and not order, ruled the universe. Nothing was fixed, nothing perfect, all was in a state of flux. Good and bad were defined only in terms of an ability to survive. The "best" of a species were those that triumphed over their weaker rivals. All of a sudden, the universe had become a harsh and uncompromising place, deprived of pre-Darwinian certainties; belief in a benevolent God was now much harder to sustain.

Thomas Henry Huxley

Darwin's most vigorous defender, the philosopher Thomas Henry Huxley (1825–1895), was one of those who could no longer reconcile science with a belief in God. While he did not reject the possibility of a supernatural power, Huxley averred that "there is no evidence of the existence of such a being as the God of the theologians." He pronounced Christianity to be "a compound of some of the best and some of the worst elements of Paganism and Judaism, moulded in practice by the innate character of certain people of the Western World."[1] Huxley coined the word *agnosticism* to express his contempt for the attitude of dogmatic certainty symbolized by the beliefs of the ancient Gnostics.[2] As propounded by Huxley, agnosticism is the doctrine that neither the existence nor the nature of God nor the ultimate character of the universe is knowable.

The most uncompromising of the evolutionist philosophers was Ernst Heinrich Haeckel (1834–1919). Originally a physician, later a professor of biology, Haeckel was the first outstanding scientist on the Continent to subscribe wholeheartedly to Darwinism. At the age of sixty-five he summarized his conclusions in a book entitled *The Riddle of the Universe*. The philosophy of Haeckel comprised three main doctrines: atheism, materialism, and mechanism. He would have nothing to do with Huxley's agnosticism; on the contrary, he dogmatically affirmed that nothing spiritual exists. The universe, he maintained, was composed of matter alone, in a process of constant change from one form into another. Life, Haeckel stated, originated from the spontaneous combination of the essential elements of protoplasm. From these earliest forms of protoplasm all the complex species of the present gradually evolved through the process of natural selection. Haeckel regarded the mind of humans as just as much a product of evolution as the body. The human mind differs only in degree from the minds of the lower animals. Memory, imagination, perception, and thinking are mere functions of matter; psychology should be considered a branch of physiology. Such was the compact philosophy of materialism and determinism which appeared to Haeckel and his followers to be a logical deduction from the new biology.

The middle classes of western Europe and the United States, disoriented by the antireligious implications of evolutionary theory, received some comfort from the writings of those who adapted Darwinian thought to the analysis of society—the so-called Social Darwinists. These thinkers argued that the apparent "success" of Western civilization was the result of its special fitness. The white race, they boasted, had proved itself superior to the black; non-Jews superior to Jews; rich superior to poor; the British Empire superior to the subject territories it controlled. If nature was a matter of competition, so was society, with the victory going to that race or nation which could demonstrate its fitness to survive by subduing others.

Though he never expressed his ideas that crudely, the English philosopher Herbert Spencer (1820–1903) extolled the virtues of competition in a way that made it easier for others to do so. Spencer grounded

---

[1] T. H. Huxley, *Collected Essays,* V (London, 1902), 142.
[2] See above, p. 68.

Herbert Spencer

Anthropology

Friedrich Nietzsche

his philosophy upon evolutionary theory. His keynote was his idea of evolution as a universal law. He was deeply impressed by Darwin's *Origin of Species* and enriched the hypothesis of natural selection with a phrase that has clung to it ever since—"the survival of the fittest." He contended that not only species and individuals are subject to evolutionary change, but also planets, solar systems, customs, institutions, and religious and ethical ideas. Everything in the universe completes a cycle of origin, development, decay, and extinction. When the end of the cycle has been reached, the process begins once more and is repeated eternally. As a political philosopher, Spencer was a vigorous champion of individualism. He condemned collectivism as a relic of primitive society, as a feature of the earliest stage of social evolution. Any so-called assistance individuals might receive from the state, Spencer argued, would result not only in their own degeneration, but in that of society as well.

If Social Darwinists could reassure some by implying the biological right of Western civilization to survive as the "fittest" within the contemporary world, anthropologists—pioneers in what was essentially a new scientific discipline—argued, on the contrary, that no culture could be perceived as "better" than any other. All societies were adaptations to a particular environment. Each society produced its own customs, which could not be declared "good" or "bad," but only successful or unsuccessful, according to the degree to which they helped that society survive. This notion of cultural "relativism" was a theme in the influential work of the English anthropologist Sir James Frazer (1854–1941). In his masterpiece, *The Golden Bough,* he demonstrated the relationship of Christianity to primitive practices and magical rites. Christianity was nothing more or less than one society's response to the craving for an explanation of the apparently inexplicable.

Christianity was challenged far more directly in the writings of the German philosopher Friedrich Nietzsche (1844–1900). Nietzsche was not a scientist, nor was he interested in the nature of matter or in the problem of religious truth. He was essentially a romantic poet glorifying the struggle for existence to compensate for his own life of weakness and misery. Born in 1844, the son of a Lutheran minister, he was educated in the classics at Leipzig and Bonn and at the age of twenty-five was made a professor of philology at the University of Basel. Ten years later repeated and severe attacks of nerves forced his retirement. He spent the next decade of his life in agony, wandering from one resort to another in a fruitless quest for relief. If we can believe his own statement, each year was made up of two hundred days of pain. In 1888 he lapsed into hopeless insanity, which continued until his death in 1900.

Nietzsche's philosophy is contained in such works as *Thus Spake Zarathustra, A Genealogy of Morals,* and *The Will to Power.* His cardinal idea was the notion that natural selection should be permitted to operate unhindered in the case of human beings as it does with plants and animals. He believed that such a constant weeding out of the unfit would eventually produce a race of supermen—not merely a race of physical giants but men distinguished above all for their moral courage, for their strength of character. Those who should be allowed to perish in the struggle were the moral weaklings, who had neither the strength nor the courage to battle nobly for a place in the sun. Before any such process of natural selection could operate, however, religious obstacles would have to be removed. Nietzsche therefore demanded that the moral supremacy of Christianity and Judaism be overthrown. Both of these religions, he alleged, glorified the virtues of the downtrodden. They exalted into virtues qualities which ought to be considered vices—humility, nonresistance, mortification of the flesh, and pity for the weak and incompetent. The enthronement of these qualities prevented the elimination of the unift and preserved them to pour their degenerate blood into the veins of the race.

His philosophy

Scientists and philosophers, as they continued to explore the various and sometimes contradictory implications of evolutionary theory, helped to undermine the comforting notion of humankind's essential superiority to the rest of the animal kingdom. The work of the Russian psychologist Ivan Pavlov (1849–1936) resulted in the discovery of the conditioned reflex. Although Pavlov experimented with animals, he insisted that his conclusions applied equally to human beings. The conditioned reflex is a form of behavior in which natural reactions are produced by an artificial stimulus. Pavlov showed that if dogs were fed immediately following the ringing of a bell, they would eventually respond to the sound of the bell alone and secrete saliva exactly as if confronted by the sight and smell of the food. This discovery suggested the conclusion that the conditioned reflex is an important element in human behavior and encouraged psychologists to center their attention upon physiological experiment as a key to understanding the mind.

Pavlov

Pavlovians inaugurated a type of physiological psychology known as behaviorism. Behaviorism is an attempt to study the human being as a purely physiological organism—to reduce all human behavior to a series of physical responses. Such concepts as *mind* and *consciousness* are relegated to the scrap heap as vague and meaningless terms. For the behaviorist nothing is important except the reactions of muscles, nerves, glands, and visceral organs. There is no such thing as an independent psychic behavior; all that humans do is physical. Thinking is essentially a form of talking to oneself. Every complex emotion and idea is simply a group of physiological responses produced by some stimulus in the environment. Such was the extremely mechanistic interpretation of human actions offered by followers of Pavlov.

Behaviorism

The other important school of psychology to make its appearance

Freud and psychoanalysis

Sigmund Freud

· *Science and religion*

after the turn of the century was psychoanalysis, founded by Sigmund Freud (1856–1939), an Austrian physician. Psychoanalysis interprets human behavior mainly in terms of the unconscious mind. Freud admitted the existence of the conscious mind (the ego), but he avowed that the unconscious (the id) is much more important in determining the actions of the individual. He considered humans as egoistic creatures propelled by basic urges of power, self-preservation, and sex. These urges are much too strong to be overcome; but inasmuch as society (the superego) has branded their unrestrained fulfillment as sinful, they are commonly driven into the unconscious, where they linger indefinitely as suppressed desires. Yet they are seldom completely submerged; they rise to the surface in dreams, or they manifest themselves in lapses of memory, in fears and obsessions, and in various forms of abnormal behavior. Freud believed that most cases of mental and nervous disorders result from violent conflicts between natural instincts and the restraints imposed by an unfortunate environment. Freud hoped that by elucidating his theory of the unconscious he could impose predictable patterns upon the irrationality that seemed to characterize so much human activity. His search for order, however, resembled that of the behaviorists by continuing to stress the extent to which men and women, like animals, were prey to drives, impulses, and reflexes over which they could exercise at best only minimal control.

Under the impact of these various scientific and philosophical challenges, the institutions responsible for the maintenance of traditional faith found themselves hard pressed. Protestantism had based its revolt against Roman Catholic orthodoxy upon the belief that men and women should seek to understand God with the aid of not much more than the Bible and a willing conscience. In consequence, Protestants had little in the way of authoritarian doctrine to support them when their faith was challenged. Some—the fundamentalists—chose to ignore the implications of scientific and philosophical inquiry altogether, and continued to believe in the literal truth of the Bible. Some were willing to agree with the school of American philosophers known as Pragmatists (Charles Pierce, William James), that if belief in a personal God produced mental peace or spiritual satisfaction, that belief must therefore be true. Truth, for the Pragmatists, was whatever provided useful, practical results. Other Protestants sought solace from religious doubt in religious activity, founding missions, and laboring among the poor. Many adherents to this "Social Gospel" were also "Modernists," determined to accept the ethical teachings of Christianity while discarding belief in miracles and the doctrines of original sin and the Incarnation.

The Roman Catholic Church was compelled by its tradition of dogmatic assertion to assist its followers in their response to the modern world. In 1864 Pope Pius IX issued a *Syllabus of Errors* condemning what he regarded as the principal religious and philosophical "errors" of the time. Among them were materialism, free thought, and "indifferentism," or the idea that one religion is as good as another. Though the *Syllabus* was generally accepted by the Church, it was condemned by some critics as a "crusade against civilization." While heated discussions continued over the *Syllabus of Errors* Pope Pius convoked a Church council in 1869, the first to be summoned since the Catholic Reformation. The most noted pronouncement of the Vatican Council was the dogma of papal infallibility. In the language of this dogma the pope, when he speaks *ex cathedra*—that is in his capacity "as pastor and doctor of all Christians"—is infallible in regard to all matters of faith and morals. Though generally accepted by pious Catholics, the dogma of papal infallibility evoked a storm of protest in many circles. Governments of several Catholic countries denounced it, including France, Spain, and Italy. The death of Pius IX in 1878 and the accession of Pope Leo XIII brought a more accomodating climate to the Church. The new pope was ready to concede that there was "good" as well as "evil" in modern civilization. He added a scientific staff to the Vatican and opened archives and observatories. However, he made no concessions to "liberalism" or "anticlericalism" in the political sphere. He would go no farther than to urge capitalists and employers to be more generous in recognizing the rights of organized labor.

The effect of various scientific and philosophical challenges upon the men and women who lived at the end of the nineteenth century cannot be measured in any exact way. Millions undoubtedly went about the business of life untroubled by the implications of evolutionary theory, content to believe as they had believed. Certainly, for most members of the middle class, the challenge of socialism was understood as "real" in a way that the challenge of science and philosophy probably was not. Socialism was a threat to livelihood. Darwinism, relativism, materialism, and behaviorism, though "in the air" and troublesome to those who breathed that air, did not impinge upon consciousness to the same degree. Men and women can postpone thoughts about their origins and ultimate destiny in a way that they cannot postpone thoughts about their daily bread. And yet the impact of the changes we have been discussing was eventually profound. Darwin's theory was not so complicated as to prevent its popularization. If educated men and women had neither the time nor inclination to read the *Origin of Species,* they read magazines and newspapers which spelled out for them its implications. Those implications induced an uncertainty that tempered the optimism of capitalist expansion.

Men and women who had never read the German philosopher Arthur Schopenhauer (1788–1860) might well have agreed with his assessment of this world as one condemned to witness the devouring of the weak by the strong. Yet their commitment to the ways of the

Roman Catholicism

Pope Pius IX

Pope Leo XIII

world prevented their acceptance of Schopenhauer's particular remedy: an escape into a life of personal asceticism and self-denial. Like the English poet and essayist Matthew Arnold, sensitive men and women might feel themselves trapped in a world resembling no more than "a darkling plain," where there was "neither joy, nor love, nor light, nor certitude, nor peace, nor help for pain."

3. THE CHALLENGE OF LITERATURE AND THE ARTS

The revolt against art as morality

Literature and the arts in the late nineteenth century continued to challenge the middle-class worldview by drawing attention to the shortcomings as well as the achievements of industrial society. By 1900, however, many artists and writers were working according to a precept even more disturbing in its implications to the educated public than a critique of social values and realities. They agreed with the writers who were protesting middle-class values that the purpose of art was not to pander or to sentimentalize. They disagreed with them, however, by declaring that art had no business preaching morality—attempting to "improve" by example. This generation of artists and writers argued that one did not look at a painting or read a poem to be instructed in the difference between good and evil, but to understand what was eternally true and beautiful—to appreciate art for its own sake. They were not so much interested in reaching a wider audience, whose standards of taste they generally deplored, as they were in addressing each other. This self-conscious desire not only to live apart but to think apart from society was reflected in their work. In 1850, educated men and women could read a Dickens novel or examine a Daumier print and understand it, even if they did not admire it or agree with its message. In 1900, men and women found it much harder to understand, let alone admire, a painting by Paul Cézanne or a poem by Paul Valéry. Artists and public were ceasing to speak the same language, a fact which contributed, as did the ideas of Darwin and Nietzsche, Pavlov and Freud, to the further confusion and fragmentation of Western culture.

Realism

These new perceptions of the artist's relationship to society did not surface to any measurable degree before the very end of the century. Until that time, the arts were dominated by what has come to be called *realism*. Realists were predominantly critics of contemporary society. Swayed by a fervor for social reform, they depicted the inequities of the human condition against the sordid background of industrial society. Like the romantics, the realists affirmed the possibility of human freedom, although realists emphasized more than romantics the obstacles that prevented its achievement. Realists differed most markedly from romantics in their disdain of sentiment and emotional extravagance. Adopting from natural science the idea of life as a struggle for survival, they tried to portray human existence in accordance with hard facts, often insisting that their characters were the irresponsible victims of heredity, environment, or their own animal passions.

Realism as a literary movement made its initial appearance in France. Its leading exponents included the novelists Honoré de Balzac and Gustave Flaubert,[3] whose work, as we have already noted, contained a stinging assessment of the dullness and greed of modern life. Émile Zola (1840–1902), another Frenchman, is often called a naturalist rather than a realist, to convey the idea that he was interested in an exact, scientific presentation of the facts of nature without the intrusion of personal philosophy. Naturalism was expected to dismiss moral values in a way that realism was not. Zola did have a definite moral viewpoint, however. His early years of wretched poverty imbued him with a deep sympathy for the common people and with a passion for social justice. Though he portrayed human nature as weak and prone to vice and crime, he was not without hope that a decided improvement might come from the creation of a better society. Many of his novels dealt with such social problems as alcoholism, poverty, and disease.

Literary realism in France

Realism in the writings of the Englishman Charles Dickens was overlaid with layers of sentimentality. Dickens was a master at depicting the evils of industrial society, but the invariable happy endings of his novels testify to his determined—and unrealistic—unwillingness to allow wrong to triumph over right. No such ambivalence marked the works of the later English novelist Thomas Hardy (1840–1928), however. In such well-known narratives as *The Return of the Native, Jude the Obscure,* and *Tess of the D'Urbervilles,* he expressed his conception that humans are the playthings of an inexorable fate. The universe, though beautiful, was depicted as in no sense friendly, and the struggle of individuals with nature was a pitiable battle against almost impossible odds. If any such being as God existed, he watched with indifference while the helpless denizens of the human ant-heap crawled toward suffering and death. Hardy pitied his fellow creatures, regarding them not as depraved animals but as specks of dust caught in the wheels of a cosmic machine.

Realism in England

Pity for humanity was a central theme in the work of the German Gerhard Hauptmann (1862–1946). Calling himself a naturalist, Hauptmann nevertheless reflected the realists' concern for suffering. His plays show the influence of Darwin in their emphasis upon determinism and environment. *The Weavers,* which depicts the suffering of Silesian weavers in the 1840s, is probably his most outstanding work. Doubtless the most eminent playwright among realists and naturalists was the Norwegian Henrik Ibsen (1828–1906). Ibsen's early dramas were not favorably received, and while still a young man he decided to abandon his native country. Residing first in Italy and then in Ger-

Realism in Germany and Scandinavia

[3] See above, p. 664.

many, he did not return permanently to Norway until 1891. His writings were characterized most of all by bitter rebellion against the tyranny and ignorance of society. In such plays as *The Wild Duck, A Doll's House, Hedda Gabler,* and *An Enemy of the People,* he mercilessly satirized the conventions and institutions of respectable life, and showed, with great insight, how these oppressed women in particular. Along with his scorn for hypocrisy and social tyranny went a profound distrust of majority rule. Ibsen despised democracy as the enthronement of unprincipled leaders who would do anything for the sake of votes to perpetuate themselves in power. As one of his characters in *An Enemy of the People* says: "A minority may be right—a majority is always wrong."

Russian literature: Turgenev and Dostoevsky

The literature of the Russians, while it came into its own during the period of realism, includes within it themes that are both romantic and idealist as well. Russia's three most outstanding novelists of this period were Ivan Turgenev (1818–1883), Feodor Dostoevsky (1821–1881), and Leo Tolstoy (1828–1910). Turgenev, who spent much of his life in France, was the first of the Russian novelists to become known to western Europe. His chief work, *Fathers and Sons,* describes in brooding terms the struggle between the older and younger generations. The hero is a nihilist (a term first used by Turgenev), who is convinced that the whole social order has nothing in it worth preserving. Dostoevsky was almost as tragic a figure as any he projected in his novels. Condemned at the age of twenty-eight on a charge of revolutionary activity, he was exiled to Siberia, where he endured four horrible years. His later life was harrowed by poverty, family troubles, and epileptic fits. As a novelist, he chose to explore the anguish of people driven to shameful deeds by their raw, animal emotions and by the intolerable meanness of their lives. He was a master of psychological analysis, probing into the motives of distorted minds with an intensity that was almost morbid. At the same time he filled his novels with a broad sympathy and with a mystic conviction that humanity can be purified only through suffering. His best-known works are *Crime and Punishment* and *The Brothers Karamazov*.

Henrik Ibsen

Tolstoy

It is generally conceded that the honor of being Russia's greatest novelist must be divided between Dostoevsky and Tolstoy. As an earnest champion of the simple life of the peasant, Tolstoy was somewhat less deterministic than the author of *Crime and Punishment.* Yet in his *War and Peace,* a majestic epic of Russian conditions during the period of the Napoleonic invasion, he expounds the theme that individuals are at the mercy of fate when powerful elemental forces are unleashed. His other most celebrated novel, *Anna Karenina,* is a study of the tragedy which lurks in the pursuit of individual desire. The hero, Levin, is really Tolstoy himself, who eventually finds refuge from doubt and from the vanities of worldly existence in a mystic love

Leo Tolstoy in His Study Dictating to His Secretary

of humanity. As Tolstoy grew older he became more and more an evangelist preaching a social gospel. In such novels as *The Kreutzer Sonata* and *Resurrection* he condemned most of the institutions of civilized society and called upon men and women to renounce selfishness and greed, to earn their living by manual toil, and to cultivate the virtues of poverty, meekness, and nonresistance. His last years were devoted mainly to attacks upon such evils as war and capital punishment and to the defense of victims of persecution.

The works of all these realists and naturalists, whatever their individual differences, shared two things in common: they contained vigorous moral criticism of present-day middle-class society, and they were written in direct and forceful language that the middle class could understand, if it chose to read or listen. The same can be said of realist painters such as Courbet and Daumier, discussed previously, and of the sculptor Auguste Rodin (1840–1917), whose style and message were neither difficult to comprehend nor easy to ignore. Realist artists were still anxious to address the public, if only to attack its members for their shallowness and insensitivity. The advent of the *impressionist* movement in painting in the 1870s marks the first significant break in this tradition. It is at this point that artists began to turn away from the public and toward each other. The movement started in France, among a group of young artists whose work had been refused a place in the annual exhibitions of the traditionally minded French Royal Academy. They had been labeled "impressionists" in derision by critics who took them to task for painting not an object itself, but only their impression of that object. The name in fact suited the personal, private nature of their work. They were painting only to please themselves, to realize their own potential as artists.

In a sense, impressionists were realists, for they were determined to paint only what they saw, and they were vitally interested in the

Realism in art

Impressionism

Monet and Renoir

See color plates following page 768

Expressionism: Cézanne

scientific interpretation of nature. But impressionist technique was different from that of the older realist painters. Scenes from the world around them were not depicted as if the results of careful study. On the contrary, the works of impressionists sought to reveal immediate sense impressions, leaving it to the mind of the observer to fill in additional details. This often resulted in a type of work appearing at first glance to be nonnaturalistic. Figures were commonly distorted; a few significant details were made to represent an entire object; and dabs of primary color were placed side by side without a trace of blending. Convinced that light is the principal factor in determining the appearance of objects, the impressionists fled from the studio to the woods and fields in an attempt to capture the fleeting alterations of a natural scene with each transitory shift of sunlight and shadow. From science they had learned that light is composed of a fusion of primary colors visible in the spectrum. Accordingly, they decided to use these colors almost exclusively. They chose, for example, to achieve the effect of the green in nature by placing daubs of pure blue and yellow side by side, allowing the eye to mix them.

Impressionism differed from realism in one other very important respect. In these new paintings artists remained detached from their subject. They did not paint to evoke pity, or to teach a lesson. They painted to proclaim the value and importance of painting *as painting*. In doing so, the artist was not deliberately setting out to exclude the viewers. It was clear, however, that the viewer must not expect to understand a painting except on the artist's terms. Probably the greatest of the impressionists were the Frenchmen Claude Monet (1840–1926) and Auguste Renoir (1841–1919). Monet was perhaps the leading exponent of the new mode of interpreting landscapes. His paintings have no structure or design in the conventional sense; they suggest, rather than depict, the outlines of cliffs, trees, mountains, and fields. Intensely interested in the problem of light, Monet would go out at sunrise with an armful of canvases in order to paint the same subject in a dozen momentary appearances. It has been said of one of his masterpieces that "light is the only important person in the picture." Renoir's subjects include not only landscapes but portraits and scenes from contemporary life. He is famous most of all for his pink and ivory nudes, which, as expressions of frank sexuality, represented a threat to middle-class sensibilities.

The freedom explicit in the work of the impressionists encouraged other painters to pursue fresh techniques and to define different goals. The *expressionists* turned upon the impressionists, objecting to their preoccupation with the momentary aspects of nature and their indifference to meaning. Expressionists were not arguing a return to meaning in the sense of "message." They were instead insisting that a painting must represent the artist's particular intellect. Here again, they were making art a private matter, removing it yet another step from the public. The artist who laid the foundations of expressionism was Paul Cézanne (1839–1906), now recognized as one of the greatest painters who ever lived. A native of southern France, Cézanne labored to express a sense of order in nature that he believed the impressionists had ignored. To achieve this end, he painted objects as a series of planes, each plane expressed in terms of a color change. While Cézanne was in this way equating form with color, he also began to reduce natural forms to their geometrical equivalents, hoping thereby to express the basic shapes of existence itself. He distorted form into geometrical regularity until abstraction became reality. In all this Cézanne was declaring the painter's right to recreate nature in such a way as to express an intensely personal vision.

Art as personal expression was the hallmark of two other painters in the so-called post-impressionist period, the Frenchman Paul Gauguin (1848–1903) and the Dutchman Vincent Van Gogh (1853–1890). Both, by their life as well as their art, declared war on traditional nineteenth-century values. Dismayed by the artificiality and complexity of civilization, Gauguin fled to the South Sea Islands and spent the last decade of his life painting the hot and luscious colors of an unspoiled, primitive society. Van Gogh, whose passionate sympathy for the sufferings of his fellow humans led him to attempt the life of a minister to poor mining families and undoubtedly contributed to his eventual insanity and ultimate suicide, poured out the full intensity of his feelings in paintings such as *The Starry Night,* which seem to swirl off the canvas.

Self-Portrait by Paul Gauguin

In the years between 1900 and the First World War, art underwent still further revolutionary development. Henri Matisse (1869–1954) greatly extended Cézanne's use of distortion, thereby declaring once again the painter's right to create according to an individual definition of aesthetic merit. This declaration was given its most ringing prewar endorsement by Pablo Picasso (1881–1973). Picasso, a Catalan Spaniard who came to Paris in 1903, developed a style, *cubism,* that takes its name from an attempt to carry Cézanne's fascination with geometrical form to its logical conclusion. Influenced both by the work of Cézanne and by African sculpture, cubism results not only in distortion but in some cases in actual dismemberment. The artist may separate the various parts of a figure and rearrange them in other than their natural pattern. The purpose is partly to symbolize the chaos of modern life but also to express defiance of traditional notions of form—to repudiate once and for all the conception of art as representational prettiness.

Cubism: Picasso

See color plates following page 768

The artistic declaration of independence from middle-class society was enunciated most dramatically by painters, but was heard also in the realms of literature and music. In France, the work of a group calling itself the symbolists, and centered upon the poetry of Paul Verlaine, Arthur Rimbaud, Stéphane Mallarmé, and Paul Valéry at-

New directions in literature and music

Girl Before a Mirror by Pablo Picasso

tempted to intensify the personal while transcending reality in a way reminiscent of the impressionists, expressionists, and cubists. In music, as well, there was a break from the romantic tradition that dominated the nineteenth century and was expressed in the works of composers such as Robert Schumann (1810–1856), Felix Mendelssohn (1809–1847), and Franz Liszt (1811–1886). Already the late romantic operas of Richard Wagner had taken vast liberties with harmony and departed from stereotypical melodic patterns, producing music that was not subject to the tyranny of form but sensitive to personal expression.

Self-imposed isolation

Whether in painting, in literature, or in music, artists sought to escape to a position from which they could learn and then express what was closest to their own consciousness. Their direct, calculated dismissal of conventional form and content declared their fundamental disdain for—more important, their complete lack of interest in—the problems of the world at large. Their self-imposed isolation served only to increase the general sense of a fragmented world that, despite its material prosperity, was at war with itself.

SELECTED READINGS

• *Items so designated are available in paperback editions.*

SOCIALISM

• Avineri, S., *The Social and Political Thought of Karl Marx,* London, 1968.
• Cole, G. D. H., *A History of Socialist Thought,* Vols. I–III, London, 1953–56.
   A comprehensive treatment of the period 1789–1914.

Gay, Peter, *The Dilemma of Democratic Socialism: Eduard Bernstein's Challenge to Marx,* New York, 1952.

Goldberg, Harvey, *A Life of Jean Jaurès,* Madison, Wisc., 1962. A good biography of the eminent French socialist.

Joll, James, *The Anarchists,* London, 1964.

Landauer, C., and E. Valkenier, *European Socialism,* Berkeley, Calif., 1959.

Lichtheim, G., *A Short History of Socialism,* New York, 1970.

• McBriar, A. M., *Fabian Socialism and English Politics, 1884–1918,* Cambridge, 1966. An extensive study of this important circle: their composition, their ideology, their methods.

Noland, Aaron, *The Founding of the French Socialist Party, 1893–1905,* Cambridge, Mass., 1956. Primarily a narrative account of the translation of ideology into political reality.

Schorske, Carl E., *German Social Democracy, 1905–1917,* Cambridge, Mass., 1955. A magnificent study of the problems of the Social Democrats in a time of imperialism and war.

SCIENTIFIC THOUGHT

• Butterfield, Herbert B., *The Origins of Modern Science,* rev. ed., New York, 1957.

Eiseley, Loren C., *Darwin's Century: Evolution and the Men Who Discovered It,* New York, 1961.

Fothergill, P., *Historical Aspects of Organic Evolution,* London, 1952.

Gillespie, C. C., *The Edge of Objectivity,* Princeton, N.J., 1960. A history of scientific ideas.

• Hughes, H. Stuart, *Consciousness and Society,* New York, 1958. Examines the reaction to Positivism and the growing interest in the irrational by considering the work of Freud, Max Weber, and others.

• Jones, Ernest, *The Life and Work of Freud,* 3 vols., New York, 1953–57. The official biography, by a close collaborator and eminent psychoanalyst.

• McKenzie, A. E. E., *The Major Achievements of Science,* Cambridge, 1960.

Singer, Charles, and A. E. Underwood, *A Short History of Medicine,* rev. ed., New York, 1962.

Wightman, W. P. D., *The Growth of Scientific Ideas,* Edinburgh, 1951.

THE ARTS

Barzun, Jacques, *Darwin, Marx, and Wagner,* Boston, 1941. Argues that these men were not so much originators of new ideas, as founders of systems which are mechanistic and pseudoscientific and therefore threatening to the human cultural heritage.

Kaufmann, Walter A., *Nietzsche: Philosopher, Psychologist, Anti-Christ,* Princeton, N.J., 1974.

Lang, Paul, *Music in Western Civilization,* New York, 1941.

Mosse, G. L., *The Culture of Western Europe: The Nineteenth and Twentieth Centuries,* Chicago, 1961.

Shattuck, Roger, *The Banquet Years: The Arts in France, 1885–1918,* New York, 1958. The emergence of modernism in French art, literature, and music.

SOURCE MATERIALS

- Arnold, Matthew, *Culture and Anarchy,* New York, 1971. Originally published in 1867. A perceptive criticism of English society and a call for an authoritarian principle in an increasingly democratic society.
- Darwin, Charles, *The Descent of Man,* Cambridge, Mass., 1964. See especially Chapter XXI.
- ———, *Origin of Species,* Cambridge, Mass., 1964. See especially Chapters IV, XV.

  Edwards, Stewart, ed., *The Communards of Paris, 1871,* New York, 1976. Annotated eyewitness reports, documents, and accounts of the Paris Commune.
- Gosse, Edmund, *Father and Son,* New York, 1963. A moving autobiography by a distinguished Victorian literary critic, this work reveals the conflict between the religious fundamentalism of the father and the skepticism of the son in the wake of Darwinian theory.

  Kohn, Hans, *The Mind of Modern Russia,* New Brunswick, N.J., 1955. An edited collection of historical, literary, and philosophical works of nineteenth- and twentieth-century Russian authors, designed to reveal the conflict between traditional and Western thought in Russia.
- Marx, Karl, *Capital,* intro. by G. D. H. Cole, New York, 1974.

  Webb, Beatrice, *My Apprenticeship,* London, 1926. Beatrice Webb was one of the leading Fabian Socialists, and in this first volume of her autobiography she explains how she, as a member of one of England's wealthier families, was converted to a socialist creed.

  Zola, Émile, *L'Assommoir,* London, 1970. Written in 1877 and set in the Paris of the 1860s, this bitterly realistic novel portrays the brutalization of the French working class by the forces of industrial change, poverty, and alcohol.

Chapter 26

THE SEARCH FOR STABILITY
(1870–1914)

Ah! What a seething there has been, . . . customs worthy of the inquisition and despotism, the pleasure of a few gold-braided individuals setting
their heels on the nation, and stifling its cry for truth and justice, under the
mendacious and sacrilegious pretext of the interest of the State!

—Émile Zola, "J'accuse"

Between 1870 and 1914, the major powers of Europe worked to
maintain both domestic and international stability. Accomplishment of this goal was facilitated by continuing industrialization. Despite periodic trade depressions, general prosperity increased for almost all classes of society at least until 1900. And
prosperity, in its turn, helped to produce stability, allowing for the establishment in many countries of social welfare systems designed to
benefit workers and their families, and thus to gain their political
allegiance. At the same time, various factors operated to make the
achievement of a generally stable Western world difficult, and ultimately impossible. First, the process of nation-building, which had resulted in the dramatic creation of a modern Germany and Italy, left
potential conflict in its wake. Second, although the majority of citizens
in most western European countries participated at least indirectly in
the governance of their country and enjoyed certain guaranteed rights,
heated debate continued as to the political usefulness of such arrangements. In France, monarchists threatened the republic; in Germany,
democrats battled imperial and bureaucratic oligarchy; in Russia, liberals rose against tsarist autocracy. And across Europe, socialists contended against the political strength of the middle classes. Finally, the
international rivalries that we have seen growing between nations as
they reached out to build empires became more heated with the coming of the new century. Nations grouped into alliances, hoping that a

The roots of instability

balance between power blocs might continue to provide the international stability that Europe had enjoyed since 1815, and that had prevented general war. Instead, the alliances produced only further tensions, and ultimately general world conflict.

1. GERMANY: THE SEARCH FOR IMPERIAL UNITY

The structure of the empire

During the years immediately following the foundation of the German Empire, Bismarck was particularly anxious to achieve imperial unity under Prussian domination. In this he was aided by the economic and military predominance of the Prussian state, and by the organizational framework upon which the empire had been constructed. All powers not granted to the central government were reserved to the individual states. Each had control over its own form of government, public education, highways, police, and other local agencies. Even the enforcement of the laws was left primarily in the hands of the state governments, since the empire had no machinery for applying its laws against individuals. Despite their apparent autonomy, however, the states were in fact subordinate to the empire, and to the emperor himself, the Prussian William I. President A. Laurence Lowell of Harvard once accurately described the German imperial units as comprised of "a lion, a half-dozen foxes, and a score of mice." The Prussian "lion" exercised authority through the person of the emperor and his chancellor. The empire was not governed by a cabinet system, in which ministers of state were responsible to a popularly elected legislature. Instead, the chancellor and other ministers were responsible solely to the emperor. And William was no mere figurehead; he was vested with extensive authority over the army and navy, over foreign relations, and over the general enactment and execution of imperial laws. He had the authority to declare war if the coasts or territory of the empire were attacked. And as king of Prussia, he controlled that country's block of one-third of the votes in the generally conservative upper house, or Bundesrat, of the imperial parliament.

The parliament was by no means a mere rubber stamp, however. All treaties had to be approved by the Bundesrat. Money for the imperial treasury had to be voted by the lower house, the Reichstag, which was elected by universal manhood suffrage and whose membership was primarily middle class. Yet these powers were essentially negative. Although the parliament could veto proposals of the kaiser (emperor) and his ministers, it could not initiate legislation on its own. Hence, although Bismarck often found himself temporarily stymied by the activities of an unsympathetic legislature, he could expect, in the end, to have his way. That way was directed toward the goal of a unified Germany under Prussian domination: essentially conservative; antisocialist, though not necessarily opposed to social welfare schemes; protectionist, and thus sympathetic to the interests of Ger-

William I of Germany

man industrialists; and, in foreign affairs, anti-French, standing firm against any threat from that longtime antagonist.

Bismarck's first campaign on behalf of imperial unity was launched against the Roman Catholic Church. Called the *Kulturkampf,* or "struggle for civilization," the attack was initiated, with some help from intellectual liberals, in 1872. Bismarck's motives were almost exclusively nationalistic. He perceived in some Catholic activities a threat to the power and stability of the empire he had just created. He resented, first of all, the support Catholic priests continued to give to the states'-rights movement in southern Germany and to the grievances of Alsatians and Poles. He was alarmed also by recent assertions of the authority of the pope to intervene in secular matters and by the promulgation in 1870 of the dogma of papal infallibility. For these reasons he resolved to deal such a blow to Catholic influence in Germany that it would never again be a factor in national or local politics. His weapons were a series of laws and decrees issued between 1872 and 1875. First, he induced the Reichstag to expel all the Jesuits from the country. Next, he forced through the so-called May Laws, which placed theological seminaries under state control and permitted the government to regulate the appointment of bishops and priests. No one was allowed to be appointed to any position in the Church unless a German citizen, and then only after a state examination. At the same time civil marriage was made compulsory, even though a religious ceremony had already been performed. In the enforcement of these measures, six of the ten Catholic bishops in Prussia were imprisoned, and hundreds of priests were driven from the country.

The Kulturkampf

Although Bismarck won some of the chief battles of the *Kulturkampf,* he lost the war. The Catholic or Center party appealed so effectively on behalf of the persecuted clergy, and adopted so enlightened an economic program, that it grew into the largest political party in Germany. In the elections of 1874 it captured nearly a fourth of the seats in the Reichstag. Recognizing that he needed this party to support other elements of his program, Bismarck gradually relaxed his persecution of the Catholics. Between 1878 and 1886 nearly all of the obnoxious legislation was repealed, and the Catholic Church restored practically to its former position in Germany.

The failure of the Kulturkampf

By the late 1870s Bismarck had declared war on German socialism, now perceived by him as a far more immediate threat to the empire than Catholicism. The Social Democratic party, under the reformist leadership of the politician Wilhelm Liebknecht (1829–1900), successor to Ferdinand Lassalle, was building a substantial following. Bismarck, his memory of the Paris Commune (see above, pp. 765) still fresh, feared socialism as anarchy, and therefore as a direct challenge to the stability and unity he was attempting to achieve within the empire. Forgetting for the moment the manner in which he had courted the socialists when he needed their support in the 1860s, Bismarck now appeared determined to extinguish them. His attack was motivated

Bismarck's antisocialism

not only by his personal perception of the socialist threat; he was by now anxious to continue to court the favor of industrialists whom he had won to his side by his policy of protective tariffs. In 1878, two separate attempts were made by unbalanced zealots on the life of the emperor. Although neither would-be assassin had anything but the most tenuous connection with the socialists, Bismarck used their actions as an excuse to secure legislation abolishing workers' rights to meet and to publish. The legislature also agreed to a law which gave the government the right to expel socialists from major cities, as was later done in Berlin, Breslau, and Leipzig.

Social welfare legislation

Bismarck was too clever a politician to suppose that he could abolish socialism solely by means of repression. He was prepared to steal at least a portion of the socialists' thunder by adopting parts of their legislative program as his own. In a speech in the Reichstag he frankly avowed his purpose of insuring the worker against sickness and old age so that "these gentlemen [the Social Democrats] will sound their bird call in vain." In addition, he had military purposes in mind. He was desirous of making the German worker a loyal soldier by safeguarding his health in some measure from the debilitating effects of factory labor. Bismarck's program of social legislation was initiated in 1883–1884 with the adoption of laws insuring workers against sickness and accidents. These acts were soon followed by others providing for rigid factory inspection, limiting the employment of women and children, fixing maximum hours of labor, establishing public employment agencies, and insuring workers against incapacity on account of old age. By 1890, when Bismarck was dismissed by the young Emperor William II, Germany had adopted nearly all the elements, with the exception of unemployment insurance, in the pattern of social legislation that later became familiar in the majority of Western nations.

Continuing spread of German socialism

Neither Bismarck's repressive nor his progressive legislation succeeded in killing German socialism, however. The Social Democratic party continued to grow. Bismarck's dismissal came in part over William's insistence that the antisocialist legislation was achieving nothing. The disagreement between the two men extended beyond the question of socialism, however. William II was determined to be his own master. Unity and stability would be the result of his personal initiative, not that of his chancellor. In this, William was expressing his belief in the divinely ordained prerogatives of the Hohenzollerns, the royal house of Prussia. He was asserting claims that—though they sat well enough with the federated princes, the large landowners, the military, and the big industrialists—were increasingly anathema to the democratic forces of the lower middle and working classes. Social Democrats and Progressives were demanding a new constitution guaranteeing control over the chancellor by the majority party in the Reichstag. To these demands the intransigent emperor remained deaf,

Bismarck and William II of Germany

further threatening the fragile stability which Bismarck's policies had attempted to encourage. In the election of 1912 the Social Democrats polled 4,250,000 votes and elected 110 members—the largest single bloc—to the Reichstag. National unity was on a collision course with class conflict. Germany was spared a domestic constitutional crisis only by the infinitely more profound international crisis of the First World War.

2. FRANCE: THE EMBATTLED THIRD REPUBLIC

Although France, in 1870, was not a newly constructed nation, like the German Empire, it was a nation sorely in need of reunification and dedication to a common set of political purposes. Its history for the past century had left it torn between various factions. Monarchists were divided between supporters of the Bourbon and Orleanist dynasties, their allegiance sustained by loyalties either to the descendents of Louis XVIII or of Louis Philippe. Bonapartists looked for political salvation to Napoleon III's son and heir Louis Napoleon. Republicans recalled the short-lived triumphs of their revolutionary ancestors. Socialists called down plagues on all political houses but their own. The result of this deep division was that not until 1875 did France have a constitution under which it could function.

Politically divided France

Following the collapse of Napoleon III's empire a provisional government was organized to rule the country until a new constitution could be drafted. Elections held in 1871 for a national constituent assembly resulted in the choice of some 500 monarchists and only about

200 republicans. Conservative political sentiment was further reinforced by the events of the Paris Commune, which occurred during the period immediately following the elections. But the apparent winners, the monarchists, could not agree among themselves as to whether their king should be a Bourbon or an Orleanist. This stalemate led to the eventual passage in 1875—by one vote—of a series of constitutive laws which made France a republic. These laws established a parliament with a lower house elected by universal manhood suffrage (the Chamber of Deputies) and an upper house elected indirectly (the Senate); a cabinet of ministers presided over by a premier; and a president. Although at first the relative powers of president and premier were not clearly established, within two years the nation had declared itself in favor of a premier at the head of a government answerable to the Chamber of Deputies. An early president, Marshal MacMahon, attempted in 1877 to dismiss a premier with whom he disagreed but who was supported by a majority in the chamber. When new elections were held, MacMahon's policy was repudiated. Henceforth, premiers of the Third Republic were answerable to the chamber and not to the president, who became a figurehead. Yet the resolution of this constitutional question failed to produce political stability, since the premier had no authority to dissolve the legislature. This meant that members of the chamber could vote a premier and his fellow ministers out of office at will, with no risk of being forced to stand for reelection. If defeated on a vote, the premier and his colleagues had no alternative but to resign. The result was no fewer than fifty ministries in the years between 1870 and 1914. The Third Republic, for all its constitutional shortcomings, nevertheless managed to last until 1940—far longer than any system of French government since 1789. Its longevity was due, as much as anything, to the stability of other French institutions—the family, the law courts, and the police, for example.

In the years after 1875, the republicans, who had been feared at first as dangerous radicals, proved themselves to be generally moderate. It

was the discontented monarchists and authoritarian sympathizers within the army, the Roman Catholic Church, and among the families of the aristocracy who took to plotting the overthrow of duly constituted governmental authority. Much of the time of successive republican governments was taken up defending the country from these reactionary radicals. In the late 1880s, a general, Georges Boulanger, gathered about him a following not only of Bonapartists, monarchists, and aristocrats, but of workingmen who were generally disgruntled with their lot and who believed, with Boulanger, that a war of revenge against Germany would put an end to all their troubles. Thanks to the general's own indecisiveness, the threatened coup d'état came to nothing. But Boulanger was a symptom of deep discontents; he appealed, like Napoleon III, to disparate groups of disenchanted citizens, promising quick, dramatic solutions to tedious problems.

One further symptom of the divisions which plagued the republic during the later years of the nineteenth century was the campaign of anti-Semitism which the reactionaries adopted to advance their aims. The fact that certain Jewish bankers were involved in scandalous dealings with politicians lent color to the monarchist insistence that the government was shot through with corruption and that Jews were largely to blame. In the face of those charges it is not strange that anti-Semitism should have flared into a violent outbreak. In 1894 a Jewish captain of artillery, Alfred Dreyfus, was accused by a clique of monarchist officers of selling military secrets to Germany. Tried by court-martial, he was convicted and sentenced for life to Devil's Island, a ghastly prison camp in the Caribbean. At first the verdict was accepted as the merited punishment of a traitor; but in 1897 Colonel Picquart, a new head of the Intelligence Division, announced his conclusion that the documents upon which Dreyfus had been convicted were forgeries. A movement was launched for a new trial, which the War Department promptly refused. Soon the whole nation was divided into friends and opponents of Dreyfus. On his side were the radical republicans, socialists, people of liberal and humanitarian sympathies, and such prominent literary figures as Émile Zola and Anatole France. The anti-Dreyfusards included monarchists, clerics, anti-Semites, militarists, and a considerable number of conservative workingmen. Dreyfus was finally set free by executive order in 1899, and six years later was cleared of all guilt by the Supreme Court and restored to the army. He was immediately promoted to the rank of major and decorated with the emblem of the Legion of Honor.

The Dreyfus affair

The history of the Dreyfus affair gave the republicans the solid ground they had lacked in order to end the plottings of the radical reactionaries once and for all. The leaders of the republic chose to attack their enemies by effectively destroying the political power of the Roman Catholic Church in France. The anticlericalism expressed in

Anticlericalism

Alfred Dreyfus Leaving His Court-Martial

this campaign was probably in part the product of a materialistic age, and of a long-standing mistrust by French republicans of the institution of the Church. Its main source, however, was the nationalism which we have already seen fueling Bismarck's *Kulturkampf*.

Anticlericalism in France reached its peak between 1875 and 1914. The great majority of the leaders of the Third Republic were hostile to the Church; and naturally so, for the Catholic hierarchy was aiding the monarchists at every turn. Clerics had conspired with monarchists, militarists, and anti-Semites in attempting to discredit the republic during the Dreyfus affair. But in the end they had overreached themselves. In 1901 the government passed a series of acts prohibiting the existence of religious orders not authorized by the state, forbidding members of religious orders to teach in either public or private schools, and finally, in 1905, dissolving the union of Church and State. For the first time since 1801 the adherents of all creeds were placed on an equal basis. No longer were the Catholic clergy to receive their salaries from the public purse. Although some of these measures were modified in later years, the Church remained in the minds of most Frenchmen under a heavy cloud of suspicion.

The republic was, during these years, pressed from the Left as well as the Right. Socialism was a political force in France, as it was in Germany. Yet the response of republicans in France to socialist pressure differed markedly from that of Bismarck. There was no antisocialist legislation. Indeed, a law was passed in 1881 abolishing "crimes of opinion," thereby extending the freedom of the press considerably. In the same year, another law authorized public meetings without prior official approval. But if there was no attempt at repression, there was little positive social reform. The largest single party in the republic, the Radicals or Radical Socialists, was really a party representing small shopkeepers and lesser propertied interests. The Radicals were willing to found and maintain a democratic compulsory educational system, but they were reluctant to respond to demands for labor legislation such as had been granted to German workers. Those laws which were passed—establishing a ten-hour workday in 1904 and old-age pensions in 1910—were passed grudgingly and only after socialist pressure. The result was a growing belief among socialists and other workers that parliamentary democracy was worthless, that progress, if it was to be made, would be made only as a result of direct industrial action: the strike. A wave of strikes swept the country for several years before 1914, including one by postal workers in 1909 and by teachers and railwaymen in 1910. The government suppressed these actions by ruthless intervention. By 1914, the republic, though hardly on the brink of revolution, remained divided and uncertain. If the threat from the radical Right had been quelled, the challenge from the Left was only just being faced.

3. GREAT BRITAIN: FROM MODERATION TO MILITANCE

During the half-century before 1914, the British prided themselves on what they believed to be a reasonable, orderly, and workable system of government. Following the passage of the Second Reform Bill in 1867, which extended suffrage to over a third of the nation's adult males, the two major political parties, Liberal and Conservative, vied with each other in adopting legislation designed to provide an increasingly larger proportion of the population the chance to lead fuller and healthier lives. Laws which recognized the legality of trade unions, allowed male religious dissenters to participate fully in the life of the ancient universities of Oxford and Cambridge, provided elementary education for the first time to all children, and facilitated the clearance and rebuilding of large urban areas, were among those placed on the books during the administrations of the two leading politicians of the period, the Conservative Benjamin Disraeli (1804–1881) and the Liberal, William Gladstone (1809–1898). In 1884, suffrage was once more widened, to include over three-fourths of the adult males, and to allow rural workingmen the chance to vote for the first time. Coupled with a previous act which instituted the secret ballot, this electoral reform bill brought Britain nearer to representative democracy.

Benjamin Disraeli

Yet Britain continued to be governed almost exclusively by a small ruling class of men drawn either from landed society or from the upper reaches of the middle class. As members of successive governmental cabinets they recognized their responsibility to Parliament and, in particular, to its lower House of Commons. It was their task, as cabinet ministers, to impose a legislative program upon the Commons. And if the House refused to agree to that program, they recognized, as well, their obligation either to resign forthwith—to make way for a cabinet of opposing party members—or to "go to the country," that is, to dissolve Parliament and order a new election to test the opinion of the voters. This system of "ministerial responsibility" meant that the cabinet retained full responsibility for the management of public affairs, subject, however, to the will of the people as represented by the House of Commons. It produced a generally stable government: Although ministries had to answer to Parliament, Parliament would think twice before voting a ministry out of office when it knew that the ministry might well appeal to the voters for support in a general election. (The lack of this particular feature was what had condemned the French Third Republic to its succession of short-lived governments.) Political stability was insured by more than the device of ministerial responsibility, however. Since both the Conservative and Liberal political leadership was drawn in large part from similar social and economic strata, there was little chance for violent change during these years. One party might espouse a particular cause—the

William Gladstone

"Ministerial
responsibility"

Conservatives imperialism, the Liberals more self-government for Ireland, for example. But both parties generally agreed upon a course steered by men whose similar background and temperament promised programs that were neither radical nor reactionary. This moderation suited the electorate, which was content to defer to politicians whose leadership was secured by the undoubted fact of Britain's general prosperity.

By 1914, however, that leadership was being seriously challenged. Prosperity, though widespread enough, did not extend to the unskilled: dock workers, transport workers, and the like. These groups formed trade unions to press their claims. Their determination encouraged other unions to assume a more militant and demanding stance. In the 1890s this activity produced a reaction in the form of anti–trade union employers' associations and a series of legal decisions limiting the right of unions to strike. Workers, in turn, reacted by associating with middle-class socialist societies to form an independent Labour party, which was born in 1901 and five years later managed to send twenty-nine members to the House of Commons. Sensitive to this pressure from the Left, the Liberals, during their ministry which began in 1906, passed a series of reforms they hoped would insure a minimum standard of living for those who had heretofore known little security. Sickness, accident, old-age, and unemployment insurance schemes were adopted. A minimum wage was decreed in certain industries. Labor exchanges, designed to help unemployed men and women find new jobs, were established. Restrictions on strikes and on the right of trade unions to raise money for political purposes were relaxed.

Liberal reforms, 1906–1914

Much of this legislation was the work of David Lloyd George (1863–1945), chancellor of the exchequer (finance minister) in the Liberal cabinet of Prime Minister Herbert Asquith. Together with another young Liberal, Winston Churchill (1874–1965), Lloyd George had hammered together legislation that was both a reflection of his own political philosophy and a practical response to the growing political power of the working class. To pay for these programs—and for a larger navy to counter a German build-up—Lloyd George proposed a budget in 1909 that included progressive income and inheritance taxes, designed to make wealthier taxpayers pay at higher rates. His proposals so enraged the aristocratic members of the House of Lords that they declared themselves prepared to throw out the budget, an action contrary to constitutional precedent. Asquith countered with a threat to create enough new peers (titled noblemen) sympathetic to the budget to insure its passage.[1] The House of Lords eventu-

Lloyd George's budget

---

[1] In Britain the monarch had the authority to elevate an unlimited number of men to the peerage. But since the crown acts only on the advice of the prime minister, it is this official who has the actual power to create new members of the House of Lords. If necessary, he could use this power to pack the upper house with his own followers.

Lloyd George and Winston Churchill on Their Way to the House of Commons on Budget Day, 1910

ally surrendered; the result of the crisis was an act of Parliament which provided that the House of Lords could not veto legislation passed by the House of Commons.

The rancor aroused by this constitutional conflict was intense. Self-proclaimed defenders of the House of Lords screamed threats in a chamber unused to anything but gentlemanly debate. Angry threats were by no means confined to the Houses of Parliament during these years, however. Throughout Britain, men and women threw moderation to the winds as they disputed issues in an atmosphere little short of anarchic. The reasons for this continued agitation were various. A decline in real wages after 1900 kept the working class in a militant mood, despite Liberal reforms, and produced an unusually severe series of strikes in 1911 and 1912. A liberal plan to grant Home Rule (self-government) to Ireland produced not only panic in the Protestant minority counties of the north (Ulster) but arming and drilling of private militias with an intensity that seemed to forecast civil war.

Perhaps the most alarming—because the most unexpected—of the militant revolts that seized Britain in the years before 1914 was the campaign for women's suffrage. The middle-class women who engaged in this struggle enjoyed more freedom of opportunity than their mothers had known. Laws had been passed easing the process of divorce and permitting married women control of their own property. Some universities had started to grant degrees to women. Contraceptive devices—and feminist propaganda defending their use—had begun to result in changed attitudes toward sexuality within the middle class. Perhaps because of these gains, many women felt their lack

Increased militance

Suffragettes

London Dock Strike, 1911. Police move to clear demonstrators from shops where they have taken refuge after having been fired upon.

of the vote all the more acutely. Although the movement began among middle-class women, it soon included some female members of the working class and the aristocracy. Agitation reached a peak after 1900, when militant suffragettes—under the leadership of Emmeline Pankhurst, her daughters Christabel and Sylvia, and others—resorted to violence in order to impress upon the nation the seriousness of their commitment. Women chained themselves to the visitors' gallery in the House of Commons; slashed paintings in museums; invaded that male sanctum, the golf course, and inscribed VOTES FOR WOMEN in acid on the greens; disrupted political meetings; burned politicians' houses; and smashed department store windows. The government countered violence with repression. When women, arrested for their disruptive activities, went on hunger strikes in prisons, wardens proceeded to feed them forcibly, tying them down, holding their mouths open with wooden and metal clamps, and running tubes down their throats. When hunger strikes threatened to produce deaths and thus martyrs for the cause, the government passed the constitutionally dubious Cat and Mouse Act, which sanctioned the freeing of prisoners to halt their starvation and then, once they had regained their health, authorized their rearrest. The movement was not to see the achievement of its goal until after World War I, when reform came largely because of women's contributions to the war effort.

Whether Britain's militant mood might have led to some sort of general conflict had not the war begun in 1914, is a question historians *Instability* continue to debate. Suffice it to say that national sentiment in the last few years before the outbreak of general hostilities was a far different

Violent Suffragette Protest. Emily Davison was killed when she threw herself in front of the king's racehorse at the Epsom Derby, June 4, 1913. Her purpose was to call attention to the suffragette cause.

one from that of the 1870s. Britain, so confident of itself and of its moderation, was proving no less a prey to instability than other European nations.

4. RUSSIA: THE ROAD TO REVOLUTION

In only one European country, Russia, did conditions pass from instability to insurrection during these prewar years. The Russian revolutionary movement had numerous forerunners. Waves of discontent broke out several times during the nineteenth century. Threatened uprisings between 1850–1860 persuaded Tsar Alexander II to grant local self-government, to reform the judicial system, and, most important of all, to liberate the serfs. Yet his government failed to sustain all these reforms; a wave of reaction followed. Radicalism revived and the number of revolutionary sects increased. Allied with them were the nihilists, who tended to condemn the whole political and social system. Although nihilism originated about 1860 as a movement to solve Russian problems by spreading enlightenment among the peasants, its failure to win general support by propagandist methods turned its leadership more and more to terrorism. The culmination of this terrorism was the assassination of the tsar in 1881.

    The years that followed the death of Alexander II marked the floodtide of reaction against the entire policy of reform. The new tsar, Alexander III (1881–1894), governed under the theory that Russia had nothing in common with western Europe, that its people had been

Reform and reaction in nineteenth century Russia

*Autocracy and
Russification*

nurtured on despotism and mystical piety for centuries and would be utterly lost without them. Such Western ideals as rationalism and individualism would undermine the childlike faith of the Russian masses and would plunge the nation into the dark abyss of anarchy and crime. In like manner, Western institutions of trial by jury, parliamentary government, and free education could never bear fruit if planted in Russian soil. With such doctrines as his guiding principles, Alexander III enforced a regime of stern and vengeful repression. He curtailed in every way possible the powers of the local assemblies, increased the authority of the secret police, and subjected villages to government by wealthy nobles selected by the state. These policies were continued, though in somewhat less rigorous form, by his son, Nicholas II (1894–1918), a much less effective ruler. Both tsars were ardent proponents of Russification and used it with a vengeance to strengthen their power. Russification was simply the more ruthless counterpart of similar nationalistic movements in various countries. Its purpose was to extend the language, religion, and culture of Great Russia, or Russia proper, over all of the subjects of the tsar and thereby to simplify the problem of governing them. It was aimed primarily at the Poles, Finns, and Jews, since these were the nationalities considered most dangerous. Inevitably it resulted in oppression. The Finns were deprived of their constitution; the Poles were compelled to study their own literature in Russian translations; and high officials in the tsar's government connived at *pogroms,* i.e., wholesale massacres, against the Jews.

Westernization

Despite these attempts to turn Russia's back to the West, however, the nation was being drawn more closely than it had ever been before into the general European orbit. Russia was industrializing, and making use of European capital to do so. Economic policies during the

A Railroad Yard in Eastern Russia, 1896

1890s, when Count Sergei Witte was the tsar's leading minister, resulted in the adoption of the gold standard, which made Russian currency easily convertible. Railways and telegraph lines were constructed; exports and imports multiplied by factors of seven and five respectively from 1880 to 1913. In addition, Russian writers and musicians contributed in a major way to the enriching of Western culture. We have already noted the singular contributions of Tolstoy, Turgenev, and Dostoevsky. The musical works of Peter Tchaikovsky (1840–1893) and Nikolai Rimsky-Korsakov (1844–1908), while expressing a peculiarly Russian temperament and tradition, were recognized as important additions to the general body of first-rate contemporary composition.

With Westernization came the growth of both the business and wage-earning classes. And with an increase in class consciousness new political parties emerged. Middle-class businessmen and professionals combined with enterprising landowners in 1903 to form a Constitutional Democratic party, whose program included the creation of a nationally elected parliament or Duma to determine and carry out policies which would further the twin goals of liberalization and Westernization. Meanwhile, two essentially working-class parties, the Social Revolutionaries and the Social Democrats, began to agitate for far more radical solutions to the problems of Russian autocracy. The Social Revolutionaries concerned themselves with the continued plight of the peasants, who, when serfdom was abolished, were compelled to purchase their land, and who were burdened with high taxes. The Social Revolutionaries wanted to equalize the landholdings of peasants within their local agricultural communes or *mirs,* and to increase the power of the *mirs* in their continuing competition with large landowners. The Social Democrats were Marxists, who saw themselves as westerners and as part of the international working-class movement. In 1903 the leadership of the Social Democratic party split in an important disagreement over revolutionary strategy. The Mensheviks, who took their name from the Russian word for minority, argued unsuccessfully for a broadly based party which, while remaining revolutionary, would nonetheless accept assistance from progressives and democrats. The Bolsheviks—the majority of the Social Democrats—favored a strongly centralized party controlled by a committee whose "party line" would be accepted at all organizational levels. The Bolsheviks reorganized the Social Democrats under the leadership of the young, dynamic, and dedicated revolutionary Vladimir Ulanov (1870–1924), who wrote under the pseudonym of N. Lenin.

Lenin was a member of the middle class, his father having served as an inspector of schools and minor political functionary. He had been expelled from the University of Kazan for engaging in radical activity, following the execution of his elder brother for his involvement in a

Growth of political parties

The Young Lenin, 1897

Lenin

plot to assassinate Alexander III. Lenin spent three years as a political prisoner in Siberia; from 1900 until 1917 he lived as a political exile in western Europe. His zeal and abilities as both a theoretician and a political activist are evidenced by the fact that he retained leadership of the Social Democrats even while residing abroad. Lenin continued to preach the gospel of Marxism and of a relentless class struggle. His treatise *What Is to Be Done?* was a stinging response to revisionists who were urging collaboration with less radical parties. Revolution was what was to be done, Lenin argued, revolution "made" as soon as possible by an elitist group of agitators working through the agency of a disciplined party. Lenin and his followers, by merging the tradition of Russian revolutionism with Western Marxism, and by endowing the result with a sense of immediate possibility, fused the Russian situation in such a way as to make eventual explosion almost inevitable.

The Russo-Japanese War

The revolution that came in 1905, however, took even the Bolsheviks by surprise. Its unexpected occurrence was the result of a war between Russia and Japan, which broke out in 1904, and in which the Russians were soundly beaten. Both countries had conflicting interests in Manchuria and Korea; this fact was the immediate cause of the conflict. On land and sea the Japanese proved themselves the military superiors of the Russians. As dispatches continued to report the defeats of the tsar's army and navy, the Russian people were presented with dramatic evidence of the inefficiency of autocracy.

The Revolution of 1905

Members of the middle class who had hitherto refrained from association with the revolutionists, now joined in the clamor for change. Radical workingmen organized strikes and held demonstrations in every important city. Led by a priest, Father Gapon, a group of 200,000 workers and their families went to demonstrate their grievances at the tsar's winter palace in St. Petersburg on January 22, 1905—ever after known as Bloody Sunday. The demonstrators were met by guard troops and many of them were shot dead. By the autumn of 1905 nearly the entire urban population had enlisted in a strike of protest. Merchants closed their stores, factory-owners shut down their plants, lawyers refused to plead cases in court, and even valets and cooks deserted their wealthy employers. It was soon evident to Tsar Nicholas that the government would have to yield. On October 30, he issued his October Manifesto, pledging guarantees of individual liberties, promising a moderately liberal franchise for the election of a Duma, and affirming that henceforth no law would be valid unless it had the Duma's approval. This was the high-water mark of the revolutionary movement. During the next two years Nicholas issued a series of sweeping decrees which negated most of the promises made in the October Manifesto. He deprived the Duma of many of its powers, and decreed that it be elected indirectly on a class basis by a number of electoral colleges. Thereafter the legislative body contained a majority of obedient followers of the tsar.

Bloody Sunday. Demonstrating workers who sought to bring their grievances to the attention of the tsar are met and gunned down by government troops, January 1905.

The reasons for this setback to the revolutionary movement are not hard to discover. In the first place, the army remained loyal to its commander-in-chief. Consequently, after the termination of the war with Japan in 1905, the tsar had a large body of troops that could be counted upon if necessary to decimate the ranks of the revolutionists. An even more important reason was the split in the ranks of the revolutionists themselves. After the issuance of the October Manifesto, large numbers of the bourgeoisie became frightened at threats of the radicals and declared their conviction that the revolution had gone far enough. Withdrawing their support altogether, they became known henceforth as Octobrists. The more radical merchants and professional men, organized into the Constitutional Democratic party, maintained that opposition should continue until the tsar had been forced to establish a government modeled after that of Great Britain. This fatal division rendered the middle class politically impotent. Finally, disaffection appeared within the ranks of the workers. Further attempts to employ the general strike as a weapon against the government ended in disaster.

The reasons for setback

But the Russian revolutionary movement of 1905 was not a total failure. The cruel vengeance taken by the tsar convinced many people that their government was not a benevolent autocracy, as they had been led to believe, but a stubborn and brutal tyranny. The uprising revealed to the masses their principal mistakes and taught them what sources of strength they should rely upon for success in the future. Moreover, some of the concessions actually obtained were not completely wiped out. The Duma was not abolished. It continued to serve

Gains from the revolutionary movement

as a means by which at least scattered opponents of reaction could make themselves heard. In addition, the revolt of 1905 persuaded some of the more sagacious advisors of the tsar that last-ditch conservatism was none too safe. The result was the enactment of a number of reforms designed to conciliate the troublesome classes. Among the most significant were the agrarian reforms sponsored by the government's leading minister, Peter Stolypin, between 1906 and 1911. These included: (1) the transfer of 5 million acres of royal land to the peasants for a price; (2) permission for the peasant to withdraw from the *mir* and set up as an independent farmer; and (3) cancellation of the remaining installments owed by the peasants for their land. Nor were the working classes altogether forgotten. Decrees were issued permitting the formation of labor unions, providing for a reduction of the working day (to not more than ten hours in most cases), and establishing sickness and accident insurance. Yet the hopes of some liberals that Russia was on the way to becoming a progressive nation on the Western model proved illusory. The tsar remained stubbornly autocratic. Few peasants had enough money to buy the lands offered for purchase. In view of the rising cost of living, the factory workers considered their modest gains insufficient. A new revolutionary outbreak merely awaited a convenient spark.

5. THE SEARCH FOR STABILITY ELSEWHERE IN THE WEST

Reforms in Italy

Other European countries generally found it just as difficult to attain internal tranquility in the late nineteenth century as did those whose history we have surveyed. Italy was plagued by squabbles among its political leaders, aggravated by the festering quarrel with the papacy over the seizure of ecclesiastical territories. Illiteracy and poverty, particular problems in the agrarian south, contributed to unrest, as did working-class radicalism in the industrial cities of the north. Attempts were made to relieve distress by the passage of social welfare legislation, including provision for nationalized life insurance. In 1912 a law tripled the electorate, instituting something approximating universal manhood suffrage. Relatively few of the newly enfranchised exercised their right to vote, choosing to register their discontent by more direct means such as strikes.

Nationalism in Austria-Hungary

Nationalist aspirations continued to be a major problem in eastern Europe. In 1867 an attempt had been made to resolve national differences in Austria by dividing the empire in two—an Austrian empire west of the river Leith, and a kingdom of Hungary to its east. Each of the two components in this so-called Dual Monarchy was to be the equal of the other, though the two were joined by the same Hapsburg monarch, by several common ministries, and by a kind of super-parliament. This solution failed to put an end to nationalist divisions, however. Czechs and other Slav minorities in both of the new terri-

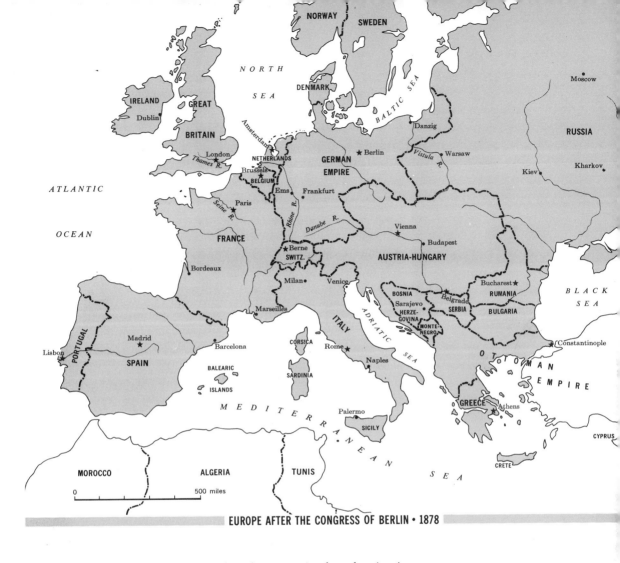

EUROPE AFTER THE CONGRESS OF BERLIN · 1878

tories nursed resentment against what they perceived as domination by alien German or Magyar culture. Despite the division of responsibilities between Austria and Hungary, the government remained centralized under the rule of the Emperor-King Francis Joseph. Social agitation was countered, as in Germany, by repression coupled with welfare measures. Universal male suffrage was introduced into Austria in 1907; in Hungary it was opposed by the Magyar majority which saw it as a device whereby the Slavic minority might increase its power.

In southeastern Europe nationalist agitation continued to rend the ever-disintegrating Ottoman Empire. Before 1829 the entire Balkan peninsula—bounded by the Aegean, Black, and Adriatic Seas—was controlled by the Turks. But during the next eighty-five years a gradual dismemberment of the Turkish Empire occurred. In some instances the slicing away of territories had been perpetrated by rival European powers, especially by Russia and Austria; but generally it

The Ottoman Empire

was the result of nationalist revolts by the sultan's Christian subjects. In 1829, at the conclusion of a war between Russia and Turkey, the Ottoman Empire was compelled to acknowledge the independence of Greece and to grant autonomy to Serbia and to the provinces which later became Rumania. As the years passed, resentment against Ottoman rule spread through other Balkan territories. In 1875–1876 there were uprisings in Bosnia, Herzegovina, and Bulgaria, which the sultan suppressed with murderous vengeance. Reports of atrocities against Christians gave Russia an excuse for renewal of its age-long struggle for domination of the Balkans. In this second Russo-Turkish War (1877–1878) the armies of the tsar won a smashing victory. The Treaty of San Stefano, which terminated the conflict, provided that the sultan surrender nearly all of his territory in Europe, except for a remnant around Constantinople. But at this juncture the great powers intervened. Austria and Great Britain, especially, were opposed to letting Russia assume jurisdiction over so large a portion of the Near East. In 1878 a congress of the great powers, meeting in Berlin, transferred Bessarabia to Russia, Thessaly to Greece, and Bosnia and Herzegovina to the control of Austria. Seven years later the Bulgars, who had been granted some degree of autonomy by the Congress of Berlin, seized the province of Eastern Rumelia from Turkey and in 1908 established the independent Kingdom of Bulgaria.

In the very year when this last dismemberment occurred, Turkey itself was engulfed by the tidal wave of nationalism. For some time the more enlightened Turkish citizens had been growing increasingly disgusted with the weakness and incompetence of the sultan's government. In particular, those who had been educated in European universities were growing more and more convinced that their country should be rejuvenated by the introduction of Western ideas of science, patriotism, and democracy. Organizing themselves into a society known as the Young Turks, they forced the sultan in 1908 to establish constitutional government. The following year, when a reactionary movement set in, they deposed the reigning sultan, Abdul Hamid II, and placed on the throne his brother, Mohammed V, as a titular sovereign. The real powers of government were now entrusted to a grand vizier and ministers responsible to an elected parliament. This revolution did not mean increased liberty for the non-Turkish inhabitants of the empire. Instead, the Young Turks launched a vigorous movement to Ottomanize all of the Christian subjects of the sultan. At the same time the disturbances preceding and accompanying the revolution opened the way for still further dismemberment. In 1908 Austria annexed the provinces of Bosnia and Herzegovina, which the Treaty of Berlin had allowed it merely to administer, and in 1911–1912 Italy entered into war with Turkey for the conquest of Tripoli.

Of all the major nations of the West, the United States probably underwent the least domestic turmoil during the several decades before

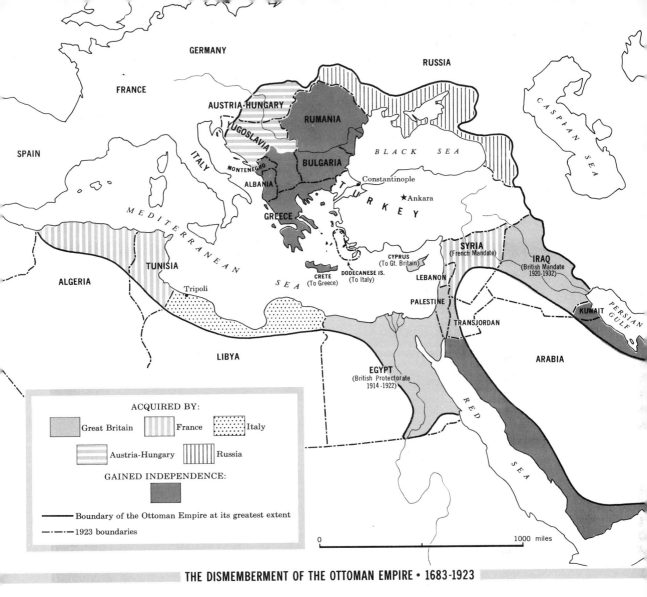

THE DISMEMBERMENT OF THE OTTOMAN EMPIRE • 1683-1923

1914. The Civil War had exhausted the country; until the end of the century the ever-expanding frontier provided an alternative for those discontented with their present lot. Yet the United States also felt, to some degree, the pressures that made stability so hard to sustain in Europe. Though the Civil War had ended, the complex moral problem of racism remained to block all attempts to truly heal the nation. Severe economic crises, particularly an economic depression in the 1890s, accompanied by the collapse of agricultural prices and the closing of factories, caused great suffering and aroused anger at capitalist adventurers who seemed to be profiting at the expense of the country as a whole. Many grew convinced that a restricted money supply had produced the depression. Demand for the issuance of paper money

Unrest in the United States

808

*The Search For Stability
(1870-1914)*

Eugene Debs

and the increased coinage of silver were at the heart of the programs of the Greenback and the Populist parties, which attracted large followings, and which campaigned as well for an income tax and government ownership of railways, and telephone and telegraph lines. Socialism of a reformist brand was espoused by Eugene V. Debs (1855–1926), leader of a mildly Marxist Socialist party. It failed to appeal to the generally un–class-conscious American worker, who continued to have faith in the dream of economic mobility. More radical was the membership of the Industrial Workers of the World, a general union whose goal was to organize the unskilled and immigrant worker. Perceived as a device of foreign agitators, the IWW was repressed both by the government and by industrial management. Characteristic of the generally moderate tone of American reformism was the Progressive movement, which captured both the imagination and votes of a vocal minority of middle-class Americans whose hostility over the accumulation of private economic power and the political corruption of urban "bosses" was balanced by their belief in the democratic process and in the possibility of continuing human progress. The movement, many of whose ideas were embodied in the programs of Presidents Theodore Roosevelt and Woodrow Wilson, was halted by the First World War, which fostered an environment hostile to the democratic process.

6. INTERNATIONAL RIVALRIES: THE ROAD TO THE FIRST WORLD WAR

The end of a century of peace

Despite the domestic instabilities and uncertainties that characterized the Western world in the years before 1914, a great many men and women retained a faith in the notion of peaceful progress. There had been an absence of multinational armed conflict—with the exception of the Crimean War—for a century. European countries—even autocratic Russia—had been moving gradually towards what most agreed was the worthy goal of democracy. Indeed, instability could be understood as the result of either an overzealous or an overdelayed movement in that direction. Above all, industrialization seemed to be providing a better standard of living for all—or at least all within the Western world. There is little wonder, therefore, that men and women reacted with disbelief as they saw their world crumbling during the days of frantic diplomatic maneuvering just prior to the outbreak of war in August 1914.

The balance of power

The key to an understanding of the coming of World War I lies in an understanding of international diplomacy during the years after 1870. Europe had prided itself on the establishment of a balance of power, which had kept any one nation from assuming a position so powerful as to threaten the general peace. During his years as chancellor, Bismarck played a diplomatic variation upon this general theme, in order to ensure that France would not engage in a war of revenge against the German victors of 1870. There was little prospect that the French would attempt war singlehanded. Therefore, Bismarck determined to isolate France by attaching all of its potential allies to Germany. In 1873 he managed to form an alliance with both Austria and Russia, the so-called League of the Three Emperors, a precarious combination that soon went on the rocks. With the League of the Three Emperors defunct, Bismarck cemented a new and much stronger alliance with Austria. In 1882 this partnership was expanded into the celebrated Triple Alliance when Italy was added as a member. The Italians did not join out of love for either Germany or Austria but from motives of anger and fear. They resented the French occupation of Tunisia (1881), a territory which they regarded as properly theirs. Moreover, Italian politicians were still at odds with the Church, and they feared that supporters of the papacy in France might gain the upper hand and send a French army to defend the pope. In the meantime, the Three Emperors' League had been revived. Though it lasted for only six years (1881–1887), Germany managed to hold the friendship of Russia until 1890.

Thus after little more than a decade of diplomatic maneuvering, Bismarck had achieved his ambition. By 1882 France was cut off from nearly every possibility of obtaining aid from powerful friends. Austria and Italy were united with Germany in the Triple Alliance, and Russia after a three-year lapse was back once more in the Bismarckian

*Bismarck's diplomatic
success*

Grand Palace, Paris Exposition, 1900. European nations continued to promote exhibitions of this sort, patterned after the Crystal Palace exhibition of 1851. Designed to celebrate the growth of Western industrialism, they also served to promote international rivalry.

camp. The only conceivable quarter from which help might come was Great Britain; but, with respect to continental affairs, the British were maintaining a policy of "splendid isolation." Therefore, so far as the danger of a war of revenge was concerned, Germany had little to fear. Bismarck's complicated structure of alliances appeared to answer the purpose for which he claimed it had been built—to keep the peace. But the alliance system was a weapon that could cut two ways. In Bismarck's hands, it kept the peace. In hands less diplomatically capable, it might become less an asset than a liability, as was the case after 1890.

A diplomatic revolution

During the years between 1890 and 1907, European nations, competing against each other across the globe for trade and territory, became more suspicious of the intentions of each other. This general international insecurity produced a diplomatic revolution that obliterated Bismarck's handiwork, and resulted in a new alignment which threatened the Germans. To be sure, the Germans had Austria still on their side; but they lost the friendship of both Russia and Italy, while Britain abandoned its isolation to enter into agreements with Russia and France. This shift in the balance of power had fateful results. It convinced the Germans that they were surrounded by a ring of enemies, and that consequently they must do everything in their power to retain the loyalty of Austria-Hungary—even to the extent of supporting that country's foreign adventures.

The Triple Entente

The first of the major results of this diplomatic revolution was the formation of the Triple Entente. In 1890 Russia and France began a political flirtation which gradually turned into a binding alliance. The secret military convention signed by the two countries in 1894 provided that each should come to the aid of the other in case of an attack by Germany, or by Austria or Italy supported by Germany. This Dual Alliance of Russia and France was followed by an Entente Cordiale between France and Great Britain. During the last two decades of the nineteenth century, the British and the French had frequently been involved in sharp altercations over colonies and trade, as in the Sudan. By 1904, however, France, fearing Germany, had buried its differences with Britain and in that year signed the Entente Cordiale. This was not a formal alliance but a friendly agreement, covering a variety of subjects. The final step in the formation of the Triple Entente was the conclusion of a mutual understanding between Great Britain and Russia. Again there was no formal alliance. The two powers simply came to an agreement in 1907 concerning their ambitions in Asia.

Two opposing camps

Thus by 1907 the great powers of Europe had come to be arrayed in two opposing combinations, the Triple Alliance of Germany, Italy, and Austria-Hungary, and the Triple Entente of Britain, France, and Russia. Had these combinations remained stable and more or less evenly matched, they might well have promoted the cause of peace. But no such condition prevailed. Each grew weaker and less stable with the passage of time. And it was this instability, rather than the al-

The Baghdad Railroad. German and Turkish officials celebrate the launching of the enterprise.

liance system itself, which was perhaps the most important contributing factor leading to the outbreak of war.

The tensions within the new alliances become more comprehensible if one considers the national aims of each of the principal European states. By 1900 six great powers in Europe—Germany, France, Russia, Italy, Austria-Hungary, and Great Britain—were competing for power, security, and economic advantage. Each had specific objectives, the fulfillment of which it regarded as essential to its national interest. Germany built its ambitions around eastward expansion. After 1890 German capitalists and imperialists dreamed of a *Drang nach Osten* (drive to the east) and planned the construction of a railway from Berlin to Baghdad to facilitate economic control of the Ottoman Empire. Austria also looked to the east, but to the Balkans rather than to any part of western Asia. Austria's hold on Trieste and other portions of the Adriatic coast was precarious, since much of this territory was inhabited by Italians. If it could carve a highway through the Balkans to the Aegean, its access to the sea would be more secure.

Aims of the great powers: Germany and Austria-Hungary

To a large degree the objectives of France were dictated by a desire to curb or counterbalance the growing might of Germany. France hoped to recover Alsace and Lorraine. But recovery of these lost provinces was not the only French objective. The French were also determined to add Morocco to their African empire regardless of the interests of other powers. The motives of the French were both economic and political. Morocco contained rich mineral deposits, and would be also valuable for strategic reasons and as a reservoir from which troops might be drawn.

Ambitions of France

A paramount ambition of Russia was to gain control of the Bosporus and the Dardanelles. Achievement of this long-desired goal would prevent the Russian fleet from being bottled up in the Black Sea in the event of war. Besides, it would give unquestioned access to the Mediterranean and probably possession of Constantin-

Ambitions of Russia

ople. Turkey would be eliminated from Europe, and Russia would fall heir to the Balkans. In addition, if the tsar's agents could get to Constantinople before the Germans, they could turn the Berlin-to-Baghdad railway into an empty dream. But the Russians had other ambitions. They coveted access to the Persian Gulf and Indian Ocean and tried for years to make Persia a Russian protectorate. They also strove for better outlets to the Pacific and attempted to extend their control over Manchuria. That each of these ambitions constituted a threat to the status quo scarcely needs emphasis.

Ambitions of Great Britain and Italy

The power policies of Great Britain and Italy were somewhat less closely related to the specific actions of other countries. The policy of Britain, in fact, was directed against almost everyone. It was no less suspicious of the Russian ambitions at Constantinople than it was of the German. Until after the beginning of the twentieth century the British distrusted France. Their cardinal aims were (1) to maintain the lifelines of their empire; (2) to keep open the sea lanes to their sources of imports and foreign markets; and (3) to preserve a balance among the nations on the Continent so that no one of them would ever become strong enough to attack Great Britain. If the actions of any other country threatened to interfere with these cardinal aims (as they often did), the hostility of Britain would instantly be aroused. The offending nation would be put in its place by diplomatic pressure, by forming an alliance against it, or by going to war, as the British finally did against Germany in 1914. Italian policy was mainly based on hopes of aggrandizement at the expense of Austria and Turkey. Austria continued to hold territories which the Italians regarded as rightfully theirs—the so-called *Italia Irredenta* (unredeemed Italy) as late as 1915—while Turkey blocked Italy's acquisition of Tripoli and other territories in North Africa.

Resulting conflicts

These often conflicting ambitions naturally placed strains on the alliances between the great powers. The Triple Alliance declined in strength because of a growing coolness between Italy and Austria. Moreover, Italian nationalists coveted territory in North Africa, notably Tripoli, which they believed they could obtain only by supporting French ambitions in Morocco. Meanwhile, the Triple Entente was threatened by discord between Britain and Russia. Because their lifeline to the East might be imperiled, the British could not view with equanimity the cardinal aim of Russia to gain control of the Bosporus and the Dardanelles and thus of Constantinople. Disharmony in the Triple Entente also increased when Britain and France refused to support Russia in its dispute with Austria over the latter's annexation of Bosnia and Herzegovina. In short, conflicts were so numerous that the members of neither alliance could be quite sure where their opposite numbers might stand in case of a real threat of a European war.

If diplomatic instability was the major cause of the war, two others must nevertheless be emphasized as well. Nationalism, particularly in eastern Europe, played an important role in heightening international conflict. Since the beginning of the twentieth century, Serbia wanted to extend its jurisdiction over all the peoples alleged to be similar to its own citizens in race and in culture. Some of these peoples inhabited what were then the two Turkish provinces of Bosnia and Herzegovina. Others included Croatians and Slovenes in the southern provinces of Austria-Hungary. After 1908, when Austria suddenly annexed Bosnia and Herzegovina, the Serbian scheme was directed exclusively against the Hapsburg Empire. It took the form of agitation to provoke discontent among the Slav subjects of Austria, in the hope of drawing them away and uniting the territories they inhabited with Serbia. It resulted in a series of dangerous plots against the peace and integrity of the Dual Monarchy.

Other causes: nationalism

In many of their activities the Serbian nationalists were aided and abetted by the Pan-Slavists in Russia. The Pan-Slav movement was founded upon the theory that all of the Slavs of eastern Europe constituted one great family. Therefore, it was argued that Russia as the most powerful Slavic state should act as the guide and protector of the smaller Slavic nations of the Balkans. Pan-Slavism was not merely the wishful sentiment of a few ardent nationalists, but was a part of the official policy of the Russian government. It went far toward explaining Russia's aggressive stand in every quarrel that arose between Serbia and Austria.

Pan-Slavism

One further expression of the growth of international instability, and hence one further cause of war, was the spread of militarism. Uncertainty as to the reliability of alliances encouraged the belief that national security depended upon the extent of military and naval preparedness. War scares produced a compulsion to build larger armies and navies. After 1870, every major European power, with the exception of Britain, had adopted conscription and universal military training. Germany and Britain strained their resources either to achieve or to maintain naval superiority. Accompanying this arms race was a growing willingness to acknowledge the place of international aggression in the conduct of world affairs. The American President Theodore Roosevelt had argued that training for war was necessary to preserve the "manly and adventurous qualities" in a nation. The German Field Marshal von Moltke and historian Heinrich von Treitschke saw in military conflict one of the divine elements of the universe and a "terrible medicine" for the human race. The French philosopher Ernest Renan justified war as a condition of progress, "the sting which prevents a country from going to sleep."

Militarism

Field Marshal von Moltke

All these factors—diplomatic instability, nationalism, and militarism—combined to produce a series of crises between 1905 and 1913. They were not so much causes as they were symptoms of international animosity. Yet each left a heritage of suspicion and bitterness that made war all the more probable. In some cases hostilities were

Moroccan crises

averted only because one of the parties was too weak at the time to offer resistance. The result was a sense of humiliation, a smoldering resentment that was almost bound to burst into flame in the future. Two of the crises were generated by disputes over Morocco. Both Germany and France wanted to control Morocco; and in 1905 and 1911 the two powers stood on the brink of war. Each time the dispute was smoothed over, but not without the usual legacy of suspicion.

Serbian crisis

In addition to the clash over Morocco, two crises occurred in the Near East. The first was the Bosnian crisis of 1908. At the Congress of Berlin in 1878 the two Turkish provinces of Bosnia and Herzegovina had been placed under the administrative control of Austria, though actual sovereignty was still to be vested in the Ottoman Empire. Serbia also coveted the territories, since they would double its kingdom and place it within striking distance of the Adriatic. Suddenly, in October 1908, Austria annexed the two provinces, in flat violation of the Treaty of Berlin. The Serbs were furious and appealed to Russia. The tsar's government threatened war, until Germany addressed a sharp note to St. Petersburg announcing its firm intention to back Austria. Since Russia had not yet fully recovered from its war with Japan and was plagued by internal troubles, Russian intervention was postponed.

Balkan Wars

Still more bad blood between the nations of eastern Europe was created by the Balkan Wars. In 1912 Serbia, Bulgaria, Montenegro, and Greece, with encouragement from Russia, joined in a Balkan alliance for the conquest of the Turkish province of Macedonia. The war started in October 1912, and in less than two months the resistance of the Turks was shattered. Then came the problem of dividing the spoils. In secret treaties negotiated before hostilities began, Serbia had been promised Albania, in addition to a generous slice of Macedonia. But now Austria, fearful as always of any increase in Serbian power, intervened at the peace conference and obtained the establishment of Albania as an independent state. For the Serbs this was the last straw. It seemed that at every turn their path to western expansion was certain to be blocked by the Hapsburg government. From this time on, anti-Austrian agitation in Serbia and in the neighboring province of Bosnia became ever more venomous.

A world at war

It was the assassination of the Austrian Archduke Francis Ferdinand by a Serbian sympathizer on July 28, 1914, that ignited the conflict. The four-year war that ensued altered the Western world immeasurably. Yet many changes which came either during or after World War I were the result, not of the war itself, but of pressures and forces we have seen at work during the prewar years. Then European power, at its height, was challenged by forces which that power had unleashed and which it proved unable to contain.

SELECTED READINGS

• *Items so designated are available in paperback editions.*

• Berghahn, Victor, *Germany and the Approach of War in 1914*, New York, 1973. Examines the domestic background of German foreign policy, especially the naval program.

Brogan, D. W., *France under the Republic, 1870–1930*, New York, 1940. An excellent survey, comprehensive and analytical.

• Dangerfield, George, *The Damnable Question: One Hundred and Twenty Years of Anglo-Irish Conflict*, Boston, 1976. A sensitive and judicious assessment of the Irish question.

• ———, *The Strange Death of Liberal England*, New York, 1935. Examines England's three major crises of the prewar period: women's suffrage, labor unrest, and Irish home rule.

Dansette, Adrien, *A Religious History of Modern France*, Vol. II, New York, 1961. Covers the period 1870–1940.

Ensor, R. C. K., *England, 1870–1914*, Oxford, 1949. From the Oxford History of England series.

• Eyck, Erich, *Bismarck and the German Empire*, New York, 1968.

• Haimson, L., *The Russian Marxists and the Origins of Bolshevism*, Cambridge, Mass., 1955.

Halèvy, Elie, *A History of the English People*, Vols. IV–VI, London, 1949–52. The best survey of the period.

Hoffman, Ross, *Great Britain and the German Trade Rivalry, 1875–1914*, Philadelphia, 1933. A perceptive account.

Jenks, William A., *Austria under the Iron Ring, 1879–1893*, Charlottesville, Va., 1965. An examination of Austria's attempts at political and social reform, set in the context of a struggle for autonomy from German domination.

Johnson, Douglas, *France and the Dreyfus Affair*, London, 1966.

• Jones, Gareth Stedman, *Outcast London*, Oxford, 1971. A remarkable book which examines the breakdown in the relationship between classes in London during the latter half of the nineteenth century.

Mack Smith, Dennis, *Italy: A Modern History*, rev. ed., Ann Arbor, Mich. 1969. An excellent survey.

• McManners, John, *Church and State in France, 1870–1914*, New York, 1972. Particularly good on the question of education and the final separation of Church and State.

• May, Arthur J., *The Hapsburg Monarchy, 1867–1914*, Cambridge, Mass., 1951.

• Mosse, W. E., *Alexander II and the Modernization of Russia*, New York, 1958.

Nichols, John Alden, *Germany After Bismarck*, New York, 1959.

Rémond, Rene, *The Right Wing in France from 1815 to De Gaulle*, Philadelphia, 1969. Traces the survival of royalism and Bonapartism in French thought and politics.

Seton-Watson, Hugh, *The Russian Empire, 1801–1917*, Oxford, 1967.

• Simon, Walter M., ed., *Germany in the Age of Bismarck*, New York, 1968.

• Taylor, A. J. P., *The Struggle for Mastery in Europe, 1848–1918*, Oxford, 1954. An excellent diplomatic history.

Thompson, Paul R., *The Edwardians: The Remaking of British Society*, Bloomington, Ind., 1975. Examines social change in England at the turn of the century and the instruments of that change.

• Thomson, David, *Democracy in France since 1870*, rev. ed., New York, 1969.

Weber, Eugen, *Peasants into Frenchmen: The Modernization of France, 1870–1914*, Stanford, Calif., 1977. Argues that the great achievement of the Third Republic was the consolidation of France, accomplished by bringing rural areas into the mainstream of modern life.

• Williams, Roger L., *The French Revolution of 1870–1871*, New York, 1969. A good narrative account.

SOURCE MATERIALS

Booth, Charles, ed., *Life and Labour of the People in London*, 9 vols., London, 1892–97. A remarkable document for its time. A street-by-street survey of London's labor and poverty. One of the most comprehensive social surveys ever.

Childers, Erskine, *The Riddle of the Sands*, New York, 1978. A best-seller in England in 1903, this novel concerns a future war between England and Germany. Its reception gives evidence of the rise of anti-German sentiment prior to World War I.

• Hamerow, Theodore S., ed., *The Age of Bismarck: Documents and Interpretations*, New York, 1973.

• Lenin, Vladimir, *What Is to Be Done?* London, 1918. Written in 1902, this is Lenin's most famous pamphlet. In it he called for the proletarian revolution to be led by elite cadres of bourgeois intellectuals, like himself.

• Mackenzie, Midge, ed., *Shoulder to Shoulder*, New York, 1975. A richly illustrated documentary history of the British movement for women's suffrage.

• Pankhurst, Emmeline, *My Own Story*, New York, 1914. The memoirs of one of the leaders of England's militant suffragettes.

• Turgenev, Ivan, *Fathers and Sons*, New York, 1966. Turgenev's greatest novel is set in Russia in the 1860s and portrays the ideological conflict between generations at the time of the emancipation of the serfs and the rise of nihilism.

• Zola, Émile, *Germinal*, New York, 1964. Zola's realistic novel describes class conflict in France's coal mining region.

Chapter 27

WORLD WAR I

Nevertheless, except you share
With them in hell the sorrowful dark of hell,
Whose world is but the trembling of a flare,
And heaven but as the highway for a shell,

You shall not hear their mirth:
You shall not think them well content
By any jest of mine. These men are worth
Your tears. You are not worth their merriment.

—Wilfred Owen, "Apologia Pro Poemate Meo"

The war that broke out in 1914 was one of the most extraordinary in history. Though it was not really the "first world war," since such conflicts as the Seven Years' War and the Napoleonic wars had also been global in extent, it had an impact far exceeding either of those. It quickly became a "people's war," in which civilians as well as soldiers in the trenches participated in violent demands for extermination of the enemy. It bore fruit in an epidemic of revolutions and sowed the dragon's teeth of new and even more venomous conflicts in the future. In such ways it set the pattern for an age of violence that has continued through most of the twentieth century.

A world at war

Historians who have studied the evidence are generally of the opinion that no one nation was solely responsible for the outbreak of war. Perhaps none of the combatants really wanted war; they would have preferred to achieve their aims by other means. But in pursuing these aims they followed policies that made war virtually inevitable. The most dangerous of national objectives were probably those of Germany. This was true not because they were more self-serving than those of other Western powers, but because they posed a more serious threat to the balance of power in Europe. As the war progressed it appeared that Germany was attempting to achieve on the Continent objectives that Britain and France had succeeded in attaining in Asia and Africa. From the beginning of the war, Germany's rulers were think-

Responsibility for war

ing in terms of a vastly enlarged German empire that would include as satellite states Poland, Belgium, Holland, the Balkans, and Turkey, establishing a great sphere of influence comparable to that of the United States in the Western Hemisphere and of Russia in the heartland of Eurasia. Fears of what this German scheme would do to the European balance of power frightened diplomats in other European capitals.

1. THE ROAD TO ARMAGEDDON

The assassination of Francis Ferdinand

It has been generally held that the assassination of the Austrian archduke was the immediate cause of World War I. Francis Ferdinand was soon to become emperor of Austria-Hungary. The reigning monarch, Francis Joseph, had reached his eighty-fourth year, and his death was expected momentarily. The murder of the heir to the throne was therefore considered in a very real sense as an attack upon the state.

Motives of the assassins

The actual murderer of Francis Ferdinand was a Bosnian student by the name of Gavrilo Princip, the tool of Serbian nationalists. The murder, though committed in Sarajevo, the capital of Bosnia, was the result of a plot hatched in Belgrade, the Serbian capital. The conspirators were members of a secret society officially known as Union or Death, but commonly called the Black Hand. What were the motives of the conspirators? If there is any one answer, it would seem to lie in the plan which Francis Ferdinand was known to be developing for the reorganization of the Hapsburg Empire. This plan, designated as *trialism,* involved a proposal for changing the Dual Monarchy into a triple monarchy. In addition to German Austria and Magyar Hungary, already practically autonomous, there was to be a third semi-independent unit composed of the Slavs. This plan was exactly what the Serb nationalists did not want. They feared that if it were put into effect, their Slovene and Croatian kinsmen would be content to remain under

The Archduke Francis Ferdinand. He and his wife are leaving the Senate House in Sarajevo shortly before the assassination, June 28, 1914.

Hapsburg rule. They therefore determined to get Francis Ferdinand out of the way before he could become emperor.

In the weeks immediately following the assassination, Austrian officials conducted an investigation which confirmed their suspicions that the plot was of Serbian origin. Consequently, on July 23, they dispatched to the Serbian government a severe ultimatum consisting of eleven demands: among them Serbia was to suppress anti-Austrian newspapers; to crush secret patriotic societies; to eliminate from the government and from the army all persons guilty of anti-Austrian propaganda; and to accept the collaboration of Austrian officials in stamping out the subversive movement against the Hapsburg Empire. On July 25, in accordance with the time limit of forty-eight hours, the Serbian government transmitted its reply. Of the total of eleven demands, only one was emphatically refused, and five were accepted without reservations. The German chancellor regarded it as almost a capitulation, and Emperor William II declared that now all reason for war had dissipated. The Austrians, however, pronounced the Serbian reply unsatisfactory, severed diplomatic relations, and mobilized parts of their army. The Serbs themselves had been under no illusions about pleasing Austria, since, three hours before transmitting their reply, they had issued an order to mobilize the troops.

Austrian ultimatum to Serbia

The Austrian intransigence vis-à-vis the Serbian response was actually the culmination of a belligerence which had been growing among European nations prior to the events which followed the assassination. As early as July 18 Sergei Sazonov, the Russian foreign minister, warned Austria that Russia would not tolerate any effort to humiliate Serbia. On July 24 Sazonov informed the German ambassador: "I do not hate Austria; I despise her. Austria is seeking a pretext to gobble up Serbia; but in that case Russia will make war on Austria."[1] In the adoption of this attitude, Russia had the support of France. About the twentieth of July, Raymond Poincaré, president of France, paid a visit to St. Petersburg. He kept urging Sazonov to "be firm" and to avoid any compromise which might result in a loss of prestige for the Triple Entente. He warned the Austrian ambassador that "Serbia has very warm friends in the Russian people. And Russia has an ally, France."[2]

Russia and France

The attitude of Germany in these critical days was ambiguous. Although the kaiser was shocked and infuriated by the assassination, his government did not make any threats until after the actions of Russia gave cause for alarm. Yet both William II and the chancellor, Theobald von Bethmann-Hollweg, adopted the premise that stern punishment must be meted out to Serbia without delay. They hoped in this way to confront the other powers with an accomplished fact. The kaiser declared on June 30: "Now or never! Matters must be cleared up with the Serbs, *and that soon.*" On July 6 Bethmann-Hollweg gave

The attitude of Germany

[1] S. B. Fay, *The Origins of the World War*, II, 300.
[2] *Ibid.*, II, 281.

Nicholas II and Raymond Poincaré, the President of the French Republic, in St. Petersburg on July 23, 1914

a commitment to the Austrian foreign minister which was interpreted by the latter as a blank check. The Austrian government was informed that the kaiser would "stand true by Austria's side in accordance with his treaty obligations and old friendship." In giving this pledge Bethmann and his imperial master were gambling on the hope that Russia would not intervene for the protection of Serbia, and that therefore the quarrel would remain a mere local squabble.

Russian mobilization

Austria declared war against Serbia on July 28, 1914. For a fleeting, anxious moment there was a possibility that the conflict might be contained. But it was quickly transformed into a war of larger scope by the action of Russia. On July 29 Sazonov and a prowar military clique persuaded Tsar Nicholas II to issue an order mobilizing all troops, not only against Austria but against Germany as well. Their argument was a logical one. Such a vast country as Russia would require considerable time to get its military machine into operation. But before the order could be put into effect, Nicholas changed his mind, having just received an urgent appeal from the kaiser to help preserve the peace.

See color map facing page 769

On July 30 Sazonov and the Russian chief of staff went to work to induce the tsar to change his mind again. For more than an hour they sought to convince the reluctant autocrat that the entire military system should be set in motion. In the end, Nicholas signed an order for immediate mobilization.

There was now no drawing back from the abyss. The Germans were alarmed over Russian preparations for war. The latest action of the tsar's government made the situation far more critical, since in German military circles, and also in French and Russian, general mobilization meant war. Upon learning that the tsar's decree had gone into effect, William II's government sent an ultimatum to St. Petersburg demanding that mobilization cease within twelve hours. On the afternoon of August 1, the German ambassador requested an interview with the Russian foreign minister. He appealed to Sazonov for a favorable answer to the German ultimatum. Sazonov replied that mobilization could not be halted, but that Russia was willing to continue negotiations. The ambassador repeated his question a second and a third time, emphasizing the terrible consequences of a negative answer. Sazonov finally replied: "I have no other answer to give you." The ambassador then handed the foreign minister a declaration of war and, bursting into tears, left the room. In the meantime, the kaiser's ministers had also dispatched an ultimatum to France demanding that its leaders make known their intentions. Premier René Viviani replied on August 1 that France would act "in accordance with her interests," and immediately ordered a general mobilization of the army. On August 3 Germany declared war upon France.

The German ultimatums to Russia and France

All eyes now turned in the direction of Britain. What would happen, now that the other two members of the Triple Entente had rushed headlong into war? For some time after the situation on the Continent had become critical, Britain vacillated. It is difficult to believe that the British would have long remained out of the war, even if the neutrality of Belgium had never been violated. In fact, as early as July 29, Sir Edward Grey, Britain's foreign secretary, had given the German ambassador in London a warning that if France were drawn into the war, Great Britain would enter also. Nevertheless, it was the invasion of Belgian territory which provided the immediate cause of

Britain enters the war

August 1, 1914. A German officer reads the declaration of war in the streets of Berlin.

Britain's entry. In 1839, along with the other great powers, Britain had signed a treaty guaranteeing the neutrality of Belgium. Moreover, it had been British policy for a century or more to try to prevent domination of the Low Countries, lying directly across the Channel, by any powerful continental nation. The Germans planned to attack France through Belgium. Accordingly, they demanded of the Belgian government permission to send troops across its territory, promising to respect the independence of the nation and to pay for any damage to property. When Belgium refused, the kaiser's legions began pouring across the frontier. The British foreign secretary immediately went before Parliament and urged that his country should rally to the defense of international law and to the protection of small nations. He argued that peace under the circumstances would be a moral crime, and declared that if Britain should fail to uphold its obligations of honor in this matter it would forfeit the respect of the civilized world. The next day, August 4, the cabinet sent an ultimatum to Berlin demanding that Germany respect Belgian neutrality, and that the Germans give a satisfactory reply by midnight. The kaiser's ministers offered no answer save military necessity, arguing that it was a matter of life and death for Germany that its soldiers should reach France by the quickest and easiest way. As the clock struck twelve, Great Britain and Germany were at war.

The conflagration spreads

Other nations were quickly drawn into the terrible vortex. On August 7 the Montenegrins joined with their kinsmen, the Serbs, in fighting Austria. Two weeks later the Japanese declared war upon Germany, partly because of their alliance with Great Britain, but mainly for the purpose of conquering German possessions in the Far East. On August 1 Turkey negotiated an alliance with Germany, and in October began the bombardment of Russian ports on the Black Sea. Thus most of the nations definitely bound by alliances entered the conflict in its early stages on one side or the other. Italy, however, though still technically a member of the Triple Alliance, proclaimed neutrality. The Italians insisted that the Germans were not fighting a defensive war, and that consequently they were not bound to go to their aid. Italy remained neutral until May 1915, when Britain and France bribed its leaders with secret promises of Austrian and Turkish territory to engage in the war on the side of the Triple Entente.

2. THE ORDEAL OF BATTLE

The "holy war" of the principal powers

In the Book of Revelation it is related that the forces of good and evil shall be gathered together on "the great day of God" to do battle at Armageddon. The author might almost have been thinking of the titanic conflict which engulfed the nations of Europe in 1914. For World War I was seldom admitted to be a struggle between rival imperialist powers or a product of nationalist jealousy. Instead, it was represented by spokesmen for both sides as a crusade against the forces of evil. No sooner had war begun than social and political leaders in England and France pronounced it a gallant effort to safeguard the rights of the weak and to preserve the supremacy of international law and morality. Prime Minister Asquith on August 6, 1914, declared that Britain had entered the conflict to vindicate "the principle that smaller nationalities are not to be crushed by the arbitrary will of a strong and overmastering Power." Across the Channel, President Poincaré was assuring his fellow citizens that France had no other purpose than to stand "before the universe for Liberty, Justice and Reason." Socialists who had, in the past, proclaimed their international solidarity and their opposition to the wars of capitalism, now in almost all cases declared themselves national patriots. Later, as a consequence of the preaching of such writers and orators as H. G. Wells, Gilbert Murray, and the American president, Woodrow Wilson, the crusade of the Entente powers became a war to redeem mankind from the curse of militarism. In the opposing camp, the subordinates of the kaiser were doing all in their power to justify Germany's military efforts. The struggle against the Entente powers was represented to the German people as a crusade on behalf of a superior *Kultur* and as a battle to protect the fatherland against the wicked encirclement policy of the Entente nations. German socialist politicians were persuaded to vote for the war on the grounds that a German war with Russia would help liberate the Russian people from the tsarist yoke.

World War I fooled military experts who believed it would end quickly. Open warfare soon disappeared from the Western Front—the battle line that stretched across France from Switzerland to the North Sea, where the fighting was concentrated for four years. Following

War of attrition

Modern Warfare. After the first few battles, the war on the Western Front settled into static or position warfare. During the four-year period, veritable cities of mud, stone, and timber sprang up behind the trenches.

Left: *British armored trucks move toward the front.* Above: *A British tank and field ambulance.*

Germany's initial advance into France, the opposing armies settled down in a vast network of trenches, from which attacks to dislodge the enemy were launched, usually in the murky hours just before dawn. These attacks always failed to achieve more than very limited gains. Protected by barbed wire and machine-guns—both making their first major appearance in a European war—defenders had the advantage. The one weapon with the potential to break the stalemate, the tank, was not introduced into battle until 1916, and then with such reluctance by tradition-bound commanders that its half-hearted employment made almost no difference. Airplanes were used almost exclusively for reconnaissance, though occasional "dog-fights" did occur between German and Allied pilots. The Germans sent Zeppelins to raid London, but they did little significant damage. Commanding officers continued to believe that the war would have to be won on the ground. Only by battering their enemies first with artillery and then with thousands of men armed with rifles, grenades, and bayonets, did they believe they could achieve the always elusive "breakthrough." On more than one occasion those in charge of the war attempted to end the stalemate by opening military fronts in other areas of the world. In 1915, Britain and France attempted a landing at Gallipoli, in Asia Minor, in the hope of driving Turkey from the war. The campaign was a disaster for the Entente powers, however, failing, as did others, to refocus the fighting or to free it from the immobility of the trenches.

Life for the common soldier on the Western Front alternated between the daily boredom and extreme unpleasantness of weeks spent *The toll* in muddy and vermin-ridden trench communities, and the occasional and horrifying experience of battle, a nightmare not only of artillery, machine-guns, and barbed wire, but of exploding bullets, liquid fire, and poison gas. Battles that accomplished almost nothing devoured

Wartime Leaders. Left: Haig, Joffre, and Lloyd George discuss strategy. Right: Reviewing a map are Hindenburg, William II, and Ludendorff, members of the German high command.

the men who fought them. Over 600,000 soldiers were killed and wounded when the Germans unsuccessfully besieged the French stronghold of Verdun, near France's eastern border, for six months in the spring of 1916. In the battle along the Somme River, which lasted from July to October 1916, and which gained the British and French no more than a few miles, the Germans lost 500,000 men, the British 400,000, and the French 200,000. Although the war, because of its stationary nature, took a relatively light civilian toll, the total numbers of dead and wounded were staggering: out of an estimated 65 million men who fought under the flags of the various belligerents, 10 million were killed and another 20 million wounded. The struggle was an endurance contest. The victory of the Entente powers came as a result of their continued control of the seas and of their ability to obtain almost unlimited supplies of money, food, and munitions from allies and neutral countries around the world.

As the conflict dragged on, more and more nations entered the war on one side or the other. Italy postponed its entry until the spring of 1915. Bulgaria joined Germany and its allies, known as the Central Powers, in September 1915, and Rumania entered on the opposite side about a year later. The event which helped greatly to tip the scales in favor of an Entente victory was the declaration of war against Germany by the United States on April 6, 1917. The United States entered the war for a variety of reasons. All sorts of moral arguments were avowed by President Wilson and other high officials of the government—to "make the world safe for democracy," to banish autocracy and militarism, and to establish a league or society of nations in place of the old diplomatic maneuvering. Undoubtedly, the primary reason, though, was the concern of the American government to maintain the balance of power in Europe. For years it had been a cardinal doctrine in the State Department and among military and naval

World War I Posters Held Back Little in Their Appeal to Emotions

The Lusitania *Leaving New York Harbor.* In February 1915 the *Lusitania* was torpedoed and sunk by a German U-boat. Among the 1,200 people drowned were 119 Americans. The disaster was one step in the chain of events which led to the entry of the United States into the war on the side of Britain and France.

officers that the security of the United States depended upon a balance of forces in the Old World. No one power must be allowed to establish its supremacy over all of Europe. So long as Great Britain was strong enough to prevent that supremacy, the United States was safe. Some authorities believe that American officials had grown so accustomed to thinking of the British navy as the shield of American security that they could hardly tolerate the thought of any different situation. Germany, however, presented not merely a challenge to British naval supremacy, but threatened to starve the British nation into surrender and to establish a hegemony over all of Europe.

Submarine warfare

The direct cause of United States participation in World War I was the U-boat, or submarine, warfare of the Germans. Once it became clear that the war would be one of attrition, the Germans recognized that unless they could break the Entente's stranglehold on their shipping, they would be defeated. The result was a campaign of submarine warfare. In February 1915, the kaiser's government announced that neutral vessels headed for British ports would be torpedoed without warning. President Wilson replied by declaring that the United States would hold Germany to a "strict accountability" if any harm should come to American lives or property. The warning had little effect. The Germans were convinced that the U-boat was one of their most valuable weapons, and they considered themselves justified in using it against the British blockade. They also believed, correctly, that the British were receiving war materiel clandestinely shipped aboard passenger ships from the United States, and continued to sink them, thus appearing to violate United States neutrality. When the kaiser's ministers announced that, on February 1, 1917, they would launch a campaign of unrestricted submarine warfare, Wilson cut off diplomatic relations with the Berlin government. On April 2 he went before a joint session of the two houses of Congress and requested and received a declaration of war.

3. REVOLUTION IN THE MIDST OF WAR

In the midst of world war came revolution. Russia, already severely weakened by internal conflicts before 1914, found itself unable to sustain the additional burden of continuous warfare. In a nation ruled as autocratically as was Russia, a successful war effort depended greatly on the determination and talents of its ruler, the tsar. Nicholas II was, by nature, irresolute and weak. His limited capabilities were further undermined by the irrationality of his wife, Alexandra, a religious fanatic, and of her spiritual mentor, the monk Rasputin. The latter had gained the tsarina's sympathy by his ability to alleviate the sufferings of her hemophiliac son, and used his influence over her to shape policy to his own self-aggrandizing ends. The tsar's incompetent direction meant that Russia's armies could not win battles, and suffered a series of humiliating defeats by the Germans. In some instances soldiers were sent to the front without rifles; their clothing supplies were also inadequate. Medical facilities were scarce. The railway system broke down, producing a shortage of food not only in the army but in the cities as well. By the end of 1916, Russia's power to resist had practically collapsed.

Incompetence of the tsar

The revolution in Russia followed a succession of stages somewhat similar to those of the French Revolution of 1789. The first of these began in March 1917 with the forced abdication of the tsar. For this the immediate cause was disgust with the conduct of the war. But there were many other factors—inflation and consequent high prices, and scarcity of food and coal in urban areas. With the overthrow of the

The March 1917 revolution

Tsar Nicholas II and His Family on the Eve of the Revolution

tsar, the authority of the government passed into the hands of a provisional ministry organized by leaders in the Duma in conjunction with representatives of workers in Petrograd, calling themselves a *soviet,* or government council. (The city had abandoned the supposedly Germanic name of St. Petersburg at the beginning of the war.) With the exception of Alexander Kerensky (1881–1970), who was a member of the rurally based Social Revolutionary party, nearly all of the ministers were bourgeois liberals. Their hope was to transform the Russian autocracy into a constitutional monarchy modeled after that of Great Britain. In accordance with this aim, they issued a proclamation of civil liberties, released thousands of prisoners, and made plans for the election of a constituent assembly.

The provisional government

The provisional government proved itself inadequate to deal with the problems it faced. Its leaders did not seem to understand the new conditions created by the war, or even some of those arising in the prewar period. Among these were overcrowding in the cities, the emergence of an urban working class, and the inevitable harshness of the class conflict in the initial stages of industrialization. Further, the heads of this provisional government made the mistake of attempting to continue the war on the basis of previous imperialist aims. They hoped to obtain Constantinople and everything else that had been promised to Russia in its secret treaties. But the masses of the Russian people were desperately weary of the years of hardship and struggle. What they wanted was peace and a chance to return to a normal life. Consequently, in May, when the leaders renewed their pledge of support for the Entente powers, opposition was so strong that they were forced to resign. A new government was organized which managed to stay in power until September. Led by Kerensky, it consisted

Scenes from the Russian Revolution. Left: Street Fighting in Petrograd, 1917. Right: Russian soldiers join the Bolsheviks in front of the Winter Palace.

Strife in Ireland, 1916. British troops raiding the office of a Dublin printer who supported the rebellion.

primarily of moderate socialists. The ultimate failure of this regime may be ascribed chiefly to the insignificant role played by the middle class in Russia at the time. In no sense can it be compared as a revolutionary force with the bourgeoisie in France in 1789. It was much smaller in size and lacked the prestige and wealth of the elements that destroyed the absolute monarchy of Louis XVI. Moreover, it had little support from the mass of the Russian people.

Triumph of the Bolsheviks

The downfall of Kerensky's regime marked the end of the first stage of the Russian Revolution. The second began immediately after, with the accession of the Bolsheviks to power under the leadership of Lenin on November 7, 1917. Soon after the overthrow of the tsar the Bolsheviks had begun to plan for a socialist revolution. They worked their way into the Petrograd Soviet, the Council of Workers' and Soldiers' Deputies, and quickly gained control of it from the Mensheviks and Social Revolutionaries. They organized an armed Red Guard and took possession of strategic points throughout the city. By November 7 everything was ready for a coup d'état. Red Guards occupied nearly all the public buildings and finally arrested the members of the government, though Kerensky himself escaped. Thus the Bolsheviks climbed to power with scarcely a struggle. Their slogan of "Peace, Land, and Bread" made them heroes to the soldiers disgusted with the war, to the peasants hungry for land, and to the urban population suffering from various shortages. As soon as possible, the Bolsheviks sued for peace with the Germans, accepting terms that included the surrender of Poland, the Ukraine, and Finland. The treaty was signed at Brest-Litovsk in March 1918.

The Easter Rebellion in Ireland

Yet another outbreak of revolution in this period was the so-called Easter Rebellion in Ireland. At the beginning of World War I, Irish nationalists, who resented the rule of their country by the British, were ripe for revolt. They had been promised self-rule on the eve of the war, but the British later reneged on the ground that a national emergency must take preeminence over everything else. This greatly angered the Roman Catholic majority of southern Ireland. They scheduled Easter Monday, 1916, as a day for revolt. British forces quelled the uprising, but not until after a hundred people had been killed. Sporadic outbreaks kept the island in turmoil for years thereafter, but were finally brought to a temporary end by an agreement constituting southern Ireland as a free republic. The northern counties, or the province of Ulster, were to continue subject to the British crown.

4. ARMISTICE AND PEACE

Peace proposals

While fighting on the several fronts raged through four horrible years, various attempts were made to bring about the negotiation of peace. In the spring of 1917, Dutch and Scandinavian socialists decided to summon an international socialist conference to meet at Stockholm in the hope of drafting plans for ending the fighting which would be acceptable to all the belligerents. The Petrograd Soviet embraced the idea and on May 15 issued an appeal to socialists of all nations to send delegates to the conference and to induce their governments to agree to a peace "without annexations and indemnities, on the basis of the self-determination of peoples." The socialist parties in all the principal countries on both sides of the war accepted this formula and were eager to send delegates to the conference, but when the British and French governments refused to permit any of their subjects to attend, the project was abandoned. That the rulers of the Entente states were not afraid of these proposals merely because they emanated from socialists is indicated by the fact that a similar formula suggested by the pope was just as emphatically rejected. Nowhere was there a disposition to take peace proposals seriously. Woodrow Wilson, as spokesman for the Allies, declared that negotiation of peace under any conditions was impossible so long as Germany was ruled by the kaiser. The Central Powers professed to regard with favor the general import of the papal suggestions, but they refused to commit themselves on indemnities and restorations, especially the restoration of Belgium.

The Fourteen Points

The best-known of all the peace proposals was President Wilson's program of Fourteen Points, which he incorporated in an address to Congress on January 8, 1918. Summarized as briefly as possible, this program included: (1) "open covenants openly arrived at," i.e., the abolition of secret diplomacy; (2) freedom of the seas; (3) removal of economic barriers between nations; (4) reduction of national armaments "to the lowest point consistent with safety"; (5) impartial adjustment of colonial claims, with consideration for the interests of the peoples involved; (6) evacuation of Russia by foreign armies; (7) restoration of the independence of Belgium; (8) restoration of Alsace and Lorraine to France; (9) a readjustment of Italian frontiers "along clearly recognizable lines of nationality"; (10) autonomous development for the peoples of Austria-Hungary; (11) restoration of Rumania, Serbia, and Montenegro, with access to the sea for Serbia; (12) autonomous development for the peoples of Turkey, with the straits from the Black Sea to the Mediterranean "permanently opened"; (13) an independent Poland, "inhabited by indisputably Polish populations," and with access to the sea; (14) establishment of a League of Nations. On several other occasions throughout 1918 Wilson reiterated in public addresses that this program would be the basis of the peace for which he would work. Thousands of copies of the Fourteen Points were scattered by Allied planes over the German trenches and behind the lines, in an effort to convince both soldiers and civilians that the Entente nations were striving for a just and durable peace.

By the close of the summer of 1918 the long nightmare of bloodshed was approaching its end. A great offensive launched by the British, French, and United States forces in July dealt one shattering blow after another to the German battalions and forced them back almost to the Belgian frontier. By the end of September the cause of the Central Powers was hopeless. Bulgaria withdrew from the war on September 30. Early in October the new chancellor of Germany, the liberal Prince Max of Baden, appealed to President Wilson for a negotiated peace on the basis of the Fourteen Points. But the fighting went on, for Wilson had returned to his original demand that Germany must agree to depose the kaiser. Germany's remaining allies tottered on the verge of collapse. Turkey surrendered at the end of October. The Hapsburg Empire was cracked open by rebellions on the part of the empire's subject nationalities. Moreover, an Austrian offensive against Italy had not only failed but had incited the Italians to a counteroffensive, with the consequent loss to Austria of the city of Trieste and 300,000 prisoners. On November 3 the Emperor Charles, who had succeeded Francis Joseph in 1916, signed an armistice which took Austria out of the war.

Germany was now left with the impossible task of carrying on the struggle alone. The morale of its troops was rapidly breaking. The

The collapse of the Central Powers

German Supplies Moving toward the Somme During the Last German Offensive in 1918

The signing of the armistice

blockade was causing such a shortage of food that there was real danger of starvation. The revolutionary tremors that had been felt for some time swelled into a mighty earthquake. On November 8 a republic was proclaimed in Bavaria. The next day nearly all of Germany was in the throes of revolution. A decree was published in Berlin announcing the kaiser's abdication, and early the next morning he was moved across the frontier into Holland. In the meantime. the government of the nation had passed into the hands of a provisional council headed by Friedrich Ebert, leader of the socialists in the Reichstag. Ebert and his colleagues immediately took steps to conclude negotiations for an armistice. The terms as now laid down by the Entente powers provided for acceptance of the Fourteen Points with three amendments. First, the item on freedom of the seas was to be stricken (in accordance with the request of the British). Second, restoration of invaded areas was to be interpreted in such a way as to include reparations, that is, payment to the victors to compensate them for their losses. Third, the demand for autonomy for the subject peoples of Austria-Hungary was to be changed to a demand for independence. In addition, troops of the Entente nations were to occupy cities in the Rhine valley; the blockade was to be continued in force; and Germany was to hand over 5,000 locomotives, 150,000 railway cars, and 5,000 trucks, all in good condition. There was nothing that the Germans could do but accept these terms. At five o'clock in the morning of November 11, two delegates of the defeated nation met with the commander of the Entente armies, Marshal Foch, in the dark Compiègne forest and signed the papers officially ending the war. Six hours later the order, "cease fire," was given to the troops. That night thousands of people danced through the streets of London, Paris, and Rome in the same delirium of excitement with which they had greeted the declarations of war.

A harsh peace

The peace concluded at the various conferences in 1919 and 1920 more closely resembled a sentence from a court than a negotiated settlement. Propaganda had encouraged victorious soldiers and civilians to suppose that their sacrifices to the war effort would be compensated for by payments extracted from the "wicked" Germans. The British prime minister, David Lloyd George, campaigned during the election of 1918 on the slogan, "Hang the Kaiser!", while one of his partisans demanded "Squeeze the German lemon until the pips squeak!". In all the Allied countries nationalism and democracy combined to make compromise impossible and to reassert the claim that the war was a crusade of good against evil. The peace settlement drafted by the victors inevitably reflected these feelings.

The conference convoked in Paris[3] to draft a peace with Germany

---

[3] The conference did most of its work in Paris. The treaty of peace with Germany, however, takes its name from Versailles, the suburb of Paris in which it was signed.

The Council of Four. Meeting to draft a peace treaty in Paris were Orlando of Italy, Lloyd George of Britain, Clemenceau of France, and Wilson of the United States.

was technically in session from January until June of 1919, but only six plenary meetings were ever held. All of the important business of the conference was transacted by small committees. At first there was the Council of Ten, made up of the president and secretary of state of the United States, and the premiers and foreign ministers of Great Britain, France, Italy, and Japan. By the middle of March this body had been found too unwieldy and was reduced to the Council of Four, consisting of the American president and the English, Italian, and French premiers. A month later the Council of Four became the Council of Three when Premier Vittorio Orlando withdrew from the conference in a huff because Wilson refused to give Italy all it demanded.

The Paris Conference

The final character of the Treaty of Versailles was determined almost entirely by the so-called Big Three—Wilson, Lloyd George, and Clemenceau. These men were about as different in personality as any three rulers who could ever have been brought together for a common purpose. Wilson was an inflexible idealist, accustomed to dictating to subordinates and convinced that the hosts of righteousness were on his side. When confronted with unpleasant realities, such as the secret treaties among the Entente governments for division of the spoils, he had a habit of dismissing them as unimportant and eventually forgetting that he had ever heard of them. Though he knew little of the devious maneuvers of European diplomacy, his unbending temperament made it difficult for him to take advice or to adjust his views to those of his colleagues. Lloyd George, the canny Welshman who had succeeded Asquith as prime minister of Britain in 1916, possessed a cleverness and Celtic humor that enabled him to succeed, on occasions, where Wilson failed; but he was above all a politician—shifty and not particularly sympathetic to particular European problems such as nationalism.

The Big Three: Wilson and Lloyd George

The third member of the great triumvirate was the aged and cynical

French premier, Georges Clemenceau. Born in 1841, Clemenceau had been a journalist in the United States just after the Civil War. Later he had won his nickname of "the Tiger" as a relentless foe of clericals and monarchists. He had fought for the republic during the stormy days of the Boulangist episode, the Dreyfus affair, and the struggle for separation of Church and State. Twice in his lifetime he had seen France invaded and its existence gravely imperiled. Now the tables were turned, and the French, he believed, should take full advantage of their opportunity. Only by keeping a strict control over a prostrate Germany could the security of France be preserved.

From the beginning a number of embarrassing problems confronted the chief architects of the Versailles treaty. The most important was what to do about the Fourteen Points. There could be no doubt that they had been the basis of the German surrender on November 11. It was beyond question also that Wilson had represented them as the Entente program for a permanent peace. Consequently there was every reason for the peoples of the world to expect that the Fourteen Points would be the model for the Versailles settlement—subject only to the three amendments made before the armistice was signed. In actuality, however, no one among the highest dignitaries at the conference, with the exception of Wilson himself, gave more than lip service to the Fourteen Points. In the end, the American president was able to salvage, in unmodified form, only four of the parts of his famous program; point seven, requiring the restoration of Belgium; point eight, demanding the return of Alsace and Lorraine to France; point ten, providing for independence for the peoples of Austria-Hungary; and the final provision calling for a League of Nations. The others were ignored or modified to such an extent as to change their original meanings.

By the end of April 1919 the terms of the Versailles treaty were ready for submission to the enemy, and Germany was ordered to send delegates to receive them. On April 29, a delegation headed by Count von Brockdorff-Rantzau, foreign minister of the provisional republic, arrived in Versailles. A week later the members of the delegation were commanded to appear before the Allied representatives to receive the sentence of their nation. When Brockdorff-Rantzau protested that the terms were too harsh, he was informed by Clemenceau that Germany would have exactly three weeks to decide whether or not to sign. Eventually the time had to be extended, for the heads of the German government resigned their positions rather than accept the treaty. Their attitude was summed up by Chancellor Philip Scheidemann in the pointed statement: "What hand would not wither that sought to lay itself and us in those chains?" The Big Three now made a few minor adjustments, mainly at the insistence of Lloyd George, and Germany was notified that seven o'clock on the evening of June 23 would bring either acceptance or invasion. Shortly after five a new government of the provisional republic announced that it would yield to "overwhelming force" and accede to the victors' terms. On June 28, the fifth anniversary of the murder of the Austrian archduke, representatives of the German and Allied governments assembled in the Hall of Mirrors at Versailles and affixed their signatures to the treaty.

The provisions of the Treaty of Versailles can be outlined briefly. Germany was required to surrender Alsace and Lorraine to France, northern Schleswig to Denmark, and most of Posen and West Prussia to Poland. The coal mines of the Saar Basin were to be ceded to France, to be exploited by the French for fifteen years. At the end of this time the German government would be permitted to buy them back. The Saar territory itself was to be administered by the League of Nations until 1935, when a plebiscite would be held to determine whether it should remain under the league, be returned to Germany, or be awarded to France. Germany's province of East Prussia was cut off from the rest of its territory, and the port of Danzig, almost wholly German, was subjected to the political control of the League of Nations and the the economic domination of Poland. Germany was disarmed, surrendering all its submarines and navy of surface vessels, with the exception of six small battleships, six light cruisers, six destroyers, and twelve torpedo boats. The Germans were forbidden to have any airplanes, either military or naval, and their army was limited to 100,000 officers and men, to be recruited by voluntary enlistment. To make sure that Germany would not launch any new attack upon France or Belgium, it was forbidden to keep soldiers or maintain fortifications in the Rhine valley. Lastly, Germany and its allies were held responsible for all the loss and damage suffered by the Entente governments and their citizens, "as a consequence of the war imposed upon them by the aggression of Germany and her allies." This was the so-called war-guilt provision of the treaty (Article 231), but it was also the basis for German reparations. The exact amount that Germany should pay was left to a Reparations Commission. In 1921 the total was set at 33 billion dollars.

The main provisions of the Treaty of Versailles

For the most part, the Treaty of Versailles applied only to Germany. Separate pacts were drawn up to settle accounts with Germany's allies—Austria-Hungary, Bulgaria, and Turkey. The final form of these treaties was determined primarily by a Council of Five, composed of Clemenceau as chairman and one delegate from the United States, Great Britain, France, and Italy. The treaties reflected a desire on the part of their drafters to recognize the principle of national self-determination. The experience of the prewar years convinced diplomats that they must draw national boundaries to conform as closely as possible to the ethnic, linguistic, and historical traditions of the people they were to contain. Yet practical, political difficulties made such divisions impossible.

The goal of self-determination

The settlement with Austria, completed in September 1919, is

ICELAND
(Denmark)

FAEROES
(Denmark)

SHETLANDS

HEBRIDES

ORKNEYS

SCOTLAND

*NORTH
SEA*

GREAT BRITAIN

IRELAND   • Dublin

ENGLAND

*ATLANTIC

OCEAN*

London ★

English Channel

NORWAY   SWEDEN

Christiania ★

Stockholm ★

GULF OF BOTHNIA

FINLAND

Helsingfors ★

Leningrad ★

G. of Finland

Tallinn ★
ESTONIA

Skagerrak   *Kattegat*

GOTLAND

ÖLAND

DENMARK

Copenhagen ★

Danzig

*BALTIC

SEA*

Riga ★
LATVIA

LITHUANIA

Kaunas ★

E. PRUSSIA
(Germany)

Brest-Litovsk •

Berlin ★

Warsaw ★

POLAND

GERMANY

NETHERLANDS
Amsterdam ★

Brussels ★
BELG.

LUXEMBURG

Rhine R.

Prague ★

CZECHOSLOVAKIA

Paris ★

Danube   R.

FRANCE

LORRAINE

ALSACE

Berne ★
SWITZ.

Vienna ★

AUSTRIA

Budapest ★

HUNGARY

RUMANIA

Bucharest ★

*BAY OF
BISCAY*

YUGOSLAVIA   Belgrade ★

Sofia ★
BUL-

PORTUGAL

Madrid ★

CORSICA
(France)

ITALY

SERBIA

MONTENEGRO

*ADRIATIC

SEA*

Lisbon ★

SPAIN

Rome ★

Tirana ★
ALBANIA

GREECE

BALEARIC IS.

(Spain)

SARDINIA
(Italy)

Aegean

*Strait of
Gibraltar*

Tangier

SP. MOROCCO

Athens ★

• Rabat

Algiers •

Tunis •

M E D I T E R R A N E A N

SICILY
(Italy)

MALTA
(Gt. Britain)

CRETE
(Greece)

MOROCCO

ALGERIA

TUNISIA

S E A

• Tripoli

0   1000 miles

LIBYA

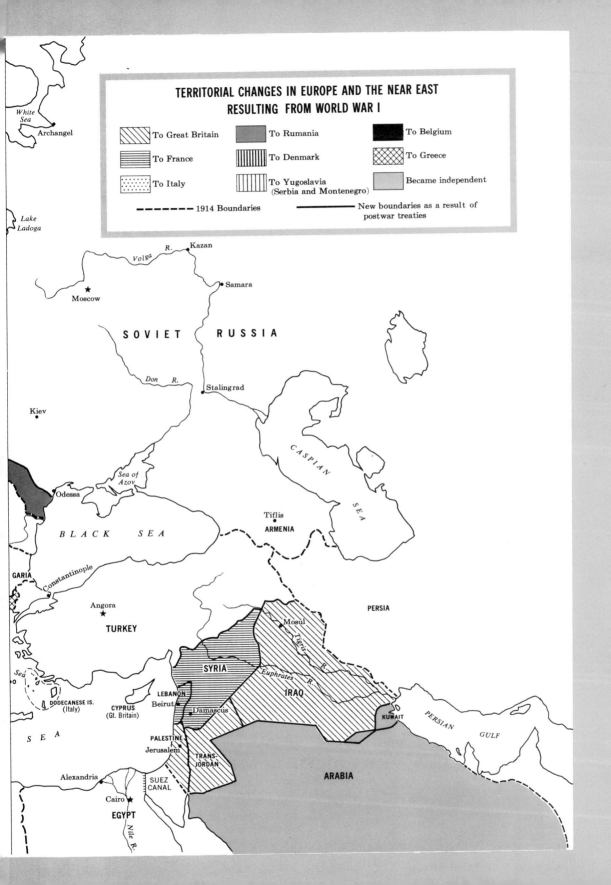

TERRITORIAL CHANGES IN EUROPE AND THE NEAR EAST RESULTING FROM WORLD WAR I

To Great Britain

To France

To Italy

To Rumania

To Denmark

To Yugoslavia
(Serbia and Montenegro)

To Belgium

To Greece

Became independent

1914 Boundaries

New boundaries as a result of
postwar treaties

White
Sea

Archangel

Lake
Ladoga

Volga R.

Kazan

Samara

Moscow

SOVIET RUSSIA

Don R.

Stalingrad

Kiev

CASPIAN SEA

Odessa

Sea of
Azov

Tiflis

ARMENIA

BLACK SEA

GARIA

Constantinople

PERSIA

Angora

Mosul

TURKEY

SYRIA

Tigris R.

Euphrates R.

IRAQ

Sea

LEBANON

Beirut

DODECANESE IS.
(Italy)

CYPRUS
(Gt. Britain)

Damascus

KUWAIT

PERSIAN GULF

SEA

PALESTINE

Jerusalem

TRANS-
JORDAN

Alexandria

SUEZ
CANAL

ARABIA

Cairo

EGYPT

Nile R.

The treaty with Austria: The compromising of national self-determination

The treaties with Bulgaria and Hungary

The Treaties of Sèvres and Lausanne with Turkey

known as the Treaty of St. Germain. Austria was required to recognize the independence of Hungary, Czechoslovakia, Yugoslavia, and Poland and to cede to them large portions of its territory. In addition, Austria had to surrender Trieste, the south Tyrol, and the Istrian peninsula to Italy. Altogether the Austrian portion of the Dual Monarchy was deprived of three-fourths of its area and three-fourths of its people. Contrary to the principles of self-determination, in several of the territories surrendered the inhabitants were largely German-speaking—for example, in the Tyrol, and the region of the Sudeten mountains awarded to Czechoslovakia. The Austrian nation itself was reduced to a small, land-locked state, with nearly one-third of its population concentrated in the city of Vienna.

The second of the treaties with lesser belligerents was that with Bulgaria, which was signed in November 1919 and called the Treaty of Neuilly. Bulgaria was forced to give up nearly all of the territory it had gained since the First Balkan War. Land was ceded to Rumania, to the new kingdom of Yugoslavia, and to Greece. Here again, self-determination was compromised. All of these regions were inhabited by large Bulgarian minorities. Since Hungary was now an independent state, it was necessary that a separate treaty be imposed upon it. This was the Treaty of the Trianon Palace, signed in June 1920. It required that Slovakia should be ceded to Czechoslovakia, Transylvania to Rumania, and Croatia-Slovenia to Yugoslavia. In few cases was the principle of self-determination of peoples more flagrantly violated. Numerous sections of Transylvania had populations that were more than half Hungarian. Included in the region of Slovakia were not only Slovaks but almost a million Magyars and about 500,000 Ruthenians. As a consequence, a fanatical irredentist movement flourished in Hungary after the war, directed toward the recovery of these lost provinces. The Treaty of the Trianon Palace slashed the area of Hungary from 125,000 square miles to 35,000, and its population from 22 million to 8 million.

The settlement with Turkey was a product of unusual circumstances. The secret treaties had contemplated the transfer of Constantinople and Armenia to Russia and the division of most of the remainder of Turkey between Britain and France. But Russia's withdrawal from the war after the Bolshevik Revolution, together with insistence by Italy and Greece upon fulfillment of promises made to them, necessitated considerable revision of the original scheme. Finally, in August 1920, a treaty was signed at Sèvres, near Paris, and submitted to the government of the sultan. It provided that Armenia be organized as a Christian republic; that most of Turkey in Europe be given to Greece; that Palestine and Mesopotamia become British "mandates," i.e., to remain under League of Nations control but to be administered by Britain; that Syria become a mandate of France; and that southern Anatolia be set apart as a sphere of influence for Italy. About all that would be left of the Ottoman Empire would be the city of Constantinople and the northern and central portions of Asia Minor. The decrepit government of the sultan, overawed by Allied military forces, agreed to accept this treaty. But a revolutionary government of Turkish nationalists, which had been organized at Ankara under the leadership of Mustapha Kemal (later called Atatürk), determined to prevent the settlement of Sèvres from being put into effect. The forces of Kemal obliterated the republic of Armenia, frightened the Italians into withdrawing from Anatolia, and conquered most of the territory in Europe which had been given to Greece. At last, in November 1922, they occupied Constantinople, deposed the sultan, and proclaimed Turkey a republic. The Allies now consented to a revision of the peace. A new treaty was concluded at Lausanne in Switzerland in 1923, which permitted the Turks to retain practically all of the territory they had conquered. Though much reduced in size compared with the old Ottoman Empire, the Turkish republic still had an area of about 300,000 square miles and a population of 13 million.

Incorporated in each of the five treaties which liquidated the war with the Central Powers was the Covenant of the League of Nations. The establishment of a league in which the states of the world, both great and small, would cooperate for the preservation of peace had long been the cherished dream of President Wilson. Indeed, that had been one of his chief reasons for taking the United States into the war. He believed that the defeat of Germany would mean the deathblow of militarism, and that the road would thenceforth be clear for setting up the control of international relations by a community of power instead of by the cumbersome and ineffective balance of power. But in order to get the league accepted at all, he felt himself compelled to make numerous compromises. He permitted his original idea of providing for a reduction of armaments "to the lowest point consistent with domestic safety" to be changed into the altogether different phrasing of "consistent with national safety." To induce the Japanese to accept the league he allowed them to keep the former German concessions in China. To please the French, he sanctioned the exclusion of both Germany and Russia from his proposed federation, despite his long insistence that it should be a combination of all the nations. These handicaps were serious enough. But the league received an even more deadly blow when it was repudiated by the very nation whose president had proposed it.

Established under such unfavorable auspices, the league never succeeded in achieving the aims of its founder. In only a few cases did it succeed in allaying the specter of war, and in each of these the parties to the dispute were small nations. But in every dispute involving one or more major powers, the league failed. It did nothing about the seizure of Vilna by Poland in 1920, because Lithuania, the victimized nation, was friendless, while Poland had the powerful backing of France. When, in 1923, war threatened between Italy and Greece, the

Kemal Atatürk

The League of Nations

Successes and failures of the league

League of Nations Buildings, Geneva, Switzerland

Italians refused to submit to the intervention of the league, and the dispute had to be settled by direct mediation of Great Britain and France. Thereafter, in every great crisis the league was either defied or ignored. Its authority was flouted by Japan in seizing Manchuria in 1931 and by Italy in conquering Ethiopia in 1936. By September 1938, when the Czechoslovakian crisis arose, the prestige of the league had sunk so low that scarcely anyone thought of appealing to it. On the other hand, the point must be made that Wilson's great project justified its existence in other, less spectacular, ways. It reduced the international opium traffic and aided poor and backward countries in controlling the spread of disease. Its agencies collected invaluable statistics on labor and business conditions throughout the world. It conducted plebiscites in disputed areas, supervised the administration of internationalized cities, helped in finding homes for racial and political refugees, and made a notable beginning in codifying international law. Such achievements may well be regarded as providing a substantial groundwork for a later effort at international organization, the United Nations, formed after World War II.

A war of waste The league, with all its failings, was seen as the one promising result of the war that many soon recognized as a hideously wasteful carnage. The price would have been enormous even if all the results which were supposed to flow from an Entente victory had really been achieved. But few indeed were the permanent gains. In fact, the war which was to "end all wars" sowed the seeds of a new and more terrible conflict in the future. The autocracy of the kaiser was indeed destroyed, but the ground was prepared for new despotisms. World War I did nothing to abate either militarism or nationalism. Twenty years after the fighting had ended, there were nearly twice as many men under arms as in 1913; and national and ethnic rivalries and hatreds were as deeply ingrained as ever.

If the war failed to make the world less of an armed camp, it nevertheless altered it drastically in other ways. In the first place, it strengthened a belief in the efficacy of central planning and coordination. To sustain the war effort, the governments of all the major belligerents were forced to manage their economies by regulating industrial output, exercising a close control over imports and exports, and making the most effective use of manpower—both civilian and military. Second, the war upset the world trade balance. With few manufactured goods coming from Europe, Japanese, Indian, and South American capitalists were free to develop industries in their own countries. When the war was over, Europe found it had lost many of its previously guaranteed markets. Third, while war was altering the patterns of world trade, it was also producing worldwide inflation. To finance their fighting, governments resorted to policies of deficit financing (spending above their income) and increased paper money which, with the shortage of goods, inflated their price. Inflation hit hardest at the middle class, those men and women who had lived on their income from invested money, and now saw that money worth far less than it once had been. Fourth, the war, while it brought hardships to most, brought freedom to many. Women were emancipated by their governments' need for them in factories and on farms. The contribution of women to the war effort undoubtedly explains the granting of female suffrage in both Great Britain and the United States in 1918 and 1920. Finally, despite this legacy of liberation, the war's most permanent contribution to the spirit of the postwar years was

Changes brought by the war

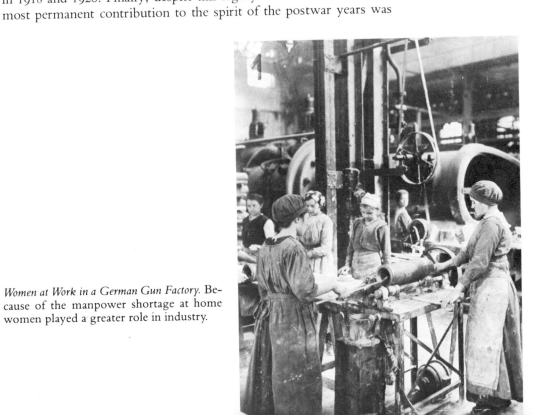

Women at Work in a German Gun Factory. Because of the manpower shortage at home women played a greater role in industry.

disillusion—particularly within the middle classes. A generation of men had been sacrificed—"lost"—to no apparent end. Many of those left alive were sickened by the useless slaughter, to which they knew they had contributed and for which they believed they must share at least part of the guilt. They were disgusted by the greedy abandonment of principles by the politicians at Versailles. Hatred and mistrust of the "old men" who had dragged the world into an unnecessary conflict, who had then mismanaged its direction with such ghastly results, and who had betrayed the cause of international peace for national gain soured the minds of many younger men and women in the postwar period. The British poet Edmund Blunden expressed this profound disillusionment when he took as the title for a poem, written to celebrate New Year's Day 1921, the Biblical verse: "The dog is turned to his own vomit again, and the sow that was washed to her wallowing in the mire."

SELECTED READINGS

• *Items so designated are available in paperback editions.*

THE WORLD WAR AND THE PEACE SETTLEMENT

• Falls, Cyril, *The Great War*, New York, 1959. A military history.
• Fay, Sidney B., *The Origins of the World War*, 2 vols., New York, 1928–30. Comprehensive.
  Feldman, Gerald D., *Army, Industry, and Labor in Germany, 1914–1918*, Princeton, N.J., 1966.
• Fischer, Fritz, *Germany's Aims in the First World War*, New York, 1967. One of the most significant historical works of the twentieth century. Thoroughly documents Germany's goal of world domination in World War I and reopens the question of war guilt.
• ———, *World Power or Decline*, New York, 1974.
• Fussell, Paul, *The Great War and Modern Memory*, New York, 1975. A brilliant examination of British intellectuals' attitudes toward the war.
  Gatzke, Hans, *Germany's Drive to the West*, Baltimore, 1950.
  Guinn, Paul, *British Strategy and Politics, 1914–1918*, Oxford, 1965.
  Hardach, Gerd, *The First World War, 1914–1918*, Berkeley, Calif., 1977. An excellent economic history of the war.
  Horne, Alastair, *The Price of Glory: Verdun, 1916*, New York, 1963.
• Lafore, Laurence D., *The Long Fuse: An Interpretation of the Origins of World War I*, Philadelphia, 1971. Argues that the war was the result of obsolete institutions and ideas.
  Lacqueur, Walter, and G. L. Mosse, eds., *1914: The Coming of the First World War*, New York, 1969. An excellent series of essays by modern scholars.
  Liddell Hart, B. H., *The War in Outline*, London, 1936. A good introduction to the military history of World War I.
  Mayer, Arno, *Political Origins of the New Diplomacy, 1917–1918*, New York,

1969. An important work which examines the advent of Wilson and Lenin into world diplomacy.

————, *Politics and Diplomacy of Peacemaking: Containment and Counter-revolution at Versailles, 1918–1919*, New York, 1967.

Moorehead, Alan, *Gallipoli*, London, 1956. A study of the British campaign.

Nicolson, Harold, *Peacemaking, 1919*, Boston, 1933. Written by a participant, provides a good account of the atmosphere of Versailles.

• Steiner, Zara S., *Britain and the Origins of the First World War*, New York, 1977. Argues that external rather than internal strains brought Britain into the war.

• Taylor, A. J. P., *English History, 1914–1945*, New York, 1965. An excellent treatment of the war and its impact on British society.

• Turner, L. C. F., *Origins of the First World War*, New York, 1970.

• Tuchman, Barbara, *The Guns of August*, New York, 1962. A popular account of the outbreak of war.

• Wheeler-Bennett, J. W., *The Forgotten Peace: Brest-Litovsk, March 1918*, London, 1939. An excellent study of personalities involved in the Russo-German peace treaty.

Zeeman, Z. A. B., *The Break-up of the Hapsburg Empire, 1914–1918*, New York, 1961.

THE RUSSIAN REVOLUTION

Carr, E. H., *A History of Soviet Russia*, Vols. I–III, London, 1950 ff. A comprehensive treatment of the Russian Revolution from 1917–1923.

• Deutscher, Isaac, *The Prophet Armed*, New York, 1954. The first volume of a magnificent biography of Trotsky; covers the years 1879–1921.

Fischer, Louis, *The Life of Lenin*, New York, 1964. A lengthy, somewhat popularized biography by a journalist who was present during the revolution.

Keep, John L. H., *The Russian Revolution*, New York, 1977.

• Pares, Bernard, *A History of Russia*, rev. ed., New York, 1953.

• Rabinowitch, Alexander, *The Bolsheviks Come to Power*, New York, 1976.

• Tucker, Robert C., *Stalin as Revolutionary*, New York, 1973. Stalin's life to 1929; a psychobiography.

• Ulam, Adam, *The Bolsheviks: The Intellectual and Political History of the Triumph of Communism in Russia*, New York, 1965.

• Von Laue, T. H., *Why Lenin? Why Stalin? A Reappraisal of the Russian Revolution, 1900–1930*, Philadelphia, 1964.

• Wolfe, Bertram D., *Three Who Made a Revolution*, rev. ed., New York, 1964. A study of Lenin, Trotsky, and Stalin.

SOURCE MATERIALS

Carnegie Foundation, Endowment for International Peace, *The Treaties of Peace, 1919–1923*, 2 vols., New York, 1924.

Gooch, G. P., and H. Temperley, eds., *British Documents on the Origins of the War, 1898–1914*, London.

Keynes, John Maynard, *The Economic Consequences of the Peace,* London, 1919. A contemporary attack upon the peace settlement, particularly the reparations agreements, by the brilliant economist who served on the British delegation to the peace conference.

Trotsky, Leon, *History of the Russian Revolution,* 3 vols., Ann Arbor, Mich., 1957.

Chapter 28

THE WEST BETWEEN THE WARS

Democracy of the West today is the forerunner of Marxism, which would
be inconceivable without it. It is democracy alone which furnishes this
universal plague with the soil in which it spreads. In parliamentarianism,
its outward form of expression, democracy created a monstrosity of filth
and fire . . .

—Adolf Hitler, *Mein Kampf*

The First World War had been waged in hopes of making the
world "safe for democracy." And for a short time after 1918,
despite the shortcomings of the Versailles settlement, it
seemed as if that elusive goal might stand a chance of success. Germany began the postwar era as a republic. Most of the new states
created by the Treaty of Versailles attempted to function under representative governments. Yet by 1939 only three of the chief powers—
Great Britain, France, and the United States—remained on the list of
democratic countries. Among the lesser states democracy survived in
Switzerland, the Netherlands, Belgium, the Scandinavian countries, a
few republics of Latin America, and the self-governing dominions of
the British Commonwealth. Nearly all of the rest of the world had
succumbed to despotism of one form or another. Italy, Germany, and
Spain were fascist; Hungary was dominated by a landowning oligarchy; Poland, Turkey, China, and Japan were essentially under military
rule. Russia, although professing to be a communist utopia, was in
fact a dictatorship.

The reasons for the decline of democracy in the West varied according to particular national circumstances. Generally, however, democracy's failure can be attributed to several major causes. First, class
conflict increased in many countries during the interwar years. The
real issue in most parts of continental Europe was whether control of
the government and economic system would continue in the possession of aristocracies, industrialists, and financiers, or some combina-

Decline of democracy

Reasons for its decline

tion of these elements. None of them were willing to surrender more than a fraction of their considerable power to the less privileged majorities which, at great sacrifice, had made major contributions to the war effort. The common people expected and had been promised that those contributions would be rewarded by greater attention to their political rights and economic needs. When they were ignored, they were naturally embittered, and hence prey to the blandishments of political extremists. Second, economic conditions worked against the establishment of stable democracies. The creation of new nations encouraged debilitating economic rivalries. War had disoriented the world's economy, leaving in its wake first inflation and then depression. Finally, nationalist sentiment encouraged discontent among minorities in the newly established states of central Europe. Countries weakened by conflicts between national minorities were an unlikely proving ground for democracy, a political system which functions best in an atmosphere of unified national purpose. Instead they turned, along with others, to totalitarianism, a system which holds out the promise of efficiency and strength of purpose, achieved by centralized authority in return for the surrender of individual liberties.

1. TOTALITARIANISM IN COMMUNIST RUSSIA

Lenin

Soon after the November 1917 revolution Russia began to succumb to totalitarian rule. The country's desperate plight—the result of wartime devastation and governmental corruption and mismanagement—compelled the Bolshevik leaders to centralize power in the hands of a few. During this transformation, Lenin assumed ultimate control of the government. He had all of the qualities necessary for success as a revolutionary figure. He was an able politician and an exceedingly effective orator. Absolutely convinced of the righteousness of his cause, he could strike down his opponents with the zeal and savagery of a Robespierre. On the other hand, he cared nothing for the luxuries of wealth or personal glory. He lived in two rooms in the Kremlin and dressed little better than an ordinary workman.

Trotsky

The most prominent of Lenin's lieutenants was the brilliant but erratic Leon Trotsky (1879–1940). Originally named Lev Bronstein, Trotsky was born of middle-class Jewish parents in the Ukraine. He was a stormy petrel of revolutionary politics during most of his life. Before the revolution he refused to identify himself with any particular faction, preferring to remain an independent Marxist. For his part in the revolutionary movement of 1905 he was exiled to Siberia; but he escaped, and for some years led a roving existence in various European capitals. He was expelled from Paris in 1916 for pacifist activity and took refuge in the United States. Upon learning of the overthrow of the tsar, he attempted to return to Russia. Captured by British

Lenin Speaking to Crowds in Moscow. To the right of the platform, in uniform, is Trotsky.

agents at Halifax, Nova Scotia, he was eventually released through the intervention of Kerensky. He arrived in Russia in April 1917 and immediately began plotting for the overthrow of the provisional government and later of Kerensky himself. He became minister of foreign affairs in the government headed by Lenin, and later, commissar for war.

No sooner had the Bolsheviks come to power than they proceeded to effect drastic alterations in the political and economic system. On November 8, 1917, Lenin decreed nationalization of the land and gave the peasants the exclusive right to use it. On November 29 control of the factories was transferred to the workers, and a month later it was announced that all except the smallest industrial establishments would be taken over by the government. Banks also were nationalized soon after the Bolshevik victory. Scarcely had the Bolsheviks concluded the war with the Central Powers, than they were confronted with a desperate civil war at home. Landlords and capitalists did not take kindly to the loss of their property. The result was a prolonged and bloody combat between the Reds, or Bolsheviks, and the Whites, including not only reactionary tsarists but also disaffected liberals, Social Revolutionaries, Mensheviks, and some peasants. The Whites were assisted for a time by expeditionary forces of British, French, and Japanese troops—hoping to defeat the Bolsheviks in order to bring Russia back into the war against Germany—and later by the armies of the newly created republic of Poland. Under the direction of Trotsky, who appealed to the Russian people both in the name of revolution and the fatherland, the Red army was mobilized to a degree that allowed it to withstand both the foreign invaders and the Russian insurgents. By 1922, the Bolsheviks had managed to stabilize their boundaries, although to do so they were forced to cede former Russian territory to the Finns, to the Baltic states of Latvia and Estonia, to Poland, and to Rumania. Internally, the Bolsheviks responded to the White counter-

The civil war

See color map following page 864

The Red Army, 1919. This scene near the southern front was the celebration of the victory over the counter-revolutionary forces.

revolution by instituting a "Terror" far more extensive than the repression that had earned that name during the French Revolution. A secret police force shot thousands as suspects or merely as hostages. The tsar and tsarina and their children were executed by local Bolsheviks in July 1918 as White forces advanced on the town of Ekaterinburg, where the family was held prisoner. That same year, a Social Revolutionary attempted to assassinate Lenin; what followed in Petrograd can only be described as a massacre. The Terror abated when the regime had satisfied itself that it had destroyed its internal opposition.

Economic and constitutional changes

The civil war was accompanied by an appalling economic breakdown. In 1920 the total industrial production was only 13 percent of what it had been in 1913. To make up for the shortage of goods, the government abolished the payment of wages and distributed supplies among the workers in the cities in proportion to their need. All private trade was prohibited, and everything produced by the peasants above what they required to keep from starving was requisitioned by the state. This system was an expedient to crush the bourgeoisie and to obtain as much food as possible for the army in the field. It was soon abandoned after the war had ended. In 1921 it was superseded by the New Economic Policy (NEP), which Lenin described as "one step backward in order to take two steps forward." The NEP authorized private manufacturing and private trade on a small scale, reintroduced the payment of wages, and permitted peasants to sell their grain in the open market. In 1924 a constitution was adopted, replacing imperial Russia with the Union of Soviet Socialist Republics. The union represented an attempt to unite the various nationalities and territories that had constituted the old empire. Each separate republic was, in theory, granted certain autonomous rights. In fact, government remained centralized in the hands of a few leaders. Further, central authority was maintained by means of the one legal political party—the Communist party—whose Central Committee was the directing force behind both politics and government, and whose organizational apparatus reached out into all areas of the vast country.

The philosophy of Bolshevism, now more popularly known as communism, was developed primarily by Lenin during these years. It was proclaimed, not as a new body of thought, but as a strict interpretation of Marx's writings. Nevertheless, from the beginning there were various departures from Marx's teachings. These changes were the necessary result of the fact that Marx had expected revolution to occur first in highly industrialized countries, whereas it had in fact broken out and succeeded in one of the least industralized nations in Europe. Marx had assumed that a capitalist stage must prepare the way for socialism; Lenin denied that this was necessary and insisted that Russia could leap directly from a manorial to a socialist economy. In the second place, Lenin emphasized the revolutionary character of socialism much more than did its original founder. Marx did believe that in most cases revolution would be necessary, but he was inclined to deplore the fact rather than to welcome it. Further, he had stated that "there are certain countries such as England and the United States in which the workers may hope to secure their ends by peaceful means." Last of all, Bolshevism differed from Marxism in its conception of proletarian rule. There is nothing to indicate that Marx ever envisaged a totalitarian state. True, he did speak of the "dictatorship of the proletariat," but he meant by this a dictatorship of the whole working class over the remnants of the bourgeoisie. Within the ranks of this class, democratic forms would prevail. Lenin, however, set up the ideal of the dictatorship of an elite, a select minority, wielding supremacy not only over the bourgeoisie but over the bulk of the proletarians themselves. In Russia this elite has remained the Communist party, whose membership has varied from 1,500,000 to 15,700,000.

The death of Lenin in January 1924 precipitated a titanic struggle between two of his lieutenants to inherit his mantle of power. Outside of Russia it was generally assumed that Trotsky would be the man to succeed the fallen leader. But the fiery commander of the Red army had a formidable rival in the tough and mysterious Joseph Stalin (1879–1953). The son of a peasant shoemaker in the province of Georgia, Stalin received part of his education in a theological seminary. Expelled at the age of seventeen for "lack of religious vocation," he thereafter dedicated his career to revolutionary activity. In 1917 he became secretary-general of the Communist party, a position through which he was able to build up a political machine. The battle between Stalin and Trotsky was not simply a struggle for personal power; fundamental issues of political policy were also involved. Trotsky maintained that socialism in Russia could never be entirely successful until capitalism was overthrown in surrounding countries. Therefore, he in-

Left: *Lenin's Casket Is Carried Through the Streets of Moscow.* It was not known with certainty until 1956 that, prior to his death, Lenin had discredited Stalin. Right: *Lenin and Stalin.* Under Stalin this picture was used to show his close relationship with Lenin. In fact, the photograph has been doctored.

sisted upon a continuous crusade for world revolution. Stalin was willing to abandon the program of world revolution, for the time being, in order to concentrate on building socialism in Russia itself. His strategy for the immediate future was essentially nationalist. The outcome of the duel was a complete triumph for Stalin. In 1927 Trotsky was expelled from the Communist party, and two years later he was driven from the country. In 1940 he was murdered in Mexico City by Stalinist agents. Lenin did not hold either Stalin or Trotsky in lofty esteem. In a "testament" written shortly before his death, he criticized Trotsky for "far-reaching self-confidence" and for being too much preoccupied with administrative detail. But he dealt far less gently with Stalin, condemning him as "too rough" and "capricious" and urging that the comrades "find a way" to remove him from his position at the head of the party.

Five-Year Plan

In his struggle with Trotsky, Stalin had insisted that Russia's first priority was economic well-being. In line with this doctrine, one of Stalin's first major reforms was the introduction of the so-called Five-Year Plan. Based upon the conviction that the Soviet Union had to take drastic steps to industrialize and thereby achieve economic parity among the nations of the world, the plan instituted an elaborate system of national priorities. It decreed how much of each major industrial and agricultural commodity the nation should produce, the amount of wages workers should receive, and the prices that should be charged for all that was sold at home and abroad. The first plan, instituted in 1928, was succeeded by others during the 1930s. In some areas goals were met, in a few they were exceeded, in some they fell short. One of the major results of the Five-Year Plans was the creation of an extensive state bureaucracy, charged with the task of organization and supervision at all levels.

Included in the first plan was a program for agricultural collectivization. The scheme was designed to bring rural farms together into larger units of several thousand acres, under the communal proprietorship of peasants. Only with this sort of reorganization, Russia's rulers declared, could the new and expensive processes of mechanization be introduced, and the country's agricultural yield thereby increased. Not surprisingly, the argument failed to win the support of the more prosperous farmers—the kulaks—who had been allowed to retain ownership of their land despite the revolution. Their opposition led to another Terror, made all the more deadly by a famine which occurred in southeast Russia in 1932. The kulaks were liquidated, either killed or transported to distant labor camps—i.e., the rural bourgeoisie was eliminated, to be replaced by a rural proletariat. Collectivization was an accomplished fact by 1939. It represented to a vast number of Russians a revolution far more immediate than that of 1917. Twenty million people were moved off the land, which, once it had been reorganized into larger units, and production mechanized, required fewer laborers. They were sent to cities, where most went to work in factories. Agricultural output did not increase during the early years of collectivization. But the scheme was nevertheless of benefit to the government. By controlling production, the central bureaucracy was able to regulate the distribution of agricultural products, allocating them for export, where necessary, to pay for the importation of much-needed industrial machinery.

As part of Stalin's campaign to put the interests of Russia ahead of those of international communism, the Bolshevik regime adopted a new and more conservative foreign policy during the 1930s. Its international goals contradicted the militant socialist internationalism of the 1920s. Lenin had supported revolutionary leftist movements in Europe, sending money and lending moral support to the radical German Marxists Karl Liebknecht and Rosa Luxemburg in 1919, and to the short-lived Soviet regime of the Bolshevik Béla Kun in Hungary in the same year. Shortly thereafter, the Third International—later called the Comintern—was formed. It declared its allegiance to international communism; its policy was to oppose cooperation or collaboration with the capitalist governments of the West and to work for their overthrow.

With Stalin's suppression of the internationalism advocated by Lenin and Trotsky, however, came a change in tactics and a revival of militarism, or nationalism, and of an interest in playing the game of power politics. The Russian army was more than doubled in size and was reorganized in accordance with the western European model. Patriotism, which the older strict Marxists despised as a form of capitalist propaganda, was exalted into a Soviet virtue. When Germany once again appeared to threaten Russian security, as it did in the 1930s, the rulers of the Kremlin decided that Russia needed friends. Along with their efforts to build up a great army and to make their own country self-sufficient, they adopted a policy of cooperation with the western European powers. In 1934 they entered the League of Nations, and in 1934 they ratified a military alliance with France.

Constitution of 1936

In 1936, the rulers of Communist Russia drafted a new constitution. It was adopted by popular vote and went into effect January 1, 1938. It continued to provide for a union of eleven (later fifteen) republics, each supposedly autonomous and free to secede if it chose. The constitution established universal suffrage for all citizens eighteen years of age and over. They were to vote not only for the local soviets but for members of a national parliament. The highest organ of state power was declared to be the Supreme Soviet of the USSR, composed of two chambers, both given equal legislative powers. To represent it when it was not meeting, the Supreme Soviet was to elect a committee of thirty-seven members known as the Presidium. This body was also empowered to issue decrees, to declare war, and to annul the acts of administrative officials which did not conform to law. The highest executive and administrative agency was to be the Council of Ministers, likewise elected by the Supreme Soviet. The constitution contained a bill of rights. Citizens were guaranteed the right to employment, the right to leisure, the right to maintenance in case of old age or disability, and even the traditional privileges of freedom of speech, of the press, of assemblage, and of religion. The constitution of 1936 was, and still is, more of a sham than a reality. Its provisions for universal suffrage, for the secret ballot, and for a bill of rights had little meaning. The explanation lies in the fact that the real power in the Soviet Union rests with the Communist party, the only party allowed to exist. The organs of the government are little more than the vocal mechanisms through which the party expresses its will.

The purges

It is noteworthy that the very period in which the constitution was being put into effect witnessed an eruption of mass arrests and executions of persons alleged to be "Trotskyists, spies, and wreckers." Collectivization and industrialization had not been achieved without bitter disagreement among Russia's political leadership. Critics on the Left and Right were disturbed by both the ends and means of Stalin's programs, and by his obvious craving for personal power. Before his critics could strike at him, Stalin struck at them. Between 1936 and 1938 more than a score of prominent Old Bolsheviks were tried, confessed publicly to having plotted against the state, were condemned either as Trotskyites or bourgeois collaborators, and put to death. Their confessions, which surprised the world at the time, were obtained, it was later learned, by means of physical and psychological torture. Some 9 million further victims of these purges were arrested, imprisoned, or sent to Siberia. By ridding the country of his opposition Stalin forestalled further revolution—not an unlikely possibility, given discontent with his policies—and solidified his position as virtual dictator of Russia.

The Soviet revolution achieved profound results. By 1939 private manufacturing and private trade had been almost entirely abolished. Factories, mines, railroads, and public utilities were exclusively owned by the state. Stores were either government enterprises or co-operatives in which consumers owned shares. Agriculture also had been almost completely socialized. No less revolutionary were the developments in the social sphere. Religion as a factor in the lives of the people declined to a place of small importance. Christianity was still tolerated, but churches were reduced in number, and were not permitted to engage in any charitable or educational activities. Furthermore, members of the Communist party were required to be atheists. Post-revolutionary communism not only renounced all belief in the supernatural but attempted to cultivate a new ethics. The cardinal virtues in this positive morality are industry, respect for public property, willingness to sacrifice individual interests for the good of society, and loyalty to the Soviet fatherland and to the socialist ideal.

Results of the Soviet upheaval

By the outbreak of World War II the Soviet regime had undeniable accomplishments to its credit. Among the principal ones were: (1) the reduction of illiteracy from at least 50 percent to less than 20 percent; (2) a notable expansion of industrialization; (3) the establishment of a planned economy, which operated successfully enough to prevent unemployment; (4) the opening of educational and cultural opportunities to larger numbers of the common people; and (5) the establishment of a system of government assistance for working mothers and their infants and free medical care and hospitalization for most citizens.

Accomplishments of the Bolshevik regime

But these accomplishments were purchased at a very high price. The program of socialization and industrialization was pushed at so frantic a pace that the good of individual citizens was overlooked. The Stalinist regime fastened upon Russia a tyranny as extreme as that of the tsar. Indeed, the number of its victims sentenced to slave-labor camps—estimated to be as high as 20 million—probably exceeded the number consigned by the tsars to exile in Siberia.

The price of revolution

2. THE EMERGENCE OF FASCISM IN ITALY

That Italy turned to totalitarianism may seem strange in view of the fact that the Italians emerged from World War I on the winning side. Italy had been the victim of frustrated nationalism for many years. Its aspirations for power and for empire had been shattered. The effect was to produce a sense of humiliation and shame, especially in the minds of the younger generation, and to foster an attitude of contempt

Frustrated nationalism in Italy

for the existing political regime. Members of the old ruling class were held up to scorn as cynical, vacillating, defeatist, and corrupt. Even before World War I there was talk of revolution, of the need for a drastic housecleaning that would deliver the country from its incompetent rulers.

The demoralizing and humiliating effects of the war

But the establishment of a dictatorship in Italy would never have been possible without the demoralizing and humiliating effects of World War I. The chief business of the Italian armies had been to keep the Austrians occupied on the Southern Front while the British, French, and Americans hammered Germany into submission along the battle lines on the Western Front. To accomplish its purpose Italy had to mobilize more than 5,500,000 men; of these nearly 700,000 were killed. The direct financial cost of Italian participation in the struggle was over 15 billion dollars. These sacrifices were no greater than those made by the British and the French, but Italy was a poor country. Moreover, in the division of the spoils after the fighting was over, the Italians got less than they expected. While Italy did receive most of the Austrian territories promised in the secret treaties, the Italians maintained that these were inadequate rewards for their sacrifices and for their valuable contribution to an Entente victory. At first the nationalists vented their spleen for the "humiliation of Versailles" upon President Wilson, but after a short time they returned to their old habit of castigating Italy's rulers. They alleged that such men as Premier Orlando had been so cravenly weak and inept that they had allowed their own country to be cheated.

Inflation, radicalism, and economic chaos

The war contributed to the revolution in a multitude of other ways. It resulted in inflation of the currency, with consequent high prices, speculation, and profiteering. Normally wages would have risen also, but the labor market was glutted on account of the return to civilian life of millions of soldiers. Furthermore, business was demoralized, owing to extensive and frequent strikes and to the closing of foreign markets. Perhaps the most serious consequence of the war, to the upper and middle classes at least, was the growth of socialism. As hardship and chaos increased, the Italian socialists embraced a philosophy akin to Bolshevism. They voted as a party to join the Third International. In the elections of November 1919, they won about a third of the seats in the Chamber of Deputies. During the following winter socialist workers took over about a hundred factories and attempted to run them for the benefit of the workers. Radicalism also spread through the rural areas, where so-called Red Leagues were organized to break up large estates and to force landlords to reduce their rents. The landowning classes were badly frightened and were therefore ready to accept Fascist totalitarianism as a less dangerous form of radicalism that might save at least part of their property from confiscation.

How much the Fascist movement depended for its success upon the leadership of Benito Mussolini is impossible to say. Mussolini was born in 1883, the son of a socialist blacksmith. His mother was a schoolteacher, and in deference to her wishes he eventually became a teacher. But he was restless and dissatisfied and soon left Italy for further study in Switzerland. Here he gave part of his time to his books and the rest of it to writing articles for socialist newspapers. He was finally expelled from the country for fomenting strikes in factories. Upon returning to Italy he took up journalism as a definite career and eventually became editor of *Avanti,* the leading socialist daily. His ideas in the years before the war were a mixture of contradictory forms of radicalism. He professed to be a Marxist socialist, but he mingled his socialism with doctrines of corporatism, adapted from the French syndicalists.

Mussolini in fact believed in no particular set of doctrines. No man with a definite philosophy could have reversed himself so often. When war broke out in August 1914, Mussolini insisted that Italy should remain neutral. But he had scarcely adopted this position when he began urging participation on the Entente side. Deprived of his position as editor of *Avanti,* he founded a new paper, *Il Popolo d'Italia,* and dedicated its columns to arousing enthusiasm for war. He regarded the decision of the government the following spring to go in on the side of the Entente allies as a personal victory.

The word *fascism* derives from the Latin *fasces,* the ax surrounded by a bundle of sticks representing the authority of the Roman state; the Italian *fascio,* means group or band. *Fasci* were organized as early as October 1914, as units of agitation to swing Italy over to the Entente cause. Their membership was made up of young idealists, fanatical nationalists, and bored white-collar workers. The original platform of the Fascist movement was drafted by Mussolini in 1919. It was a surprisingly radical document, which demanded, among other things, universal suffrage; abolition of the conservative Senate; the establishment by law of an eight-hour day; a heavy capital levy; a heavy tax on inheritances; confiscation of 85 percent of war profits; acceptance of the League of Nations; and "opposition to all imperialisms." This platform was accepted more or less officially by the movement until May 1920, when it was supplanted by another of a more conservative character. Indeed, the new program omitted all reference to economic reform. On neither of these platforms did the Fascists achieve much political success.

The Fascists made up for their initial lack of numbers by disciplined aggressiveness and strong determination. As the old regime crumbled, they prepared to take over the government. In September 1922, Mussolini began to talk openly of revolution and raised the cry, "On to Rome." On October 28 an army of about 50,000 Fascist militia, in blackshirted uniforms, occupied the capital. The premier resigned, and the following day the king, Victor Emmanuel III, invited Mussolini to form a cabinet. Thus, without firing a shot the blackshirts had

Left: *"On to Rome."* Mussolini (wearing a suit) and uniformed Fascists march into Rome in October 1922. Right: *Mussolini Addressing a Crowd of His Followers from the Balcony of the Palazzo Venezia in Rome*

gained control of the Italian government. The explanation is to be found not in the strength of fascism, but in the chaos created by the war and in the weakness and irresolution of the old ruling classes. By the end of the next three years Mussolini's revolution was virtually complete. He had abolished the cabinet system, made the political system a one-party system, and reduced the functions of the parliament to ratifying decrees.

The leading doctrines of Italian fascism may be summarized as follows:

(1) Totalitarianism. The state incorporates every interest and every loyalty of its members. There must be "nothing above the state, nothing outside the state, nothing against the state."

(2) Nationalism. The nation is the highest form of society ever evolved by the human race. It has a life and a soul of its own apart from the lives and souls of the individuals who compose it. There can never be a real harmony of interests between two or more distinct peoples. Internationalism is therefore a perversion of human progress.

(3) Militarism. Strife is the origin of all things. Nations which do not expand eventually wither and die. War exalts and ennobles man and regenerates sluggish and decadent peoples.

Declaring his allegiance to these principles, Mussolini began to build what he called the corporatist state. The Italian economy was placed under the management of twenty-two corporations, each responsible for a major industrial enterprise. In each corporation were representatives of trade unions, whose members were organized by the Fascist party, the employers, and the government. Together, the members of these corporations were given the task of determining working conditions, wages, and prices. In fact, however, the decisions of these bodies were closely managed by the government. In 1938 the last vestiges of democratic control were removed in Italy. The Chamber of Deputies was replaced by the Chamber of Fasces and Corporations, whose members were appointed by the government.

Corporatism did little to lessen Italy's plight during the years of worldwide depression which occurred in the 1930s. Although he managed to make his country appear more efficient—his admirers often bragged that he had at last "made the trains run on time"— Mussolini failed to solve its major problems, particularly those of the peasantry, whose standard of living remained desperately low. Mussolini's fascism was little more than illusion. It is a measure of the Italians' disgust with their past leaders that they were so ready to be taken in.

Its failure

3. THE RISE OF NAZI GERMANY

Germany succumbed to totalitarianism later than Italy. For a brief period following World War I, events seemed to be moving the country to the Left. Most of the leading politicians in the immediate postarmistice government were socialists, members of the Social Democratic party. Their reformist policies, which had seemed radical enough to many prior to the war, now appeared too mild to a group of extreme Marxists who had been encouraged by the revolution in Russia. Calling themselves Spartacists,[1] and led by the able Rosa Luxemburg and Karl Liebknecht, they attempted an uprising in 1919 designed to bring the proletarian revolution to Germany. Despite assistance from the Russian Bolsheviks, the rebellion was crushed; Liebknecht and Luxemburg were killed by soldiers while being taken to prison. In engineering the Spartacists' defeat, the German government had recourse to private vigilante groups headed by disillusioned former army officers, men whose true sympathies lay no more with democratic socialism than with Russian communism, and whose discontent would soon focus on the government they had helped to salvage.

Germany: the Spartacists

With the Spartacist revolt only just behind them, the leaders of a coalition of socialists, Catholic Centrists, and liberal democrats in 1919 drafted a constitution for the new German republic reflecting a generally progressive political and social philosophy. It provided for universal suffrage, for women as well as men; the cabinet system of government; and for a bill of rights, guaranteeing not only civil liberties but the right of the citizen to employment, to an education, and to protection against the hazards of an industrial society. But the republic set up under this constitution was beset with troubles from the start.

The Weimar Republic

[1] After the Roman, Spartacus, who led a slave revolt.

Karl Liebknecht (center) *and Rosa Luxemburg*

Reactionaries and other extremists plotted against it. Moreover, the German people had had little experience with democratic government. The Weimar Republic (named for the city where its constitution was drafted) did not spring from the desires of a majority of the nation. It was born of change forced upon Germany in its hour of defeat. Its instability made it a likely victim of the forces it was desperately attempting to tame.

Causes of German totalitarianism: (1) defeat in war

The factors which led to the eventual triumph of German totalitarianism were many and various. First was the sense of humiliation arising from defeat in the war. Between 1871 and 1914 Germany had risen to lofty heights of political and cultural prestige. German universities, science, philosophy, and music were known and admired all over the world. The country had likewise attained a remarkable prosperity, by 1914 surpassing Britain and the United States in several fields of industrial production. Then came the crushing blow of 1918. Germany was toppled from its pinnacle and left at the mercy of its powerful enemies. It was too much for the German people to understand. They could not believe that their invincible armies had really been worsted in battle. Quickly the legend grew that the nation had been "stabbed in the back" by socialists and Jews in the government. Though there was no truth in this charge, it helped to salve the wounded pride of German patriots. Those in search of a scapegoat also blamed the laxity and irresponsibility that appeared to distinguish the republican regime. It was alleged that Berlin had displaced Paris as the most frivolous and decadent city of Europe. What the country seemed to need was authoritative leadership to spearhead a campaign to regain the world's respect.

Another major reason for the appeal of totalitarianism was the inflation that Germany suffered in the 1920s. When the country began to experience severe unemployment, the government increased the supply of paper money—eventually to a flood—in order to finance programs of unemployment insurance and to try to provide its citizenry with the economic wherewithal to stay alive. The result was a period of wild inflation, particularly demoralizing to the middle class. Salaries could not keep up with the vast increase in the cost of living. Those who existed on fixed incomes—pensioners, stockholders—saw their security vanish. As they lost their faith in the ability of the government to come to their aid, these men and women began, as well, to lose whatever faith they may have had in the republic. Germany recovered from inflation in the late 1920s, thanks, largely, to the scaling down of reparations payments and to foreign loans and investments. But the middle class, traumatized by its experience of inflation, continued its search for a government that promised attention to its needs and sympathy with its problems. That search intensified with the advent of the Great Depression of 1929. As we shall see, the depression was a major disaster for most of the world. In few countries, however, were its effects more keenly felt than in Germany. Farmers were angered by the collapse of agricultural prices and by their burden of debts and taxes. University students saw little prospect of gaining a place in already overcrowded professions. Six million workers were unemployed. Once again the middle class saw its savings vanish.

(2) economics

One political result was a swing on the part of many workers to the German Communist party. The Spartacist failure had, for a time, quelled middle-class fears of a leftist takeover. But in the presidential election of 1932, the Communist party polled about 6 million votes, or over one-seventh of the total. As had happened in Italy, a number of capitalists and property-owners were alarmed at what they regarded as a growing danger of Bolshevik revolution and lent their support to a different sort of totalitarianism as the lesser of two evils.

(3) fear of Bolshevism

The origins of German totalitarianism go back to 1919 when a group of seven men met in Munich and founded the National Socialist

Depression in Germany. Following the defeat in World War I, inflation was rampant and food in short supply. Here a fallen horse is torn to shreds by hungry citizens.

The founding of the Nazi party; the early career of Hitler

The Nazi revolution

German Workers' party.[2] Presently the most obscure of the seven emerged as their leader. He was Adolf Hitler, born in 1889, the son of a petty customs official in the Austrian civil service. Hitler's early life was unhappy and maladjusted. Rebellious and undisciplined from childhood, he seems always to have been burdened with a sense of frustration. He was a failure in school and decided that he would become an artist. With this purpose in view he went to Vienna in 1909, hoping to enter the Academy. But he failed the required examinations; for the next four years he was compelled to eke out a dismal existence as a casual laborer and a painter of little sketches and watercolors. Meanwhile he developed some violent political prejudices. He became an ardent admirer of certain vociferously anti-Semitic politicians in Vienna; and since he associated Judaism with Marxism, he hated that philosophy also. When World War I broke out, Hitler was living in Munich, and though an Austrian citizen, he immediately enlisted in the German army. Following the war, he joined with other disaffected Germans to denounce the Weimar Republic. In 1923, Hitler led an attempt in Munich by the Nazis' private army, the Brownshirts, to stage a "putsch," or sudden overthrow of the government. The revolution was proclaimed in a beer hall, with Hitler firing a revolver into the ceiling. The Brownshirts were quickly dispersed, and Hitler sentenced to a term in prison, where he composed a declaration of his beliefs, *Mein Kampf* (My Struggle). In this rambling treatise he expressed his hatred of Jews and communists, his sense of Germany's betrayal by its World War I enemies, and his belief that only with strong leadership could the country regain its rightful place within the European concert of nations.

Hitler's message appealed to an ever-growing number of his disillusioned and economically threatened countrymen and women. In the election of 1928 the Nazis won 12 seats in the Reichstag. In 1930, they won 107 seats, their popular vote increasing from 800,000 to 6,500,000. During the summer of 1932 the parliamentary system broke down. No chancellor could retain a majority in the Reichstag, for the Nazis declined to support any cabinet not headed by Hitler, and the communists refused to collaborate with the socialists. In January 1933, a group of reactionaries—industrialists, bankers, and Junkers—prevailed upon President Paul von Hindenburg to designate Hitler as chancellor, evidently in the belief that they could control him. It was arranged that there should be only three Nazis in the cabinet, and that Franz von Papen, a Catholic aristocrat, should hold the position of vice-chancellor. But the sponsors of this plan failed to appreciate the tremendous resurgence of mass feeling behind the Nazi movement. Hitler was not slow in making the most of his new opportunity. He persuaded von Hindenburg to dissolve the Reichstag and to

[2] The name of the party was soon abbreviated in popular usage to Nazi.

One Step Away from Power. President von Hindenburg followed by Hitler, Göring on the extreme right, and other Nazi party members.

order a new election on March 5. When the new Reichstag assembled, it voted to confer upon Hitler practically unlimited powers. Soon afterward the flag of the Weimar Republic was hauled down and replaced by the swastika banner of the National Socialists. The new Germany was proclaimed to be the Third Reich, the successor of the Hohenstaufen Empire of the Middle Ages and of the Hohenzollern Empire of the kaisers.

Within a few months, other and more sweeping changes occurred. Germany was converted into a highly centralized state with the destruction of the federal principle that had been a feature of Bismarck's imperial scheme. All political parties except the Nazi party were declared illegal. Totalitarian control was extended over the press, over education, the theater, the cinema, radio, and many branches of production and trade. Drastic penalties were imposed upon the Jews: they were eliminated from government positions, deprived of citizenship, and practically excluded from the universities. With the passing of the years, the entire regime seemed to shift more and more in a radical direction. The new tendency approached its climax in 1938 with the extension of party control over the army and with the institution of a fanatical crusade against the Jews to expel them from the Reich or to annihilate them entirely.

Consolidation of Nazi rule

So far as its ideology was concerned, German totalitarianism resembled the Italian variety in a great many of its essentials. Both were collectivistic, authoritarian, nationalistic, militaristic, and anti-intellectual. Yet there were some outstanding differences. Italian fascism never had a racial basis. True, after the formation of the Rome-Berlin Axis, an alliance made in 1936, Mussolini issued anti-Jewish decrees.

Nazi racism

But race was not a central theoretical pillar of Italian fascism as it was of German National Socialism. The Nazis argued that the so-called Aryan race, which was supposed to include the Nordics as its most perfect specimens, was the only one ever to have made any notable contributions to human progress. They contended further that the accomplishments and mental qualities of a people were determined by blood. Thus the achievements of the Jew forever remained Jewish, or Oriental, no matter how long he or she might live in a Western country. It followed that no Jewish science or Jewish literature or Jewish music could ever truly represent the German nation. Obviously, most of this racial doctrine was mere rationalization. The Nazis persecuted the Jews because Hitler was himself rabidly anti-Semitic and because they needed a scapegoat upon whom they could place the blame for their nation's troubles. Before this extremism had run its course, millions of Jews had been rounded up, tortured, and murdered in concentration camps. Other representatives of "imperfect" racial and social groups—homosexuals, gypsies, and anti-Nazi intellectuals—met a similar fate. The extremism of Hitler's anti-Semitic campaigns underscores the fact that National Socialism was more fanatical than Italian fascism. It was comparable to a new religion, not only in its dogmatism and its ritual, but in its fierce intolerance and its zeal for expansion.

Dissimilarities with Italian fascism

Despite the fact that Germany was one of the most highly industrialized countries in the world, National Socialism had a peculiar peasant flavor which Italian fascism did not possess. The key to Nazi theory was contained in the phrase *Blut und Boden* (blood and soil). The word *soil* typified not only a deep reverence for the homeland but an abiding affection for the peasants, who were considered to embody the finest qualities of the German race. No class of the population was more generously treated by the Nazi government. This high regard for country folk came partly no doubt from the circumstance that they had the highest birthrate of the nation's citizens and therefore were

A Nazi Party Rally. Hitler at the height of his power, followed by other Nazi party officials.

most valuable for military reasons. It was explainable also by the reaction of the Nazi leaders against everything that the city stood for—not only intellectualism and radicalism but high finance and the complicated problems of industrial society. In its attempt to control all aspects of national life, Nazism resembled not only Italian fascism but all totalitarian regimes. Trade unions were replaced by the government-controlled National Labor Front. Public works programs—including reforestation and housing and highway construction—were begun. A policy of rearmament led to further industrial organization, and helped reduce unemployment.

The significance of German and Italian totalitarianism is still a subject of controversy among students of modern history. Some argue that it was simply the enthronement of force by big capitalists in an effort to save their dying system from destruction. It is true that the success of both movements in gaining control of the government depended in some measure upon support from great landowners and captains of industry. A second interpretation would explain German and Italian totalitarianism as a reaction of debtors against creditors, of farmers against bankers and manufacturers, and of small businessmen against high finance and monopolistic practices. Still other students of the movement interpret it as a revolt against communism, a reversion to primitivism, a result of the despair of the masses, a protest against the weaknesses of democracy, or a supreme manifestation of nationalism. Undoubtedly it was all of these things combined. An increasingly popular view in recent years holds that fascism and Nazism were extreme expressions of tendencies prevalent in all industrialized countries. If official policies in most Western countries in the 1930s took on more and more of an authoritarian semblance—a tightly controlled economy, limitation of production to maintain prices, and expansion of armaments to promote prosperity—it was because nearly all nations in that period were beset with similar problems.

*The complex significance
of German and Italian
totalitarianism*

4. THE DEMOCRACIES BETWEEN THE WARS

The histories of the three Western democracies—Great Britain, France, and the United States—run roughly parallel during the years after the First World War. In all three countries there was an attempt by governments to trust to policies and assumptions that had prevailed before the war. The French, not surprisingly, continued to fear Germany and to take whatever steps they could to keep their traditional enemy as weak as possible. Under the leadership of the moderate conservative, Raymond Poincaré, who held office from 1922 to 1924, and again from 1926 to 1929, the French pursued a policy of deflation, which attempted to keep the price of manufactured goods low, by restraining wages. This policy pleased businessmen, but was hard on the working class. Edouard Herriot, a Radical Socialist who

Class conflict in France

served as premier from 1924 to 1926 was, despite his party's name, a spokesman for the small businessman, farmer, and lower middle class. Herriot declared himself in favor of social reform, but he refused to raise taxes in order to pay for it. Class conflict lay close to the surface of French national affairs throughout the 1920s. While industries prospered, employers rejected trade unionists' demands to bargain collectively. A period of major strikes immediately after the war was followed by a sharp decline in union activity. Workers remained dissatisfied, even after the government passed a modified social insurance program in 1930, insuring against sickness, old age, and death.

Britain's economic difficulties

Class conflict flared in Britain as well. Anxious to regain its now irretrievably lost position as the major industrial and financial power in the world, Britain, like France, pursued a policy of deflation, designed to lower the price of manufactured goods and thus make them more attractive on the world market. The result was a reduction in wages which undermined the standard of living of many British workers. Their resentment helped to elect a Labour party government in 1924 and 1929. But its minority position in Parliament left it little chance to accomplish much of consequence, even had its leader, Prime Minister J. Ramsay MacDonald, been a more adventurous socialist than he was. In 1926 British trade unions grew increasingly militant because of the particularly distressing wage levels in the coal mining industry, and because the Conservative government, returned to power under Prime Minister Stanley Baldwin in 1925, refused to be deflected from its deflationary stance. The unions staged a nationwide general strike which, though it failed as an industrial strategy, turned the middle class more than ever against the workers.

Conservatism in the U.S.

The United States was undoubtedly the most impregnable fortress of conservative power among the democracies. The presidents elected during the 1920s—Warren G. Harding, Calvin Coolidge, and Herbert Hoover—upheld a social philosophy formulated by the barons of big business in the nineteenth century, and the Supreme Court used its power of judicial review to nullify progressive legislation enacted by state governments and occasionally by Congress.

Labor Troubles in Britain. Mounted police escorting delivery wagons through a mob of angry strikers during the general strike of 1926.

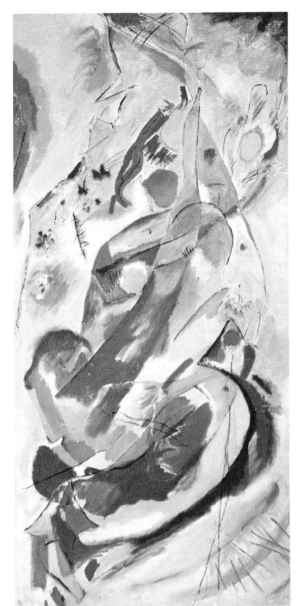

Panel (3), Wassily Kandinsky (1866–1944). The Expressionist painters carried their explorations of the psychological properties of color and line to the point where subject matter was deemed unnecessary and even undesirable. (Museum of Modern Art)

Nude Descending a Staircase, Marcel Duchamp (1887–1968). An example of the impact of film on painting. The effect is that of a series of closely spaced photographs coalescing to create motion. (Philadelphia Museum of Art)

The Table, Georges Braque (1881–1963). An example of later cubism showing the predominance of curvilinear form and line instead of geometric structure. (Museum of Modern Art)

I and the Village, Marc Chagall (1889–   ). The subject refers to the artist's childhood and youth in Vitebsk, Russia. The profile on the right is probably that of the artist himself. (Museum of Modern Art)

The Persistence of Memory, Salvador Dali (1904–   ). The Spaniard Dali is the outstanding representative of the surrealist school. Many objects in his paintings are Freudian images. (Museum of Modern Art)

Barricade, José Clemente Orozco (1883–1949). The Mexican muralist Orozco was one of the most celebrated of contemporary painters with a social message. His themes were revolutionary fervor, satire of aristocracy and the Church, and deification of the common man. (Museum of Modern Art)

Sea and Gulls, John Marin (1870–1953). A native of New Jersey, Marin was a gifted abstract painter. His objects are sometimes recognizable, sometimes not. He painted not the likeness of nature, but *about* nature. (Museum of Modern Art)

Around the Fish, Paul Klee (1879–1940). Klee is recognized as the most subtle humorist of XX-cent. art. The central motif of a fish on a platter suggests a banquet, but many of the surrounding objects appear to be products of fantasy. (Museum of Modern Art)

Above: *Little Big Painting*, Roy Lichtenstein (born 1923). Oil on canvas. (The Whitney Museum of American Art). In the 1960's and early 1970's, American artists dominated the new movements, particularly "Pop," "Op," and "the New Realism." The works on this and the following page are by some of the best-known contemporary artists.

Left: *Summer Rental No. 2*, Robert Rauschenberg (born 1925). Oil on canvas. (Collection Whitney Museum of American Art). Gift of the Friends of the Whitney Museum of American Art.

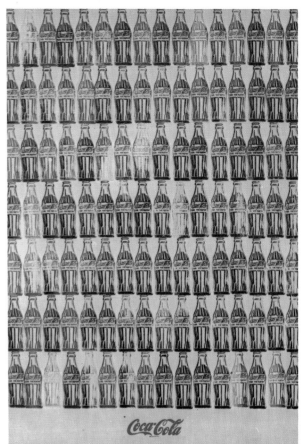

Top Left: *Girl in Doorway*, George Segal (born 1924). A life-size construction in plaster, wood, glass, and aluminum paint. (Collection Whitney Museum of American Art). Top Right: *Green Coca Cola Bottles*, Andy Warhol (born 1931). Oil on canvas. (Collection Whitney Museum of American Art). Gift of the Friends of the Whitney Museum of American Art. Left: *Gran Cairo*, Frank Stella (born 1936). Synthetic polymer paint on canvas. (Collection Whitney Museum of American Art). Gift of the Friends of the Whitney Museum of American Art.

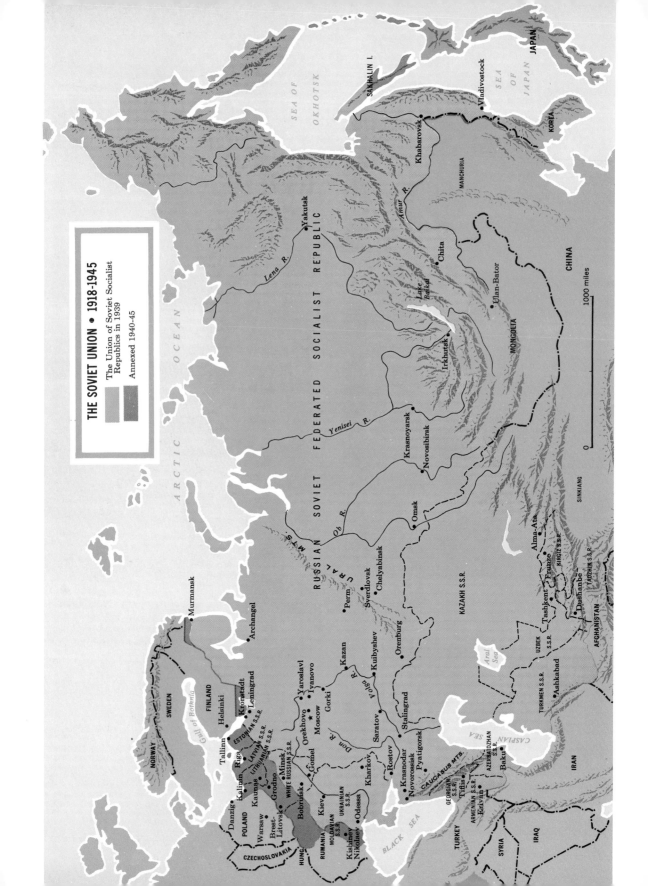

THE SOVIET UNION • 1918-1945

The Union of Soviet Socialist
Republics in 1939

Annexed 1940-45

ARCTIC OCEAN

SEA OF OKHOTSK

SEA OF JAPAN

JAPAN

SAKHALIN I.

Vladivostock

KOREA

Khabarovsk

MANCHURIA

Amur R.

Yakutsk

Chita

CHINA

Lena R.

Lake Baikal

Irkutsk

Ulan-Bator

MONGOLIA

1000 miles

0

RUSSIAN SOVIET FEDERATED SOCIALIST REPUBLIC

Yenisei R.

Krasnoyarsk

Novosibirsk

Omsk

SINKIANG

Ob R.

URAL MTS.

Perm

Sverdlovsk

Chelyabinsk

Orenburg

KAZAKH S.S.R.

Alma-Ata

Frunze

KIRGIZ S.S.R.

Tashkent

Dushanbe

TADZHIK S.S.R.

AFGHANISTAN

UZBEK S.S.R.

Aral Sea

Murmansk

Archangel

TURKMEN S.S.R.

Ashkabad

Kazan

Kuibyshev

Volga R.

Saratov

Stalingrad

CASPIAN SEA

IRAN

SWEDEN

FINLAND

Helsinki

Gulf of Bothnia

Kronstadt

Leningrad

Tallinn

ESTONIAN S.S.R.

Riga

LATVIAN S.S.R.

LITHUANIAN S.S.R.

Yaroslavl

Ivanovo

Orekhovo

Moscow

Gorki

Don R.

NORWAY

Kalinin

Kaunas

Grodno

Minsk

WHITE RUSSIAN S.S.R.

Bobruisk

Gomel

Kiev

UKRAINIAN S.S.R.

Odessa

Kharkov

Rostov

Krasnodar

Novorossisk

Pyatigorsk

CAUCASUS MTS.

GEORGIAN S.S.R.

Tiflis

AZERBAIDZHAN S.S.R.

Baku

ARMENIAN S.S.R.

Erivan

TURKEY

Danzig

POLAND

Warsaw

Brest-Litovsk

RUMANIA

MOLDAVIAN S.S.R.

Kishinev

Nikolaev

HUNG.

CZECHOSLOVAKIA

BLACK SEA

SYRIA

IRAQ

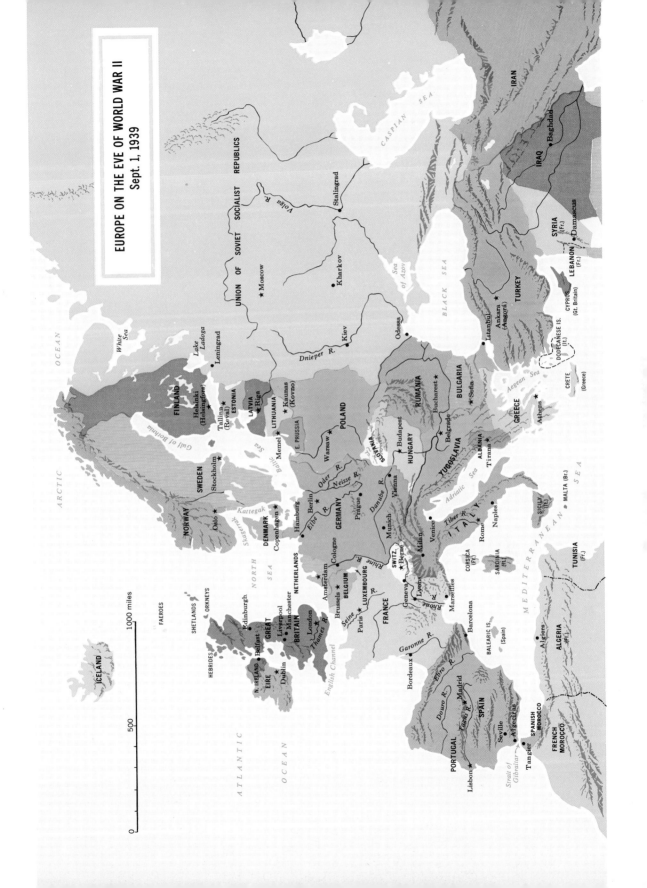

EUROPE ON THE EVE OF WORLD WAR II
Sept. 1, 1939

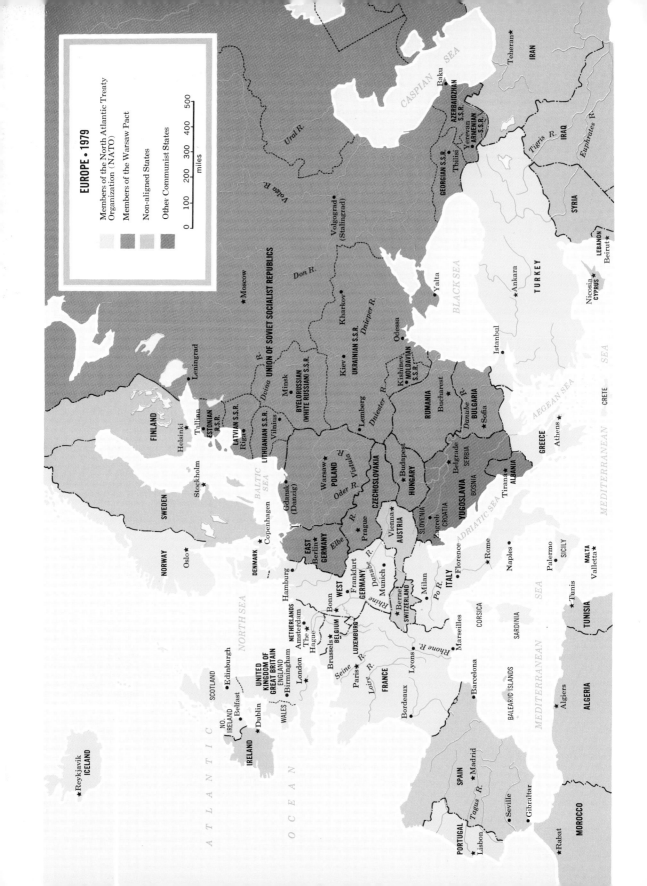

EUROPE · 1979

Members of the North Atlantic Treaty
Organization (NATO)

Members of the Warsaw Pact

Non-aligned States

Other Communist States

miles
0 100 200 300 400 500

ICELAND
★Reykjavik

ATLANTIC OCEAN

NORTH SEA

IRELAND
Dublin●
NO. IRELAND
Belfast●

SCOTLAND
Edinburgh●
UNITED KINGDOM OF GREAT BRITAIN
WALES
Birmingham●
ENGLAND
London●

FINLAND
Helsinki★

SWEDEN
Stockholm★

NORWAY
Oslo★

Leningrad●

UNION OF SOVIET SOCIALIST REPUBLICS
Moscow★

Ural R.

Volga R.

Volgograd (Stalingrad)●

Don R.

ESTONIAN S.S.R.
Tallinn●

LATVIAN S.S.R.
Riga●

LITHUANIAN S.S.R.
Vilnius●

Duna R.

Minsk●
BYELORUSSIAN (WHITE RUSSIAN) S.S.R.

Kharkov●

Kiev●
UKRAINIAN S.S.R.
Dnieper R.

Odessa●

Lemberg●

Dniester R.

Kishinev●
MOLDAVIAN S.S.R.

Yalta●

BLACK SEA

GEORGIAN S.S.R.
Tbilisi●

Baku●
AZERBAIDZHAN S.S.R.

Yerevan●
ARMENIAN S.S.R.

CASPIAN SEA

Teheran★
IRAN

IRAQ
Tigris R.
Euphrates R.

SYRIA

LEBANON
Beirut●

Ankara●
TURKEY

CYPRUS
Nicosia★

AEGEAN SEA

CRETE

MEDITERRANEAN SEA

DENMARK
Copenhagen★
Hamburg●

BALTIC SEA

Gdansk (Danzig)●

POLAND
Warsaw★
Vistula R.
Oder R.

EAST GERMANY
Berlin★
Elbe R.

WEST GERMANY
Bonn★
Frankfurt●
Munich●

NETHERLANDS
Amsterdam●
The Hague★

BELGIUM
Brussels★
LUXEMBOURG★

FRANCE
Paris★
Seine R.
Loire R.

Bordeaux●

Lyons●
Rhône R.

Marseilles●

CORSICA

SARDINIA

SPAIN
Madrid★
Barcelona●
Seville●
Gibraltar●
BALEARIC ISLANDS

PORTUGAL
Lisbon★
Tagus R.

MOROCCO
Rabat★

ALGERIA
Algiers★

TUNISIA
Tunis●

CZECHOSLOVAKIA
Prague★

AUSTRIA
Vienna★
Danube R.

SWITZERLAND
Berne★

Rhine R.

ITALY
Milan●
Po R.
Florence●
Rome★
Naples●

MEDITERRANEAN SEA

SICILY
Palermo●

MALTA
Valletta★

HUNGARY
Budapest★

YUGOSLAVIA
Belgrade★
SLOVENIA
Zagreb●
CROATIA
BOSNIA
SERBIA

RUMANIA
Bucharest★
Danube R.

BULGARIA
Sofia★

ALBANIA
Tirana★

ADRIATIC SEA

GREECE
Athens★

Istanbul●

The Stock Market Crash, October 24, 1929. Crowds milling outside the New York Stock Exchange on the day of the big crash.

The course of Western history was dramatically altered by the advent of worldwide depression in 1929. We have already mentioned this event as it contributed to the rise of Nazism. But all countries were forced to come to terms with the economic and social devastation it produced. The Great Depression had its roots in a general agricultural slump in the 1920s, the result of increased postwar production which drove down the price of grain and other commodities to the point of bankrupting farmers, though not far enough to benefit the urban poor. To chronic agricultural distress was added the financial crisis that began with the collapse of prices on the New York stock exchange in 1929. With a drop in the value of stocks, banks found themselves short of capital and forced to close. International investors called in their debts. Industries, unable to sell, stopped manufacturing and started laying off workers. Unemployment further contracted markets—fewer people had money with which to buy goods or services—and that contraction led to more unemployment.

The results of the depression took varied forms throughout the West. In 1931 Great Britain abandoned the gold standard, and the government of the United States followed suit in 1933. By no longer pegging their currencies to the price of gold, these countries hoped to make money cheaper, and thus more available for programs of public and private economic recovery. This action was the forerunner of a broad program of currency management, which became an important element in a general policy of economic nationalism. By way of illustration, President Franklin D. Roosevelt informed the London Economic Conference of 1933 that "the sound internal economic system of a nation is a greater factor in its well-being than the price of its currency in changing terms of the currencies of other nations." As early as 1932 Great Britain abandoned its time-honored policy of free trade. Protective tariffs were raised in some instances as high as 100 percent.

The Great Depression

Results of depression: economic nationalism

Léon Blum

Domestic policies

The New Deal

Its achievements

Domestically, Britain moved cautiously to alleviate the effects of the depression. A national government, which came to power in 1931 with a ministry composed of members from the Conservative, Liberal, and Labour parties, was reluctant to spend beyond its income, as it would have to in order to underwrite effective programs of public assistance. Of the European democracies, France adopted the most advanced set of policies to combat the inequalities and distress that followed in the wake of the depression. In 1936, responding to a threat from ultraconservatives to overthrow the republic, a Popular Front government, under the leadership of the socialist Léon Blum (1872–1950), was formed by the Radical, Radical Socialist, and Communist parties, and lasted for two years. The Popular Front nationalized the munitions industry and reorganized the Bank of France so as to deprive the 200 largest stockholders of their monopolistic control over credit. In addition, it decreed a forty-hour week for all urban workers and initiated a program of public works. For the benefit of the farmers it established a wheat office to fix the price and regulate the distribution of grain. Although the threat from the political Right had for a time been quelled by the Popular Front, conservatives were generally uncooperative and unimpressed by its attempts to ameliorate the conditions of the French working class. The anti-Semitism that had surfaced at the time of the Dreyfus affair resurfaced; Blum was both a socialist and a Jew. Businessmen saw him as the forerunner of a French Lenin, and were heard to opine, "better Hitler than Blum." They got their wish before the decade was out.

The most dramatic changes in policy after the depression occurred, not in Europe, but in the United States. The explanation was twofold. The United States had clung longer to the economic philosophy of the nineteenth century. Prior to the depression the business classes had adhered firmly to the dogma of freedom of contract and insisted upon their right to form monopolies and to use the government as their agent in frustrating the demands of both workers and consumers. The depression in the United States was also more severe than in the European democracies. Industrial production shrank by about two-thirds. The structure of agricultural prices and of common stocks collapsed. Thousands of banks were forced to close their doors. Unemployment rose to 15 million, or to approximately 33 percent of the total labor force. An attempt to alleviate distress was contained in a program of reform and reconstruction known as the New Deal. The chief architect and motivator of this program was Franklin D. Roosevelt (1882–1945), who succeeded Herbert Hoover in the presidency on March 4, 1933.

The aim of the New Deal was to preserve the capitalist system, by managing the economy and undertaking programs of relief and public works to increase mass purchasing power. Although the New Deal did assist in the recovery both of individual citizens and of the country, through programs of currency management and social security, it left the crucial problem of unemployment unsolved. In 1939, after six years of the New Deal, the United States still had more than 9 million jobless workers—a figure which exceeded the combined unemployment of the rest of the world. Ironically, only the outbreak of a new world war could provide the full recovery that the New Deal had failed to assure, by directing millions from the labor market into the army and by creating jobs in the countless factories that turned to the manufacture of war materiel.

5. INTELLECTUAL AND CULTURAL TRENDS IN THE INTERWAR YEARS

The First World War, which proved so disillusioning to so many, and the generally dispiriting political events which followed in its train, made it difficult to hold fast to any notion of a purposeful universe. Philosophers, to a greater degree than their predecessors, declared that there was little point in attempting to discover answers to questions about the nature of ultimate reality. These antimetaphysicians discarded the search for God or for the "meaning" of life as a hopeless and therefore pointless task. Probably the most influential of these thinkers was the Viennese Ludwig Wittgenstein (1889–1951), founder, with the Englishman Bertrand Russell (1872–1970), of the school of Logical Positivism. Developed further by the so-called Vienna Circle, whose leader was Rudolf Carnap, Logical Positivism emerged as an uncompromisingly scientific philosophy. It is not concerned with values or ideals except to the extent that they may be demonstrable by mathematics or physics. In general, the Logical Positivists reject as "meaningless" everything that cannot be reduced to a "one-to-one correspondence" with something in the physical universe. In other words, they reduce philosophy to a mere instrument for the discovery of truth in harmony with the facts of the physical environment. They divest it almost entirely of its traditional content and use it as a medium for answering questions and solving problems. They are concerned especially with political theory, regarding that subject as particularly burdened with unproved assumptions and questionable dogmas.

Antimetaphysics

Sociologists reinforced philosophers in denying the value of metaphysics. One of the most important was the German Max Weber (1864–1920), who, in his book *The Protestant Ethic and the Spirit of Capitalism* (1905), argued that religion must be understood as a cultural force, in this case assisting directly in the spread of capitalism. By making work a cardinal virtue and idleness a supreme vice, Protestantism had encouraged the work ethic, which, in turn, had fueled the energies of early capitalist entrepreneurs. When he turned to a study of

Bertrand Russell

the contemporary world, Weber concluded that societies would inevitably fall more and more under the sway of ever-expanding and potentially totalitarian bureaucracies. Recognizing the extent to which such a development might threaten human freedom, Weber posited the notion of "charismatic" leadership as a means of escaping the deadening tyranny of state control. A term derived from the Greek word for gift, "charisma" was, according to Weber, an almost magic quality which could induce hero worship and which, if properly directed by its possessor, might produce an authority to challenge bureaucracy. Weber himself recognized the dangers as well as the attractions of charismatic authority, dangers which the careers of Hitler and Mussolini soon made all too apparent. Another thinker who treated religion as a powerful social and psychological force, rather than as a branch of metaphysics, was the Swiss psychologist Carl Jung (1875–1961). Originally a student and disciple of Freud, Jung broke with his intellectual mentor by proclaiming the existence of a force behind individual id, ego, and superego: the "collective unconscious." Jung's literary background and his personal penchant for mysticism helped persuade him of the enduring psychological and therapeutic value of myth and religion, something Freud refused to acknowledge.

The writings of some philosophers during the interwar years not only reflected a sense of crisis and despair but, because of the influence of those works, contributed to it as well. Foremost among these were the Italian Vilfredo Pareto (1848–1923) and the German Oswald Spengler (1880–1936), who agreed in their contempt for the masses, in their belief that democracy was impossible, in their anti-intellectual viewpoint, and in their admiration for strong and aggressive leaders. Spengler was, in many respects, more extreme than Pareto. Although he completed in about 1918 an erudite and in some respects brilliant philosophy of history, which he entitled *The Decline of the West,* his later writings reflected totalitarian prejudices. In his *Hour of Decision,* published in 1933, he fulminated against democracy, pacifism, internationalism, the lower classes, and nonwhite peoples. He sang the praises of those "who feel themselves born and called to be masters," of "healthy instincts, race, the will to possession and power." Spengler despised the old, analytical reasoning of urban intellectuals and called upon men to admire the "deep wisdom of old peasant families." Human beings, he maintained, are "beasts of prey," and those who deny this conclusion are simply "beasts of prey with broken teeth."

Literary movements during the interwar period showed tendencies similar to those in philosophy. The major novelists, poets, and dramatists were deeply concerned about social and political problems and about the hope and destiny of humanity. Like the philosophers, they were disillusioned by the brute facts of World War I and by the failure of victory to fulfill its promises. Many were profoundly affected also by revolutionary developments in science and especially by the probings of the new science of psychoanalysis into the hidden secrets of the mind. Much of the literature of the interwar period expressed themes of frustration, cynicism, and disenchantment. It was an era dominated by those whose ideals had been shattered by the events of their time. Its mood was set by the early novels of the American Ernest Hemingway (1899–1961), by the poetry of the Anglo-American T. S. Eliot (1888–1965), and by the plays of the German Bertolt Brecht (1898–1956). In *The Sun Also Rises,* Hemingway gave the public a powerful description of the essential tragedy of the so-called lost generation and set a pattern which other writers, like the American F. Scott Fitzgerald, were soon to follow. In his poem *The Waste Land* (1922), T. S. Eliot presented a philosophy that was close to despair. Once you are born, he seemed to be saying, life is a living death, to be ground out in boredom and frustration. The German, Brecht, in plays written to be performed before the proletarian patrons of cabarets, proclaimed the corruption of the bourgeois state and the pointlessness of war.

The works of many writers in the interwar period reflected to an increasing extent the isolation of self-conscious intellectuals and the constricting of their audience that, as we have seen, characterized the years before the First World War. While Brecht carried his revolutionary messages into the streets of Berlin, other writers wrote primarily for each other or for the small elite group who could understand what they were saying. Eliot crammed his poetry with esoteric allusions. The Irishman James Joyce (1882–1941), whose ability to enter his characters' minds and to reproduce their "stream-of-consciousness" on paper made him a writer of the very first order, nevertheless wrote with a complexity that only few could appreciate. The same was true, though to a lesser extent, of the novels of the Frenchman Marcel Proust (1871–1922) and the Englishwoman Virginia Woolf (1882–1941). In her novels and essays, Woolf was an eloquent and biting critic of the ruling class of Britain, focusing in part on the enforced oppression of women even in that class.

The Great Depression of the 1930s forced a reexamination of the methods and purposes of literature. In the midst of economic stagnation and threats of totalitarianism and war, the theory evolved that literature must have a political purpose, that it should indict meanness, cruelty, and barbarism, and point the way to a more just society. It should also be a literature addressed not to fellow intellectuals, but to common men and women. The new trend was reflected in the works of a diversity of writers. The American John Steinbeck (1902–1968), in *The Grapes of Wrath,* depicted the sorry plight of impoverished farmers fleeing from the "dust bowl" to California only to find that all the land had been monopolized by companies that exploited their workers. Pervading the novels of the Frenchman André Malraux

T. S. Eliot

Intellectual isolation

Virginia Woolf

Influence of the depression

Jean-Paul Sartre

Existentialism

George Orwell

John Maynard Keynes

(1901–   ) was the strong suggestion that the human struggle against tyranny and injustice is that which gives meaning and value to life. Young British writers such as W. H. Auden, Stephen Spender, and Christopher Isherwood declared, as communist sympathizers, that artists had an obligation to politicize their art for the benefit of the revolution. They rejected the pessimism of their immediate literary forebears for the optimism of political commitment to a common cause.

In this they differed radically from their French contemporary, Jean-Paul Sartre (1905–1980), whose pessimistic philosophy of Existentialism was receiving its first hearing at this time. Sartre was a teacher of philosophy in a Paris *lycée* and subsequently a leader of the French resistance movement against the Germans. His philosophy takes its name from its doctrine that the *existence* of human beings as ·free individuals is the fundamental fact of life. But this freedom is of no help to humanity; instead it is a source of anguish and terror. Realizing, however vaguely, that they are free agents, morally responsible for all their acts, individuals feel themselves strangers in an alien world. They can have no confidence in a benevolent God or in a universe guided by purpose, for, according to Sartre, all such ideas have been reduced to fictions by modern science. The only way of escape from despair is the path of "involvement," or active participation in human affairs. It should be noted that in addition to the atheistic Existentialism of Sartre, there was also a prior Christian version, which had its origin in the teachings of Søren Kierkegaard (1813–1855), a Danish theologian of the mid–nineteenth century. Like its atheistic counterpart, Christian Existentialism also teaches that the chief cause of human agony and terror is freedom, but it finds the source of this freedom in original sin.

Another writer who refused to allow himself the luxury of political optimism was the Englishman George Orwell (1903–1950). Although sympathetic to the cause of international socialism, Orwell continued to insist that all political movements were to some degree corrupted. He urged writers to recognize a duty to write only on the basis of what they had themselves experienced. Above all, writers should never simply parrot party propaganda. Orwell's last two novels, *Animal Farm* and *1984,* written during and immediately after the Second World War, are powerful expressions of his mistrust of political regimes—whether of the Left or the Right—that profess democracy but in fact destroy human freedom.

Optimism during the 1930s was generally the property of those writers who were prepared to advocate a violent change in the social order, most notably men and women sympathetic to the doctrines of communism and the achievements of Soviet Russia. An exception to this rule was the British economist John Maynard Keynes (1883–1946), who argued that capitalism could be made to work if governments would play a part in its management, and whose theories helped shape the economic policies of the New Deal. Keynes had served as an economic adviser to the British government during the 1919 treaty-making at Paris. He was disgusted with the harsh terms imposed upon the Germans, recognizing that they would serve only to keep alive the hatreds and uncertainties that breed war. His dismay did not induce him to turn his back on the world and its problems, however. Keynes was very much a man of the world, among other things a successful financial speculator in his own right. Keynes believed that capitalism with its inner faults corrected could provide all the justice and efficiency reasonable people could expect. Capitalism, though, would require a "face-lifting" that some of its more conservative defenders would consider drastic. First, the idea of a perpetually balanced budget would need to be abandoned. Keynes never advocated continuous deficit financing. He would have the government deliberately operate in the red whenever private investment was too scanty to provide for the needs of the country. But when depression gave way to recovery, private financing could take the place for most purposes of deficit spending. He favored the accumulation and investment of large amounts of venture capital, which he declared to be the only socially productive form of capital. Finally, Keynes recommended monetary control as a means of promoting prosperity and full employment. He would establish what is commonly called a "managed currency," regulating its value by a process of contraction or expansion in accordance with the needs of the economy. Prosperity would thus be assured in terms of the condition of the home market, and no nation would be tempted to "beggar its neighbor" in the foolish pursuit of a favorable balance of trade.

Trends in art tended to parallel those in literature. For much of the period, visual artists continued to explore aesthetic frontiers far re-

John Maynard Keynes

Big Julie by Fernand Léger. Note the artist's fascination with industrial shapes and images.

Mountain, Table, Anchors, Navel by Jean Arp

See color plates following page 864

Trends in art

Art and the depression

moved from the conventional taste of average men and women. Picasso followed his particular genius as it led him further into cubist variations and inventions. So did others, such as the Frenchman Fernand Léger (1881–1955), who combined devotion to cubist principles and a fascination with the artifacts of industrial civilization. A group more advanced, perhaps, than the cubists, the expressionists argued that since color and line express inherent psychological qualities which can be represented without reference to subject matter, a painting need not have a "subject" at all. The Russian Wassily Kandinsky (1866–1944) carried the logic of this position to its conclusion by calling his untitled paintings "improvisations," and insisting that they meant nothing. A second group of expressionists rejected intellectuality for what they called "objectivity," by which they meant a candid appraisal of the state of the human mind. Their analysis took the form of an attack upon the greed and decadence of postwar Europe. Chief among this group was the German George Grosz (1893–1959), whose cruel, satiric line has been likened to a "razor lancing a carbuncle." Another school expressed its disgust with the world by declaring that there was in fact no such thing as aesthetic principle, since aesthetic principle was based on reason and the world had conclusively proved by fighting itself to death that reason did not exist. Calling themselves dada-ists (after a name picked at random, allegedly, from the dictionary) these artists, led by the Frenchman Marcel Duchamp (1887–1968), the German Max Ernst (1891–   ), and the Alsatian Jean Hans Arp (1887–1966), concocted "fabrications" from cut-outs and juxtapositions of wood, glass, and metal, and gave them bizarre names: *The Bride stripped bare by her Bachelors, even* (Duchamp), for example. These works were declared by critics, however, to belie their professed meaninglessness, to be, in fact, expressions of the subconscious. Such certainly were the paintings of the surrealists, artists such as the Italian Giorgio de Chirico (1888–1978) and the Spaniard Salvador Dali (1904–   ), whose explorations of the interior of the mind produced irrational, fantastic, and generally melancholy images.

For a time in the 1930s artists, like writers, responded to the sense of international crisis by painting to express their pain and outrage directly to a mass audience. Among the chief representatives of the new movement were the Mexicans Diego Rivera and Jose Clemente Orozco, and the Americans Thomas Hart Benton, Reginald Marsh, Edward Hopper, and Grant Wood. The fundamental aim of these artists was to depict the social conditions of the modern world and to present in graphic detail the hopes and struggles of peasants and workers. While they scarcely adhered to any of the conventions of the past, there was nothing unintelligible about their work; it was intended to be art that anyone could understand. Much of it bore the sting or thrust of social satire. Orozco, in particular, delighted in pillorying the hypocrisy of the Church and the greed and cruelty of plutocrats and plunderers.

Mural of Kansas City, Missouri by Thomas Hart Benton. The mural protests the corruption of American politics and the depression misery and degradation of farm workers and industrial laborers. The man in the armchair is the political boss of Kansas City in the 1930s, Tom Pendergast.

It was inevitable that music should reflect the spirit of disillusionment that reached a climax following World War I. The more original developments were closely parallel to those in painting. Most fundamental of all was the revolt against the romantic tradition, especially as it had culminated in Wagner. Many, although by no means all, composers went so far as to repudiate the aesthetic ideal entirely, relying upon complexity and novelty of structure or on a sheer display of energy to supply interest to their works.

The chief trends in contemporary music

Deviations from the classical and romantic formulas have been generally of two types, designated broadly as impressionism and expressionism. The former seeks to exploit the qualities of musical sound to suggest feelings or images. The latter is concerned more with form than with sensuous effects and tends toward abstraction. The most perfect exponent of impressionism was Claude Debussy (1862–1918), its originator. Even in France impressionism did not prove to be an enduring school. With Maurice Ravel (1875–1937), most celebrated of the composers who reflected Debussy's influence, it became less poetic and picturesque and acquired a degree of cold impassivity together with greater firmness of texture.

Musical impressionism

Expressionism, more radical and more influential than impressionism, comprises two main schools: atonality, founded by the Viennese Arnold Schoenberg (1874–1951), and polytonality, best typified by the Russian Igor Stravinsky (1882–1971). Atonality abolishes key. In this type of music, dissonances are the rule rather than the excep-

Musical expressionism: atonality

Igor Stravinsky

Development of functional architecture

tion, and the melodic line commonly alternates between chromatic manipulation and strange unsingable leaps. In short, the ordinary principles of composition are reversed. The atonalists attempt, with some success, to let musical sound become a vehicle for expressing the inner meaning and elemental structure of things.

Polytonality, of which Stravinsky is the most famous exponent, is essentially a radical kind of counterpoint, deriving its inspiration partly from baroque practices of counterpoint that were placed in the service of new ideas. However, it does not simply interweave independent melodies which together form concord, but undertakes to combine separate keys and unrelated harmonic systems, with results that are highly discordant. While the atonalists have retained elements of romanticism, the polytonalists have tried to resurrect the architectural qualities of pure form, movement, and rhythm, stripping away all sentimentality and sensuous connotations.

Architects during this period were also intent upon denying sentimentality. Between 1880 and 1890 certain architects in Europe and America awoke to the fact that the prevailing styles of building construction were far out of harmony with the facts of modern civilization. The result was the launching of a new architectural movement known as functionalism. Its chief pioneers were Otto Wagner (1841–1918) in Germany and Louis Sullivan (1856–1924) and Frank Lloyd Wright (1869–1959) in the United States. The basic principle of functionalism is the idea that the appearance of a building shall proclaim its actual use and purpose. There must be no addition of friezes, columns, tracery, or battlements merely because some people consider such ornaments beautiful. True beauty consists in sincerity, in an honest adaptation of materials to the purpose they are intended to serve. Functionalism also includes the idea that architecture shall express either directly or symbolically the distinguishing features of contemporary culture. Ornamentation must therefore be restricted to such elements as will reflect an age of science and machines. Modern men and women do not believe in the Greek ideas of harmony, bal-

Taliesin East by Frank Lloyd Wright. A famous example of the functional style, with the pattern of the house conforming to the natural surroundings.

Contrasting Architectural Styles in Germany Between the Wars. Left: The Bauhaus by Walter Gropius. This school in Dessau, Germany, is a starkly functional prototype of the interwar "international style." Right: The Chancellery in Berlin by Albert Speer. Note the massive qualities of the Nazi state style.

ance, and restraint or in the medieval virtues of piety and chivalry, but in power, efficiency, speed, and comfort. These are the ideals which should find a place in architecture.

The functional style of building construction is one of the most significant architectural developments since the Renaissance. Among all of the styles which have been adopted during the last 300 years, it is the only one that is really original. Known also as modern architecture or the international style, it is the best approach that has yet been made to an efficient use of the tremendous mechanical and scientific resources of the contemporary world. It permits an honest application of new materials—chromium, glass, steel, concrete—and tempts the builder's ingenuity in devising others. One of the pioneer practitioners of the functional or international style was the German Walter Gropius (1883–1969), who, in 1919, established a school—the *Bauhaus*—to serve as a center for the theory and practice of modern architecture. Gropius and his followers declared, as good functionalists, that the aesthetic content of a building can only be expressed legitimately in terms of its purpose.

Gropius was one of the multitude of German intellectuals—both Jewish and non-Jewish—to leave their country after Hitler's rise to

The significance of functional architecture

power. Nazism had its own cultural aesthetic, which it imposed upon Germany. Functionalism, which celebrated the qualities of material, line, and proportion, had no place in a totalitarian regime, where the arts were obliged to advertise the virtues of the state, its tradition, and the aspirations of its people. Instead of Gropius, Hitler had Albert Speer, an architect of unimpressive talents, who produced for him grandiose designs whose vacuous pretentiousness was an unconscious parody of Nazi ideology. Atonality in music was banished along with functionalism in architecture, to be replaced by the mystical and heroic nationalism of Wagner.

Art was an important part of the new and cultural arm of totalitarianism: propaganda. Never before had so many of the world's people been able to read. Nineteenth- and twentieth-century governments had encouraged literacy, fearing an ignorant working class as a revolutionary threat. Now totalitarian regimes used education unashamedly as a means of indoctrination. Books critical of the state were banned, their places on school and library shelves taken by others specifically written to glorify the present leadership. Youth programs instructed children in the virtues of discipline and loyalty to the state. Mass gymnastic displays suggested the ease with which well-trained bodies could be made to respond to the military needs of the nation. Propagandizing was made more effective by the advent of mass-circulation publishing, the radio, and the motion picture. Newspapers which printed only what the state wanted printed reached a wider audience than ever before. Party political broadcasts, beamed into homes or blared through loudspeakers in town squares, by their constant repetitiveness made people begin to accept—if not believe—what they knew to be untrue. Films could transform German youths into Aryan gods and goddesses, as they could Russian collective farms into a worker's paradise. Sergei Eisenstein (1898–1948) the Russian director, rewrote Russian history on film to serve the ends of the Soviet state. Hitler commissioned the filmmaker Leni Riefenstahl to record a political rally staged by herself and Speer. The film, entitled *Triumph of the Will,* was a visual hymn to the Nordic race and the Nazi regime. (And the comedian Charlie Chaplin riposted in his celebrated lampoon, *The Great Dictator,* an enormously successful parody of totalitarian pomposities.)

In Western democracies, although the media were not manipulated by the state as they were elsewhere, their effectiveness as propagandizers was nevertheless recognized and exploited. Advertising became an industry when manufacturers realized the mass markets that newspapers, magazines, and radio represented. Much that was printed and aired was trivialized by writers and editors who feared that serious or difficult material would antagonize the readers or listeners upon whom they depended for their livelihood. This is not to say that the new media were uniformly banal, or that artists and per-

A Scene from John Ford's film of Steinbeck's *The Grapes of Wrath*

formers were unable to use them to make thoughtful protests. The film version of Steinbeck's *Grapes of Wrath,* directed by John Ford, though an exception to the normal run of escapist Hollywood comedies and adventures, was perhaps as stinging an indictment of capitalism as the novel, and it reached far more people. During these years popular culture, whatever else it was, remained a powerful and alarming new fact of life: powerful in terms of its vast audience; alarming because of its particular applicability as a means of controlling the minds of men and women.

SELECTED READINGS

• *Items so designated are available in paperback editions.*

GENERAL

Galbraith, John Kenneth, *The Great Crash, 1929,* Boston, 1955. An entertaining and informative account by the celebrated economist.

• Hamilton, George Heard, *Painting and Sculpture in Europe, 1880–1940,* Baltimore, 1967. An excellent survey.

Hughes, H. Stuart. *Contemporary Europe: A History,* Englewood Cliffs, N.J., 1971. A good general text.

Laqueur, W., and G. L. Mosse, eds., *The Left-Wing Intellectuals between the Wars, 1919–1939,* New York, 1966. Recent essays by modern historians.

• Passmore, John A., *A Hundred Years of Philosophy*, New York, 1968.
• Rothschild, Joseph, *East Central Europe between the Two World Wars*, Seattle, 1975. An authoritative survey; does not include Austria.
  Shapiro, Theda, *Painters and Politics: The European Avant-Garde and Society, 1900–1925*, New York, 1976. An analysis of the political and social attitudes of a revolutionary generation in the arts.

THE SOVIET UNION

  Carr, E. H., *A History of Soviet Russia*, Vols. IV–VII, London, 1950 ff. Comprehensive analysis of the period 1923–26.
• Daniels, Robert U., *The Conscience of the Revolution*, Cambridge, Mass., 1960. Discusses the opposition to Bolshevism in the 1920s.
• Deutscher, Isaac, *The Prophet Unarmed*, London, 1959. Trotsky, 1921–1929.
• ———, *The Prophet Outcast*, London, 1963. Trotsky in exile, 1929–1940.
  ———, *Stalin: A Political Biography*, New York, 1949.
  Fainsod, Merle, *How Russia Is Ruled*, Cambridge, Mass., 1967.
  Nettl, J. P., *The Soviet Achievement*, New York, 1967.

FASCISM

• Bracher, Karl Dietrich, *The German Dictatorship: The Origins, Structure, and Effects of National Socialism*, New York, 1970. A penetrating and exhaustive study of the Nazi state by a political scientist.
• Bullock, Alan, *Hitler: A Study in Tyranny*, rev. ed., New York, 1962. The standard biography.
  Conway, John S., *The Nazi Persecution of the Churches*, London, 1968. A thorough and judicious account.
• Dahrendorf, R., *Society and Democracy in Germany*, Garden City, N.Y., 1967.
  Delzell, Charles F., *Mussolini's Enemies: The Italian Anti-Fascist Resistance*, Princeton, N.J., 1961.
• Eyck, Erich, *History of the Weimar Republic*, 2 vols., Cambridge, Mass., 1962. A sympathetic account by a prominent German liberal.
• Gatzke, Hans, *Stresemann and the Rearmament of Germany*, Baltimore, 1954. Details German rearmament in violation of the Treaty of Versailles and secret agreements between Weimar Germany and Soviet Russia in the 1920s.
  Gay, Peter, *Weimar Culture: The Outsider as Insider*, New York, 1968. Examines the failure of commitment to the Weimar Republic by German intellectuals.
  Kirkpatrick, Ivone, *Mussolini: A Study in Power*, New York, 1964. The standard biography.
• Mosse, G. L., ed., *Nazi Culture*, New York, 1966.
• Nolte, Ernst, *The Three Faces of Fascism*, New York, 1966. A difficult but rewarding study of Germany, Italy, and France, from a philosophical perspective.
• Schoenbaum, David, *Hitler's Social Revolution: Class and Status in Nazi Germany, 1933–39*, Garden City, N.Y., 1966.
• Waite, R. G. L., *The Psychopathic God*, New York, 1977. An intriguing if not always successful attempt to explain Hitler's character and actions with the aid of psychoanalytic theory.

- ———, *Vanguard of Nazism: The Free Corps Movement in Postwar Germany, 1918–1923,* New York, 1952. An important monograph which describes the mentality of violence within elements of German society.
- Weiss, John, *The Fascist Tradition: Radical Right-Wing Extremism in Modern Europe,* New York, 1967.
- Wiskemann, Elizabeth, *Fascism in Italy: Its Development and Influence,* New York, 1969.
- Zeman, Z. A. B., *Nazi Propaganda,* New York, 1973. Examines an important bulwark of the authoritarian state.

THE DEMOCRACIES

Bullock, Alan, *The Life and Times of Ernest Bevin: Trade Union Leader, 1881–1940,* London, 1960. An excellent study of the British trade unionist and the political and social history of Britain between the wars.
- Burns, James M., *Roosevelt: The Lion and the Fox,* New York, 1956.

Curtis, Michael, *Three Against the Third Republic: Sorel, Barres, and Maurras,* Princeton, N.J., 1959. The attack from the French Right.
- Graves, Robert, and Alan Hodge, *The Long Week-End: A Social History of Great Britain, 1918–1939,* London, 1940. A striking portrait of England in the interwar years.
- Greene, N., *From Versailles to Vichy: The Third Republic, 1919–1940,* New York, 1970.

Harrod, R. F., *The Life of John Maynard Keynes,* New York, 1951.

Hughes, H. Stuart, *The Obstructed Path: French Social Thought in the Years of Desperation, 1930–1960,* New York, 1968.

Joll, J., *Intellectuals in Politics: Three Biographical Essays,* London, 1960. Léon Blum, Walther Rathenau, and Filippo Marinetti.
- Leuchtenburg, W. E., *Franklin Roosevelt and the New Deal, 1932–1940,* New York, 1964. A good introduction.

Lorwin, V. R., *The French Labor Movement,* Cambridge, Mass., 1954.

Lyman, Richard W., *The First Labour Government,* London, 1957.
- Mitchell, Broadus, *Depression Decade: From New Era through New Deal, 1929 to 1941,* New York, 1947.

Mowat, Charles L., *Britain between the Wars, 1918–1940,* Chicago, 1955. A detailed political and social history, especially valuable for its extensive biographical footnotes.
- Schlesinger, Arthur M., Jr., *The Age of Roosevelt,* 3 vols., Boston, 1957–1964. An extensive biography by an admirer of Roosevelt.
- Taylor, A. J. P., *English History, 1914–1945,* New York, 1965. The best survey of the period. Witty, provocative, insightful.
- Thomson, David, *Democracy in France since 1870,* rev. ed., New York, 1969.
- Weber, Eugen, *Action Française: Royalism and Reaction in Twentieth-Century France,* Stamford, Conn., 1962. The best study of this protofascist movement.

SOURCE MATERIALS

Cole, G. D. H., and M. I. Cole, *The Condition of Britain,* London, 1937. A contemporary analysis by English socialists.

• Greene, Nathanael, comp., *European Socialism Since World War I,* Chicago, 1971. A collection of contemporary accounts.

• Hitler, Adolf, *Mein Kampf,* New York, 1962. Hitler's autobiography, written in 1925. Contains his version of history and his vision for the future. Especially important for his insight into the nature of the masses and the use of propaganda.

Noakes, Jeremy, and Geoffrey Pridham, *Documents on Nazism, 1919–1945,* New York, 1975. An excellent sourcebook. Comprehensive and annotated.

• Speer, Albert, *Inside the Third Reich,* New York, 1964. The self-serving but informative memoirs of one of the leaders of Nazi Germany.

Tucker, Robert C., ed., *The Great Purge Trial,* New York, 1965. An annotated edition of the transcript of one of the Soviet "show-trials" that so puzzled Western observers.

• Woolf, Virginia, *Three Guineas,* New York, 1938. The brilliant analytical work in which Woolf takes apart both the motivation for war and the oppression of women in modern society.

Chapter 29

WORLD WAR II

The President [Roosevelt] and the Prime Minister [Churchill], after a complete survey of the world situation, are more than ever determined that peace can come to the world only by a total elimination of German and Japanese war power. This involves the simple formula of placing the objective of this war in terms of an unconditional surrender by Germany, Italy, and Japan.

—Franklin D. Roosevelt, Casablanca, January 24, 1943

In September 1939, Europe plunged again into war. The peace of 1919–1920 turned out to be no more than an armistice; once more millions of people were locked in a conflict that surpassed any that had occurred heretofore. As had happened in 1914–1918, the new struggle soon became worldwide. Although World War II was not merely a continuation of, or a sequel to, World War I, the similarity in causes and characteristics was more than superficial. Both were precipitated by threats to the balance of power, and both were conflicts between peoples, entire nations, rather than between governments. On the other hand, there were notable differences. The methods of warfare in World War II had little in common with those of the earlier conflict. Trench warfare was largely superseded by bombing and by sudden aerial (Blitzkrieg) attacks, with highly mobile armies, on both civilian populations and military installations. Because so many were now vulnerable to the ravages of warfare, it seems safe to say that the distinction between soldiers and civilians was more completely obliterated in the second conflict than it had been in the first.

A comparison of the two world wars

1. THE CAUSES OF THE WAR

The causes of World War II were related to the failure of the peace terms of 1919–1920. Those terms, while understandable in view of the passions and hatreds engendered by the First World War, created almost as many problems as they solved. By yielding to the demands of the victors for annexation of territory and the creation of satellite states, the peacemakers sowed new seeds of bitterness and conflict. By proclaiming the principle of self-determination while acquiescing in the distribution of national minorities behind alien frontiers, the treaties raised expectations while at the same time frustrating them. Perhaps most important, by imposing harsh terms on Germany, the treaty-makers gave the Germans what seemed to many to be legitimate grievances, by depriving them of their rightful share of international power and saddling them with the entire burden of war "guilt."

The role of power politics in causing World War II is undeniable. Although Woodrow Wilson and other sponsors of the League of Nations had acclaimed the league as a means of eliminating power struggles, it did nothing of the sort. It merely substituted a new and more precarious balance for the old. The signatures on the peace treaties had scarcely dried when the victors began the construction of new alliances to maintain their supremacy. A neutralized zone consisting of the Baltic states, Poland, and Rumania was created as a buffer against Soviet Russia. A Little Entente composed of Czechoslovakia, Yugoslavia, and Rumania was established to prevent a revival of Austrian power. These combinations, together with a Franco-Belgian alliance and a Franco-Polish alliance, would also serve to isolate Germany. Thus the old system of power politics was reconstituted along essentially the same lines it had had before World War I. Even the league itself was fundamentally an alliance of the victors against the vanquished. That there would be fears and anxieties over a disturbance of the new power arrangement could hardly be unexpected. The first sign of such a disturbance appeared in 1922 when Germany and Russia negotiated the Treaty of Rapallo. Though disguised as a mere trade agreement, it opened the way for political and, according to some accounts, even military collaboration between the two states.

Diplomats made various attempts to preserve or restore international amity during the 1920s and 1930s. Some saw in disarmament the most promising means of achieving their purpose. Accordingly, a succession of conferences was called in the hope of limiting at least the competition in armaments. The results were negligible. In 1925 representatives of the chief European powers met at Locarno and acted on the suggestion of the German foreign minister, Gustav Stresemann, that Germany and France pledge themselves to respect the Rhine frontiers as established in the Versailles treaty. They agreed also that they would never go to war against each other except in "legitimate defense." More widely celebrated than the Locarno Agreements was the Pact of Paris, or Kellogg-Briand Pact of 1928. Its purpose was to outlaw war as an international crime. Eventually, nearly all the nations of the world signed an agreement renouncing war as "an instrument

Members of the Council of the League of Nations. In the front row, from the right, are Chamberlain of Britain, Vandervelde of Belgium, Stresemann of Germany, and Briand of France

of national policy" and providing that the settlement of international disputes "of whatever nature or of whatever origin" should never be sought "except by peaceful means." Neither the Locarno Agreements nor the Pact of Paris was much more than a pious gesture. The signatory nations adopted them with so many reservations and exceptions in favor of "vital interests" that they could never be effective instruments for preserving peace. Had the League of Nations they set up been better organized, it might have relieved some of the tensions and prevented clashes between nations still unwilling to relinquish their absolute sovereignty. It was not a league of all nations, however. Both Germany and Russia were excluded, at least for a time, thereby pushing them into the role of outsiders.

Economic conditions were a third important cause of the outbreak of war. The huge reparations imposed upon the Germans, and the French occupation of much of Germany's industrial heartland, helped, as we have seen, to retard Germany's economic recovery and bring on the debilitating inflation of the 1920s. The depression of the 1930s contributed to the coming of the war in several ways. It intensified economic nationalism. Baffled by problems of unemployment and business stagnation, governments resorted to high tariffs in an attempt to preserve the home market for their own producers. The depression was also responsible for a marked increase in armaments production, which was seen as a means of reducing unemployment. Despite the misgivings of some within the governments of Britain and France, Germany was allowed to rearm. Armaments expansion, on a large scale, was first undertaken by Germany about 1935. The results in a few years were such as to dazzle the rest of the world. Unemployment disappeared and business boomed. It would have been too much to expect that other dissatisfied nations would not copy the German example. Similarly, the depression resulted in a new wave of militant expansionism directed toward the conquest of neighboring territories as

Economic conditions

The Krupp Shipworks in Germany. Seen here are German submarines in the final stages of assembly.

a means of solving economic problems. Japan took the lead in 1931 with the invasion of Manchuria. The decline of Japanese exports of raw silk and cotton cloth meant that the nation as a consequence was unable to pay for needed imports of coal, iron, and other minerals. Japanese militarists were thus furnished with a convenient pretext for seizing Manchuria, where supplies of these commodities could then be purchased for Japanese currency. Mussolini, in part to distract the Italians from the domestic problems brought on by economic depression, invaded and annexed Ethiopia in 1936. Finally, the depression was primarily responsible for the triumph of Nazism, whose expansionist policies contributed directly to the outbreak of war.

Nationalism

Nationalism was a further cause of the general discontent that helped increase the chances for world war. In eastern Europe, national and ethnic minorities remained alienated from the sovereign states into which the treaty-makers had placed them. This was particularly the case of the Sudetenland Germans, who had been included in the newly created state of Czechoslovakia. That country could in fact boast no national majority, including as it did Czechs, Slovaks, Poles, Ruthenians, and Hungarians, as well as Germans. Although it possessed an enlightened policy of minority self-government, the patchwork state of Czechoslovakia remained unstable. And its instability was to prove a key factor as the tensions mounted in the late 1930s.

Appeasement

A final cause of war was the policy of "appeasement" which was pursued by the Western democracies in the face of German, Italian, and Japanese aggression. The appeasers' strategy was grounded in three commonly held assumptions. The first was that the outbreak of another war was unthinkable. With the memory of the slaughter of 1918 fresh in their minds, many in the West embraced pacifism, or at any rate adopted an attitude that kept them from realistically addressing the implications of Nazi and fascist policies and programs. Secondly, many in Britain and the United States argued, as the years passed, that Germany had been mistreated in the Versailles treaty, that the Germans had legitimate grievances which should be acknowledged and resolved. Finally, the appeasers were, for the most part, staunch anticommunists. They believed that by assisting Germany to regain its former military and economic power, they were constructing a bulwark to halt the westward advance of Soviet communism. When Japan invaded Manchuria, the West refused to impose sanctions against the Japanese through the League of Nations, arguing that Japan, too, could serve as a counterweight to Russia.

Hitler took advantage of this generally tolerant attitude to advance the expansionist ambitions of Germany. As the country rearmed, Hitler played upon his people's sense of shame and betrayal, proclaiming their right to regain their former power within the world. In 1933, he removed Germany from the League of Nations—and thus from any obligation to adhere to its declarations. In 1935 Hitler tore up the disarmament provisions of the Treaty of Versailles, announcing the revival of conscription and the return to universal military training. In 1936 he repudiated the Locarno Agreements and invaded the Rhineland. Britain and France did nothing to stop him, as they had done nothing to prevent Mussolini's invasion and conquest of Ethiopia the previous year.

Hitler's aggressive moves

In 1936 civil war broke out in Spain; a series of weak republican governments had proved unable to prevent the country's political disintegration. Although they had signed a pact of nonintervention with the other Western powers, Hitler and Mussolini both sent troops and equipment to assist the forces of the rebel fascist commander, Francisco Franco. Russia countered with aid to the communist troops serving under the banner of the Spanish republic. Again, Britain and France did nothing. The Spanish Civil War lasted three years, with the forces of the fascists finally victorious over those of the republicans. The conflict engaged the commitment of many young European and American leftists and intellectuals, who saw it as a test of the West's determination to resist totalitarianism. The fighting was brutal; aerial bombardment of civilians and troops was employed for the first time on a large scale. Hence the Spanish war has often been seen as a "dress rehearsal" for the much larger struggle that was shortly to follow.

The Spanish Civil War

In March of 1938, Hitler annexed Austria, declaring it his intention to bring all Germans into his Reich. Once more, there was no official reaction from the West. Hitler's next target was the Sudetenland in Czechoslovakia. With Austria now a part of Germany, Czechoslovakia was almost entirely surrounded by its hostile and rapacious neighbor. Hitler declared that the Sudetenland was a natural part of the Reich and that he intended to occupy it. The British prime minister, Neville Chamberlain, determined to negotiate, but on Hitler's terms. On September 28, Hitler agreed to meet with Chamberlain, Premier Édouard Daladier of France, and Mussolini in a four-power

Munich and after

The Munich Conference, 1938. Left: Prime Minister Chamberlain of Britain and Hitler during the Munich conference. Right: Chamberlain addressing a crowd on his return from the Munich conference. In his speech, September 30, 1938, he proclaimed that "peace in our time" would result from the agreement.

conference in Munich. The result was another capitulation by France and Britain. During the next few months Hitler not only annexed the Sudetenland (as the Munich agreement had permitted him to do), but he annihilated the entire Czech republic. This action intensified the crisis. The Soviet government was convinced that the Munich settlement was a plot by Britain and France to save their own skins by diverting Nazi expansion eastward. In August 1939, Stalin and his colleagues, having failed to persuade Britain and France to ally with them on their terms, entered into a pact of their own with the Nazi government. Its effect was to give Hitler the green light for an attack on Poland. There was an understanding that the two dictators would divide Poland between them. In going to Munich, Britain and France had thought of their own interests; Russia would now look after its own.

See color map following page 864

2. THE OUTBREAK OF HOSTILITIES

Beginning of the war

Following the extinction of Czechoslovakia, Hitler demanded the abolition of the Polish Corridor, a narrow strip of territory connecting Poland with the Baltic Sea. The corridor contained a large German population, which Hitler declared must be reunited with the Fatherland. Convinced finally that Hitler's appetite for power was insatiable, Chamberlain announced that Britain would give Poland armed assistance. Soon afterward he declared that his government would come to the aid of any country that felt itself menaced by Hitler's ambitions. In the weeks that followed, both Britain and France gave definite guarantees not only to Poland but to Greece, Rumania, and Turkey. Hitler, judging Britain and France by past performance, believed these pledges were worthless. With the Soviets drawn into his camp, he expected that Poland would quickly capitulate, and that the Western allies would back down once more as they had done at Munich. When Poland stood firm, Hitler decided to attack. On September 1, 1939, a long column of German tanks crossed the Polish border. Upon learning of the attack, Britain and France sent a joint warning to Germany to cease its aggression. To this there was no reply. September 3 brought a radio announcement by Neville Chamberlain that Britain was at war with Germany. He spoke of the "bitter blow" it was to him that his "long struggle for peace" had failed. He asserted that it was evil the British nation would be fighting against—"brute force, bad faith, injustice, oppression, and persecution." Later the same day France also entered the war.

The conflict with Poland proved to be a brief encounter. In less than three weeks the Polish armies had been routed, Warsaw had been captured, and the chiefs of the Polish government had fled to Rumania. For some months after that the war resolved itself into a kind of siege, a "phony war" or "sitzkrieg," as it was sometimes called. Such fighting as did occur was largely confined to submarine warfare, aerial raids on naval bases, and occasional battles between naval vessels. In the spring of 1940 the sitzkrieg was suddenly transformed into a Blitzkrieg, or "lightning war." The Germans struck blows at Norway, Denmark, Belgium, the Netherlands, and France, conquering them one after another. In France a puppet government loyal to the Germans was established at Vichy under the leadership of the aged World War I hero, Marshal Henri-Philippe Petain.

The "phony war"

Following these conquests the war entered a new stage, the so-called Battle of Britain. Before launching an invasion across the Channel, the Nazis decided to attempt the reduction of Britain's military strength and civilian will by air raids. From August 1940 to June 1941

The Battle of Britain

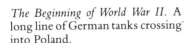

The Beginning of World War II. A long line of German tanks crossing into Poland.

A German V-2 Rocket. Used in the later years of the war, it was the forerunner of the early space launch vehicles.

thousands of planes smashed at British ports, industrial centers, and air defenses throughout the country. Despite the fact that whole sections of cities were laid in ruins and more than 40,000 civilians killed, the British held firm. Winston Churchill had by this time succeeded Neville Chamberlain as prime minister of Britain. A maverick Conservative, who had served in Britain's World War I government as a Liberal, Churchill was not trusted by his party's leadership, particularly since he had been one of the few who had spoken out in favor of British rearmament during the years of appeasement. Now that his warnings had proved true, he was given direction of the war as head of a national government composed of ministers from the Conservative, Liberal, and Labour parties. Churchill, an exceedingly compelling orator, used the radio to persuade his countrymen and women—and the rest of the free world—that Britain must not, and would not, surrender to the Nazis. His friendship with President Roosevelt, and the latter's conviction that the United States must come to Britain's aid, resulted in the shipment of military equipment and ships to the British under the so-called Lend-Lease Act passed by the U.S. Congress in 1941.

Meanwhile, Germany moved eastward into the Balkans, subduing the Rumanians, Hungarians, Bulgarians, and Yugoslavs. The Italians, less successful in their campaigns in Greece and North Africa, required German assistance to accomplish their missions. Scornful of Mussolini's military inadequacies, Churchill called him Hitler's "jackal." Frustrated in his attempt to subjugate Britain, Hitler broke with his erstwhile ally Russia, and turned eastward, on June 22, 1941, with a massive invasion. Before the end of the year his armies had smashed

Left: *London During the Blitz.* This picture conveys a vivid impression of the agony which the British capital suffered during the Battle of Britain, which lasted from August 1940 to June 1941. Behind the tumbling ruins brought down by firebombs is St. Paul's Cathedral. Right: *French Refugees Driven from Their Homes During the Early Years of the Nazi Occupation.*

Pearl Harbor, December 7, 1941. This photo shows American battleships sunk at their moorings, following the Japanese raid on what President Franklin D. Roosevelt declared was "the day that will live in infamy."

their way to the gates of Moscow but never actually succeeded in capturing it.

The war was converted into a global conflict when Japan struck a deadly blow at Pearl Harbor on December 7 of the same year. The Japanese had been involved in a costly war with China since 1937. To wage it successfully they needed the oil, rubber, and extensive food resources of the Netherlands Indies, the Malay Peninsula, and Southeast Asia. They had allied with Germany in 1940. Now, before attacking south, they considered it necessary to lock the back door by crushing American naval and air power on the base of Pearl Harbor. The next day the United States Congress recognized a state of war with Japan, and on December 11 Germany and its allies declared war upon the United States.

Pearl Harbor

The course of the war was marked by several turning points. The first was the stubborn defense of Moscow by Stalin's armies in November and December 1941. The second was the defeat of the Germans under General Erwin Rommel in North Africa in 1942, which opened the way for the Allied invasion of Italy and the overthrow of Mussolini in the following year. The third was the Battle of Stalingrad in 1943, when the Germans failed in their attempt to cut northern Russia off from the food-producing region of the Ukraine and from the oil resources north and south of the Caucasus. The turning points in the Pacific war came during the spring of 1942 with the defeat by the United States Navy of Japanese forces in the battles of the Coral Sea and of Midway. These defeats spelled the doom of Japanese attempts to capture Australia and the Hawaiian Islands and thereby deprive the United States of advance bases for a counteroffensive against Japan.

The war's turning points

By the winter of 1944–1945 World War II was nearing its end. On June 6, 1944 (D-Day), Allied forces had crossed the English Channel and landed successfully in northern France. On August 25 Paris was liberated. In September advance detachments drove to the Rhine, and

Left: *D-Day.* Cargo ships are seen pouring supplies ashore during the invasion of France. Balloon barrages float overhead to protect the ships from low-flying enemy planes. Right: *Signing the German Surrender, May 7, 1945.*

End of the war in Europe

eventually whole armies penetrated to the heart of Germany, an advance necessitated by Hitler's refusal to surrender unconditionally. At the same time, Soviet troops were approaching from the east. On April 21, 1945, they hammered their way into the suburbs of Berlin. During the next ten days a savage battle raged amid the ruins and heaps of rubble. On May 2 the heart of the city was captured, and the Soviet red banner flew from the Brandenburg Gate. A few hours earlier Adolf Hitler killed himself in the bomb-proof shelter of the Chancellery. On May 8 representatives of the German High Command signed a document of unconditional surrender. Peace had come at last to an exhausted Europe after five years and eight months of slaughter.

The concentration camps

It was only then that the world began to learn the extent of German tyranny. When Allied armies opened the concentration camps in Germany and elsewhere in what had been German-occupied Europe, they found the starved, diseased, and brutalized remnants of a total of six million prisoners, those who had been able to survive the ghastly experience of Nazi persecutions. Most of the men, women, and children who had been imprisoned, tortured, and killed, were Jews, although Poles, Russians, gypsies, homosexuals, and other "traitors" to the Reich had been incarcerated, used for forced labor, and executed also.

The atomic bomb; Japan's surrender

The end of the war in the Pacific was delayed for another four months. Victory over the Japanese Empire had to be achieved by savage naval battles and by bloody assaults upon almost impregnable islands. In June 1945, Okinawa was taken, after eighty-two days of desperate fighting. The Americans now had footholds less than 500 miles from the Japanese homeland. The government in Tokyo was nervously anticipating an invasion and calling upon the citizens for supreme endeavors to meet the crisis. On July 26 the heads of the United States, British, and Chinese governments issued a joint proclamation calling upon Japan to surrender or be destroyed. In the absence of a reply the highest officials of the United States government resolved to make use of a new and revolutionary weapon to end the war quickly. This weapon was the atomic bomb, recently developed in secrecy by Allied scientists. Many high military and naval officers contended that use of the bomb was not necessary, on the assumption that Japan was already beaten. Harry Truman, who had succeeded Roosevelt following the latter's death in April 1945, decided otherwise. On August 6, a single atomic bomb was dropped on Hiroshima, completely obliterating about 60 percent of the city. Three days later a second bomb was dropped, this time on Nagasaki. These actions, like the fire-bombing of Dresden and Tokyo, insured that the Allies would share the responsibility for the carnage of the war, and that, unlike the First World War, this one would take a heavy toll of civilian lives. President Truman warned that the United States would continue to use the atom bomb as long as might be necessary to bring Japan to its knees. On August 14, Tokyo transmitted to Washington an unconditional acceptance of Allied demands.

3. THE PEACE SETTLEMENT

The war was over. To fight it, governments had been compelled, to an even greater degree than during the First World War, to mobilize their entire populations. Both sides used mass propaganda techniques to maintain popular commitment to their cause. As Wilson had spoken of a war "to end wars," so the Western leaders promised a peace that would rid the world of conflict. The first statement of Allied objectives in the event of victory was the Atlantic Charter,

The Atlantic Charter and the United Nations declaration

Victims of the Nazi Concentration Camp at Belsen, Germany. Photographed in 1945.

View of Hiroshima After the First Atom Bomb Was Dropped, August 6, 1945. This photo, taken one month later, shows the utter devastation of the city. Only a few steel and concrete buildings remained intact.

issued by Roosevelt and Churchill on August 14, 1941. Its essential principles were as follows: (1) no territorial changes that do not accord with the wishes of the people concerned; (2) the right of all peoples to choose the form of government under which they will live; (3) all states to enjoy access, on equal terms, to the trade and raw materials of the world; (4) freedom to traverse the seas without hindrance; (5) disarmament of all nations that threaten aggression. The Atlantic Charter acquired a broad significance when it was reaffirmed by the United Nations declaration on January 2, 1942. Twenty-six nations signed this declaration, including Great Britain, the United States, the Soviet Union, and the Republic of China. Subsequently about fourteen others added their signatures. The declaration resembled Wilson's Fourteen Points: both were ringing affirmations of international peace and freedom; both were designed to bolster Allied morale; and both fell victim to the realities of power politics.

As the war progressed, high officials of the leading United Nations met in various conferences for the purpose of determining the conditions of peace. The first of outstanding importance was the conference that met in Cairo in November 1943, to discuss the fate of the Japanese Empire. The participants were Roosevelt, Churchill, and the Chinese leader, Generalissimo Chiang Kai-Shek. They agreed that all of the territories taken by Japan from China, with the exception of Korea, were to be restored to the Chinese Republic. Korea was to become free and independent. They agreed, further, that Japan was to be stripped of all the islands in the Pacific which it had seized or occupied since 1914 and of "all other territories which she had taken by violence

The Cairo Declaration

or greed." What disposition was to be made of these islands and territories was not specified.

The second important conference to determine the conditions of peace met at Yalta, in the Crimea, in February 1945. This time the chief participants were Roosevelt, Churchill, and Stalin. A formal report issued at the close of the conference declared that the Big Three had agreed upon plans for the unconditional surrender of Germany, upon methods of controlling Germany and its allies after the war, and upon the establishment of a United Nations Organization to keep the peace. In addition, it was announced that Poland would surrender its eastern provinces to Russia and be compensated by "substantial accessions of territory" in the north and west—to be taken, of course, from Germany. The existing government of Poland, set up under Soviet auspices, was to be reorganized with the inclusion of democratic leaders from among the Poles. The government of Yugoslavia was also to be broadened in similar fashion. Regarding the Far East, it was agreed that Russia should enter the war against Japan and receive as its reward all the territories taken from it by Japan in the Russo-Japanese war of 1904–1905.

The Yalta agreement

The Yalta agreement reflected the idealism of the Atlantic Charter in its provision for a United Nations. It also foreshadowed the tension between East and West which in a few years, would take the shape of a "cold war" between Russia and its political satellites, on the one side, and the Western powers, on the other. Stalin, a determined power politician, was anxious to protect Russian interests. Hence his insistence on a Polish settlement that would insure a strong, pro-Soviet bulwark against Germany. Although Stalin promised free elections there, he refused to agree to an international commission to supervise them.

The implications of the Yalta agreement

The surrender of Germany required yet another conference of the victorious powers. On July 17, 1945, Stalin, Churchill, and Truman, met in Potsdam, a suburb of Berlin. Before the Potsdam Conference had finished its work, Churchill had been replaced by Clement Attlee,

The Yalta Conference. Churchill, Molotov, Secretary of State Stettinius, at the left, and Stalin, in the center, with glasses raised in a toast. Roosevelt is also to Stalin's left.

The Potsdam Conference. Churchill, a cigar in his mouth, is seated in the back to the left; Stalin is at the right; Truman is seated with his back to the camera.

The Potsdam agreement

the new Labour prime minister of Great Britain. The most important provisions of the formal declaration, issued on August 2, were as follows: (1) the territory formerly known as East Prussia was to be divided into two parts, the northern part to go to the Soviet Union, and the southern part to be assigned to Poland; (2) Poland was to receive the former free city of Danzig; (3) all German territory east of the Oder and Neisse rivers would be administered by Poland, pending a final settlement; (4) the military power of Germany would be totally destroyed; and (5) Germany would be divided into four occupation zones, to be governed, respectively, by the Soviet Union, Great Britain, the United States, and France. In November 1945, a trial of major Nazi leaders, conducted by an inter-Allied tribunal, began in Nuremberg, Germany. In September of the following year, eighteen of the twenty-two defendants were found guilty of "war crimes," receiving sentences ranging from ten-years' imprisonment to death.

The peace treaties

After the end of the war the victorious states drafted peace treaties with Japan and with Germany's satellites. The treaty with Japan deprived the Japanese of all the territory they had acquired since 1854—in other words, their entire overseas empire. They gave up the southern half of Sakhalin Island and the Kuril Islands to Soviet Russia, and the Bonins and Ryukyus to control by the United States. They also renounced all rights to Formosa, which was left in a status still undefined. They yielded to the United States the right to continue maintaining military installations in Japan until the latter was able to defend itself. The treaty went into effect in April 1952, against the opposition of the Russians, who had hoped that Japan would be crippled by more drastic punishments and thereby left an easy convert to communism.

As in the case of the Versailles treaty one of the most significant elements in the World War II settlement was its provision for an international organization. The old League of Nations had failed to avert the outbreak of war in 1939, and in April 1946 it was formally dissolved. Allied statesmen had long recognized the need for a new organization. In February 1945, they agreed at Yalta that a conference to implement that need should be convoked for April 25 in San Francisco. Despite the sudden death of Roosevelt two weeks earlier, the conference met as scheduled. A charter was adopted on June 26, providing for a world organization to be known as the United Nations and to be founded upon the principle of "the sovereign equality of all peace-loving states." Its important agencies were to be (1) a General Assembly composed of representatives of all the member states; (2) a Security Council composed of representatives of the United States, Great Britain, the Soviet Union, the Republic of China, and France, with permanent seats, and of six other states chosen by the General Assembly to fill the nonpermanent seats; (3) a Secretariat consisting of a secretary-general and a staff of subordinates; (4) an Economic and Social Council composed ot eighteen members chosen by the General Assembly; (5) a Trusteeship Council; and (6) an International Court of Justice.

Establishment of the United Nations

Although the United Nations has failed to live up to the hopes of its founders, it continues to function as the world's longest-lived international assembly of nations. By far the most important functions of the new organization were assigned by the charter to the Security Council. This agency has the "primary responsibility for the maintenance of international peace and security." It has authority to investigate any dispute between nations, to recommend methods for settlement, and, if necessary to preserve the peace, to employ diplomatic or economic measures against an aggressor. If, in its judgment, these have proved, or are likely to prove, inadequate, it may "take such action by air, naval, or land forces" as may be required to maintain or restore international order. The member states are required by the charter to make available to the Security Council, on its call, armed forces for the maintenance of peace.

The Security Council

The Security Council was so organized as to give almost a monopoly of authority to its permanent members. It was the belief of the Big Three who assembled at Yalta, and of President Roosevelt especially, that the peace of the world depended upon harmony among the states primarily responsible for winning the war. Accordingly, they agreed that when the Security Council should be set up, no action of any kind could be taken without the unanimous consent of Great Britain, France, the United States, the Republic of China, the Soviet Union, and two other members besides. This absolute veto given to each of

The veto power of the Big Five

the principal states had none of the hoped-for effects. Instead of bolstering the peace of the world, its chief result was to cripple the council and to render it helpless in the face of emergencies. The primary cause of this was the growth of distrust between Soviet Russia and the West.

Other agencies of the U.N.

The remaining agencies of the U.N. were given a wide variety of functions. The Secretariat, composed of a secretary-general and a numerous staff, is chiefly an administrative authority. Its duties, though, are by no means routine, for the secretary-general may bring to the attention of the Security Council any matter which, in his opinion, may threaten international peace. The functions of the Economic and Social Council are the most varied of all. Composed of eighteen members elected by the General Assembly, it has authority to initiate studies and make recommendations with respect to international social, economic, health, educational, cultural, and related matters, and may perform services within such fields at the request of U.N. members. Under its jurisdiction are such specialized agencies as the World Health Organization (WHO), which works to control epidemics and to assist underdeveloped nations in stamping out cholera, typhus, and veneral disease, and in raising standards of health and sanitation; and the Food and Agriculture Organization (FAO), which seeks to promote increases in food production by finding remedies for agricultural depressions, for plant and animal diseases and insect pests, and by projecting plans for mechanizing small farms and for the more efficient distribution of food.

Failures of the U.N.

During the first three decades the work of these agencies helped the U.N. achieve a modestly impressive record of accomplishment. But against its successes must be recorded major failures as well. The U.N. failed in its efforts to establish control of nuclear weapons. And it was powerless in the face of any determined effort by a major power to have its own way, as in the case of the Soviet suppression of a revolt in Hungary in 1956; or the massive intervention by the United States in Vietnam. If the United Nations acted upon occasion to defuse potentially explosive world situations, it failed to achieve the lofty peace-making and peace-keeping goals set for it by its ambitious and idealistic founders.

SELECTED READINGS

• *Items so designated are available in paperback editions.*
  Aron, Raymond, *The Century of Total War,* New York, 1954.
  Carr, E. H., *The Twenty-Years Crisis,* London, 1942. Stimulating, though
    somewhat dogmatic.
• Carr, Raymond, *The Spanish Tragedy: The Civil War in Perspective,* London,
    1977. A thoughtful introduction to the Spanish Civil War and the evolu-
    tion of Franco's Spain.

- Churchill, Winston S., *The Second World War,* 6 vols., London, 1948–1954. His history and apologia. Particularly useful is Volume I, *The Gathering Storm.*
- Divine, Robert A., *Roosevelt and World War II,* Baltimore, 1969. A diplomatic history.
- Feis, Herbert, *Churchill-Roosevelt-Stalin: The War They Waged and the Peace They Sought,* Princeton, N.J., 1957.

  Géraud, André, *The Gravediggers of France,* Garden City, N.Y., 1944. A critical and impassioned account of the fall of France.

  Gilbert, Martin, and R. Gott, *The Appeasers,* Boston, 1963.
- Hersey, John, *Hiroshima,* New York, 1946.

  Hilberg, Raul, *The Destruction of the European Jews,* Chicago, 1961. Exhaustive.

  Holborn, Hajo, *The Political Collapse of Europe,* New York, 1951. Examines Europe's position in light of the rise of Russia and the United States as superpowers.
- Jackson, Gabriel, *The Spanish Republic and the Civil War, 1931–1939,* Princeton, N.J., 1965.
- Lafore, Laurence D., *The End of Glory: An Interpretation of the Origins of World War II,* New York, 1970.

  Milward, Alan S., *War, Economy, and Society, 1939–1945,* Berkeley, Calif., 1977. Analyzes the impact of the war on the world economy and the ways in which economic resources of the belligerents determined strategies.

  Neumann, W. L., *After Victory: Churchill, Roosevelt, Stalin, and the Making of the Peace,* New York, 1967.
- Paxton, Robert D., *Vichy France: Old Guard and New Order,* New York, 1972. A bitter account.
- Payne, Stanley, *The Spanish Revolution,* New York, 1970.
- Reitlinger, G., *The Final Solution: The Attempt to Exterminate the Jews of Europe, 1939–1945,* New York, 1968.

  Snell, J. L., *Illusion and Necessity: The Diplomacy of Global War, 1939–1945,* Boston, 1963.
- Taylor, A. J. P., *The Origins of the Second World War,* New York, 1962. A controversial but provocative attempt to prove that Hitler did not want a world war.
- Wright, Gordon, *The Ordeal of Total War, 1939–1945,* New York, 1968. Particularly good on the domestic response to war and the mobilization of the resources of the modern state.

SOURCE MATERIALS

- Bloch, Marc, *Strange Defeat: A Statement of Evidence Written in 1940,* London, 1949. An analysis of the fall of France, written by one of France's greatest historians, who later died fighting for the resistance.
- Churchill, Winston, *Churchill in His Own Words: Years of Greatness; The Memorable Wartime Speeches of the Man of the Century,* New York, 1966.
- De Gaulle, Charles, *The Complete War Memoirs,* New York, 1964.

  Noakes, Jeremy, and Geoffrey Pridham, *Documents on Nazism, 1919–1945,* New York, 1975.

Part Seven

THE EMERGENCE OF
WORLD CIVILIZATION

*Western civilization, as we have described and analyzed it, no longer
exists today. Instead, we speak in terms of a world civilization, one that
owes much of its history and many of its most perplexing problems to the
West, but one which is no longer shaped by those few nations that for so
many centuries dominated the globe.*

*The great powers of the nineteenth century—Britain, France, and Ger-
many—are powers now only insofar as they have agreed to pool their interests in an all-European Common Market. The mid–twentieth century
superpowers, the United States and the Soviet Union, after two decades of
confrontation, have begun to understand the limitations of their power and
to adjust their expectations accordingly. Power, and with it the attention of
the world, is shifting from the West to the emerging nations of Africa, the
Middle East, Asia, and Latin America. Their vast natural resources are
affording many of them the chance to play the old Western game of power politics, and in a world arena wider than ever before. The equally vast dimensions
of their internal problems—economic, racial, nutritional, and political—suggest that their solution will have to be worldwide as well. We are all,
as the American designer Buckminster Fuller has said, partners for better or
worse on "spaceship earth."*

POLITICS	SCIENCE & INDUSTRY

1945

Truman Doctrine, 1947
Independence of India, 1947
Communist regimes established in eastern Europe,
    1947–1948
Marshall Plan, 1948
Division of Germany, 1949
Victory of Chinese communists, 1949
NATO, 1949
Korean war, 1950–1953

Death of Stalin, 1953

Hydrogen bomb, 1952
Discovery of polio vaccine, 1953

Discovery of DNA, 1953

Hungarian revolt, 1956
Suez crisis, 1956

Sputnik launched, 1957

1960

Conflict in the Congo, 1960

Berlin wall, 1961

Cuban missile crisis, 1962
Assassination of John F. Kennedy, 1963
War in Vietnam, 1964–1975
Assassination of Malcolm X, 1965
Civil war in Nigeria, 1966–1970
Arab-Israeli war, 1967
Assassination of Martin Luther King, Jr., 1968

Manned U.S. spacecraft lands on moon, 1969
Advent of automation, 1970s

1970

Civil war in India, 1971
First SALT agreements signed, 1972
Arab-Israeli war, 1973
Egyptian-Israeli peace treaty, 1979
Shah of Iran deposed, 1979

ECONOMICS & SOCIETY	ARTS & LETTERS	

	Abstract expressionism in art, mid-1940s	**1945**
	Albert Camus, *The Plague,* 1947	
	Simone de Beauvoir, *The Second Sex,* 1949–1950	
	Samuel Beckett, *Waiting for Godot,* 1952	
European Common Market established, 1958		
Black civil rights movement, United States, 1960–1968	Lorraine Hansberry, *A Raisin in the Sun,* 1959 "Pop" art, 1960s	**1960**
Frantz Fanon, *Wretched of the Earth,* 1961 Youth "revolution," 1960s	Francois Truffant, *Jules and Jim,* 1961	
Women's liberation movement, 1960s–1970s	Arthur Penn, *Bonnie and Clyde* (1967)	
		1970
	Aleksandr Solzhenitsyn, *The Gulag Archipelago,* 1973	

Chapter 30

NEW POWER RELATIONSHIPS

Africa, all I ask from you is the courage to know: to look about you and
see what is happening in this old and tired world; to realize the extent and
depth of its rebirth and the promise which glows on your hills.

—W. E. B. Du Bois, *Autobiography*

W orld War II left the political world of Europe, Asia, and the
United States in a state of disorder. As victory approached,
wartime allies began to mistrust each other and to protect
themselves against those whom they now perceived as prospective
rivals. In addition, the war spawned nationalist revolts throughout the
world. Many of these struggles were attempts by colonies to gain independence. Although these wars were often no more than local, they
threatened to lead to major conflict and, because of the increasing proliferation of nuclear weapons, to general holocaust. This threat, if it
did not reduce tensions, may in fact have operated to prevent nations
from pursuing their interests to the point of no return.

*Tensions in the postwar
world*

1. SOVIET-AMERICAN WORLD RIVALRY

As a result of the Second World War, world power relationships were
drastically altered. Germany, Italy, and Japan had been defeated so
overwhelmingly that they seemed for a time destined to play a subordinate role in world affairs. Officially, the list of great powers included five states—the Soviet Union, the United States, Great Britain,
France, and the Republic of China. These were the Big Five that, as
the war ended, seemed fated to rule the world. China was soon overwhelmed by a communist revolution, however, while Britain and
France became increasingly dependent upon the United States. As a
consequence, the world of nations, during the ten years after 1945,
took on a bipolar character, with the United States and the Soviet

*Changing power
relationships*

The United States after World War II

Russia's strengths and weaknesses

Russia in eastern Europe

Union contesting for supremacy and striving to draw the remaining states into their orbits.

From the standpoint of economic power, the United States had far outdistanced the rest of the nations. Since 1939 Americans had doubled their national income and quadrupled their savings. Though they constituted only 7 percent of the world's population, they enjoyed over 30 percent of the world's estimated income. For the first time in its history the United States was in a position to be the arbiter of the destinies of at least half the earth. Japan was virtually its colony; the U.S. controlled both the Atlantic and Pacific Oceans, policed the Mediterranean, and shaped the development of international policy in western Europe. Until 1949, America had a monopoly of death-dealing atomic weapons. When the Soviet Union cracked this monopoly U.S. policy-makers remained convinced that their assumption of superior strength was still valid. All that was now necessary was to add new and more deadly weapons, thereby making sure that no rival could successfully challenge the United States.

Soviet Russia emerged from World War II as the second strongest power on earth. Though its navy was small, its land army and possibly its air force by 1948 were the largest in the world. Soviet population was climbing rapidly toward 200 million and this in spite of the loss of 7 million soldiers and about 8 million civilians during the war. In mineral wealth Russia's position compared favorably with that of the richest countries. After 1946 it claimed a large percentage of the world supply of petroleum. On the other hand, there can be no doubt that its industrial machine had been badly crippled by the war. No fewer than 1700 Russian cities and towns had been totally destroyed and about 40,000 miles of railway and 31,000 factories. Stalin declared in 1946 that it would probably require at least six years to repair the damage and rebuild the devastated areas.

It seems reasonable to suppose that much of the hostility displayed by the USSR in its dealings with other nations during the years after 1945 was attributable in some measure to the losses sustained during the war. Resentful of the fact that they had been compelled to make such sacrifices, the Soviets became obsessed with security as a goal that must be attained regardless of the cost to their neighbors. Fearful that poverty and hardship might make their own people rebellious, Russia's rulers encouraged their people to think that their country was in imminent danger of attack by capitalist powers. Following the end of the war, the Russians were determined to maintain the influence their military advance had secured for them in eastern Europe. Building on the agreements reached at Yalta, the Soviet Union remained as an occupying force throughout that area, working meanwhile to establish "people's republics" sympathetic to the Soviet regime. By 1948, governments which owed allegiance to Moscow were established in Poland, Hungary, Rumania, Bulgaria, and Czechoslovakia. Albania and Yugoslavia, liberated by their own anti-Nazi forces, were not directly linked to Russia as satellites, although the governments of those two countries were also communist. The nations of eastern Europe did not succumb without a struggle. Greece, which the Russians wished to include within their sphere of influence, was torn by civil war until 1949, when with Western aid its monarchy was restored. Perhaps the most direct challenge to the Yalta guarantee of free, democratic elections occured in Czechoslovakia, where in 1948 the Soviets crushed the coalition government of liberal leaders Eduard Beneš and Jan Masaryk.

The United States countered these aggressive moves with massive programs of economic and military aid to western Europe. In 1947, President Truman proclaimed the so-called Truman Doctrine, which *The Marshall Plan* provided assistance programs to prevent further communist infiltration into the governments of Greece and Turkey. The following year, the Marshall Plan, named for Secretary of State George Marshall who first proposed it, provided funds for the reconstruction of western European industry. The plan was notable in two respects: first, it represented an attempt by the United States to restore the strength of its most serious economic competitors, and of its former enemy Germany, under the notion that an economically independent Europe would be less likely to fall prey to Soviet domination. Second, it relied upon a willingness on the part of the western European nations to coordinate their economic efforts, substituting, at least to some degree, cooperation for competition.

At the same time, the U.S. moved to shore up the military defenses of the West. In April 1949, a group of representatives of North Atlantic states together with Canada and the United States signed an agreement providing for the establishment of the North Atlantic Treaty *NATO* Organization (NATO). Subsequently Greece, Turkey, and West Germany were added as members. The treaty declared that an armed attack against any one of the signatory parties would be regarded as an attack against all, and that they would combine their armed strength to whatever extent necessary to repel the aggressor. It was decided also that the joint military command, or NATO army established in 1950, should be increased from thirty to fifty divisions in 1953, and that West Germany should be rearmed and invited to contribute twelve of the divisions. It was thereby hoped that NATO would be ready for an emergency that might arise as a consequence of the expansionist policies of Soviet Russia.

The Russians reacted with understandable alarm to the apparent determination of the United States to strengthen western Europe economically and militarily. They were particularly concerned when *The Berlin Blockade* U.S. money began to flow into those areas of western Germany occupied by British, French, and U.S. forces. In 1946, the joint administration of Germany by the four powers collapsed. Russia remained in

Crises in Berlin. Left: The Berlin Airlift, 1948. For fifteen months the United States, Britain, and France airlifted over two million tons of supplies into West Berlin, around which the Russians had imposed a land blockade. Right: The Berlin Wall, 1961. Thirteen years after the blockade, the East German government constructed a wall between East and West Berlin to stop the flow of escapees to the West.

control of its satellite, which eventually became the nominally independent German Democratic Republic (East Germany), while the Western powers continued to support the industrial recovery of that area under their control—in its turn to emerge as the Federal Republic of Germany (West Germany). A crisis arose in 1948 when, in retaliation for the reunification of the western zones of control under one authority, the Russians closed down road and rail access from the west to Berlin. Berlin, though within the territory of East Germany, was administered by all four powers. The Western powers countered with an airlift of food and other necessary supplies which prevented the collapse of the city into Soviet hands. After almost a year the Russians lifted the blockade. For many years to come, however, Berlin was to remain one of the hottest spots in the ongoing "Cold War," as it came to be called, between Russia and the West.

The most serious armed clash of the immediate postwar period was the Korean war of 1950–1953. At the end of World War II it had been agreed that Korea, under Japanese rule since 1910, was to become an independent and united country. The United States and the Soviet Union left occupying forces there until 1949, however, the Americans south of the thirty-eighth parallel, the Russians to the north of it. During this period of occupation, the Soviets refused to cooperate with the United Nations–sponsored plan to hold free elections for the entire country. Instead, they established in the north a people's republic similar to those they had erected in eastern Europe. In June 1950, troops

The Korean war

from this republic crossed the thirty-eighth parallel and invaded the south. Taking advantage of a temporary Russian boycott of the United Nations, the United States was able to avoid a Soviet veto of its plan to counter this invasion by sending a contingent of troops to oppose it. The troops, though nominally under United Nations command, were largely American, directed and supplied by the United States. Initial military gains by this force were countered in November by the invasion into Korea of troops from the newly established People's Republic of China (see below, p. 912), sent to aid the North Koreans. A stalemate ensued, President Truman and his advisors being as unwilling to widen the conflict into China—fearing a third world war—as they were to abandon their South Korean allies. After two years of military and diplomatic deadlock, a peace settlement was concluded, recognizing the existence of both North and South Korea and abandoning any scheme for their reunion.

The Korean war adversely affected relationships between the United States and the nations of the Far East. While Japan had welcomed American intervention as a sign of its determination to halt the spread of communism, other countries had looked on America's role with suspicion. The United States claimed to be acting in accordance with United Nations principles. Powers such as India, Burma, and Indonesia, however, saw the war as a neocolonialist intrusion by America on behalf of its client state, South Korea. China's determination to understand the war in this light contributed greatly to the deep hostility that characterized Sino-American relations during the next twenty years.

Effects of the Korean war

The tensions between the United States and Russia eased somewhat during the late 1950s and 1960s. America, it is true, continued to adhere to a policy of Soviet "containment," seeking as allies those most willing to oppose by military force, if necessary, the spread of international communism. And Russia was never afraid to risk Western military reaction when suppressing revolts within the countries of its satellite allies. Yet the period has not incorrectly been labeled one of "thaw." A change in direction was signaled by the death of Stalin in 1953 and the accession to power after a brief interregnum of Nikita Khrushchev (1894–1971) in 1955. Khrushchev created the impression that the Soviet Union was prepared to pursue a new diplomatic line: for example, he denounced Stalinist tyranny and continued the program of destalinization begun after Stalin's death. In addition, he and his colleagues announced their approval of the doctrine of "more than one road to socialism." In accordance with this new attitude, the Russians concluded peace with Austria and withdrew their occupying troops. In 1955 they agreed to a "conference at the summit" with the chiefs of government of Great Britain, France, the United States, and the USSR as the participants.

The "thaw"

Nikita Khrushchev

This change in policy was undoubtedly prompted in part by discontent within the country. The Russian people had no desire for another

Reasons for the "thaw"

Continued tensions

war, and were weary of the restrictions and rigidities imposed by the Stalin regime. They believed that the time had come for less emphasis on expanding the production of heavy industry and armaments and more on providing the amenities of life. This switch in emphasis would mean a lessening of the Soviet role as overlord of the socialist world. Khrushchev was disposed to sympathize with the demands of the Russian people. The new policy, however, soon ran into trouble. The first sign of change was the Soviet suppression of revolts in Poland and Hungary in 1956. The Poles escaped serious repressions when they promised to remain within the Soviet orbit in return for permission to make various modifications in their socialist system. The Hungarians, however, were repressed with bloody violence when they attempted not merely to change the economic system but to break all ties with the Soviet Union.

At the beginning of another "summit" conference in Paris in May 1960 with President Dwight D. Eisenhower (1890–1969), Premier Khrushchev erupted violently when he learned that the Russians had shot down an American high-altitude reconaissance plane far over Soviet territory, whose mission was to discover the location of bases and other military installations. Though at first Washington officials denied these flights, they later admitted them and sought to justify them as necessary for the military security of the United States. The summit conference terminated immediately, with nothing but a poisoned atmosphere to mark its effects, despite the subsequent suspension of these flights. Yet Khrushchev was not ready to completely abandon his policy of conciliation. Later in 1960 he enunciated his principle of "peaceful coexistence." Though he did not renounce the ultimate triumph of communism, insisting that "we will bury you," he refused to admit that this triumph must be accomplished by force of arms.

With respect to Germany, Soviet leaders remained unyielding. They nurtured the fear that Germany might launch a new war, aided and abetted by its capitalist allies. For this reason they staunchly op-

Revolt in Hungary. By 1956 discontent with Soviet domination manifested itself in several of the satellite states. Violent revolt broke out in Poland and Hungary. Left: The photograph indicates the extent of the violence in Budapest. Right: A group of Hungarian freedom fighters.

The Occupation of Czechoslovakia. In 1968 the liberalized regime of Alexander Dubček was suppressed by the Soviets. The violent response by the citizens was put down by military force.

The Berlin Wall

Arms limitation

posed unification of the country and insisted upon recognizing East Germany as one of their satellites. In 1961 the East German government built a high wall separating the two sectors of Berlin, in order to cut off the escape of thousands of East Germans to West Berlin and thence to western Germany. Many did make their escape, but the wall remained as a symbol of Soviet determination to prevent the formation of a united Germany. Khrushchev eventually fell prey to political rivals and was deposed in 1964, reduced to the level of a "non-person." The reins of power passed into the hands of a joint dictatorship of Aleksei Kosygin as premier and Leonid Brezhnev as secretary of the Communist party. The government did not return to Stalinist policy, but some of the new trends moved noticeably in that direction. A cardinal example was the occupation of Czechoslovakia in 1968. The Soviet dictators accused the Czechs of flirtation with West Germany to such an extent as to threaten the Soviet system and weaken its ties over eastern Europe. In particular, they resented the economic and social privileges allowed by the Czech government to its own citizens. Accordingly, they sent in armored troops and puppet rulers to take over the country. They followed this action by issuance of the Brezhnev Doctrine, which asserted the right of Moscow to interfere in the affairs of any satellite that strayed from the path of Soviet leadership.

During the 1970s, the Soviets showed, by their intervention in the affairs of newly emerging nations of the so-called Third World—Africa, Asia, and Latin America—that they remained vitally interested in extending their sphere of influence wherever they could. At the same time, they continued to adhere to a policy which allowed for a further easing of tensions, a policy pursued with some enthusiasm, as well, by American diplomats. Henry Kissinger, secretary of state under Presidents Richard Nixon and Gerald Ford in the 1970s, proclaimed détente with the Russians as his goal, and devoted much time to negotiations aimed at defusing potentially explosive areas of conflict between the two nations. Both countries were particularly concerned to curb the spread of nuclear weapons and to limit, if possible, the apparently endless expansion of their own arsenals. The Strategic Arms Limitation Treaty (SALT) talks, in which the Russians and Americans engaged during the 1970s, were an indication of mutual willingness to recognize and tackle a problem of awesome dimensions, even if their initial attempts to solve that problem resulted in at least temporary stalemate.

The European Common Market

Meanwhile, developments in Europe assisted in altering the balance of power and hence the nature of the international rivalry between the United States and Russia. European economic recovery led in 1958 to the establishment of a Common Market, or tariff union. By the mid-1970s, most of the major western European nations, including Britain, France, and West Germany, were members. Although the market was by no means the equivalent of a United States of Europe, its formation and continuing operation declared the existence of a new and important power bloc which, while more generally sympathetic to U.S. than to Soviet aims, nevertheless was determined to speak with a voice of its own.

2. IMPERIAL DECLINE IN ASIA AND THE MIDDLE EAST

The Third World

Probably more significant in the long run than U.S.-Soviet rivalry in the postwar period has been the decline of the Western imperial powers and the concurrent emergence of the Third World. Many of these countries have established themselves in territories which were formerly part of European empires. Others—China and the various nations of the Middle East, for example—while nominally independent of the West before 1945, nevertheless existed under European hegemony and were forced to acquiesce to European demands. Such is the case no longer. Although many of these so-called emerging nations are poor, and although the people of the Third World are by no means a united bloc, they represent a new and increasingly independent factor in the world power equation.

Relations with the West

Many of these countries are rich in natural resources. Nations in the Middle East, Venezuela in South America, and Nigeria in Africa, possess oil in quantities sufficient to make their every move of vital importance to the West. Other African nations, Zaire and Angola, for example, are immensely rich in many mineral resources. Population is both a liability and an asset in the Third World. The people of China, by their sheer numbers (roughly 1 billion in 1979), constitute an implicit threat to the balance of power at all times. The people of India, again by their sheer numbers, and lack of food, represent a perpetual threat to the stability of their own country and hence to all Asia. Every

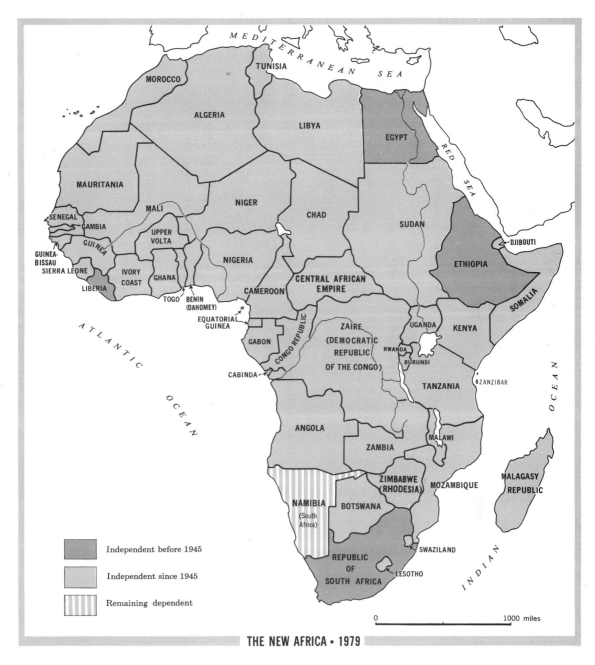

THE NEW AFRICA • 1979

Legend:
- Independent before 1945
- Independent since 1945
- Remaining dependent

area in the Third World is a potential "trouble spot." This is so not only because the problems of racism, poverty, hunger, and overpopulation make them particularly vulnerable to violent civil conflicts. It is so, as well, because the superpowers—the United States, Russia, the European nations, and China itself—are prepared to engage each other through the medium of Third World adversaries,

Ayatollah Khomeini

Mao Tse-tung. A photograph taken in 1933 when he was the leader of the radical left opposition to the Kuomintang under Chiang Kai-shek.

thus increasing the possibility of conflict by their willingness to encourage it. To protect themselves from direct confrontation with each other, these developed nations interfere in the civil wars of others, on opposite sides and with an intensity that frequently belies their declared interest in avoiding general world war.

A final general observation concerning the Third World: Although the governments of most countries have pursued the twin goals of industrialization and urbanization, this policy has not gone unchallenged. In the spring of 1979, for example, the extremely repressive regime of one of the Third World's most devoted "Westernizers," the shah of oil-rich Iran, was overthrown by the revolutionary forces of a religious fanatic, the Ayatollah Khomeini, whose explicit policy was to turn his country's back not only on the West but on "progress" as the West had defined that term for the past two hundred years.

The most radical Third World change resulting from the events of World War II was the Chinese revolution. A civil war had raged in China since 1927, when the forces of the nationalists, under Chiang Kai-shek (1887–1975), had engaged in battle first in the south, then the north with communist insurgents under the leadership of Mao Tse-tung (1893–1976), a former teacher and union organizer. A truce in 1937 had allowed both sides to wage common battle against the Japanese. At the end of World War II, however, the communists, still led by Mao Tse-tung, refused to surrender the northern provinces under their control, and civil war broke out again. The United States intervened, first as mediator, then with massive military assistance, as an ally of Chiang—all to no avail. The nationalists, corrupt and unrepresentative of the people, surrendered in 1949 to the communists and decamped to the island of Taiwan. Intensely hostile to the capitalist West, the Chinese communists soon found themselves engaged, as well, in a series of skirmishes, verbal and otherwise, with their erstwhile Marxist co-revolutionaries, the Russians. The Sino-Soviet rivalry, and the willingness of the United States in the 1970s to reach an accommodation with the Chinese in order to capitalize on that rivalry, suggest that however much power has shifted since World War II, power politics remains a game nations believe themselves compelled to play—if necessary, in opposition to their ideological commitments.

The Second World War, which had assisted the course of Chinese revolution by dissolving older power structures, served the same purpose within the colonial empires of the West. The first major British colony to establish self-government after World War II was India. Rebel movements had harassed the representatives of Britain in that country throughout the nineteenth century. The flames of revolt burned more fiercely during World War I and after; World War II added more tinder. By 1945 anti-British resentment had reached such a pitch that the country was ripe for revolution. Resolutions by na-

Gandhi and Nehru at a Meeting of Indian Leaders in 1946

tionalist bodies such as the Indian National Congress called upon Britain to "quit India." The congress had taken the position that India would fight only as a free nation without limitations imposed by the mother country. Protests and disturbances mounted more strongly than ever. It is noteworthy, however, that the foremost Indian nationalist leader, Mohandas K. Gandhi (1869–1948) did not approve of attacks on rulers and their institutions by violence. His methods were noncooperation and civil disobedience. By 1947, he and his comrade and disciple, Jawaharlal Nehru (1889–1964), had gained such support that the British found it expedient to grant autonomy to India and its neighboring area, Pakistan. In 1950 the two countries organized themselves as independent republics. Disorders continued to plague the two countries, however, finally resulting in a bloody war in 1971. One outcome of this conflict was the establishment of the independent republic of Bangladesh, formerly East Pakistan.

Indian independence

In recent years India has struggled to maintain itself as a democracy in the face of mounting economic and social problems. In the mid-1970s, Prime Minister Indira Gandhi (the daughter of Nehru), assumed authoritarian powers after declaring the country in a state of emergency. Her defeat, in free elections which she sanctioned following more than a year of virtual dictatorship, and her subsequent partial political comeback, leaves unresolved the question of whether a country as dominated by the internal problems of poverty, illiteracy, over-population, and near-starvation as India can afford what many Third World leaders claim is the luxury of a slow-moving and comparatively inefficient democracy.

Indian democracy

Having surrendered India, Great Britain was further constrained to give up most of the remaining portions of its empire. Over a period of years Britain liberated Ceylon, Malaysia, Mauritius, Fiji, Singapore, and Nauru, among others, together with the Caribbean colonies of

Guyana, Trinidad and Tobago, Jamaica, and Antigua, and, as we shall see, significant territories in sub-Saharan Africa as well. More significant for the world picture was its forced departure from Egypt. In 1951 Egyptian nationalists compelled the British to withdraw all their troops from Egyptian territory. A year later a clique of nationalist army officers seized control of the government. They deposed the playboy king, Farouk, alleged to be subservient to the British, and proclaimed the state a republic. Soon thereafter the government passed under the control of Lieutenant Colonel Gamal Abdel Nasser (1918–1970), who ruled as a virtual dictator until his death, when he was succeeded as president by Anwar al-Sadat. With the collapse of British power in India and Egypt, to say nothing of the long chain of smaller dependencies, little was left of the grand empire on which "the sun never set."

In contrast to the relatively rapid British retreat from empire, that of the French has been marked by lengthy conflict. The North African colony of Algeria was inhabited by about 1,000,000 immigrants, mainly French, of a total population of 10,300,000. These immigrants monopolized not only the government positions but also the best economic opportunities in industry, trade, and finance. The Arab and Berber inhabitants were chiefly peasants and laborers, though some, of course, maintained small shops in the native quarters of the large cities. In 1954 Arab and Berber nationalists rose in revolt when their demand for equal status with the French was denied by the government. The revolt continued its bloody course for seven years. It was complicated by the fact that many of the European settlers hated the French government almost as much as they did the Algerian nationalists. They were determined to keep Algeria "French" and feared a sellout by President Charles de Gaulle (1890–1970) that would make

Anti-Imperialist Revolt in Algeria, 1960. At Dar-es-Saada, Moslems take furniture from the homes of Europeans and burn it in the streets.

the former colony independent and subject the immigrant governing class to the rule of the Arabs and Berbers. The upshot was a revolt by four French generals. They seized government buildings, arrested French officials, and threatened to invade France. De Gaulle proclaimed a state of emergency and ordered a total blockade of Algeria. In the face of such determined opposition the revolt collapsed. On a promise of self-government the nationalists laid down their arms in 1962, and Algeria soon after achieved independence.

Additional sections of the French empire in North Africa were also whittled away after World War II. In 1955 the French gave up their protectorate over Morocco and allowed it to be organized as an independent kingdom. A short time afterward they renounced their protectorate over Tunisia, except for a naval and air base at Bizerte. The Tunisian government resisted and after a brief interval the U.N. commanded the French to give up the Bizerte base.

Morocco and Tunisia

The loss by the British and French of Egypt and Algeria came at a time of mounting tension in the Middle East, an area fated to become one of the most troubled in the postwar world. The conflicts in the Middle East focused upon the creation and continued existence of the state of Israel. When World War I ended, the country now known as Israel was a province of Turkey. Its population was about 70 percent Arab and 30 percent Jewish and Christian. By the defeat of Turkey in 1918, it was made a mandate of the League of Nations under the guardianship of Great Britain. In the meantime, Zionists in Britain and the United States worked zealously to convert Palestine into a national home for the Jewish people. In return for their labors the British government issued the Balfour Declaration promising to view their goal with favor. At the same time provision would be made for safeguarding the rights of non-Jewish communities in Palestine.

The rise of active Zionism

On the basis of the Balfour Declaration, Britain accepted the mandate for Palestine. The British wanted not merely to establish a Jewish national home, but "to secure the preservation of an Arab National Home and to apprentice the people of Palestine as a whole in the art of self-government." It was an optimistic ambition, but at the time optimism seemed justified. In fact, for a period of ten years there was every reason to expect that the undertaking would be successful, as Palestine prospered as never before in its history.

The bright prospects of the early years

By 1929, however, evidences of disharmony had begun to appear in the land that was holy to three great religions. The Jews were prosperous and well-educated and were arousing the envy and fears of the Arabs by their high standard of living and their more strenuous competition. Their purchases of land, in many cases from absentee owners, had resulted in the displacement of thousands of Arab farmers and had thrown them into the cities at a time when the Great Depression was beginning to make unemployment a serious problem. But the major cause of Arab foreboding was the steady increase in the Jewish population. The opportunity to emigrate to Palestine had offered a

The development of conflicts between Jews and Arabs

Immigration to Palestine. Left: British soldiers guard the shore as a ship loaded with unauthorized refugees attempts to land in 1947. Right: A view of the unbearably crowded conditions aboard ships bringing refugees to Palestine.

greater temptation than the Arabs had expected. As a consequence, some of them foresaw a relentless advance and expansion of Europeans and Americans, backed by foreign capital and flaunting a culture that was alien to the ways of the Arab majority. In 1929, 1930, and 1931 armed attacks were waged upon Jewish settlements followed by terrorist murders.

Rebellion of the Arabs against the mandate

But these episodes paled into insignificance when compared with the bloody violence that followed. When the mandate was established, no one could have foreseen the desperate plight that was to overtake the European Jews with the accession of the Nazis to power in Germany. As news of the persecutions spread, it was inevitable that pressure should be brought upon the British government to relax the barriers against immigration into Palestine. During the period 1933–1935 the admission of more than 130,000 Jewish immigrants was authorized, and uncounted thousands more came in illicitly. From this time on Palestine was a seething cauldron of violence and warfare. The Arabs rose in open rebellion against the mandate. Organized terrorism swept the country. Guerrilla attacks in the rural areas and looting, burning, and sabotage in the towns and cities kept the whole population in turmoil. By 1938 Britain had 20,000 troops in Palestine, and even these were unable to maintain order.

Termination of the mandate and establishment of the State of Israel

Little progress toward a lasting settlement had been achieved when, in April 1947, the British government referred the Palestine problem to the United Nations and announced that a year later it would terminate the mandate and withdraw all its troops from the country. On May 15, 1948, the British mandate came to an end, and on the same day a Jewish provisional government proclaimed the establishment of an independent state of Israel. Elections were held for a Constituent Assembly, which met in February of the following year and adopted a temporary constitution for a democratic republic.

Meanwhile, from the day of proclaimed independence until the spring of 1949, Israel and its Arab neighbor countries were at war. United Nations efforts brought about truces several times, but nothing lasting was achieved until Israel and Egypt signed a general armistice agreement in February 1949; Jordan and Syria also signed armistices in April. The United Nations peace effort was at first under the direction of Count Folke Bernadotte of Sweden; when he was assassinated in September 1948, by Israeli extremists in Jerusalem, it was continued by Dr. Ralph Bunche of the United States. The status at the ceasefire was regarded as a victory for Israel and a defeat for the Arab powers; neither, however, accepted it as final. Violent incidents continued to occur, including retaliatory massacres.

The Arab-Israeli wars

Despite its troubles with the Arabs, Israel strengthened its economy, and many new industries were created. Large sums of money flowed into the country as a result of West German restitution for the outrages of Nazism. Yet the fate of Israel was not a happy one. Israel agreed to participate in an attempt by the British and French to invade Egypt, following Nasser's nationalization of the Suez Canal Company in 1956. Israel's role is this extraordinarily mismanaged and ill-fated venture not only increased the enmity of its Arab neighbors, it did little to enhance Israeli prestige in the world at large.

Progress of Israel

Trouble brewed in Sinai in 1967 until President Nasser resolved to teach the Jewish nation a lesson. He formed alliances with Jordan and Syria and vowed that Israel must be wiped from the map. Nasser closed Aqaba, Israel's only direct outlet to the Red Sea. The Israelis responded with a lightning war against Egypt and its Arab allies. The Egyptian and Syrian forces were routed in six days, and the Syrians accepted a ceasefire a short time later. But ceasefire did not spell peace.

The Six-Day War

Israeli Tanks Move into Jerusalem. A scene during the Arab-Israeli War of June 1967.

Future peace prospects

New outbreaks flared sporadically for more than two years. The conditions for peace were really nonexistent. The Arabs were tormented by loss of confidence and fearful of their own future as a result of their staggering defeat. The Israelis were obsessed with security and determined to preserve it regardless of cost. It was an impasse from which no one could be sure of a way of escape.

Another war of longer duration in 1973 once again failed to resolve the impasse. In that conflict, the Arabs threatened to withhold their immense oil reserves from the West, in hopes that the West would in turn put pressure on the Israelis to negotiate. This tactic succeeded only to the extent of convincing Europe and America of its dependence on Arab oil, and of their need to escape from that dependence. Since that time, prospects for peace have improved somewhat. In 1978, President Sadat traveled to Jerusalem in a dramatic bid to break the deadlock. And in the fall of that year U.S. President Jimmy Carter, having persuaded Sadat and Israeli President Menachem Begin to meet with him at Camp David outside Washington, engineered their agreement to a treaty draft, which was signed in final form by Israel and Egypt in Washington in 1979. Yet factors such as Israel's reluctance to surrender Arab territory in the Sinai peninsula and the continuing terrorist campaigns of non-Jewish Palestinians deprived of a homeland by the Israelis, guaranteed that peace would not come easily or soon to the Middle East. Behind these specific troublesome areas of contention lay the fact of Western dependence upon the Arabs for oil. The Organization of Petroleum Exporting Countries (OPEC), formed in the 1970s, was dominted by Middle Eastern Arab nations, who were determined to extract a high price—both economic and political—in return for the oil which the West, despite its resolves to develop alternative energy sources, continues to rely upon. The oil

On the Path to Peace in the Middle East. From left to right, Egyptian President Anwar Sadat, U.S. President Jimmy Carter, and Israeli Prime Minister Menachem Begin shake hands at the announcement of the Camp David accord which laid the groundwork for a peace treaty between Egypt and Israel.

reserves of the Middle East will dictate, as much as anything, the affairs of that part of the world in the years immediately ahead.

3. THE RISE OF BLACK AFRICA

For some years after World War II it appeared that the most volatile countries of the world would turn out to be the new states of Africa. Most of them were imbued with a new consciousness of their importance and determined to win for themselves a place befitting their destiny. They had been influenced by talk of independence at the end of the war and by the success of several struggles for self-rule in other parts of the world.

African revolts against colonialism

If any one country could be considered the leader of the African colonial revolt, it was Ghana, formerly called the Gold Coast, a colony of Great Britain. In 1954 Britain granted self-government, and in 1960 Ghana became a republic. Leadership of the Ghana independence movement was at that time supplied by Kwame Nkrumah (1909–1972). The son of an illiterate goldsmith, he was a gifted student and obtained an education in the United States and in England. Nkrumah returned to his homeland in 1948 and became a nationalist agitator. Though he classified himself as a Marxist, he denied being communist. Yet he admired Lenin and generally looked to Moscow for support of his policies, rather than to London or Washington. Nkrumah considered it preposterous that the Central Africans, with their proud traditions and ancient culture, should be ruled by Europeans. Nkrumah ruled benevolently even after converting the nation into a one-party state. He established hospitals and schools and raised literacy standards. Accused of extravagance and corruption, and of fostering a "cult of personality," he was deposed by a revolt of army officers in 1966, which, it was subsequently learned, was actually supported by the U.S. Central Intelligence Agency. He was driven from his homeland and forced to take refuge in Guinea, where he died in 1972.

Kwame Nkrumah (center, seated) and Members of His Government in Ghana

One of the most violent of the revolts in Central Africa occurred in the Congo. Conditions in the Congo, a colony of Belgium, had been for a number of years very unstable. In 1960, fearing an outbreak of violence among disaffected colonial subjects, Belgium granted the Congolese independence. This was the signal for the beginning of a series of rebellions and assassinations that raged for more than five years. A chief cause of the flaming disorders centered in the southeastern province of Katanga, the location of rich copper resources controlled by Belgian capitalists. At one time the copper mines of Katanga had produced revenues sufficient to defray 50 percent of the costs of the Belgian colonial government. In July 1960, Katanga seceded and attempted to gain control of the entire country. In the course of the revolt several former premiers and other high-ranking officers were murdered, including the leftist Congolese leader Patrice

Conflict in the Congo

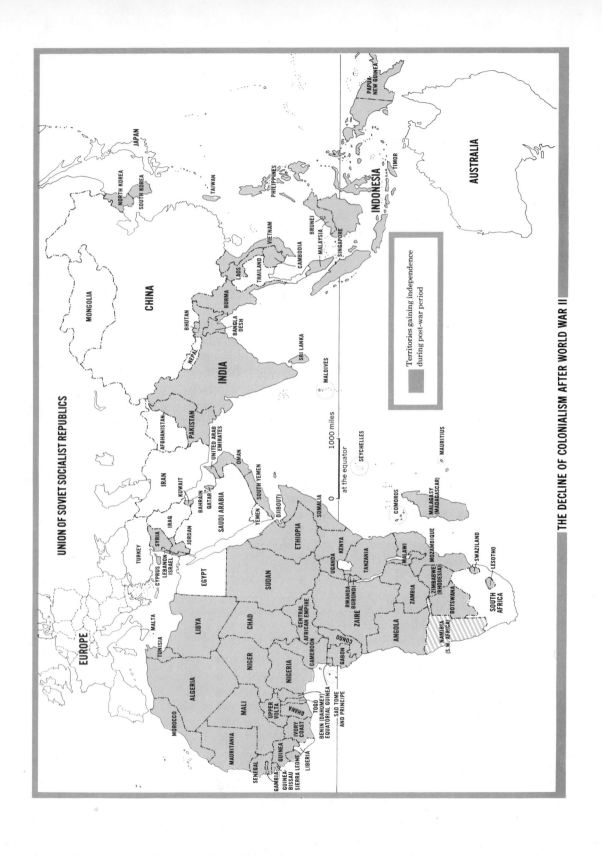

THE DECLINE OF COLONIALISM AFTER WORLD WAR II

Territories gaining independence
during post-war period

0   1000 miles
at the equator

Lumumba, whose assassination was arranged with the aid of the American C.I.A. The U.N. Security Council sent a contingent to guard against revival of civil war. Strong-man rule was revived by President Mobutu, who changed the name of the country to Zaire in 1971, and a degree of stability was ultimately restored. The continued willingness of both the United States and Russia to interfere in the affairs of emerging African nations is a measure of their desire to extend their power while avoiding direct confrontation.

Other African countries—especially Kenya and Nigeria—seemed to promise a smoother transition to independence. Both were former British colonies. Some authorities held that British colonial administration was wiser than that of most other European empires. Whereas the French and Belgians withheld self-government as long as they could, and then granted it suddenly, the British brought their colonies to independence more gradually. Many local leaders were trained in administration and knew how to deal with intricate problems before they actually arose. Yet again in Nigeria the familiar charges of corruption and inefficiency, whether true or not, led to the murder of the premier and the overthrow of the government in 1966. After more assassinations a military government seized control. Within a year the eastern region seceded and proclaimed itself the Republic of Biafra. Civil war followed and harassed the country for three years. The total of casualties was enormous. More than 1 million people lost their lives. Thousands were killed in battle, but many more died of starvation. The rebels capitulated in 1970. From every standpoint the war was a tragedy. Nigeria is one of the most richly endowed of African countries. Its natural resources include oil and natural gas, coal, and the world's greatest abundance of columbium (used in steel manufacturing).

Kenya did not achieve independence without violence. A country of East Africa lying athwart the Equator, Kenya, unlike Nigeria, is a poor country. The whole northern three-fifths of the territory is barren and almost waterless. Sections can be found in which there is no rainfall whatever for years at a time. The only well-watered sections are in the south and along the coast. It follows that agricultural resources are limited. World War II brought in thousands of Indians as settlers in Kenya. They did not become farmers or artisans, but settled in the cities and towns as petty traders. By 1970 there were 65,000 Indians in Kenya in a total population of 10,500,000.

The most serious conflict with regard to the Kenyan struggle for independence broke into the open in 1952 when the Mau Mau rebellion occurred. The Mau Mau were a secret terrorist organization made up of members of the Kikuyu tribe who instituted a reign of terror throughout the country against white settlers and all Kikuyu who refused to join the Mau Mau. By 1958 the revolt was suppressed, and five years later the country obtained independence.

Jomo Kenyatta Addressing an All-Africa Congress in London

The struggle in Rhodesia

The leader who did most to promote the growth and progress of Kenya was the Kikuyu tribesman Jomo Kenyatta, president of his country from 1963 until his death in 1978. Kenyatta devoted a long career to the defense of his homeland against white exploitation. In 1953 he was thrown into prison for seven years as a Mau Mau leader and a dangerous enemy of the state. His imprisonment seems to have done more to educate him in the realities of politics than to imbue him with hatred of his captors. While in prison he developed his philosophy of African socialism. Although for a time Kenyatta had studied at Moscow University, he adopted almost none of the trappings of Soviet communism. Instead his socialism bore a closer resemblance to that of the British or the Scandinavian countries. He urged his followers to forget the wrongs of the past and to concentrate on building a better world for the future. This future would be found in avoiding affiliations with either the East or the West. The African way, Kenyatta declared, has little in common with either capitalism or communism. The sharp antagonisms of class that exist in Europe and America have not been conspicuous elements in the African tradition. African socialism, according to Kenyatta, cannot be based on a dictatorship of the proletariat or any other form of class rule. Rather, its aim should be to prevent the seizure of power by individuals or groups armed with economic power. Its aim should be to enable every mature citizen to participate fully and equally in political affairs. Such is the essence of democracy and also of African socialism, according to Kenyatta's conception.

The brief national histories described here suggest the tremendous problems and the various solutions to those problems that have characterized the emergence of the African nations, and that will probably continue over the next several decades. Whatever the eventual outcome of the political struggles on the continent, it seems safe to say that they will all succeed in establishing black majority rule. Two nations in Africa—Rhodesia and the Republic of South Africa—have set themselves in determined opposition to this general trend. Rather than see power transferred to the blacks in Rhodesia, its prime minister, Ian Smith, in 1965 declared his country's unilateral independence from the British Commonwealth, that loose confederation of sovereign states which still maintains economic ties with Britain. Smith held firm in his determination to resist black rule until 1977, when combined pressure from the United States and Britain appeared finally to budge him. The compromise plan he favored, which promised gradual increase in black political power, and resulted in the election of Rhodesia's first black president in 1979, failed to satisfy the more militant rebel forces who claimed that the elections had been rigged, and that whites would continue to exercise real power in Rhodesia.

Meanwhile, South Africa continued to oppose all appeals from concerned governments and international organizations to relax its racial

Apartheid in South Africa. A policeman and an interpreter check the passports of black men coming to work in the mines of Johannesburg.

policy of "apartheid," which has for years decreed a separate and desperately inferior existence for its black and mixed-race population. In 1976, blacks rioting to protest racial inequality in the Johannesburg ghetto of Soweto were suppressed by the police, leaving a death toll of over 200. The following year Steve Biko, a powerful black leader and advocate of nonviolent protest, died under extremely suspicious circumstances in jail following his intensive campaign against apartheid practices. Because many countries and many internationally powerful corporations have large investments in South Africa, the weapon of economic boycott, though threatened, has not been employed to try to force the government to change its racial policy. Political power may change hands, but the power of money remains a prime mover in the affairs of the world.

South African "apartheid"

4. THE LIMITS OF POWER

Although the world's leading nations retained or acquired enormous power in the postwar years, they often found themselves unable to exercise that power as they once had, or as they might want. Possession of nuclear weapons did not necessarily mean that a nation could impose its will upon another. Fear that their use might unleash a war that would destroy civilization forced nations to keep their powder dry.

A nuclear balance of power

The issue had been raised first during the Korean war, when the United States government deliberately refrained from extending the war into China, for fear that such a move might lead irrevocably to a nuclear world war. This policy puzzled and angered many Americans, however, accustomed to the concepts of all-out war and unconditional surrender. Especially galling to them was the fact that President Harry

Cuban missile crisis

Fidel Castro

The war in Vietnam

Ho Chi Minh

Truman saw fit to fire General Douglas MacArthur, hero of the Pacific theater in World War II and now commander of the United Nations forces, because MacArthur refused to fight a limited war. In 1962, the United States and the Soviet Union were again forced to ask themselves how much they were willing to risk in order to protect their own strategic interests. During the early 1960s, United States President John F. Kennedy (1917–1963) and his advisors grew increasingly concerned about the activities of Premier Fidel Castro of Cuba. Castro was a communist revolutionary who had led a successful revolt against a repressive Cuban dictatorship. He had subsequently arranged to have the Russians supply him with "offensive" missiles and other war materiel. In October 1962 Kennedy ordered a naval blockade of the island to prevent a delivery of promised equipment. The Soviet government, alarmed by the threat of war, agreed to withdraw and to remove the bombers and missiles already on Cuban soil. The incident posed an extremely difficult question for the two superpowers: How could one nation convince another of its determination to brook no further interference with its plans, if its adversary could be fairly certain that because of the fear of nuclear war, the threat was no more than a bluff?

In this instance, the Russians chose not to call America's bluff, if bluff it was, and war was averted. The United States' major excursion into foreign affairs in the 1960s—the Vietnam war—was not blessed with equal success. After the defeat of Japan in 1945, France had sought to recover its lost empire in the Far East. These efforts ended in failure, however. The French were immediately confronted by a rebellion of Vietnamese nationalists under the leadership of Ho Chi Minh (1890–1969). The rebels resorted to guerilla warfare and inflicted such costly defeats upon the French that the latter decided to abandon the struggle. An agreement was signed at Geneva in 1954 providing for the division of Vietnam into two zones, pending elections to determine the future government of the entire country. Ho Chi Minh became president of North Vietnam and established his capital at Hanoi. His followers, who came to be called Viet Cong, were numerous in both halves of the country. Had elections been held as provided by the Geneva Agreement, Ho Chi Minh would probably have been elected president of all of Vietnam. But the government of South Vietnam, backed by the United States, refused to permit elections to be held.

From this point on, involvement by the United States in the Vietnamese civil war steadily increased. President Kennedy was convinced that the Chinese Communist juggernaut would soon roll over all of Southeast Asia. The first victims would be Vietnam, Laos, Cambodia, Malaysia, and Singapore. Then would come Thailand, Burma, and India. How far Kennedy would have gone in his crusade against communism had he escaped assassination in 1963 is impossible to say with

War in Vietnam. Confronted with a new kind of warfare, the American military sought to adapt its methods to the Vietnamese situation.

certainty. Kennedy's successor, Lyndon B. Johnson (1908–1973), hoped that a relatively small force of perhaps 100,000 men would be sufficient to defeat the Viet Cong and drive them back into their own country. Little consideration was given to the fact that these forces were solidly entrenched in both states of Vietnam, and that they had been waging a bitter national struggle for upwards of eighteen years. They had succeeded in driving out the French in 1954 and were not likely to surrender to a new invader, as they conceived the Americans to be. The Viet Cong and the North Vietnam regulars, though less well-equipped, nevertheless fought the South Vietnamese and their American allies to a standstill on several occasions. During the Tet offensive of 1968 they came close to capturing Saigon, the South Vietnamese capital.

Kennedy's intrusion into Vietnam

Exasperated by failure to win an easy victory in South Vietnam, the American civilian and military chiefs determined upon aerial bombing. A series of incidents in 1964 provided the justification. Reports, of doubtful veracity, indicated that North Vietnamese ships had attacked American naval vessels in the Tonkin Gulf. President Johnson pronounced these incidents acts of war and immediately obtained from Congress authorization to use whatever measures necessary to repel communist aggression. Soon afterward the first American bombers unloaded their first cargoes upon towns and villages occupied by the North Vietnamese and the Viet Cong. Although evidence accumulated which cast doubt on the efficacy of these raids, they continued to be used. It has been estimated that at least as much tonnage in nonnuclear bombs was dropped on tiny Vietnam as was unloaded by the Allied forces on all of Germany in World War II. But still the deadly onslaught continued. The only answer of those responsible for strategy in Washington and Saigon seems to have been "Cover up the failure by escalating the war." As the struggle entered its fifth year,

President Johnson escalates the war

with no end in sight, disillusionment spread throughout the United States. Criticism of President Johnson was so harsh in 1968 that he was forced to abandon his plans to run for a second term.

The Nixon policies

Johnson's successor, Richard M. Nixon, was elected on the strength of promises to end the war. But this turned out to be a shadowy promise. While ground troops were being withdrawn from Vietnam, in May 1970, the United States invaded Cambodia and a few months later the kingdom of Laos. In April 1972, the North Vietnamese, with massive aid from Russia and China, launched a powerful counteroffensive with the apparent objective of conquering South Vietnam and driving all foreign armies out of the country. A number of South Vietnamese strongholds were captured and the offensive seemed more dangerous than the famous Tet offensive of 1968. Nixon countered with increased bombing of North Vietnam's factories and railroads and by mining its harbors, including savage raids while negotiations were underway in December 1972.

The limits to power

A ceasefire, early in 1973, did no more than postpone the inevitable. Two years later, South Vietnam fell to the Viet Cong and the North Vietnamese. The massive intervention had proved a ghastly failure. The lesson of Vietnam—that in a nuclear age there are limits to national power—was one that the United States, Russia, and other countries of the world were beginning to learn in the 1970s. The Soviet Union had suffered its share of setbacks too: in Cuba, as we have seen, in border clashes with China, and in its attempts to penetrate the governments of the Third World. An ability to accommodate goals to limitations was a talent difficult for the superpowers to master. Yet it remained their best hope for a continuing, if uneasy, peace.

SELECTED READINGS

• *Items so designated are available in paperback editions.*
• Barnett, A. Doak, *A New U.S. Policy Toward China*, Washington, D.C., 1971.
  Berger, Earl, *The Convenant and the Sword: Arab-Israeli Relations, 1948–1956*, London, 1965. An impartial account.
• Brzezinski, Z. K., *The Soviet Bloc: Unity and Conflict*, rev. ed., Cambridge, Mass., 1967.
• Degler, Carl N., *Affluence and Anxiety: The United States Since 1945*, Glenview, Ill., 1968.
• Dehio, Ludwig, *Germany and World Politics in the Twentieth Century*, London, 1959. A series of essays assessing Germany's twentieth-century drive for European hegemony.
  Ehrmann, Henry W., *Politics in France*, Boston, 1968. French politics since 1958.

• Erikson, Erik, *Gandhi's Truth: On the Origins of Militant Nonviolence,* New York, 1969. An analysis of Gandhi by a modern psychologist.
• Fairbank, J. K., *The United States and China,* rev. ed., Cambridge, Mass., 1971.
  Fall, Bernard B., *The Two Vietnams: A Political and Military Analysis,* rev. ed., New York, 1967.
• Fanon, Frantz, *The Wretched of the Earth,* New York, 1968. The extraordinary and brilliant delineation of the oppression of Third World peoples.
• Halpern, Manfred, *The Politics of Social Change in the Middle East and North Africa,* Princeton, N.J., 1963.
  Henderson, W. O., *The Genesis of the Common Market,* Chicago, 1963.
  Hoffman, Stanley, et al., *In Search of France,* Cambridge, Mass., 1963. Essays providing perceptive analyses of postwar French politics and society.
• Khouri, F. J., *The Arab-Israeli Dilemma,* Syracuse, N.Y. 1968.
• Knapp, Wilfrid, *Unity and Nationalism in Europe Since 1945,* Elmsford, N.Y., 1969.
  Kolko, Gabriel, *The Politics of War: The World and United States Foreign Policy, 1943–45,* New York, 1969. Argues that the blame for the Cold War rests with the Western allies.
• Moore, Barrington, *The Social Origins of Dictatorship and Democracy: Lord and Peasant in the Making of the Modern World,* Boston, 1966.
• Oliver, Roland, and J. D. Fage, *A Short History of Africa,* New York, 1963.
  Reischauer, Edwin O., *Beyond Vietnam: The United States and Asia,* New York, 1968.
  ———, *The United States and Japan,* Cambridge, Mass., 1965.
• Rotberg, Robert I., *The Rise of Nationalism in Central Africa,* Cambridge, Mass., 1965.
  Schwartz, Benjamin, *Chinese Communism and the Rise of Mao,* Cambridge, Mass., 1967.
  Seabury, Paul, *The Rise and Decline of the Cold War,* New York, 1967.
• Worsley, Peter, *The Third World,* Chicago, 1964.
• Wylie, Laurence, *Village in the Vaucluse,* rev. ed., Cambridge, Mass., 1974. Analyzes the social structure of French rural life in 1950. An afterword reveals the changes wrought by the intrusion of modern life in the ensuing twenty years.

SOURCE MATERIALS

Adenauer, Konrad, *Memoirs, 1945–53,* Chicago, 1966. Adenauer served as chancellor of the Federal Republic of Germany from 1949 to 1963 and sought both American support and the reunification of dismembered Germany.
Barnes, Thomas G., and Gerald D. Feldman, comps., *Breakdown and Rebirth: 1914 to the Present,* Boston, 1972. An excellent documentary collection of contemporary history, primarily European.
Brandt, Conrad, Benjamin Schwartz, and John Fairbank, eds., *A Documentary History of Chinese Communism,* Cambridge, Mass., 1952.

• Caputo, Philip, *A Rumor of War,* New York, 1977. The best memoir of the American experience in the Vietnam war.

De Gaulle, Charles, *Memoirs of Hope: Renewal and Endeavor,* New York, 1971.

Kennan, George F., *Memoirs, 1925–1950,* New York, 1967. Kennan, a career diplomat, was America's leading expert on Russia and instrumental in the formation of the containment policy.

Chapter 31

PROBLEMS OF WORLD CIVILIZATION

> This conjunction of an immense military establishment and a large arms industry is new in American experience. The total influence—economic, political, even spiritual—is felt in every city, every statehouse, every office of the federal government. . . . We must guard against the acquisition of unwarranted influence, whether sought or unsought, by the military-industrial complex. The potential for the disastrous rise of misplaced power exists and will persist.
>
> —Dwight D. Eisenhower, "Farewell Address"

T he writing of a final chapter in a text book of this sort is, for the authors, a difficult task. Not only are they called upon to attempt an instant analysis of their own society and time; they are expected as well to discern in present events patterns that will continue to be of some consequence five to ten years hence. In other words, they are called upon to pick historical winners, to decide not what *has* mattered, which is difficult enough, but what *will* matter. Historians, whose job it is to acknowledge the way in which human idiosyncrasies make prediction a tricky business, are particularly loath to single out this movement or that trend and to pronounce it "significant" in terms of the future. We shall therefore merely content ourselves with a discussion of some of the most serious problems confronting society in the 1970s, calling attention at the outset to the fact that these problems are rooted in many of the historical developments—industrialization, urbanization, and international competition, for example—that we have traced in the preceding chapters.

The present as history

1. THE GROWTH OF CENTRALIZED GOVERNMENT AND ITS CONSEQUENCES

Centralization and social welfare

The responsibilities central governments assumed, and the power they arrogated to themselves to discharge those responsibilities, increased significantly around the world after World War II. In almost all countries, successive administrations either intitiated or expanded social welfare programs, insuring that entire populations would receive protection from the depredations of unemployment, sickness, and old age. Building upon the examples set by Germany and Britain before World War I, Western nations instituted increasingly comprehensive national programs for health and social security. Socialist and Third World countries likewise moved, in some cases with remarkable speed, to alleviate the problems and disabilities of people who for generations had been denied the chance of a healthy and secure existence.

Reasons for the increase

This movement to expand social welfare systems resulted in an increased tendency on the part of governments to manage and control their citizenry. Programs of social insurance were designed to benefit and hence to regulate the lives of all classes of men and women, not just the destitute. New agencies, staffed by armies of newly recruited bureaucrats, imposed rules while they dispensed assistance to a clientele that grew to include the entire citizenry. Many of those responsible for the institution of these programs were motivated by a genuine desire to provide a decent life to all citizens, regardless of economic class. An equally powerful incentive, however, was the conviction of governments that without a strong and generally satisfied population a country was doomed to recurring unrest, that social insecurity would contribute to rapid national decline into domestic inefficiency and international ineffectiveness.

The role of international competition

Concern to improve or at any rate to stabilize a nation's international position, within a world in which power relationships were constantly shifting, contributed further to the growth of centralized government. New nations wanted to attain some new measure of international power. Older nations wanted to retain whatever measure had been theirs. In either case, governments recognized the importance of a stable economy and a strong military defense. Few countries, old or new, managed to attain those twin goals in the 1970s to the extent they deemed necessary. Inflation in particular proved an intractable obstacle to their achievement. Nevertheless as nations strained to assert themselves, their governments tightened their hold on the economy, working to do so with the forces of both management and labor, while investing enormous sums in the most sophisticated and up-to-date armaments of war. The result of these activities was a further growth of the power and control of government.

What have been the consequences of such growth? Some observers have argued that the general worldwide increase in the authority of central governments is a symptom of a decline in the importance of political and economic ideology. Whether a nation declares itself to be a capitalist democracy (as does the United States), a socialist commonwealth (as does the Soviet Union) or something in between (as do many of the nations of western Europe), all appear to some degree to have blunted ideological differences as they have attempted to rationalize—or nationalize—their industries, manage their economies, provide for the well-being of their citizens, and arm themselves against the possibilities of future war. Fewer socialists now advocate collective ownership of the means of production; they have become instead exponents of the welfare state. Defenders of capitalism still exist in theory but few would recognize it if they saw it in full swing. Capitalist economies are no longer free enterprise systems but "mixed" economies, involving government controls, managed currencies, and forced distribution of profits. Small-time capitalists are permitted to enjoy their gains only until they turn them over to the government to finance its wars, armaments, and social welfare programs.

*Political reaction to
centralization*

To suggest that there has been some ideological blurring in the movement toward more generally accepted goals does not mean, however, that men and women do not continue to call themselves capitalists or socialists, or that those terms have lost their meaning. Nor should it imply that there is not continuing and heated debate about both ends and means. During the mid-1970s a reaction of some magnitude occurred in several Western countries against the notion that governments should manage the lives of their citizens to the extent they were. Social reform, critics said, has cost too much, and has not really achieved what it was supposed to. There is still poverty and misery. Admit that they will always exist, these people argued, and moderate your goals accordingly; in the process, put an end to big government. This viewpoint was occasionally translated into political victory. The socialist government of Sweden, in power for decades, was succeeded by a conservative one. Margaret Thatcher, arch-conservative leader of Britain's Tory party, became the first woman prime minister of that country in 1979, as well as the first woman head of state of a Western nation, on a platform which blamed her country's economic decline in the 1970s on the fact that the government had overextended itself. In the United States there was a relatively successful campaign by citizens to curb government activity by limiting taxation.

*Critics of bureaucratic
centralization*

This debate has been carried on not only in the political arena but in the writings of thoughtful and angry critics of modern society. Two of the most powerful voices raised against the growth of worldwide governmental expansion and authoritarianism were those of Alexsandr Solzhenitsyn and Herbert Marcuse. Solzhenitsyn, an exiled Russian novelist, attacked the brutal methods employed by the Soviet Union in its rapid climb to world power. His *Gulag Archipelago,* published in 1973, is a fictionalized account of the fate of those whose

Margaret Thatcher

Alexsandr Solzhenitsyn

President Nixon Resigns. Here Nixon bids his last farewell to the White House in the wake of his resignation.

willingness to stand in the way of Soviet "progress" sentenced them to life in Siberian labor camps. Marcuse, an American, charged that authoritarianism was just as much a fact of life under capitalism as under communism. He argued that industrial capitalism had produced a "one-dimensional" society, in which the interests of individual citizens had been ruthlessly subordinated to those of the powerful corporate interests which were the true governors of the world.

Marcuse urged the adoption of revolutionary measures to accomplish the overthrow of authoritarian capitalist imperialism. Those unwilling to follow him to that extreme nevertheless concurred in his denunciation of the manner in which big government and big business together appeared to be draining power from individual citizens. Indeed, as devoted a capitalist as Dwight D. Eisenhower, general in the U.S. Army during the Second World War and president of the United States in the 1950s, warned in his farewell presidential address of the growing might of what he called "the military-industrial complex." In those countries calling themselves democracies, democracy seemed to many to have less and less meaning, as people appeared to enjoy little control over their government and hence over their lives. Concerns of this sort received apparent confirmation in the late 1960s and early 1970s, when the United States was at war in Vietnam. Evidence subsequently published showed that the democratically elected Congress was misled by President Lyndon Johnson and his advisors into believing that hostile North Vietnamese attacks on American ships had compelled U.S. intervention, whereas the attacks had instead been "manufactured" to allow the government to pursue its own aggressive policies. Concern about the arrogance of governmental power reached its peak in the United States during the Watergate investigations leading to the resignation of President Richard Nixon in 1974, when it was learned that Nixon had authorized domestic spying in the name of national security but without proper regard for the constitutional rights of American citizens. Following that dramatic episode came revelations about the role played in secret by the U.S. Central Intelligence Agency in subverting leftist Third World governments, along with the intervention of giant multinational corporations and the C.I.A. together in assisting to overthrow a democratically elected socialist government in Chile. Knowledge of these events brought home the extent to which centralized authority in supposedly democratic governments had removed itself from popular control and accountability.

2. COMMITMENT: THE GROWTH OF BLACK CONSCIOUSNESS

Partly in response to revelations of this sort, partly as a result of long-standing grievances and dissatisfactions, groups that had hitherto lived as subordinates in society, kept powerless and in large part silenced, raised their voices in the 1960s and 1970s, demanding not only to be heard but to have their demands met. At the very time when democracies were being charged with ignoring the wishes of their constituents, blacks, youth, and women, in particular, began to assert their right to equality.

*U.S. blacks after the
Civil War*

The growth of insurgency among American blacks has to some extent paralleled the rise of black nations in Africa and the Caribbean. Through most of the years from the Civil War to 1900, black people were condemned, in the North as well as the South, to a subordinate role within a predominantly white culture. The emancipation of slaves, and the Thirteenth and Fourteenth Amendments to the Constitution brought little change in a quality of existence which was centuries-old and which was underwritten by the racist attitudes and practices of most whites. These attitudes and practices were realized in substandard education, lack of jobs, poor housing, inequality under the law, lynching of both black men and women, and other conditions of life with which black people were faced. Any changes in this reality might have been indefinitely postponed had it not been for the spread of black political consciousness and the rise of a number of black leaders, both male and female, during the course of the twentieth century. Black political consciousness and black leaders were not unknown before the turn of the century: Harriet Tubman, Sojourner Truth, Frederick Douglass, Nat Turner, and others, were eloquent and powerful spokespeople and activists. But with the twentieth century came a massive emigration of blacks from the South to the North. Although the North shared most of the attitudes of the South, there were more opportunities for blacks in the industrial cities than in the primarily agrarian South. Many thousands of black people emigrated to the North during the years of the First World War, when the lack of white labor created a need for their services; it should also be mentioned that over 400,000 blacks were made to serve in the war even though, in most parts of the United States, they were essentially disenfranchised citizens. During the postwar depression, however, black workers were the first to suffer and to lose their jobs. But the emigration brought a changed political consciousness for black people; more voted, for example.

In 1910 the National Association for the Advancement of Colored People was founded and contributed to this political progress and the growing awareness among black people that they were an oppressed group and that this should be changed. The work of the NAACP was supplemented in 1911 with the founding of the National League on Urban Conditions Among Negroes (later known as the National Urban League). The work of black leaders of this time—for example, Ida Wells-Barnett (1862–1931), A. Philip Randolph (1889–1979), W. E. B. Du Bois (1868–1963), Mary Mcleod Bethune (1875–1955)—who were visible and vocal opponents of lynching, promoters

W. E. B. Du Bois

Marcus Garvey

The Black Muslims

Martin Luther King, Jr.

of educational opportunities for blacks, and labor union organizers, kept this movement toward equality and against oppression a vital force in American history, which would culminate in the civil rights movement of the 1960s.

The year 1919 saw the rise to prominence of another important black leader, Marcus Garvey (1887–1940), a native of Jamaica. Garvey's political base was Harlem in New York City, a major black ghetto. Garvey emphasized the African origins of black Americans and taught his followers to refer to themselves as "black" rather than "Negro." He claimed his people were the descendents of the "greatest and proudest race who ever peopled the earth," and generated a movement of black emigration from America to Africa. Garvey encouraged and influenced an important black literary movement, the so-called Harlem Renaissance of the 1920s. Several of its leaders derived inspiration from him, notably Langston Hughes and Countee Cullen.

Garvey's philosophy also extended indirectly to the Black Muslim movement, through his influence on the father of its most vigorous proselytizer, Malcom X (1925–1965). Malcolm X was converted in prison by his brother to the religion of Islam. After his release he became a spokesman for Elijah Muhammad, founder of the movement. Most of his followers were people of the same background who had flocked to Garvey's standard—recent migrants from the South who now lived in poverty in the black ghettos of northern cities. Malcolm X attempted to overcome their feeling of helplessness by giving them a new religion to take the place of the white man's Christianity and by restoring black pride. This new religion was Islam, which Malcolm X described as the true faith of Africans. Though he and his followers were firm believers, they were not fanatics. They did not renounce worldliness as a life of sin. They urged blacks to pool their resources and establish black-owned businesses. This would lead to economic independence and a heightened sense of self. The Muslims taught their adherents to avoid aggression and to fight only when attacked. Their charismatic minister broke with the Black Muslims in 1964. In February 1965 he was assassinated as he started to speak at a rally in Harlem.

In the meantime black consciousness was being expressed through other forms. One was the Congress of Racial Equality (CORE), founded by James Farmer in 1942. His announced aim was to translate "love of God and man" into specific crusades against injustice. By 1960 CORE had combined its efforts with those of other political organizations seeking to end discrimination against blacks. It helped in promoting "freedom rides" for civil rights into the South and boycotts against racist shopkeepers. After 1955 Farmer often collaborated with Martin Luther King, Jr. (1929–1968), a young Baptist minister. Like Farmer, King also embraced the Gandhian philosophy of nonviolence. For more than ten years he was widely regarded—and feared—as the most effective defender of black rights. His career was brought to a tragic end by an assassin's bullet as he stood on the balcony of a motel in Memphis in 1968.

Important successors to King, Farmer, and in a sense the Black Muslims, were the Black Panthers. Their movement began during the civil rights confrontations of the 1950s and 1960s in Alabama and Mississippi. From there it rapidly spread northward and about 1968 established its headquarters in Oakland, California. Its leaders—such men as Huey Newton, Bobby Seale, and Eldridge Cleaver—adopted for their party the name of Black Panthers. They saw in the panther an animal slow to take the initiative of aggression but fierce in retaliation when attacked by its enemies. The Panthers differed from other black activists in a number of ways. First of all, they were frankly revolutionary and not nonviolent. They believed that only by seizing power could they redress society's wrongs against black people. Second, the Black Panthers, unlike some of their forerunners, did not advocate a return to Africa, but sought an end to racism in America. The Black Panthers also professed a kind of internationalism similar to that of other revolutionaries.

The Black Panthers

Black movements in the 1970s to some degree retreated from militant commitment. Even the Black Panthers declared their willingness to work within the existing system for reform. Civil rights laws enacted under the Johnson administration in the 1960s have brought U.S. blacks some measure of equality with regard to voting rights— and, to a much lesser degree, school desegregation. In other areas, such as housing and job opportunities, blacks continue to suffer disadvantage and discrimination, as a result of white racism, which underwrites the belief that blacks should be satisfied with the gains they have made, and the general recalcitrance of administrations following Lyndon Johnson's domestically innovative one. These problems are not confined to the United States. In Great Britain, for example, where there has been a large immigration of blacks from former colonies, extreme discrimination in jobs and housing menaces the chances for early or satisfactory integration. Because the momentum for reform has slowed, black leaders are less able than in the 1960s to chart their movement's direction. Meanwhile black people derive continued strength not only from the conviction that the battle for equality is both justified and still to be won, but from the example of African and Caribbean nations emerging into independent statehood.

Blacks in the 1970s

3. COMMITMENT: YOUTH AND WOMEN

The years from 1964 through 1972 were marked by a protest and upheaval by the younger generation more rampant than the world had witnessed in many decades. They were committed, as were blacks, to

Vietnam Protest, 1971. Veterans of the U.S. Armed Forces march on the capitol to protest continued U.S. involvement in the war in Vietnam.

The youth rebellion

the assertion of their right to be heard. In the United States this rebellion was fueled by the war in Vietnam. Young men, drafted to fight in a war they despised, rebelled against the idea that it was their "duty" to serve. Together, young men and women proclaimed instead their duty to question anew the presuppositions that had led the U.S. into its unhappy military predicament. Science antagonized them because of its association with war-making. Knowledge that was not "relevant" to the world's problems was questioned with regard to its worth. Young leaders urged their peers to leave their college books and address the problems of the "real" world: overpopulation, industrial pollution, mistreatment of blacks and other minorities. It was this rebellion that exposed the inhumanity of the American adventure in Southeast Asia. Long before adult liberals spoke out against the bombing raids and body-counts of that war, students in colleges and universities stormed the institutions of the Establishment in angry protest. Although they did not stop the war, they helped to bring about President Johnson's retirement in 1968. Their *compères* in France, who rioted in May 1968, contributed to the defeat of President Charles de Gaulle.

Radicalism in the 1970s

Political radicalism no longer shapes the mind of the West's youth as it did in the late 1960s, a fact explained in large part by the end of hostilities in Vietnam. Radicalism's much-distorted reflection, however, appears in the activities of terrorist gangs such as that which in 1978 abducted and eventually killed the moderate Italian political leader Aldo Moro. Hoping their extremist tactics would help divide Italy and somehow produce a revolution, the gang's leaders discovered instead that they had conducted a sterile exercise in terror for its own sake.

Not all young rebels in the 1960s and 1970s committed themselves to a life of radical political activism. Some turned for spiritual or psychological comfort to fundamentalist religious movements. Some declared their disgust with the world by "dropping out," living in communities of their own design apart from society. Others devoted themselves to a counterculture reflected in the intensely personal music and lyrics of young popular musicians, in the custom of drug-taking, and in the freedom to live with each other without marriage. Social rebellion of this sort infected various countries to various degrees. It was primarily a movement of urban middle-class youths. Though in some cases their rejection of older values was the result of deeply held and enduring convictions, in many others their declaration of independence was short-lived, amounting to little more than the customary behavior of uncertain and impatient adolescents.

Youthful counterculture

Women, like blacks and young people, began to assert themselves during the 1960s and 1970s. As was the case with the youth rebellion, the women's movement began in the United States and was first directed from within the middle class. Some women in western European countries joined in the struggle for equal rights; by the mid-seventies the movement had spread worldwide, including the Third World nations, and was no longer limited to the middle class. Many of the early activists within the movement had been part of the youth rebellion during its most intense phase in the sixties. Their activism, in part, stemmed from a realization that even in a radical political atmosphere, women were relegated to second place. Women's position within society had changed radically since the nineteenth century. The assumption that the middle-class woman's place was in the home had been challenged by the ever-increasing demand for women workers and by the need experienced by more and more women to hold a job—either for financial reasons or because housework was for a growing

The women's movement

Students of the University of Paris During the Uprisings of 1968

Margaret Sanger, a Leader in the Movement to Awaken the World to the Necessity of Birth Control

number an unfulfilling occupation. The increased availability and social acceptance of birth-control devices meant that women were having fewer children, and that they could begin to exercise more control over the pattern of their lives.

Yet society seemed loath to acknowledge the implication of these changes: that women are equal to men. Women were paid less than men for similar work. Women with qualifications no different from men were turned down because of their gender when they applied for jobs. Women with excellent employment records were forced to rely on their husbands to establish credit. Political action helped alleviate some of these inequities in the late 1960s and the 1970s. The U.S. government instituted programs of "affirmative action" which mandated the hiring of qualified women as well as members of racial minority groups. The campaign for equality did not meet with universal approval, however. A particularly volatile subject was a woman's right to an abortion. Feminists argued that women must enjoy the freedom to plan for their future unencumbered by the responsibilities of motherhood if they choose, and that their bodies are theirs to govern. Their

Abortion as a central issue

opponents, which included members of the so-called right-to-life movement, countered with the argument that abortion encouraged sexual irresponsibility; some declared that abortion is the equivalent of murder. By the end of the seventies the campaigners for women's equality, though still battling in the United States for passage of a constitutional Equal Rights Amendment, had a good many successes to their credit. Unlike the youth rebellion, which had run its course by that time, the women's movement, like that of black people, was based not on the disaffections of only one generation, but on a history of discrimination experienced by great numbers and recognized as unjust by a sizable proportion of majority opinion.

4. LITERATURE AND ART AS REFLECTIONS OF CONTEMPORARY PROBLEMS

Postwar authors

Not surprisingly, the work of many of the West's leading writers reflect the difficulties and commitments we have been surveying. During the immediate postwar years novelists concerned themselves with the horrors of war and of the totalitarian systems which had spawned the conflict of the 1940s. The Americans James Jones and Norman Mailer, in *From Here to Eternity* and *The Naked and the Dead,* portrayed the coarseness and cruelty of military life with ruthless realism. The German Günter Grass's first and probably most important novel, *The Tin Drum,* depicted the vicious and politically diseased life of Nazi Germany in the 1930s. In France, Jean-Paul Sartre, as a result of his own and his country's wartime experiences, recommitted himself in his novels, plays, and other writings to a life of active political

involvement as a Marxist. Whereas he had previously defined hell in terms of individual hostilities, he now defined it in terms of class inequality. Unlike Sartre, his compatriot Albert Camus (1913–1960) was unable to construct a secular faith from his own perceptions of the world and its apparent absurdities. Though idealist enough to participate in the French resistance movement against the German occupation in World War II, and though proclaiming the virtues of rebellion, Camus remained tortured in novels such as *The Fall, The Plague,* and *The Rebel* by the problem of humanity's responsibility for its own miserable dilemma and by the limitations placed upon the ability of men and women to help each other.

The theme of individual alienation and helplessness, a reflection of the problems arising from the growth of state power, was one which writers addressed themselves to with increasing frequency in the 1960s and 1970s. The Russian Boris Pasternak, in his novel *Dr. Zhivago,* indicted the Soviet campaign to shape all its citizens to the same mold. Although both Pasternak and his compatriot Solzhenitsyn were awarded the Nobel Prize for literature, the former in 1958 and the latter in 1970, their works were condemned by the Soviet government and Solzhenitsyn was sent into exile. Western novelists dealt with the threat to individuality as well, building upon a prewar tradition most forcefully expressed in the writings of the Austrian Franz Kafka (1883–1924). Kafka's novels present a vision of humans in a hostile universe, hopelessly striving to come to terms with a remote and unknown power. It is not so much a dream as it is a nightmare composed of weird, fantastic details brought together in a terrifying pattern. His best-known work, *The Castle,* is at once a satire on bureaucracy and a philosophical representation of the isolation of the individual in the universe. The American novelist Saul Bellow (1915–   ) was concerned with many of these same themes, though Bellow spoke with a far gentler, if less compelling, voice than Kafka. He chose the modern city as the milieu for his fiction. His heroes in novels such as *The Adventures of Augie March, Henderson the Rain King,* and *Mr. Sammler's Planet* were all men trapped in a world turned upside down, condemned to seek personal understanding—indeed to maintain their sanity—in an environment at worst savage, at best absurd.

Women authors wrote not only of the general loneliness of the human condition, but of the particular plight of women trapped in a world not of their own making. The Frenchwoman Simone de Beauvoir (1908–   ) in *The Second Sex,* a germinal study of the female condition, denounced the male middle class for turning not only workers but also its own women into objects for its own ends. American writers like Adrienne Rich, Tillie Olsen, and the philosopher Mary Daly helped define the politics and culture of the women's movement.

The specific issues that drove men and women to committed action

Alienation and helplessness

Simone de Beauvoir

Women writers

James Baldwin

Black women authors

The absurd and fantastic

in the mid-1960s compelled writers to take sides as well. Günter Grass, in *Local Anaesthetic,* published in 1970, wrote of student unrest and political involvement. The movement for black equality encouraged a tradition in America that had burgeoned in the wake of the depression and World War II. One initiator of this tradition was Richard Wright (1908–1960), who grew up amid the rural poverty and violent racism of Mississippi. As a youth Wright drifted to Chicago and became a resident of and spokesman for the black ghetto. In his novel, *Native Son,* and his autobiography, *Black Boy,* he portrayed with scathing realism the oppression of working-class blacks. Despite the pretensions of the New Deal, he found that the burdens of that group had not been appreciably lightened. One of the most effective articulators of black aspiration and disenchantment in the 1960s was James Baldwin, the son of a Harlem clergyman. Living under the dual stigmas of his blackness and his homosexuality, Baldwin remained a self-exile in Paris for ten years following the Second World War. He returned to the United States to warn, in his most powerful book, *The Fire Next Time,* that unless whites awoke soon to the extent and pervasiveness of their racism, American society would be consumed by its own animosities.

Not only black men, but black women also wrote of the oppression and struggle of their race. Zora Neale Hurston (c. 1901–1960) was a novelist, anthropologist, and folklorist. In both her novels and anthropological studies Hurston wrote eloquently of the history of black people, their language and traditions. Her major novel, *Their Eyes Were Watching God* (1937), is about the strength of one black woman and her belief in her own strength and in herself. The poet Audre Lorde and the novelist Toni Morrison are two black women writers who also deal in detail and with an assured sense of history with the experience of black people, particularly with the black female experience. One of the most sensitive of contemporary black women writers was Lorraine Hansberry (1930–1965). A poet and dramatist, Hansberry won distinction in her tragically brief lifetime for her play *A Raisin in the Sun,* specifically the story of one black family in Chicago but actually the story of many black families existing under racism. Her dramatic talent was displayed even more clearly in *To Be Young, Gifted, and Black,* produced four years after her death. Hansberry wrote with defiance and anger, and sometimes in bitterness, when the beauty she saw in life was dimmed by bigotry and extinguished by repression.

Some authors, although they agreed with indictments of contemporary civilization, believed the human condition too hopeless to warrant direct attack. These writers expressed their despair by escaping into the absurd and fantastic. In the plays of Samuel Beckett (1906–   ), an Irishman who wrote in French, and of the Englishman Harold Pinter (1930–   ), nothing happens. Characters speak in the banalities that have become the hallmark of modern times. Words which are meaningless when spoken by human beings nevertheless take on a logic of their own; yet they explain nothing. Other authors, less willing, perhaps, to attempt to make a statement out of nothingness, have invaded the realms of hallucination, science fiction, and fantasy. The novels of the Americans William Burroughs and Kurt Vonnegut convey their readers from interior fantasizing to outer space. Significantly one of the most popular books among the youth of the sixties and seventies was *The Lord of the Rings,* a pseudosaga set in the fantasy world of "Middle Earth," written before the Second World War by the Englishman J. R. R. Tolkien.

Filmmakers, in the decades after the Second World War, made films which mirrored the problems and concerns of society, with a depth and artistic integrity seldom attempted or achieved previously. The *Film* Swede Ingmar Bergman, the Frenchmen Jean-Luc Godard and François Truffaut, the Italians Frederico Fellini and Michelangelo Antonioni, to name but a few of the most gifted directors, dealt in their films with the same themes that marked the literature of the period: loneliness, war, oppression, and corruption. One important factor facilitating the achievement of artistic quality was the general willingness on the part of censors—state or industry sponsored—to reflect public taste by permitting filmmakers great license in the handling of themes such as racism, violence, and sexuality. While there is no question that this relaxation led to exploitation, it cleared the way for extraordinarily powerful film statements, such as the American Arthur Penn's *Bonnie and Clyde* (1967) and the Italian Bernardo Bertolucci's *Last Tango in Paris* (1972), shocking declarations about humanity made possible by explicit depictions of violence and sex. Film, while gaining a general maturity it had heretofore lacked, did not desert its role as entertainment. The international popularity of the British rock-and-roll group, the Beatles, was translated, for example, into equally successful films, charming, slapstick escapism which nevertheless proclaimed the emancipation of youth from the confining formalities and conventions of their elders.

Unlike writers or filmmakers, the majority of postwar artists did not use their work as a vehicle to express either ideological commitment or a concern for the human situation. Following trends es- *Fine arts* tablished by the impressionists and cubists, they spoke neither about the world or to the world, but instead to each other and to the extremely small coterie of initiates who understood their artistic language. Foremost among the postwar schools of art was abstract expressionism, whose chief exponents were the painters Jackson Pollack (1912–1956), William deKooning (1904–   ), and Franz Kline (1910–1962). Their interests lay in further experimentation with the relationships between color, texture, and surface, to the total exclusion of "meaning" or "message" in the traditional sense. Jasper

Mahoning by Franz Kline. A work representative of the abstract expressionists' desire to explore the varieties of light, texture, and surface.

Johns's painting of the American flag insisted that the viewer see it not as *a* painting—that is, something to be interpreted—but instead as painting, the treatment of canvas with paint. Robert Rauschenberg, in revolt against the abstract expressionists, exhibited blank white panels, insisting that by so doing he was pressing art to the ultimate question of a choice of medium. Painters fought the notion that their work in some way expressed disgust with an empty civilization. "My paintings are based on the fact that only what can be seen is there," declared the American Frank Stella, who painted stripes on irregularly shaped canvases. "Pop" art, a phenomenon of the late sixties which took as its subject everyday objects such as soup cans and comic-strip heroes, was likewise, according to its practitioners, not a protest against the banality of industrialism but another experiment in abstractions.

Rothko

See color plates following page 864

Even the remote and yet extraordinarily compelling abstractions of Mark Rothko (1903–1970), glowing or somber rectangles of color imposed upon other rectangles, were said by the artist himself to represent "nothing but content—no associations, only sensation." Only with the coming, in the 1970s, of the so-called hyper-realists, artists such as the American Duane Hanson, who recreates his invariably depressing human subjects in plastic down to the last eyelash, can we perhaps say that some artists are making a statement not only about technique but about what they perceive as the vacuity of life.

5. THE CRISIS OF ECOLOGY AND POPULATION

Pessimism about the human condition derived not only from concern for the problems of the present that we have been considering. It stemmed as well from a fear about the future, the future of the earth's human beings, of the earth itself, and of what is termed its ecology. The word "ecology" is often used primarily to refer to human beings and their environment, but it is much broader than that. Ecologists think of humans as a link in a vast chain of life which extends all the way back through mammals, amphibians, invertebrates, and the simplest microorganisms, which may be either plants or animals. In popular usage ecology may be synonymous with pollution problems. Again this is an oversimplification. The causes and prevention of pollution make up important elements in the study of ecology, but they are not the whole subject. Equally important is the use of our environment in ways that will safeguard the heritage of fertile soil, pure air, fresh water, and forests for those who come after us.

Ecological violations consist not merely of poisoning the atmosphere and contaminating oceans, rivers, and lakes by dumping wastes into them, but of any assault upon them that makes them less valuable for human survival. The excessive construction of dams, for example, causes the silting of rivers and the accumulating of nitrates at a faster rate than the surrounding soil can absorb. The use of insecticides, especially those containing DDT, may result in upsetting the balance of nature. An example in the recent history of Malaysia illustrates such an occurrence. The Malaysian government resorted to extensive spraying of remote areas with DDT in the hope of stamping out malaria-carrying mosquitoes. The DDT killed the mosquitoes but also poisoned the flourishing cockroaches. The cockroaches in turn were eaten by the villages cats. The cats died of the DDT poison. The net result was a multiplication of rats formerly kept from a population explosion by their natural enemies, the cats. So badly disturbed was the balance of nature that a fresh supply of cats had to be airlifted from other regions. Other assaults upon the balance of nature have been even more serious. The Aswan High Dam of Egypt, undoubtedly valuable for increasing the water supply of that country, has at the same time cut down the flow of algal nutrients to the Mediterranean, with damaging effects on the fishing industry of various countries. From the ecological standpoint the rapid development of industry in modern times is almost an unmitigated disaster. For thousands of years the human race introduced into the environment no more waste substances than could easily be absorbed by the environment. But modern technology has introduced into nature a variety of wastes never abundant before. Among them are carbon monoxide, sulfur dioxide, and nitrogen oxides. And this is to say nothing of the discharge into nature of pesticides, the great host of synthetic products that are not biologically degradable, and the fruits of nuclear weapons testing.

The ecological problem is caused not simply by the dumping of harmful and nondegradable products. It is also the result of wastage of land as our most valuable natural resource. In many parts of the world

Industrial Pollution. This photo shows steel mills in Westfalenhuette, West Germany. While polluting gases and particular matter are released into the air, industrial wastes, both thermal and chemical, are released into nearby waters.

Diminishing land resources

rivers run brown because they are filled with earth washed from the fields bordering them. In some of the largest American cities two-thirds to three-quarters of the land area is paved with streets and parking lots. Meanwhile, the nation's crop land is shrinking at an alarming rate. Ecologists say that much of this land will probably have to be abandoned.

Ecology and the population explosion

A close link exists between the problems of ecology and the population explosion. Indeed, if population control had remained a reality, the problems of ecology might well have passed unnoticed for many years. For example, New York City on the eve of the Civil War had a total population of 700,000. The area was not essentially smaller than what it is now. Yet the inhabitants of the five boroughs constituting the city have multiplied ten times over. This increase has been accompanied by physical transformations that have facilitated crowded living by masses of people. Oil lamps were replaced by gaslight and then by electricity, horse-drawn wagons and carriages by trolley cars, automobiles, subways, and buses. While some of these inventions eliminated a few forms of pollution, the general effect was to multiply sources of contamination and abuse of the natural environment. The example of New York City can be duplicated in many other overcrowded areas, not only in America but especially in Asia. Calcutta now has a population of 7 million, compared with 3 million in 1961. Tokyo has grown from 9 million to over 11.5 million in little more than fifteen years.

As the population increases, human beings create more and more problems and the damage done by each person escalates rapidly. Conditions in Los Angeles illustrate the danger. Despite excellent laws, the city makes little progress in carrying them out. Increases in the number of smog-producers nullify every victory the smog-control experts succeed in gaining. The worst offenders in vitiating ecological progress are the big industrial powers. They combine exhaustion of natural resources with contamination of the environment by industrial poisons, and consume hundreds of times more natural products than do most of the inhabitants of the Third World. The oil shortages of the 1970s, produced by the uncertain political state of the Middle East, forced the West—and particularly the United States—to become aware of its wasteful ways. Whether those shortages will also compel the West to expend its resources less extravagantly remains to be seen.

Most nations of the contemporary world are in danger of being overwhelmed by a population explosion. Its major cause has been what the experts call the demographic revolution. By this is meant an overturning of the ancient balance between births and deaths, which formerly kept the population on a stationary or slowly rising level. This balance is a biological condition common to nearly all species. For thousands of years humankind was no exception. It is estimated, for example, that the total population of the earth at the beginning of the Christian era was about 250 million. More than sixteen centuries passed before another quarter-billion had been added to the total. Not until 1860 did the population of the globe approximate 1 billion. From then on the increase was vastly more rapid. The sixth half-billion, added about 1960, required scarcely more than ten years.

What have been the causes of this radical imbalance known as the demographic revolution? Fundamentally, what has happened has been the achievement of a twentieth-century deathrate alongside a medieval

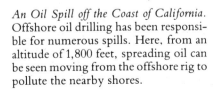

An Oil Spill off the Coast of California. Offshore oil drilling has been responsible for numerous spills. Here, from an altitude of 1,800 feet, spreading oil can be seen moving from the offshore rig to pollute the nearby shores.

birthrate. Infant mortality rates have markedly declined. Deaths of mothers in childbirth have also diminished. The great plagues, such as cholera, typhus, and tuberculosis, take a much smaller toll than they did in earlier centuries. Wars and famines still number their victims by the millions, yet such factors are insufficient to counteract an uncurbed rate of reproduction. Though the practice of contraception has been approved by the governments of such nations as India, China, and Japan, only in the last decade have the effects been worthy of notice. In some countries poverty, religion, and ignorance have made the widespread use of contraceptives difficult. Leaders in Third World countries charge that attempts by Western powers to encourage them to limit population growth, either by contraceptive devices or by sterilization, is a not-so-subtle form of genocide.

The demographic revolution has not affected all countries uniformly. Its incidence has been most conspicuous in the underdeveloped nations of Central and South America, Africa, and Asia. Whereas the population of the world as a whole will double, at present rates. of increase, in thirty-five years, that of Central and South America will multiply twofold in only twenty-six years. An outstanding example is that of Brazil. In 1900 its population was estimated to be 17 million. By 1975 this total had grown to 98 million, more than a fivefold increase. Mexico and Venezuela have two of the highest birthrates in the world. The population of Asia (excluding the USSR and Japan) grew from 813 million in 1900 to approximately 2 billion in 1975. By way of summary, at mid-century, the population of the underdeveloped portions of the globe was more than twice that of the developed portions. Their total land areas were about equal.

6. ACHIEVEMENTS AND LIMITATIONS OF SCIENCE AND TECHNOLOGY

The magnitude of the world's problems has encouraged doubt and pessimism among some of its most creative thinkers. Yet the majority of those charged with the responsibility of finding solutions to the problems—primarily politicians and civil servants—remain cautiously optimistic. For solutions they have continued to turn, paradoxically, to those agencies responsible, in many cases, for the creation of the problems: science and technology. Scientists and technicians invented and perfected the internal combustion engine and the chemical DDT. Now other scientists and technicians are seeking ways to combat their deleterious effects. Scientific research has been responsible for the medical advances which have helped to produce worldwide population increase. No one would argue, of course, that the research should not have taken place, or that the continuing battle against disease is not one of humanity's most worthwhile engagements. Most would agree, however, that science must move as quickly as possible to come up with a safe and simple method of controlling birth, as it continues to fight to prolong life.

The achievements of science in the field of health during the past half-century have been truly remarkable. Two discoveries of great importance have enabled scientists to understand more clearly the ways in which the human body receives and transmits disease. The discovery of viruses was the result of experimentation conducted chiefly by the American biochemist Wendell Stanley in the 1930s. Viruses are microscopic organisms which show signs of life—including the ability to reproduce—only when existing inside living cells. They are the cause of many human diseases, including measles, poliomyelitis (infantile paralysis), and rabies. Not until the nature of viruses was understood could scientists begin to develop means of treating and preventing the virus-produced illnesses in human beings. A second most important discovery that has increased our understanding of human life occurred in 1953, when the Englishman F. H. C. Crick and the American James D. Watson further unlocked the mysteries of genetic inheritance that had been explored by Gregor Mendel at the end of the nineteenth century. Crick and Watson successfully analyzed deoxyribonucleic acid, or DNA, the chemical molecular structure that occurs in the nuclei of gene cells. They discovered that DNA is composed of smaller molecules of four different kinds, linked together in spiral chains. The arrangement of these molecules in each cell forms a

The discovery of viruses; DNA

The Decoding of DNA. Left: F. H. C. Crick and James D. Watson discuss their efforts to analyze the molecular structure of DNA. Right: A model of the molecular structure of DNA. The dual spiral chains are called a double helix.

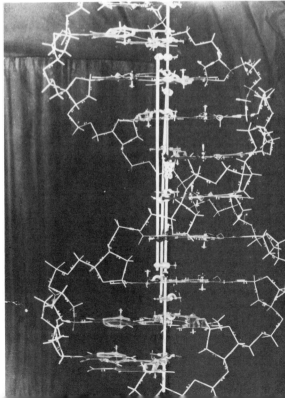

distinct chemical message which determines the character of the genes and therefore of the human organism of which they are a part. The knowledge gained through analysis of DNA has enabled scientists and doctors to understand the causes of hereditary disease and also, by altering a patient's body chemistry, to prevent it. Despite the great benefits that have resulted from this recent discovery, scientists and others have warned that an understanding of the workings of DNA could lead to dangerous tampering with the genetic processes, as, for example, in attempts to produce artificially a breed of more "perfect" human beings.

Medical advances: sulfa drugs, antibiotics, tranquilizers

Experimentation based upon a fuller understanding of the causes of disease has led to the discovery of new medicines to treat it. In 1935 a German named Gerhard Domagk discovered the first of the sulfa drugs, which he called sulfanilamide. Soon others were added to the list. Each was found to be marvelously effective in curing or checking such diseases as rheumatic fever, gonorrhea, scarlet fever, and meningitis. About 1930, the Englishman Sir Alexander Fleming described the first of the antibiotics, which came to be known as penicillin. Antibiotics are chemical agents produced by living organisms and possessing the power to check or kill bacteria. Many have their origin in molds, fungi, algae, and in simple organisms living in the soil. Penicillin was eventually found to be a drug that could produce spectacular results in the treatment of pneumonia, syphilis, peritonitis, tetanus, and numerous other maladies hitherto frequently fatal. Scientists used knowledge obtained through the analysis of DNA to strengthen the cultures used to develop penicillin. In the 1940s the second most famous of the antibiotics—streptomycin—was discovered by the American Dr. Selman W. Waksman. Streptomycin seems to hold its greatest promise in the treatment of tuberculosis, though it has been used for numerous other infections that do not yield to penicillin. Another category of so-called miracle drugs is tranquilizers. Introduced in 1955, they came to be used frequently in the treatment of mental disorders such as manic-depression and have achieved success in making violent patients more tractable. Although these drugs do not themselves effect cures, they help make patients more accessible to other forms of therapy and enable them in many instances to lead relatively normal lives outside institutions in which they would otherwise be incarcerated. That tranquilizers have been misused by men and women indiscriminately as a dangerously simple method of achieving a desired state of mind is no more than further confirmation of the fact that science continues to create new problems as it solves old ones.

Dr. Jonas Salk in His Laboratory

As important as the discovery of new drugs to treat disease has been the development of new means of preventing it. Sir Edward Jenner discovered the first successful vaccine, used to prevent smallpox, in 1796. But not until the 1950s were vaccines found that could protect from diseases such as mumps, measles, and cholera. One of the most exciting breakthroughs occurred with the development of an innoculation against poliomyelitis by the American Dr. Jonas Salk, in 1953. Still to be discovered are effective agents for the successful treatment of two of the world's most deadly killers, heart disease and cancer. The technique of transplanting a heart from a recently dead human being to a live but ailing heart patient, first perfected by the South African, Dr. Christiaan Barnard, has proved of limited usefulness. More effective have been operations substituting plastic valves for defective arteries leading to the heart, and the insertion of electrical devices—"pacemakers"—to steady or stimulate heartbeat. Testing has produced a definite link between cancer and cigarette smoking, as well as industrial and urban pollution—another example of the way in which technology generates difficulties as it resolves others. Doctors continue to experiment with cancer treatment by X-ray and chemical therapy. But despite the dedication of researchers and the expenditure of large sums to assist their work, a cure eludes them.

Vaccines, heart disease, and cancer

Few would today oppose continued campaigns by scientists intent upon eradicating disease. Governments have found it increasingly difficult, however, to justify the spending of vast sums of public money on programs designed to facilitate the exploration of outer space. From their inception, these "experiments" have resembled international competitions between the United States and the Soviet Union as much as they have scientific and technological investigations. On October 4, 1957, the government of the Soviet Union rocketed the first artificial satellite into space at a speed of about 18,000 miles an hour. Though it weighed nearly 200 pounds, it was propelled upward higher than 500 miles. This Russian achievement gave the English language a new word—Sputnik, the Russian for satellite or fellow traveler. A month later the Soviet scientists surpassed their first success by sending a new and much larger Sputnik to an altitude of approximately 1,000 miles. These Sputniks were the forerunners of others of greater significance. In April 1961, the Russians succeeded in sending the first man into orbit around the earth. Meanwhile, scientists and military specialists in the United States had been competing to match the Soviets' achievements. After a number of successes with animals and "uninhabited" capsules, and the suborbital journey of a manned capsule, they succeeded, on February 20, 1962, in launching the first American manned spaceship into orbit around the earth. The successful astronaut was Lieutenant-Colonel John H. Glenn, Jr., who circled the globe three times at a top speed of over 17,000 miles per hour. In 1966 a United States Navy officer left the cabin of his spacecraft and walked in space for forty-four minutes, hundreds of miles above the earth. His feat was surpassed in July 1969, when Neil Armstrong, a civilian astronaut, left his lunar landing module and became the first man on the moon's surface. All over the world these successful voyages and those that followed were hailed as events of capital importance. They did promise an extension of our knowledge of outer space and could doubtless prepare the way for exploration of the

Space exploration

The First Lunar Landing. Astronaut Edwin E. Aldrin, Jr., is photographed walking near the lunar module of Apollo 11. Astronaut Neil Armstrong, who took the picture, and part of the lunar module are reflected in Aldrin's face plate.

moon and eventually of distant planets. But by the mid-1970s, both the United States and the Soviet Union had drastically cut back their space programs in response to demands on their economies from other quarters. Plans for a space "shuttle" and laboratory, plus continuing experiments of a minor nature, kept the programs alive. But their value was being questioned, in view of the billions required to keep them operational.

Nuclear science: Einstein's discoveries

Undoubtedly it was in the area of nuclear science that the largest and most disturbing questions arose as to the capabilities, limitations, and implications of science and technology. Most of the eventual twentieth-century developments in this area were based upon the pioneering work of the physicist Albert Einstein (1879–1955). In 1905 Einstein began to challenge not merely the older conceptions of matter but practically the entire structure of traditional physics. The doctrine for which he is most noted is his principle of relativity. During the greater part of the nineteenth century, physicists had assumed that space and motion were absolute. Space was supposed to be filled with an intangible substance known as *ether,* which provided the medium for the undulations of light. But experiments performed by English and American physicists near the end of the century virtually exploded the ether hypothesis. Einstein then set to work to reconstruct the scheme of the universe in accordance with a different pattern. He maintained that space and motion, instead of being absolute, are relative to each other. Objects have not merely three dimensions but four. To the familiar length, breadth, and thickness, Einstein added a new dimension of *time* and represented all four as fused in a synthesis which he called the *space-time continuum*. In this way he sought to explain the idea that mass is dependent upon motion. Bodies traveling at high velocity have proportions of extension and mass different from what they would have at rest. Included also in the Einstein physics is the conception of a finite universe—that is, finite in space. The region of matter does not extend into infinity, but the universe has limits. While these are by no means definite boundaries, there is at least a region beyond which nothing exists. Space curves back upon itself so as to make of the universe a gigantic sphere within which are contained galaxies, solar systems, stars, and planets.

The Einstein theories had a major influence in precipitating other revolutionary developments in physics. By 1960 it had been discovered that the conception of the subatomic world as a miniature solar system was much too simple. The atom was found to contain not only positively charged protons and negatively charged electrons, but *positrons,* or positively charged electrons; *neutrons,* which carry no electric charges; and *mesons,* which may be either negative or positive. Mesons, it was discovered, exist not only within the atom (for about two millionths of a second) but are major components of the cosmic rays that are constantly bombarding the earth from somewhere in outer space.

Albert Einstein

Several of the developments in physics outlined above helped to make possible one of the most spectacular achievements in the history of science, the splitting of the atom to release the energy contained within it. Ever since it became known that the atom is composed primarily of electrical energy, physicists had dreamed of unlocking this source of tremendous power and making it available for man. As early as 1905 Einstein became convinced of the equivalence of mass and energy and worked out a formula for the conversion of one into the other, which he expressed as follows: $E = mc^2$. E represents the energy in ergs, m the mass in grams, and c the velocity of light in centimeters per second. In other words, the amount of energy locked within the atom is equal to the mass multiplied by the square of the velocity of light. But no practical application of this formula was possible until after the discovery of the neutron by the Englishman Sir James Chadwick in 1932. Since the neutron carries no charge of electricity, it is an ideal weapon for bombarding the atom. It is neither repulsed by the positively charged protons nor absorbed by the negatively charged electrons. Moreover, in the process of bombardment it produces more neutrons, which hit other atoms and cause them in turn to split and create neutrons. In this way the original reaction is repeated in an almost unending series.

Releasing the energy within the atom

In 1939 two German physicists, Otto Hahn and Fritz Strassman, succeeded in splitting atoms of uranium by bombarding them with neutrons. The initial reaction produced a chain of reactions, in much the same way that a fire burning at the edge of a piece of paper raises

The development of the atomic bomb

the temperature of adjoining portions of the paper high enough to cause them to ignite. Scientists in Germany, Great Britain, and the United States were spurred on by governments anxious to make use of these discoveries for military purposes during the Second World War. The first use made of the knowledge of atomic fission was in the preparation of an atomic bomb. The devastating weapon was the achievement of scientists working for the War Department of the United States. Some were physicists who had been exiled by Nazi or Fascist oppression. (Einstein himself, a native of Germany and a Jew, had left that country in the 1930s for the United States.)

The hydrogen bomb

Even more disturbing than the results of the bombs dropped on Japan at the end of World War II were the first tests of a hydrogen bomb by the United States Atomic Energy Commission in November 1952. The tests were conducted at Eniwetok Atoll in the South Pacific; an entire island disappeared after burning brightly for several hours. The hydrogen bomb, or H-bomb, is based upon fusion of hydrogen atoms, a process which requires the enormous heat generated by the splitting of uranium atoms to start the reaction. The fusion results in the creation of a new element, helium, which actually weighs less than the sum of the hydrogen atoms. The "free" energy left over provides the tremendous explosive power of the H-bomb. The force of hydrogen bombs is measured in *megatons,* each of which represents 1,000,000 tons of TNT. Thus a 5-megaton H-bomb would equal 250 times the power of the A-bombs dropped on Hiroshima and Nagasaki.

Clearly the scientists had, at the behest of their government, unleashed a weapon of devastating proportions upon the world. By the 1970s, not only the United States, but the Soviet Union, China, Brit-

An H-Bomb Mushrooms. The cloud spreads into a huge mushroom following a 1952 explosion of a hydrogen bomb in the Marshall Islands of the Pacific. The photo was taken 50 miles from the detonation site at about 12,000 feet. The cloud rose to 40,000 feet two minutes after the explosion. Ten minutes later the cloud stem had pushed about 25 miles. The mushroom portion went up to 10 miles and spread 100 miles.

Calder Hall. Built in 1956 in England, this was the world's first large-scale atomic power station. The two towers on the left are for cooling. Since this time such power plants have proliferated around the world. However, the near-catastrophic accident at the Three Mile Island Power Station close to Harrisburg, Pennsylvania, in March 1979 has spurred opponents to press even harder for a reexamination of the use of nuclear power.

ain, France, India, Israel, and other nations either possessed atomic weapons or were in the process of developing the technology to do so. Science was once and for all proved to be something other than "pure," that is, without practical and political implications. The application of its discoveries had become a burdensome fact of life for humanity the world over.

The proliferation of nuclear weapons

Governments experimented with schemes to harness nuclear energy for peaceful purposes. Some progress has been made in the development of atomic power as an alternative source of domestic and industrial fuel. But the dangers of radiation as a by-product suggest that this scheme may prove of limited value. During the late 1970s, when the West's supplies of oil were threatened, heated debate continued between advocates of further construction of atomic power plants and those who argued in favor of other energy forms—among them solar—as safer and cheaper alternatives. Meanwhile, technologists working for private industry made use of discoveries in atomic physics to pioneer the field of electronics. Electronics derives from that branch of physics which deals with the behavior and effects of electrons, or negative constituents within the atom. Electronic devices have multiplied in staggering profusion since World War II. Among them are devices to measure the trajectory of missiles, to give warnings of approaching missiles or aircraft, to make possible "blind" landings of airplanes, to store and release electrical signals, to amplify and regulate the transmission of light and sound images, and to provide the power for photoelectric cells that open doors and operate various automatic machines. The spacecraft industry, which has made possible the exploration of outer space, is closely dependent upon electronics.

The uses of atomic energy; electronics

The Age of Television. Left: The first working television pickup camera, 1929. Right: The Telstar communications satellite. Weighing only 170 pounds, and measuring 34 inches in diameter, it is powered by 3,600 solar cells. It circles the earth at a speed of 1,600 miles per hour, at a height of from 500 to 3,000 nautical miles.

Automation

The use of electronic devices for radio reception led to initial progress in automation. Automation should not be confused with mechanization, though it may be considered the logical extreme of that process. More correctly conceived, automation means a close integration of four elements: (1) a processing system; (2) a mechanical handling system; (3) sensing equipment; and (4) a control system. Though all of these elements are necessary, the last two are the most significant. Sensing equipment performs a function similar to that of the human senses. It observes and measures what is happening and sends the information thus gained to the control unit. It employs such devices as photoelectric cells, infra-red cells, high-frequency devices, and devices making use of X-rays, isotopes, and resonance. It operates without fatigue and much faster and more accurately than do the human senses. Moreover, its observations can be made in places unsafe for, or inaccessible to, human beings. A control system receives information from a sensing element, compares this information with that required by the "program,'" and then makes the necessary adjustments. This series of operations is continuous, so that a desired state is constantly maintained without any human intervention, except for that initially involved in "programming." This revolution has been greatly extended by the invention of lasers. A laser is a device for amplifying the focus and intensity of light. High-energy atoms are stimulated by light to amplify a beam of light. Lasers have demonstrated their value recently in medicine. They have been used effectively in arresting hemorrhaging in the retina in eye afflictions. Through automation, expensive and complicated machines are constantly taking the place of much human labor. Data processing machines and electronic computers are employed to control switching operations in railroad yards, to operate assembly lines, to operate machines that control other machines, and even to maintain blood pressure during critical operations in hospitals.

Electronic inventions have proved no more an unmixed blessing than have the other discoveries and developments of scientists and technicians. One obvious problem generated by devices that can do the work of humans is that they put humans out of work. Technological unemployment has become an important problem for the modern world. Though new industries absorbed many workers, others were bound to be displaced by automation. While the demand for skilled labor remained high, the so-called entry jobs performed by the unskilled were fast disappearing. They were being eliminated not by computers so much as by fork-lift trucks and motorized conveyors and sweepers. Mechanization of agriculture also eliminated thousands of jobs for unskilled and uneducated workers.

Technological Unemployement

Science and technology provide no panaceas for the problems of the world. If those problems are to be solved, men and women, not machines, will have to do the work. They will be better equipped to do so if they possess some sense of their own past. The lesson of history is not that it repeats itself. The lesson is, rather, that the present can be clearly perceived, and the future intelligently planned for, only when those responsible for the world's destiny understand the workings of human nature. And for knowledge of that extraordinarily complicated and fascinating mechanism, there is no better source than history.

SELECTED READINGS

- *Items so designated are available in paperback editions.*
- Banfield, Edward C., *The Unheavenly City: The Nature and Future of Our Urban Crisis*, rev. ed., Boston, 1974.
- Bell, Daniel, *The End of Ideology: On the Exhaustion of Political Ideas in the Fifties*, Glencoe, Ill., 1960.
  Beynon, Huw, *Working for Ford*, London, 1973. A recent analysis of England's industrial and labor problems. Stimulating and perceptive.
  Collins, Doreen, *The European Economic Community, 1958–72*, London, 1975. A thorough analysis of the Common Market, emphasizing the social policies that have emerged in Europe since 1958.
- Erlich, Paul, *The Population Bomb*, New York, 1968.
- Galbraith, John Kenneth, *The New Industrial State*, Boston, 1967. A penetrating analysis of the changes in capitalism wrought by advanced technology.
- Harrington, Michael, *The Other America: Poverty in the United States*, New York, 1962.
- Heilbroner, Robert, *The Future as History*, New York, 1960.

• ———, *An Inquiry into the Human Prospect,* New York, 1975, 1980.

Infeld, Leopold, *Albert Einstein: His Work and Its Influence on Our World,* New York, 1950. A general introduction.

Lerner, M., *The Age of Overkill,* New York, 1962.

• McKenzie, A. E. E., *The Major Achievements of Science,* New York, 1960.

• Marcuse, Herbert, *Counterrevolution and Revolt,* Boston, 1972.

• Popper, Karl, *The Open Society and Its Enemies,* rev. ed., London, 1962. A vigorous comparison of the totalitarian and democratic philosophies by a libertarian.

Rosenberg, Harold, *The Anxious Object: Art Today and Its Significance,* New York, 1964.

• Shonfield, Andrew, *Modern Capitalism: The Changing Balance of Public and Private Power,* New York, 1965.

• Toffler, Alan, *Future Shock,* New York, 1971. An extended essay on the consequences of rapid change in modern industrial society.

Von Laue, T. H., *The Global City: Freedom, Power and Necessity in the Age of World Revolutions,* Philadelphia, 1969.

SOURCE MATERIALS

Bowges, Hervé, comp., *The Student Revolts: The Activists Speak,* London, 1968. Interviews with participants of the student riots of May 1968 which shook France and almost toppled the government.

• Jackson, George, *Soledad Brother: The Prison Letters of George Jackson,* New York, 1970.

• Rich, Adrienne, *On Lies, Secrets, and Silence,* New York, 1979. Essays by a leading feminist thinker.

Snow, C. P., *The Two Cultures and a Second Look: An Expanded Version of the Two Cultures and the Scientific Revolution,* Cambridge, 1965. Argues that in the modern world the great divergence between science and the humanities has been a disastrous process.

• Solzhenitsyn, Alexsandr, *The Gulag Archipelago, 1918–1956,* New York, 1974–75. An account of prison camps during the Stalinist era by the exiled Russian novelist.

RULERS OF PRINCIPAL EUROPEAN STATES SINCE 700 A.D.

The Carolingian Dynasty

Pepin, Mayor of the Palace, 714
Charles Martel, Mayor of the Palace, 715–741
Pepin I, Mayor of the Palace, 741; King, 751–768
Charlemagne, King, 768–814; Emperor, 800–814
Louis the Pious, Emperor, 814–840

MIDDLE KINGDOMS

Lothair, Emperor, 840–855
Louis (Italy), Emperor, 855–875
Charles (Provence), King, 855–863
Lothair II (Lorraine), King, 855–869

WEST FRANCIA

Charles the Bald, King, 840–877; Emperor, 875
Louis II, King, 877–879
Louis III, King, 879–882
Carloman, King, 879–884

EAST FRANCIA

Ludwig, King, 840–876
Carloman, King, 876–880
Ludwig, King, 876–882
Charles the Fat, Emperor, 876–887

Holy Roman Emperors

SAXON DYNASTY

Otto I, 962–973
Otto II, 973–983
Otto III, 983–1002
Henry II, 1002–1024

FRANCONIAN DYNASTY

Conrad II, 1024–1039
Henry III, 1039–1056
Henry IV, 1056–1106
Henry V, 1106–1125
Lothair II (of Saxony), King, 1125–1133; Emperor, 1133–1137

HOHENSTAUFEN DYNASTY

Conrad III, 1138–1152
Frederick I (Barbarossa), 1152–1190
Henry VI, 1190–1197
Philip of Swabia, 1198–1208 ⎤
Otto IV (Welf), 1198–1215 ⎦ Rivals
Frederick II, 1220–1250
Conrad IV, 1250–1254

INTERREGNUM, 1254–1273

EMPERORS FROM VARIOUS DYNASTIES
Rudolf I (Hapsburg), 1273–1291

Adolf (Nassau), 1292–1298
Albert I (Hapsburg), 1298–1308
Henry VII (Luxemburg), 1308–1313
Ludwig IV (Wittelsbach), 1314–1347
Charles IV (Luxemburg), 1347–1378
Wenceslas (Luxemburg), 1378–1400
Rupert (Wittelsbach), 1400–1410
Sigismund (Luxemburg), 1410–1437

HAPSBURG DYNASTY

Albert II, 1438–1439
Frederick III, 1440–1493
Maximilian I, 1493–1519
Charles V, 1519–1556
Ferdinand I, 1556–1564
Maximilan II, 1564–1576
Rudolf II, 1576–1612
Matthias, 1612–1619
Ferdinand II, 1619–1637
Ferdinand III, 1637–1657
Leopold I, 1658–1705
Joseph I, 1705–1711
Charles VI, 1711–1740
Charles VII (not a Hapsburg), 1742–1745
Francis I, 1745–1765
Joseph II, 1765–1790
Leopold II, 1790–1792
Francis II, 1792–1806

Rulers of France from Hugh Capet

CAPETIAN KINGS

Hugh Capet, 987–996
Robert II, 996–1031
Henry I, 1031–1060
Philip I, 1060–1108
Louis VI, 1108–1137
Louis VII, 1137–1180
Philip II (Augustus), 1180–1223
Louis VIII, 1223–1226
Louis IX, 1226–1270
Philip III, 1270–1285
Philip IV, 1285–1314
Louis X, 1314–1316
Philip V, 1316–1322
Charles IV, 1322–1328

HOUSE OF VALOIS

Philip VI, 1328–1350
John, 1350–1364
Charles V, 1364–1380
Charles VI, 1380–1422
Charles VII, 1422–1461
Louis XI, 1461–1483
Charles VIII, 1483–1498
Louis XII, 1498–1515
Francis I, 1515–1547

Henry II, 1547–1559
Francis II, 1559–1560
Charles IX, 1560–1574
Henry III, 1574–1589

BOURBON DYNASTY

Henry IV, 1589–1610
Louis XIII, 1610–1643
Louis XIV, 1643–1715
Louis XV, 1715–1774
Louis XVI, 1774–1792

AFTER 1792

First Republic, 1792–1799
Napoleon Bonaparte, First Consul, 1799–1804
Napoleon I, Emperor, 1804–1814
Louis XVIII (Bourbon dynasty), 1814–1824
Charles X (Bourbon dynasty), 1824–1830
Louis Philippe, 1830–1848
Second Republic, 1848–1852
Napoleon III, Emperor, 1852–1870
Third Republic, 1870–1940
Pétain regime, 1940–1944
Provisional government, 1944–1946
Fourth Republic, 1946–1958
Fifth Republic, 1958–

Rulers of England

ANGLO-SAXON KINGS

Egbert, 802–839
Ethelwulf, 839–858
Ethelbald, 858–860
Ethelbert, 860–866
Ethelred, 866–871
Alfred the Great, 871–900
Edward the Elder, 900–924
Ethelstan, 924–940
Edmund I, 940–946
Edred, 946–955
Edwy, 955–959
Edgar, 959–975

Edward the Martyr, 975–978
Ethelred the Unready, 978–1016
Canute, 1016–1035 (Danish Nationality)
Harold I, 1035–1040
Hardicanute, 1040–1042
Edward the Confessor, 1042–1066
Harold II, 1066

ANGLO-NORMAN KINGS

William I (the Conqueror), 1066–1087
William II, 1087–1100
Henry I, 1100–1135
Stephen, 1135–1154

Angevin Kings

Henry II, 1154–1189
Richard I, 1189–1199
John, 1199–1216
Henry III, 1216–1272
Edward I, 1272–1307
Edward II, 1307–1327
Edward III, 1327–1377
Richard II, 1377–1399

House of Lancaster

Henry IV, 1399–1413
Henry V, 1413–1422
Henry VI, 1422–1461

House of York

Edward IV, 1461–1483
Edward V, 1483
Richard III, 1483–1485

Tudor Sovereigns

Henry VII, 1485–1509
Henry VIII, 1509–1547
Edward VI, 1547–1553
Mary, 1553–1558
Elizabeth I, 1558–1603

Stuart Kings

James I, 1603–1625
Charles I, 1625–1649

Commonwealth and Protectorate, 1649–1659

Later Stuart Monarchs

Charles II, 1660–1685
James II, 1685–1688
William III and Mary II, 1689–1694
William III alone, 1694–1702
Anne, 1702–1714

House of Hanover

George I, 1714–1727
George II, 1727–1760
George III, 1760–1820
George IV, 1820–1830
William IV, 1830–1837
Victoria, 1837–1901

House of Saxe-Coburg-Gotha

Edward VII, 1901–1910
George V, 1910–1917

House of Windsor

George V, 1917–1936
Edward VIII, 1936
George VI, 1936–1952
Elizabeth II, 1952–

Prominent Popes

Silvester I, 314–335
Leo I, 440–461
Gelasius I, 492–496
Gregory I, 590–604
Nicholas I, 858–867
Silvester II, 999–1003
Leo IX, 1049–1054
Nicholas II, 1058–1061
Gregory VII, 1073–1085
Urban II, 1088–1099
Paschal II, 1099–1118
Alexander III, 1159–1181

Innocent III, 1198–1216
Gregory IX, 1227–1241
Boniface VIII, 1294–1303
John XXII, 1316–1334
Nicholas V, 1447–1455
Pius II, 1458–1464
Alexander VI, 1492–1503
Julius II, 1503–1513
Leo X, 1513–1521
Adrian VI, 1522–1523
Clement VII, 1523–1534
Paul III, 1534–1549

Paul IV, 1555–1559
Gregory XIII, 1572–1585
Gregory XVI, 1831–1846
Pius IX, 1846–1878
Leo XIII, 1878–1903
Pius X, 1903–1914
Benedict XV, 1914–1922

Pius XI, 1922–1939
Pius XII, 1939–1958
John XXIII, 1958–1963
Paul VI, 1963–1978
John Paul I, 1978
John Paul II, 1978–

Rulers of Austria and Austria-Hungary

*Maximilian I (Archduke), 1493–1519
*Charles I (Charles V in the Holy Roman Empire),
    1519–1556
*Ferdinand I, 1556–1564
*Maximilian II, 1564–1576
*Rudolph II, 1576–1612
*Matthias, 1612–1619
*Ferdinand II, 1619–1637
*Ferdinand III, 1637–1657
*Leopold I, 1658–1705
*Joseph I, 1705–1711
*Charles VI, 1711–1740
Maria Theresa, 1740–1780

*Joseph II, 1780–1790
*Leopold II, 1790–1792
*Francis II, 1792–1835 (Emperor of Austria as
    Francis I after 1804)
Ferdinand I, 1835–1848
Francis Joseph, 1848–1916 (after 1867 Emperor
    of Austria and King of Hungary)
Charles I, 1916–1918 (Emperor of Austria and King
    of Hungary)
Republic of Austria, 1918–1938 (dictatorship
    after 1934)
Republic restored, under Allied occupation, 1945–1956
Free Republic, 1956–

*Also bore title of Holy Roman Emperor.

Rulers of Prussia and Germany

*Frederick I, 1701–1713
*Frederick William I, 1713–1740
*Frederick II (the Great), 1740–1786
*Frederick William II, 1786–1797
*Frederick William III, 1797–1840
*Frederick William IV, 1840–1861
*William I, 1861–1888 (German Emperor after 1871)

Frederick III, 1888
William II, 1888–1918
Weimar Republic, 1918–1933
Third Reich (Nazi Dictatorship), 1933–1945
Allied occupation, 1945–1952
Division into Federal Republic of Germany in west
    and German Democratic Republic in east, 1949–

*Kings of Prussia.

Rulers of Russia

Ivan III, 1462–1505
Basil III, 1505–1533
Ivan IV, 1533–1584
Theodore I, 1584–1598
Boris Godunov, 1598–1605

Theodore II, 1605
Basil IV, 1606–1610
Michael, 1613–1645
Alexius, 1645–1676
Theodore III, 1676–1682

Ivan V and Peter I, 1682–1689
Peter I (the Great), 1689–1725
Catherine I, 1725–1727
Peter II, 1727–1730
Anna, 1730–1740
Ivan VI, 1740–1741
Elizabeth, 1741–1762
Peter III, 1762

Catherine II (the Great), 1762–1796
Paul, 1796–1801
Alexander I, 1801–1825
Nicholas I, 1825–1855
Alexander II, 1855–1881
Alexander III, 1881–1894
Nicholas II, 1894–1917
Soviet Republic, 1917–

Rulers of Italy

Victor Emmanuel II, 1861–1878
Humbert I, 1878–1900
Victor Emmanuel III, 1900–1946
Fascist Dictatorship, 1922–1943
    (maintained in northern Italy until 1945)

Humbert II, May 9–June 13, 1946
Republic, 1946–

Rulers of Spain

Ferdinand {
    and Isabella, 1479–1504
    and Philip I, 1504–1506
    and Charles I, 1506–1516
}
Charles I (Holy Roman Emperor Charles V),
    1516–1556
Philip II, 1556–1598
Philip III, 1598–1621
Philip IV, 1621–1665
Charles II, 1665–1700
Philip V, 1700–1746
Ferdinand VI, 1746–1759
Charles III, 1759–1788
Charles IV, 1788–1808

Ferdinand VII, 1808
Joseph Bonaparte, 1808–1813
Ferdinand VII (restored), 1814–1833
Isabella II, 1833–1868
Republic, 1868–1870
Amadeo, 1870–1873
Republic, 1873–1874
Alfonso XII, 1874–1885
Alfonso XIII, 1886–1931
Republic, 1931–1939
Fascist Dictatorship, 1939-1975
Juan Carlos I, 1975-

Index

i

teleological universe, concept of, 131
Tempest, The (Shakespeare), 445
Ten Commandments, 71, 78, 86, 253
Ten Lost Tribes of Israel, 74
Tennis Court Oath, 599
terrorism, 799, 916, 919, 921
Tess of the D'Urbervilles (Hardy), 779
tetanus, 948
Tet offensive of 1968 (Vietnam War), 925, 926
Tetzel (Dominican friar), 465
Teutonic Knights, 534
Texas, 739
textile industry, 628–29, 634, 635, 648, 649, 657
Thailand, 924
Thales (thā′lēz) of Miletus, 125, 132
Thatcher, Margaret, 931
Thebes, 33, 113, 124, 155
Their Eyes Were Watching God (Hurston), 940
Theocritus (thē′ŏk′rĭ-tus) of Syracuse, 159
Theodora (thē′ŏ-dō′ra), Empress, 236
Theodoric (thē-ŏd′ŏ-rik) the Ostrogoth, 229–30, 235
Theodosius (thē-ō-dō′shĭ-us) I (the Great), Emperor, 212, 217, 218, 226, 227, 231, 232, 236
Theophrastus (thē′ō-frăs′tus), 161
Thessalonica (thĕs′a-lŏ nĭ-ka), 252
Thessaly, 115, 145, 806
Third Crusade, 341–42
Third International, 851, 854
Third Punic War, 177
Third Reich, 861
Third Republic (France), 791–94, 795
  anticlericalism, 793–94
  constitutional shortcomings, 792
  coup d'etat, 792
  elections of 1871, 791–92
Third World nations, 913, 926, 945, 946
  emergence of, 910–12
  Soviet intervention in, 909
Thirteenth Amendment, 933
Thirty Years' War, 483, 529, 537–40, 543, 544
  cause of, 538
  events leading to, 537–38
  results of, 539–40
Thomas, Sidney Gilchrist, 737
Thrasymachus (thră-sĭm′a-kus), 127
Thucydides (thŭ-sĭd′ĭ-dēz), 137, 159, 255, 420
Thus Spake Zarathustra (Nietzsche), 774
Tiberius, tribune of Rome, 179
Tiber River, 170
Tigris-Euphrates Valley, 18–19, 21, 55, 89, 90, 101
  Mesopotamian civilization, 45–61
Tigris River, 47, 61
timocracies, 114
Tin Drum, The (Grass), 938
Tintoretto (tēn′tŏ-rĕt′to), 425
Tiryns (tĭ′rĭnz), 93, 99
tithe, 462

Titian (tĭsh′an), 425, 440, 570
Tobago, 914
To Be Young, Gifted, and Black (Hansberry), 940
Togo, 754
Tokyo, 890–91, 944
Toledo, 274, 440
Toleration Act, 524
Tolkien, J. R. R., 941
Tolstoy, Leo, 257, 780–81, 801
Tom Jones (Fielding), 572
Tonkin Gulf incident, 925
Tories (England), 525, 677, 678, 679, 684, 695, 931
totalitarianism, 514, 846–63, 885, 938
  in communist Russia, 846–53, 876
  Italian fascism, 853–57
  Nazism, 857–63, 875–76
Toulouse, 375
towns, growth of, 296, 304
Townshend, Viscount Charles "Turnip," 504–505
Toynbee, Arnold J., 18, 102
trade, revival of, 302–8; *see also* under the names of countries
trade unions, 307, 686–87, 863, 864
  labor riots, 769, 794, 796
traditionalism, 254–55
Trafalgar Square riot (1887), 769
Trajan (trā′jăn), Emperor, 187, 188, 192, 201
tranquilizers, 948
transportation, 646–47
  coming of railways, 636–39
  impact of electricity on, 738
transubstantiation, doctrine of, 346, 349, 479
Transvaal (trans-väl′), 755
Transylvania, 838
Travels (Benjamin of Tudela), 247
Treasury of Merits, doctrine of, 458
Treatise of Civil Government (Locke), 551
Trebizond, 252
Treitschke (trīch′kĕ), Heinrich von, 813
trialism, 818
trial jury system, 318
Trianon (trē′ä′nôn′), Palace, Treaty of, 838
Tribonian, 237
Trieste (trē-ĕst′), 831, 838
trigonometry, 272
Trinidad, 616, 914
Trinity (Masaccio), 423
Trinity, doctrine of the, 219, 359, 481
Triple Alliance, 809, 810–11, 812, 822
Triple Entente, 810, 812, 821, 823, 824, 840
Tripoli, 806, 812
Tristan (Gottfried von Strassburg), 364
Triumph of the Will (motion picture), 876
Trojans, 95
Trojan War, 133
Trojan Women, The (Euripides), 136
Troppau (trôp′ou) Conference, 676
Trotsky, Leon, 846–47, 849–50, 851

Trotskyites, 852
troubadours (trōō′ba-dōorz), 362–63
Trouvères (trōō′vâr′), 363
Troy, 92, 93, 100
Truce of God, 339
Truffaut, François, 941
Truman, Harry, 891, 893–94, 905, 923–24
Truman Doctrine, 905
Trusteeship Council (United Nations), 895
trusts, 746
Truth, Sojourner, 933
tuberculosis, 271, 946, 948
Tubman, Harriet, 933
Tudor dynasty, 396, 441, 446, 475, 515, 516
Tunisia, 176, 809, 915
Turgenev (tōōr-gyä′nyĕf), Ivan, 780, 801
Turkey, 61, 90, 100, 209, 236, 268, 818, 831, 835, 838, 845, 887, 905
  see also Constantinople
  Crimean War, 717
  Russo-Turkish War (1877–1878), 806
  World War I, 822, 831, 915
Turks, 275, 337, 530
  Byzantine invasions, 250, 251, 258
Turner, J. M. W., 704
Turner, Nat, 933
Tuscany, 720, 721
Tutankhamen (tōōt′ängk-ämĕn), Pharaoh ("King Tut"), 33
Twelfth Dynasty (ancient Egypt, 27–28
Twelve Tables, 173, 197
Two Sicilies, Kingdom of the, 311, 537, 540, 673, 676, 720, 721; *see also* Naples; Sicily
Tyler, Wat, 381
typhus, 946
Tyre, 80, 101
Tyrol (tē-rōl), 838
Tyrtaeus (tûr-tē′us), 115

U-boat warfare, 826
Ukraine, 649, 829, 846, 889
ulama, 269, 270
Ulanov, Vladimir, *see* Lenin, Nikolai
Ulpian, 197, 204
Ulster, 797, 830; *see also* Ireland
Umar, Caliph, 263, 265
Umayyad caliphate, 265–67, 269
unemployment, 740, 859, 865, 866, 867, 883, 955
unemployment insurance, 796
Union or Death (society), 818
Union Pacific Railroad, 726
Union of Soviet Socialist Republics (U.S.S.R.), 260, 326, 870, 882, 884, 885, 892, 899, 911, 921, 931, 946, 952
  see also Bolshevik Revolution; Russia (before 1917)
  agriculture, 851, 852, 853, 876
  Five Year Plans, 850–51
  industrialism, 848, 853